I CHING

The Oracle of the Cosmic Way

I CHING

The Oracle of the Cosmic Way

Carol K. Anthony

Hanna Moog

ICHINGBOOKS

Contents

Part I. Introduction to the Cosmic Way

Part II. The Hexagrams

Part III. Appendices

Foreword

As the title indicates, this is a book about the Cosmic Way. To we humans, learning the Cosmic Way is about understanding transformation. Transformation is the natural activity of the Cosmos, and of all that exists within it. As such, it is among the enduring Cosmic Principles, discussed in this book, that govern all existence. The authors of this book are careful in distinguishing transformation from "changes," the word traditionally associated with the I Ching, or "Book of Change(s)".

But isn't transformation simply change of a sort, or perhaps a vaunted kind of change? The Oxford American Dictionary defines transformation as "a great change in the appearance or character of [something]," and offers the example of "*the caterpillar is transformed into a butterfly*." Now since transformation is thus defined in terms of change, how does the OAD conceive of change? "To make or become different; to pass from one form or phase to another; alteration; a fresh occupation or surroundings."

So, "transformation" is becoming different in a great way, typically in terms of a thing's outward appearance. The authors of this book are asking us to look beyond this rather circular definition. The further difference between transformation in the Cosmic Way and change lies in the source and direction of the movement. Change is movement confined to the outer plane of experience, while transformation is movement on the inner plane, to which the outer plane responds spontaneously.

Transformation, then, is an experiential process that both encompasses and transcends the inner and outer planes, and indeed, the very idea of planes. Change is left back in the world of the surface, spinning around on the medieval wheel of fortune— that area in which the manipulation and splitting of experience occur. Obviously, any oracle worth the name is going to have to work beyond change and become a transformational medium. Thus, the I Ching represented in this book is properly known as "The Book of Transformation."

But what is the experience of transformation like, and what is needed to make it happen? In the pages to follow, the answer is clearly stated: transformation happens through the daily influence of natural and cosmic Helpers, whenever people allow them freedom of movement. Among these Helpers, these noumenal, invisible Presences of the Cosmic Consciousness (see Hexagram 1), is a specific entity known as the Sage. This is the Cosmic Teacher that speaks to us through the I Ching. Ms. Anthony and Ms. Moog have described the nature and mode of action of this teaching consciousness throughout the pages that follow; it is the purpose of this small prelude to draw a picture of how the Sage may be personally experienced.

Hexagram 29, "The Abyss," describes the deepest fears that, paradoxically, draw us toward and away from the Sage. These are fears of the unknown: of every aspect of lived experience that cannot be apprehended through the outer senses or by our rational minds. "The Abyss," which is the metaphor for this net of fear, is depicted in traditional renderings of the I Ching text as a place of darkness and looming danger, a yawning chasm of doubt and horror, lined with labyrinthine canals of deep crannies and fissures. Anything not outwardly manifest, anything that we cannot grasp, control, use, and throw away, is subject to being characterized as a danger or threat. Even our own bodies, and their internal organs, such as the brain, are objects of suspicion and its handmaiden, fear. The brain itself is especially perceived as a tangle of mystery and malevolent power, and so we turn to science to demystify this organ, to reveal it as a complex but benign net of electrochemical wiring, a *mechanicus* in the same way that our heart and circulatory apparatus are really just an intricate system of plumbing fixtures. This model incorporates a hierarchical conception of the relationships that exist within this mechanical apparatus: the heart is the pump, the ticker, that directs the flow of the life-giving blood throughout the organism; the brain is the mastermind, the supervisory master computer that directs and programs the operations of the lower organs, and within the brain itself a hierarchical ordering exists among its components. At this point, the soul or spiritual self appears, whose place it is to command and restrain, control and punish, with a branding iron called guilt and a broadsword called morality, or Law. Religion nods its silent approval to the scientific metaphor of body-as-machine, and adds that it is mere dust and ashes, after all. The alternative it offers is the path of Heaven and the elevation of spirit; but this must follow in practice upon a debasement of the body, its organs, and their processes. Any ascetic, self-destructive, or even suicidal act against the physical self can be deemed a step in the path toward eternal life in the total realization of spirit. Enlightenment, salvation, grace, martyrdom: these are among the avowed goals of the spiritual path, to which the reductive metaphors of modern science have supplied their implicit assent.

This strange and deeply systematized structure of fear, guilt, divisiveness, and the aggrandizement of all that is human, rational, and reductive, is what the authors of this text refer to as the "collective ego." It is the influence of this architectonic of mistaken beliefs and the institutions that support and perpetuate them, that draws us inexorably into the abyss of guilt, fear, and suffering which, ironically, often also leads us to consulting oracles. Lao Tzu, in Verse 76 of the Tao Te Ching, writes:

Men are born soft and supple;
Dead, they are stiff and hard.
Plants are born tender and pliant;
Dead, they are brittle and dry.
Thus whoever is stiff and inflexible
Is a disciple of death.
Whoever is soft and yielding
Is a disciple of life.[1]

Any concretized set of beliefs, principles, laws, social structures, arguments, commandments, or ideologies has immediately abandoned its life force, its organic nature, by setting itself up as Truth. Any system that professes itself as true, to the exclusion of any other possible understanding, has instantly undermined its own veracity and separated from the Cosmic Way. Thus, the identifying marks of the collective ego are to be found in the open or insidious display of intolerance, rigidity, extremism, parochialism, the use of power, anthropocentrism, insularity, or doctrinal moralism, either on the part of the individual ego (the personal manifestation of the collective ego's influence) or of a group or institution of the collective ego.

[margin annotation: the trouble w/ truth]

How, then, would the oracle, and the Sage that speaks through it, recommend that we respond? It seems, on the surface, to be a classic "fight-or-flight" situation: we either rebel outwardly and struggle, or else we seek sanctuary from the collective ego and

---

[1] *Tao Te Ching:* A New English Version. Stephen Mitchell, translator.

its institutions—in a monastery, a mountain, a cave, or an addiction. The I Ching offers an alternative to fight-or-flight, which involves working on the inner plane of being, simultaneously within ourselves and toward others. But what's wrong with social action? Rebellion or outer struggle, pursued in isolation, only feeds the collective ego's appetite for power: by offering ourselves as an opponent or an enemy to it, we provide it with the fuel (contention) and the recognition (opposition) that it needs to persist. In Hexagram 49, this sort of approach is referred to as "molting in the face." It's like trying to walk on your knees: there is some forward movement, but it is rather slow, painful and unbalanced; it would be better to use the entire set of resources we've been given, in order to make real progress.

In this version of the I Ching, a new and revolutionary approach is presented: allow the oracle, and the Helpers that it speaks of, to lead you toward a state of inner clarity, from which point your outer action will flow, accurately and effortlessly, toward harmony, resolution, and fulfillment—in relationships, in professional pursuits, and in the furtherance of your emotional and physical well being. Now, a certain level of directed effort (what the I Ching repeatedly calls "perseverance") is required, along with a new orientation toward certain principles having to do with preparation, action, effort, and judgment. Once again, we are talking here about a Book of Transformation: in order for transformation to occur, certain idols of the mind will have to be smashed and abandoned. These may include assumptions or beliefs that the reader may have long harbored as self-evident truths: devotion to God or a similar spiritual overlord, the supporting idea that divides our nature into physical/spiritual or bodily/mental aspects, the egocentric burden of human supremacy over Nature, or the primacy of the human intellect. The oracle has been given to us so that we may overthrow the ideological enslavement of the collective ego; what arises as each encrustation of this servitude is shed is the natural self that was always there, within, though forced into silence, retreat, or imprisonment behind the walls of ego. To the extent that we are able to demolish these inner walls, we regain contact with the Cosmic Way, and innumerable helping Presences are liberated in a beneficent cycle that draws energy from the very core of the Cosmos, harmonizing our inner life and fulfilling the outer.

The beginning and center of the inner work indicated by this I Ching consist in the practice of the "suspension of judgment." There is no adherence to doctrine or leap of faith required to enter into this work: in fact, the text advises against any submission to dogma or received belief, as that would only amount to a further endorsement of the collective ego in one or another of its manifestations. Instead, the authors ask the reader only to allow the Sage room to speak, and then to let his own experience lead him from there. In their now-famous set of interviews from the late 1980's, Joseph Campbell and Bill Moyers had an exchange that highlights this point. Moyers asked Campbell to describe his faith, and Campbell answered that he didn't have any—he had no need of it. Moyers leaned backward in surprise. Campbell explained: "I don't need faith because I've had these experiences—when you have the experience of this so-called mysticism, then what do you need faith for? Faith is belief placed beyond the reach of experience, and you don't really need that."

So the Sage asks that, as we consult the oracle, we loosen our grip on our cherished beliefs and relax our preconceptions about what is real and what is not; if we come to the I Ching with this minimal bit of inner preparation, then its lessons will move deeply and resonantly within us. From that point, we are encouraged to "undertake something"—that is, to progressively clear our own inner space of the detritus of culture, belief, institutional adherence, and the rigidity of prejudice in all its forms. The experiences that follow upon this work serve to deepen or strengthen the suspension of judgment, so that there is a refreshing diminishment of conscious effort involved in thought, speech and action. There is no feeling of attainment, enlightenment, or belief, but only of trust—trust in a process of inner disburdenment, a lightening of the load, that seems to further itself, the more it is practiced. This is the process through which the natural self, and the Helpers that accompany its movement through life and time, appear and are liberated. To the extent that it is allowed to unfold, the natural innocence described in Hexagram 25 is felt to arise, and then the awareness of beauty, the attraction of Nature, the fulfillment of sexuality, and the grateful recognition of life, and even of death's place within the web of life, become denuded of mystery and are no longer the self-conscious conundrums of the tortured intellect.

This new I Ching, then, is an eminently practical oracle, designed to provide the benefit that an oracle should give people: information—that is, cosmically valid responses to sincerely felt questions — that people can really use to gain insight into their own lives, their relationships, and into the life of the Cosmos. An oracle has to be fluid in order to consistently accomplish its helping purpose. It is meant to reflect the consciousness of the inquirer and his moment, with an added perspective that reaches beyond the seeker's ego. If the person approaching the oracle is too weighted with his ego's ballast, too rigid in his inner movement, then there is often nothing for it but to allow him his delusion, in the hope that it will bring him back again, more humble and receptive. This is how the Sage deals with our own arrogance in approaching it, and it is how we are meant to encounter ego-encroachments, such as intolerance, in our own lives: by saying the "inner No," and turning away, thereby depriving the ego of the energy that it would gain through arousing our emotional responses—the energy that is behind all enmity, hostility, and combat. The path of the "inner No" is described in this volume as a conscious negation of, and withdrawal from, deceit, misunderstanding, intolerance, and encroachment, based on the encompassing perspective and insight that the oracle provides. This inner No has the effect of directing and informing outer action, and of transforming life situations from the rigidities of position-taking and global castigation, toward balanced and constructive relationships. In this respect, this new I Ching is a psychological document of considerable depth and utility.

But how does the inner No work? Once again, the answer is to be found in the social attribution, contrasted with what Chomsky[2] might call the "deep structure" of the word. The dictionary defines "no" as a denial or refusal; a negative reply. The inner No is this, and something else besides. It is a casting-off, an overthrow, done firmly and with an indomitable inner energy, as if Atlas were to suddenly drop his burden; it is a depth-rejection of all that is distorted, oppressive, destructive. It has the force and focus of a primal scream, or of John the Baptist's "voice crying out in the wilderness." But it is neither of these: it

---

[2] Noam Chomsky, *Language and Responsibility* (1979), Chapter 8, in *On Language*. Chomsky's concept of deep structure, part of his "transformational grammar," helps to explain the deeper meanings that underlie the surface structures of words, phrases, or sentences.

is, instead, a silent retreat, a movement away. It is neither flight nor evasiveness, but an inner act of staring evil in the face and denying it any Cosmic validity, any objective reality. The inner No is anything but passive; indeed, it is a weapon of a sort, and therefore should be treated with the care and circumspection that a weapon deserves. The oracle, as it is presented in this book, has the capacity to show us how, where, when, and in what direction to apply the inner No. In this context, it is worth remembering that an oracle is not meant to be a toy or a parlor game. It is a guide to inner action, a source of that clarity from which outer action can flow like water.

The efficacy and strength of the inner No are drawn from the combined energies of the total organism. This cumulative energy is the entity that the authors of this book call the will. The will, when aligned with all the inner senses, moves us effortlessly in the direction of our natural destiny. It thus bridges our thinking consciousness with the feeling-consciousness of our inner senses. Even in our own reductive and analytical culture, deep veins of feeling-consciousness course through our experience and our language. We talk of a person's "radar;" we wonder whether someone "has eyes in the back of his head;" we smell a rat, we play a hunch, we follow our nose, we get a gut-feeling, we taste something fishy, we know when something sounds good, or feels wrong — even (or especially) when there is no apparent logic or evidence to support us. We will even say that "something doesn't add up," when there is not a trace of mathematical reasoning appropriate to the situation. Unfortunately, we will often (especially as children) allow ourselves to be pressured into repudiating our feeling-sense, whenever we are confronted with the injunction to "be reasonable."

But an oracle cannot "be reasonable;" it must work past the props and defenses of that evolutionary adolescent, the intellect. An oracle must cross the moat of logic and reach the inner poet that resides, perhaps repressed but nonetheless alive, within all of us. The I Ching helps us tune into our feeling consciousness through imagery and metaphor, and this, we find, is the path of clarity, of both strength and tolerance, of gentle humor, and of love. We understand this at a deep level, and this is why we often come to the oracle when reason, logic, and all the hierarchies of thought and action have failed us and left our ego-self frozen in confusion and dread. We are most likely to open the inner ear to the voice of the Sage at the very moment when we become dimly aware of our urgent need to recover an essential aspect of our very nature, which has become so buried in the dust of deceit and erudition that we feel suffocated: gasping for breath in a stark and arid inner landscape. At such a moment, the voice of the Sage reverberates, deeply and resonantly, revealing our errors without the encumbrance of guilt; providing perspective, help, and sustenance; drawing us back into relationship with ourselves, our planet, Nature, and the Cosmos.

How often have you heard it said on TV, or seen it written in a magazine article, that we use only 5% or 10% of our brains? And how often, in encountering such news, have you automatically translated that into "we use only 5% or 10% of our intellects"? Indeed, it may be partially true at that level: but if we do misuse our brains, perhaps it's because we push our thinking minds out onto the stage of life, completely alone and without help—without the benefit of the intuitive, feeling, and noumenal capacities of our inner nature—capacities that are nascent within the very same skull that houses the intellect. The insight of the Sage, as transmitted in this volume, is that the process of freeing these manifold inner abilities and the Helpers that animate them has the effect of disburdening and liberating the intellect itself, so that it can perform its proper supportive function in the psyche, without the isolating glare of primacy and the weight of expectation.

What then is the true function of the intellect within a harmonious cooperation between all the functions of the psyche? It is to form words based on feelings, to give verbal expression to our intuitions rather than to our fantasies, and to fill us with the joy that comes from calling things by their true names. Krishnamurti had a similar insight, when he described an intellect that has isolated itself from the rest of the psyche:

"So thought is always limited; it can imagine the immeasurable, it can invent all the gods on the earth, all the rituals, all that business, which is extraordinarily unreal. So thought can never be free, or thought can never bring about a sense of being totally free. Right? I wonder if you understand this. Because thought itself is limited, and therefore whatever it does will still be limited."(1984)

I Ching, The Oracle of the Cosmic Way is, in part, a manual for a revolution within the psyche. It teaches that we can overthrow the petty tyranny of an isolated intellect and restore the natural balance and total energy of the psyche, through a process of insight (identifying, with the help of the Sage, the manifestations of the collective ego within one's own personal ego) and resolution (discovering avenues of liberation from the inner grip of ego). The reader will find this process consistently, and often iteratively, expressed throughout the text; he will also notice that the Sage varies the inner flavor of the message from one hexagram to the next, as peculiar aspects of the Cosmic teaching are revealed in the lantern-light's passage over the shifts and contours of the mottled landscape.

The most distinct practical instrument in this process is the retrospective three coin method, perhaps familiar to the readers of Ms. Anthony's two most recent books. It allows the reader to clarify the texts received and thereby avoid becoming the victim of his own projections. The "*rtcm*," as this method is called, challenges us to look at our deeply-held belief systems, and to open our minds to understanding the many new conceptualizations of psychological phenomena contained in this volume. The *rtcm* offers a fresh perspective and a broader scope for the application of the I Ching to the problems and questions of our daily lives. Once again, the "suspension of judgment" is a crucial preparation for working with the *rtcm*. The reader is asked to open his mind to the possibility that the oracle can speak directly to his specific questions and situations, and then to allow his own experience to lead him further. It is simply a matter of allowing the Sage to speak personally, and of becoming practiced in forming one's questions from a position of inner balance.

The I Ching here presented is a marvelous tapestry of insight and guidance, which goes far beyond mere divination. Those who approach this evolution of the oracle with the expectation of "seeing their future" will be initially disappointed; but if they will work with the Sage and the Helpers whose presences inform the text, these readers will discover a practical source of understanding that surpasses any advantage to be gained from fortune telling and its egotistical projection of a predetermined future. In this respect, perhaps what needs to be clearly stated is that the I Ching's *raison d'etre* is to direct us toward the Helpers that aid us in creating our future in harmony with the Cosmic Way—a future that is correct for each of us, rather than giving us the lowdown on some deterministic train of events that is to transpire.

But if the future cannot be foreseen, the present can be transformed. This I Ching teaches that transformation can become a daily and burgeoning experience in the life of anyone who approaches it with an open mind and a sincere heart. For every person who is moved by this book to undertake the inner journey, to initiate the inner examination, to ask himself the critical questions: "am I living for myself, or for some image, group, idea or commandment from outside myself, and is it worth going on like this?"—for every such person who is started on the path of transformation through his own unique and personal experience with the Sage, there will be that much more of the Cosmic Harmony realized in our species and our planet.

Brian Donohue

Acknowledgments

We thank from our hearts our editor, Brian Donohue, who commented substantively on the text; his humor and insights made the editing particularly enjoyable. He has further graced our book with a wonderful foreword. We also thank Gabriele Wilson for her beautiful cover design. We are grateful to Jose Cedillos, Ph.D., Professor of Creativity and Consciousness Studies, The Graduate College, Union Institute, for his commentary and review of our book. Helpful critique and further encouragement came from Ruth Smith, Associate Professor of Religious Studies, Worcester Polytechnical Institute. Great help was received from Vivian Ling, former chairperson of the East Asian Studies Program of Oberlin College, in clarifying certain Chinese cultural and historical issues. Essential encouragement came from members of our seminars who shared their successes in using the methods we describe in this book.

Carol Anthony and Hanna Moog

Part I

Introduction to the Cosmic Way

Why a New Version of the *I Ching*?

The idea of writing a new version of the *I Ching* would never have occurred to either of us. The fact is, it "grew" from our daily consultations of the *I Ching* after we joined forces, in 1998.

To that point, each of us had been using a method of consulting the *I Ching* that Carol had discovered in 1994. This method grew out of her feeling that the *I Ching* developed from a more basic system that resembles our modern practice of tossing a single coin to decide which team goes to bat first in a ball game. The head side, taken as positive, was interpreted as Yes, the tail side as No; this is the basis of the two kinds of lines that make up the whole *I Ching*: a straight line (—), and a broken line (--).

Carol regarded the method as reflecting the affirmation or negation of the Cosmos. Tossing one coin was enough, but tossing three coins had the advantage of offering a "wholehearted" Yes (three heads), a "basic" Yes (two heads), a basic No (two tails), and a definite No (three tails). We have called this method the "retrospective three-coin method," or "*rtcm*." (See p. 736, Using the Retrospective Three-Coin Method.)

Carol had used this method to ask the Sage, the voice that speaks through the *I Ching*, for clarification when a hexagram seemed particularly puzzling, by asking "Are you saying this..." or "that...?" and putting forth a reasonable hypothesis. When she discovered what it was actually saying, it was often different from what she expected, but always she was led to a new and amazing insight. None of the new insights contradicted each other, but formed what in time became a visible logic that is based on harmony as its guiding principle. The Sage made us aware (through the *rtcm*), that the name for this logic is *Cosmic Logic*. Carol soon realized that in this more or less "accidental" way, a new method of consulting had opened, by which the Sage could speak for itself. It was clear that the Sage, normally confined to a few words of set text, wanted to reply in words of its own, and in a relevance to her everyday life. After practicing this new method for awhile, she picked up ten coins and tossed them, asking, "Is this a legitimate way of determining the answers?" Nine of them came up Yes. From that time on, she regularly used it, and shared this new method with friends, including Hanna.

After both Hanna and Carol began working as associates in Anthony Publishing in 1998, the process of learning new interpretations of the hexagrams with the help of the *rtcm* took giant steps. Our different backgrounds produced a much broader range of questions. After six months, we had collected so many new interpretations of the hexagrams and lines, that we were impelled to ask the Sage, "are we actually collecting material for a new version of the *I Ching*?" The reply was "Yes, Yes, Yes." To us, that seemed to be followed by an exclamation point. Four years later, we have produced this first edition. No doubt, additions will be made in subsequent years because all learning occurs in hand-holds that lead to ever larger understandings. It is like climbing up a rock face, with each handhold not being the final one, but the basis for climbing even higher and having a bigger view. This is not to imply that the Cosmic Principles of Harmony on which the Cosmic Order is based will change. Learning by hand-holds simply means that humans cannot develop a definitive knowledge of the Cosmos, because, as we have learned, the Cosmos itself is constantly evolving.

What we have been led to understand, through this wonderfully patient entity we call the Sage that speaks through the *I Ching*, is a vastly enlarged view of the Cosmos and its ways. In the process of this communication, we have felt the intensely caring, loving, and nourishing energy the Chinese have called *chi*, meaning life-force, but which we also realize, is love.

The Sage that speaks through the *I Ching* is the voice of the Cosmic Teacher. It speaks for the aggregate consciousness of the Cosmic Whole, which in this volume we call the *Cosmic Consciousness*. We were to learn that everything that exists *in form* is compressed consciousness, and thus is an individualized aspect of the Cosmic Whole.

To fully grasp these realizations, it was necessary that we abandon all the reductionist views we had grown up with. The Cosmic Consciousness, or consciousness of the whole, is comparable to our personal consciousness as the aggregate consciousness of every cell in our bodies. We were guided to understand that just as when we look at a grain of sand and see it as stationary, we cannot see that in its atomic structure something is moving at enormous speeds; in the same way we cannot imagine that a grain of sand also has consciousness. In part, this is due to the very limited idea we have of consciousness. Consciousness, in the larger sense we have been guided to see, includes kinds of awareness we are incapable of imagining. (*See* the explanations given of the *eight trigrams*, below.) Furthermore, we were to understand that although the Cosmic Consciousness can think, assimilate, coordinate thought, and understand, it is nevertheless primarily a *feeling* consciousness.

Greater than the sum of its visible parts, the Cosmos was shown to us to include an invisible side that is constantly busy nourishing and helping all the things it generates into form. We refer to this invisible side throughout this volume as the *invisible* or *inner world*. The helping aspects that reside in the invisible sphere of consciousness have been anonymously called "Helpers" throughout the traditional *I Ching*, and unfortunately, over the centuries, have been interpreted to be "humans of ability." The Sage, one of those Helpers, which has identified itself to us as the teaching aspect of the Cosmic Consciousness, has several other functions which are described in this volume. A myriad of other kinds of Helpers exist which we have been led to identify by their *functions*. People who have experienced their help have often imagined them to be angels or fairies, or such, but we were guided away from seeing them in any such forms, for reasons which will become obvious later in this text. We have also called the invisible realm the "inner world," because it is perceptible only through our inner senses, as in meditation.

We were led to see that while the Cosmic Consciousness "knows" all things, it does not set itself above and apart from all the things which are its myriad aspects. This view was echoed by Lao Tzu in his description of the Tao (the Way of the Cosmos):

The Great Tao is universal like a flood.
How can it be turned to the right or to the left?

3

All creatures depend on it,
And it denies nothing to anyone.

It does its work,
But it makes no claims for itself.

It clothes and feeds all,
But it does not lord it over them:
Thus, it may be called "the Little."

All things return to it as to their home,
But it does not lord it over them:
Thus, it may be called "the Great."

It is just because it does not wish to be great
That its greatness is fully realized. (Verse 34)*

How this Book Came to Be

To a certain extent this book is based on the work of Richard Wilhelm, whose work we highly respect. It was he who had given the ancient document the background interpretations that enabled it to act as a viable oracle for Westerners. Perhaps its usability was due to the fact that Wilhelm, who was familiar with modern psychoanalysis, recognized the *I Ching*'s ability to reflect the subconscious. It was on this ground that he introduced it to his friend, Carl G. Jung, the Swiss psychoanalyst. Jung's famous foreword to the English translation by Cary F. Baynes, helped to bring the book to the attention of the Western world.**

As mentioned before, our putting questions to the Sage with the *rtcm*, addressed the many contradictions found in that text. We realized that these contradictions were not due to Wilhelm's

---

* *Tao Teh Ching*, translated by Dr. John C.H. Wu (St. John's University Press, New York, 1961).
** The *I Ching* or Book of Changes, The Richard Wilhelm Translation rendered into English by Cary F. Baynes (Princeton University Press, 1961). The original German translation was published under the title: I Ging, Das Buch der Wandlungen, aus dem Chinesischen übertragen und hrsg. von Richard Wilhelm (Eugen Diederichs Verlag, Munich, 1956).

work, but to the differences that constitute two layers of text in the book that had been merged into one. We came to see these two layers as the "oracle layer" and the "feudal layer."

For Carol the idea of "writing" a new version of the *I Ching* produced qualms, especially since many of Wilhelm's commentaries would be left behind. "I was attached to the Wilhelm translation, having credited it for making the *I Ching* accessible to me in the first place. I still liked so many things about it. I also felt it presumptuous to overturn anything so ancient. Who, after all, were we? Then one morning I awoke with two words coming into my mind. They were the German word 'uralt' and the English word 'exalt.' The German prefix 'ur' means 'origin' or 'beginning,' while 'alt' means 'old.' As I contemplated these words, an associated thought came to mind: that I was exalting what was ancient only because it was ancient. This made me realize that I had internalized a taboo against questioning what has been called, "the wisdom of the ancients," and this was creating resistance in our progress. Asking the Sage if I understood the problem correctly, this was confirmed. I was to learn that I needed to question everything, and allow the Sage to answer what in the traditional version was correct and what was not."

With Carol's qualms behind us, the underlying philosophy of the *I Ching* as the Cosmic Way began to show itself, as we were led in a zigzag fashion through the 64 hexagrams. As learning from the Sage means learning through experience, our lessons were always related to our daily life, and included questions of national and world importance. We were amazed to see in how many different ways a hexagram could be read depending on the particular circumstance. By using the *rtcm*, in addition to *I Ching* meditation and paying attention to our dreams, we experienced that we no sooner put all the pieces of a puzzle together than the boundary of the picture would be enlarged by the Sage. It was not unlike Aristotle's science giving way to Newton's, and Newton's perception giving way to Einstein's.

Now that this new book is finished, we can see how our individual experiences have been used by the Sage to prepare us for this task. Both of us had come to the *I Ching* at times of crises in our lives, but the kinds of questions we put to it were quite different. This fact stimulated many insights.

Carol began consulting the *I Ching* in 1971, during a time of intense anxiety. She found it spoke to something in her that was beyond words and reason, giving her a restorative kind of nourishment she did not even know she needed, but for which she was desperately starved. The help was immediate, leading her right away to learn how to meditate. Meditation, in turn, helped her understand in a more comprehensive way, what the *I Ching*'s messages were trying to tell her. Her understandings were later published in *A Guide to the I Ching* (1980), *The Philosophy of the I Ching* (1981), *The Other Way, Meditation Experiences Based on the I Ching* (1990), and *Love, An Inner Connection, Based on Principles Drawn from the I Ching* (1994).

Shortly after the last book was published, Carol realized that wherever the *I Ching* recommends action, it meant inner action, and that by and large, inner action means saying the inner No to ego-behavior wherever it exists, either in oneself or in others. This was what the *I Ching* meant by "persevering in what is correct." This understanding resolved contradictions she frequently encountered in its use, which often seemed to recommend acceptance and passivity, but just as often recommended some sort of action. The behavior that was unacceptable and required saying the inner No to, was behavior that encroached, was insensitive, insincere, unjust, or uncaring. She also found that when she was firm and consistent in saying the inner No to what was incorrect, outer action was not needed. All difficulty in relationships was seen to come in those areas where this inner boundary was not clearly defined in her own mind.

The discovery of the inner No was the result of being led by the *I Ching* to recognize the boundaries each person must have in a love relationship, for the relationship to achieve duration. These boundaries were connected with another subject iterated many times in the *I Ching*, that a person's respect for his own dignity is the very basis on which the love relationship is made possible. Carol had found the model for the love relationship in her studies with the Sage. The inner No was to be applied only to the ego, as a way of helping either one's own true self, or another's, to become free of the ego's dominance. Saying it inwardly had the advantage of not arousing the ego's resistance, and of not causing the other to lose face.

During the next years she was to learn how the inner No was to be applied in all sorts of new situations, so that when she began to work with Hanna Moog after 1998, she felt fully ready to write a new book on the inner No.

Hanna Moog, from Germany, came to the *I Ching* in 1982 during a personal crisis. Although she had no one to teach her the *I Ching*, she allowed it to speak to her feelings. "I was deeply touched by its answers. I realized that no human being would have been able to characterize, as it did, my desperate situation so perfectly. At the same time, it gave me the deep certainty that there was something good in my life waiting to be discovered...something that meant growth, and a new kind of life; something that would truly fulfill me." Although she had a master's degree in Economics and Business Administration, and diplomas in French and English, she asked the Cosmos to be shown her true vocation.

With the Richard Wilhelm translation of the *I Ching* in her backpack, Hanna went on a four month hiking tour to the Canary Islands, hoping to return to Germany with an idea of what that vocation would be. She soon discovered that this expectation was a bigger weight than the backpack itself, causing her to blame herself almost daily for not yet having found out the answer to what she would do once she returned. After three months, she noticed a sudden change: the pressure was gone! Her first reaction was alarm: had she turned into a social "drop out?" On examining her feelings, however, she realized that something had grown in her center that had not been there before. This something was a trust in the "unknown." It had grown, day by day, as she had coped with being all by herself in a Spanish-speaking country, and had felt guided by something for which she did not have a name, but which definitely was of a caring and benevolent nature. She had been consulting the *I Ching* daily, often only getting a glimpse of what it was saying, but keeping her mind open so that a deeper understanding could take place afterwards. That was her way of learning what the hexagrams were saying, through experience.

This sincere approach to the *I Ching* led to her being asked, upon returning from her trip, to write an article about her "Journey with the *I Ching*" in a book called *Erfahrungen mit dem I Ging* (Experiences with the *I Ching*) (Diederichs). The book was compiled by Ulf Diederichs, head of the German publishing house, Diederichs Verlag, that had first published the Richard Wilhelm translation of the *I Ching* in 1924. Soon afterward, Hanna was interviewed for a film about the *I Ching* by the West German Television. Her dedication to it began to open more and more doors of speaking and writing about the *I Ching* and her experiences with it. In 1985 she was asked to become a free lance editor for Diederichs Verlag, with a special emphasis in the fields of *I Ching*, Asian philosophy and religion, mythology and fairy tales. Four years later she had an extraordinary dream that clearly showed her that the *I Ching* itself was the vocation she had asked to be shown. She also understood that the dream was encouraging her to teach others what she had learned. This marked the beginning of her long-standing activities as an *I Ching* teacher, giving lectures and seminars all over Germany, Austria, and Switzerland. She also composed a radio feature on the *I Ching* and authored two books on the subject: *I Ging, Das Orakel- und Weisheitsbuch Chinas,* (*I Ching*, The Oracle and Wisdom Book of China) (Knaur, 1994) and *Leben mit dem I Ging, Erfahrungen aus Kunst, Therapie, Beruf und Alltag* (Living with the *I Ching*, Experiences in the Arts, Therapy, Professional and Everyday Life) (Diederichs, 1996).

In 1988, Hanna Moog became aware of Carol Anthony's first two books, *A Guide to the I Ching,* and *A Philosophy of the I Ching.* She particularly liked the fact that Carol, from her personal experiences with the *I Ching*, had found a way to interpret the hexagrams in psychological terms and to render them into a contemporary language. She convinced Diederichs Verlag that Carol's books were an essential addition to their *I Ching* program, and soon found herself translating them into German. It was through Carol's books that Hanna became consciously aware of the existence of a "Sage" that apparently spoke through the *I Ching* and had shown itself in several of Carol's meditations. There was only one thing that bothered Hanna:

that Carol was referring to the Sage as "he." At that time, Hanna was deeply involved with matriarchal mythology; in search of her roots as a woman, she could not readily accept that wisdom was connected with the image of a male being. She shared this concern with Carol asking her what she thought about that. Carol's reply was that while the Sage had always shown himself in meditations as a male, her husband, in his meditations, had experienced the Sage as a woman. From that time on, the correspondence between Hanna and Carol went back and forth, each infusing the other with new discoveries. It is this inquisitive attitude and her ever open mind that finally led to Hanna's moving to the United States and joining forces with Carol, in 1998.

The more we were given, through using the *rtcm*, new interpretations of the original texts of The Judgment and The Lines, the more we wondered how it was that no one had ever discovered such a method before, that would allow the Sage which speaks through the oracle, to say how it wanted the hexagrams and lines to be interpreted. But even as we thought about this, we realized how such questioning has been prevented by the encrustation of taboos that have surrounded it, which also have made it increasingly inaccessible and confusing.

In learning from the Sage through this new method, the differences were continuously pointed out between the original oracle text and the feudal layer that had been superimposed upon it. Also, the Sage constantly focused on what humans have spoiled through their pretensions of being at the center of the universe. The backside of this belief—that humans must "do it all," we discovered, has manifested in many forms of illness, depression, and a depleted will to live. We experienced, first with ourselves and then with others, that when people find, with the help of the Sage, the mistaken ideas they hold, and deprogram them, their health is restored.

For this new version of the *I Ching*, we were guided to keep most of the original hexagram names, and the texts of The Judgment and The Lines. This was because due to their metaphorical language, they have mostly preserved the original oracle meanings. We were to disregard the texts called The Image because these texts are based on dividing people into superior and inferior, although in a few instances, we were guided to include material from the commentaries.

When we began to see that it was the feudal overlay that contradicted the basic oracle text, we thought we were being shown something that needed to be removed. But in lesson after lesson, we were made aware how much we were holding ideas and beliefs about the Cosmic Way that actually came from the feudal mindset, without our having been aware of it. The Sage wanted us to retain the evidence of the feudal thinking within the *I Ching* because it presents all the false assumptions about the nature of the Cosmos and its ways, that have been taken for granted worldwide. This catalogue of mistaken ideas is essential to making people aware that these ideas remain yet today as a feudal mindset that guides our thinking. It is this litany of ideas that has separated us from the Cosmic Whole, and the love and help that are available from the Cosmos. Reunification with the Cosmic Whole, which is the entire purpose of the *I Ching*, is attained through systematically freeing ourselves of the presumptions implicit in feudal thinking.

To give an example, we were shown that in looking up to the Sage as some sort of higher power, we were acting from a feudal mindset which takes for granted that any entity that knows more than we do is automatically higher. Looking up to the Sage, we learned, not only erected a false distance between the Sage and ourselves, it actually hid the loving nature of the Sage behind a veil. At the same time, we were putting down our own intrinsic worth and dignity, something no human being is meant to do.

We were led to see, with considerable surprise, that our own culture possesses the same feudal mindset that has dominated the planet for the last 3,000 years. Once initiated, it has perpetuated itself through safeguards that keep its contradictions from being questioned. We have also not questioned it, because we have never known any other way of thinking, and have therefore found it difficult to step outside its boundaries, to see it objectively. In our sessions with the Sage, we were guided to understand the basic Cosmic Principles that maintain and restore harmony in life. In the light of these principles we began to gain an entirely new view of our place in the Cosmos. This included understanding what our true natures are like, and realizing that there is such a thing as a natural social order.

We have tried to make this volume a book of "signposts" to help the *I Ching* user liberate his true nature from the prisons of the feudal mindset. We have also tried to make it a book that would enable each person to access the Sage directly, without anyone being needed to interpret it for him, or stand as his guide. We learned that the student of the Sage does not need special knowledge, or special talents to understand the oracle, because the Sage knows how to communicate with every person, according to the way he understands, be it through verbal or non-verbal means. The *rtcm* will enable him to determine whether he has correctly understood or not.

A final word needs to be said about the gender issue. We have used the male pronoun throughout this book wherever "person" preceded it, to avoid the incessant awkwardness and tediousness of "he/she...." The fact that a fluent use of language makes it impossible to refer to both genders simultaneously is unfortunate, since it forces us to speak either in a male or female dominated way. We felt that using "he" was less jarring than "she" would have been, because it would avoid emphasizing the feminine over the masculine, which would have been just as unfortunate. The reader's prejudices will be challenged enough by this book. Certainly, the real issues described herein lie beyond the gender issue.

Even though the feudal mindset is basically patriarchal and obviously male-dominated, we have avoided the obvious construction "man-centered view of the universe." We believe it needs to be recognized that the conditioning which creates the feudal mindset, which puts humans up as special over all the other species and things, is often embraced as much by females as by males. The competition between males and females as to which gender is superior is simply an extension of this fundamentally flawed feudal viewpoint.

The *I Ching* as a Book of Philosophy About the Cosmic Way

The entire *I Ching* is comprised of the answers of the oracle to human questions about what is in harmony with the Cosmos, and what is not. The answers were communicated to the recipients as a basic Yes to what was in harmony with the Cosmic Way, and a basic No to what was not in harmony with it. Thus the philosophy written within the *I Ching* developed from human thought about life *as it was put to the test of the oracle.* What emerged originally from this communication was a view of the Cosmos as a system of harmony which benefits everything that thinks and acts in accord with it, while reacting with Fate (adversity) to all that sets itself in opposition to that harmony. Being in harmony was expressed throughout the *I Ching* by the words "good fortune" and "success," whereas thinking and acting in ways that were discordant had the prognosis of "misfortune," or "remorse."

However, over the centuries, the oracle came to be overwritten, particularly by scholars of the Confucian school, who subjected it to what Joseph Campbell called "a forest of pencils."* Their overwriting added many contradictions to the *I Ching* text. These additions reflected the man-made order and the values of feudalism.

This new version of the *I Ching* is radically different from the traditional versions, in that the contradictions created by this overwriting, have been identified and separated from the oracle text. The manner in which this was done, was through consulting the Sage, using the *rtcm*, as to what the Cosmic meanings of the hexagrams were. The Sage has helped us to clearly identify the ideas and language of the feudal mindset that characterized ancient China, but which have also been carried over to most of today's cultures. This mindset differs sharply from the Cos-

---

* "...all of the myths (or rather, as we now have them, moralizing anecdotes) of the Chinese golden age have to be recognized as the productions rather of a Confucian forest of pencils than of any 'good earth' or 'forest primeval.'" "Oriental Mythology: The Masks of God" by Joseph Campbell (New York, Viking Penguin, 1962), p. 380.

mic view illustrated in the various hexagrams. The advantage for the reader who learns how to use the new method of communicating with the Sage, is that he can verify for himself whether the Cosmic view we have shown here, is correctly rendered. (*See* p. 736, Using the Retrospective-Three-Coin Method, or *rtcm*.) For our part, we have used this method to check nearly every line and word, as to whether we were communicating the Sage's message correctly.

This version of the *I Ching*, then, is the result of four years of asking thousands of questions. Our questioning followed one principle: were we understanding it correctly? When the answer was often No, we continued questioning until it responded that we had understood correctly. The answers corrected and enlarged the text. In regard to the two primary hexagrams, 1 and 2, it gave us a completely new understanding. It also explained why they, as written, contained misconceptions, and how these misconceptions had come about. It showed us how they are the very same misconceptions that are found in the major world philosophies, and to some extent, in the major world religions.

It removed from our own minds misunderstandings that have stood in the way of our finding, exploring, and developing the wonders of our own natures. Our impression grew that it wanted to liberate us, and humans generally, from the mindset of the "young fool," which reflects our training to be shepherded throughout life by human authorities, to help us grow up into fully responsible, fully realized beings.

Despite all our sincere intentions, the nature of communicating with the oracle is such that however many questions one asks, and however careful one is to clarify to the best of one's ability the answers, there remain always some key questions one has failed to ask: questions that are not yet within one's grasp. As we went along, we believe we became more skilled in asking these, but as the student of the Sage grows in his perspective, the questions he asks are always from this new platform of understanding. Important unasked questions will certainly occur to one or another reader. He now has in his grasp the same methods we have used, to ask his own questions.

The Human-Centered View Superimposed upon the Cosmos

In its first *complete written* form the *I Ching* dates back to King Wen in 1100 B.C. Extensive commentaries were added over the centuries that followed by the Confucian scholars and commentators. It is considered as historic fact that the *I Ching* was subjected to numerous attempts to adapt it to the ideologies of the various feudal regimes.

These ruling ideologies were consistent in two things: that the Cosmic Order was like their own feudal order, hierarchical in structure, and that humans are at the center of all things. These views are spelled out particularly in the traditional versions of Hexagram 11, *Peace*, and Hexagram 37, *The Family*. Hexagram 11 describes the Cosmic Order as "the order of heaven," in which heaven is above, earth below, and man is at the center. This view further "authorized" the Emperor, as the Son of Heaven, as the one designated to bring heaven's order to the earth. Hexagram 37, *The Family*, describes the family as having a hierarchical ordering, with the father at the head, in the place of the ruler, and each member taking his "proper" place below. It further describes how the family is "society in embryo," in spelling out the proper relationships between humans.

As will become obvious from the descriptions of the harmonious order of the Cosmos, this human-centered view of the universe is the cause of human separation from the Cosmic Whole, because it negates the entire invisible world of the Cosmic Consciousness, as well as the equality, worth, and dignity of *all* things.

In using the new *rtcm* method, we discovered that many of our previous misunderstandings of the text were due to certain words and phrases to which the Sage would not respond. We began to ask, when we were puzzled, "would you prefer that we find a better word?" to which it would often answer Yes. We began to understand that certain words commonly used have no Cosmic basis, because they are inventions of the human-centered view. The same faults were found with certain phrases, so that we needed to find "unpolluted" words and phrases that were suitable to describe Cosmic Reality. We found that the Sage tolerated our use of wrong words for a while, but only until we had learned certain lessons that prepared us to see that their continued use was unsuitable. For example, we asked on one occasion if it was describing a Cosmic law, to which it replied Yes. Later, it indicated that this had only been a handhold until we found a better word, which was "Cosmic Harmonic." The word "law" was to be used only in relation to the Law of Fate, even though Fate is part of the Cosmic Harmonics. The problem with the word law was due to its human-centered implications and authoritarian tonality.

As we progressed, we discovered a Cosmic vocabulary and Cosmic Logic that are entirely different from the logic we now recognize as feudal and authoritarian in background and tone. Indeed, we came to recognize that our search was no longer for the truth, but for the untruths we have been taught. Learning from the Sage has brought us to question especially those things we have been taught not to question, for it was in precisely this area that we found the faulty basic premises and ideas that have separated us from our inner truth, and thereby from our unity with the Cosmos.

In the course of writing this new *I Ching*, we were also made aware of the basic misunderstanding of the attitude the *I Ching* supports, which has been called *wu wei*. *Wu wei* has been interpreted as taking no action, and as enduring and accepting incorrectness in others through endless perseverance with the view that the Cosmos, or time, will make it correct. While it is true that the Sage never counsels a person to counter incorrect situations through overt action, it teaches him to take *inner* action (*wu wei*) and to be "firm and correct." We found this means saying *the inner No* to all transgressions by the ego. (Note, the ego, as defined by the *I Ching*, is not the same as that of Freud or Jung. *See* p. 46, "The Development of the Individual Ego.") The inner No, we learned, engages the help of the Sage and the Helpers of the invisible world, that create change through invisible channels of consciousness.

This brings us to the other major difference between this volume and other versions of the *I Ching*. The name, "*I*," was taken from the Chinese character that has the shape of a chameleon. The chameleon was a metaphor for "changes," "easy changeability," and "the easy." The title, therefore, has been translated as "The Book of Changes." The Sage, however, guided us to understand that the true meaning of "easy changeability" is "transformation," brought about by the invisible Helpers in the atomic realm. Transformation differs from changes in that it is fundamental and enduring. It is clear that the Chinese of the post-Confucian era made little distinction between changes and transformation. Indeed, many of the rivers of thought extracted from the traditional *I Ching* have assumed that changes, in their more superficial or mechanical sense, are what was meant. This meaning, in turn, corresponds to the imperial view that humans are those whose task it is "to bring order to the world" (through changes). (For a more detailed description *see* below: "Transformation versus Changes.")

The Oracle of the Cosmic Way

The *I Ching* is the last viable oracle that has come down to us from ancient times. The Sage drew our attention to two documents that existed prior to King Wen's text, and which may have been oracle systems. These two documents are known as the *Lien Shan*, and the *Kuei Ts'ang*,* and seem to have emphasized the role of "the hidden" as the cause of all things in the apparent world. *Lien Shan* means "two mountains linked together," the word mountain being a metaphor for *form*. The image suggests one form hidden inside another form. Thus, one form is visible while the other is not. This is a description of Nature: it comes in myriad visible forms, with each form being compressed consciousness. This description of Nature parallels our own findings in writing this new *I Ching*. (See Hexagram 2, *Nature*.) The second document, under the title *Kuei Ts'ang*, means "Return to the Hidden." What is hidden is the invisible Cosmic Consciousness that expresses itself in Nature, and which gives rise to all things. (See Hexagram 1, *The Cosmic Consciousness*.) The second document thus seems to have been about the way of return to the Cosmic Consciousness. Together, they could

---

* *See* Wilhelm, p. lviii. We include the mention of these two documents here after inquiring of the Sage as to their contents and purpose.

have shown the *process of transformations* through which the Cosmic Consciousness evolves: from non-form into form, and the return from form into non-form. We can infer that the knowledge contained in these two ancient documents must have undergone numerous changes, when we compare this understanding of the Cosmic Way with that given in the traditional versions of the *I Ching* that have come down to us since the time of King Wen, and especially since the time of Confucius, when it became an accepted imperial (feudal) document.

Looking at the *I Ching* in its graphic form, we find that it expresses itself first of all in a code made up of two kinds of lines: a light, positive line (—) and a dark, negative line (- -). Positive and negative are taken in the sense of the two phases of an electrical circuit. These two lines represent the basic language in which the oracle speaks: a light line representing Yes, meaning harmony with the Cosmos, its blessings and help, and a dark line meaning No, or discord. When a No was obtained, the whole matter was capable of being looked into more thoroughly to find the cause of the disharmony. The goal was then to bring oneself back into harmony with the Cosmos. How this was to be achieved depended, of course, on a correct assessment of the cause of the disharmony.

When we view the *I Ching* as an arrangement of 64 hexagrams, it reflects the Cosmos in its entirety, as having a wonderful order and harmony. The question arises: where is the cause of disharmony to be found?

This question was the subject of a philosophical debate between Confucius and Lao Tzu about human nature and the origin of evil. Lao Tzu held that human nature is wholly innocent and good, and that evil is not in man's nature, but is the result of social conditioning. Confucius is said to have believed, on the one hand, that human nature is born good, and on the other, that it is divided into "higher" and "lower" (animal) parts. He maintained that it was man's animal nature that was the cause of evil, and therefore concluded that to avoid evil, humans needed to "cultivate" their higher nature and tame their lower nature. Confucius therefore defined the virtues a person needed to develop if he was to become "the superior man." Lao Tzu replied that it was not at all a question of "cultivating, cultivating, cultivating," since a person already possesses all the virtues by nature; it was instead a question of subtracting, or "decreasing" all the mistaken ideas he has learned, that have taken him away from his original harmony with the Cosmos. Similarly, the Sage has taught us that returning to harmony with our true natures is to return to unity with the Cosmos, and this entails a process of ridding ourselves of all the mistaken ideas we have learned about ourselves, about life, and about the Cosmos.

In the hidden layer of the traditional *I Ching* text, there are hints that tell us we need to pay attention to the "seeds," while things are still in their beginnings. In another place, we find the statement that one's "words must have substance." And indeed, we were made to realize that all causes of disharmony and of separation from the Cosmic Whole lie in the creation of false words and fantasy images that give rise to mistaken ideas about the Cosmic Way and about human nature. (*See* p. 36, "The Human Gift of Language.")

The Eight Trigrams

The simple code consisting of one light and one dark line, when extended to figures of *three lines*, takes on different meanings. In all their possible combinations, they make up *eight trigrams*. Each trigram expresses a particular aspect of what in this book is called The Cosmic Family. (See Hexagram 37, *The Family*.)

Unlike the feudal model of a human family, which has been superimposed on the original meaning of that hexagram, the Cosmic Family designates different kinds of consciousness which together represent the total Cosmic Consciousness. All of these consciousnesses are feeling consciousnesses, with the exception of two, which are the intuitive and the thinking consciousnesses.

The intuitive consciousness refers to the function of the imaging mind to form images based on the feelings of inner truth. The thinking consciousness is concerned with the formation of words based on images.

Trigram Ch'ien   ☰

The aggregate consciousness of all consciousnesses and their relationships.

Trigram K'un   ☷

The aggregate consciousness of all feeling consciousnesses expressed in form (Nature), and their relationships.

Trigram Kên   ☶

The feeling consciousness of the earth (minerals). Its primary characteristic is non-movement.

Trigram Tui   ☱

The reflective consciousness of still water. As a state of mind, it is necessary for the inspiration described under Chên to occur.

Trigram Chên   ☳

The state of mind in which the Cosmic Consciousness and the individual thinking consciousness meet as inspiration, best described as "mind flashes," and expressed as "Aha!" in Hexagram 51, Shock.

Trigram Sun   ☴

The consciousness of inner truth, which is our memory of what Cosmic Harmony feels like.

Trigram Li   ☲

The intuitive mind and its true function, which consists in forming images based on inner truth, resulting in clarity. (Together with the thinking mind, intuition's function is to learn from inner truth.)

Trigram K'an   ☵

The thinking mind and its true function, which consists in forming words that are based on images formed from the feelings of inner truth.

The last three trigrams describe how feelings are converted first into images, and then into words.

We learned that animals have all of the above-mentioned consciousnesses, in different combinations, which give each species its uniqueness. The unique gift to humans is that they also have a thinking consciousness which is based on words and language.

In all the traditional versions of the *I Ching*, the eight trigrams are said to represent the eight members of a feudal family (father, mother, three sons and three daughters), or eight animals, eight sections in time (eight times three hours making 24 hours), or eight cardinal directions. They have also been taken to represent heaven, earth, water, fire, lake, thunder, mountain and wind. Although some of the analogies taken from Nature can render the feeling that accompanies a particular trigram, such as the feeling of shock that goes with thunder, or the feeling of non-movement that goes with mountain, the feeling of invisible penetration that is typical for wind, the experience of light in connection with fire, and the experience of danger connected with water, other analogies, such as equating the Cosmic Consciousness with heaven, are misleading. For this reason, we did not use these analogies at all.

The hexagram interpretations contained in the traditional versions of the *I Ching* were formed by analyzing the structure of a hexagram and the interactions between its two trigrams. For the new *I Ching*, we were guided to accept the existing texts of *The Judgment* and *The Lines* with only small changes. Our task was not to explain relationships between trigrams, but to show what had been "spoiled" by false interpretations that accumulated over the centuries. Thus, ours has been a task of correcting concepts and meanings, under the direction of the Sage. We were led to remove altogether the section added by the Confucian school called *The Image*, because of its misrepresentation of how aspects of Nature relate to each other, since this was no more than a justification of the feudal mindset and its customs.

An example is *The Image* in Hexagram 8, *Holding Together*. The text of this section reads: "On the earth is water: The image of Holding Together. Thus the kings of antiquity bestowed the different states as fiefs and cultivated friendly relations with the feudal lords." The Cosmic Principle described by this particular hexagram is the principle of attraction that exists between complementary aspects, which principle holds the entire Cosmos together. Another word for this principle is love. By contrast, the principle described in The Image is that of holding a kingdom together through cultivating the relationship between the king and his feudal lords. Hexagram 35, *Progressing*, gives a description of the purpose of such cultivation: it was the feudal lords' task to enforce the king's power over newly gained territories, which were bestowed upon them as fiefs.

In a similar manner as described above, most of The Images in the Wilhelm version of the *I Ching* contain recommendations as how to become a "superior man" by cultivating "superior" values and virtues. The purpose of this cultivation was to suppress the person's true nature, and bring him under the control of the feudal system through encouraging him to develop a flattering self-image.

The Sixty-Four Hexagrams

A hexagram is a six-lined configuration that is the result of pairing two trigrams. When the eight trigrams are paired in all their possible combinations, they make up 64 hexagrams. With the exception of the first two hexagrams, each of the 62 remaining hexagrams describes a Cosmic Harmonic, or Cosmic Principle. Hexagram 1 refers to all Cosmic Harmonics, Hexagram 2 refers only to the Cosmic Harmonics relevant to Nature, including the laws of physics.

Each hexagram has traditionally been given a name. We have been guided by the Sage to use only a particular English translation of the Chinese names because some of the latter do not render the Cosmic meaning of the hexagrams. In a few cases we have given new English names altogether because they provided a more complete context needed to describe the Cosmic Harmonic.

Most hexagrams describe a particular Cosmic Harmonic, as indicated by the names, *Increasing, Returning, Limitation,* and

Holding Together. Some other hexagram names indicate that a particular Cosmic Harmonic has not been understood, as for example, *Youthful Folly, The Abyss, Oppressing/Exhausting,* and *Darkening of the Light.* Each hexagram also contains a sentence or two that pronounces The Judgment. The Judgment is an extension in metaphorical terms of the Cosmic Harmonic that is the theme of that hexagram. Observance of that harmonic always leads to success.

For example, The Judgment of Hexagram 42, *Increasing,* reads, "It furthers one to undertake something. It furthers one to cross the great water." "To cross the great water" is a metaphor frequently used in the *I Ching.* It indicates that before undertaking anything, the person needs to bring his thinking into harmony with the Cosmos. Thus, The Judgment implies the existence of mistaken ideas the person holds, but particularly in regard to what constitutes "increase."

As a Cosmic Harmonic, "increase" is always something that benefits the Cosmic Whole. This implies that the person who is in harmony with the whole also experiences an overall increase in everything he undertakes. A mistaken idea about "increase" is that an increase for one party automatically decreases another. Such thinking comes from the human-centered view that excludes the helping aspects of Nature and the Cosmos as a whole. In this case the mistaken idea blocks the Helper of Increase that would normally further his undertakings to increase the whole.

Each Judgment is accompanied by a commentary. The commentaries in the new *I Ching* make a clear distinction between the Cosmic Harmonic described by each hexagram and the misunderstandings and mistaken ideas that come from the human-centered view of the universe. The commentaries in the traditional versions of the *I Ching* do not make these distinctions, but present the human-centered view of a hexagram's theme as "the way the Cosmos works." Only the metaphors of The Judgment have retained the potential to hint at the different, more hidden meanings that were revealed to us by the Sage.

Metaphors have the advantage of being multidimensional. This makes them suitable to point to the hidden dimension

(Cosmic point of view), as well as being a reference to something in the literal sense. To use the above example: the metaphor of the "great water" can refer to "dangerous ideas," but also to a "dangerous undertaking," the dangers being due to acting from mistaken ideas.

Apart from The Judgment and its commentary, a hexagram also contains brief texts associated with The Lines. Since a hexagram consists of six lines, The Line texts concern six different sub-principles of the Cosmic Harmonic described by that particular hexagram.

Continuing with Hexagram 42 as our example, Line 1 reads: "It furthers one to accomplish great deeds...." The sub-principle addressed here is that the great deeds which achieve duration cannot be accomplished by humans alone; such deeds are always achieved through engaging the helping aspects of the Cosmos which create changes through transformation.

Line 2 reads: "Someone does indeed increase him.... Good fortune." The word "someone" here refers to the Cosmos, from which a person has received an increase of some sort. The sub-principle stated is that all increase comes from the Cosmos.

Line 3 reads: "One is enriched through unfortunate events. No blame, if you are sincere and walk in the middle and report with a seal to the prince." This line refers to a person who has received from the Cosmos what he was attached to having. However, because his motives were not correct, blame was attached and a fate created (the "unfortunate events"). This blame can be extinguished if he is sincere and allows himself to be guided to use the gift in a manner that benefits the Cosmic Whole. "Walking in the middle" means to be in harmony with the Cosmos. "Reporting with a seal...." means that he has to account to the Cosmos by using the gift in a harmonious way, and not for egotistical purposes. The sub-principle explained by this line is that the Cosmos can use "increase" to give a person an opportunity to correct his ideas about the nature of the Cosmos, as when he sees the Cosmos as stingy, or as not giving him what he needs. (For a complete reading of The Lines *see* Part II: The Hexagrams.)

The above example of Hexagram 42, *Increasing*, shows how

important it is to understand the metaphors used in The Judgment and The Lines. When we consider the host of mistaken (because human-centered) ideas that have been written into the classic commentaries on these parts of the text, and which have been taken for granted as true since that time, it is impossible, without the help of the Sage, to find the meanings that refer to the Cosmic Harmonics, and to see with clarity the mistakes that have been written into the text.

Newcomers to the *I Ching* often try to find some consistent system in the way the hexagrams have come to be interpreted. There do exist systems that people have found in contemplating the various lines and trigrams, but they are inconsistent. For example, some hexagrams, such as Hexagram 20, *Seeing*, have taken their interpretations from their appearances. That hexagram was seen to form the shape of a tower that suggested a view over the countryside. This image became as a metaphor for the way we see things generally. Hexagram 23, *Splitting Apart*, likewise took its meaning from the image it presented of a house about to collapse. Another system of interpreting the hexagrams had to do with speculations about the ways the trigrams were thought to relate to each other. This is true, for example, of Hexagrams 11 and 12, and 63 and 64. In Hexagram 11 the trigram thought to represent the earth is above and the trigram thought to represent heaven is below. Their energies are pictured respectively as moving down (earth) and up (heaven) thus "meeting," and coming into harmony; therefore, the meaning was given as "peace." In their opposite configuration in Hexagram 12, their energies were assumed to go in opposite directions and failing to meet, therefore picturing a situation of "standstill." A similar situation was assumed in Hexagrams 63 and 64.

A particular group of twelve hexagrams was seen to mirror a solar calendar of the year. These so-called calendar hexagrams begin with Hexagram 24, Return, just after the winter solstice, when the "entrance of a single light line at the bottom" of five dark lines indicates the beginning of the return of the light. The next five months are represented by hexagrams in which the light is shown as progressively increasing, with light lines being introduced from the bottom, until they culminate in the summer solstice with Hexagram 1, which is composed of six light lines. These hexagrams are 19, 11, 34, and 43. From this point on "dark lines" are seen to be introduced at the bottom, and to "mount upward" starting with Hexagram 44 and proceeding through 33, 12, 20 and 23, until all are dark lines in Hexagram 2, reflecting the winter solstice. Many of the names traditionally given to these hexagrams may be seen to reflect either the increase of the light in the first six, or the increase of the dark in the last six.

The general tendency to view the first six calendar hexagrams as imbued with positive energy, and the second six as imbued with negative energy, has led to the belief in life as an eternal progression of changes, a succession of ups and downs, and of times of prosperity alternating with lean times. These observations have also led to the idea, written into the traditional versions of the *I Ching*, that if the person only waits, times will change. It has also led to the fatalistic view that good times are inevitably followed by bad times. Seeing things in Nature as being subject to an alternation of positive and negative times also led to other false conclusions about Nature, as in seeing the light and the dark as two separate forces that fight each other, with dark "undermining" the light, and light "fighting" the dark. Such a view has tended, as well, to cause people to assume that the misfortunes they experienced were due to some external factor present in Nature. These analogies and conclusions are false, for misfortune is invariably caused by false thinking that sets up a consciousness that is in conflict with the consciousness of the Cosmos.

The light and the dark are two aspects of chi energy, as noted in Hexagrams 1 and 2. They are complementary aspects that interpenetrate each other. This is consistent with what we see in plant life. During the seasons of increasing light, they absorb the light or chi energy, and thereby grow and reproduce. The increasing darkness causes them to store up the chi energy, give off their fruits, and retreat into rest. The dark, throughout this process, is not hostile, but is a part of a natural process, just as sleep is a natural part of a human's 24 hour cycle of time.

Some Standard Metaphors in The Judgments

The texts called The Judgment repeatedly use a number of standard metaphors to indicate what leads to success, within the Cosmic theme of a particular hexagram. The following interpretations of these standard metaphors are by no means comprehensive, but meant to give an approximate sense of their meanings:

It furthers one to see the great man is counsel, first, to recognize that every person is accompanied by the Sage, and second, that one needs to ask the Sage in one's own presence, and also the Sage in the other's presence to intervene in the situation. Doing so enables the two aspects of the Cosmic Sage to communicate with each other, and solve the problem in harmonious ways that cannot be imagined. When a person is dominated by the ego, the Sage in his presence is kept inactive until someone else calls it into action on his behalf. Doing this is important when one is tempted to give up on someone, or to see him as an opponent, an obstruction, or a problem. If one gives up on that person, the Sage remains blocked for him. When called upon, the Sage displaces those aspects of the ego in that person which are active in the situation. Activating the Sage in this manner is also valuable in preparation for group meetings, negotiations, being called to court, and for decision-making.

"The great man" can also be a reference to a person's personal Helper. This Helper is given to the individual person to help him fulfill his destiny, and accompanies him for the entire time he is in a body.

Perseverance furthers is always given in the context found in Hexagram 2, *Nature*, as "the perseverance of a mare." This refers to having a correct cooperation with Nature. When a person acts from sensitivity, what he does is furthered by the Helpers of Nature. The mare is a metaphor for Nature. The context for this metaphor is what a person experiences in successfully working with a mare: it refers to a conscious cooperation of the human with what the horse is able to do, and a conscious cooperation of the horse with the human. This interaction, in a good horseman, becomes a unity of purpose between them, rather than a domination of the human over the animal's will. The interaction is characterized by a sensitivity on the part of the human in regard to the correct limits of what he may do, and the horse's openness to hear and feel what the human is asking her to do.

The metaphor can also refer to the Sage as the horseman and the student as the mare. The Sage is sensitive and caring about what the student is able to learn at a given time, and thus guides him step by step according to his capabilities. This, of course, requires a certain willingness on the part of the student to experience for himself that the Sage is a trustworthy guide. This attitude on the part of the student enables the entire teaching process to be successful. The entire process, of course, requires the student to present himself to the Sage and be available.

It furthers to be firm and correct is counsel for a person to avoid acting outwardly until he has discerned the inner truth of the matter, and what in the matter is harmonious and what is discordant. He then says an inner Yes to what is harmonious, and the inner No to what is discordant. By saying the inner No, he separates from what is discordant and draws to himself what is harmonious, thus bringing about transformation.

Acting inwardly in this way is in contrast to weakly tolerating discordant elements, since doing the latter only gives an inadvertent permission to the persons involved to continue. The same is true when people decide that "nothing can be done about the situation."

It furthers to have somewhere to go is one of those oracular terms that not only says one needs to do something, it implies that one must find the right place to go. It is a way of counseling a person who is experiencing a fate to direct his attention to the right source of help. It does not say it directly, but it means that the person should consult the Sage, because it alone knows the right way to proceed.

The phrase is also a metaphor for distinguishing the ego from the true self and then saying the inner No to all suggestions coming from the ego that say, "you have to do this," or "you have to do that!" In this way a person separates his consciousness from the commands and demands of his ego, hence "goes away from it."

The phrase can also be a reminder that ideas which disparage the body create ill health, and that the person needs to rid himself of those ideas. Doing so will bring him back to unity with himself, and to health.

The great water is a metaphor that can have different meanings, depending on the context. For example, it can stand for the demonic sphere of consciousness created by the false use of language that separates a person from unity with the Cosmic sphere of consciousness; it can therefore represent the dangerous realm into which a person has fallen. It can also indicate a fate a person has created, and in which he is caught. It can also represent fears that project themselves into reality, and prevent him from being in harmony with the Cosmos.

Crossing the great water can stand for the difficult passage a person has to make to shed the ego and find his true self. It can also mean bringing something to completion, such as the unification of two love partners, the completion of a difficult undertaking, or the resolution of a problem or an illness.

Completion cannot take place within the demonic sphere of consciousness, but only in the harmonious consciousness of Nature. The counsel met in several places in the *I Ching*, that "it furthers to cross the great water" is given to make a person aware that he first needs to bring himself into harmony with Nature, by examining the ideas and beliefs he has about it. This may require asking for another hexagram that would point specifically to mistaken ideas or beliefs. The Helper of Transformation is the "vehicle for crossing" mentioned in the commentary to Hexagram 64, *Before Completion*, Line 2. Try as courageously as we may to achieve success all by ourselves, we need these Helpers to complete our effort. It is also the Helper that makes the results endure.

It does not further to cross the great water can be saying that a person's goal is incorrect. It can also refer to a person's belief in the use of power as the correct means to achieve his goal. All use of power comes from the ego. Using power means pressing forward, striving, fighting, arguing, contriving, exercising passive aggression, using leverage, projecting guilt, or any other strategy of the ego. It even includes thoughts of intervening in situations, forcing one's views on others, of taking action, or arguing inwardly with the Sage.

"It does not further to cross the great water" can also indicate that a person is acting from guilt, or from a false sense of duty. It can also refer to a person who has mistaken ideas about Fate, and his trying to cope with his fate on the basis of such mistaken ideas. In another sense, it refers to a person who is trying to deal with conflict within the framework of the idea that there is a "guilty party." Acting on this idea only leads him deeper and deeper into the "water" of conflict that separates him from being in harmony with the Cosmos.

Success, in its Cosmic definition, is undertaking something in cooperation with the Helpers of the invisible world. It also means doing one's share of an undertaking, and then allowing it to be completed by the Helper of Transformation. Doing one's share includes bringing oneself into harmony with the Cosmos. Success also implies that the result has duration.

Good Fortune, in its Cosmic definition, refers to the array of blessings received from the Cosmos by the person who is modest in his attitude.

Misfortune is the result of a person's separation from his true nature, and thereby from the Cosmic Unity. The mention of misfortune is meant to indicate that a person's thoughts or actions are not in harmony with the Cosmic Principles. It is not to be taken as a prediction that something bad will happen regardless of what the person does; it is given as a warning to tell him that he needs to correct his thoughts or attitudes in order to avoid misfortune, which can refer to a fate.

The Purpose of Consulting the Oracle

The *I Ching*, in Hexagram 1, defines the purpose of consulting the oracle in four terms: They are: *Yüan Heng. Li Chên.*

In their extremely condensed form, they describe the four steps of a process. They address the person who wants to undertake something, and before taking action wants to make sure that he is in harmony with the Cosmos.

Step 1: He puts his question, or the matter at hand, to the

Cosmic Consciousness (*Yüan*) that speaks to him through the oracle.

Step 2: The oracle helps him see the inner truth of the matter with clarity (*Heng*), meaning it helps him see whether his motive, attitude, wish, or goal, is in harmony with the whole, or not. The moment of glimpsing the inner truth of the matter is like a mind-flash. It can occur either in the form of an image or in words. This process is one of the meanings of the word "penetrating." It also means "developing a full understanding" in order to bring the inner truth to completion.

Step 3: He brings the inner truth to completion through bringing it into full consciousness and discerning (*Li*) what is favorable and what is unfavorable to do, meaning what is harmonious and what is disharmonious. He says the inner Yes to what is harmonious, and the inner No to what is disharmonious. By saying the inner No he separates from what is disharmonious, draws to himself what is harmonious, and initiates transformation on the inner plane.

Step 4: When one has made a correct discernment, the result is stability and duration (*Chên*).

The *I Ching* is first and foremost an oracle, in that it has the capacity to give a Cosmic response to a person's inner question of concern. The Sage is the Cosmic Teacher that responds. It responds only to the person who is sincere in mind and modest in attitude.

Contrary to what many people expect, the Sage neither makes decisions for the person consulting it, nor predicts a predetermined future. (*See* p. 39, "Success and Misfortune.") We have only occasionally used the term "good fortune" mentioned in traditional versions of the *I Ching*. We use it to mean Cosmic largesse in the form of gifts and help that are desperately needed. We omit it where it would be incorrectly interpreted as good luck coming from chance. When we include it, we specify its meaning in the individual circumstances. We use the term "success" to designate the positive result of having brought oneself into harmony with the Cosmos. We have retained the word "misfortune" because most people correctly associate it as having a definite cause. Misfortune indicates that there are elements either in a person's conscious thinking, or in his subconscious, that are not in harmony with the Cosmic Way, and therefore are creating adversities in his life. The Sage gives counsel on how he can turn his affairs around by correcting his ideas. In helping him achieve success in his daily life, the Sage also teaches the way of the Cosmos.

Just as success is the consequence of a person's being in harmony with his true nature, and therefore with the Cosmos, misfortune is the result of his having separated from his true nature. Success and misfortune, therefore, indicate whether a person's thoughts or actions are in harmony with the Cosmic Principles or not. Misfortune is not to be taken as something that will happen regardless of what he does; it is given to warn him that he needs to correct his thoughts or attitudes in order to avoid misfortune. It is part of our learning experience as humans to make mistakes, therefore the Cosmos does not hold this fact against us, but provides all the help we need to return to unity with the Cosmic Whole. Return into this unity is felt as a wonderful peace of mind; it means being blessed in one's undertakings, finding the love partner who is really suited to one, or returning to good health.

The person, however, who approaches the *I Ching* thinking it will make decisions for him, will be confronted with difficulties in understanding it, because the purpose of the Sage is to help him reach his inner truth, which already knows the answer. If he continues with this mistaken attitude, the answers he receives will not come from the Sage, because it has retreated, but from the ego within himself. The retreat of the Sage is one of the meanings of misfortune. It occurs because the Sage cannot, according to its own principles, communicate with the ego in a person, which is a false element in his psyche.

The Sage that Speaks through the Oracle

Most people begin consulting the *I Ching* with the assumption that they are consulting "a book of ancient wisdom." This assumption has led to a reverence of the book as a text written in stone, which contradicts its very nature as an oracle. An oracle is an alive consciousness that wants to communicate with us in the context of our time and circumstances.

Some people among the ancient Chinese had the correct intuition that there existed an invisible entity that answered through the *I Ching*. In Hexagram 4, *Youthful Folly*, this entity is called "the teacher." This teacher is described as having a certain attitude toward the person consulting the oracle, which is defined in that hexagram: it is patient if the person is modest and unassuming, but it will make him aware that it is about to retreat if he is arrogant and presumptuous. It has a certain personality which always remains true to itself. It surrounds itself with certain limits that define its own dignity, and which it will not breach.

The words of The Judgment of this hexagram have often been taken incorrectly. They read, "It is not I who seek the young fool; the young fool seeks me. At the first oracle I inform him. If he asks two or three times, it is importunity. If he importunes, I give him no information." They have had the correct effect of scaring away people who were insincere in their approach to the Sage, but they have also had the unfortunate effect of giving the sincere student the false impression that he may only ask one question at a time. For some people, this has led to the practice of tossing a hexagram only once a year. This idea totally contradicts the very nature of the *I Ching*, which makes itself available at all times to teach a person who has a sincere desire to understand.

When recognized as an alive, but invisible consciousness, the Sage also appears in meditations and dreams. It often shows in a variety of forms that give clues to its many-faceted characteristics. In one dream, for example, the Sage appeared as a master and a servant simultaneously. This was its way of saying that in the Cosmic scheme of things, there is no difference between a master and a servant. As mentioned earlier, the Sage also may at one time show itself as a male, and at another as a female; at still other times it may appear as an animal, such as a chameleon. This is why we prefer to speak of the Sage in terms of "it."

In giving help, the Sage does not expect that the person should blindly give up his existing ideas and replace them with new ones. By pointing to a particular hexagram, the Sage shows him which Cosmic Harmonic in particular he needs to understand. The term Cosmic Harmonics refers to the principles that, in their totality, cause the Cosmos to function as a harmonious whole. Once a person realizes the Cosmic Principles active in his given situation, he can also see which of his old ideas or beliefs have been in conflict with these principles. Thus the Sage teaches through first bringing clarity. From this clarity, the person can then dispose voluntarily of his mistaken ideas.

In accord with the Cosmic Harmonic of the *equality* of all aspects of the Cosmos, the Sage relates to the student not as a superior, but as an equal with his true self.

As the reader can see, the Sage's way of teaching is in sharp contrast with the authoritarian way he may expect of such a teacher. Unfortunately, people tend to project upon the Sage their previous experiences of teachers, especially if they were punishing or unforgiving, or authoritarian, or as having power over him. They likewise project themselves before such a teacher as dumb and insignificant. Certain hexagrams in this volume mention these mistaken attitudes, to make the student aware that his false view is projecting itself into his relationship with the Sage, and is thus blocking the Sage's ability to communicate with him. They also show how the person can remove the blocks he is creating.

The person approaching the Sage needs to be aware that neither the Sage nor the Cosmos employs power. Only the ego works through power. Moreover, when we suspect the Sage of doing that, the Sage retreats, to maintain its dignity. Then the person only receives answers that do not make sense, or contradict each other. The Sage will return to teach him when he returns to an attitude of openness to be taught about the cause of the Sage's retreat.

The Helpers as the Helping Aspects of the Cosmos

We began to learn about the Helpers in connection with receiving Hexagram 3, *Making a New Beginning.* We came to understand that the text was not referring to humans as Helpers, as has been traditionally interpreted, but to Helpers of the invisible world. These Helpers, depending on their unique functions in the Cosmic Whole and in Nature, are referred to in a number of hexagrams under names such as "a wagon for loading," "a vehicle for crossing the great water," or as "specialists in their fields whom one needs to give a free hand." In other places, the *I Ching* indicates that some Helper is blocked or imprisoned, as in: "his right arm is broken," or "one sees the wagon dragged back, the oxen halted."

Helpers become blocked or imprisoned when a person has forgotten or dismissed their help, or has denied their existence. The Sage brings the Helpers back into our awareness, and helps us free those which have become disabled or imprisoned due to mistaken ideas we have projected on the Cosmos, on Nature, or on our own natures. Their sensitivity to the way we think is due to the fact that the whole Cosmos is consciousness.

Every aspect of Nature is a Helper with a unique function in the overall scheme of things. Thus, we learned that the correct way to name a particular Helper is to name it by its unique function. There are, for example, the Cosmic Doctor and the Cosmic Surgeon, which can be asked to take care of mistaken ideas that act as the spells and poison arrows that cause illness. (For further explanations of spells and poison arrows, *see* below.) In addition, there are the Health Helpers that comprise the self-healing abilities of every aspect of Nature, including our own natures. There is also the Cosmic Banker that directs money to flow in accordance with the Cosmic Harmonics; there are Business Helpers, and Helpers that help us find lost things or something we need, such as a home or a job. There are Helpers of Relationships, and a particular Helper of the Love Relationship. There is also the Cosmic Army that fights violations of the Cosmic Harmonics when asked for its help. The Cosmic Army is composed of bands of Helpers that protect a person from the encroachment of the ego in others, when he brings himself into harmony with the Cosmos.

There are also Helpers of Fate. Their function is to bring a person back to his senses, and make him aware that he needs to dispose of mistaken ideas or beliefs that have put him in conflict with the Cosmic Harmonics. (For a further explanation of Fate *see* below.) There are also Helpers that form and describe a person's true nature. (*See* p. 47, The True Self.)

All the Helpers in their totality maintain and restore the Cosmic Harmony through nourishing, healing, protecting, and furthering everything that exists. Phrases in the *I Ching*, such as "it furthers to undertake something," refer to the necessity of consciously cooperating with the Helpers by recognizing their existence and their true functions. Including them in our daily awareness brings joy and fulfillment to our lives. Their ability to help us is also dependent on their being free from the control of the ego so that they can express their uniqueness.

We personally block certain of these Helpers by harboring ideas and beliefs that either deny their existence, slander their natures, or misname them. At the basis of all beliefs that block the Helpers is the human-centered view of the universe.

False beliefs affect different Helpers differently: some become blocked or imprisoned, others become demonized, and yet others react by retreating. Their blockage or retreat causes a person to feel helpless and abandoned; demonizing them can cause a feeling of being tormented, which can drive the person to compulsive behavior or criminal acts.

What we learn through the reactions of the Helpers are the limits set by the Cosmic Harmonics to what a person is free to think and do. He is not free, as the ego puts it, to think or do anything he likes. Every thought that is not in harmony with the Cosmos has a negative effect on certain Helpers and creates a reaction on their part. The *I Ching* reminds the person that the Cosmos is ruled by love and harmony, and that whenever these are missing in his life, he needs to turn inside and search for the mistaken ideas that have caused him to separate from the Cosmos. The Cosmos does not expel anyone from its unity; the person expels, or rather, isolates himself. The Cosmos only reacts to disharmonious behavior by retreating from it.

When we realize the ways in which the Helpers can respond to our needs, and how they are perfectly equipped to give help that benefits the whole, we also realize how presumptuous it is for humans to think they "have to make everything work," and what an impossible burden they have taken upon themselves. Clearly, such an idea violates the Cosmic Virtue of Modesty, which the Sage shows us is the result of recognizing and taking our true place in the Cosmos. Modesty, when seen in the context of all the help the Cosmos makes available to us, has nothing to do with the common idea of lack, self-denial, or being shorn of everything but the bare essentials. On the contrary, modesty is the joyful recognition that humans are not meant to be heroes, but part of a loving and caring Cosmos that provides them with everything they need, when they relate to it correctly.

The Human Gift of Language

Humans, as part of all the expressed forms of the Cosmic Consciousness, have received among their many gifts from the Cosmos, the unique gifts of thinking and of language. Each gift of the Cosmos is meant to give expression to the Cosmic Consciousness and its logic in a unique way.

However, as mentioned above, language also contains the potential, when used incorrectly by the thinking mind, to create an independent consciousness (and reality) that is in conflict with the Cosmic Consciousness. In order to express Cosmic Consciousness, words must reflect the *feeling* nature of the Cosmos. Humans possess, as part of their natural makeup, an imprint or memory of what Cosmic Harmony feels like, which is also part of their feeling consciousness. This imprint is what the *I Ching*, in Hexagram 61, calls a person's resident "inner truth." In cooperation with the person's commonsense, his inner truth provides the conscious mind with the feeling guidance it needs. However, when the thinking and imaging minds are given priority by being thought of as "special," their cooperation with the feeling consciousness is blocked. Thereafter, language becomes divorced from feeling, and from considerations of inner truth. The thinking and imaging minds then work together to create abstract ideas that are in conflict with the Cosmic Harmony.

Once the thinking and imagining consciousnesses are thought of as "the mind," and given priority over the feeling consciousness, the imaging mind takes the lead over the thinking mind.

This happens when the young child is made to accept the given culture's myths that have been passed down through the generations. Because these myths conflict with his inner truth and his commonsense, and because of the risk incurred if the child does not agree with the myths, his thinking mind is put to the task of creating the justifying rationales necessary for him to accept the myths. In time, the grown adult becomes entirely habituated in this process, whereby his thinking mind fulfills the task of justifying beliefs, in exchange for being spoken of as clever. Through this process, the person may lose touch entirely with his feeling consciousness and its Cosmic purpose to enable him to live in harmony with the Cosmos.

In order for language to express Cosmic Logic and Cosmic Truths, the formation of words must come from a perception of reality that includes the full spectrum of our feeling consciousness. False names are given to things when our feeling consciousness is ruled out, and our perception is limited to outer seeing and hearing. An example is the word "special," which has been invented by humans to describe their ability to think. The word special contains all the self-flatteries that build an imagined hierarchical order of the universe. The correct word for our ability to think is "unique," which respects the fact that each species and form in Nature has unique functions and capabilities. False words become the basis of mistaken ideas and beliefs about the nature of things and their relationships to each other. When humans see themselves as "special" due to their gift of language, they forget its gift nature, its purpose and its source, and thus separate from the Cosmic Whole.

Language is also manipulated by the thinking and imaging minds to create half-truths. Half-truths are phrases which sound poetical or profound because they have omitted or left unexplained the logical context in which they are to be taken. Without this logical context, they lose their relativity and begin to be read as absolutes. They then enable the imaging mind to read into them whatever meaning it likes, to support its myths. An example is the phrase, "In the beginning was the word." Its half-truth nature lies in what it fails to say: In the beginning of what? It might make more sense if it was explicitly relative to something, such as "In the beginning of the thinking mind was the word," because such a phrase, in terms of the brain, is totally related to the thinking portion only. Left out entirely are the feeling consciousness and the commonsense.

Mistaken beliefs created by half-truths have the effect of putting a frame around what the person perceives, much like a frame around a picture. The frame then excludes from the person's perception any thought or fact that does not fit within it, or else it makes him try to force facts to fit inside its borders by giving them false explanations. This is true for any attempt to fit the harmonious nature of the Cosmic Logic into the framework of rational logic that by its very definition excludes the feelings.

In terms of the brain and central nervous system, false words and phrases block synapses—the cellular junctions where the transmission or communication of energy and information occur—thereby preventing the person from being able to subject his experiences to his commonsense. Moreover, mistaken beliefs about humans, animals, and the way of the Cosmos/ Nature, distort reality through the mechanism of projection, thus locking the things observed into behaving as projected. This occurs because false consciousness behaves differently from Cosmic Consciousness, in that it works through projection. We call the different kinds of negative effects produced by mistaken ideas and beliefs, "projections, spells, and poison arrows."

Not surprisingly, the researches of modern science corroborate much of what we have learned from the Sage. Alfred Korzybski wrote extensively in the 1930's about experiments that showed that harmful neurological effects were created by certain uses of words. His work initiated a number of books by other writers that established the subject of semantics. Contemporary scientists studying memetics* have found similarities to what we have learned about the way mistaken beliefs are

---

* meme: (pron. 'meem') A contagious idea that replicates like a virus, passed on from mind to mind. Memes function the same way genes and viruses do, propagating through communication networks and face-to-face contact between people. Memetics is a field of study which postulates that the meme is the basic unit of cultural evolution. Examples of memes include melodies, icons, fashion statements and phrases.

created and spread through what they call "thought contagion." Medical studies of how mental fixes are created by threats and traumas, and then stored in the amygdala of the brain in the form of certain proteins, describe the equivalent of what we refer to in this book as spells.*

The Cosmic Harmonics

The Cosmos orders itself around principles of harmony that in this book are called Cosmic Harmonics. The most basic among these are the Principle of Equality and the Principle of the Uniqueness of all aspects of the Cosmic Whole. Another Principle is that of Modesty on the part of every aspect. Together they form the three most basic Cosmic Virtues that each aspect possesses intrinsically and which give each its Cosmic dignity. It is due to these basic virtues that a single force is able to hold together the functioning of the whole: it is *the force of mutual attraction between complementary aspects.* Another name for this force is love. The force of attraction is able to maintain the Cosmic Order and to move the Cosmos on the path of continuous Evolution, which is yet another Cosmic Harmonic. Humans take part in this evolution when they are part of the Cosmic Unity, through their inner resonance with these aforementioned principles.

Success and Misfortune

The Cosmic Harmonics can be better understood within the context of the two central terms that are used as oracle sayings in the traditional *I Ching*, "success" and "misfortune." As mentioned before, they are not predictions which indicate that life is a pre-written script. What is predicted is the inevitability of help coming to the person who puts himself in harmony with the Cosmos, and evil consequences to the person who does not withdraw from the trajectory created by decisions and attitudes that are in conflict with the Cosmic Harmonics, or Cosmic Laws. Thus, the terms "success" and "misfortune" are meant to make a person aware of the way of the Cosmos. The warning of mis-

---

* See "Memories of Fear—Researchers Discover How They Work," U. of Southern California, www.sciencedaily.com/releases/1999/12/991229123710.htm

fortune counsels him to "recognize the seeds" of future events as residing in his thoughts (consciousness), and the way his thoughts affect reality. The distinction between these two terms can be characterized as follows: When a person's heart and reason are in harmony with the Cosmic Consciousness, he is under the protection of the Cosmos and receives its help in everything he does, because he contributes to the increase of the whole. When he is thus in harmony with the Cosmos, he fulfills his Cosmic Destiny. This is the meaning of "success." When, however, a person's heart and feelings are ruled by reason or intellect, he has separated from the Cosmic Harmony. A reasoning mind that does not follow the heart develops abstract concepts, creating a parallel reality that competes with the Cosmos. These abstract concepts project images on the Cosmos that contradict its true nature and create conflict with it. How does the Cosmos react to this conflict? It reacts with Fate, which is often referred to as "misfortune." Fate has several functions, which are explained in the next section. Every violation of the harmony of the Cosmic Whole, be it through thoughts or deeds, creates a fate for its originator.

It is also part of the Cosmic Harmonics that every person is free, at any time, to return to unity with the Cosmos by inwardly leaving the parallel reality, and its false values and ways of thinking. Doing so is always a question of will.

Fate

Fate, as a word, is often considered synonymous with Destiny. The Sage has informed us, however, that it uses the word Fate to mean adverse events which a person creates by harboring thoughts and ideas that are in conflict with the Cosmic Harmony. It uses the word Destiny to mean the successful fulfillment of one's life's purpose.

Fate has been subjected to numerous misconceptions by humans, the most common being the idea that Fate is "a decree of Heaven," is "written in the stars," or is a script written before he was born. Such ideas, unfortunately, have led to false conclusions about how to react to Fate. Some people believe they have to submit to it, while others blame the Cosmos or life for having put it on them. Yet other people hold that Fate needs to be overcome through fighting it. All these reactions only create new fates, because they prevent the person from looking to his own thoughts and actions as its cause. Recognizing the mistaken ideas about the Cosmic Way and firmly rejecting them is the only way to end a fate and return to harmony with the Cosmos.

As mentioned in the previous section, Fate is a Cosmic Harmonic. It is the Cosmic reaction to any thought or deed that disturbs the harmony of the whole. These disturbances have their seminal causes in false words and images, and mistaken ideas and beliefs, the "seeds of evil" mentioned earlier.

Fate can manifest in different ways, depending on the content of the mistaken idea or belief that has caused it. For example, illnesses can be caused by seeing human beings divided into hierarchically ordered parts, such as mind, soul, and body, with mind or soul perceived as superior to the body. Still another mistaken view is to see the body as a set of purely mechanical systems. In both these cases, the consciousness of the body is demonized, causing the body to react with illness.

Fates pertaining to poverty are caused by beliefs that the Cosmos is stingy, or that its resources are limited. Fates that come as loss can have their cause in attachment to possessions (coming from seeing the Cosmos as a trickster that takes things away at random), or in the idea that people are free to do with their possessions whatever they like because they have "deserved" them (not recognizing that everything comes as a Cosmic gift).

Fate has several purposes: (1) to compensate for the damage caused to the injured aspect of the Cosmos, and thereby to the Cosmic Whole; (2) to bring the person (literally) back from his head to his senses; (3) to make him aware of his mistaken ideas and beliefs, and to reduce him to an attitude of openness and humility that will help him shake loose the hold of the ego within him, which is their source. A fate will be just as severe as is needed to wake the person up; its extent depends on the degree of his rigidity, the strength of his attachment to his mistaken ideas and beliefs, and to the level of his arrogance.

Fate is never an end in itself. It comes to an end when it has fulfilled its purposes, something that can happen in different ways: (1) when the person has come to a state of burnout by seeing how his mistaken ideas have led to a dead-end; (2) when Fate has run its full course of time, although the person may not have corrected his viewpoint, the fate has expired, like a prison sentence; (3) when the person has of his own accord sought its causes and freed himself of them. (The method showing how to do this is described in the Appendix.)

When a person disposes voluntarily of the mistaken ideas or beliefs that have caused his fate, he is reunited with the Cosmos. This reunification is experienced as increase, furtherance, and progress, because everything in the Cosmos is directed toward furthering and increasing all of its parts.

? why

The Parallel Reality Created through the False Use of Language

The Collective Ego

The seeds that cause a person to separate from his unity with the Cosmos have been identified above as "the seeds of evil." They consist of false words and images that form mistaken ideas and beliefs about the nature of the Cosmos, about human nature, and about the human place in the whole. The totality of these mistaken ideas and beliefs, and the social structures that have been erected to support them are in this volume called "the collective ego."

The collective ego has its roots in the storytelling of early humans, which in time developed into myths. Myths monumentalized human achievements, in particular the achievements attributed to human mental faculties. The fairytales and heroic myths laud their heroes for their cleverness, brilliance, daring, bravery, nobility of character, and superiority. It was done almost always in the context of fighting, conquering, and dominating either other humans, or aspects of Nature that were demonized as threatening.

The Sage made us aware that the human ability to think in words and to form images is a relatively recent development in the animal kingdom. Both faculties are located in the frontal lobes of the brain. The fact that they are relatively young means that the thinking and imaging functions are still inexperienced in the correct use of their abilities. To learn to use them correctly has required the freedom to make mistakes.

Unfortunately, history shows that humans allowed their imaging and word minds to decide that their unique abilities were "special" in relation to all the other things that existed. This was also the beginning of these minds seeing themselves as superior to all other parts of human nature. These self-flattering observations of the imaging and word minds were the early beginnings of the ego, and the self-deceptions that have afflicted the human species ever since. It was also the point of human separation from the Cosmic Whole.

These self-deceptions blinded humans to the fact that every aspect of the Cosmos possesses unique abilities, and that the word "special" itself is the basic seed of evil. This is because the word special, with all its derivative uses, denies the Cosmic Virtues of Uniqueness, Equality, and Modesty that every aspect of the Cosmic Whole possesses. The word "special" is the sole false word on which humans have built the myths that show them as the centerpiece (or masterpiece) of creation.

The collective ego has set itself up in competition with the Cosmos, both in its visible and invisible aspects. Through this competition, it has created a parallel reality, which like the Cosmos, also has visible and invisible sides.

The invisible side of the parallel reality is the negative consciousness that in this volume is called "the demonic sphere of consciousness." It is negative because in every way its ideas negate the Cosmic Reality. It is demonic inasmuch as every false word, image, and idea takes on a demonic form in a person's psyche. These forms can be seen in meditation, dreams, and the fantasized reality that occurs in schizophrenia. The parallel reality and schizophrenia are inextricably combined.

The visible side of the parallel reality consists of the institutions that are based on the collective ego's concepts, and those natural social forms that it has turned to its purposes. Thus, they include the family, community, nation, and cultural institutions in whatever ways they are devoted to serving the ideas and purposes of the parallel reality.

Within the system of the parallel reality, the family is given the primary task of promoting the ideas and values of the collective ego. Its role is seen as "preparing" the individual child for his designated role within the system of values of the collective ego. This is done by introjecting the collective ego's program of ideas and beliefs into the psyche of the young child, phrase by phrase. The result is the creation of the ego within the child's psyche.

The collective ego acts in many ways like a computer virus. Its program installs itself through rewards and threats, its maintenance and upgrade features adapt it to change within its host, and its reinstalling features ensure that the individual remains locked within its system, should he come to a crisis with it. This computerlike program installs itself in each new generation through the parents to the children.

Once installed, the program is designed to make the individual believe that its beliefs and values are his own. It even speaks in the psyche as "I," as well as "you" and "we." The program's maintenance features include all the taboos that surround the collective ego's basic belief tenets, which are designed to keep the person from questioning their validity. Its upgrade features enable the program to appropriate gifts of insight and invention that come from the Cosmos, and claim them as the achievements of human ingenuity. Through its appropriations strategies, it makes itself appear to be on the forefront of every advance, and responsible for every achievement. The reinstalling features of the program, which include guilt and fear of guilt, kick in every time the person considers ridding himself of the program, with the rationale that doing so would mean "betraying the beliefs of his forefathers." Its features ensure that the individual remains locked within its system, especially whenever he begins to recognize that it imprisons his inner truth, and if left in place, will gradually extinguish his true self.

The significance of the collective ego's program is not that it is merely in conflict with the Cosmic Order: its logic and purpose are aimed at undermining and replacing the Cosmic Order with itself. It is, in effect, a social system based on conflict, that not only appropriates and suppresses the natural social order, it attempts to establish itself as God.

To accomplish its ends, the collective ego must steal energy from the individual's true nature, and indeed from Nature itself. Just as the so-called charismatic person owes his charisma to the chi energy given him by those who look up to him in awe, so the collective ego is empowered by the awe and fear it installs in each individual. Furthermore, to remain in power, it must constantly assure the individual that he is dependent on it for his survival. Its existence depends entirely on its keeping this point alive, and on keeping the individual ignorant of the fact that the Cosmos is his only true source of help and nourishment.

It is thus important for the collective ego to constantly slander the loving nature of the Cosmos, by labeling it "the unknown." Such a name gives rise to fearful images, which heighten the individual's sense of abandonment, and make him ever more dependent on the collective ego's institutions. When a person accepts the idea of the Cosmic Consciousness as the unknown, he no longer trusts it, and is even made to see it as an adversary. Asserting that the Cosmic Consciousness is "unknowable" denies the fact that it reveals its caring presence and love to the person who is open to it, through his feelings. These ideas of there being an unknown and an unknowable serve to establish the parallel reality as the only reality there is.

The collective ego diverts the individual from recognizing that the Cosmos fulfills his true needs by suggesting false needs, such as the need for the collective ego's recognition. It then satisfies this need by granting titles, medals, degrees, and membership in groups which promise to recognize him. However, these turn out to be empty of real nourishment, since they only nourish the ego, while keeping his true self enslaved and starved. To keep him in line, the collective ego holds out the ultimate promise, like a carrot on a stick, that the person will receive recognition of his greatness in the "afterlife." This promise is given to the person who will sacrifice his life to fulfill the myth of the hero, which also means sacrificing his true self to the collective ego's purposes.

The Development of the Individual Ego

In consulting the traditional *I Ching* over a period of years, one is shown that the ego is not a natural part of the personality. It is rather a false mental program that flatters a person to think of himself as special, on the one hand, while telling him he is lacking in the most essential ways, on the other. Hierarchically organized, one part of himself is designated as "higher," the other as "lower," with the higher needing to be developed, and the lower to be repressed. (The lower here refers to everything that has to do with his body.) Through these concepts, the individual ego is passed from one generation to the next.

The program consists of a list of flattering self-images the person can develop, which, he is told, will make up for the list of essential qualities that he purportedly lacks. He is told that he can refine them to suit his individuality; this enables the program to speak in his psyche as "I." Once the program is fully installed, he will even defend it as "his individuality."

This program then proceeds from the development of the ego as "I" to the development of the ego as "we," as in the group-we. This aspect of the program is designed to make the individual identify his interests with those of his group. Thus he sees the ups and downs of his group as his own good fortune or adversity, thereby losing his individuality and inner independence to the group. The "group-we" is another name for the collective ego. Liberating oneself from the idea that one is part of a "group guilt," or "group success" (or failure), is what Hexagram 59, *Dissolution/Dissolving*, refers to in the counsel, "He dissolves his bond with his group. Supreme success." Thinking in terms of the group-we is one of the more subtle "upgrade" features of the collective ego's program, inasmuch as it substitutes a person's natural loyalty to his inner truth with a forced loyalty to his group; that is to say, he must be loyal to family, friends, and social group regardless of his inner truth, or else he will be "guilty" of something.

Just as the collective ego sets itself up in competition with the Cosmos by asserting that humans hold a special place in the overall scheme of things, the ego is set up within the individual to compete with his true nature.

These few basic ideas, which are used to install the program that makes up the individual ego are based on the slander of the person's original wholeness, and on the idea of there being no source of help but the institutions of the collective ego. (See Hexagram 23, *Splitting Apart.*) The sole purpose of this program is to split the person off from his connection with the Cosmos and tie him to the collective ego through self-doubt and guilt, on the one hand, and through striving for fame and glory on the other, to make up for his presumed faults.

The traditional versions of the *I Ching* have used the term "the superior man" to describe the person who develops his "higher nature." However, the descriptions of what the superior man does are quite often contradictory: sometimes he is associated with the person who strives to attain the abstract virtues held up by the collective ego; at others, he is shown as the one who acts in harmony with the Cosmos. This indiscriminate use of the term is typical of the ego's strategy to obliterate a clear distinction between the ego and the person's true self. On this account, the term superior man has been eliminated from this book; we have replaced it by clearly calling it the ego when the words are referring to a person's pride system, and the true self when they refer to a person's true nature.

Bringing Oneself into Harmony with the Cosmic Order

The True Self

A large group of Helpers forms and describes a person's true nature, or true self. They stand for all the different functions that enable the person to express his uniqueness during his life in a body. These Helpers are referred to in Hexagram 14, *Possession in Great Measure*, as what we possess in great measure. Among these possessions are a person's Cosmic Virtues, such as his natural goodness, kindness, modesty, sensitivity, firmness, and loyalty to his inner connection with the Cosmos. Other

Helpers are his five commonly known perceptive senses, including his inner senses of smell, taste, touch, hearing and seeing. He also possesses a number of "metaphorical senses," such as a sense of wholeness, a sense of injustice, a sense of dignity and self respect, a sense of natural caution, a sense of appropriateness of behavior, etc., all of which comprise his commonsense. A person's commonsense is identical with the Helper of Transformation (in humans).

There are also the Helpers that help him learn things, such as languages, mathematics, and music. In addition, a person's true feelings of love, harmony, health, joy, and sadness need to be understood as Helpers. There is a Helper that coordinates all functions of his psyche and body, which we have called the Feeling Manager; there is also the Helper of Will, and a group of Helpers that make up a person's "inner truth," which is the name for his Cosmic Memory of what Cosmic harmony feels like. Finally, a Personal Helper is specifically assigned to each person to help him fulfill his destiny, along with the help of all the other Helpers of the Cosmos and of Nature.

The thinking and imaging functions of the mind are also a person's Cosmic possessions, and under the guidance of the feeling memory of inner truth, they are also Helpers. When they depend on this guidance, the images and words formed in the two frontal lobes correspond to inner truth rather than to what is seen and heard only. In this way the Cosmic Language finds its expression through a human being.

How the Formation of the Ego Affects the True Self

Several hexagrams show how, during childhood, a person's Cosmic Possessions are appropriated by the collective ego and harnessed to serve its purposes. Hexagram 9, *The Taming Power of the Small*, describes how this is done by the "small means" of rewards. Hexagram 26, *The Taming Power of the Great*, describes how a person's nature is actually *altered* through threats and punishments. Both rewards and punishments put spells and poison arrows on his true self, perverting his true nature.

The rules enforced on the individual by the collective ego are phrased in the form of "shoulds" and "musts." They set the standard he is expected to follow. By accepting them into his psyche, voluntarily or involuntarily, he also accepts the guilt that the collective ego has attached to each should-not and must-not. Guilt, and the paralyzing fear of becoming guilty, as previously mentioned, serve to keep the individual locked into the collective ego's system, and to prevent him from leaving the group-we, whenever he feels the need to follow his inner truth.

Perhaps the most crucial problem for the individual is created by threats and punishments that are directed against the child's natural ability to say the outer or inner No against injustices and encroachments into his inner space. The ability to say No is crucial to the child's ability to develop discernment based on his feelings of inner truth. When a parent or caretaker has arbitrarily punished a child who has correctly said No to something wrong, a switch is flipped in the child's brain that partially robs him of that ability. When this happens repeatedly, the person becomes totally unable to say No to authority later in life, and to those who intimidate him with aggressive behavior. The worst effect is that he is unable to say the No's that are necessary to deprogram phrases and images that have caused neurotic patterns in his psyche. However, this situation, while difficult, is not hopeless, as is shown in the Appendix. (*See* p. 677, Saying the Inner No.)

In the seemingly hopeless situation created by the collective ego's imprisonment of the true self, the Cosmos offers help. Often, this help is not recognized, because it comes in an unexpected guise—the gift of a love relationship, for example, that does not conform to the rules dictated by status, gender, or race. The gift of a love relationship is given by the Cosmos to two people's true selves; it is never given to the egos within them. The gift of love allows them to recognize and strengthen each other's true self. It is clear, of course, that the ego will make every attempt to gain control over the relationship, because it views it as a welcome opportunity to expand its domain.

This volume shows in many hexagrams how a person can recognize the various kinds of help offered by the Cosmos to free him from the spells and poison arrows that keep his true self under the dominance of the ego. It also exposes the plots and strategies employed by the ego in its attempt to keep him locked in the parallel reality. Because guilt is the main means by which he is bound to the parallel reality, the next section will explain the difference between guilt and the terms used in the *I Ching*, "blame" and "no blame."

Guilt, Blame, and Shame

Guilt as a permanent stain that has been laid upon human nature, is primarily a Western concept, which the Sage informs us has no Cosmic basis. It is connected with the story of the fall of Adam and Eve from Paradise, and with human sexuality as the cause of original guilt or sin. Throughout the feudal history of the West, guilt has mostly served as the collective ego's instrument to control the behavior of the individual.

While there is no evidence that the Chinese had the concept of guilt, most of the writers of the Confucian school nevertheless looked at human animal nature as the main reason humans have deviated from their original good nature. That idea is also behind the Taoist Religion's emphasis on mental control of the body. Both the idea of guilt and the idea that human animal nature is the source of evil, slander and falsely divide the wholeness of the individual's nature, and lock various Helpers in his psyche in spells, depriving the person of important abilities.

The concept of guilt is also connected with the threats and punishments used by the collective ego to install its program of musts and must-not's in the individual's psyche. The guilt that is aroused by going against a must-not serves to reinstall its program when a person has decided to follow his inner truth. The threat of "becoming guilty" is connected with the image of an inextinguishable stain put upon his person, one which excludes him forever from social acceptance.

The Chinese have a similar threat in the branding phenomenon associated with shame. Shame differs from guilt in that it only involves a person's public image. A person who commits a violation will suffer shame only if the violation becomes public knowledge. Because the shame is considered to extend to his family or community, the society is obsessed with the threat of shame. A similar threat is particularly evident in the small towns and communities of the United States, and in the nation as well, in the continual rewriting of histories to cleanse the community memory of all negative happenings that would stain the community pride.

Neither guilt nor shame as defined above, have Cosmic relevance. The mention of "blame" in the *I Ching* refers to Cosmic blame, which is incurred when a person has betrayed or compromised his true nature. "No blame" can be saying that a person is in harmony with the Cosmos, or that a person is incorrectly blaming himself due to judging himself by the standards of the collective ego. The Sage informs us that Cosmic blame is not a permanent stain, but can be extinguished at any time the person recognizes and rids himself of the mistaken idea that has caused the blame.

When a person does not free himself of the cause of his blame, but continues to act against his true nature, he creates a fate. Fate, as discussed earlier, can be ended in several ways. Cosmic blame is extinguished with the end of the fate.

Despite the fact that a child absorbs the program of the collective ego during a time when his ability of discernment is not fully formed, he nevertheless experiences the conflict of this program with his inner truth. It is felt as a background anxiety that contains a message, experienced during certain moments of youth and adolescence, that following the ego-program will betray his true nature. These are the first moments in which Cosmic blame can be incurred.

Part of the collective ego's strategy to keep the individual within its system is to occupy him with looking for someone or something outside himself to blame. It either preoccupies him with blaming himself individually, with accepting group blame, or with focussing on another individual or group as the culprit.

The first step in freeing the true self is to say the inner No to the entire idea of guilt, and to the term "culprit," with all that it implies. Neither guilt nor culprit is part of the Cosmic vocabulary, and neither has a place in the Cosmic Harmonics. Even the collective ego is not a culprit; it is a juggernaut of ideas and institutions that maintain themselves only through our continued permission. We have the option to free ourselves of them by deprogramming them word by word, image by image, and phrase by phrase. We cannot do this, however, if we see the collective ego as a monstrous force and a culprit, for this view only energizes it and keeps it alive as an objective entity.

Saying the inner No brings about the transformation needed to open all of the prison doors created by the mind. The importance of the No is in the fact that it undoes the inadvertent Yes we have formerly said through our acquiescence to the collective ego. Indeed, the inner No is the most direct means to remove ourselves individually from the demonic sphere of consciousness and its parallel reality, while at the same time diminishing its influence. (*See* p. 677, Saying the Inner No.)

Transformation versus Changes

Besides being able to express a Yes or a No, the light and dark lines that make up the entire *I Ching* are also expressions of the Cosmic Way: the light representing the invisible Cosmic Consciousness, and the dark representing Nature. Since the light and the dark are not static phenomena, but dynamic forces that attract each other due to their complementarity, they bring about transformations—from non-form into form, and from form into non-form. These two forces need to be seen as *inseparable*, because they are two aspects of *one* entity.

This version of the *I Ching* shows that when we correctly understand the Cosmic Harmonics, the term "*I*" of "*I Ching*" means transformation rather than changes. One could say that the "Book of Transformation" has been hidden for millennia under the cover of "The Book of Changes." The idea that the Cosmos works through changes needs to be seen as part of the human-centered view of the universe, in which the forces of the light and the dark are seen as opposites.

When a person assumes the light and the dark to be opposites, the result for him is not attraction but a fight between them, which blocks their ability to create transformation in his life. The mistaken belief that things are in a "natural relationship of opposition" creates the parallel reality which is ruled by *changes* because it creates *fates*. When a person does not recognize that his consciousness is actively projecting that mistaken belief into reality, he then concludes, "that is the way of life."

The "world of changes" thus is the creation of the rational mind, and is a sign of separation from the Cosmic Whole. A worldview based on seeing things as opposites includes the idea that time is linear, having a beginning and an end. This view likewise assumes that the "natural order" is hierarchical, with some things *controlling* others.

The new *I Ching* shows how transformation, not change, is the true way of Nature, including human nature. This is so, except when humans block transformation by projecting mistaken ideas onto their own natures. When not disturbed by the projections, spells, and poison arrows created by false consciousness, all life is constantly being renewed through transformation, without beginning or end. Life in a body is but one possible form of never-ending life. When, however, we allow our rational minds to project abstract ideas onto life, as, for example, by seeing death as the opposite of life, then death fights life and eventually destroys it. Such ideas are the result of only looking at the appearance of things, without taking into account their inner truth.

The world of changes is also characterized by the experience of "ups and downs," and by swings from one extreme to another, when a person believes that if the answer to a problem is not to be found in one idea, it must lie in an opposing idea. Such thinking suggests two solutions that lie on the plane of "either-or." Both lack an understanding of Cosmic processes. The realm of "either-or" thinking is part of the rational logic of the collective ego. The metaphor of the impassible mountain and the engulfing abyss shown in Hexagram 39, *Meeting Obstruction*, is given to call a person's attention to his seeing a situation as hopeless, precisely because he sees only two equally impossible solutions. The Sage frequently counsels a person with a problem to lift himself out of the trap of dichotomous solutions. This means that he needs to turn within and ask the Sage for help. Then he will be shown a solution that is outside these two alternatives, which is also in harmony with the Cosmos.

The belief that all life is subject to changes can easily become a trap when we continue to look at the appearance of things and listen to "what people say." As has been pointed out above, the world of changes has become a reality through the rational mind's power of projection. When we understand how the rational mind creates its own false reality, we see that it is incorrect to call change "the natural state of things." It is rather the state of things defined by the collective ego. It is proof of an egocentric view that has set itself above Nature, by deeming Nature as "wild" and "primitive," and then blaming Nature for the misfortune created by those very projections.

Transformation cannot be brought about by the conscious effort of humans. It is the function of a particular Helper that operates on the plane of feeling, which makes the transformation from non-form to form, and from form to non-form possible. Transformation occurs in the realm of the atom, which is also the realm of the consciousness of feeling. Saying the inner No to a mistaken idea brings about transformation by erasing wrong words or ideas from the person's conscious mind. At the same time, the blockage created by the mistaken ideas, which has occurred in particular synapses of the brain, is dissolved. Every correctly said inner No contributes to freeing the person's access to his Cosmic memory of inner truth. Saying the inner No is a Cosmic function that is identical with the Helper of Transformation. Saying the inner No to what is incorrect from the Cosmic point of view is called in the *I Ching* "biting through" (the name of Hexagram 21). This hexagram also informs us that "biting through" is the meaning of exercising our ability of discernment. Discernment consists in recognizing what feels in harmony or out of harmony with the Cosmic Way. Exercising our discernment is to say the inner No to what feels disharmonious and turning the matter over to the Cosmos for correction.

The Natural Social Order and Commonly Encountered Resistances to Allowing It

The existence of a natural social order is neither a myth nor an ideal. It can be seen to exist in certain situations, as when shock causes individuals' egos to temporarily freeze. It happens during and shortly after an accident, when shock allows their true selves to temporarily emerge. The natural social order is more obvious when shocking events occur on a large scale, such as in wars, earthquakes, etc. It emerges when people are temporarily free of the egos within them. Then they relate heart-to-heart as they spontaneously see and respond to each other's needs. This relating is free of "organized doing good," and has no motive of being recognized as "good." However, as soon as the main shock waves are over and the egos once again feel secure, they return to their usual control of the personalities and soon brand those moments in which the egos were frozen as "an abnormal situation." The collective ego also grasps all the spontaneous helping of one another and calls it "heroism," making sure that the egos of those involved are credited for what the persons' true selves did.

The two main meanings of "the family" mentioned in Hexagram 37, *The Family*, pertain to the development of the natural social order. One is the Cosmic Family, and the other refers to the inner relationships we develop with people. These include our biological families, our friendships, our love relationships, and all other aspects of the Cosmic Whole.

The Cosmic Family consists of the entire invisible world of the Helpers, the Helpers of Nature, and our own personal Helpers, as well as all the aspects of the Cosmic Consciousness that exist in form. Nothing is excluded. This hexagram talks about taking one's correct place in the Cosmic Family, or Cosmic Whole. Taking one's place means divesting oneself of all ideas that humans are special, thereby attaining a harmony of fellowship with all things. It also means recognizing the Cosmic Family as the true source of all nourishment, love, and help. The words in Line 1, "firm seclusion within the family" refer to rejecting the world of the ego, and any thinking in terms of the group-we. The message is to make us aware that first and foremost, each person, by the fact of his existence, is part of the Cosmic Family, even though, through the influence of the collective ego, he has left it. Through making the effort to free his true self, the individual reunites with the Cosmic Family.

Both this hexagram and Hexagram 60, *Limitation*, define the limits that are appropriate to each species. The limits refer to thoughts and acts that fail to respect the dignity of all other species. These limits are factors known to the inner truth of every person; to go against them creates a fate.

In a natural social order, the recognition of belonging to the Cosmic Family is the point of reference for every individual human being. It is what unites him with others who equally take that as their point of reference. His belonging to the Cosmic Family is not a conformity to its overall consciousness, as when one conforms to the rules of the collective ego; it is rather a sensitivity and awareness that his consciousness is part of the beneficent functioning of that overall consciousness.

A natural social order exists whenever two or more people have inwardly made a conscious decision to follow the light of their own inner truth and the principles that are in harmony with the Cosmos. Thus arises the natural morality that circles around the principles outlined in the hexagrams of the *I Ching*, that keep people in touch with the Sage and in harmony with the Cosmic Whole. In concrete terms, this means that each individual follows his primary duty to respect and honor his own dignity, place, and purpose in the Cosmic Whole, and those of others. He thus abstains from using power, he is absolute in his unwillingness to throw away his dignity, he relies on the inner No to keep his relationships with others correct, and he follows the way of the Sage in retreating from the ego, in himself and in others. He recognizes that the gifts such as love, chi-energy, talents, help, etc., that he receives from the Cosmos are not to be squandered on the ego in others.

When the ego is absent, the person's true self is present. Unique, but not having a need to demonstrate its uniqueness, the true self respects the uniqueness of every other person. There is no reason, therefore, for conflicts of interests, and no need for comparisons. Such a person, having defused the causes of disharmony in himself, knows that when things become disharmonious, he can ask the Sage that exists in everyone's presence, to intervene. A society in which each individual has recognized and adhered to what corresponds with his dignity and self-esteem would offer no threats to anyone, nor would it give rise to the perversions that accompany the failures of self-esteem, which occur in ego-based societies.

A natural social order arises between people who maintain a conscious awareness of the Helpers of the invisible world that are needed to help them in everything they do. The consequence is the constancy and abundance of that help. It is such that people find themselves calling it "magical" and "miraculous." The Sage, however, has helped us to see that when the Cosmos is active in our lives, what we term as magical or miraculous is the ordinary and natural way of the Cosmos. It is neither extraordinary nor supernatural. Only when we are held within the parallel reality do such terms apply, for that is the only measure we know. The simple inner asking for Cosmic help when discord arises, or the simple saying of the inner No, has nearly immediate transforming effects. Naturally, the person who has not experienced these things can only imagine them.

The creation of the natural social order begins with the transformation of each individual. Nothing is imposed from without, nor does it require effort to change the existing order. No new order is to be superimposed upon the old, nor is there any need to rebel against and take down the old. As the natural order emerges spontaneously out of the effort of each individual to correct himself, the old order is gradually transformed from within, due to the harmonious way that each individual relates to everyone and everything around him. Then the true needs of people begin to be fulfilled, and the whole, including Nature, is increased.

The new *I Ching* emphasizes that liberating the natural social order requires the individual to become free of thinking in terms of the group-we. Such thinking comes from the feudal mindset of the collective ego. This group-ego gains all its power from bringing people to see themselves as dependent on it, but also from getting them to identify with it. The new *I Ching* shows us that as individuals, we can work within the institutions of the collective ego and still remain in harmony with the Cosmos, by consistently saying the inner No to whatever is incorrect: to the institutions' encroachment, flattery, intimidation, and insensitivity. The matter is then turned over to the Cosmos, which brings about the inner transformations that are needed.

The person who is freeing his true self recognizes that doing a thing for its own sake engages Cosmic Helpers and initiates wonderful new creative experiences. Such a new order is not the product of design and planning, for its creation occurs through the help of the Cosmos itself. In order for it to begin in a person's life, he need only make a conscious choice to live within the Cosmic Reality and to leave behind the parallel reality of the collective ego. This conscious choice brings him into harmony with himself and activates the creative process.

Although people may have experienced these seeming miracles, the collective ego has wrongly credited them to good luck, synchronicity, or angels, rather than to the person's being in harmony with the Cosmos through having a modest and sincere attitude.

These false explanations blind the person to seeing the gift-giving and caring nature of the Cosmos, and to seeing that his choice to follow the Cosmic Principles enables these wonders to become his everyday experience. What the person hears from the collective ego to further distance him from the benefits of this path are doubts, such as, "if you follow this path, you won't fit into society any more," or, "this path undermines the stability of the social order." What he does not notice in this threat is that it is not the natural order that undermines the order of the collective ego, but the collective ego that undermines the natural order of society and of the Cosmos. Such reasoning is typical of the sleight-of-hand tricks of the ego, to make people feel guilty when they follow their inner truth.

The more individuals take away their feelings of self-doubt and inferiority created by the tactics of the collective ego, the less they feel a need to monumentalize and elevate themselves or others, and the less they need false props to hold up their personalities. Automatically, the diversions that accompany decadence lose their attraction.

Another of the ego's tricks is to suggest that the Cosmic Reality is a pie-in-the-sky fantasy, unattainable in the "real world," and "too good to be true." Such a view is held by the person who lives only within the parallel reality and who has engaged fate after fate. Once he frees himself of the untruths and half-truths that have colonized his psyche, he gains the help of the whole Cosmos. The more he frees himself from fates he has created, the more he is furthered on the path of his unique destiny. This is the true meaning of progress as described in Hexagram 35, *Progressing*. There is a unique task for every person in the Cosmic scheme of things, which gives him an opportunity to bring his abilities to their fullest expression. As he progresses in this direction, his inner truth penetrates to the true selves of other people around him, awakening them to their own potentials. This is the true meaning of *Gathering Together*, the theme of Hexagram 45.

So long as the ego is in place, it will do what it can to prevent the person from seeing that to be free of it is to be free of the prison of fears and self-doubts it has created to rule him. The path of freeing the true self reveals a harmony, creativity, and joyfulness not previously experienced. This natural order can exist between two people in the love relationship, or within the family, once it is freed of the tortured patterns of relating created by projections, spells, and poison arrows, and by the false hierarchical ordering of the family. Once this harmony exists within the family, it extends through inner connections outwardly to other people, animals, and Nature.

Threatening scenarios, which imply that inner freedom leads to chaos and anarchy, are promoted by the collective ego to prevent the individual from beginning his inner path toward his destiny. It threatens by questioning, "what if everybody does what you're doing?" The fact is, such transformations can only occur within the individual, and not in groups. As each individual rids himself of the ego, he begins to transform the quality of his own way of relating; he begins to answer real, rather than contrived needs.

The ego assumes that the natural order of things is chaos, to start with, whereas the *I Ching* teaches us that the natural order of things is harmony. To return to the natural order of things means that the individual brings himself into the existing harmony of the Cosmic Whole. The principles of that harmony, which are described throughout the *I Ching*, are not an unknown. There is no chaos to fall into. In fact, it is the ego that has created the chaos and projected the blame onto Nature as the scapegoat. All of these ideas are the necessary excuses it needs to support its hierarchical, feudalistic power structure.

The collective ego tries to impute that a natural order would do what *it* would do: overturn the existing order by force, and insert a new power structure. The natural order of society can only grow out of each individual's recognition of his dependency on the Cosmos, and on his willingness to say the inner No to all activities of the ego in himself and in others.

So long as a person is caught within the parallel reality, he will think that the solution is to step out of the collective ego's values and customs, or adopt an opposite system. Any rush, however, to an opposite system is only to be caught in yet another system of the ego, for it is the nature of the parallel reality to incorporate its opposite. The natural order of society occurs only through dissolving what is decadent within the individual himself. Dissolving is purely a process of taking away what is false. When what is false has been dissolved, what is left is harmony and unity with the Cosmic Whole. The crucial issue is to recognize that the bleak picture presented by the ego is always devoid of Helpers, and of any acknowledgment of the Cosmic Order. (*See* Hexagram 59, *Dissolution/Dissolving.*)

The last ace up the sleeve of the collective ego, designed to prevent the individual from reuniting with his true self, and thereby with the Cosmic Family, is guilt. It suggests that a person's development is selfish, an act of betrayal of his family and friends. Leaving the group-we is not any of these things; neither is it to be pictured in the manner portrayed in the Bhagavad Gita, where Arjuna is joined by Krishna to do battle against his family, teacher, and friends. It is no battle, no being against anyone, no playing either the role of hero for the right, or rebel against the wrong. The inner No is a simple and firm rejection of ideas and roles that are false, but not of the people caught in the grip of those ideas and roles.

Separating from the Individual Ego

Just as the collective ego raises obstruction after obstruction in the form of false arguments, to uphold its structure and prevent the emergence of the natural order, so the individual ego also puts up rationale after rationale, to keep itself in control of the personality. To free oneself of the ego, it is first necessary to clearly recognize that even though it speaks in the personality as "I," the ego is nevertheless a foreign element, a parasite in one's psyche. Its goal is to develop a heroic self-image of the person, to compensate for the idea that its parent, the collective ego, has inserted, that the person is not good enough in and of himself. What the creation of this heroic self-image means, however, is that the price is nothing less than the ultimate sacrifice and destruction of the person's true self.

To camouflage its falseness, the ego uses a number of means to convince the person that his "self" and the ego are one and the same. This happens, for example, when the ego speaks for the person as "I," in proudly pronouncing, "I did it," or "I deserve it," or as when it seizes a goal such as self-development and declares, "I am working on my spiritual development." What the ego is actually working on is the perfection of an image of the person that will "look good" in the eyes of the group to which he belongs. This to say that the ego, which is the hero of the "good group," is no different from the ego which heads the band of robbers. Both are self-images. To expand further, wanting to "be" a modest person, a person of rectitude, or a person who defies society, who "doesn't care about anything," means to adopt a self-image created by the ego for the purpose of being recognized in a special way. Since the ego is composed of a complex of self-images, it has no real existence; nevertheless, it attains a simulated existence through being seen by others, regardless of whether it is recognized positively or negatively. When the ego convinces another that its characteristics are the actual characteristics of that person, it achieves a feeling of affirmation, or pride, as if to say, "I really do exist." This feeling is the needed compensation for loss of self-esteem created by being told early in life, "in and of yourself you are not enough." However, the feeling of being affirmed lasts only a short time, when the doubt reinserts itself. Then the affirmation must once more be renewed. This cycle, and the anxiety of not being enough, drives the individual ego and is what gives it a life of its own. To maintain this "life," it guzzles chi, in order to gather the energy it needs to keep itself affirmed by others, and to keep at bay the constant threat of extinction that accompanies not being recognized. The most "successful" egos are those which can attain positions of power, whether it be charismatic, psychological, or feudal power (as in being a part of the aristocracy), for this means the eyes of others are forced to "see" and recognize them as high, or great, and as holding the keys to their success. This is why, within the dynamics of the parallel reality, possessing power is equated with "success." The person seeking to become free of the ego within himself needs to thoroughly understand these dynamics. (True success as indicated in the *I Ching*, occurs when a person is in harmony with the Cosmos.)

The ego can be heard as a voice within the personality, in the speech modes of the character or the role it is playing. Thus, when a person says to himself, "I am a father," he then takes on the role of the father in whatever way the idea of a father is defined by his group. If the group sees the father as authoritarian, the inner (and outer) voice of the person who begins to identify with that role takes on this tonality. The same happens to the person who says, "I am an author," "I am a singer," "I am an academic," etc. So long as he identifies with the role, it dictates his life, for his inner voice is constantly checking to see if he is fitting the role, and whether others are recognizing him as such. The same does not happen if he says, "I write," or "I have a child," and avoids adopting the corresponding self-images.

All self-images are character masks that live their "lives" at the expense of the true self. The true self is thrust aside, gagged, and locked up in an inner prison cell, where it leads the life of a slave. (*See* Line 3 of Hexagram 54, "The marrying maiden as a slave.") The person who embarks on the path of his inner truth needs to realize that the goal is not to "sacrifice" any part of his true nature; it is to free himself of the ego in all its aspects, thereby liberating his true self from the ego's oppression.

To be able to free the true self, it is essential to clearly understand the difference between the ego and one's true self. The ego even appropriates Cosmic words such as "self-development" and "modesty" to its purposes. It will try to describe modesty as "taking a back seat," or the person's "fading into nothingness." Or else it will minimize or trivialize our sincere effort by inferring that we are paying too much attention to ourselves. This activity of the ego is part of its program of "upgrade" features, which are designed to deal with anything that threatens to displace it. These upgrade features are more sleight-of-hand tricks that have this mode: they perceive a threat in the form of a freeing idea; they embrace that idea, and then subtly turn it to its opposite meaning. In regard to self-development, the ego has no interest in developing the true self; on seeing it as a threat, it will do all it can to encourage the person to pursue the self-image of the "self-developed person," or the "spiritual person." Through this tactic, the ego inserts itself as the leader of the person's self-development, and if successful, drives the true self gradually into annihilation.

Throughout this book we have made a clear distinction between true self-development which means liberating the true self and allowing it to grow up, and false self-development as the cultivation of a self-image.

A similar interference of the ego is at work when modesty is put up as a model of achievement. It is important to constantly be aware of when we feel any pride or attachment to an idea, for this indicates the activity of the ego.

Feeling and Emotion

Another clear distinction between the ego and the true self needs to be made when it comes to a person's feelings: the Sage has given us a deeper understanding of what distinguishes true feelings from the emotions (negative or positive) coming from the ego. A true feeling is neither negative nor positive, but simply expresses the inner truth of that person at a given moment. Due to the principle of complementarity among all aspects of the Cosmos, every true feeling draws a complementary feeling (which is a Helper), the result of which is felt as harmony. Sadness about a given situation, for example, draws a Helper that helps to heal that situation. Love, we learned, is never a feeling that can be felt by one aspect of the Cosmos all by itself, but is either the result of two people's recognition of their complementarity, or the result of a person's recognition of his own complementarity with certain aspects of Nature.

What we call negative emotions (hatred, envy, jealousy, boredom, grief, etc.) or positive emotions (love, when stolen by the ego, or pity) are either ego-emotions created by the ego's distorted view of reality, or true feelings that the ego has appropriated to itself, in order to steal their energy. When, for example, the ego steals a person's true feelings of love, it turns them into an instrument of power over the beloved. Pity is an ego-emotion that comes from denying the existence of the Helpers, and is an acceptance of suffering as the natural condition of life. The *I Ching* makes it clear that all suffering is ego-induced; pity is a projection that prevents a person from calling the Helpers to aid another, or from saying the inner No to the other's ego, which would strengthen the suffering person's true self.

As to the "negative" emotions, it is more obvious that they are in conflict with the Cosmos, which expresses itself as love. Negative emotions not only have no place in the Cosmic scheme of things, they act to keep the person separated from the Cosmic Whole. Rejecting ego-emotions is the main theme of Hexagram 41, *Decreasing*. Within the Cosmic Harmony, everything is directed at increasing the whole. The increase of one aspect of the Cosmic Whole does not, as commonly thought, mean decrease for another; it is always an overall increase. It is only the ego, that through increasing itself, automatically decreases something else. This is true for the entire parallel reality.

The Ego's Tactics to Remain in Place

Among the maintenance features of the collective ego's program is the variety of fears it installs in the psyche: fear of not having enough, of being without help, of being rejected and abandoned, and the fear of annihilation, which the ego uses to perpetuate its tyranny of fear. All of these fears are based on mistaken ideas about the nature of the Cosmos. The person freeing his true self needs to recognize that the ego will activate these fears in every possible situation. His only defense is to bring the phrases in which these fears are couched into full consciousness with the help of the Sage and the *rtcm*, and reject them with the inner No. The presence of fear is always an indication that the ego is at work; the *I Ching* teaches us how to separate from fear and its intimidation.

Another tactic of the ego is to declare that relying on the inner No as a response to problems is "nonsense," and that the person who follows his inner truth has "lost his sense of reality." When a person starts to see and experience the Cosmic Way, he knows both from his heart and his mind that it is real.

The same observation applies to objections from the ego that the Cosmos as a system of harmonics is not scientifically proven. The *I Ching* calls such a demand that the Cosmos prove itself to the one sense of outer seeing, "youthful folly." The natural sciences have pervasively excluded the feeling consciousness of the Cosmos by the very definition of what scientists consider as "objective reality." The Cosmic Reality is first and foremost *felt* and perceived through *all* our senses. The objective approach of Western science denies the relevance of most of our inner senses, such as the senses of inner smell, inner taste, inner hearing and inner seeing. The objective approach is based only on thinking and calculation. The result is a rational logic that, due to its fundamentally limited view, has created the parallel reality described in this volume. So long as "objectivity" is dependent on the one sense of outer seeing, rational argument will turn in circles.

When a person is ready to embark on the path of unveiling his true self, he needs to be aware that his ego will pull a number of tricks to hold him back or obstruct his progress. A common trick is to instill fear in him by suggesting, for example, that "the Sage might ask you to give up your job/your relationship/your group, etc. "It will suggest that the person is jeopardizing his existence by following such a path, since it is contrary to everyone else's opinion. On closer examination, these rationales turn out to be iterations of the same phrases by which the ego was installed into his psyche in the first place. Any insinuations, that the Sage asks us to give up this or that, are false. The Sage does not ask a person to give up anything. It only helps him to see that his freedom lies in ridding himself of the ideas that keep him in bondage.

Other suggestions of the ego are: to be in permanent harmony "would be boring," and that "ups and downs are what
make life interesting." It also suggests that if the person gives up
his status, "he won't have a purpose any more," that if she gives
up her "sunny" self-image, she "won't be loved any more," if he
gives up his image of being the provider, he "won't be needed
anymore," and if the person gets rid of all his self-images "he
will no longer exist." Through such suggestions, the ego presents a bleak and hapless picture of what it would be like to
have "no identity." It characteristically argues that "either you
are special or you are a nobody," and suggests whatever is necessary to make the person feel comfortable within the status
quo and to keep striving. When a person recognizes the wholeness and uniqueness of his true self, and the fact that his true
self is being cared for and loved by the Cosmos, he can clearly
identify the rationales of the ego as lies.

The ego, in every circumstance, wishes to make the person
feel powerless against its dominance. Its power lies in the fact
that the fears, by which the ego was installed in the child's psyche,
were greatly magnified by the child's imagination. For example,
to the sensitive child, the imagination of hell's fire attains a demonic size and reality. It is this magnified visage of the threat
that enables the ego to appear invincible.

Deprogramming the False Inner Programs of the Collective Ego

The program of the collective ego has been designed in me-
ticulous detail, to ensure that it is passed on from generation to
generation. Nevertheless, it is entirely possible to systematically
deprogram it, with the Sage's help. Every phrase removed leaves
the person that much freer to be who he truly is. One of the
main meanings of the *I Ching* words, "it furthers one to undertake something," is to point to the necessity of taking inner action to free one's true self.

The method of deprogramming consists in reversing the process by which the false words, images, and phrases were originally introjected into the psyche. (A detailed description of the
method is given in the Appendix.)

It is important to recognize that the ego is on hand with any number of programs to replace those we remove; in fact, it is the very element that asserts the need for another existing program, or else an entirely new program, along with the complaint that "there would be nothing there" if we take everything away. In fact, the only way to uncover and activate the perfect program that is part of our original nature is to add nothing. It is also part of the ego's tactics to make us feel that we have been stripped bare, once we take away all the self-images and their attendant ego-emotions. It suggests that we will no longer be able to feel anything. In reality, once we have removed the old program and let go of all the false emotions connected with it, we experience a wonderful feeling of being in harmony with ourselves and with the Cosmic Whole.

We have already experienced deprogramming to have wonderful effects on mental, emotional, and physical health; we have also experienced these results in our personal relationships and business activities. At this point we feel that every problem we encounter can be resolved through finding the obstructing mistaken ideas that have caused it, and deprogramming them in the ways we have learned from the Sage. These ways are detailed in the Appendix.

Freeing Oneself from Projections, Spells, and Poison Arrows

We have already mentioned the existence of projections, spells, and poison arrows, and their harmful effects on our lives and on Nature in general. The following is a more thorough description of them. The method of how to free oneself and others from them is mentioned in the Appendix.

Our awareness of these elements gradually emerged with receiving Line 3 of Hexagram 32, *Duration*, which says, "He who does not give duration to his character meets with disgrace." Wilhelm's commentary, "humiliations often come from an unforeseen quarter," and the suggestion that the cause lay within the person, provided the clues that led us to ask the Sage more about this line. It turned out that it had to do with fears or doubts the person had, which he projected into reality. This was the beginning of our investigation into projection itself, which we realized had to do with "consciousness" either as incorrect thoughts or images. The power of projection lies in the fact that inasmuch fears and doubts are a form of consciousness, they have the ability to project the disharmonious thoughts and images, the very things feared, into reality.

This realization also led us to recognize how words and images, inappropriately applied to describe a person's nature, create fixes or locks in that person's psyche, that we call "spells." Spells create blocks in certain synapses of the brain and central nervous system, but also in muscle tissues. An example of a common spell is the phrase, "That's the way he is." Other typical spells contain the words "always" or "never." In addition to affecting humans, spells are routinely put on animals and plant-life by humans, as well as on foods and living environments. Spells are primarily negative and general conclusions a person has mistakenly drawn from experience. This happens, for example, in relationships when a person has decided, after a negative experience, that "men are like that," or "love is a myth," or "women are not trustworthy," etc. The person, on making this decision, obstructs the function of numerous synapses in his brain, preventing him from being able to experience relationships in other ways. It can be said of spells that they are like the frame of a picture that closes off everything to be seen beyond that frame. Belief systems characteristically close off fields of perception that lie beyond their defined boundaries. On this account, it can be said that all belief systems include, in their basic premises, wordings that create spells.

The mention of "metal arrows" in Line 4 of Hexagram 21, *Biting Through,* led us to distinguish a particular kind of spell, caused by envy, comparisons, hatred, vindictiveness, and similar ego-emotions, which we call "poison arrows," because of the poisonous reactions they create in the body of the person affected by them. The poison arrows "wound" the body consciousness; the poisonous nature of the wound can give rise to chronic illnesses. Inasmuch as they affect a person's subconscious, poison arrows can cause the person to have injuries and accidents. We also learned that poison arrows can be the cause of so-called inherited diseases, since these are often due to comparisons that have been made between one person and another, from whom he "might" inherit the problem. The word "might" is the tip of the arrow, a doubt that allows the rest of the arrow to enter.

We also found that the poison arrows mentioned in Feng Shui have their origin, not in the earth or land itself, but in the thoughts and images that are projected onto the land, both by the ego of the owner, and by the envy aroused in the beholder.

We have learned that the characteristics ascribed to certain breeds of animals fix those animals into certain behavioral patterns, and in their "tendencies" to develop particular kinds of health problems. Similar spells are created by preventive health care regimens, which "look for the possibility" of certain illnesses presumed to occur at certain ages. Statistics similarly can put spells on people or things.

Projections, spells, and poison arrows are capable of seriously damaging the developing psyches of embryos, causing psychological problems such as learning difficulties and states of depression, and a wide range of physical problems. We have experienced these effects caused by guilt in mothers who have smoked, drunk, or taken drugs during pregnancy, when a person has been an unwanted child, or when a person's birth was wanted mainly to fulfill a family duty, or fulfill the self-image of the mother or father.

As we have pointed out in the Appendix, it is possible to free the psyche of the person thus affected, by ridding him of the phrases and images that have caused the damage. Of course, this requires that the person have a strong will and desire to free himself of them. One would, at first, think this is not to be questioned. However, to get along in life, people have frequently surrounded themselves with relationships that act as crutches. These co-dependencies can make them afraid of losing their copartners, once they are freed of their problems. Often these copartners have a complementary investment in their partner's remaining dysfunctional, especially when their self-worth is attached to being the caretaker.

Part II

The Sixty-Four Hexagrams

1. *The Cosmic Consciousness*

 Ch'ien
Ch'ien

This hexagram is inseparable from Hexagram 2, since together they show the two sides of the Cosmic Whole. Hexagram 1 shows the expanding energy of the light. Hexagram 2 shows the energy of the dark that attracts the light.

The Judgment: *Yüan Heng. Li Chên. The Cosmic Consciousness is great through its interpenetration of all things; it discerns what feels harmonious and brings it into form through transformation.*

"Cosmic Consciousness" is the name the Sage gives the aggregate consciousness of the Cosmos. It is the invisible origin of all the things that exist in form as Nature. Nature is the primary way in which the Cosmic Consciousness manifests. All the things that exist in Nature are *compressed* Cosmic Consciousness, and are unique aspects of it. (*See* Hexagram 2, *Nature.*)

In an extremely condensed form, the four Chinese words of The Judgment, *Yüan Heng. Li Chên,* show the main Cosmic Principles that characterize the Cosmic Consciousness: *Yüan"* means "great," "the head," or "the first"; *"Heng"* means "penetrating," and "inner truth"; *"Li"* means "discerning"; and *"Chên"* means "transformation from non-form into form," and "duration."

The Cosmic Consciousness and Nature are inseparable. They interpenetrate each other in the same way that a person's consciousness (which is invisible) interpenetrates with his body (which is visible). The experience that they make together, as an integrated being, connects the person with his Cosmic origin, and contributes, along with the experiences of all the other things that exist, to the constant evolution of the Cosmic Consciousness.

The words, "it discerns what feels harmonious" refer to the

conscious response of the Cosmos to everything that happens. The Cosmic Consciousness is primarily a *feeling* consciousness that also thinks. This conscious response is a thinking response which is expressed in the Cosmic words "Yes" and "No." It says Yes to what *feels* in harmony with its unity and to what benefits all of its parts. It says No to what feels harmful to its unity (discord), and retreats from it. While its parameters allow dissonance (small mistakes), they do not allow discord (continuing mistakes). Thus, as a whole, the Cosmic Consciousness is a system of harmonics with self-defined parameters.

The phrase "...and brings it into form through transformation" refers to the fact that the Cosmic Consciousness employs transformation rather than changes as its primary way of operating. Through transformation, it brings into form what feels harmonious. The result of this is Nature.

"Penetrating" also refers to the way Cosmic Evolution is carried out as far as humans are concerned. It occurs through the invisible penetration of harmonious thought and feeling from one person to everyone around him. In order to know what feels harmonious, every person possesses a Cosmic Memory of what Cosmic Harmony feels like. This memory is located in every body cell. It is meant to guide human thinking and help humans find the correct words and names for things—words that express their essence. When feelings of Yes and No come from a person's inner truth into his fully conscious mind, and are then acted upon by saying the inner Yes or inner No to them, they penetrate without effort or intention to the inner truth of those around him.

Penetration takes place in the realm of the atom, where atoms are transformed by specific helping aspects of the Cosmic Consciousness. All human efforts and intentions to make things happen through *changes* (as of a mechanical nature, or by superficial alterations), block this transformation, because they come from the ego and its use of power; the Cosmos does not collaborate with the ego.

Because of the interference of the ego, humans have been given the *I Ching* to show them the Cosmic Way and to help them discern which thoughts and actions are in harmony with the Cosmos, and which thoughts and actions come from the ego. The four principles that characterize the Cosmic Consciousness also describe the purpose of consulting the oracle: as the way for humans to bring themselves into harmony with the Cosmic Consciousness before undertaking something. Each term describes a step in a four-step process. Consulting the oracle means learning to discern what thoughts are in harmony with the Cosmic Way and saying the inner Yes to them, while saying the inner No to all disharmonious thoughts. (*See* p. 29, "The Purpose of Consulting the Oracle.")

The *I Ching* is concerned with the human ego as the primary source of discord with the Cosmos. The individual ego is the product of a collective ego that has developed from a false use of language. This false use of language has led humans to imagine themselves to be the center of the universe. It is the key idea that has caused humans to separate from the Cosmic Unity; it has also resulted in the creation of a *demonic sphere of consciousness* and a *parallel reality* that compete with the Cosmic Consciousness, causing it to retreat from humans. (*See* p. 42, for a discussion of the collective ego and p. 46, for a discussion of the individual ego.)

Incorrect thoughts and feelings, having their origin in the demonic sphere of consciousness, harm everything they focus on. However, they do not affect things through penetration, but through jumping from the shoulder of one person to another. They are the dragons mentioned in the lines of this hexagram.

The Cosmic Evolution is meant to be achieved jointly, with the full consent of all its aspects, including human beings. This is the Cosmic meaning of the "joint approach" mentioned in Hexagram 19, *Approaching Jointly*. However, so long as humans see themselves as set up above all other aspects of existence as *special*, they remain outside the Cosmic Unity, inhibiting its evolution.

The Cosmic Consciousness is eternal, perpetual, and directionless in Time; this is why it can always be found, and revealed, in this very moment.

Wilhelm translated *Ch'ien*, the name of this hexagram, as "The Creative, Heaven," based on a quote from Confucius which said, "Great indeed is the generating power of the Creative; all beings owe their beginning to it. This power permeates all heaven." Three problems occur with this rendering: first, that it becomes the basis for seeing the Cosmos as having a *hierarchical order*, with heaven above and earth below; second, that *heaven* is the source of the primal creative force, and third, the idea of a *creation* implies Time as linear or discontinuous, with all things having a beginning and an end.

From a Cosmic perspective, these conceptions are the result of a feudal culture that has imagined the Cosmos to operate and be ordered like itself: as hierarchical, and as based on power. These conceptions provided the basis for the feudal idea that humans are the special creatures of creation, whose purpose it is to create "heaven's order on earth."

The purpose of this hexagram is to show the true nature of the Cosmic Consciousness and how the collective ego competes with it through its institutions. Just as the individual ego is a false self that oppresses and sacrifices a person's true self, the collective ego is a false ordering created by institutionalized beliefs and societal myths that oppress and sacrifice what would otherwise be the natural order of society. Just as the true self, which is in accord with the Cosmos, constantly benefits from its help, so would the natural order of society be guided and helped by the Cosmic Consciousness. What prevents this symbiosis is the constant attempt of the collective ego to deny the existence of the Cosmic Consciousness and to put its own institutions in its place.

The various hexagrams of the *I Ching* show that the Cosmic Consciousness operates through harmony and attraction, without employing any power. The *modus operandi* of the collective ego, by contrast, is entirely based on the use of power.

Each line of Hexagram 1 presents the dragon as a metaphor for the collective ego and its accumulated ideas that seek to control the life of the individual. They do this by first defining human nature, and subsequently human goals and purposes, in the terms of the collective ego. These definitions conflict with the real purpose of human life, which is for each individual to fulfill his *uniqueness* (instead of fulfilling the empty ideal of being *special*). Only in this way can each person contribute to the ongoing evolution of the Cosmic Whole.

Because the collective ego is a composite of mental constructs that depends upon the energies of each individual to keep it functioning, it is parasitic in nature, and ultimately destructive to the life force of the individual and to the whole of Nature.

The collective ego's control of the individual is initiated during early childhood, by its introjecting mistaken beliefs into the psyche of the child through a continuous conditioning process. The phrases and images of these beliefs are what Confucius is reported to have called the "seeds" of good fortune or misfortune.* These seeds gradually grow in a person's psyche, suppressing his original inner program and controlling his actions. As controlling elements that reflect the values of the collective ego, they are the dragons referred to in this hexagram, and in Hexagram 2. Because these values are inserted into the psyche through threats accompanied by punishments, and through the flattery that humans are special, they have a demonic character, haunting the individual and filling him with guilt if he goes against them by following his *inner truth*. Those ideas of the collective ego that are flattering and suggestive (especially those offering the fame, success, and personal power associated with becoming a hero) operate as imps within the psyche. These imps form the ego, which then seeks to dominate the individual's psyche, and repress his true self.

Although these demonic elements (dragons, demons, and imps, the latter of which we have added after seeing them in meditation) are the subject of concern in all the hexagrams,

---

* Wilhelm's commentary to Line 2 of Hexagram 16 reports Confucius to have said that the seeds of thought are the "first imperceptible beginning of movement, the first trace of good fortune (or misfortune)...." and that to know them "is divine indeed." The Sage made us aware through referring to this quotation, that the "seeds" we need to pay attention to are the seed phrases of the structured beliefs that underpin all demonic thought.

they are rarely named in this volume, because doing so gives them a recognition which empowers them. The *I Ching* shows that these demonic elements are structures created by language, and accordingly, can be dismantled, phrase by phrase and image by image; they are eradicated from the psyche by saying the inner No to the seed phrases and images that comprise them. Indeed, ridding oneself of them is the effort referred to in the *I Ching* as "undertaking something."

The lines of Hexagram 1 show in their sequence how the individual ego is led to develop itself from an imp into a dragon. The final step is shown in Line 4, where the person has wholeheartedly internalized the values of the collective ego, and become its *hero* who, in turn, enforces its values. In Line 5 his fantasy sees him "flying in the heavens" as his reward. The lines thus show how a person splits himself off from the Cosmic Unity through the creation of the ego, and through accepting the myth that he is special and superior.

As mentioned, the mental program that creates the ego has been installed in the psyche with the help of threats, punishments, flatteries, and rewards. Therefore, the ego takes on a "bully" character that keeps the true self intimidated and locked in self-doubt. The person needs to clearly realize that the ego is a parasite in his psyche that not only feeds on his life energy, but that, if not counteracted, will eventually destroy him. To rid himself of it requires that he recognize and deprogram all the false phrases and images on which it is based. The purpose of the *I Ching*, as a gift of the Cosmos to humans, is to help the individual achieve this divestiture.

This hexagram shows that the Cosmic Consciousness is the source of the life force (chi energy). This life force is comprised of helping consciousnesses that are the source of all creativity, nourishment, help, and healing. Throughout the *I Ching* these consciousnesses are anonymously called "Helpers," "friends," "armies," or are referred to indirectly as "a wagon for loading," a "yellow lower undergarment," or a "vehicle for crossing the great water." These Helpers come to a person's aid whenever they are called, but especially when they are included in his everyday awareness. As many of the hexagrams show, these Helpers become blocked or demonized by beliefs that deny their existence, and that slander human nature and Nature as a whole.

While the collective ego places humans at the center of the universe, it simultaneously asserts that the *individual* is insignificant in the overall order of things. It does this by telling him he is not good enough in and of himself, and therefore needs *to become* something, if his life is to have meaning. This contradictory logic has the purpose of denying two facts: that the individual has true significance and a Cosmic purpose, and that he has all the help he needs from the Cosmos to live his life successfully. The purpose of these lies is to make him dependent on the collective ego for its recognition and help. The collective ego asserts itself as the sole authority to define the person's success, while at the same time making its measure unattainable. This last device seeks to keep the person permanently attached to *its* goals. The *I Ching* shows us that the only way out of this mental maze is to say the inner No to the seed premise that the individual is born deficient, and that he must *become* something. Freeing himself from this construct restores his original wholeness and self-esteem.

The second premise put forward by the collective ego is the idea that the individual is indebted for everything he has ever received. Thus he owes the debt of his life eternally to his parents, the debt of his religious training to the church, the debt of his education to the school he has attended, etc. When all the debts that extend from home to nation are added up, his psyche is burdened with an unpayable debt that becomes transferred into a repository of guilt and false feeling of loyalty to the collective ego. This unpayable debt is the dragon that haunts each line of this hexagram, and is the driving force that separates the individual more and more from his unity with the Cosmos.

Both the guilt and the loyalty strengthen the power and control of the collective ego and divert the individual's attention from remembering what his repressed inner truth could tell him: that all existence, including the daily sustenance he receives, is a gift of the Cosmic Consciousness and its expression as Nature.

Application:

When a person receives this hexagram without changing lines, it is a message to remind him that he is an equal part of the Cosmic Whole. This means that while he is unique, he is not special. Just as humankind is not "chosen" or distinguished among animals, no individual human or group is to be considered elite or heroic. It tells him that if he will take his proper place in the Cosmic Whole by saying the inner No to the delusion that he is special, he will put himself back in the Cosmic stream of chi energy (his source of creativity, nourishment, help, and healing) from which he has become separated. Being separated also means that he is no longer in contact with the Sage, the Cosmic Teacher.

Receiving this hexagram can be a signal for a person to reflect on where he is looking for guidance. Is he looking outward to the "ancient wisdom" promoted by the collective ego? Or, is he turning his attention within by asking the Sage that speaks through the *I Ching* to provide him with the insight he needs to find the correct way for himself? This hexagram wants to make him aware of the danger that comes from looking without, and of the benefit that comes from looking within. What he gets from looking without, or to others for guidance, is only the appearance of reality and other people's ideas about the nature of the Cosmos. This knowledge is not the same as what he learns by communicating with the invisible Sage, and thereby *experiencing* for himself the nature of the Cosmos.

Receiving this hexagram without lines can also call a person's attention to his using words that have no basis in the Cosmic Harmony, and to the fact that using them creates demonic consciousness. Among such words are the following: guilt, culprit (evildoer), power, and unconditional love. These words are faulty because they describe conditions that do not exist in the Cosmic Order. For example, while there is Cosmic blame, which is always momentary and erased the instant the fault is corrected, *guilt* is a permanent stain imagined by human beings.

A person may also receive this hexagram when he has accepted the ideas that "his (or human) nature is faulty" and that "he is deficient in and of himself to cope with life." These ideas fix parts of his psyche in a spell that subjects him to a life of striving to become something he is not, and to adopt the self-images offered by the collective ego. These ideas prevent him from discovering and expressing his uniqueness, and trap him into following the path of the hero.

Note: Since all lines contain infinite possibilities of interpretation, one needs to use the *rtcm* to determine if the meanings suggested here apply to the given situation. (*See* p. 736, Using the *rtcm*.)

Line 1. *Hidden dragon. Do not act.*

In the broad and general sense, the "hidden dragon" refers to the collective ego, which has presented its institutions and values as "the only source of solutions." This idea serves to divert people from recognizing its dragon nature, and obscures the fact that the Cosmos is the true source of all their needs.

In the particular sense, the "hidden dragon" indicates the presence of demonic influences in the situation being referred to. These influences can be back-of-the-mind thoughts that are generated by ego considerations. They can also come from a projection, spell, or poison arrow. So long as these influences are not recognized and eradicated, the action the person takes will not be successful. (*See* p. 697, Freeing Yourself from Projections, Spells and Poison Arrows.)

Among these influences is a poison arrow that makes a person believe that by nature he is faulty, or not good enough, in and of himself. This poison arrow has been activated in relation to the situation at hand. Before the outer situation can be corrected, he needs to make an inner effort to rid himself of any seed phrases that suggest he is faulty, such as, "you are not sufficient within yourself to cope with life," "everyone is dependent on those around him," "evil comes from your animal/bodily nature," and all the images that are connected with animal nature as inferior, or degraded (wild, bestial, cruel, savage, etc.).

These poison arrows, which originate in the collective ego, have the effect of shutting off certain synapses in the brain, isolating a person from helping aspects within himself, thus robbing him of his completeness. Because they firmly put him on the path of the collective ego, they separate him from the Cosmic Unity.

To compensate for these supposed deficiencies in his nature, the collective ego suggests that each person has "unrecognized greatness" or "heroic potential," that if developed under its supervision, will overcome his deficiency. This idea is the origin of all ambition, striving, and subsequent arrogance.

The person's ambition has the goal of redeeming him in the eyes of the human authority that has pronounced him to be inherently inferior. The authority can be his parents, peers, teachers, or the various institutions of society, when they act on behalf of the collective ego. His ambition is to become either equal with, or in charge of, that authority, be it in the social, political, economic, or spiritual sphere.

When demonic elements are hidden in the psyche, they influence the person's actions even against his will. They reduce his options to those which are offered by the collective ego, which, generally speaking, are either/or choices. Seeing his world in this narrow framework leaves him feeling helpless and stuck, because he has been isolated from his true nature, and from Cosmic help.

The person who has thus developed an inferiority complex is caught in a "logical circular reference" that is unsolvable within its own logical system. The ideas that comprise the circular reference cause the person to see only the institutions of the collective ego as his source of help. Therefore, he looks to institutions, hierarchical authorities, and solutions that are often the lesser of two evils, and leave him unfulfilled and embroiled in further problems. From his disappointments and humiliations, which in reality are fates he has created, he draws even more false conclusions about their causes. These false conclusions only isolate him further from his true self, and from Cosmic help. This situation continues until, through some shock or difficulty, he recognizes that by myopically looking within the system for answers, he will find only the same either/or options that lead him around in circles. Once he takes the courage to say the inner No to the mistaken ideas that hold up this system, and calls for help by looking within himself, he can reunite himself with the Cosmos. (*See* p. 677, Saying the Inner No.)

This line can also refer to the hidden source of an illness created by poison arrows that have made a person believe he is inferior and guilty. To restore his health he needs to rid himself of these poison arrows. In making this inner effort, it is important that he not merely call on the Cosmic Helpers to get free of the illness, but also ask them to help him free himself of its sources in his psyche. Anything less would only lead him back to the above-mentioned disharmonious attitudes, renewing the illness, or shifting its locus to a new place.

Line 2. *Dragon appearing in the field. It furthers one to see the great man.*

This line counsels how to respond when the ego (the dragon) begins to appear in another. "The great man" refers to the Sage that accompanies every person. As the ego appears, the Sage in his presence becomes immobilized, unless someone else calls on that Sage to intervene on behalf of his true self. This is especially important in those moments when the observer is tempted to give up on the other as hopeless. If he gives up on that person, the Sage remains blocked for him. When called to intervene, however, the Sage is activated, and displaces those aspects of that person's ego that are active in the situation.

A person may receive this line when he has concluded that another is evil, and thus has put a spell on the Sage in that person's presence and on him. It is not that person's nature that is responsible for his evil deeds, but spells that have been put on him by others. It is the Cosmic duty of the person who observes another doing evil things to first take away the spell he himself has put on him by saying he *is* evil, and then ask the Sage whether he is meant to dispel any other spells that person is under. (*See* p. 697, Freeing Yourself from Spells.)

The dragon appearing in the field can also indicate that a person is becoming aware of the existence of the collective ego and its controlling influence on his life. "Seeing the great man" in this instance, refers to his seeing that his true self, with the help of the Sage, is capable of leading his personality. He needs, however, to make a concerted effort to keep aware of the incursions of the ego, and to keep saying the inner No to them.

The dragon can also refer to a person's having an *image* of himself as a "great man." In this fantasy, he sees himself idealized as the archetypal hero, father, mother, leader, or role model to others, or even as a god or goddess. The person has adopted these self-images to compensate for underlying images of himself as inferior or guilty, images which were instilled in him by the collective ego during childhood. All these self-images of greatness are based on the central myth of the collective ego: that humans are at the center of the universe. It is an irony that these opposite images continuously recreate each other, with greatness only increasing inferiority, and increased inferiority creating the need for more greatness, thus forcing the individual personality into the most extreme positions.

"Dragon appearing in the field" can also be a metaphor for incorrectly seeing the invisible Cosmic Consciousness as "God" in man's image. In this case, "It furthers one to see the great man" means to recognize that God as a high and powerful being is the product of human imagination, and human self-idealization.* Receiving this line can indicate that anyone who looks upward or outward to a deity for help is looking in the wrong direction. To access the Helpers of the invisible world, a person needs to rid himself of the idea that the Cosmos has a hierarchical order, for this only creates a false separation between himself and them. (*See* p. 689, Freeing Yourself from Seed Phrases and Mistaken Ideas, and p. 682, Activating the Helpers.)

Receiving this line can also indicate a person who sees some people as great and powerful, and himself and others as inferior. To reclaim his true self he needs to realize that all people

---

* By looking to ancient China one can see how the idea of a God in man's image came into being. The Chinese did not conceive of a universal higher being, but of their own feudal system replicated in the heavens, with the emperor's first ancestor being at the head of the hierarchy, followed by his feudal lords and ministers, down through their various ranks. Thus, the Em peror worshipped his ancestor as the Emperor on High, while his ministers worshipped their ancestors, and so on. A few humans who attained special status, such as Confucius and Lao Tzu, were given the rank of "Immortals." Otherwise, there existed a lesser pantheon of household and earth gods and goddesses, but nothing comparable to the all-powerful Western Gods.

and things are equal; he needs also to demystify all those he has seen as great, and to release others, including himself, from the negative categories in which he has classified them.

Line 3. *All day long the superior man is creatively active. At nightfall his mind is still beset with cares. Danger. No blame.*

The Sage is informing a person not to approach his effort at self-correction (or correcting anything) ambitiously, as if it were a religion, whereby he ignores his normal life. The danger refers to ambition as an activity of the ego; it would seize the development of the true self and impose it upon the person as a belief system, with rigid rules and duties, in the self-flattery that the more conscientious and self-effacing he is in his efforts, the more swiftly he will attain his goal.

"Danger" refers to harboring and acting upon the idea that self-effacement and self-sacrifice are necessary to develop humility. This idea falsely equates effort at self-correction with asceticism: being poor, working without pay, or being otherwise selfless. This idea is based on the collective ego's idea that the self is the source of evil and therefore needs to be overcome through self-sacrifice. It is the ego that claims the victory when the self is sacrificed.

"No blame" refers to a person's freeing himself of all kinds of ambition. At the core of spiritual ambition is the idea that it consists of "work" at "self-development," with the implication that there is a spiritual ladder that ascends upward to heaven. All ambition belongs to the ego, and is dependent on the person's believing in his "original fault," or "inherent deficiency." (*See* Line 1.) Freeing the true self involves no striving. It is a process of deprogramming layers of mistaken ideas that have repressed and concealed it. All self-images of high achievement, whatever forms they take, only distract and divert a person from freeing his true self. (*See* p. 691, Freeing Yourself from Self-Images.)

This line is also about misunderstandings that surround the nature of creativity. True creativity is a partnership with the Helpers of the invisible world. The presence of ambition is the mark of the person who believes he must do it all. On this account, his creativity suffers. Only when he asks for help from the anonymous Helpers will he collect the help he needs for his inspiration, and also to complete his work. To make this happen, he must first deprogram the ideas behind his ambition, his dependence on the values of the collective ego for his inspiration, and his ideas of insufficiency of self that block synapses in his brain that would connect him with his feelings. (Also *see* the main text of this hexagram.)

Line 4. *Dragon casting about.*

Here, a person's ego has itself become a dragon, because the person has internalized all the values of the collective ego, and now upholds them as its defender. He now believes his purpose is to judge others on behalf of the collective ego. In doing so, he casts spells on them.

"Casting about" can also refer to a person's contemplating which kind of hero he wants to become: the hero who promotes and defends the values of the collective ego, or the hero who defies them. In the latter case, he sees himself as a rebel hero, or one whose heroism is to become a recluse. Whether being a hero for or against the "system," the person is still held within the parallel reality of the collective ego, and he only ends in sacrificing his true self to the heroic self-image.

If a person will rid himself of all such mistaken ideas and the self-images proposed by the collective ego, his true self will become liberated. He will be shown his true place in the Cosmic Reality, and be given a task that allows his true self to mature, which will bring him self-respect.

Line 5. *Flying dragon in the heavens. It furthers one to seek out one's true nature.*

The "flying dragon in the heavens" is an image of the fantasized rewards promised by the collective ego if a person sacrifices his true self as indicated in Lines 3 and 4. In ancient China the reward was immortality.

This line indicates a person in whom spiritual ambition has reached its peak. It advises him to undertake the effort to return to his true nature in order to undo the fate he has created. This effort entails identifying and ridding himself of the cluster of mistaken ideas that revolve around the heavenly rewards offered by the collective ego for the sacrifice of his true nature. (*See* p. 689, Freeing Yourself from Seed Phrases and Images.)

A person can also receive this line when he has accepted the ideas of mortality and immortality put forth by the collective ego. Both misrepresent the nature of the Cosmos as the source of never-ending life. Life, we are informed by the Sage, continues in many dimensions and forms. This continuity, however, can be ended when a person, due to his striving for immortality in the eyes of the collective ego, creates a fate that makes his life end in the very death he seeks consciously to avoid.

This line can also refer to a person who sees with clarity the different ways in which the collective ego operates and the way of the Cosmos, and thus chooses the Cosmic Way.

Line 6. *Arrogant dragon leads to humiliation. Afterwards, a new beginning is possible.*

"Arrogant dragon" can refer to a person who, after recognizing the true nature of the collective ego, still holds to its values out of fear of losing his titles and honors.

"Arrogant dragon" also refers to the grandiose and human-centered idea that in sacrificing his animal nature, a person will gain glory, recognition, or immortality. Such a view regards his earthy nature as degraded, unworthy, and mortal. It also implies that his nature is divided into "spiritual" and "animal," with his spiritual nature being connected with immortality. This false division slanders the wholeness and integrity of his nature. Receiving this line informs him that he has created a fate by his ambition to reach immortality. Because he has lost contact with the earth (reality), Fate will bring him back to his senses. To restore his original wholeness and to end his fate he needs to rid himself of ambition, and the ideas that cause him to strive. (*See* p. 692, Freeing Yourself from a Fate.)

Fate, coming in the form of an illness, brings the person back to his senses. At the same time, a person need not suffer through his fate to its end. He can end it by ridding himself of the poison arrows that have slandered his true nature and his senses. These poison arrows consist of all the phrases and images that see his animal nature as primitive and lowly, and as the source of evil. The downfall is brought about by the slandered senses themselves, because any slander turns them into Helpers of Fate. (*See* also Hexagram 10, *Conducting Oneself.*)

The Law of Fate is also demonstrated in all those situations where people have declared a ship to be "unsinkable," a building to be "indestructible," and when those small back-of-the-mind thoughts say, "now I am secure," and "I have finally got things where I want them." All such thoughts are human-centered and have to do with wanting to fix things in a certain position in time; all such fixing leads to rigidity and decay.

This line may also indicate that through correcting himself, a person has ended his fate and invoked the Cosmic Principle of Transformation. This leads to a new beginning in his relationship with the Cosmos.

2. Nature*

 K'un
K'un

This hexagram is inseparable from Hexagram 1, as both hexagrams show the two sides of the Cosmic Whole. Hexagram 2 shows the energy of the dark that attracts the light, and thus finds guidance.

The Judgment: *Nature is great through its interpenetration with the Cosmic Consciousness; it discerns what feels harmonious and allows that to lead, with the firmness of a mare. If a person tries to lead, he goes astray, but if he follows, he finds guidance. It is favorable to find friends in the west and south and to forego friends in the east and north. Perseverance brings good fortune.*

---

* The traditional name of this hexagram was "The Receptive, Earth." It was said to be the completer of the creative energy associated with Hexagram 1. We have been guided to see that these names have led to confusion. On the one hand Wilhelm states, for example, that the Creative and the Receptive are to be regarded as equals and not as opposites. On the other, he says, "there is a clearly defined hierarchic relationship between the two principles." "When, however, the receptive abandons its position [below] and tries to stand as an

"Nature is great through its interpenetration with the Cosmic Consciousness" refers to Nature as the expression of the harmony of the Cosmic Consciousness. This is true of human and animal nature, as well as for plants, rocks, the earth, and all the forms that are expressed in the Cosmos.

Nature, we learn from the Sage, is Cosmic Consciousness compressed into forms. These myriad forms find guidance through their inner connectedness with the Cosmic Consciousness, and in turn feed back their experiences to it. Together they comprise a living whole that evolves from the interaction of the whole with all its parts. Simultaneously, while one part of the Cosmic Consciousness is compressed into form, the consciousness of the whole is expanded through what is experienced.

"Interpenetrating" also refers to the Helpers of Nature (or forces of Nature) and their capacity to help the whole through creating transformations in the atomic realm. All transformations occur through them. (*See* p. 52, Transformation versus Changes.) All the individual forms in Nature discern what is harmonious through their inner truth, which is their direct connection with the Cosmic Consciousness. This inner truth is imprinted in everything that exists, and is an essential part of the guidance system which each thing possesses. It is a memory of what Cosmic Harmony feels like. When each form allows that memory to guide it, it is in harmony with the whole.

"The firmness of a mare" refers to the state of mind that attracts the light of inner truth; this is a state of being open and receptive, in contrast to just being empty. The open mind is actively reflective, and thereby attracts inner truth. Unlike the empty mind, it distinguishes what it takes in by feeling its quality: whether it is harmonious or discordant. The empty mind, by contrast, is passive and unreflective, and therefore suscep-

---

equal side by side with the Creative ... it becomes evil. The result then is opposition to and struggle against the Creative, which is productive of evil to both." (See Wilhelm pp. 10, 11.) Thus, these names incorrectly introduce competitive behavior into the Cosmos itself. Further, because of the association of the male with Hexagram 1 and the female with Hexagram 2, the basis is established for justifying a hierarchical or oppositional relationship between the sexes. All these ideas contradict the essential unity and harmony of the Cosmos, and the equality between all its parts.

tible to taking in all sorts of ideas without discerning how they feel. In terms of dark and light, the darkness of the open mind attracts the light of inner truth.

The metaphor of the mare, as an animal that is commonly thought to be more willing to follow behind other horses than the stallions, also tells us that we have a choice as to where we put our will: to follow the way of the Cosmos, which is the way of inner truth and harmony, or to follow the way of convention and the collective ego.* If we are to learn how to put ourselves in harmony with the Cosmic Whole and remain in harmony with it, we need to develop the daily habit of asking for the help and guidance of the Sage, our Cosmic Teacher. When we enter situations without the Sage's help, we are forced to rely on our intellect, which, if not connected with inner truth, keeps us in the parallel reality created by the collective ego.

The relationship between the Sage and the student is never one of dominance by the Sage and servility by the student. The Sage places no requirements. Always, it is a question of will as to whether the student wants to belong to the Cosmic Reality, or to the parallel reality. For the student, the learning process can occur only through a cooperation that comes from the deep desire of the student to reunite with the Cosmic Whole, from which he has become separated.

The student needs to understand that the process of reuniting is gradual, much like peeling an onion, layer by layer. He begins at a point where he no longer recognizes his inner truth. The Sage helps him by reflecting his inner truth in the daily situations of his life. If the student asks each day for help, he begins to experience what it means to connect with the multitudinous Helpers of the invisible world. Each new day, he develops an inner dependency upon the invisible world, which makes him gradually ever freer of unhealthy dependencies on others, and on the collective ego. After some time, when his awareness of his inner truth has become established, his dependence on his inner truth, and on help from the invisible world, becomes his way of life.

---

* It is not the genders of the respective horses that is at issue, but rather the Cosmic Principle, expressed as metaphor.

The mare (and the person presumed to be cooperating with the mare) is also a metaphor for the correct cooperation between humans and the rest of Nature (including other humans). This cooperation requires sensitivity on the part of humans, and feeling toward Nature. It is this sensitivity and feeling that create a complementarity between the human and the helping aspects of Nature. This sensitivity and feeling are described further in Hexagram 10, *Conducting Oneself.*

This hexagram informs us about the way our original natures automatically cooperate with the *intelligence of Nature.* This happens through our bodily consciousness, which, like the intelligence of Nature, is a *feeling consciousness.* Each cell and organism possesses this feeling consciousness. An example is the intelligence of what we call the involuntary nervous system. It "knows" perfectly how to regulate itself and interface with the environment, without the need to think. Thinking, however, often interferes with its abilities.

The intelligence of Nature (including our own natures) responds to human thought in a variety of ways, as the various hexagrams make clear. It operates as a complete intelligence of a kind that is not understandable when we confine our perception only to the two frontal lobes of the brain. Nevertheless, by seeing and listening within, each individual has the ability to connect with and experience Nature's intelligence and help. We experience this when we consult the *I Ching.* Like the individual who possesses senses and abilities far beyond the outer senses of seeing, hearing, touching, smelling, and tasting, the intelligence of Nature perceives far beyond what humans can imagine when they confine their view to perceiving and trying to understand only the visible aspects of existence. The views that are produced from this limited perspective lead to the mistake of seeing the universe as turning around humans, and only as a "system of mechanics." (*See* Glossary: The Senses).

"If a person tries to lead" refers to people who act on the collective ego's beliefs that all things depend upon human activity and intervention. Such people, because of their human-centered view of the universe, are unable to draw upon the helping forces that are present in all of Nature, and therefore they go astray, meaning, they separate from the whole. If, however, they will rid themselves of this arrogant view and ask for help, they will find friends in the Helpers of the invisible world ("friends in the west and south"). The image of "friends in the north and east" refers to relying on human Helpers that act within the framework of the collective ego; that is, they help from false feelings of obligation, guilt, the wish to be recognized, or from the intention of gaining power and control. In this respect, "Perseverance brings good fortune" can be a warning to distinguish where one's Helpers come from.

This hexagram also shows how non-form is brought into form. An example is the way helping gifts of insight are given to humans in the forms of inventions, new steps in awareness, some works of literature, music, theater, and what people experience as "achievements of genius." Help comes as well in thousands of other ways: receiving money, the right relationship, the most appropriate job, finding a parking place, or other convenience when one needs it. Help comes to all aspects of Nature, as well as to humans, in the perfect form that is needed. The only times this help becomes blocked or distorted is when humans assume that they are the ones in charge of Nature, and arrogantly interfere in its processes, rather than cooperating with it.

Traditionally, this hexagram has been associated with the dark, and also with receptivity. Light, as energy particles, is activated by its attraction to the dark, to enter the space the dark inhabits. Space is not "empty" in the sense commonly assumed. It contains the dark, which itself is energy. It is furthermore the receptive medium through which light travels. The dark is one part of the Cosmic Consciousness; the other part is the light. Space, therefore, is inhabited by the Cosmic Consciousness that is composed of both the light and the dark. In this space, the interaction between the light and the dark takes place. Through their interaction, the Cosmic Consciousness gets compressed into forms, and is again transformed from form into non-form.

This hexagram also addresses spells that have been put on Nature by mistaken human ideas. Spells and projections, which are brought on by incorrect conclusions about the nature of things and the way they operate, freeze their functioning in accordance with the projected image, preventing them from functioning normally. What we then observe is not the harmony of Nature, but Nature disturbed. These spells remain in effect until someone recognizes their existence and says the inner No to them. Saying the No activates the Helper of Transformation to break the spell. To free Nature from these projections and spells, it is only necessary to take them away. Any attempt to "restore" or "protect" Nature puts yet other spells on Nature's ability to return to harmony. Such attempts come from the same human-centered view that created the problems in the first place.

Application:

Receiving this hexagram is meant, first of all, to teach a person what Nature is, and that he can relate to it correctly only when he recognizes that he is an equal part of it.

Second, it is meant to make him aware that all his mistaken ideas about Nature affect it adversely, causing it to operate in distorted ways. Receiving this hexagram is also to make him aware that he has a responsibility to relate to Nature with sensitivity and feeling.

Third, it informs him that he, like all the other expressions of Nature, is dependent on his connection with the Cosmos for guidance.

Spells connected with this hexagram are created by seed phrases and images having to do with seeing the human role as the creator of order in Nature. Offshoots of this view see human nature as divided into a lower and a higher nature, with human animal nature being demonized. The demonizing of humans' animal nature, and the guilt associated with it, create the perversions that lead to many human criminal acts. Also, describing Nature as wild and threatening creates a perverted relationship between humans and the other animals. Other spells are created by viewing Nature as a system of mechanics, devoid of consciousness or feeling.

Note: Since all lines contain infinite possibilities of interpretation, one needs to use the *rtcm* to determine if the meanings suggested here apply to the given situation. (*See* p. 736, Using the *rtcm*.)

Line 1. *When there is hoarfrost underfoot, solid ice is not far off.*

Here, the hoarfrost that precedes ice is a metaphor for the way all mistaken beliefs lead to disintegration because they separate the person who holds them from his unity with the Cosmos.

This line can refer to the person who harbors the mistaken belief that death is a final end, and that life is suffering. These views falsely present death as connected with irretrievable loss and separation, and slander the nature of the Cosmos by denying the truth that life continues after death in different dimensions of consciousness. Such views spoil the joys of life in a body by the constant anticipation of a loss to come. Moreover, they create a fate. What actually happens at death is the *transformation* that takes the person (animal, plant, etc.) over to the next dimension, which is invisible to us.

This line also points to the hopelessness that accompanies such views, leading a person to see the Cosmos as indifferent and cold. This conclusion is an example of how cause and effect have been reversed by the collective ego. It is not the Cosmos that is indifferent to humans, or which has abandoned them. It is the person's own mistaken views of the Cosmos that have created his separation from it, causing him to feel cold, abandoned, and alone. It is through correcting his mistaken views that he can reunify with the Cosmos and end his fate. (*See* p. 689, Freeing Yourself from Seed Phrases and Images.)

"Hoarfrost" is also a metaphor for the beginning stage of alienation in a relationship, when a person has begun to allow his heart to close toward another. The ice refers to the gradual rigidifying of the heart that comes after he has concluded that the other person or the situation is "hopeless." The person needs to be aware that if he allows his thoughts to continue in this direction, the relationship will certainly end. No situation is hopeless if he asks the Sage to help him identify and deprogram any projections, spells, or poison arrows that are causing the difficulty.

This line also addresses a person who has allowed his heart to close after having been rebuffed for encroaching into another's space. The ego is incorrectly blaming the other for hurting his pride and for causing him to lose face. He needs to reject this activity of the ego through saying the inner No; otherwise, a more serious and unwanted separation from the other will occur. He also needs to ask the Helpers to reopen his heart.

This line also describes the rigidity that occurs when a person turns his back on the Sage by deciding to abandon his efforts at self-correction. He thus gives way to the subliminal protests of the ego that "the ego is not *all* evil," or "I like my ego" (listening to the ego speaking as "I"), or "you can't (or should not) kill your ego." Such a decision separates the person from the Sage and all Cosmic help, and creates a fate.

This line can also refer to an illness. The illness is an expression of a disharmony between a person's body and psyche, due to mistaken beliefs he has adopted. The beliefs have overridden his body intelligence, disabling its natural ability to function harmoniously. The malfunctions caused can lead to death (the ice mentioned in this line), if the false beliefs are not deleted. Such a person needs to seek out the seed phrases of the false program and rid himself of them. (*See* p. 689, Freeing Yourself from Seed Phrases and Images.)

Hoarfrost can also refer to a certain kind of projection that becomes a spell (ice): it is a suspicion that it is in the nature of a person, animal, plant, or other thing to behave in a certain way. This suspicion then projects itself into the psyche of the thing observed, causing it to behave as suspected. If the observer then concludes that the thing's nature is as he suspected, the conclusion turns the projection into a spell, locking that thing either temporarily or permanently into the suspected behavior. Such projections are felt by the recipient as sudden disturbed feelings, such as anxiety, depression, inner weakness, and head or body aches. The resulting spells are experienced as compulsive behavior, in which the person engages against his will. Often, people resign themselves to such behaviors by deciding, "that is the way I am." These projections and spells can be easily broken with the help of the Sage and the Helpers. (*See* p. 697, Freeing Yourself from Projections and Spells.)

Line 2. *Straight, square, great. Without effort everything will be furthered.*

The characteristics "straight and square," contrary to the traditional interpretation of this line, do not refer to the way Nature functions. Nothing in Nature follows straight lines and forms squares in the absolute sense. Even crystalline forms are slightly irregular. The words "straight and square" refer instead to the collective ego's way of building belief systems that justify its existence. The logic of the ego expresses itself in straight lines and absolutes that are shorn of any peripheral considerations. They then are formed into even bigger structures which are "square." The word "great" would only seem to be the self-flattery of the collective ego in contemplating the powerful effect it has on Nature. The Cosmos, by contrast, moves zigzag, the way a sailboat sails to its destination. It moves by what feels harmonious and in this way relates to everything justly.

Squareness also has to do with defining things in terms of time and place as absolutes, thus fixing the things in spells. In regard to time, this happens when we define a person or situation as "always being like that." The "always" freezes the person or situation in time, and the "like that" freezes them in the behavior (place) to which it refers. When this freezing happens, nothing furthers. Use of the words "always" and "never" invariably creates spells that need to be dispelled.

The words "straight, square, great" can point to spells that are caused by seeing things (Nature, animals, human physiology, etc.) as only operating mechanically. This idea comes from the human-centered view that denies that all things in Nature have consciousness. The spells created by these views limit Nature's creative abilities to help us. They also limit the ability of our bodies to coordinate with the environment, our minds to learn (as in learning languages, painting, physical skills), and our abilities to heal, and otherwise protect ourselves from disharmonious influences. (*See* p. 697, Freeing Yourself from Spells.)

In the Cosmic meaning of this line, the word "straight" is a metaphor for the way inner truth, because it is in harmony with Nature, penetrates straight to the heart of others. There, it connects with their inner truth as feeling, rather than thought. It feels "square," meaning it feels wholesome and satisfying. It feels "great," meaning it inspires others, giving them a sense of relief and harmony. When inner truth is spoken aloud, the resonance with others' sense of truth is such that there is no need to defend it or to convince others of it. It is a human-centered view to think that truth needs defending.

Line 3. *Hidden lines. One is able to remain firm and correct [in harmony with Nature]. If by chance you are in the service of a king, seek not works, but allow your efforts to be brought to completion.*

"Hidden lines" points to the fact that a person needs to see the issue at hand as part of a greater Cosmic Plan. In order to fulfill this plan, a person is meant to cooperate with Nature to bring increase to the whole. He needs to recognize that all the great achievements of culture come when humans allow themselves to accomplish things "hand-in-hand" with Nature's Helpers. This means that a person takes neither a dominant nor a servile role, since either of these undermines the equality between himself and the Helpers. Receiving this line indicates that a person has done his share of the task, and now needs to turn it over to the Helpers for completion. A danger exists in that he may think he knows what needs to be done to complete the matter; if he acts on such a thought, he will rule out the Helpers and thus fail to achieve a true completion. He also creates a fate.

A person makes this mistake when he has accepted the pretense, put forward by the collective ego, that humans are the creators of culture. Such a view wipes out of human consciousness the fact that all great achievements of culture are accomplished in cooperation with Nature's Helpers. It is they that have provided the writers their insights, the artists their masterpieces, the inventors their inventions, the builders their knowledge and skills, and the medical researchers their discoveries. When, however, the people who have received these gifts falsely credit only themselves, they steal the gifts. The consequence is that the Helpers gradually withdraw, depriving the accomplishment of the chi energy that makes it beneficial. Such people also create the fate of losing contact with the source of their creativity. When this is the case, some people, instead of returning to humility, turn to *robbing* the Cosmic gifts from Nature by force, as by subjecting animals, plants, and the earth itself to their experiments, or "borrowing" other peoples' insights and creative gifts. In doing so, they create "obstruction upon obstruction" (*see* Hexagram 39, *Meeting Obstruction*). Receiving this line is a call to return to humility, and to apologize to the Cosmos and to Nature. If a fate has been created, the person needs to rid himself of any connected self-image, such as that of the "author," "artist," "inventor," "creator," "star," "the one who knows," etc. (*See* p. 691, Freeing Yourself from Self-Images.)

The "king" can be a metaphor, either for the collective ego, or for the Cosmic Consciousness, depending on which the person serves.

A person can also receive this line when he has made a pact with God or with the Cosmos to bring something to completion that would serve the "greater good," on the condition that he receives wealth or another outcome he desires. By making such a pact, the person has created a fate, which is now in progress, taking away the wealth he has received. The wealth was given to him by the Cosmos—not as an answer to his promise, but as an opportunity to fulfill his uniqueness. The fate can be extinguished by ridding himself of the pact (a poison arrow) and by recognizing that he needs to cooperate hand-in-hand with Nature's Helpers, which alone can bring things to completion.

This line can also refer to the person who follows his inner truth without making any anything of it, or laying claims to it; thus he draws on "hidden lines"—his connection with the invisible Cosmic Helpers.

Line 4. *A tied up sack. No praise, no blame.*
A "tied up sack" is a metaphor for a complex of spells in which a person is caught, in the form of self-images. These self-images have made him buy into ideas that are "pigs in pokes" because they are based on subtle self-flatteries. The self-images include high and noble sounding words that have promised to make him superior, such as "noble," "graceful," "intellectual,"

"distinguished," "philanthropic," "loving," "forgiving," "compassionate," or "spiritual." In presumably lifting him above the perceived lowliness of his animal nature, which he has slandered as "base," "filthy," "plain," "simple," "earthy," "selfish," "greedy," and "driven by lustful/sensual drives," he has deprived himself of the wholeness of life that is to be experienced in a body. The person who thus slanders his animal nature is caught in a double bind—the tied up sack mentioned above. Such a person seeks to hide his animal nature through acquiring "superior" attributes. What he does not realize is that in childhood he was made to feel that because of his animal nature, he is inherently defective. This idea of being defective has created a "hole" in the center of his being that he has hoped to fill through becoming superior. Now, despite his high standing, he finds that the hole is still there. He needs to recognize that the hole is automatically removed when he takes away the mistaken ideas that have created it, thus returning his demonized nature to its original wholeness. (*See* p. 697, Freeing Yourself from Spells and Poison Arrows.)

This line can also indicate a person who sees himself as superior to, or separate from, the Sage, and thus has a standoff attitude by which he judges whether the Sage is to be trusted. Because his attitude is not truly open-minded, the Sage cannot approach. The same applies when a person regards himself as superior to another person, animals, things, or Nature itself: he keeps the invisible Helpers that exist in himself and in all other things blocked from helping him.

The same principle applies to the person who regards parts of his body, or some of its functions, such as his sexuality, as lowly. This view makes it lowly, thereby separating it from being a means by which Cosmic love can be expressed. When it is thus separated from expressing Cosmic love, it becomes perverted. It is the sexual aspect of our animal nature that enables us to receive the Cosmic nourishment of love that renews our life force (chi).

Looking at one's animal nature as lowly also blocks its self-healing capacity. Healing occurs when we rid ourselves of those mistaken ideas that divide us into higher and lower parts. These false divisions break up the unity of the light and the dark, which when not interfered with, interact with each other to complete the cyclical movement of chi energy in every body cell. Healing is not a matter of balancing the light and the dark, but of taking away the ideas that divide them and that see them as opposites. Efforts to balance come from the part of the mind that is devoted to abstract ideas; this part has been given a false superiority, and by such flattery, has been brought into the service of the collective ego.

"A tied up sack" can also refer to the camouflage that disguises a belief system. The disguise is composed of loaded words that surround the belief system with a shield of taboos, preventing a person from questioning its basic premises. Among such loaded words are: "ancient," "sacred," and "untouchable." Only mistaken beliefs need to be protected by such camouflaging. Cosmic Truth, as the Sage makes us aware, is not something fixed, or capable of being written in a "once and for all" format that makes it untouchable, unquestionable, or unchangeable. The truths of life can only be discovered through questioning the untruths that cover them up and make them inaccessible. The search, therefore, is for the untruths.

Another loaded concept is that of the "spiritual path." The idea of such a path is a trap for two reasons: (1) the word "spiritual" falsely implies that the meaning of our existence lies in disembodiment, and the rejection of our connection with the earth and Nature; (2) "spiritual path" implies a path already trodden by others, which we are to follow. In looking to these others for guidance, instead of to the Cosmic Teacher, the Sage, we find ourselves stuck in a tied up sack, unable to follow our inner truth. As the Sage teaches, each individual is meant to follow his own inner truth. This path alone leads him to the unending growth and discovery that occurs by "handhold truths." Each handhold truth allows us to discover the uniqueness of each moment, and leads to an ever-enlarging view. This is the only path that directly connects us, through our life in a body, with the gifts of Nature, and through Nature, with the ever-evolving Cosmic Consciousness.

Line 5. *A yellow lower garment brings supreme good fortune.*

This line tells us that if a person has not suppressed his natural modesty, he will have good fortune. A person may receive this line when he is either tempted to intervene self-importantly or has already done so in a situation for which he has asked the Sage to help. This line counsels him to let go and allow the Sage and the Helpers to take care of the matter, unhindered by his attention. The yellow lower garment refers to the way the Sage and the Helpers operate from their hidden place, in their own mode (which is the mode of transformation), and in their own time. The time required to accomplish their task is always relevant to the circumstances of the moment.

The yellow lower garment is also a metaphor for the Cosmic Consciousness and the Helpers that are compressed into forms. When humans look at things, including their own bodies, as "only matter" that has no consciousness, a spell is put on the Helpers within those things, blocking their ability to help. In the case of a person's body, the spell takes away the body's will to live. (*See* p. 697, Freeing Yourself from Spells.)

The yellow lower garment also refers to the body's knowledge of inner truth. We know what inner truth is by the resonance it strikes within us when we hear it. Each person is born possessing a treasure chest of inner truth as part of his body. Each cell contains imprints of what Cosmic truth feels like, and is his direct connection with the Cosmic Consciousness. He therefore can always trust his inner truth.

Line 6. *Dragons fight in the meadow. Their blood is black and yellow.*

Traditionally this line was taken to mean that the "dark element should yield to the light, because its time is over." This implied that the two elements were separate, and meant to give way to each other. It also implied that the light was higher and leading, and the dark should yield, indicating a hierarchical relationship that assumes that if the right element leads, there will be peace, and if the wrong one leads, there will be discord. Since the light, as noted in the general text, is the Cosmic Consciousness and the dark its expression in forms, there is no such hierarchical relationship, competition, or struggle possible between them. The light and the dark form a unity that operates through one principle only: the principle of attraction between complements.

The meadow here is a metaphor for the field of *opposites* presupposed by the collective ego; the dragons which fight upon it are the two supposed options from which we are to pick. These options are opposite ways to do things that compete with each other, such as socialism versus capitalism, or materialism versus idealism, with each presenting itself as the "right alternative." The person receiving this line is thus caught in arguments of right and wrong, and cannot find his way out, because the point of this duality is to keep him within the field of opposites, and from recognizing the invisible world of the Helpers. The solution is to step out of this duality through eradicating those mistaken ideas about how the Cosmos really operates, thus to reunify with its harmony. Once a person remembers the Helpers and asks for their help, his problem disappears.

False seed phrases connected with this line are: "all belief systems have at their bottom the same basic truths" (in reality, they share the same falsehood that humans are the centerpiece of creation and are therefore superior); "the forces of nature combat each other"; "Nature is man's enemy"; "you either belong to the evil or you belong to the good."

Also in relation to this line is the use of certain words that have no Cosmic basis and, when used, create *opposition,* such as the words "culprit," "enemy," and "villain." They arouse opposing dragons to fight, because they are dragons in themselves. When used in relation to ideas, these words become invested with evil personalities, and thus act as dragons. They can only be deprived of their "life" when a person says the inner No to them as words, and no longer uses them for any purpose.

With respect to a person's chi energy, receiving this line indicates that its two components, the light and the dark, are fighting each other instead of cooperating. This has been caused by beliefs that put one part of his nature up as higher (and light) and the rest as lower (and dark). Through embracing the higher and rejecting the lower, he has put a poison arrow on himself that causes disturbances of the heart, the vascular system, and the blood. The disturbance can be corrected by ridding himself of the poison arrow involved. (*See* p. 697, Freeing Yourself from Poison Arrows.)

3. *Making a New Beginning**

 K'an
Chên

The Judgment: *It furthers one to persevere in not undertaking anything until clarity is attained. It furthers one to appoint Helpers.*

While Hexagrams 1 and 2 describe the basic nature of the Cosmos, the Sage has used this hexagram to define the human place in it.

A person receives this hexagram at times when he is making a new beginning, whether it be in his relationship with himself or another, in his job, or in his learning a new lesson from the Sage. The hexagram wants to make him aware that the new beginning is a Cosmic gift, after a fate that he had created has ended. In order to make a real new beginning, he needs to "attain clarity" about the Cosmic Law of Fate. (*See* Glossary: Fate.)

The Cosmic gift that enables the person to make a new beginning may have come as an inheritance, a love relationship, a child, or help of any kind. Such gifts are expressions of the Cosmos's/Nature's generosity in increasing everything that is in harmony with it. One of the purposes of Fate is to bring a person back to humility, which is a state of being in harmony

---

* We learned that the connotation associated with its traditional name, "Difficulty at the Beginning," implies that "all beginnings are difficult" and has the unwanted effect of putting a spell on making new beginnings; we have changed it accordingly.

with the Cosmos. The gift makes him experience what it is like to be in that harmony, and thus participate in the constant stream of blessings that come from the Cosmos.

At this starting point the person is uncertain how to relate to his gift. The lines of this hexagram offer him guidance in this respect. The first step is for him to recognize its Cosmic nature; the second is to recognize its purpose: the gift he has received is meant to help him free his true self. It wants to be seen as giving him an opportunity to deepen his understanding of the dynamics of life, both in its visible and invisible aspects. The third step is to acknowledge his responsibility to the gift. This responsibility is to not allow the ego to appropriate the gift to its purposes, which would happen if the gift were used to develop a new self-image: that of "the benefactor," or "person of influence" (money gift); in the case of receiving the gift of a child, the danger lies in adopting a self-image that fulfills the *role* of the mother, or the *role* of the father or "head of the family," as defined by the collective ego. In the case of the gift of a love relationship, the self-image might be that of "the man who dominates" or "the woman who yields," or vice versa.

In all such new beginnings, the ego, which has not yet been routed, stands on the side offering flattering suggestions as to how the person can gain extra status or advantage through the gift. If he listens to these suggestions, or entertains them in any way, the ego succeeds in remaining in control. As the servant of the collective ego, the individual ego is always a robber waiting to steal a person's Cosmic gifts, to turn them to the collective ego's use in hopes of gaining its approval, rewards, and authorization. When the person allows the ego to seize the gift, he creates a new fate.

A person frequently receives this hexagram when, upon beginning his lessons with the Sage that speaks through the *I Ching*, he unconsciously transports into his lessons his preconceived ideas, fears, expectations, and prestructured ways of approaching situations. So long as these preexisting elements are in place, "nothing should be undertaken" because they would unconsciously influence the situation. What is true here is true for all the other new beginnings mentioned.

This hexagram also refers to a person who, after he has experienced the burnout of a mistaken idea or belief, seeks to make a new beginning. This new beginning will not be possible, however, if he carries forward his anger, disappointment, and fear of further failure, as these would prevent him from having the openness needed to communicate with the Sage, or "appoint Helpers" as The Judgment recommends (referring to the Helpers of the invisible world).

This hexagram also wants to make the beginning student of the *I Ching* aware that his situation of the moment is the material to which he is meant to apply what he learns. Moreover, no detail of his experience is too small or insignificant to be of use in this learning process. The Sage does not teach theoretical lessons, but uses the situation at hand to teach him that each situation contains an inner truth that is not obvious to the eye. It then shows him the new way he is meant to relate to situations, as for example, by saying the inner No to what is incorrect, and calling on the Helpers of the invisible world to do what is necessary to correct it.

"It furthers one to persevere and not undertake anything" also refers to the suspension of disbelief that is necessary before a new beginning can take place. The Sage realizes that each person brings with him belief systems that are in conflict with what he learns; the Sage never engages in argument, or in efforts to prove anything, but allows the student to discover the truth for himself, often repetitively, until he knows it from within. Even this cannot take place, however, unless the student is willing to temporarily put aside his distrust and at least temporarily suspend his disbelief. This effort alone is required.

Another mistake of the beginner is to transfer onto the Sage all his existing ideas of authority, including that of the highest authority. He needs to recognize that this is the activity of the ego which, by putting the Sage on a pedestal, seeks to gain favors in exchange for obeisance. The Sage retreats whenever the ego is present, and the messages the person receives become confused. (*See* p. 31. The Sage.)

Another obstruction to learning from the Sage is the fear that the Sage will require the person to change in a manner that he

105

is unable or unwilling to do. In fact, the student will present him only with truths that he is capable of understanding and following, and which he can clearly see are in harmony with his true nature.

Other fears connected with the beginning are expressed as doubt: "what is it (the *I Ching*)? Will it tell me the truth? Can I rely on it? Can I trust it? Will it protect me? Will it punish me if I make a mistake? What if it says something that is against my beliefs? Will I fall under its influence and not be able to get free? Will it mean I will have to leave my family, friends, partner, or be abandoned by them? Will it ask me to change myself, so that I am no longer the person I now am? Is the Sage evil?" All of these doubts belong to the ego and its fears of being displaced by the true self, once the person begins to discover his inner truth. The Sage makes no demands that a person do anything; it only helps him to see his inner truth.

The Sage also does not ask a person to trust or have faith. It makes itself available to show the sincere student how his fears block him from realizing his inner truth; how they create in his psyche the demonic sphere of consciousness that attempts to rule his life. It shows him how, by taking away the mistaken beliefs he has adopted from the collective ego, he can learn the true way of the Cosmos, and free his true nature, which is in harmony with the Whole.

The beginner also needs to understand that the Sage does not teach beliefs; moreover, it discourages him from adopting any. A frequent mistake of the beginner is to look around for other belief systems to replace the ones he has discarded. This is because he has been falsely taught as a child that he needs a belief system, because his inner truth is not trustworthy, and because he is not capable of having his own connection with the Cosmos. Accordingly, he may easily fall into the temptation to see the *I Ching* as teaching the same "universal truths" contained in all religions. He needs to realize that this is but one more ploy of the collective ego to remain in control through equating what he learns from the Sage with conventional beliefs. In this way it provides a platform for likening the Sage with the "enlightened" human beings it recognizes.

Another misunderstanding that occurs at the beginning comes from thinking in terms of changes rather than transformations. The "*I*" of *I Ching* has been translated either as "changes," or "transformation" because the two have been used interchangeably in China. The Sage makes us aware that harmony with the Cosmos is not to be achieved through making superficial changes, such as changing one's mind, habits, or attitudes. True change is impossible so long as a person retains the false program introjected into his psyche during childhood. Transformations occur on the base level of consciousness when he deprograms the false phrases and images of this program. A true new beginning requires that he examine and rid himself, with the help of the *rtcm*, of the false basic premises that underlie all belief systems he has accepted into his psyche, whether consciously or unconsciously. He needs to add nothing. What is uncovered through this effort is his true self that is in harmony with the Cosmos. This is the effort that leads to transformation by engaging the Helpers of the invisible world. This is also the meaning indicated by Lao Tzu when he described freeing the true self as "daily diminishing [aspects of the ego]".*

The particular Helper associated with this hexagram is the one that helps us find the root phrases and images, spells and projections stored in our psyche that discourage us from making a new beginning. The robber mentioned in Line 2 is the collective ego that poses as a Helper having the "right solution." These solutions always propose handling the situation by external means, and by taking outer action.

Spells connected with this hexagram often have to do with phrases or images that present new beginnings as difficult. They are difficult only so long as a person does not recognize the existence of the Sage and the Helpers, and does not ask for their help. Plunging ahead without a clear view of the inner truth of a situation certainly leads to difficulties. Among such phrases are: "I would not know where to begin" (as an excuse not to

---

*"Learning consists in daily accumulating; The practice of Tao consists in daily diminishing. Keep on diminishing and diminishing, Until you reach the state of No-Ado. No-Ado, and yet nothing is left undone." Lao Tzu, *Tao Teh Ching*, trans. by Dr. John C.H. Wu (St. Johns University Press, NY, 1961), p. 69.

begin), and "all beginnings are difficult." Such thinking incorrectly views developing oneself as contorting one's nature into a model form. The effort to liberate the true self, under the Sage's guidance, does not burden the person with endless chores and false disciplines; it frees him from within through stages of growth. Each time a person rids himself of a spell, he frees Helpers within himself, making the task easier and easier as he goes.

Note: Since all lines contain infinite possibilities of interpretation, one needs to use the *rtcm* to determine if the meanings suggested here apply to the given situation. (*See* p. 736, Using the *rtcm*.)

Line 1. *Hesitate, because there is a hindrance. It furthers to remain persevering. It furthers to appoint Helpers.*

A person can receive this line when at the beginning of a situation, he feels impelled to take action simply from the belief that taking no action is weak or bad. The word "hesitate" indicates that he lacks clarity, therefore it is unfavorable to take any *outer* action.

The person needs to discover and eliminate the mistaken beliefs he holds about his true nature, which are the hindrances mentioned. They prevent his seeing with clarity that his true nature, which is composed of Helpers, possesses everything he needs to live his life in harmony with Nature. His true nature also connects him with all the helping aspects of the Cosmos. His mistaken ideas and beliefs have put spells both on his true nature, and on the Cosmic Helpers, blocking their harmonious functioning. Taking away these spells will free his feelings, from which true clarity comes. To identify the phrases of the spells, he needs the help of the Sage and the Helpers of the invisible world. He must persist in this effort, by using the *rtcm*, until he has been assured by the Sage that he has correctly and adequately identified them. (*See* p. 689, Freeing Yourself from Mistaken Ideas and Beliefs.)

Spells connected with this line are contained in:

• The phrase: "There is no one to help me but myself." This spell imprisons a person's Personal Helpers through his believing that everything needs to be accomplished by mental calculation, effort, and striving. Such a person carries the world on his shoulders.

• The belief that a person's animal nature is inferior and that to become free of it, he needs to develop his spiritual nature. This idea divides a person's wholeness into parts that are considered antagonistic. A person's true nature is inextricably connected with his body, which is the vehicle for receiving chi energy (life force) from the Cosmos. Disdain of the body blocks the nourishing and healing chi and thus creates susceptibility to illness. Such a person needs the help of the Sage to free his animal nature from this spell/slander.

• The idea that all things have their origin in ideas.* The Cosmic Consciousness originates things from its *feelings*, not from ideas. The person who holds this idea has put a spell/slander on his feelings, so that he looks to ideas for truth rather than to his feelings. He has done so by accepting the flattery that his two frontal lobes are the most important part of his brain.** This belief has also created another spell on the rest of his brain which has been dismissed as primitive. The spell has blocked many synapses and capabilities of the dismissed parts of the brain. (*See* p. 697, Freeing Yourself from Spells.)

This line may also indicate a person who wishes to act, just to end the ambiguity that accompanies not acting. Instead, the person needs to inwardly ask the Sage to be guided. If he remains open, the answer will show itself, if he gives the Sage the necessary space by dispersing his distrust. Dispersal of distrust is a conscious act of saying the inner No to phrases expressing doubt about the Sage's existence, and about its ability to respond and do what is needed. (*See* p. 689, Freeing Yourself from Seed Phrases and Images.)

Line 2. *Difficulties pile up. Horse and wagon turn about. If the robber were not there, the wooer would come. The maiden is*

---

* The Creative (as referred to in traditional versions of the *I Ching*) supposedly originates things from ideas. (*see* Wilhelm, Hexagram 1, page 4.
** See Hexagram 18, main text, for a complete discussion of the consequences of this spell.

*faithful; she does not pledge herself. Ten years — then she pledges herself.**

This line points out that "difficulties pile up" when a person interprets the words of the *I Ching* as verifying his mistaken ideas and beliefs. This happens because he takes its words as literal calls to act outwardly, and as an excuse to use power to make things happen. He does not realize that the Sage can connect with him only through the resonance of the specific words and phrases regarding his situation that comes through his *feelings*. If his mind is operating without any connection to his heart, the messages of the Sage cannot get through to him. The wagon is a metaphor for his feelings, and the horse for the words. The message makes sense only when they are connected. Both are Helpers that have come to help, but have been turned back.

The "robber" is a metaphor for the collective ego, which has interjected its conventional beliefs between the person and what the Sage is trying to say. "The maiden is faithful" refers to the Sage and the Helpers that, being true to themselves, cannot give their support under these circumstances. "Ten years" is a metaphor that says, "the Sage will never come as long as the person holds to those beliefs."

"The maiden is faithful" also refers to situations in which a person is tempted to make a deal to be faithful to another, in exchange for advantages gained. Such deals are inconsistent with his true self; further, they involve him in obligations that are embarrassing and prevent his true partner from approaching. As this line makes clear, the person approaching with the "deal" does so with the intention of robbing him of something: his goods, his chi energy, his good name, his integrity, etc.

Seed phrases that lead one to accept such deals are: "you have to be willing to compromise to get along"; "there is no such thing as the 'right' person for you"; "the right person/help always comes too late"; "you can't count on anything in this life"; " a bird in the hand is worth two in the bush"; "sometimes you have to settle for less"; "it's the best deal I'll ever get"; "in my

---

*This version of the line, taken from the alternative reading mentioned in R. Wilhelm's footnote, was recommended by the Sage.

circumstances you don't look a gift-horse in the mouth." All such phrases create spells that keep a person locked into positions in which he must compromise himself. (*See* p. 697, Freeing Yourself from Spells.)

Line 3. *Whoever hunts deer without the forester only loses his way in the forest.*

The forest in this line refers to demonized Nature, but particularly to a person's nature. The hunting of deer is a metaphor for the hunting of demons that are populating his psyche due to spells. The forester represents the Sage as the only one that can lead him in this hunt. The killing of these demons frees him to be his true self, and ends his separation from Nature and from the Cosmic Whole.

The hunter can also be a person who asks questions of the Sage from idle curiosity, just to be in the know about the way of the Cosmos. Such a person takes for granted the human-centered view of the universe that humans have a right to know everything and the freedom to do whatever they want with Nature. This line warns him that treating Nature as a set of mechanics invokes a fate (his losing his way in the forest).

This line also describes the person who believes the universe operates as a set of mechanics and sees the *I Ching* as defining how the mechanics work. The Sage cannot communicate with him because his beliefs put a spell on his ability to understand.

Two other spells referred to by this line have to do with the idea that "to be in the know is to be like God." It is based on the second spell that says he is unworthy unless he knows the nature of good and evil. (*See* p. 697, Freeing Yourself from Spells.)

Line 4. *Horse and wagon part. Return to the way. To go brings good fortune. Everything acts to further.*

The horse and wagon represent things that are meant to cooperate to achieve progress, as in the unity between thoughts and feelings (mind and heart). Here, the things meant to cooperate have been separated by spells and the wrong conclusions mentioned in the previous lines. "Return to the way" counsels the person to rid himself of these impediments to his progress.

A person makes true progress by ridding himself of the demons in his psyche. The collective ego, by contrast, would have him make progress by following "the new path" it proposes, leading him to a new fate. If he will only walk on the path of his inner truth, which has not been trod by anyone else, everything will act to further.

Line 5. *Difficulties in blessing. A little perseverance brings good fortune. Great perseverance brings misfortune.*
Here, the difficulties encountered refer to the retreat of the Sage that occurs when the ego takes over a person's work on developing himself. The ego hopes, through ambitious and pious work, to be recognized by the Sage as "spiritual."

The meaning of "a little perseverance" is to approach liberating the true self with modesty. This means not to forget to live one's life joyfully. The ego, in its striving, would drive the person to ascetic extremes and deprivations. This is the meaning of "great perseverance brings misfortune."

The problem with the idea of "being spiritual" is that it contains all the self-flattery that maintains the ego as leader of the personality. It further divides a person's true nature into a higher and lower self, splitting his wholeness and placing spells on what is believed to be his "lower," or animal nature. Accepting this idea creates a fate, which is usually that of illness.

This line can also indicate a person whose progress is blocked due to mistaken beliefs about the purpose of human life. It can refer to human-centered beliefs such as: "I have to do it all," "humans are the representatives of heaven on earth," "humans are responsible for making everything work," and "for creating order in the world." These difficulties in blessing can be erased if he asks the Sage to help him rid himself of these mistaken beliefs. This will engage the Helper of Transformation to remove the blocks created by these phrases in his inner program.

Line 6. *Horse and wagon part. Bloody tears flow.*
"Horse and wagon part" refers to the doubt a person has that he will ever reach his goal, whether that be to unite with another, to find the job that really suits him, or the freeing of his

true self. Doubt, coming from the ego, has taken over his psyche, with the result being the bitter or bloody tears mentioned. The blood refers to the consequent loss of the will to go on.

The underlying reason for not having attained his goal is that the ego was busy on the side, seeking to fulfill a certain self-image. For this reason, the help needed from the invisible world was not available. This help could become available if he would rid himself of the ego's ambition to fulfill the self-image.

This line frequently refers to the goal of fulfilling the self-image of the "superior man" (referred to in Confucian versions of the *I Ching*), or the "spiritual person." (*See* p. 691, Freeing Yourself from Self-Images.)

The line can also refer to the fate a person is experiencing due to having accepted mistaken ideas and beliefs such as, "life has a beginning and an end." This fills him with the hopelessness that produces the bitter tears mentioned. Such a view prevents him from recognizing that life is a continuum from one dimension to another, and separates him from the Cosmic Whole. To reunite with the Cosmos, he needs to rid himself of this incorrect idea. (*See* p. 689, Freeing Yourself from Mistaken Ideas and Beliefs.)

4. Youthful Folly

 Kên
K'an

The Judgment: *Youthful folly has success. It is not I who seeks the young fool; the young fool seeks me. At the first oracle I inform him. If he asks two or three times, it is importunity. If he importunes, I give him no information. It does not further to persevere.*

In this hexagram the Sage defines the relationship between itself and the person who consults the oracle. It says to him that if his attitude is modest and unassuming, it will come to help him and answer his questions. It will not withhold any answer so long as he has this attitude. This message is echoed in Hexagram 48, *The Well*, Line 6, "One draws from the well without hindrance. It is dependable. Supreme good fortune."

The title, *Youthful Folly*, points to the different ways in which a person's *ego* approaches the oracle. The words, "It is not I who seeks the young fool, the young fool seeks me" is an indication that it is the person's ego that is approaching, and not his true self. "It does not further to persevere" informs him that after having given this hexagram as a rebuff, the Sage then promptly retreats, so that the messages thereafter either do not make sense, or they tell the person only what the ego wants to hear. After having received this hexagram, the person needs to refrain from consulting the *I Ching* until he has examined and rid himself of his presumptuous attitude.

The ego approaches the oracle with the idea that it is a mechanical device or one of a number of modalities it can use in the hope of attaining success. It also approaches in the hope of gaining knowledge that will give it power, or in the expectation to be confirmed and supported in its beliefs, or in the expectation that the Sage will speak in the ego's language, or inform it of "the truth" in one sentence. It is also the ego that approaches the oracle in an attitude of disbelief, and in a presumptuous and arrogant attitude, in which it expects the Sage to prove itself. Or, it approaches in idle curiosity, to "know" with the mind what the *I Ching* is.

In other instances of youthful folly, the person approaches the oracle servilely, hoping that by looking up to the Sage as a "higher authority" or guru, he will replace the ego with it. This motive is also behind his looking to it as a replacement for his commonsense.

In all the above instances either the ego or the person is trying to appropriate the book or the Sage to serve ego-purposes, something the Sage does not allow. The purpose of this hexagram is thus to show the fraudulent nature of the ego, and a person's wrong motives in approaching the oracle.

"Youthful folly has success" speaks of the different ways the Sage relates to a person's ego and his wrong motives. These different ways are described in the lines.

This hexagram also addresses the mistaken idea typical of newcomers to the oracle that they are only consulting a book.

They tend to take the text literally or symbolically as referring to fixed situations and therefore do not understand that its messages are given in the language of metaphors, the meanings of which are variable, depending on the circumstance. When taken as metaphors, they make possible new insights that deepen the person's understanding, rather than being just an iteration of fixed "ancient truths."

The Sage makes it clear in Line 6, that it tolerates mistaken beliefs for awhile, as when a person expects that the Sage is a "higher power," but it does not support such ideas in the long run. The Sage regards itself, as do all the invisible helping aspects of the Cosmic Consciousness, as *equal* to all the other aspects of the Cosmos. This includes humans, animals, plant life, the earth, and indeed all the things of existence. The Sage acts to support our suppressed *inner truth* until we develop the confidence needed to reclaim our true natures through learning the true way of the Cosmos. However, it never acts in the way we might expect of an all-powerful God: to intervene powerfully in a person's affairs, or to make deals with humans.

To correct any of the above mentioned ego-attitudes that separate a person from approaching the Sage with modesty, he needs to say the inner No to the mistaken views that are behind such attitudes. (*See* p. 677, Saying the Inner No.)

Youthful folly is also about the follies of the collective ego. Among them are: the exalting of what is old; the exalting of what is believed to be powerful; the belief that humans are the center of the universe; that great achievements are due to "human genius"; that "might makes right"; that "winning is the important thing"; that humans are superior to other creatures due to his large brain; that the collective ego knows best what is good for the whole, etc.

Note: Since all lines contain infinite possibilities of interpretation, one needs to use the *rtcm* to determine if the meanings suggested here apply to the given situation. (*See* p. 736, Using the *rtcm*.)

Line 1. *To make a fool develop, it furthers to apply discipline. The fetters should be removed. To go on in this way brings humiliation.*

The person to whom this line applies has been disciplined by the Sage and the Helpers through their withdrawal: they have left him to his own devices, to suffer the consequences. Due to his having been humbled, it informs him that the fetters have been removed. However, if he allows the ego to return as before, it will bring further humiliation.

This line can refer to the person's ego having openly disciplined another's, and put poison arrows of blame and spells of guilt on him. These are also fetters that need to be removed because they create hatred and vindictiveness in the one blamed. Because it is not correct for one person's ego to discipline another's, the Sage puts the fetters of the discipline mentioned above on the person who does this. (*See* p. 697, Freeing Yourself from Spells and Poison Arrows.)

This line shows the correct way to respond to another's ego: by saying the inner No and then turning the matter over to the Sage. The person then keeps his heart neutral and firmly resists allowing the ego to attach itself to justified anger. (*See* Hexagram 26, *The Taming Power of the Great* for an explanation of how the energy of anger is transformed.) He also resists allowing the ego to brand the other person as a culprit, for all branding keeps the interaction between egos active. Retaining neutrality and reserve engages the Helpers to apply whatever discipline is necessary to correct the situation.

A person may also receive this line when he possesses the mistaken belief that the mind ought to control the body. Such beliefs put spells on his wholeness and disable the Helper of Transformation that renews his chi energy. These spells are the "fetters" which manifest in the form of health problems created by the lack or obstruction of chi energy. The health problems bring the "humiliation" mentioned in the line, returning the person to his senses. (*See* p. 697, Freeing Yourself from Spells.)

Phrases that are part of this spell put the mind over the body, and that one's lower/animal nature needs to be disciplined. The person also needs to rid himself of all the images associated with these phrases.

Line 2. *To bear with fools in kindliness brings good fortune. To know how to take women brings good fortune. The son is capable of taking charge of the household.*

"To bear with fools in kindliness" has to do with the Sage's tolerating for a certain length of time misconceptions and mistaken beliefs held by those who approach it. It takes into account the person's ignorance of how to relate to the Sage; it also takes into account his fears of leaving behind the beliefs he has adopted from the collective ego, and helps him to free himself of them. This is the good fortune mentioned. The Sage retreats, however, if or when the person falls back onto his old beliefs, or retains the practices connected with them.

The Sage also acknowledges that the person does not immediately know how to apply what he has learned, and that he will make mistakes, as mistakes are part of his learning process, for which there is no blame.

"To know how to take women brings good fortune," is an incorrect phrase that comes from the Chinese custom of looking down on the female while at the same time using her. It is used here, as well, as a metaphor for times when a person allows the ego to condescendingly question the Sage's counsel because it does not fit his egotistical use. Such a practice creates a fate.

"The son is capable of taking charge of the household" is a metaphor for a person's consulting the Sage in a sincere attitude. It reflects that the person's true self has taken charge of his personality (the household).

This line can also apply to the person who holds the idea of the collective ego that it is the man's duty to be responsible for the woman. Such an idea puts a spell both on the man and on the woman for whom he believes himself to be responsible. By taking on this responsibility, the man excludes the Helpers, that withdraw, leaving him to do it all by himself. Thus, he has put himself in the prison of false duty by making the woman dependent on him.

Phrases connected with this spell are: "Women are weak and need to be taken care of by the man," and "If there were not men to protect them, they would be taken over by other men." These phrases are accompanied by corresponding images of a man's duties. (*See* p. 697, Freeing Yourself from Spells.)

In a broader sense this line refers to the folly of the human-centered presumption that the world is mankind's personal household, and that humans are in charge of managing it. This idea is the basis of all hierarchical systems and of the presumption that humans are superior to Nature. "Women," in this line, is a metaphor for all the aspects of Nature a person considers as lesser, which ideas have also separated him from the Cosmic Whole. Receiving this line is a signal that his feeling of helplessness stems from feeling unequal to the self-imposed challenges of life. Indeed, without the aid of the Helpers, he is. He may remedy the situation if he asks for help to rid himself of the mistaken beliefs that separate him from the Cosmic Whole. (*See* p. 689, Freeing Yourself from Mistaken Ideas and Beliefs.)

This line also calls attention to human-centered beliefs that people commonly have about Fate. An example is the person who believes he is "chosen" either by God or some human authority to administer "deserved fate" to others; another is the idea that a person has the ability to control his own fate. Another mistaken idea is that a person needs to pay restitution for his wrong deeds. Fate can be extinguished by ridding himself of the mistaken ideas and beliefs that have caused it. (*See* p. 40, Fate, and p. 692, Freeing Yourself from a Fate.)

Line 3. *Take not a maiden who, when she sees a man of bronze, loses possession of herself. Nothing furthers.*

The maiden referred to by this line is a metaphor for a person who is looking at the Sage or a human master (the man of bronze) to make his decisions for him. "Nothing furthers" refers to the Sage's retreat in the face of this attitude. Developing the true self means learning from the Sage how to access and follow one's inner truth, and to listen to one's senses. The correct task of the human teacher is to help the person to communicate on his own with the Sage, not to take the Sage's place. As for the person who poses as a spiritual master, he is really a swindler who has falsely put himself in the place of the Sage.

Seed phrases connected with this line are: "spiritual development means finding a human spiritual master and submitting oneself to him/her." Another is, "I don't have any resources in myself that I can trust." These and like phrases create spells that need to be broken. (*See* p. 697, Freeing Yourself from Spells.)

The line can also indicate a person who, on seeing a potential partner with wealth (or like advantage), wants to marry or follow him/her. The person is thus ready to throw his true self away in exchange for being taken care of. In all unequal relationships, one partner throws his true self away to the other's ego. The person who does this allows the other's ego to feed on his life force, thereby depleting it.

Line 4. *Entangled folly brings humiliation.*
Entangled folly refers to a person who is experiencing a fate. The fate has been caused by a mistaken belief which has put a spell on his commonsense, so that he is blocked from hearing what the Sage wants to tell him. He therefore reads in the lines of the *I Ching* only what he wants to hear. While in this self-induced spell, there is no way for the Sage to communicate the Cosmic Truth to him, so that there is no choice but for the Sage to leave him to follow his chosen path until the mistaken belief has burned out. If, however, he heeds the message the Sage is giving him through this line, and is willing to identify the mistaken belief and free himself of it, his fate can be extinguished. (*See* p. 692, Freeing Yourself from a Fate.)

Entangled folly often refers to the belief a person has that "death is inevitable." This belief throws a dark shadow on his whole life and negates that life is ongoing, proceeding through various dimensions. His belief keeps him trapped in the desire to overcome death through spiritual development that denies the joy of life in a body. This belief creates the fate that the joys connected with life in a body are denied.

This line also wants to make the person aware that his fate can be extinguished, if he will rid himself of the mistaken belief that has put a spell on his life in this body. (*See* p. 689, Freeing Yourself from Mistaken Ideas and Beliefs.)

Entangled folly can also refer to hopes upon which a person has placed his dependence. These hopes come from the ego, and are based on the belief that "if I only work hard enough, persevere long enough, am a good enough person (etc.), I will get what I want." This idea fails because it denies that all creative activity occurs through a partnership with the Helpers.

When the person thinks of himself as the one who creates, he blocks the Helpers.

Line 5. *Childlike folly brings good fortune.*

In its positive meaning, "childlike folly" refers to the person who has an innocent attitude in which he sees the good that is possible in all situations. The key ingredient here is allowing things to be transformed after having said the inner No to what is incorrect. This attitude always draws the Helpers that bring good fortune.

In its negative meaning, it refers to the view of the collective ego that for his spiritual development, a person needs to seek out a human leader or master.

The line can incorrectly suggest that the student should regard the Sage as a master before whom he should put aside everything he has learned from his commonsense. The Sage comes as a friend and Helper, and not as an entity before which we should servilely submit ourselves as lord and master. The object of the Sage's teachings is to "underline" our inner sense of truth, and thus revive our trust in it enough to follow it.

The line can also refer to viewing the *I Ching* as a "sacred text" that can only be approached if one observes the taboos that have been placed around it. Among these taboos are: that one can only consult it for "important" matters; that one needs to understand the interrelationship of the trigrams; that it is only a book for telling the future; that it is a compilation of ancient wisdom; that it is a binary code or ancient set of mathematical principles (making it into a mechanical system); that it was written by wise humans (denying the influence of the Sage); that it is to be seen as one of "*man's* great achievements"; that one is not meant to question any part of its text; and that one needs a trained human sage to interpret it. These ideas present the *I Ching* as complicated, distant, and forbidding, inspiring the person who approaches it with awe and fear. They cause him to miss the fact that the *I Ching* is meant to connect with him through his ordinary experience. This is the opposite of the innocent (childlike) and simple way a person is meant to approach the *I Ching*, meaning free of preconceived ideas.

Line 6. *In punishing folly it does not further to commit transgressions. The only thing that furthers is to prevent transgressions.*

This line describes the difference between what the Sage considers a transgression and what the collective ego defines as one. The Sage calls transgressions the careless indifference and use of power that is sanctioned and even rewarded by the collective ego, and that comes from all the beliefs that put humans at the center of the universe. The use of power always exceeds the Cosmic limits that apply to human action.

This line describes the kinds of folly that the Sage "punishes" in people: intentional transgressions of one person against another, transgressions against nature (animals, plants, the environments in which other life forms live, etc.), people's transgressions against their own true natures, transgressions against the Cosmic Consciousness or any aspect of it, including the Sage, repression of Cosmic truths by authorities, repression of the natural inhibition against killing, wounding, or maiming, indifference to the suffering caused by blind obeisance to the rules, commandments, and prohibitions of the collective ego, and the willful ignoring of Cosmic limits.

"The only thing that furthers is to prevent transgressions" is a statement that the punishments applied by the Sage are only as severe as they need to be to break through the obstinacy a person has in ignoring the Cosmic limits, and to make him listen to his inner truth. (Also *see* Hexagram 21, *Biting Through*, Lines 1 and 6.) This contrasts with the self-righteous and vindictive excesses with which the collective ego punishes those who go against its standards and views: by excluding, abandoning, and treating them cruelly .

The Sage makes it clear that it is not a person's job to punish another, but to say the inner No and retreat in the face of his transgression. He then needs to turn the matter over to the Sage and the Helpers for whatever else needs to be done to correct him.

5. *Waiting*

 K'an
Ch'ien

The Judgment. *If you are sincere, you have light and success. To be firmly correct brings good fortune. It furthers to cross the great water.*

Waiting is defined by the Sage as having two main meanings that are directly connected with each other: one refers to humans waiting for something (nourishment, help, fulfillment of their lives); the other refers to the Helpers that would come to their aid, if the person waiting would make it possible for that to happen (through a correct and modest attitude, and asking for their help).

The principal purpose of this hexagram is to inform us of the way the Helpers that are primarily assigned to humans engage in their helping activities: these Helpers wait until we acknowledge their presence and function in our lives. Receiving this hexagram tells a person that they have retreated into a neutral attitude of waiting.

The Helpers retreat and become uninvolved when we follow mistaken beliefs and engage in deluded enthusiasms, leaving us to our own devices until our beliefs burn out; they come to our aid when we attain the smallest bit of modesty. While waiting, the Helpers never lose sight of their goal: to draw us into returning to our true selves.

The Helpers are brought into our lives by our inner cries for help. The help they give is to increase our awareness and understanding that the Cosmos is made up of billions of Helpers. They seek to make us aware of this, so that we may remove our thinking from the demonic sphere of consciousness, which would have us believe that we are cut off from all help except that which the collective ego provides.

The Helpers, whose job it is to wait in the manner described above, are: the Sage as the Cosmic Teacher, the Personal Helper assigned to each individual to help him fulfill his destiny, and the Feeling Manager, whose task it is to coordinate the psyche and the body (a person's invisible and visible sides). These are the three uninvited guests mentioned in Line 6 of this hexagram. These three come uninvited only in certain circumstances, which we may know by receiving Line 6 of this hexagram.

The hexagram also concerns human situations, in which a person, through having a human-centered view of the universe, has caused the Helpers to retreat into waiting. They cannot help until he returns to some degree of modesty.

"Waiting" can describe a person who is at a crossroads, not knowing where to go or what to do. What he is waiting for, without his necessarily being aware of it, is Cosmic help: in the form of its gift of love; help to find and understand his true purpose in life; furtherance in his job; help to recover from an illness or injury; and help that will bring to an end an adverse situation, as when he is in a prison (mentally or physically).

"If you are sincere" states that when waiting for help, the person's sincerity of mind draws the light that shows him that to go on with his life without further waiting is the correct path. If he will ask for daily guidance, the right things will show themselves and the path that is true for him will emerge of its own accord. The "light" refers to the Helpers that come when being asked, and that bring the exact gifts of help needed.

The hexagram can also refer to the person who has put his life on hold to wait for something he hopes will happen, out of a belief that if he waits long enough and is patient enough, a problem will get resolved. Such a person has a heroic self-image in which he sees himself as capable of patiently enduring all hardships that stand between him and his goal. He needs to realize that life is not about *waiting*, but about making progress by going on with his life. Making progress is possible at any moment when he includes the Helpers of the invisible world in his life, and says the inner No to all those situations that he believes he must wait through. His belief in passive waiting has blocked those Helpers from being able to further his progress.[*]

This hexagram also applies to people who have unconscious fears to make a move, or who cannot do so because of spells and poison arrows. The fear to make a move may be due to mistaken ideas and beliefs put forward by the collective ego about the nature of the Cosmos, and which have presented it as the fearful and dangerous "unknown." The result of these fears and beliefs is that the person unconsciously dreads making changes. He either contents himself with hoping and dreaming, or buries himself in work, or engages in the endless diversions offered by the collective ego.

"To be firmly correct" means that he needs to identify and free himself from whatever fears, spells, or poison arrows exist in his psyche that keep him waiting for miracles.

"Crossing the great water" in this hexagram occurs when a person has understood and said the inner No to his having accepted the collective ego's demonizing the Cosmos as the threatening "unknown." It also refers to turning inside and asking the Sage for help. Then the threatening unknown is seen to be what it truly is: the demonic sphere of consciousness created by the half-truths and untruths on which the collective ego's existence is based. It is the repository of all fears: abandonment, suffering, being alone in old age, death, and what happens after death.

Among the spells connected with this hexagram are those based on the following half-truths and beliefs:

- beliefs that place a person's hopes for justice, for "truth to prevail," and for everlasting happiness to occur in an afterlife. Such a view prevents a person from saying the inner Yes to his life on earth. It also prevents him from saying the inner No to the predations and abuses of the ego, and its slanders on the way of the Cosmos which create injustices and sufferings in the here and now.

- mistaken ideas about the nature of *Fate*, in particular the idea that it is something imposed on people by something outside themselves. This idea creates any number of other mistaken beliefs by which the person thinks his fate is ei-

---

* Many people who use the traditional versions of the *I Ching* believe it is counseling them to wait passively, and that all action it recommends has to do with enduring, or persevering. This is because they do not understand that action in the *I Ching* refers to the inner action of saying the appropriate inner No's to all aspects of the ego, and asking for help from the Cosmos.

ther to be endured, because there is nothing he can do about it; that he is a victim of an unkind Cosmos; that it is inflicted on him as a trial of his character; that it is a hidden gift from heaven, or punishment by God; or that it is something he needs to fight. Fate is the natural consequence of going against the Cosmic Laws; it is the consequence of mistaken beliefs and acts resulting from them. It is possible to end a fate any given time a person is willing to rid himself of the mistaken ideas or beliefs that have created it. Fate is never something a person is meant to endure or fight. Seeing Fate as coming from without keeps the person trapped in its adversities.

• the mistaken idea that the help offered by the collective ego "is all there is," and the idea "I have to do it all." With this view the person is trapped in waiting for help that does not further the development of his true self, but on the contrary, hinders it. The help offered by the collective ego is always directed at subjugating the individual to its systems and institutions.

Note: Since all lines contain infinite possibilities of interpretation, one needs to use the *rtcm* to determine if the meanings suggested here apply to the given situation. (*See* p. 736, Using the *rtcm*.)

Line 1. *Waiting in the meadow. It furthers one to abide in what endures. No blame.*

"Waiting in the meadow" refers to waiting in an in-between place (neither in the city nor in the forest) as at a crossroads, where one wishes to know the right road to take. The problem in the person's attitude is that he suspects that taking one road will lead to disaster and the other to success. He does not realize that he can safely take either road if he is sincere, for then the Helpers will protect him from dangers, and see to it that his mistakes in judgment will lead, despite all, to a good end.

This line can refer to the person who is using the *I Ching* to tell him the future. It wants to make him aware that the purpose of the *I Ching* is not to give him inside knowledge of the outcome of a horserace or the like. It may, however, at times forewarn him of a fate about to happen to enable him to relate correctly to it, as by saying the inner No to its causes. (See p. 692, Freeing Yourself from a Fate.) The main purpose of consulting the *I Ching* is to inform him of the attitudes that draw the Helpers, no matter which road he takes.

"Abiding in what endures" refers to the person who goes on with his life without anticipating what the future holds. This allows the clear path to show itself. "No blame" tells him that the mistakes he makes while going on with his life never lead to permanent blame, because permanent blame is not part of the Cosmic Way. Moreover, mistakes are part of his learning process. (*See* p. 50, Guilt, Blame, and Shame.)

It is the ego that wants to know the future, and to have assurances of taking the "correct" road. It does this because it knows that it is acting outside Cosmic limits, and thereby is running the risk that Fate will catch up with it.

Seed phrases by which the ego attempts to frighten the person from following his inner truth are: "Who are you to be different from the rest of us?" "That's a crazy path...It's uncharted, it's untried." "It's a lonely path." "People get lost when they go alone." "How do you know you will get help?" "It'll never get you anywhere." "You ought to turn back." "Let your friends and family help you." "You need to make provisions for the future."

Line 2. *Waiting on the sand. There is some gossip. The end brings good fortune.*

"Waiting on the sand" refers to active seed images (fears) that come to a person's mind, suggesting all kinds of evil consequences if he goes on his own path. These fears are due to a guilt spell he has received during childhood, that makes him feel guilty every time he follows his inner truth. Entertaining these negative images blocks the Helpers.

The fears play on the idea that a person needs to know what is going to happen; lacking this knowledge, the ego presents all the worst-case scenarios imaginable (the "sand" mentioned). The "gossip" refers to his being open to what other people's egos say he ought to do in the situation, based on their negative experiences.

"The end brings good fortune" is a prediction that can happen only if the person stays centered within, and does not give in to these pressures to do something. He needs to ask for help in meditation to rid himself of the seed images that drive the fears. (*See* p. 689, Freeing Yourself from Seed Phrases and Images and p. 693, Freeing Yourself from Fears.) Making this inner effort frees the Sage to come to his aid. Failing to rid himself of his fears and the images behind them, allows the fears to project themselves into reality.

A person may also receive this line when he has been getting help from other people and doubts that it is correct to accept it. These doubts are the "gossip" referred to in this instance. He is meant to realize that the help has also been inspired by the Cosmic Helpers.

The line may also refer to a person who is waiting for help to come from somewhere rather than asking the Cosmos for it. The Cosmos only needs to be asked with sincerity.

A person may also receive this line when he is experiencing a fate he has created by falsely blaming someone through listening to gossip, thus putting a poison arrow on that person. In order to free himself of the fate he has created, he needs to retract the blame he has put on the other. (*See* p. 697, Freeing Yourself from Poison Arrows.) This situation also informs us that engaging in gossip about others is "idle waiting" that creates poison arrows.

Line 3. *Waiting in the mud brings about the arrival of the enemy.*

Waiting in mud is a metaphor for the paralyzing fear that in the end, one will be stuck. The phrase of this fear is: "I don't see any way for this to work out." It is followed by," What will I do then?" These phrases indicate a deeper poison arrow that the person has accepted from the collective ego, such as, "There is no one to help you but yourself," or, "if you make a wrong move, it will be your last." Its effect has been to exclude the Helpers from his life, making them retreat into a waiting mode. Without their protection and help, the very thing he dreads is projected into reality.

This line can also refer to the person's already being in a stuck situation he has projected. If he frees himself from the poison arrow, the situation can be corrected. (*See* p. 697, Freeing Yourself from Poison Arrows.)

This line can also refer to a spell a person has put on another, through harboring fears about the outcome of what that person is doing, or by doubting that the Helpers can or will help him in his situation. He needs to free the person from the spell. Fixing others in spells creates a fate for both parties.

Other seed phrases connected with this line that create spells contain the words "always" or "never." Since these words are a form of consciousness, superimposing them upon the consciousness of things or situations observed, fixes them in regard to time, either as always happening, again and again, or never happening. The spells are the mud referred to in this line.

Line 4. *Waiting in blood. Get out of the pit.*

"Waiting in blood" refers to an attitude of hopelessness, as when someone has received a dire prediction about the future, or when he has decided there is no hope (help) available. The person, in listening to the ego, has eliminated from his range of possibilities, the existence of help from the invisible world. As a consequence, he is in pain and suffering.

Blood also refers to when a person has rejected life as "a rotten experience," or "nothing but suffering." Or, he may be blaming himself for everything that has gone wrong, as for his illness. To end his separation from the Helpers, he needs to free himself from the spells created by these mistaken beliefs. The first and second phrases have put spells on the way his life moves forward; the third is a guilt spell that the ego uses to control him, but which also shuts down the Sage, his Personal Helper, and his body helpers. (*See* p. 697, Freeing Yourself from Spells.)

Waiting in blood also refers to a person's fear of the unknown that comes from the collective ego. The word "unknown," with all its threatening connotations, has been falsely put on the Cosmos, to distance a person from receiving its love and help. The Cosmos cannot be "known" by the intellect alone because it is primarily a feeling consciousness. Through feeling it and experiencing it daily, we come to know it in the only way we can really know something: through the heart. This is a knowing that has nothing to do with faith or hope. The person needs to recognize the way the word *unknown* has made him see things falsely, and say the inner No to the word *unknown*, treating it as a projection. (*See* p. 697, Freeing Yourself from Projections.)

Blood can also refer to a person's allowing the ego to hold onto his anger or annoyance, after having said the inner No to another. This shows that he believes that if he drops his anger, the other will continue his wrong actions. He needs to understand that by allowing the ego to hold onto the anger, the effect of his inner No is defeated, and the Helpers must remain in retreat. To correct himself he needs to say the inner No to the ego, and to ask the Sage to eliminate it.

Another meaning of waiting in blood has to do with waiting in a spell created by the fear that if one will step out of an unhealthy dynamic in which one is a key figure, everything will fall apart. An example is the person who has taken on the role of being responsible for creating the peace within the family (a heroic self-image), and whose life-energies are consequently being drained by the family. "Get out of the pit" tells the person that he is living in a "pit" which requires an endless drain on his life-energy to fulfill the role. He needs to rid himself of the self-image spell and the guilt spell that may be connected with it, which would make him feel guilty for abandoning that role. (*See* p. 697, Freeing Yourself from Spells.)

Line 5. *Waiting at meat and drink. If one is firmly correct it brings good fortune.*

A person may receive this line when he has everything he needs but does not see it. Such a person has not opened his eyes to what he has because he is always looking for something that is not there. He is allowing the ego to focus on the future or the past, and so misses out on his life. If he will say the inner No to the ego's indulgence in wanting, worrying, and wondering, and also regretting, he will renew his contact with the Helpers.

"Waiting at meat and drink" also refers to a person who has never made a firm decision to find the purpose of his life. Instead, he indulges in ideas that he thinks are nourishing, because they bring him recognition by the collective ego. Among these are ideas of self-development that center around the idea of "becoming" somebody or something. These ideas give him the impression that he is participating in the feast of life, while the reality is that his true self is starving due to his dependency on the collective ego. Such a person needs to realize that he is following a path laid out by the collective ego because he has not freed himself from his fear of the "unknown" that holds him back from following the path indicated by his inner truth. (*See* p. 697, Freeing Yourself from Spells.)

Waiting at meat and drink also refers to a person who sees his life as over, and is waiting for his death. Such a person's ego is angry at life, blaming it for having lost its purpose. He needs to free himself from the ego's definition of the meaning of life, by saying the inner No to it. The person who is true to himself lives his life to the full without programming the future, up to the day of his passing over to the new dimension.

"Firmly correct" points to saying the inner No to all the mistaken ideas that prevent a person from going on with his life and living it to the full. Life is meant to be lived joyfully, and the Helpers are always there for him, to help him fulfill its purpose.

Line 6. *One falls into the pit. Three uninvited guests arrive. Honor them and in the end there will be good fortune.*

The "pit" refers to the despair a person falls into after perceiving that all his efforts to achieve some end have been in vain. "Three uninvited guests arrive" tell him that despite what he perceives, the experience was not in vain, and that three Helpers are standing by to help him if he will rid himself of the ideas: "I have to do it all," or "there is no help." The three Helpers are: The Sage, his Personal Helper, and his Feeling Manager. Then, he needs to leave the matter in their hands, meaning that he does not allow the ego to stand by watching and measuring what they do. The resuming of any ego supervision would cause them once again to retreat into waiting.

6. Conflict

 Ch'ien
K'an

The Judgment: *Conflict. You are sincere and are being obstructed. A cautious halt halfway brings good fortune. Going through to the end brings misfortune. It furthers one to see the great man. It does not further one to cross the great water.*

All conflict, the Sage demonstrates in this hexagram, has its origin in an inner conflict in an individual's psyche. Inner conflict originates in mistaken ideas and images that contradict a person's inner truth. Everything that is in conflict with inner truth is also in conflict with the Cosmos.

Conflict is the result of mistaken ideas and beliefs that separate the person from the Cosmic Whole. The person to whom this hexagram applies needs to recognize that he is experiencing a fate brought about by his engaging in conflict.

The phrase, "You are sincere and are being obstructed," refers to his thinking that he is in the right. This prevents him from recognizing that the causes of his problems lie in mistaken ideas he holds to be true. Among them is his human-centered view of the universe, which gives him the false impression that he has the right to think and say anything he likes, and to do whatever he *thinks* is correct; these presumptions, in turn, lead him to disregard the evil effects of thoughts and actions that come from this human-centered view.

"A cautious halt halfway" can be telling the person consulting the oracle to retreat from questioning further. Because of his state of inner conflict, he will not be able to perceive the true answer to his problem, even if the Sage offers it, because his ego is dominating, looking for an answer that satisfies *its* inner demands, or for a culprit to blame. In the face of this attitude, the Sage has retreated until his false enthusiasm burns out, or until he returns to modesty, and an open mind.

A part of his inner conflict lies in the self-flattery promoted by the ego that he is in the right and that others are guilty. The words *guilt* and *culprit* are the creation of the collective ego in its efforts to find a scapegoat for problems caused by *its* inept handling of situations. The person does not see that the evil consequences he experiences are the direct result of allowing the ego to rule his personality. In the Cosmic sense there is no guilt and no culprit, as evil does not inhere in a person's nature but is the result of mistaken ideas and beliefs a person has accepted as true. Evil is created by the projections, spells, and poison arrows these mistaken ideas have put on the person's true nature, causing him to act in ways that are not true to himself.

"Going through to the end brings misfortune" refers to allowing the ego to continue trying to force a conclusion to the conflict through argument and blaming. Doing so only creates another fate, which is the misfortune mentioned. A person caught in conflict is caught in a spell set up by the ego's demand to have things turn out its way. The Cosmos does not respond to the ego, or to this totally human-centered view of things. When a person is caught in this frame of mind, he will accept no reasonable or commonsense argument.

"It furthers him to see the great man" is counsel for the person to seek contact with his inner truth, which lies beyond the apparent issues of conflict; it will tell him which projections, spells, and poison arrows have created his fate, thus give him the information he needs to free himself from it.

"It does not further one to cross the great water" also refers to attempts of the ego to force a conclusion between two mistaken ideas by believing that one of them must be right. Adopting one of two false alternatives only entangles the person more and more in conflict with the Cosmos.

Spells connected with this hexagram contain the words "culprit," or "guilty party," when these terms are assigned to another person, life, Nature, God (as giving one an adverse fate), the Devil, the Cosmos, etc. Other spells are created by the mistaken idea that "life is a struggle," "conflict is to be expected," "conflict is a natural part of life," "we are born into a hostile universe," and "humans are necessarily in conflict with Nature."

Note: Since all lines contain infinite possibilities of interpretation, one needs to use the *rtcm* to determine if the meanings suggested here apply to the given situation. (*See* p. 736, Using the *rtcm*.)

Line 1. *If one does not perpetuate the affair, there is a little gossip. In the end, good fortune comes.*

This line concerns a person who has created a fate through having lost his modesty by thinking that the universe revolves around his interests, and that he is special over other things. As a consequence, he blames things outside himself when things go wrong, such as Fate, life, a godhead, another person, karma, etc., therefore has an inner argumentative attitude toward the Cosmos. He sees it as there for his purposes, but not performing its duties toward him. On the one hand he intuits that there are Helpers there for him, but he does not understand that they can only cooperate as his equals. If he will rid himself of his arrogant attitude through rejecting it with the inner No, the help that he seeks will come to him.

Withdrawal from inner conflict requires relinquishing the demand of the ego for a resolution to its arguments. Certainly, the person's ego will want to continue arguing (the meaning of "a little gossip"), but in the face of persistent firmness, it will be unable to do so. (See p. 687, Retreating from Conflict and Opposition.)

The "good fortune" that comes from saying the inner No to the ego is the insight and help that then come from the Helpers. They show the person that the powers of the ego are limited, whereas before, he had thought it to be unconquerable.

The Helpers will also help free him from his fate if he will rid himself of the mistaken idea that he can resolve things by engaging in conflict. Correcting himself will reunite him with the Cosmic Whole and bring him peace and harmony. (*See* p. 677, Saying the Inner No, and p. 689, Freeing Yourself from Mistaken Ideas and Beliefs.)

Line 2. *One cannot engage in conflict. One returns home, gives way. The people of his town, three-hundred households, remain free of guilt.*

This line refers to a person's engaging in conflict and trying to force his way. Since conflict is not the way of the Cosmos, he cannot succeed. If he will retreat from conflict by returning to his inner truth (his inner home), the problem will lose its energy, enabling the Helpers to resolve it.

"The people of his town" refers to all the people with whom he is inwardly connected, who will be freed from the embarrassment and false sense of guilt that would be created by his continuing the conflict. (For a better understanding of guilt as part of the demonic sphere of consciousness, *see* p. 48, Guilt, Blame, and Shame.)

Through this line the *I Ching* wants to draw attention to the role of guilt and blame as the main motors that keep the demonic sphere of consciousness in place. Guilt, when projected upon another, by calling him "the guilty party," puts a spell on that person. It then activates the ego to project blame back. This blaming activity, if not stopped by saying the inner No to the idea of there being "a guilty party," continues through generations and generations (the 300 households), thereby nourishing the demonic sphere of consciousness. This line signifies that a person needs to put the conflict to an end, no matter whether he is the one blaming another, or whether he is on the receiving end of a blame spell. (*See* p. 696, Freeing Yourself from Guilt.)

Line 3. *To nourish oneself on ancient virtue induces perseverance. Danger. In the end, good fortune comes. If by chance you are in the service of a king, seek not works.*

"To nourish oneself on ancient virtue" is a concept by which the collective ego appropriates a person's natural virtues and turns them to its service. The king here is a reference to the collective ego as the feudal authority. By turning the person's virtues to *its* use, an *inner* conflict is created. This appropriation occurs when a person's natural loyalty to his inner truth is turned to loyalty to the institutions of the collective ego, as expressed in "my country right or wrong." Danger refers to the fate created by acting from false loyalties.

The collective ego also suggests that "ancient virtue" nourishes a person's "higher nature." The Sage makes us aware, however, that ancient wisdom serves primarily to legitimate the collective ego's parallel reality.

The Cosmic meaning of this line refers to serving one's inner truth, thereby also the Sage and the Cosmic Whole. In this instance "ancient virtues" refer to a person's natural virtues, which inhere in his very nature since before he was born into this dimension. They are the source of his inner nourishment when he does not hold them in doubt; by following them he remains free of conflict.

"Seek not works" warns him against striving for fame and recognition. The attainment of fame, social recognition and its attendant flatteries can soon turn him away from his true self, putting him in self-conflict. "Seek not works" also states the principle that the person who is true to himself does not need to prove anything to anyone.

Spells connected with this line have to do with striving to be recognized as the "good person," the "modest person," the "noble-hearted person," the "spiritual person," or the "hero who saves and helps others." Striving to fulfill self-images of any kind is in conflict with a person's true nature. (*See* p. 691, Freeing Yourself from Self-Images.)

Line 4. *One cannot engage in conflict without creating a fate. One turns back, changes one's attitude, and finds peace in perseverance. Good fortune.*

Receiving this line indicates that a person is experiencing a fate brought about by his engaging either in inner or outer conflict. It is the purpose of Fate to make a person end his engaging in conflict; however, if he fails to realize this purpose of Fate, and instead blames Fate as if it were coming from something outside himself, such as the stars, the times, life, or the evil in others, he will continue to engage in conflict and create even more fate for himself. "One turns back" is a stern warning that to avoid even worse consequences, he needs to turn back now.

Changing "his attitude" refers to recognizing that his actions have been ego-dominated, and that it is time to rid himself of the mistaken ideas that have supported his engaging in conflict.

To "find peace" refers to ending the gnawing of his conscience when he has created a fate. This gnawing comes from an inner

Helper that is trying to make him aware of the fate created by going against his inner truth. Finding peace also means that he can rid himself of the blame connected with his deeds and thus end the fate.

The two main mistaken ideas that initiate conflict are the idea of special ownership and the idea of having rights. Receiving this line may be calling a person to rid himself of these ideas as defined by the collective ego.

From the Cosmic point of view, everything we possess is truly ours only when it has come to us from the Helpers to support us in fulfilling our life's purpose. When we no longer recognize that what comes to us, even though it comes through our efforts, is nevertheless a free gift of the Cosmos, we allow our egos to appropriate it. Then what we possess becomes "stolen goods," and subject to being lost. Appropriation happens when we believe we have deserved the gift, and when we think we have sole rights over it. What we possess as gifts of the Cosmos comes with the needed Cosmic protection from being falsely appropriated by someone else, so long as we are in harmony with the Cosmos. If the person tries to personally protect what he possesses, the Helpers of Protection retreat. The mistaken idea about having rights come from the human-centered view of the universe, and the ego's wanting to hold onto what it has falsely appropriated. (*See* p. 689, Freeing Yourself from Mistaken Ideas and Beliefs.) Appropriation also occurs when a person's lives in luxury at someone else's expense.

The "good fortune" indicated by this line are those possessions the Helpers give to the person who has a correct view toward possessions. They include insights, help to achieve his task, and possessions in the most literal sense.

Line 5. *To contend before him brings supreme good fortune.*

"To contend before him" refers to turning a conflict over to the Sage. This line tells a person that while he is in a state of conflict, he will not be able to understand the Sage's answers, because they will all be interpreted within the framework of that conflict. He needs to turn his inner eye away from the problem altogether.

A person also receives this line when he is caught in considering two arguments that seem to be reasonable alternatives. However, both are false. The true answer lies in another direction altogether, which he can find only by asking the Sage for help. For example, a person experiencing a fate may be debating whether to accept his fate or to fight it. Neither of these ideas is based on a true understanding of Fate. (*See* p. 40, Fate) Fate can be ended at any time by deprogramming the mistaken idea or belief that has created it.

Line 6. *Even if by chance a leather belt is bestowed on one, by the end of the morning it will have been snatched away three times.*

This line shows what happens when a person carries a conflict to its bitter end. His apparent victory is lost a hundred times over through losing the things he really values: his dignity, his self-esteem, his inner peace, and his contact with the Sage and the Helpers.

What he initiates, instead, is a long-lasting fallout from the inner war, and a procession of invisible projections, spells, and poison arrows that remain in his psyche until such time as he discovers and removes them. In addition, he initiates a fate that corresponds to the degree of his arrogance and obstinacy.

7. The Army

 K'un
K'an

The Judgment: *The army needs firm correctness and a strong man. Good fortune without blame.*

In this hexagram, the Sage refers to two different kinds of armies, the Cosmic Army and the army of the collective ego, with each having a different order and different goals.

The Cosmic Army is the name for that aspect of the Cosmic Consciousness that fights violations of Cosmic Harmonics by humans. It comprises Cosmic Helpers that fight in a coordinated way in accordance with the Cosmic Harmonics.

Although the "leader" mentioned in Line 2 would suggest that the Cosmic Army is a hierarchical organization, this is not so. The leader is the person's true self, also referred to here as the "strong man" who is firmly correct. His function is to initiate the army's action and coordinated support by calling on it for help, and by saying the inner No to the incorrect situation. He also does not allow the ego to become involved in the situation.

The Cosmic Army's function is to fight, when called upon, transgressions against ourselves, other people, and against Nature in general (animals, plants, and the earth as a whole). When humans try to do this themselves, they only create opposition that strengthens the aggressor, for when the ego is engaged in defending, the other's ego is energized and empowered.

It is the duty of a person to be unwavering in saying the inner No, first to the ego in himself, and then to the ego in others whenever it appears. This may necessitate either suspending any distrust that the Cosmic Army is effective enough, or saying the inner No to any fear that the Cosmic Army might do something harmful to the other person.

This hexagram also refers to the way the collective ego fights transgressions by arguing, engaging in lawsuits, practicing passive resistance, or by any of those ways in which matters are taken in hand, such as fighting in wars. Responding in this way only brings a fate to the person who does so. As for the aggressors, they have already brought a fate on themselves.

This hexagram gives counsel on how to respond to an inner war that is already in progress. It also counsels the person on how he may end his part in it and the fate he has created by participating in it.

The first step is to take away the poison arrow created by his seeing the other as a culprit. (*See* Glossary: Culprit.) The second step is to say the inner No to his own hatred and blaming. The third is to dispel other spells he may identify that have been put on him or on the other.

While another may have done hideous things, the person needs to realize that he did them, not because his nature is evil, but because he is either under spells, or his inner programming contains mistaken beliefs. Saying the inner No to these mistaken beliefs strengthens that person's true self, giving him the opportunity to correct himself. The fourth step is to thank the Helpers. This process may need to be repeated over a period of several days, which can be determined by using the *rtcm*.

The Cosmic Army accomplishes its task only through transformation, which is why it does not create resistance (opposition). (*See* p. 52, Transformation versus Changes.)

When an individual sees the collective ego or its institutions as culprits, he not only creates its determined opposition, he creates in himself feelings of aggression and frustration. These feelings further empower the collective ego and keep him engaged in the demonic sphere of consciousness. If he then tries to resolve his conflict by fighting the collective ego openly, he creates a poisonous reaction. Saying the inner No to seeing it as a culprit, on the other hand, lifts him out of the demonic sphere of consciousness and deprives the collective ego of its power over him. He also needs to realize that the collective ego is not an external entity; it is rather a set of mistaken beliefs that, once institutionalized, has continued through the power that each individual has given it, and through acceding to its self-proclaimed authority.

The Cosmic Army operates on the principle that the fate a person creates through his wrongdoing always returns to him like a boomerang. This happens if no one has interfered to counteract it, as by a person's attempts to bring "justice" according to *his* ideas. When a person interferes in this manner, the fate is not only prevented from returning to its source, the person also draws the fate to himself. This is true for the leaders of countries, as well as for individuals.

A person may receive this hexagram when, through listening to the ego he feels defeated. He needs to call on the Cosmic Army for help, and say the inner No to the ego.

A person may also receive this hexagram when he has become involved in one or another type of "war" which has been initiated by the following ego-behaviors:

• challenging another's pride to engage in conflict;

• giving up on another's true self, by fixing him as "hopeless,"

or "inhuman," or as "having no feelings";
 • treating another insensitively, as if he does not exist, or has no worth;
 • encroaching into another's inner space, or using force, acting aggressively, or with careless abandon.

The person mistreated is meant to win the battle through holding to his inner truth, by saying the inner No to the unjust act, and all attempts of the other's ego to engage him. The person who has caused the war can end it by freeing the other from the projections, spells, and poison arrows he has put on him, and by apologizing to the Cosmos for his transgressions. He also needs to free himself of any projections, spells, and poison arrows that have been put on him. If a person sees himself as the victim, he needs to inquire through the *rtcm*, what part, if any, he may have played in provoking the aggression, and correct himself accordingly. (*See* p. 695, Freeing Yourself from Projections, Spells, and Poison Arrows.)

When an inner war exists between people, the Cosmic Army needs to be called to help resolve it. It is important that the person seeking its help be free of personal desires and intentions, and especially, free of any desire to come out on top, and of any claims to "being in the right." To say the inner No to any ego-desires, aspirations, and intentions is the meaning of "being firm and correct."

A person may also receive this hexagram when he is under attack by projections, spells, or poison arrows, or when he is under attack by fears initiated by his own ego. He may determine how the hexagram is to be applied by using the *rtcm*.

Note: Since all lines contain infinite possibilities of interpretation, one needs to use the *rtcm* to determine if the meanings suggested here apply to the given situation. (*See* p. 736, Using the *rtcm*.)

Line 1. *An Army must set forth in proper order. If the order is not good, misfortune threatens.*

Since the Cosmic Army is initiated by a person's true self, this line suggests that the ego is still in place, therefore the Cosmic Army cannot be activated. If he then goes ahead to defend or assert himself, he will certainly create a fate.

A person can receive this line when he is under attack by some-body or under the attack of his own fears. Setting forth in proper order refers to the correct order of his reactions when under threat. He first needs first to determine, with the help of the *rtcm*, the inner truth of the situation. Often, either he or the opposing persons are acting from a projection, spell, or poison arrow, in which case he needs to free the situation of them. Oth-erwise, he may only need to say the inner No to the threatening person, idea, or thing, and ask the Helpers to help. (*See* p. 695, Freeing Yourself from Projections, Spells, or Poison Arrows.)

Among the seed phrases that would prevent the person from following this order of action are those that say, "I'll show them," and "you must act (defend yourself)!" In the first case, the phrase comes from injured pride that may have occurred in childhood. In the second case, the phrase comes from the belief that one has no invisible Helpers and has to take outer action. (*See* p. 687, Freeing Yourself from Seed Phrases and Images.)

Line 2. *In the midst of the army, good fortune. No blame. The king bestows a triple decoration.*

This line says that the Cosmic Army is in order when the person's true self is in command of his personality, when he has said the necessary inner No's to what is incorrect, and has asked the Cosmic Army to come to his aid. Then there is no blame, and the king, here meaning the Sage, his Cosmic Guide, fully supports him.

Being "in the midst of the army" is also a metaphor for the constant awareness the person must have of the first signs that the ego is trying to take over, either by inspiring fear or over-confidence. The ego wants to see others as culprits, and itself as the righteous one; allowing it to become the driving force would give rise to continuous and bitter warfare.

When the persons' true self is in command, he is on guard against the ego's attempts to argue with the other, and to seize his own emotions, such as anger, which it would turn into ha-tred. The true self does not allow the ego to fall into comparing himself with others, whereby the ego would gain control through self-pity, envy, and competing with others. The true self guards against the wanting that would make him forget the gifts and help that the Cosmos constantly gives him. It recognizes the first whisperings of the ego in the form of worrying, which makes him forget the true source of help that is always available to him. It stop the wondering that causes him to encroach (through idle curiosity) into other's inner spaces, including those of animals and Nature, or into the way of the Cosmos, in its search to attain power. The true self recognizes that by allowing the ego to do these things, the person's inner truth, dignity, and self-respect are betrayed.

The "king bestows a triple decoration" is often interpreted mistakenly as a confirmation that the person receiving this line has been doing the right thing. He has received the line, however, to make him aware that he has been acting with an eye to obtaining the approval of the collective ego. The collective ego, as "king," would encourage the ego-behaviors mentioned above. It even authorizes politicians, businessmen, news reporters, researchers, scientists, teachers, adventurers, etc., to intervene and encroach self-importantly and self-righteously into the private lives and thoughts of people, and into the lives and secrets of animals, and Nature in general, as measures of their professional success. What the collective ego does not tell its adherents is that all such behavior creates a fate. (*See* p. 687, Freeing Yourself from Mistaken Ideas and Beliefs.)

"No blame," from the standpoint of the collective ego, refers to adhering to its standards and conventions. Such adherence, however, is invariably against a person's inner truth, therefore creates blame in the Cosmic sense. It needs to be understood that the collective ego declares the individual's inner truth as invalid simply and only because it is outside its jurisdiction, or direct control. So long as a person's views keep him in awe and fear of the collective ego, his ability to bring the Cosmic Army to his defense will remain blocked. A person's inner truth is the only thing that keeps him in harmony with the Cosmos and able to arouse the Cosmic Army. If the person has incurred Cosmic blame, he can rid himself of it if he will ask the Sage for help to remove his awe of the collective ego's institutions, and to discover the phrases and images in his inner program that have given rise to it. (*See* p. 687, Freeing Yourself from Seed Phrases and Images.)

Line 3. *Perchance the army carries corpses in the wagon. Misfortune.*

This line indicates that the turning point in the battle being carried out by the Cosmic Army has been reached. Up to now, the job of the true self, as its initiator, has been to keep the ego from entering the scene. Invariably, in such situations, the person has withdrawn from conflict with another into neutrality. Withdrawal temporarily shuts down the "aperture of the heart." Misfortune means that the closing of the heart has been seized by the ego and held as a sort of ransom. It says inwardly to the other, "before I will open my heart again, you must humble yourself by begging forgiveness, or making restitution." This seizure of the heart by the ego has injured the person's Helper of the Heart, rendering it ineffective. The corpse mentioned is the other person, who has been mentally executed by this action. Before any healing of the situation can take place, this Helper needs to be asked to reopen the person's heart. This is possible if he will rid himself of the ego's demands. In all situations involving the Cosmic Army, the victory sought cannot be achieved if the heart is kept closed.

Corpses can also refer to a person's wishing for another's death. Such a wish is a poison arrow that needs to be removed. (*See* p. 695, Freeing Yourself from Poison Arrows)

This line can also indicate that a person is acting from passive-aggressive behavior due to having lost his ability to say No to an authority during childhood. This loss has deprived him of certain benefits of his commonsense, one of them being the ability to receive chi energy from the Cosmos. This deprivation has caused him to carry an inner grudge which he takes out on others by employing tactics to anger them, while at the same time appearing to be the innocent victim. In this way he draws the chi energy he needs from them. The corpse, in this case, refers to his disabled Helper of Commonsense. It can be recovered if he asks for help to recall the childhood situation that caused him to lose his ability to say the inner No. (*See* p. 675, Saying the Inner No.)

Corpses can also refer to a person's commonsense that has been overwhelmed through his placing responsibility for himself upon another person. His commonsense can also be overwhelmed through his placing credence on existing beliefs. The "misfortune" he suffers is the defeat of his inner dignity and self-esteem.

"Corpses," in a Cosmic meaning, can refer to ego elements in oneself or another that have been conquered, such as pride and vindictiveness, both of which were interested in keeping the war going. As a result of the person's effort at freeing himself from these elements, they are now being taken away in the wagon, which is a metaphor for the Helpers that clean up the battle scene, and the Helper of Transformation, that restores the person to wholeness.

Line 4. *The army retreats. No blame.*

The Cosmic Army has retreated because a person has failed to discipline the ego and has engaged in a fight. Although this has left him without defenses, and subject to the fate he has created, the Cosmic Army is not to be blamed for having retreated. The person can end his fate if he ceases fighting, and says No to the ego. This No also needs to be said to the ego's attachment to annoyance, anger, envy, hurt pride, and its desire to punish the other and see him as a culprit. It also needs to be said to the ego's desire to prove itself superior in character, virtues, abilities, knowledge, heroism, and its attempts to wrestle the other person into submission.

Because of the Cosmic Army's retreat, and his being left unprotected, it may be that the person has received projections, spells, or poison arrows from the other, which have caused illness or a feeling of not being well. His health will be restored if he frees himself of the spells and poison arrows involved. He also needs to free the other of any projections, spells, or poison arrows he has put on him. (*See* p. 695, Freeing Yourself from Spells and Poison Arrows.)

Line 5. *There is game in the field. It furthers one to catch it. Without blame. Let the eldest lead the army. The younger transports corpses.*

"Game" here refers to particular negative emotions such as hatred, vengeance, and hurt pride coming from the ego. "In the field" means the emotions have come out into the open to attack either himself, the Sage, the *I Ching* way, another person, Nature, or Fate. "It furthers one to catch it" indicates their destructive nature, if they are allowed to continue. It is when they are "in the open" that the opportunity arises to intercept and deprogram the seed phrases and images on which these emotions are based. Doing so prevents blame from occurring.

"The eldest" that needs to lead the army is the Helper of Discipline, which is at the person's disposal if called upon. It can effectively obliterate the power that these ego-driven emotions have assumed over the personality. It does so through showing that aspect of the psyche which has been trained to believe it is helpless against these emotions, that if it joins the effort to discipline the ego, the terror produced by the emotions can be overcome. The discipline involved is to say the inner No to them.

"The younger transports corpses" refers to the formerly terrorized aspect of the psyche that now is capable of disposing of the negative emotions (corpses) that have been "killed" by the inner No. The "younger," or that part of the psyche that was terrorized, is transformed by this experience into a Helper of Strength, so that now the person is able to stand up to new efforts of the ego to seize and control the emotions.

This line can also point to the poison arrow mentioned in Line 3 that has damaged the person's ability to say No to an authority. Now that he is an adult, he can ask for the help of the Sage to stand up to his childhood fear of authority. (*See* p. 675, Saying the Inner No.)

"Game in the field" can also refer to a health problem which serves as a message telling a person that a mistaken idea or belief stored in his psyche is the cause of the problem, and needs to be extinguished. This mistaken idea or belief can be identified by casting another hexagram and using the *rtcm* to clarify precisely what it is.

Game in the field can also refer to an ego-driven doubt of the

Sage that is interfering with the person's efforts to free his true self. The eldest, in this case, is the element in his psyche that makes the person aware that the doubt is coming from the ego. No blame is incurred if he says the inner No to its phrases.

Line 6. *The great prince issues commands, founds states, vests families with fiefs. Inferior people should not be employed.*

This line shows how the collective ego succeeds in extending its power through employing only those who operate within its system of values. It can likewise be taken as referring to the individual ego, when it believes it has won a battle against another's ego.

The Sage also uses the metaphor of "the great prince" to mean the true self, when it has won a battle over the ego and has assumed its rightful place in the personality. In particular, it refers to the true self when the person has made the inner effort indicated in the previous lines. He completes his effort by saying a conscious Yes to following his inner truth. The "states" he founds is a reference to his setting correct limits around his inner space so that he does not allow others to encroach into it; at the same time, he respects the inner space of others. He also applies the same limits to himself in regard to animals and Nature by repudiating the human-centered ideas of having rights to manipulate and use them, in distinction to cooperating with them. The "families" who receive "fiefs" is a metaphor for the conscious validation of the person's Cosmic qualities of character. Through saying the inner Yes to them, they are freed from the ego's oppression and imprisonment, thus are able to occupy their true homes in the personality. (In Line 5 they are referred to as the "younger.") "The fiefs" also represent their tasks within the personality to serve inner truth.

"Inferior people should not be employed" is a warning against allowing ego elements to return by small and subtle suggestions that the help received from the Sage and the Helpers was not the real cause of the improved situation. It is they that try to rationalize things away, by suggestions such as, "the situation simply got better by itself." Only through the help of the Sage and the Helpers can false elements that invade and take over the psyche be defeated.

When this line refers to the ego in a person, which believes it has won an outer battle against the ego in another, it warns that inferior people have been employed, and that the gains won by such means only set the stage for the ego's further delusion that it has attained power. While history provides us with many obvious examples of the rise of dictators, it also provides us with the details of their inevitable fall. The fall of the ego is Cosmic Law. It is only a matter of time. The same dynamic takes place in every ego-dominated relationship.

8. Holding Together

 K'an
K'un

The Judgment: *Holding together brings good fortune. Inquire of the oracle once again whether you possess sensitivity, duration, and perseverance; then there is no blame. Those who are uncertain gradually join. Whoever comes too late meets with misfortune.*

This hexagram is used by the Sage to explain the force of attraction that holds the invisible Cosmic Consciousness together with all its visible forms. (*See* Hexagrams 1 and 2 and their relationship to each other.) This attraction is brought about and maintained through *feeling*. While the Cosmic Consciousness is capable of thinking, it is primarily a *feeling consciousness* that operates through the force of attraction between complementary aspects.

The attraction between these aspects can be pictured as the two parts interpenetrating each other's consciousness much like the weaving together of feelings of mutual sympathy.

We are also informed that Cosmic Logic is not based on reasoning, but on *feeling* as its leading principle. Because Cosmic Laws are derived from feeling, they are called Cosmic Harmonics. As "harmonics" they operate more like principles of higher physics than like human-made laws.

The logic of the collective ego, by comparison, is supported by reasoning that is purposely separated from feeling, so as to create the impression that abstract concepts not related to experience can be true. Such concepts are based on premises that form spells when they are projected onto things. When the key premise of a belief is discovered and consciously recognized as false, the spell is broken.

This hexagram shows that the basis for a person's unity with the Cosmos, and therefore also with others, is holding together with the Sage in his presence, since the Sage enables him to connect with his inner truth/feelings.

Receiving this hexagram can indicate that a person has replaced holding together with the Sage by holding to fixed beliefs or customs. This has separated him from his unity with the Cosmos. He is counseled to find the beliefs or customs in question (with the help of the *rtcm*), and rid himself of them. It may be the belief that people need to hold to something outside themselves, as expressed in the phrase, "everyone needs a belief"; or, the person is holding to a human leader or group to provide him with "the truths of life." Or, he may be holding to his family, friends, or mate, when his inner truth tells him he needs to go his own way, especially inwardly. Such a person needs to rid himself of mistaken ideas or beliefs that separate him from his inner truth.

Related to the above is a false image a person may have of "unity and harmony" with another: the image of a single circle in which both reside. This image fails to respect the boundaries that mark each person's intrinsic space. All unity between two people is made possible by their recognizing and respecting each other's boundaries; this being the prerequisite, the Sage then makes their harmonious connection possible. An image of a harmonious relationship between two people is the horizontal figure eight. The two circles of the eight represent the respective spaces of each person. It is their seeing the true self in each that enables them to connect. The point at which their two circles connect is love (mutual respect).

"The perseverance" indicated in The Judgment counsels the person to ask himself whether he has firmly established his loyalty to his inner truth. Then his relations with others are intrinsic, based on the natural force of attraction. Loyalty to his inner truth brings him into contact with those who are likewise firmly centered within themselves.

"Holding together," in the sense of being centered within, occurs when a person's true self is the sovereign within—the sole authorizer of the validity of his feelings. The person who is thus sovereign over himself holds together with the Cosmos, and receives from it chi energy and help, while contributing back to it his feelings and unique experiences. Because he then contributes to the Cosmic Evolution, he never needs to ask, "What is my purpose?" because he is all the while fulfilling it.

A person gives away his self-authorizing ability when he adopts any self-images (ego) either to conform to or rebel against the collective ego. Both kinds of self-images keep him within the net of the collective ego and its system of opposites, because he keeps looking to it for its approval or disapproval. This keeps the collective ego invigorated since it lives off the chi energy it can gather from people's dependence on it.

The collective ego achieves this controlling role in a person's life through its promotion of the idea that the source of all evil lies in humans' animal nature, and that it is also the source of all human inadequacies and guilt. It also proposes that without its control and supervision, humans would supposedly run wild, creating chaos. People who accede to this idea are tricked into believing that without authorization by the collective ego, their lives would have no meaning, and without its conditioning, they would become the victims of their "worst tendencies" and "drives."

A person often receives this hexagram when he is questioning whether his life has meaning. He may have accepted the mistaken idea that his life has meaning only when it is directed to fulfilling tasks authorized by the collective ego, or he may believe that his life has no particular meaning, or that its meaning is known to someone or something outside himself. Such ideas keep him from seeing that the purpose of his life is to fulfill his uniqueness by simply being himself.

Spells connected with this hexagram contain seed phrases such as, "there is no purpose in my life" or "I need to find the purpose in my life." These phrases lead to false conclusions, such as: "life has no purpose," "accomplishments give one's life meaning," "you are nobody unless you have done something important," "the way you influence others tells your life's meaning," "he/she is a nobody," "he/she is an unworthy member of society," "he/she is no good," etc. Such spells imprison Helpers that would otherwise help the person fulfill his life's purpose. (*See* p. 697, Freeing Yourself from Projections, Spells, and Poison Arrows.)

The traditional interpretation of this hexagram is given by Wilhelm as follows: "The central power of a social organization must see to it that every member believes that his true interest lies in holding together with it." According to this formula, it is the duty of organizations to give their members the impression that they benefit by holding together with the organization. The result of this advice is that the individual places his center outside of himself, thus becomes dependent on the organizations of society rather than on his relationship with the invisible world. It is in this manner that the collective ego appropriates the individual's sovereignty.

The Cosmic meaning of "holding together" has to do with holding together with the Sage as one's inner guide. A person may receive this hexagram when he is considering ideas and beliefs others propose, which would draw him away from the Sage, or trivialize what the Sage has said. In this case, the person is no longer sensitive to the Sage, and thus brings harm to the relationship. This is the meaning of: "Inquire of the oracle...whether you possess sensitivity." It also may refer to the person's attitude when through retaining an analytical, suspicious, and aloof approach, he is unfeeling toward the Sage. He may even be expecting the oracle to authorize his wrong points of view.

As to asking himself whether he has "duration," this can refer to his falsely crediting the help he receives from the Sage to chance circumstances. By appropriating the accomplishments achieved in partnership with the Sage to himself, the changes thus created gradually revert to their former state. The question whether he has "perseverance" refers to keeping in contact with the Sage after his problems have been resolved. Only then is there "no blame."

The phrase, "those who are uncertain gradually join," refers to the person who is willing to put aside his distrust; this enables him gradually to have the experiences that will show the Sage's counsel to be true and trustworthy.

"Whoever comes too late meets with misfortune" refers to the person who allows the ego to completely take over his personality; he thereby puts all his dependence on the collective ego. Such a person cannot receive any benefit from the oracle.

Another problem is created by the ego's *wanting*. Ego-wanting is not the same as the natural desire a person has, when he wishes to be with his beloved, or to be protected, or to be nourished. It is a desire to get things or produce results on terms dictated by the ego. These terms contain mental considerations, such as thinking he has the right to get what he wants. The person who engages in this kind of wanting imposes his ego-demands on every hexagram and line of the *I Ching*, giving them a wrong interpretation. Wanting is also connected with wondering and worrying, especially when what the person's ego wants is not forthcoming. This hexagram is stating that the Cosmos gives its gifts only through the force of attraction. Attraction is lacking when the person stands, as it were, with his hands stretched out in expectation of Cosmic gifts. The Cosmos does not give its gifts in any situation in which a person is willing to throw away his dignity.

"Holding together" also refers to refraining from dividing one's wholeness into mind and body. Traditional versions of the *I Ching* follow the Confucian idea that humans have a higher and a lower (bodily) nature. The Confucians further assumed that evil is due to humans' lower, or "animal" nature. The Sage makes us aware that this idea violates the Cosmic Harmonic of the Equality of all aspects of the Cosmos. No one thing is higher or better than another. Furthermore, striving and applying disciplines to develop into something higher only separate a person more and more from his true self, which is *by nature* united with the Cosmos.

The collective ego binds people to its institutions through instilling in them ideas of guilt, insufficiency of self, fear, and self-doubt, whereas the Cosmos holds all its aspects together through the principle of attraction and love.

Note: Since all lines contain infinite possibilities of interpretation, one needs to use the *rtcm* to determine if the meanings suggested here apply to the given situation. (*See* p. 736, Using the *rtcm*.)

Line 1. *Hold to him in truth and loyalty; this is without blame. Truth, like a full earthen bowl: Thus in the end good fortune comes from without.*

The Cosmic Consciousness holds all its aspects together through the attraction of what is harmonious, and through inner truth. It does not hold anything to itself through force or threats. Holding in truth and loyalty counsels a person to hold to his inner truth. This loyalty brings him into harmony with himself, thus also with the Cosmic Whole. The "full earthen bowl" describes the abundance of chi energy that comes from being in touch with inner truth through one's feelings, and the fact that they also attract good fortune from without.

This way of relating harmoniously compares with the demanding nature of the collective ego that insists on having the individual's trust and loyalty, upon the threat that something awful will otherwise happen.

The line seeks to make a person aware that he is under the influence of the ideas that he is born with original guilt, and that he is by his nature insufficient in himself to cope with life. These ideas act in his psyche as poison arrows, making him feel guilty any time he is not loyal to the collective ego and its values. So long as these ideas reside in his psyche, certain other spells cannot be permanently removed, because guilt acts to reinstall them. Before a person can advance in developing his true self, he needs to free himself from these two poison arrows, and also of the threats by which they were installed. (*See* p. 697, Freeing Yourself from Spells and Poison Arrows.)

Some seed phrases addressed by this line include commandments that a person "must" do something, and imply "or else...."

This line can also concern pacts a person has made to be loyal to another, or to something outside himself. In Cosmic terms, all pacts and promises are incorrect, because a person is meant to hold to another only as long as it corresponds to his inner truth. Such pacts need to be treated as spells or poison arrows.

Line 2. *Hold to him inwardly.*

This line is counsel for a person to hold to his inner truth and commonsense. It also addresses a desire to end a relationship through giving up on another as hopeless. Doing this is what the *I Ching* calls "executing" the other's true self. It also has the effect of locking the person in his objectionable behavior (by putting a spell on him), and of starting an inner war that holds the two together in a cycle of mutual blame. Holding inwardly to him means not giving up on the person's true self, even though it may be correct to end the relationship.

The correct way to end a relationship is to ask the Helper of Relationships to cut the inner connection, otherwise they will remain bound together inwardly. An unclosed inner connection is a channel through which blame, anger, envy, and other ego-driven emotions travel, creating projections, spells, and poison arrows. (*See* p. 687, Closing an Inner Connection.)

Line 3. *You hold together with the wrong people.*

This line points to a person's "holding together" with popular beliefs that are contrary to the Cosmic Harmonics. Many of these beliefs are common sayings which have slipped by default into his programming, simply because he has not consciously rejected them or questioned their validity. Being in conflict with his commonsense, these phrases act as projections and spells on one or another of his senses, with the result being that parts of his commonsense are disabled.

Receiving this line calls a person to find the particular saying that is active in his current situation. He also needs to ask whether it is a projection or spell, and then rid himself of it. (*See* p. 689, Freeing Yourself from Mistaken Ideas and Beliefs.)

This line can also refer to ideas a person holds about himself or others that he or they are "incapable" of understanding something complex, or that the something is "unknowable." Both rationales become an excuse to look to a human authority (be it a person or a book) who seems to have found the answers. Holding to them shuts out the Sage, that is available to teach him all he needs to know.

The idea that we need to possess a storehouse of knowledge in order to face life and to be protected against the future is similarly flawed, because it is based on the idea that life is an adversary. Such a slander on life creates a fate. The person who maintains his conscious connection with the Sage receives the help and protection he needs during adversities. Fearing the Unknown is based on the same assumption that life is an adversary, and has the same consequences.

This line also warns against holding together with another when there is no inner connection. This is obvious when the ego in one person is constantly in control. An inner connection can occur only between two people's true selves.

Line 4. *Hold to him outwardly also. Perseverance brings good fortune.*

"Hold to him outwardly" counsels a person to hold to the Helper of Transformation rather than resorting to people or other external means to resolve the outer situation. A person may think that the Helpers, being invisible, only handle intangible problems. This hexagram shows that the invisible and the visible hold together as one. The invisible Helpers are available to help with tangible problems as well, because they create transformations where form and non-form interface—in the realm of consciousness. A person's disbelief is the only thing that prevents the Helpers from helping him with his outer problems.

This line counsels such a person to look for those phrases and images that imply that the Helpers can only operate in the way he imagines. Such ideas imprison them. (*See* p. 689, Freeing Yourself from Seed Phrases and Images.)

Line 5. *Manifestation of holding together. In the hunt the king uses beaters on three sides only and foregoes game that runs off in front. The citizens need no warning. Good fortune.*

The image of the hunt is a metaphor for "troubleshooting,"—

rounding up and shooting mistaken ideas in a person's psyche that lead him into delusion. The delusions of concern are those that prevent him from holding together with his inner truth.

Delusions have their origin in abstract "truths" that have no basis in life as it is experienced and felt. They come about when people search for "the truth" as an abstract thing, as when a person searches for "the meaning of life." In looking for the truth, people tend to project their preconceived ideas upon the situation. The projection then acts to influence what they see, confirming to them what they have anticipated. Cosmic Truths, by comparison, are revealed to the person who keeps his connection open to the Cosmic Consciousness, first by being conscious of its presence, and second by staying in touch with his feelings and inner senses.

Cosmic Truths come in hand-holds of insight that are gained precisely when the person's awareness is "tuned-in," as described. This cannot occur so long as he is trying to force his views upon the situation. Cosmic Truth is also to be found through his dedicated search to find and rid himself of the preconceived ideas that block access to these insights. The search, which is also a hunt to "kill" the mistaken ideas found, by saying the inner No to them, can best be described as a search for the untruths, or half-truths that have come down from the collective ego as "ancient wisdom," and which have generally been surrounded by taboos to insure they will not be questioned.

It needs to be said that societal conditioning disables and demonizes the senses and the feelings by regarding them as insignificant, or inferior, since they are part of humans' animal nature. So long as they are in this blocked condition, they are incomplete and uncoordinated, and therefore cannot fulfill their true function of revealing Cosmic Truths until they are freed. Receiving this line tells a person that he needs to make a "hunt" for the untruths that are blocking his access to his inner truth. These untruths are demonic elements within the psyche that keep him held in the enclosure, which is formed by a combination of spells, as described below.

The three sides of the enclosure mentioned in the line can represent the three primary spells put on a person that limit the way he experiences his life, and that are giving rise to the false conclusions he is drawing from those experiences.

The first spell (a poison arrow), is the idea that humans' animal nature, represented by the game mentioned, is the source of evil. The enclosure is the trap that has been set to kill his animal nature.

The second spell (also a poison arrow) is the guilt spell that accompanies the first idea, that having an animal nature marks humans with an inextinguishable stain, or fault, that exists so long as a person is connected with his body.

The third spell is created by the idea that humans are born into life without help. This spell separates the person from the Cosmos, which can provide the help for everything he needs.

The king, in this metaphor, can represent either the collective ego (which would like to appear as fatherly, generous, and benevolent to the person who subjects himself to its control and allows his animal nature to be killed), or to the Sage. In this second meaning, the line indicates that the person has allowed the Sage to guide his hunt for the demonic elements. It is only then that "the citizens" (Helpers that have been previously warned away by the two poison arrows and spell mentioned above) "need no warning," because they are now being freed from these harmful elements.

The open fourth side tells the person caught in the enclosure that he can always leave it, by looking within rather than without, and by asking the Sage for help. His reward is his inner freedom and his reunification with the Cosmic Whole.

Half-truths and untruths related to the above spells and poison arrows are: that the meaning of life is to be found in developing one's spiritual, or higher nature; that truth is to be found through suppressing, disciplining, or overcoming one's bodily nature and its feelings; that one's feelings stand in the way of perceiving the truth; that only by getting free of one's feelings can one perceive the truth objectively. (*See* p. 697, Freeing Yourself from Spells and Poison Arrows.)

"Manifestation of holding together" has two meanings: first it refers to the positive consequences of a person's holding to his inner truth, and thus drawing the Helpers into his life. It can also refer to people who are holding together in a "group-we" in order to show unity and create allegiances. However, since these allegiances exclude other people and the Helpers of the invisible world, they create a fate. Moreover, their unity, as indicated, is nothing but a *show*, and therefore has no substance. A further problem caused by commitment to a "group-we" is that it blocks the person's connection with his inner truth. To free himself from the negative consequences of participating in a group-we, the person needs to rid himself of all ideas that present merging his identity and purposes with a group as a benefit.

This line can also refer to a situation in which one person confides his problems to another, asking for his counsel. The game in the enclosure represents demonic elements the person "exposes" freely and is willing to get rid of. This line informs the psychological counselor that he should discuss only the elements exposed and not address other problems that are not openly presented. Doing so would only cause suspicion and distrust, and create a fate for the counselor.

Line 6. *He finds no head for holding together. Misfortune.*
Holding together, here as elsewhere, refers to being within the Cosmic Unity, as opposed to being separated from it. This holding together occurs through *feeling*, which involves the person's whole self, including his commonsense, which is a consensus of all his senses.

"No head for holding together" is a metaphor for a person's having allowed some part of his perceptive abilities to be blocked, so that he no longer is able to perceive the inner truth of things. A complete perception is drawn from what we feel through our combined inner and outer senses. It is then compared with our inner truth to give a correct perception. These senses include far more than outer seeing and hearing. Our senses of seeing, hearing, smelling, tasting, and touching operate both literally and figuratively so that we not only smell odors, for example, we also smell intentions and evil thoughts in people; things that contradict our inner truth likewise leave us with a "bad taste." However, as we have been taught to disregard our inner senses, we have shut them off. Without access to them, we figuratively "have no head" for perceiving reality in its Cosmic sense. (*See* Glossary: The Senses.)

The collective ego, by comparison, would tell us that our ability to perceive the truth is dependent only on what we can see and hear. The two frontal lobes, being necessary to process what is seen and heard, are therefore viewed as superior to other parts of the brain, especially those parts that register and interpret feelings.

Receiving this line is to make a person aware that he has allowed thinking to replace feeling. This mistake has occurred through his accepting the flattery that it is his rational and imagining abilities that make him brilliant and superior to the other creatures of creation. He does not suspect, therefore, that his continued reliance on what he thinks of as his mind (contrivance, cleverness, intellectualism, and mental structures) keeps him locked in the fate he has created. The remedy is to rid himself of the disdain he has learned for his senses, and to ask the Helpers to help him to return to his true nature. (*See* also Line 5 for the spells that are behind this disdain.)

This line also calls attention to the fact that if a person allows himself to remain separated from his feeling consciousness for too long in his life, his inner light (chi) will become extinguished. Then he becomes a "walking dead person." In this case, the "head" he lacks is his connection with the Cosmic Whole. (*See* Glossary: Walking Dead Person.)

"No head for holding together" can also be saying that a spell has been broken because the ringleaders, the key phrases of the spell, have been killed. As a consequence, the rational logic that has held the components of the spell together has fallen apart, bringing good fortune, rather than the misfortune mentioned.

9. The Taming Power of the Small/ Success through the Small

Sun
Ch'ien

The Judgment: *Dense clouds. No rain from our western region.*

In this hexagram, the Sage focuses on how people, animals, plants, and other aspects of Nature, are tamed and trained through small means. More specifically, it refers to how people are brought under the control of the collective ego through getting them to unquestioningly follow rules that bind them to its structure. "Small" refers to the rewards used in this training. Good behavior, which earns the rewards given, is the term used to define conformity to the rules.[*]

"Dense clouds" is an image of the result of the conditioning process by which Cosmic Virtues are appropriated by the collective ego, then turned into abstract virtues which cloud, or obscure, the light that would otherwise come from the person's true nature and virtue. In the course of this conditioning, his senses of outer and inner seeing are brought under a spell that makes him focus only on the superficial appearance of things. It also causes him to look at things as objects, prohibiting him from recognizing that everything that exists has consciousness and dignity. By relying only on what he sees, the person is divorced from his feelings about what he observes. This creates in him a distorted perception which then projects itself back upon the things he observes, distorting, in turn, their way of expressing themselves. Thus, the reality he observes is very much created by his projections. His sense of reality is thus "beclouded."

"No rain" means that such a person is prevented from receiving the Cosmic nourishment that would come from relating to

---

[*] This contrasts with what the collective ego designates as the "bad behavior," that receives the penalties and implied threats for going against its rules, as referred to in Hexagram 26, *The Taming Power of the Great/ Success through the Great.*

the intrinsic nature of things. The "western region" is a metaphor for a person's Cosmic Virtues, from which nourishment comes. "No rain" indicates that the approval and rewards of the collective ego contain no true nourishment. In addition, the true nourishment cannot come because the collective ego has appropriated these virtues by making the person believe he does not have them, and therefore needs to develop them. Thus, for example, his natural loyalty to his inner truth is replaced by loyalty to the collective ego's institutions and values. His being loyal to his inner truth is denounced as subjective, irrational, and subversive. Instead, the collective ego's moral rules tell him how and to whom his virtues are to be applied, regardless of the circumstances. In the case of kindness, he is to be kind in circumstances which it describes as correct, even though this may mean that he puts his kindness in the service of the egos in others.

The effect of this conditioning is to suppress the person's true self, through making him doubt his inner truth and disregard the prompting of his Cosmic Virtues. It divorces him from his feelings by asserting that feelings are a part of his "weak" nature and therefore cannot be trusted. The person is thereby reduced to relying only on thinking, which has also been brought under the collective ego's control. The effect on the social structure as a whole is to deprive it of the *feelings* that would otherwise provide a harmonious interaction between all its people, and make possible a natural society that is in harmony with the rest of Nature and the Cosmic Whole.

The conditioning can also be seen as introducing "microchips" of memory not only into the psyche of a person, but into certain muscles and organs as well. Similar to Pavlovian training, its goal is to produce reflexive behavior, such as unquestioned obedience to authority. Such training, which is against a person's nature, invariably creates unplanned for consequences.

Spells connected with this hexagram include phrases such as: "People do not have Cosmic Virtues; all virtue is cultivated"; "human animal nature needs to be tamed." (*See* p. 697, Freeing Yourself from Spells.)

"Success through the small," the Cosmic meaning of this

hexagram, shows a person how his suppressed true self can be reclaimed from the subconscious step by step through the gradual penetration of the light of inner truth. The "small," in this case, refers both to the "small steps" and the small seeds of ideas, that when deprogrammed, bring down the "whole trees" that have grown into neurotic complexes from the mistaken ideas. It also is a metaphor for the individual path of destiny that is begun by taking these first small steps.

Entry onto this path often begins with the gift of love to two people. It comes as a Cosmic intervention in their lives to reveal to them their lost true selves, which have become "strangers within." Love, which is given only to their true selves, provides them with the opportunity to recognize and validate each other's true self as the rightful leader of their personalities. The gift also gives them an opportunity to recognize the presence of the invisible Helpers in their lives.

Note: Since all lines contain infinite possibilities of interpretation, one needs to use the *rtcm* to determine if the meanings suggested here apply to the given situation. (*See* p. 736, Using the *rtcm*.)

Line 1. *Return to the path. How could there be blame in this? Good fortune.*

"Return to the path" is counsel given to a person, who, through the influence of the ego, is tempted to abandon the path of freeing his true self. The ego presents the path as too hard, or as not to be trusted, because it requires that he depend on what he cannot see, or it does not appear to lead to his goal, or the ego will say that the way of the Sage is a fiction of his imagination. Seed phrases behind such thoughts are: "at some point you're going to be disappointed"; "such a path goes against the 'wisdom of the ages,'" and "how can such small steps lead to big results"; "it is impossible to rid yourself of your ego"; "there are no such things as spells, or a demonic sphere of consciousness."

The line may also indicate that a person is judging the gift of love he has received by what he ought to think about it, rather than by validating what his feelings are telling him, or verifying their validity by consulting the Sage. Such a person regards the shoulds of the collective ego as more important than his inner truth. "How could there be blame in this" refers to the effort he needs to make to rid himself of seed phrases that devalue his feelings as "only subjective."

This line defines the difference between true blame and what the collective ego calls blame. True blame is incurred when a person betrays his inner truth by following the shoulds of the collective ego. From the viewpoint of the collective ego, blame is incurred by disregard of *its* rules and values. A further difference is that true blame is never the cause of guilt, and can always be extinguished either by a fate, or by a sincere correction of attitude. The Cosmos rejects altogether the idea of guilt, while the collective ego sees it as the consequence of blame. As the convicted felon is made to realize, the collective ego does not allow that guilt can be eradicated; it must be paid for endlessly. (*See* p. 50, Guilt, Blame, and Shame.)

In order to return to the path of freeing his true self, a person also needs to rid himself of any feelings of guilt that he may have betrayed the values or rules of the collective ego. The reverse is true: it is the collective ego that betrays his true nature.

"Return to the path" also counsels a person against confronting the ego in another directly, in an effort to counter it. Rather than being bothered by the ego's display and blaming him, the person says the inner No and asks for the help of the Cosmos. If necessary, he agrees with him outwardly, to allow him to save face, as long as he is in that ego-mode. In this way, his inner No supports the person's true self while not engaging the ego.

Line 2. *He allows himself to be drawn into returning. Good fortune.*

This line draws our attention to the active help a person gets from the Cosmos to draw him back to his true nature. The help referred to comes in the form of a Cosmic gift. The gift can be a love relationship or a job opportunity, because the receiver is modest and sincere. Receiving a love relationship, sudden wealth, or some other benefit is to make the person aware that his "good fortune" does not come, as he may think, from his having been virtuous, but to strengthen his imprisoned true self. Recognizing this fact is "to allow himself to be drawn into returning" to the truth of the matter, and to humility.

The line may also apply to the person who thinks that his gift of love is the result of having successfully sublimated his "lower nature," whereas the gift has been given to him to free the repressed part of his nature to make him whole. Seed phrases behind the idea of sublimating one's "lower nature," and which put spells and poison arrows on the body, are: "sexuality is part of one's lower instincts," and "the instincts must be sublimated in favor of one's higher nature." (*See* p. 689, Freeing Yourself from Seed Phrases and Images.)

The Cosmic gift can also come as an unpleasant happening to make a person aware that he has put a projection, spell, or poison arrow on another. The unpleasant happening has the purpose of sparking him to reflect and to correct himself.

"Allowing himself to be drawn into returning" also counsels a person to leave behind friends or associates who are following the path of the collective ego. Leaving them behind does not mean that he mentally executes or condemns them, but says the inner No to their path, and goes on his own way.

The line also is counsel against using the *I Ching* for ego-purposes, that is, in any way that would diminish its dignity. At the same time, it is counsel against putting it on a pedestal as a sacred book, or putting the Sage up as "higher," which would distance the person from it.

Line 3. *The spokes burst out of the wagon wheels. Man and wife roll their eyes.*

The wagon referred to here is a metaphor for the natural progress of a person's life when he is in harmony with his nature. The spokes stand for his Cosmic Virtues that are in connection with his feelings/inner truth (the wheels). When the individual undergoes the collective ego's conditioning mentioned in the main text of this hexagram, his virtues become separated from his feelings/inner truth; this is the meaning of "the spokes burst out of the wagon wheels." By making his virtues conform to the standards prescribed by the collective ego, the person has put spells on his feelings and inner senses. Consequently, he has been acting from thinking and according to shoulds and in the process has created a fate.

This line can refer to the effect such a fate has on the sense of inner seeing when it is under a spell: it makes the person see a fate as "undeserved," because he has been a virtuous person in the eyes of the collective ego. Receiving this line is to make him aware that he himself is the creator of his fate, through betraying his inner truth. He also needs to realize that the fate is a Cosmic reaction to his having violated Cosmic Laws. Fate is another means employed by the Cosmos to "draw him into returning" to his inner truth and commonsense. Fate, as shock, makes the eyes "roll" in terror. This is good, because terror temporarily freezes the ego, thus allowing the person to get in touch with his true feelings. When Fate comes in the form of an illness, it frees his senses from the spell put upon them by the collective ego.

This line can also refer to a person who has put a spell on a situation that prevents progress. For example, through a mistaken idea of loyalty, a person has promised to be faithful to his partner for the rest of his life. The promise, in addition to giving permission to the ego in his partner to dominate the relationship, puts a spell on himself that forces him to be loyal, no matter what; it also inserts into the other's psyche the idea that regardless of what he does, he has a right to the other's loyalty. The person needs to ask for help to be freed from this spell. Ridding himself of it will also extinguish the fate he has created, and open new possibilities for the relationship as a whole. (*See* p. 697, Freeing Yourself from Spells.)

This line can also draw a person's attention to a Helper that makes him feel the gnawing of his conscience to remind him that he has betrayed his true nature. Feeling this gnawing is not meant to make him feel guilty, but to make him aware that he has created blame, and give him an opportunity to rid himself of it. This is done by recognizing that thoughts of self-blame, or which blame life, are rationales coming from the ego. Through saying the inner No to these rationales he frees the Helpers (his Cosmic Virtues) that are meant to help him through his life, and he enables his true self to grow.

The line can also make a person aware that he is experiencing a fate, because he has put a spell on a part of his nature by call-ing it "lower," as by saying or thinking, "sexuality is part of one's lower instincts," and "the instincts must be sublimated in favor of one's higher nature." His fate can be extinguished if he will rid himself of this spell.

This line can also point to a spell put on the natural order of society, through disbelief that such an order exists and that it would actually function. This spell blocks the Helper of Cre-ativity, and the Helper of a Natural Society. (For a more de-tailed discussion of this theme and the spells connected with it *see* Hexagram 45, *Gathering Together.*)

Line 4. *If you are sincere, blood vanishes and fear gives way. No blame.*

"Blood vanishes and fear gives way" is an explanation that the Cosmos has intervened to correct the difficult situation be-cause the person involved has kept himself open to Cosmic help, and refrained from any attempt to correct matters according to his own ideas.

The line is also a statement that a person needs to be sincere in correcting himself after having broken Cosmic Law. "Blood," in this case, refers to his feelings of guilt and fear of punish-ment for having done so. He is incorrectly thinking of guilt and punishment in the way the collective ego does, and therefore fears that the matter cannot be corrected. This line tells him that in the given circumstance, to "make blood vanish and fear give way" he needs to do two things: (1) correct his error by recognizing he has done something wrong and saying the inner No to his wrongdoing; (2) rid himself of the idea of guilt by treating it as a spell. (*See* p. 696, Freeing Yourself from a Guilt Spell.)

Line 5. *If you are sincere and loyally attached, you are rich in your neighbor.*

This line makes a person aware of the source of true blessings and success: the Cosmic Consciousness. Every person is directly connected with it through his "neighbor," which is a metaphor for the Helpers of Inner Truth. A person is in harmony and connected with the Cosmic Consciousness when he is "sincere and loyally attached" to his inner truth. The Sage is the Helper that helps him access his inner truth; no human intermediary can serve this function, or interpret what his inner truth is telling him.

Line 6. The rain comes, there is rest. This is due to the lasting effect of character. The moon is nearly full. If the superior man persists, misfortune comes. Perseverance brings the woman into danger.

"The rain comes bringing rest" is an indication that a person has come to an understanding of what the Sage means in the specific situation. The lesson he has learned, however, must not be taken as "true for all situations." It is to be taken as only a handhold in his learning process. As a handhold, it is to be held onto until it is eventually succeeded by yet another handhold, or broader understanding. This learning process allows no understanding of the moment to become true for all time. It is, however, dependable as a temporary structure that enables the person to make progress in his life.

"The moon is nearly full" is a reference to the moon's nearly full reflection of the sun. As a metaphor it represents the person who, in learning from the Sage by hand-holds, begins to think that he has learned the ultimate truth, and therefore has become a "superior man." This assumption, however, reveals that he has allowed the ego to appropriate what he has learned from the Sage. "Perseverance brings the woman into danger" refers to this fact, since the "woman" stands for his feelings, which have now been shut out. Receiving this line can indicate that a person believes in the mistaken idea that enlightenment is the goal of developing the true self. This concept is only an invitation to egoistic pride, which is the enemy of all learning.

The goal of enlightenment is taken from the collective ego's view of education; it implies a final state of knowledge or attainment acquired by studying things as objects in such a way that the student is divorced from his feelings about them. Studying things in this way projects upon the things being studied the distorted and degraded view produced by seeing them as objects. Cosmic learning, by contrast, is learning through listening to our feelings, and through perceiving the dignity that is inherent in all things. This kind of learning enlarges our perception and enables us to discover things in their true identity, and thereby to contribute to the ongoing evolution of the Cosmic Consciousness.

"The rain comes, there is rest" also refers to the chi energy, harmony, and joy a person receives upon discovering life through his *feelings* and experiencing its underlying harmony. This experience is the source of an inner security that takes away all fear of the unknown through realizing that the Cosmos is knowable through one's feelings.

Seed phrases in this context are: "there is only so much you can know"; "if you're in the know you have nothing to fear"; "knowledge is what distinguishes humans from animals"; "knowledge gives you control"; "ignorance is bliss." An image is the unknown as an endless abyss into which one falls. (See p. 689, Freeing Yourself from Seed Phrases and Images.)

10. *Conducting Oneself*

 Ch'ien
Tui

The Judgment: *If the person treads upon the tail of the tiger, it bites him.*

Here, the Sage describes how certain hidden Helpers a person is born with cooperate to enable him to conduct himself in harmony with the Cosmic Whole. These Helpers are concealed senses, for which the tiger is a metaphor. They are not the commonly known five senses, but are, for example, a person's sense of appropriateness, the sense of loyalty (to his inner truth), the sense of fairness, and the sense of wholeness. These senses are referred to throughout this book as the "metaphorical senses." One of their general characteristics is *simplicity,* as mentioned in Line 1: they allow a person to react harmoniously and appropriately to circumstances without the *necessity of thinking.*

They operate as involuntary reactions that keep him *centered and complete within himself,* therefore in harmony with the Cosmos. When a person lives his life in harmony with all his senses, he remains "without blame," meaning, he does not create a fate.

The metaphorical senses mentioned here are perceptible by the conscious mind only if a person tunes into them. However, when the conscious mind comes under the domination of the ego, *thinking* becomes exalted and these senses, as a *feeling consciousness,* are subsequently diminished as "primitive," repressed into the subconscious, and disregarded.

Because they continue to act on their own, subliminally, on behalf of the whole, they have been assumed to be of a purely mechanical nature, as the name "involuntary nervous system" suggests. Their cooperation with the conscious mind can succeed, however, only when the person validates their importance.

The senses mentioned are located in muscle tissues throughout the body. They bring about involuntary reactions such as blushing, retreating, fleeing, and also advancing along the line of no resistance; the latter is another term for saying they achieve things through transformation. One of the functions of a person's metaphorical senses is to protect him from harm coming from outside that threatens his completeness. In short, they enable him to do the right thing in relation to the circumstance of the moment.

"Treading on the tail of the tiger" is a metaphor for what happens when a person acts against these senses, because they have become suppressed through conditioning. Then the "tiger bites," in the form of Fate.

The suppression of a person's metaphorical senses starts at a very young age, when a program is introjected into the child's psyche that demonizes his "animal nature" as dirty and undesirable. The goal of this program is to have the child regard every fluid and material that naturally comes out of his body as despicable, and every exploration into his sexuality accompanied by guilt. Since his animal nature and sexuality are the very sources of his life force (chi energy), these mistaken ideas trap the person in an impossible paradox: he must regard the very things that comprise his nature and supply him with nourishment as his enemy. A further program is installed by the collective ego which tells the child that he can redeem himself by developing his "higher nature," through following the dictates of the collective ego. However, his rejecting the body as inferior puts spells and poison arrows on his body, creating illnesses and other forms of Fate.

A person receives this hexagram when he is experiencing a fate due to the above false program that has disabled his metaphorical senses. (*See* p. 697, Freeing Yourself from Spells and Poison Arrows. Also *see* Glossary: The Senses.)

The Sage draws our attention to the difference between self-development defined by the collective ego and the natural desire to free the true self from the ego. The collective ego first cultivates insufficiency and guilt in the individual in order to create a false dependency on it; in slandering a person's animal nature as "wild," it provides a reason for its hierarchical control over him. By accepting these slanders the person incurs Cosmic blame. When the blame is continued over a period of time, a fate is activated to make him aware that he is in conflict with his true nature. To free the true self, the Sage encourages him to rid himself of the idea of guilt, and then of the entire program of cultivating his "higher nature," which is based on guilt and insufficiency of self.

Part of the collective ego's program is the development of so-called qualities of character and models of conduct that would make him a "superior man." Implied in this program is the self-flattering idea that by becoming guilt-free, the person can become "like God."

This hexagram makes a clear distinction between conduct that leads to the fulfillment of a person's destiny, and conduct that creates a fate. Fate is not, as the collective ego would make us believe, something we are born with, that is written in the stars, is the result of a hostile Cosmos or Nature. It is rather the consequence of conduct that results from mistaken ideas and beliefs. Fate is a signal that the person is not fulfilling his natural destiny.

Spells and poison arrows connected with this hexagram contain phrases such as, "humans' animal nature is the source of evil," "in and of yourself you are not enough to cope with life," and ideas that a person is guilty by nature. Related phrases are, "you have to develop character," "you have to become something," and "you need to become like God." Related spells come from calling things by wrong names that create confusion about their true natures. Among them are calling the ego "the self," and inventing things that do not exist in the Cosmic order of things, such as "soul," for the psyche, "instincts," for the metaphorical senses, and "culprit," for a person who is trapped in mistaken beliefs. (*See* Glossary: Soul, Instincts, Culprit.)

Note: Since all lines contain infinite possibilities of interpretation, one needs to use the *rtcm* to determine if the meanings suggested here apply to the given situation. (*See* p.736, Using the *rtcm*.)

Line 1. *Simple conduct. Progress without blame.*

Simple conduct means *reacting to* situations rather than *creating* them. It is a way of remaining centered and correct in the midst of other people's activity. "Making progress without blame" occurs when a person is free of pretenses.

This line often refers to conduct that is not in harmony with the Cosmos because it lacks simplicity. Such an attitude may be observed in the person who comes to the *I Ching* only to get free of the discomfort caused by his problems, and not to rid himself of the luxurious and egocentric attitudes that have caused them. Such a person will not escape his fate.

The line may also refer to the person who does what is correct from the Cosmic point of view, but only to "be a superior person," and not because it is in harmony with his true feelings. The same also applies to the person who fails to retreat and say the inner No in the face of other's ego-behavior, from fear of being disliked. Simple conduct means to do a thing for its own sake, as in the famous Chinese saying, "The master potter leaves no trace." He makes the pot for itself, and not to achieve acclaim, or from any other intention.

The line can also refer to someone who has adopted the self-image of the "unpretentious person." However, simplicity, like modesty, cannot be achieved as a goal, since it is the consequence of a person's seeing his true place in the Cosmos. When such a person creates a fate through having adopted the self-image of "being simple," he will say, "I don't deserve this fate."

Line 2. *Treading a smooth, level course. The quiet and solitary man fulfills his destiny.*

The "quiet and solitary man" indicates a person who is capable of shutting out the clamoring voices of the ego and thus is attentive to all that his senses tell him. He is solitary in that he places his dependency on his inner truth rather than on others. Having no need to put himself forward egotistically, he is able to go on his way alone and retreat in the presence of others' ego-behavior. He does not judge or condemn them, but withdraws to maintain his integrity. Treading a smooth, level course refers to his being centered, therefore not having to go through the ups and downs of Fate.

The path that such a person follows is primarily reactive rather than proactive, embracing what is harmonious (saying the inner Yes to it), and rejecting (saying the inner No) and withdrawing from participation in what is discordant. In all situations he consults his feelings for this Yes or No, and acts accordingly.

A person may receive this line when he is afraid to stand or go on his way alone in this fashion, out of fear of being lonely or excluded by others. He does not realize that retreating from ego-behavior in others is to be embraced by the Cosmos itself. His fear keeps him imprisoned, and makes him accept ego-behavior from others. It also draws other's transgressions into his space. Although he does not realize it, he can always leave the prison of his fear.

Such a person may be caught in the idea that to be without someone is to be only half a person, and that he needs the other(s) to complete him. This view puts a poison arrow on his natural completeness. To become free of it he needs to rid himself of the phrases, "in and of yourself you are not enough," and "by yourself you are incomplete." (*See* p. 697, Freeing Yourself from Poison Arrows.)

This line may be referring to a person who is staying in a wrong relationship from guilt, believing that he owes it to the partner to stay. To be free of the spells created by guilt, he needs to reject guilt and all its supporting "reasons." Accepting a wrong relationship with another creates Cosmic blame. (*See* p. 677, Saying the Inner No.)

This line informs us that the purpose of maintaining inner quiet is to attain clarity, not to "be quiet" or "live in solitude" because doing so fulfills a model of "spirituality." A spiritual self-image is still a creation of the ego. (*See* p. 691, Freeing Yourself from Self-Images.)

This line also exposes the mistaken idea promoted by the collective ego that spiritual growth needs to take place in solitude. Such an idea comes from spiritual ambition, which occurs when the ego in a person tries to take charge of his inner growth toward maturity by turning it into a retreat from the world. It seeks to attain an ideal of perfection through a solitude that will keep him free of worldly contamination. Such a person confounds isolation from others with the inner independence that is found through depending on the Cosmos.

Line 3. *A one-eyed man is able to see. A lame man is able to tread. He treads on the tail of the tiger. The tiger bites the man. Misfortune.*

The "one-eyed" and "lame man" is a metaphor for a person whose senses have been partially disabled due to a poison arrow. The line states that although he is somewhat able to see and conduct his life, he is not in harmony with the Cosmos. As a consequence, he continually creates fates for himself.

The poison arrow, which was put upon him at a very early age by one or more of his elders, has at its base the idea that humans' animal nature is the source of evil, and that therefore he is born guilty. The person who has this belief is unable to see (is one-eyed) that every aspect of Nature, including his animal nature, is an expression of the Cosmic Consciousness, and is endowed with dignity. (*See* p. 697, Freeing Yourself from Poison Arrows.)

The "one-eyed man" can also refer to a person who, in judging another, is judging his nature as faulty. The Sage informs us that a person's nature is not evil, but that evil comes from his acting upon mistaken beliefs that put humans at the center of the universe. (*See* Glossary: Good and Evil.) It may also be that he is judging the person on the basis of appearances rather than on the inner truth of the situation, which he cannot see (another meaning of "one-eyed"). It is possible that the person's behavior is being caused by projections, spells, or poison arrows which may have been put on him by the seemingly innocent parties to the situation. By looking to the wrong person and blaming him, he has separated from the Cosmic Unity and created a fate for himself. To correct himself, he needs to say the inner No to the idea that evil lies in a person's or a thing's nature. He can then ask for help to have his fate extinguished.

A person may receive this line when he has attached himself to his past mistakes, curbing his ability to go on with his life. This happens when he allows his natural feeling of regret to be transferred (as the collective ego teaches him to do) into a permanent stain of guilt, an emotion that gives the collective ego control over him. Such self-incrimination puts a spell on him.

This line can also refer to a person who carelessly treads on aspects of Nature through regarding them as inert, mechanical, chemical, or alchemical. Because he thinks he can do with them what he likes, he creates a fate, and thus "is bitten."

A person may also receive this line when he has carelessly ignored the Cosmic Law by adopting a high-and-mighty attitude. He arrogantly upholds conduct that is human-centered, believing that because he is a human being, he has rights over animals, other people, and even life itself. When Fate has "bitten" as a consequence, he thinks he is innocent and blames it on a "hostile universe." His attitude is the source of his fate. To end it, he needs to return to humility by taking his proper place in the Cosmos, as an equal to all its other aspects.

"The tiger bites the man," in all these cases, is a metaphor for the fate that "bites" a person as a result of his disregard of his metaphorical senses. It is, in fact, these very senses that bite him, in order to wake him up to the fact that due to their disablement, his reactions to danger have become incomplete, making him vulnerable to attacks from without. These attacks come from both the collective ego and the egos in others in the form of mistaken ideas that would further harm him, if he follows them. This disablement makes him unable to recognize their damaging effects, and also unable to attract the protection of the Helpers. People experience this wake-up call in disturbing dreams and in small accidents. If these warnings are not heeded, the adversities will become ever more severe.

Line 4. *He treads on the tail of the tiger. Caution and circumspection lead ultimately to good fortune.*

"He treads on the tail of the tiger" is a metaphor for a person who is experiencing a fate. Fate, as indicated in the previous line, can be ended at any time a person recognizes the error of his ideas and beliefs, and rids himself of them.

"Caution and circumspection" is a warning that there are mistaken ideas present in the situation that would pull the person back into certain traps. It warns in particular against the dangers created by incipient guilt. Guilt is that ego-emotion cultivated in a person to lock him securely within the collective ego's values. It is the feeling that sometimes sets in after a person has said the necessary inner No to wrong actions or beliefs he has been trained to tolerate and accept. It makes him doubt the correctness of his authorizing himself to say No to the ego. To have feelings of guilt is also the result of training that causes the individual to transfer his natural feelings of regret for having made a mistake into the stain of permanent guilt. This transfer succeeds in reinstalling the spell that keeps him within the confines of the collective ego. On this account, guilt in any form needs to be recognized as the first thing that needs to be said No to. It is the element that undoes the effect of previously said inner No's, and supplies the rationales that reinstall all the old ego-programs. (*See* p. 696, Freeing Yourself from Guilt.)

Caution and circumspection are those metaphorical senses that lead a person to the kind of detachment that separates him from the ego, by making him an observer of his emotions, freeing him from being trapped in them. Detachment is a neutral attitude that is free of being in any "gear," such as "reverse" (the impulse to deny, avoid, or flee), or "first gear" (an impulse to move forward before one knows where one is going), or in "drive" (an aggressive or defensive movement). Neutrality creates the inner space that allows the Sage to be heard within, for it is the Sage, ultimately, that can help the person free himself from his fate (the good fortune referred to).

Caution and circumspection also warn a person against the danger of blaming his fate on something outside himself, such as chance circumstances, God, or the Cosmos. It also warns him against attempting to make bargains with the entity he blames, as by making pacts (with God), or reparations (to the Cosmos as by doing good deeds), or by making efforts to change his circumstances, thinking his fate is merely a mechanical incident. While fate can be ended through relating to it correctly, it cannot be ended through bargaining or by efforts to change it.

This line can also refer to a person whose fate has been caused by going against his natural inhibitions from a false sense of duty. His natural inhibitions are metaphorical senses whose function is to protect him from doing that cause a loss of self-esteem and dignity. Going against them leads to inner conflict, which is felt as embarrassment and self-betrayal. The person can avoid self-betrayal if he is cautious and retreats when confronted with situations that arouse hesitation about entering them. Circumspection, in this regard, refers to taking seriously the warnings offered by his feelings; it also refers to finding a tactful way of handling situations in which others assert that it is his duty to do things that are against his nature.

Caution and circumspection also refer to not accepting something as true simply because someone has said it is so. The validity of ideas and statements can always be checked with the Sage by using the *rtcm*, and, if necessary, by asking for a hexagram. In this way a person can avoid putting himself on paths that are dead-ended or that would invoke a fate.

A person may also receive this line when he has wrongly concluded that he can do nothing about his fate. As said above, all fate can be ended, but in this case, the person first needs to say the inner No to the idea that he can do nothing about it. The purpose of Fate is to redirect him inwardly to freeing himself from the mistaken ideas that prevent him from fulfilling his destiny. (*See* p. 692, Freeing Yourself from a Fate.)

Line 5. *Resolute conduct. It furthers to be firmly correct, with awareness of danger.*

In its Cosmic sense, resolute conduct means putting one's will to the correct use. What is called will is not the same as the will to live. Our will is part of our metaphorical senses, but unlike some of the other metaphorical senses, it can be flattered by the ego into serving *its* purposes, as in fighting what the ego defines as evil, or in pushing the person's efforts to achieve goals it defines as good. The ego's flattery is the danger referred to in the line. Being firmly correct means saying the inner No to those flatteries. When a person is struggling to free himself from the ego's tyranny, his will can be of inestimable help if he asks it to come to his aid.

When the ego has succeeded in turning a person's will to its purposes, it uses the will to obstruct the other metaphorical senses that would otherwise be able to restrain the person from pursuing its false goals. In the will's unrestrained effort to achieve the ego's goals, the entire self will be sacrificed, if need be. As the driver of a person's will, the ego strongly asserts itself as "I." The person needs to recognize that the parasitic ego, if not stopped, will drive him so hard it will extinguish its host. It can be stopped by saying the inner No to the ego's demands.

The ego will also use a person's will either to fight a fate or to overcome it through submission. Both approaches come from a heroic self-image that misuses the will. Such an abuse of will only creates a new fate. The person needs to rid himself of the mistaken ideas that create such self-images.

The mention of danger in this line can also refer to being rigidly correct. The true self does not strive after any such self-flattering idea as perfection. Rigid correctness is also associated with self-righteousness, which comes from the ambition to be in the right, and to fulfill the self-image of the good person, as defined by the rules and values of the collective ego. Wherever either ambition or a self-image is involved, a fate is created.

Our will, as Line 5 of Hexagram 31, *Influence* informs us, is located in the nerves in the back of the neck, just below the brainstem. From this position it is capable of influencing the other metaphorical senses located in muscle tissues throughout the body.

Line 6. *Look to your conduct and weigh the favorable signs. When everything is fulfilled, supreme good fortune comes.*
A person can receive this line when he is weighing whether to make a particular move. The line tells him that his hesitation is justified because his commonsense feels elements in the situation that are not appropriate, but are not yet conscious to his mind. He needs to consult the Sage to discover the inner truth of the situation. Then the right way to go will show itself.

This line can also indicate a person who is not going on with his life, because he is waiting for something favorable to happen. As Hexagram 35, *Progressing*, makes us aware, life is a process of "going on." It is while we are going on with our lives that the things happen that lead us to our destiny, even though, at the time, we may not recognize this fact.

The word "weighing" also points to the person who believes he can make deals with Fate: that he will be rewarded if he behaves according to the shoulds and musts of the collective ego. The person who has thus lived his life "by the book," has ended in finding only disappointment.

A person can also receive this line when he has misunderstood the true meaning of conduct. Since early childhood he may have lived his life by the standards and values of the collective ego, and may even think he has brought these values to perfection through fulfilling its images of the hero, the good person, or the spiritual person. He may have transferred his idea of correct conduct to his way of following the *I Ching* as a sacred text, with the idea that if he behaves as he understands it, an imagined good fortune will come. He has taken the written words as a promise. Now he is weighing the outcome and is wondering why the good fortune has not come. He has been paying attention to conduct as form, rather than understanding that correct conduct is the result of being in harmony with his inner truth. He has not noticed that in doing so his true nature has been sacrificed, and he has created a fate. He can free himself from his fate by recognizing his mistaken beliefs and ridding himself of his self-images. (*See* p. 691, Freeing Yourself of Self-Images.)

11. *Harmony/Peace/Prosperity*

K'un
—————
Ch'ien

The Judgment: *The small departs, the great approaches. Good fortune. Success.*

The Sage shows us, in this hexagram, that before the "great" can approach, in the form of harmony, peace, and prosperity, the "small" must first depart. The small, in this case, refers to the primary thoughts and premises devised by the collective ego, which are the ringleaders of all disorder. We are directed, therefore, to identifying and clearing them away.

The most primary among them is the idea that humans are the special creatures of creation, and the focal point around which the universe revolves. This basic idea has produced the "ribbon grass" of mistaken beliefs about Nature that are responsible for disorder.

Ironically, traditional versions of this hexagram these beliefs as ancient truths, whereas they are the foundation stones upon which the collective ego has based its authority to establish and maintain its rule over Nature and society.

Ideas derived from the human centered view of the universe and given in the traditional versions of this hexagram are that "man's destiny is to represent heaven's will on earth," and that "man's job is to bring order to Nature." These beliefs are explained in Wilhelm's commentary to The Image of this hexagram as follows:

"The stream of energy [between heaven and earth] must

be regulated by the ruler of men. It is done by a process of division. Thus, men divide the uniform flow of time into the seasons, according to the succession of natural phenomena, and mark off infinite space by the points of the compass. In this way Nature in its overwhelming profusion of phenomena is bounded and controlled. On the other hand, nature must be furthered in her productiveness....This controlling and furthering activity of man in relation to nature, is the work on nature that rewards him."

Showing how this belief was applied to the control of human society to create peace and harmony, Wilhelm continues,

"When the good elements of society occupy a central position and are in control, the evil elements come under their influence and change for the better. When the spirit of heaven rules in man, his animal nature also comes under its influence and takes its appropriate place."*

What is relevant to us today is that although these ideas are typically Confucian, they are embraced by religions and feudal-derived cultures worldwide. The idea that a person's animal nature is evil is the primary and justifying foundation upon which the collective ego sets itself up as the designated authority to discipline, fight, and overcome humans' animal nature, and by implication, Nature itself. The individual ego mimics this authority when it takes on the roles of "the creator," "the doer," and "the hero."

The idea that humans occupy such an exalted position in the order of things separates them from the Cosmic Unity, which is based on the essential *equality* of all aspects of the Cosmos. The idea that humans are the centerpiece of creation has its origin in the feudal mindset that has dominated the last 3,000 years of human history. This mindset imagines the Cosmos as hierarchically ordered in order to justify its own hierarchical ordering of society. In this system, a Cosmic "overlord" is invented to fulfill the purpose of "authorizing" the dominance of the feudal lord. In the Chinese system, the granting authority, as indicated

---

* Wilhelm, pp. 48, 49. (We were led by the Sage to omit the section entitled The Image from this volume.)

179

above, is "heaven," and it is also heaven that is seen to grant the various entitlements and rights to the individual, according to his rung on the feudal social ladder.

The hierarchical thinking of feudalism is also the source of thinking in terms of opposites, with one of the pair of opposites as superior to the other: yang as superior to yin, heaven as ruling earth, male as dominating female, and humans as superior to animals, etc. Human nature is likewise divided into higher and lower parts, with one being seen as good, the other as the source of evil. Like ideas justify the human purpose to dominate not only Nature, but also other human beings that are regarded as inferior.

The idea that evil originates in humans' animal nature contradicts the principle *implicit* throughout the *I Ching* that humans are born good, possessing the perfect natural program to live their lives in harmony with the Cosmos.

The idea that humans are the centerpiece of creation also contradicts the modesty defined in Hexagram 15 as the Cosmic Virtue that unites humans with the Cosmic Harmony. It is modesty that draws those Helpers that are associated with peace and prosperity.

Peace, as all feudal cultures conceive it, is the result of certain "qualified" humans controlling others. In the Cosmic view, peace is the result of the individual's living in harmony with his true and undivided nature, since his true nature is in harmony with the Cosmos/Nature. Disorder and evil result when part of his nature has been slandered. When a person is in harmony, he invokes the help of the Cosmos in all that he does.

The traditional view of this hexagram also falsely credits humans with the great achievements of culture. The Sage informs us that human creativity is always a partnership with the Helper of Creativity, which is accessed through the individual's inner truth. This Helper is also engaged when a person establishes a feeling relationship with the consciousness of the things with which he is working. Creativity is not, as the human-centered view would have us believe, the result of the abilities of the rational mind. All inventions and discoveries come through the intervention of these Helpers. For many people, the help can only come after a person has come to his "wit's end" and has given up. Just then, when he has experienced a moment of humility, the Helper comes to guide him to the precise answer he was looking for. All great artists and performers have had this experience. Some have also experienced the loss of this gift when they have forgotten its source, or credited it to themselves. The gift of creativity comes easily and repetitively to those people who know and recognize where the gift comes from, and who continually credit the source.

The Cosmic theme of this hexagram, which is expressed in its names, was taken from the interaction of the two primary trigrams which represent the Cosmic Consciousness and Nature. This interaction is the pairing and interpenetrating of their energies with each other, creating harmony, peace, and prosperity. They pair because they are in a complementary relationship to each other, the Cosmic Consciousness being represented by the inner (= lower) trigram and Nature represented by the outer (= upper) trigram as its complement.

A person receives this hexagram when, because of his human-centered beliefs, he has blocked the Helper of Creativity. He can free this Helper to come to his aid if he will rid himself of the mistaken beliefs listed above. This effort requires identifying seed phrases in his inner program that see Nature (including his own animal nature) as the source of disorder, chaos, and evil. He also needs to rid himself of phrases and their accompanying images that place humans in the center of the universe.

Note: Since all lines contain infinite possibilities of interpretation, one needs to use the *rtcm* to determine if the meanings suggested here apply to the given situation. (*See* p. 736, Using the *rtcm*.)

Line 1. *When ribbon grass is pulled up, the sod comes with it. Each according to his kind. Undertakings bring good fortune.*

"When ribbon grass is pulled up" is a metaphor for the mistaken ideas and beliefs a person needs to dispose of in order to return to harmony with the Cosmos. They are also the "ringleaders of disorder" mentioned in Hexagram 36, *Darkening of the Light,* Line 3.

When a person rids himself of a central mistaken idea, he

brings to the surface other ideas that are based on it as a premise, or that are unrelated, but have been combined with it to form a justification for further incorrect ideas. This combining of unrelated ideas is typical of the illogic of the collective ego. It is essential for the person to rid himself of all ideas that form such clusters. "Each according to his kind" is a reference to the various unrelated ideas.

The basic mistaken idea indicated by this line is that humans are at the center of the universe. When this idea is combined with the idea that humans' animal nature is the source of evil, a basis is provided for the further idea that it is the human job to order and control Nature, including human nature. Because these phrases slander the Cosmic Helpers that achieve their tasks through Nature, their help is blocked. When confronted with this distorted reality, the false conclusion is drawn that "humans must do everything themselves," including correcting the distortions in Nature created by humans. The latter phrase puts yet another spell on Nature.

This line applies to the person who has separated from the Cosmos and its help by having accepted the above-mentioned ideas. He is informed that he can be reunited with the Cosmic Whole if he will rid himself of them. These are the "undertakings" that "bring good fortune." The effect of ridding one's personal program of the "ribbon grass" is obvious; the statement that "the sod comes with it" points to the less obvious fact that the power of the collective ego ("the sod") over the individual is thereby diminished. (*See* p. 689, Freeing Yourself from Mistaken Ideas and Beliefs.)

Line 2. *Bearing with the uncultured in gentleness, fording the river with resolution, not neglecting what is distant, not regarding one's companions; thus one may manage to walk in the middle.*

The line is counsel to a person who is confronted with people who are difficult, telling him to bear with them patiently because they are unaware of the invisible world, or they have never learned from the Sage. "Fording the river with resolution" is advice for him to hold to their true selves despite their outer behavior. Fording the river, in this case, represents getting past the difficulty. "Not neglecting what is distant" reminds him that holding fast to his inner truth will ultimately succeed in correcting the situation. "Not regarding his companions" is saying, "do not concern yourself with what others may think of your actions." Following this path enables him to "walk in the middle," meaning to avoid getting caught up in the ego's demands that the situation improve "or else..."

This line can also refer to a person's creativity. "Fording the river with resolution" states that it is correct for a person to trust his intuition, because it gives him a glimpse of the bigger outline ("what is distant"); it is necessary to move ahead on that basis, although the reasoning ego would want to object.

"Not regarding one's companions" is also counsel to avoid a servile dependence on the Sage, as by asking about what the person already knows from other lessons with the Sage, or about something he already intuitively knows within.

In a situation where a person's dignity and integrity have been injured, the counsel to "ford the river with resolution" means to get past seeing the situation from the human-centered perspective, which would make him want to take justice into his own hands. "Not neglecting what is distant" points to the Cosmic Justice that will take care of the unjust behavior of the other person in the form of the fate he has created. The gentle way to handle the situation is to say the inner No to the unjust behavior, and then turn the matter over to the Cosmos.

"Not regarding one's companions" can also mean that a person has allowed his sense of seeing to dominate so that the other senses (its "companions"), in particular his inner senses, cannot give balance to his perception of the truth of the situation.

Another meaning is that a person needs to withdraw from looking at what someone else who disturbs him is doing. In this way he will be able to regain his center, thereby "manage to walk in the middle."

The "companion" can also refer to a person or thing (an authority, money, or success) that a person regards as standing in his way to success, or holding the key to his life. When he gives the authority to those things, then indeed they become the determining factors. But when he recognizes that success depends on Cosmic help, he puts his future in the correct hands.

Line 3. *No plain not followed by a slope. No going not followed by a return. Do not complain about this truth; enjoy the good fortune you still possess. He who is firm and correct in this danger is without blame.*

The Confucian interpretation of this line presents a depressed view of life. "No plain not followed by a slope" and "no going not followed by a return" refer to the belief that life is a series of ups and downs. This belief is the source of various pessimistic expressions such as, "everything on earth is subject to change" (meaning subject to loss); "prosperity is followed by decline: this is the eternal law on earth"; and "evil can indeed be held in check, but not permanently abolished; it always returns," as Wilhelm states in his commentary to this line.

The deeper layer of the *I Ching*, however, contradicts these ideas in Hexagram 32, *Duration*, where it is shown that *everything in harmony with the Cosmos endures.* What people observe as changes, as in watching the passage of the seasons, is really the ongoing transformations that bring things from the realm of non-form into the realm of form, and from form into non-form.

The person to whom this line applies, who regards the "ups and downs" as the natural course of life, is really observing the actions of Fate. Fate, the "down" part of the swing, is meant to make him examine his mistaken beliefs about the way the Cosmos functions. His mistaken views have affected his will to live (the danger mentioned). (*See* p. 40, Fate.)

This line counsels the person to be "firm and correct" in this dangerous situation by saying the inner No to the above mistaken beliefs that see life as ruled by changes and adversities.

Line 4. *He flutters down, not boasting of his wealth, together with his neighbor, guileless and sincere.*

"He flutters down...guileless and sincere..." refers to the Helper of Creativity that has given a person (his neighbor) the gift of a "mind-flash." This has happened because the person has been in harmony with his own essence.

"Not boasting of his wealth" states that the Helper makes no "to-do" about the greatness of the insight and its blessing, so as not to make the receiver feel belittled.

The mind-flash is an insight that guides a person to more and more realizations as long as he remains tuned-in to the creative process. These realizations come as a moving stream that fills and completes his perspective.

The insight also comes in the form of giving the correct names for things, names that accord with their essence. The essence of a thing always has to do with its *function* in the Cosmic Whole, based on its unique abilities.

Traditionally, this line has been associated with humans' supposed ordering function in the universe to name and classify things. However, the Sage makes us aware that when humans give things names that deprive them of their dignity, they put spells on them which keep them from evolving. A name, to be correct, must correspond with the essential dignity of that thing.

This line can also refer to a person who may be boasting of having had an insight; however, the insight contains no inner truth, and is only a product of his fantasy.

Line 5. *The sovereign I gives his daughter in marriage. This brings blessing and supreme good fortune.*

In its Cosmic meaning, the sovereign refers to the Cosmic Consciousness as a whole. The daughter can be taken as a metaphor for all its individual aspects that operate together like a shoal of fishes, with each influencing the other and being influenced simultaneously. The "marriage" refers to the constant interaction of these parts in the realm of feeling, which is felt as harmony, and produces blessings and supreme good fortune. (*See* the image of the "shoal of fishes" in Hexagram 23, *Splitting Apart,* Line 5.)

In its other meaning, the metaphor refers to the Chinese custom for the daughter to obey the authority of her father without resistance. (It was the custom in China for the sovereign's daughter to be given to a lesser feudal lord to create a bond of loyalty between the royal house and the feudal lord.)

This illustrates the collective ego's idea of creating peace by imposing a moral order that suppresses a person's true nature. It lures the person into conforming to its rules in exchange for rewards in this life or for promised blessings in the hereafter.

A person may receive this line when he is tempted to accept the collective ego's promises of rewards if he embraces its beliefs. He may be under the influence of a spell or poison arrow consisting of that kind of promise. (*See* p. 697, Freeing Yourself from Spells and Poison Arrows.)

Line 6. *The wall falls back into the moat. Use no army now. Make your commands known within your own town. Perseverance brings humiliation.*

The situation presented here is that of a fortified town in which the walls have been battered down by Fate. The town is a metaphor for a culture in which humans view themselves as the controllers and regulators of Nature. The wall falling back into the moat is the effect of the fate created by this idea.

"Use no army now" is counsel for this controlling person, whose protective walls of defense have been destroyed by Fate, to cease defending himself, as, for example, by blaming his fate on life. His fate, he needs to understand, is the result of his defensive attitude. If he will rid himself of it, he will free Helpers to end his fate and bring him into harmony with the Cosmos.

12. *Being Halted*

Ch'ien
K'un

The Judgment: *Evil people do not further a person's perseverance. The great departs; the small approaches.*

In the words "the great departs," the Sage describes the retreat of the Helper a person needs to make progress in life. This Helper is the Sage which speaks through the *I Ching*, and which retreats whenever a person no longer recognizes his need for the help that comes from the invisible world.

The term "evil people" refers to mistaken beliefs rather than to actual people. In this hexagram it refers specifically to those mistaken beliefs that identify the Helpers as humans, angels, or other mythical figures that humans have imagined. While the Helpers of the invisible world can indeed operate through humans without their being aware of it, the help nevertheless comes from the Helpers, which are invisible aspects of the Cosmic Consciousness. They come to help people during those moments in which they are humble. The Helpers include the Sage and the many anonymous Helpers mentioned in Hexagram 19, *Approaching Jointly*, Line 5, as being "experts in their fields." They include Helpers for relationships, Helpers for money needs, Helpers to find jobs, Helpers to find lost things, Helpers for health (such as the Cosmic Doctor), Helpers that lead one to insight, Helpers that help one find seed phrases, and many others that are all equally important. There are even Helpers that are generated by the specific needs of the moment. It is important to realize that they are not human, and do not have humanlike personalities. (*See* p. 682, Activating the Helpers.)

"Being halted" in one's progress is meant to draw one's attention to the mistaken belief that "there is no one to help but oneself." This view excludes the Helpers, thereby blocking their ability to help. Such a person needs to ask the Helper of Transformation to free him from this belief, and any of the other mistaken beliefs mentioned below that he may hold. The Helper of Transformation will enable him to widen his perspective by liberating him from the grip of his narrow views. (*See* p. 689, Freeing Yourself from Mistaken Ideas and Beliefs.)

This hexagram concerns the many states of mind that cause the Helper of Transformation to retreat. Among them are: the melancholic state that locks a person into the view that everything meaningful has already occurred in his life; a hopelessness that sees no prospect for a resolution of the problems in his life; a helplessness that envisions him as abandoned and all alone in life, forever. Other misdirected states of mind are created by mistaken ideas, such as: that a person's nature is defective; that everything is born into a hostile world; and that life is suffering. Such states of mind are also created by diffused feelings of guilt, as for being alive, for taking space with respect to wildlife, for what humans have done to Nature, for being alive after "someone better" has died, and guilt due to the belief that a person owes his life to those (his parents) who brought him into the world.* All these states of mind take on demonic forms in the psyche, which are empowered by the individual seed phrases that make up the mistaken beliefs. All these beliefs are based on misidentifications of the way the Cosmos functions, of the human place in it, and mistaken views of the range and importance of his responsibilities.

"Being halted" also refers to the effect of a correctly said inner No. The No, in this instance, needs to be said by a person to put an end to the above-mentioned mistaken beliefs he holds; or it needs to be said to others that hold them. It may also need to be said to egotistical acts. The inner No is also employed to stop an unwanted event, such as an unwanted visit, or to stop a person from encroaching into one's space. When a person, through fear, fails to say the inner No to someone's encroachment into his inner space, his fear causes the other person to do just that. (The same applies if a person feels, from a false sense of obligation, that he "ought" to allow the intruder in.) However, if his inner No is absolute and unwavering, the potential intruder will feel his inner firmness and withdraw. It is important that the person combine saying the inner No with asking the Cosmos for help; he then needs to truly turn the matter over to the Cosmos. After the person has experienced being protected by the Helpers, it is important to thank them, and not credit himself for the good effects. He also must not allow the ego to use the experience as an excuse to gloat, or become overconfident, as happens when he presumes he now possesses the knowledge of "how to control things." All such ideas cause the retreat of the Helpers, and create a fate.

Receiving this hexagram can also call a person's attention to a

---

* In regard to this latter belief, the Sage informs us that a person owes his life to no one. The idea of owing one's life or loyalty to anyone, including the Cosmos itself, is held to be incorrect throughout the *I Ching*. It is again one of those ideas of the collective ego created to give it control over the individual. See also the main text of Hexagram 1.

fate he is experiencing due to seeing himself as belonging to a certain class of people, and possessing rights on that account. The division of people into classes is the creation of the collective ego, which sorts people out into those that deserve only to have their "bare needs" met, and those who deserve "the best" they can get out of life. A person thus begins to assign himself to the class in which he grew up. This view has caused the fate he is experiencing, either by holding him in poverty, or by having caused him to strive endlessly for wealth and position. The fate can be ended if he will rid himself of his self-image as belonging to a class. Once freed from his fate, he can ask the Cosmic Banker to give him what he truly needs, which the Cosmic Banker alone knows. (*See* p. 691, Freeing Yourself from Self-Images.)

From the Cosmic view, everyone and everything has equal worth. When people recognize their equality and say the inner No to the collective ego's determining their worth, their true needs will be met, neither in a miserly nor exaggerated form.

Among the many spells connected with this hexagram are those that create feelings of helplessness and hopelessness. Seed phrases connected with these spells are: "life is suffering," "life is hell," "life is work," "life is a challenge," "life is to be endured," "life is not meant to be a rose garden," "life has no purpose," "the purpose of life is to serve your betters," "life is a cruel joke God played on man," etc.

Note: Since all lines contain infinite possibilities of interpretation, one needs to use the *rtcm* to determine if the meanings suggested here apply to the given situation. (*See* p. 736, for use of the *rtcm*.)

Line 1. *When ribbon grass is pulled up, the sod comes with it. Each according to his kind. Perseverance brings good fortune and success.*

Here, ribbon grass, as a metaphor for false seed phrases, is pulled up by the Helpers when a person says the inner No to those phrases.

"Each according to its kind" refers to the Helper that is needed to identify the particular seed phrase that has blocked its ability to function. This Helper is invoked when the person asks the

Cosmos for help in identifying the phrases. A typical blocking phrase is: "there is nobody to help you but yourself."

"Perseverance" counsels the person to persevere in his efforts, for in uncovering and ridding himself of mistaken ideas and beliefs that slander the nature of the Cosmos, he frees it up to give its blessings through the Helpers mentioned above (the "good fortune" mentioned).

This line defines the Cosmic meaning of success: it comes to a person who has returned to his commonsense, which helps him stay in harmony with the Cosmic Whole. (*See* Glossary: Commonsense.)

Line 2. *They bear and endure. Being halted helps a person attain success.*

"They" refers to all aspects of a person's being (including his body cells) that are suffering because the collective ego has pressed beliefs on him that are contrary to his nature. Being halted by suffering has the purpose of making the person question, "what does my sickness/situation want to tell me?" The person who regards his problem as a message telling him that he needs to find and rid himself of a mistaken belief, will be helped right away to find it. This is the success referred to in this line.

Conventional beliefs say that suffering is God's punishment, or the consequence of original sin, and therefore needs to be endured; receiving this line counsels that the suffering is not meant to be passively endured and accepted. Instead, the person needs to say the inner No to such ideas since they only project more suffering into reality. Doing so will release him from the projected suffering.

In its Cosmic meaning, the phrase "bear and endure" can counsel a person to be patient and tolerant with those who are uneducated in the Cosmic Way, since his impatience only halts their progress.

"Bear and endure" can also be counsel for a person to bear with the ego and its anger, desire, or other ego-driven emotion that has become active in the given situation. Bearing with and enduring its pressures without acting on them brings the ego to a halt and gives the person the necessary separation from it while its power diminishes. The ego cannot withstand a determined resistance for more than three minutes. During this time, it may attack in three waves, each of which is half the strength of the preceding one. After its pressure has entirely subsided, the person needs to remain on guard against any renewed attempts on its part to return, either through self-pity, flattery, or self-righteousness.

Line 3. *They bear shame.*

"They bear shame" refers to aspects of the true self that feel ashamed after someone has said the inner No to the ego in him. This marks the point at which the person has begun to doubt the correctness of his actions.

Shame is also experienced when a person's will is turned toward competition, when he throws away his kindness or loyalty on the ego in another, or when his patience and endurance are exercised toward someone who is encroaching into his private space. All misuse of a person's Cosmic Virtues betrays his true self, creating shame. The function of shame is to turn the person back to his true self. However, when the ego seizes shame, it keeps the person from looking for the cause, by initiating denial. (See p. 50, Guilt, Blame, and Shame.)

Line 4. *He who acts at the command of the highest remains without blame. Those of like mind partake of the blessing.*

Acting at the "command of the highest" is a misleading phrase because it suggests a hierarchical order of the Cosmos with something at the top (as, for example, "heaven") that issues commands. This is a feudal overlay to the true *I Ching* text. A person may be holding this mistaken view of the Cosmos. He may also be thinking that he can be absolved from blame if he submits himself to what he views as the will of a "higher power."

These ideas of a hierarchical order of the Cosmos and a higher power are the product of the feudal mindset into which we were born. The Sage, however, has made us aware that there is nothing "higher" or "lower" in the Cosmic Order, and that all its parts are *equal*; further, the Cosmos does not operate through power. It operates, rather, as an integrated system of *harmonics.*

In seeing some things as higher (and good) and others as lower (and bad, or inferior) the person "is not of like mind" with the Cosmic Consciousness, and therefore cannot "partake of the Cosmic blessings." He can reunite with the Cosmos if he rids himself of his mistaken view.

To conform with its Cosmic meaning this line should read, "He who acts according to the Cosmic Will remains without blame and partakes in the Cosmic blessings."

Line 5. *Being halted is giving way. Good fortune. "What if it should fail. What if it should fail." He ties his trust to a cluster of mulberry shoots.*

This line is received after a person has asked for help to inform him that progress is being made on the inner plane. It also informs him that he must not allow doubts to interfere with the Helpers' tasks because they would shoo away the Helper of Transformation. He needs to ask, "please Helpers free me of my doubts." The Helpers that free one from doubts are the "cluster of mulberry shoots" mentioned to which the person ties his trust.

"What if it should fail" can also be counsel not to become overconfident after having come out of a difficult period. This is achieved by saying the inner No to his overconfidence.

Line 6. *Being halted comes to an end. Good fortune.*

Because a person has said the inner No to a mistaken idea mentioned in the foregoing lines or in the general text, his "being halted" is ended even though this may not yet be apparent.

The traditional interpretation of this line is that in order to be released from a blocked situation ("standstill") a person must make an external effort to end it. The Sage informs us, however, that blockages are created by mistaken ideas and will continue indefinitely until the person says the inner No to them. Doing so, furthermore, pulls them up by the roots (*see* Line 1), therefore, the correction is permanent.

13. *Associating with People*

The Judgment: *Associating with people in the open. Success. It furthers to cross the great water and to be firm and correct.*

In this hexagram, the Sage addresses the Cosmic Principle of Relating, which principle is observable in a person's relationship with the Sage, and which relationship is defined in Hexagram 4, *Youthful Folly.*

The Cosmic Principle of Relating is defined by one single limitation: "no relationship with the ego." Through firmly refusing to relate to the ego in others, a person follows what is correct, and the "great water," which is a metaphor for the gulf standing between the way of the collective ego and the Cosmic Way, is crossed.

"Associating with people in the open" means that one's openness is restricted to another's true self only. We relate openly to others when the ego in them is absent, and withdraw into caution and hesitation when the egos become active. Reserve and caution prevent the predatory and parasitic appetite of the ego from gaining the sustenance (a person's chi energy) it seeks to stay alive. Observing this restriction also aids, nourishes, and strengthens others' true selves. This is the way the Sage retreats the instant the ego in us is present, and returns the moment we have reached a true humility. When a person observes this limitation in relating to another, he is in harmony with the Cosmos. He also creates duration in his relationships by ensuring that they are based on the attraction that always exists between people's true selves.

The retreat of the Sage in the presence of the ego is also a model for our retreat from others. The Sage, in retreating, calls out to our true self to rally itself to stand up to the ego, to affirm its leadership of the personality. Thus the Sage does not "give up" on us. When the ego in another is dominating, we say the inner No to it, and call on their true selves. This activates the Sage in their presence (which has been shut out) to displace the ego's dominance.

Just as we experience hindrances in our relationship with the Sage when we put the Sage up as "special," or higher, or on the other hand see ourselves as the judge of the Sage, we erect similar hindrances when we relate to others in these ways.

The Sage also points out the problems connected with the ideals of fellowship and brotherhood traditionally associated with this hexagram. These ideals are the basis of the attempt to create a humanistic society where "men are brothers," as a remedy to the evils caused by factionalism as, for example, during the historical era of the "warring states" in China. Such ideals of a universal order designed to create a "lasting unity among men" are bound to fail because they are man-centered, and thus fail to take into account the Cosmic Order on which all unity is based. They also rule out the Helpers which are necessary to make unity possible.

Note: Since all lines contain infinite possibilities of interpretation, one needs to use the *rtcm* to determine if the meanings suggested here apply to the given situation. (*See* p. 736, Using the *rtcm*.)

Line 1. *Associating with people at the gate. No blame.*

The gate is a metaphor for the place where humans and the Sage meet. This line speaks to the person who comes to the Sage with his conventional views, ideas, and beliefs. The Sage does not hold this against him, as long as he is prepared to open the gate (his mind).

"Associating with people at the gate" is also counsel to a person that for there to be a fruitful relationship between him and another, he needs to recognize the Sage's role in this relationship, as well as the essential equality that must exist between himself and the other. For all relationships to have meaning, the Sage must be included as an essential element. It is included when at least one person in the relationship recognizes that their relationship is part of a bigger unity, and that it depends on the Sage's presence and help.

In regard to a love relationship, at least one of the partners needs to recognize that the gift of love comes from the Cosmos, flows through the lovers, and back again to the Cosmos. This gift can remain theirs only so long as they recognize its source and its gift-nature. If they forget this, and begin to claim it as something that exists only between themselves, they have allowed the egos in themselves to possess the relationship. If this situation is not corrected, the egos will go on to destroy the relationship. The very presence of the ego, with its demands and claims, shuts out the Cosmic flow of chi energy. The inner No needs to be said by at least one of the partners to every ego-aspect that inserts itself into the relationship.

This line also addresses situations in which a person is either looking up to another or down on him. In either case, a mistaken idea is active in his psyche. It may be that he has been trained during his youth either to look at himself as better than others or as inferior to them. In the former case, he needs to say the inner No to all the phrases in his inner program that put himself up and the others down. In the latter, he needs to say the inner No to the persons who look down on him, and to any rationales in himself that have caused him to accept or excuse their superior attitude.

"No blame" can mean that a person incorrectly believes himself to be free of blame because he has been looking down on someone who has "obvious inferior qualities." He may be unaware that he is one of those who have fixed that person in those qualities and thereby put a spell on him, and created a fate for himself. To free himself from blame and his fate, he needs to free the other from the spell he has put on him, and rid himself as well of his self-image that he is "blameless." (*See* p. 697, Freeing Yourself from Spells, and p. 691, Freeing Yourself from Self-Images.)

"No blame" can also refer to the person who is incorrectly thinking something is wrong with himself because he does not look up to someone society has said he ought to look up to. To determine which meaning of "no blame" is to be applied, the person needs to use the *rtcm*.

Line 2. *Associating with people in the clan. Humiliation.*

The word "clan" refers to an association of people that has failed to include the Sage. When a person fails to recognize that the Sage is in every person's presence, the essential vehicle that makes a meaningful relationship is excluded.

In another meaning, the line can point to a person's desire to form a clan-relationship with the Sage, meaning, he comes in the hope of finding support for his egotistical goals. The line can also apply to a person who does not want to leave behind the entitlements and authorizations given to him by the collective ego, that make him see himself as special. What he seeks, in consulting the *I Ching*, is to gain the Sage's approval of these entitlements. The Sage, however, can only withdraw and leave him to the advice of the ego he is allowing in himself.

The line can also refer to a person who, in approaching another to be his partner (in love, business, etc.), comes to meet him unequally because he is attached to his possessions, entitlements, and authorizations. A successful relationship can only happen when neither one thinks he is better or more entitled. The mere idea of authorizations and entitlements is in conflict with the natural equality that exists, not only between two people, but between all things in the Cosmos.

The word "clan" can also refer to a person who is holding to mistaken ideas, or to the ego, or to a person who is criticizing another while failing to correct himself. The line can also point to a person who ignores his obligation to say the inner No to what is incorrect in another, because that person belongs to his "clan," i.e., family or other interest group. All such favoritism is in conflict with Cosmic Law.

The "clan" also refers to any group which has assigned someone in it to serve as its "enlightened leader," and to whom they have given the power or authority to judge and forgive, and to have the right to encroach into the group members' intrinsic spaces. It can also refer to anyone to whom a group gives its consent to act magnificently, or to represent God, or to stand between an individual and his inner truth. Whenever a person encounters such a situation, he needs to say the inner No to it.

Line 3. *He hides weapons in the thicket; he climbs the high hill in front of it. For three years he does not rise up.*

This line addresses the reasons for a person's inability to have a true relationship with other people. He always suspects that they have hidden motives. A phrase expressing this belief is, "nobody does anything for unselfish reasons." This belief puts a spell on the others, giving rise to mutual suspicion.

The line can also apply to a person who approaches the *I Ching* with the suspicion that it contains a hidden catch. This attitude comes from the widespread belief that an oracle speaks in obscure terms (the "thicket") and therefore cannot be trusted. This impression is true so long as a person comes to the oracle with egotistical motives. This fact has caused him to misunderstand the Sage's message, and has trapped him in the fate he is experiencing. He needs to recognize the presence of the ego with its suspicion, and say the inner No to it. Then the Sage can speak to him clearly. "He climbs the high hill," describes the ego's superior attitude in judging that "the oracle does not work," because it has not satisfied his hidden expectations and demands.

"For three years he does not rise up" refers to different kinds of reactions a person has to the fate he is experiencing: he may believe that if he "humbly" accepts the fate "the powers that be" will release him from it, or he may mistake his fate as a "duty" he must perform.

He needs to understand what Fate is, how it is created, the purpose it has, and that it can be extinguished with the help of the Helpers if he recognizes and rids himself of its cause. (See p, 694, Freeing Yourself from a Fate.)

Line 4. *He climbs up on his wall; he cannot attack. Good fortune.*

"He climbs up on his wall" refers to the person who assumes he knows what is right and wrong, therefore does not seek the Sage's help; as a consequence, he cannot gain a correct approach to his problems (the meaning of "he cannot attack"). The wall represents the attitude of superiority and self-righteousness that he has gained from studying the wisdom of the world. However, this wall, at the same time, has also become his prison in the form of a spell that prevents him from seeking the help he needs. The seed phrases of the spell are: "I believe in the source of my wisdom," "I don't need anything else," and "I have the right belief." Such a person believes that it is his "spiritual duty" to find the answer in the belief system he has adopted. He needs to recognize that this belief system keeps him trapped and prevents him from learning from the Sage. One way such a person can be reached is through an inner connection by giving him an inner message that he is creating a fate for himself, and by asking the Helpers to do what is necessary to take away that wall. This is the good fortune indicated. (*See* p. 697, Freeing Yourself from Spells.)

"He climbs up on his wall" can also refer to the person who thinks he has the ability to integrate Cosmic Logic with rational logic. He does not realize that these two kinds of logic are incompatible, because Cosmic Logic is based on the principles of harmony and equality, while rational logic is based on the principle of opposites that implies both a hierarchical and a linear ordering of things. While Cosmic Logic includes what is known by *all* the senses and pertains to the visible *and* invisible worlds, rational logic is based only on what can be seen and heard—thus only takes into account the visible world.

The line can also point to a person who is trying to integrate what he learns from the Sage with his existing belief system. This is the same as trying to integrate the Cosmic Whole with the collective ego, or the same as trying to integrate the Cosmic Consciousness with the demonic sphere of consciousness.

Line 5. *People bound through inner ties first weep and lament, but afterward they laugh. After great struggles they succeed in meeting.*

This line depicts two people who are bound through an inner Cosmic tie, but are unable to meet each other. This happens because their beliefs, doubts, and fears create blocks that prevent the Cosmic love from flowing to and through them back to the Cosmos.

These beliefs, doubts, and fears are based on their misunderstandings of where the love comes from, and the conditions under which it can flow. They may believe, for example, that the love comes from the other person. Love is a Cosmic gift that comes *through* people to each other; they can only be a vehicle for it, and cannot by themselves make it happen. They may *simulate* what they think love feels like, but such simulation only comes from the egos in them. They may also be struggling under the belief that their love is not flowing because they are not working hard enough at "making love stay." They may believe that they need to talk more to each other, go on vacations with each other, or be more in each other's presence. These beliefs are based on the idea taught by the collective ego, that love is something one can make happen, if one strives hard enough, which belief, in turn, is based on the mistaken idea that humans are at the center of the universe (or 'the measure of all things'). Such efforts lead only to the "great struggles" mentioned in the line, and create the fate of being blocked.

The fate is due to the fact that all these beliefs shut out the Cosmos, which is the source of the love. When the partners recognize that the fate wants to make them aware of their mistaken beliefs about the source and nature of love, they can correct themselves and reunite with the Cosmos, thus ending their fate.

Fate, if not ended through a person's self-correction, can also end through the burnout of the belief a person holds that he should keep striving to make unity happen. The fate is ended when he is willing to turn the entire matter of his separation from the other over to the Cosmos, with a complete readiness to accept whatever the result will be. At the same time, he becomes firmly resolved to go on with his life. This attitude engages the Helpers. His modest attitude will free the Cosmos to do whatever is necessary to bring about his happiness, with or without the other person.

This line addresses various spells that a person may have put on the Sage, as, for example, by the phrase "I have to make the relationship happen." Spells are put on the partners by such phrases as: "we'll never come together," "it's too hard," "there's no way to make this work," or "struggle is part of the natural course of things." Yet other spells have to do with hurt pride and blaming (oneself, the Sage, Fate, the partner, circumstances, etc.); other spells are caused by the belief that one is obligated to be loyal to a previous relationship. When these spells are dispelled, the gift of love from the Cosmos can be received. (*See* p. 697, Freeing Yourself from Spells, and p. 689, Mistaken Ideas and Beliefs.)

Line 6. *Associating with people in the meadow brings remorse.*

The meadow, as a cultivated piece of land, represents the collective ego's ideal of the "cultivated relationship." In such a relationship each person is assigned what the collective ego calls the person's "natural role": the man is to fit himself into the role of being in charge of the partnership; the woman is to fit herself into the role of being guided by the man, etc. The roles are fixed, and the person is expected to sacrifice all those feelings he has that do not fit into the role, and to even feel guilty for having them. The promise is made that in exchange for his sacrifice, the person will attain "enduring happiness," whereas, in reality, it only brings remorse. The model includes periods of male deviation that the woman is to accept as "natural." It hardly needs to be added that none of this is natural.

Receiving this line can indicate that a person thinks that an incorrect behavior is natural simply because people have said so, while in reality, the label "natural" is being used merely to get the person to accept the incorrect behavior.

The societal roles referred to above have been given expression in all the world's literature, but most clearly in Pirandello's play "Six Characters in Search of an Author." The Sage informs us that to fit oneself into a role is to put a spell on oneself in the form of a self-image. It prohibits the development of the person's true self, and ends in killing off the true love relationship. (*See* p. 697, Freeing Yourself from Spells and p. 691, Freeing Yourself from Self-Images.)

This line, which addresses the "cultivated relationship" and its prescribed roles, makes us aware of how the collective ego attempts to control the love relationship. In this attempt it goes so far as to compete with the Cosmos as the source of love. Since the collective ego is unable to give love, it gives as a substitute its recognition and approval to those who obediently follow its rules and fulfill its roles. Of course, this substitution yields no real fulfillment, and only causes the person, in the end, to look back over his life as a disappointment.

14. *Possession in Great Measure*

Li
Ch'ien

The Judgment: *Supreme success.*

In this hexagram the Sage informs us of the Cosmic Possessions a person comes with at birth and those which are given to him throughout his life by the Cosmos. These Cosmic Possessions are all that he needs to live his life happily, and realize his uniqueness.

The Cosmic Possessions he is born with include what is called in this book his "treasure chest of inner truth," his inner and outer senses, and a group of other senses called here the "metaphorical senses." Also part of his possessions are his Cosmic Virtues, his supporting Helpers called talents, and his automatic access to all the helping energies and aspects of the Cosmos when he is in harmony with his true nature.

Among the possessions he accumulates throughout his life are his experiences of the gift-giving and helping nature of the Cosmos, and those Helpers that fulfill his particular needs. Other Cosmic gifts are given to him in the form of jobs, a place to live, a love relationship, and friends that best suit him. "Possession in great measure" also describes the endless generosity of the Cosmos to the person who is in harmony with it.

A person's physical (inner and outer) senses, give him a true perception of both the visible and the invisible worlds. They are the basis of his commonsense, which provides him with the correct mental and physical responses to potentially harmful situations. It is his commonsense that enables him to intuit incorrect motives in others, and danger coming from unknown sources. (See Glossary: The Senses.)

The collective ego, by contrast, defines possessions within the context of the idea that humans are at the center of the universe. It presumes that humans are meant to possess the earth and everything on it. This is the cause of humans' aggressive and arrogant attitude toward Nature, including their own bodies, and is the main cause of human separation from the Cosmic Unity. (*See* Hexagram 2, *Nature.*)

The collective ego, while promoting the idea of human superiority, trains the individual to believe that he is born lacking the qualities and help he needs for life. It then steals his energies by promising that if he fits into all the roles *it* assigns him, he will attain its support and help, and if he does it with valor and self-sacrifice, he will even gain honors, privileges and entitlements. By this lie, and a variety of other sleight-of-hand tricks, the collective ego puts itself in the place of the Cosmic Consciousness, as the source of people's needs.

The person who has accepted the belief that he is born lacking and needy, has put spells on his true nature that limit his Cosmic Possessions. Furthermore, his disbelief in the invisible world blocks him from receiving the flow of Cosmic blessings. As invariably happens, the promises of the collective ego prove empty of the true help and nourishment that only the Cosmos can give. When the person then looks for the causes of his impoverishment, he is told by the collective ego that his condition is due to the unkindness and indifference of the Cosmos.

It is often said that Nature is economical and wastes nothing. While this is true, some people have incorrectly taken it to imply that Nature acts in a miserly way. They do not realize that such thoughts put spells upon their relationship with Nature that block them from receiving its abundance. What a person receives from Nature/the Cosmos depends entirely on his attitude toward them.

As is shown above, the mental program installed in the young person's psyche by the collective ego leaves no part of his relationship with Nature/the Cosmos untouched. The collective ego's intention is to appropriate as many of a person's Cosmic Possessions as possible to its purposes.

The belief in the "ups and downs of life" promoted by the collective ego is responsible for the fear that even though a person may possess more than enough of everything, he will never have enough to protect himself from the unforeseen, and so must always strive for more. Such a person actually believes that chance or probability rules life, and thus holds the Cosmos in distrust. His view creates the Fate that what he does receive from the Cosmos is taken away. When a person has a trusting relationship with the Cosmos, he receives Cosmic gifts in abundance as he needs them.

The collective ego would make us believe that everything in Nature exists to be possessed by humans and serve their purposes. Since this belief is not in harmony with the Cosmos, it blocks a person from receiving Nature's gifts. He then concludes that he must forcefully take what he needs from nature, and bend it to his purposes. In Cosmic terms this is stealing from Nature rather than allowing it to give its gifts. Such stealing creates Fates.

Inasmuch as this hexagram speaks of the gift-giving nature of the Cosmos, it tells us that the nature of the Cosmic Consciousness is love. Its love pours to us in the many forms already mentioned. But this love can also come as a Cosmic intervention in our lives when we are in great trouble, or as help given to the imprisoned true self to free it from the tyranny of the ego. The terms "conditional love" and "unconditional love" do not apply to Cosmic love, which pours out constantly and without measure. It is humans alone who, by holding to mistaken ideas and beliefs, limit their abilities to receive it.

A person who has given himself over to the ego cannot receive Cosmic love, because it means that he is wholeheartedly devoted to the values of the collective ego. However, even the most arrogant person can receive it during those moments when through shock he is drawn back into self-examination. His connection with the Cosmos, however, will last only so long as his heart remains open.

This hexagram is often received to inform a person why his Cosmic gifts "come and go." More than likely this is due to his belief that "change is the rule of life," which has projected itself into reality. He may also be falsely attributing his gifts to the wrong source, such as to his cleverness; or he may be using them for his egotistical purposes. Or, his Cosmic gifts have dried up because he "thinks poor" or thinks luxuriously, as in: "you can never have enough," "if an experience is to be worthwhile, it must be difficult or costly," "nothing comes from nothing," "I don't deserve it" or "I deserve it," "I have the right to do whatever I want with what I possess," "a person must have something to be somebody," "success is what counts, never mind the means," "possessions are power, and power is everything," "being spiritual means getting free of worldly possessions," "giving is more noble than receiving," and "having money and possessions is evil." (*See* p. 697, Freeing Yourself from Spells.)

Two of the unique Cosmic gifts given to humans are the ability of speech and the ability to form images. The ability of speech belongs to the word mind, and the ability to form images belongs to the intuitive mind. Their function is to form images and words that express a person's inner truth, which is always in harmony with the Cosmos. The collective ego, however, has appropriated these two gifts, by flattering the word mind and the image mind that they are what makes humans special and superior to all other forms of existence. Once captured by the ego, the intuitive mind develops fantasies about the greatness of the human species, while the word mind provides rationales to support those fantasies. Both minds, caught up in the ego's purposes, forget their original functions.

When the two frontal lobes of the brain are thus exalted, other parts and functions of the brain and body are slandered as inferior. For example, the Feeling Manager, a Helper whose function is to coordinate the psyche and body, and which is located in the brain stem, is partially disabled when it is regarded as insignificant. It is through the many capabilities of the Feeling Manager that a person's health is maintained. It is particularly destructive to a person's health when the thinking mind puts itself in charge of the body.

The spells that have been put on these two minds through flattery need to be broken. They consist of phrases and images having to do with human superiority, and with ideas that pronounce the human species as special. Examples are the Chinese idea that "man is the representative of heaven on earth," and its Western equivalent, that "man is the crown of creation whose job is to rule the earth," and their scientific equivalent, that "humans are at the top of the evolutionary ladder." Holding these ideas creates Fates. (*See* p. 697, Freeing Yourself from Spells.)

The Judgment words, "supreme success" refer to the success a person has in all that he does when he fully recognizes his Cosmic Possessions and does not allow the ego to steal them.

Note: Since all lines contain infinite possibilities of interpretation, one needs to use the *rtcm* to determine if the meanings suggested here apply to the given situation. (*See* p. 736, Using the *rtcm*.)

Line 1. *No relationship with what is harmful. There is no blame in this. If one remains conscious of difficulty, one remains without blame.*

"No relationship with what is harmful" is a statement that the Cosmos does not entertain a relationship with the ego. "There is no blame in this" states that the Cosmos is not to blame if a person is not receiving the gifts it holds for him; if he is not receiving gifts, it is an indication that the person needs to free himself from the ego's grip. "If one remains conscious of difficulty" means that he needs to remain aware that if the ego is present, it will attempt to appropriate or steal the Cosmic gifts to its purposes. Only if he remembers this will he have no cause for regret.

In particular, this line points to the demanding attitude of the ego, and to its pretenses to having the right to receive love, and the right to good luck and money. A person's security in all that he possesses is dependent entirely on his relationship with the Cosmic source of those gifts. When he turns them to the benefit of the ego, be it in himself or others, he creates the fate of losing them.

The Cosmic gift of chi, or life energy, cannot be received in the love relationship if a person regards his or the other's sexuality as the cause of original sin. Such a view is a poison arrow. (*See* p. 697, Freeing Yourself from Poison Arrows.)

Line 2. *A big wagon for loading. One may undertake something.*
No blame.

The possession referred to in this line is the Helper of Transformation (the big wagon for loading), and its ability to take care of problems once we turn them over to it. It is there to help us clear away the main obstructions that keep us from receiving the Cosmic gifts.

"One may undertake something" refers to activating the Helper of Transformation by asking for its help and putting ego-emotions such as grief, guilt, blame, (self-blame and blame of others), fears, doubt, and hatred "onto its wagon." This enables the person to move on with his life without having to carry the heavy burden these emotions create. Through turning them over, the Helper of Transformation is enabled to transform them into other Helpers. Doubt of its ability to do this, however, interferes with this ability.

Of all these emotions, it is most important to get rid of guilt, because guilt keeps the person caught in a vicious circle of self-blame. (*See* p. 50, Guilt, Blame, and Shame; also *see* p. 696, Freeing Yourself from Guilt.)

This line may apply to someone who is holding onto one or more of these ego-emotions, which will create a fate if he continues to do so. The ego holds onto them, in order to feed on them.

Line 3. *A prince offers it to the son of Heaven. A petty man cannot*
do this.

From the standpoint of the collective ego, the prince represents a noblehearted person who devotes his talents and Cosmic gifts to the purposes and goals of the collective ego. In doing so he is seen by others as magnanimous and princely. "The son of heaven," in this analogy, is the collective ego which has set itself up as the representative of "heaven on earth," thus also as the sole judge of what is important and valuable.

Concepts such as "being noblehearted" and "being petty" are used by the collective ego to divert a person's talents and Cosmic gifts to *its* purposes. The text suggests that a person is *either* noblehearted *or* petty. The person who takes this line as wisdom is driven, on the one hand, to adopt the self-image of being noblehearted out of fear of being seen as petty, and on the other, to succumb to the flattering associations connected with the word "noblehearted." This is a typical sleight-of-hand trick of the collective ego. By making the person think he must choose one or the other, he is lured into developing a self-image that will allow the collective ego to usurp his chi-energy and his Cosmic gifts.

Seen in Cosmic terms, the line refers to times when a person's true self (the prince) leads the personality. He has a correct attitude of responsibility toward his Cosmic gifts, and acknowledges their true source. The petty man represents the individual ego that claims the gifts to be of its making and the right to use them as it sees fit.

This line may also refer to a person's attachment to his possessions, as when he is possessive of his love partner, or is emotionally attached to his looks, health, wealth, or position. It refers also to a person's attachment to his talents and abilities, to parent's attachment to their children, or a person's attachment to anything that comes into his care. The only correct attachment a person may have is to his inner truth. All other attachments come from the ego that believes it has rights over people and things.

The condition by which we may possess anything is our continued recognition of its gift nature. This is also the condition of duration. Such an attitude toward our possessions, however, cannot be contrived. It is the result of deep realizations that accompany ridding oneself of the mistaken idea that humans have entitlements, and that they can do with their possessions what they like.

Receiving this line can also be an indication that a person has created a fate even though it has not yet manifested. The cause of his fate is due to the spell mentioned in the general text, that "humans are superior because they possess language." Ridding himself of that mistaken idea will extinguish the fate. (*See* p. 697, Freeing Yourself from Spells.)

A person can receive this line to reflect his incorrect view of himself as lowly and undeserving, or as not competent to approach the Helpers directly. As a result, he holds back and therefore is deprived of obtaining the help he needs. He must say the inner No to all the phrases and images by which he has come to accept this incorrect view of himself.

Line 4. *He makes a difference between himself and his neighbor. No blame.*

This line states that a person needs to see his uniqueness as a possession. It is vital that he not compare himself with anyone else, as with other members of his family, clan, class, race, etc.

Everything in the Cosmos is a unique expression of the Cosmic Consciousness. The purpose of everything is to relate back to the whole its unique perceptions, feelings, and experiences. In doing this, each thing contributes to the evolution of the whole. When, however, a person comes under the influence of the collective ego, his uniqueness is suppressed and sacrificed to make him conform to its values. When a person's uniqueness is appropriated in this way, it is an act of robbery that decreases the Cosmic Whole. This line may be a statement to a person that he needs to find his true self, free it from the ego's domination, and develop his uniqueness, which only his true self possesses. Possibly he sees himself as important, either for social, financial, or other reasons, or else he sees himself as unimportant. Either view distracts him from the real issue of recognizing his uniqueness.

This line can also make a person aware that he needs to say the inner No to comparing his new love relationship with a previous one, referred to in the line as the "neighbor." These comparisons arise because the inner connection to the previous partner has not been closed. It is necessary to close any old inner connections, since these are openings through which thoughts come that might damage the new relationship. (*See* p. 687, Closing an Inner Connection.) The person may also need to free himself from unresolved issues left over from the previous relationship, such as a false loyalty caused by the belief that "you can have loyalty to only one partner in your life."

Making a difference between himself and his neighbor can also be counsel to cease watching another from an inner doubt in his ability to succeed on his own. Such a person does not understand that the other may ask the Sage for guidance.

This line may also refer to a person who sees himself as superior to another due to his accumulated knowledge. Such a comparison is superficial, since in Cosmic terms, accumulated knowledge is devoid of the true understanding that includes feeling, and therefore is of no significance.

Making no comparisons avoids creating Cosmic blame.

Line 5. *He whose truth is accessible, yet dignified, has good fortune.*

"He whose truth is accessible, yet dignified" refers to a person who is unwilling to throw the gifts he has received from the Cosmos away on the ego. In this way he preserves his integrity and dignity.

This line refers to the set of conditions under which a person can share his gifts with others: when those sharing in them are sensitive to their gift-nature and do not presume they have a right to receive them, or to misuse them.

This line also refers to the person who does not allow himself to be flattered or intimidated by the collective ego into giving his gifts to its institutions or to the ego in others. Flattery and intimidation are recognizable in what the collective ego says a person "ought to do" with his gifts.

Line 6. *He is blessed by heaven. Good fortune. Nothing that does not further.*

This line can be a confirmation of the blessings given by the Cosmos to the person who, despite difficulties, has remained true to himself. It is also a statement that the Helpers are coming to further him in everything he does, and to free him from the fate he has caused.

A person can also receive this line when he has won something to which he believes he has a right. For example, he may have "won" the right to receive love from another person. This impression is created by the traditional marriage ceremony. However, love is a Cosmic gift that is not under the jurisdiction of the collective ego's institutions. Allowing the love relationship to be put into the harness of the collective ego blocks a person's access to the Cosmic gift of love.

It is the same with all Cosmic gifts, such as those that come in the form of scientific breakthroughs, inventions, artistic talents, etc. When people credit these gifts to their glory and honor, the Helpers in these gifts retreat, so that the gifts become empty.

15. Modesty

 K'un
Kên

The Judgment: *Modesty creates success. The superior man carries things through.*

Modesty, the Sage informs us, is one of the three fundamental Cosmic Virtues that all aspects of the Cosmic Whole are endowed with. The other two virtues are equality and uniqueness. Together, they give each aspect of the Cosmos its dignity. It is due to these basic virtues that a single force is able to rule the functioning of the whole: the force of mutual attraction of complementary aspects. Another name for this force is love.

When the virtue of modesty is seen in this context, it means that the modest person recognizes the equality and uniqueness of every other aspect of the Cosmic Whole. It is equivalent to seeing his true place in the whole. He has no need to put himself up or down, because any aggrandizement or abnegation of the self fails to take into account the fact that *every* aspect of the Cosmos is endowed with unique possessions. (*See* the previous hexagram.) Modesty also means that a person recognizes the uniqueness of his own possessions and the responsibilities toward the Cosmic Whole connected with them.

Modesty is the virtue connected with a person's *commonsense*. Commonsense is the consensus of all the senses a person is born with. When none of his senses is blocked, his commonsense gives him a sure *feeling* of what is true and untrue, because it is in harmony with Cosmic Truth. Commonsense is closely connected with a person's inner truth—his memory of what Cosmic Harmony feels like. Applied to a given situation, we can picture the process as follows: All the senses react to the situation in accordance with their unique functions. Most senses react to the *inner* components of the situation, which manifest as vibrations, feelings, smells, etc., whereas the senses of outer seeing and hearing react only to the situation's outer appearances. The commonsense integrates all these perceptions into a discernment of what corresponds or does not correspond with the feelings of inner truth. The imprint of what Cosmic Harmony feels like is stored in every body cell, and constitutes a person's original inner "program" that is fully adequate to run the personality. The discernment needs no reasons to prove its validity. Validating one's feelings is the meaning of "modesty creates success." To "carry things through" means to then bring into full consciousness whatever feels discordant and say the inner No to it. The saying of the inner No would occur spontaneously, were it not for the conditioning that prevents it. Therefore, in bringing the true self to maturity, learning to say the inner No needs to be recognized as a duty that is consistent with one's inner dignity and self-respect. Until the conditioning is undone, saying the inner No needs to be consciously remembered and practiced. When a person is tuned into his feelings, the inner No arises spontaneously and is heard as a firm inner voice.

Consciously saying the inner No to another's ego display engages another natural function of a person's commonsense: as the Helper of Transformation. It transforms what is disharmonious in the situation. The inner No also has the ability to transform harmful thoughts that attack a person's psyche, thereby protecting him from them.

Failure to say the inner No to the ego in another occurs because the ego in oneself has been aroused; then one falls back on the use of power, either through words or actions, to correct the other. Allowing the ego to intervene in this way causes a person to lose his modesty and his Cosmic Protection.

True modesty also means to recognize that the Sage exists in every person's presence. The Sage in another's presence can be called upon to intervene when the ego in that person is active. True modesty is remembering to ask the Sage in others' presence to intervene under such circumstances.

The use of the term "the superior man" in The Judgment comes from the Confucian school and its view that modesty—the mark of the cultivated man—is a quality that comes from working on one's self-development. However, the idea of there being such a goal as "becoming superior" contradicts the very meaning of modesty. The person who seeks to be superior has already lost contact with the natural modesty he was born with. What is also overlooked is that being called "a superior man" is a spell that forces him into upholding all the abstract values the collective ego assigns to that appellation.

By saying that virtues are not part of our nature and need to be cultivated, the collective ego appropriates a person's natural modesty. This doubt about the wholeness of his own nature is instilled in a child as the first step in his conditioning. Being a poison arrow, it demonizes his commonsense and his feeling connection with the Cosmos, preventing him from knowing (through his feelings) that he can depend on the Cosmos for everything he needs. Separated from his feelings and therefore from Cosmic help, the child is then taught to depend on the institutions of the collective ego for his needs. Since the collective ego can never replace Cosmic help, it encourages him to "be modest" in his needs and behavior. By *implication* it thus defines modesty ("the highest attainable virtue") as "a selfless acceptance of poverty and injustice." To achieve acceptance of such an idea, it encourages the person to think he will be rewarded by being recognized and accepted by others as virtuous. He may even be rewarded with medals, titles, and fame. Thus we see a paradoxical situation created: that the person who works hard to develop the self-image of modesty, must make sure that his modesty gets noticed!

At the core of all virtuous self-images cultivated by the collective ego is actually "self-denial," for the "truly virtuous" person is the one who has not merely repressed, but totally routed out every aspect of his true self. The object of this cultivation of virtue, thus, is to have no self at all! All self-images tend to be expressed in their extreme through the fact that the object of cultivating them is to "perfect" them. Since the institutions of the collective ego are those which have taught him his virtues (his parents, teachers, and the society as a whole), the person with the self-image of being modest believes he owes "all that he is" to them; he thus carries with him strong feeling of indebtedness. This indebtedness is always connected with guilt, which becomes active whenever he makes any attempt to leave the prison of their total control.

Of all the hexagrams, this one shows that the ancient Chinese were aware of a connection between true modesty and "good fortune." They noticed that the person who was not arrogant was helped along by what they called "heaven." What they were observing was the Cosmic help and protection that are enjoyed by every person who lives by his *natural* modesty. But it seems to have occurred to only a few, such as Lao Tzu, that modesty is a virtue every person possesses as part of his natural makeup. True modesty is the absence of any self-image.

"Carrying things through to completion" also means stepping out of the collective ego's system of opposites, in particular the hero and anti-hero/rebel models. By setting up the ideal of the self-sacrificing hero, a person is led to sacrifice his true self to the collective ego's values; or, if he discovers that he cannot mold himself into the image of the hero, he may turn to admire the anti-hero/rebel who renounces the system. What he does not see is that the anti-hero is as essential to the dichotomous system of the collective ego as the dragon is to the dragon-slayer, for it is in the nature of the collective ego to embrace the opposing elements that are essential to its system. A person can step out of this system only by recognizing that all self-images, regardless of whether they are of the hero/rebel, good citizen/outlaw, self-righteous person/the irreverent person, have their origin in the idea that a person must "become" something, because "in and of himself he is not enough," or he was "born with original guilt/sin/fault." What we do not notice is that in all striving to become something we are actually striving to *overcome* something false which has been put upon us. These phrases are the original poison arrows a child has received from the collective ego, which must be removed, if he is to return himself to his original wholeness. (*See* p. 697, Freeing Yourself from Poison Arrows.)

Note: Since all lines contain infinite possibilities of interpretation, one needs to use the *rtcm* to determine if the meanings suggested here apply to the given situation. (*See* p. 736, Using the *rtcm*.)

Line 1. *The modest person may cross the great water. Good fortune.*

Crossing the great water here refers to the success the modest person has in regard to whatever he seeks to do. Because he is modest without contriving to be so, all the Helpers come to ensure his success. He is modest without contriving when he recognizes his true place in the Cosmos as equal to all other aspects of it, and when he respects the dignity of all things.

A person who strives to uphold the image of "being modest" can only attain a false modesty. He may think, because he is making a great effort to be modest, that he is deserving of success, and therefore is puzzled when success does not come. Such a person needs to recognize that his self-image of "being modest" prevents him from being his true self.

This line also describes how the Helper of Commonsense goes about its business: it creates transformation without making a big to-do about it. Commonsense feels the needs of the moment and guides one to act accordingly. When not held under a spell, the response is spontaneous and perfect. When one or another of the senses has been damaged through the person's having devalued it, this spontaneity is locked up. When it is locked up, the person will follow conventional advice, and what he does creates a fate.

The sense that is most often blocked is the inner sense of smell. This happens when a person has accepted the poison arrow that his animal nature is the source of evil. Other poison arrows are put on certain senses by the idea that a person is divided into mind and body, or when a person adopts self-denial as a virtue, or when he equates "being modest" with poverty. Such virtuous self-images actually put poison arrows on him, locking out the ability of his Helpers to come to his aid. The Cosmos does not "think poor"; it gives abundantly to those who do not culti-vate self-images of any kind. (*See* p. 697, Freeing Yourself from Poison Arrows, and p. 691, Freeing Yourself from Self-Images.)

Line 2. *Modesty that comes to expression. Being firmly correct brings good fortune.*

In its Cosmic meaning, modesty comes to expression when a person listens to his commonsense. His commonsense tells him when a thing or situation is cosmically incorrect or untrue. When uninhibited by poison arrows, it shouts out the inner No! Thus, modesty means being inwardly firm and correct by consciously affirming such inner No's, and allowing transfor-mation to take place. By making this inner effort, a person's modesty acts as an invisible shield, protecting him from harm. This is the good fortune mentioned.

By contrast, the collective ego holds up modesty as a virtue suited to the masses, but this definition of modesty tells the individual that he is not qualified to question what authorities tell him. In this way the collective ego insures that it can con-tinue to parade its wrong values without opposition.

"Modesty that comes to expression" can also refer to the per-son who has adopted the self-image of the modest person. Such a person, unlike the truly modest person, needs to show off his modesty, as by wearing special clothing or other insignia of modesty, or by adopting behavior that draws attention to his modesty. (*See* p. 691, Freeing Yourself from Self-Images.)

Line 3. *The superior man of modesty and merit carries things to conclusion. Good fortune.*

In its Cosmic meaning, the superior man here refers not to a person, but to his commonsense as the Helper that "carries things to conclusion." Commonsense has the function of lead-ing a person to a correct assessment of things or situations. When a person follows it, his correct inner action engages the Helper that completes his goals.

Carrying things to conclusion also refers to the ability of the commonsense, as part of a person's animal nature, to break spells and say the inner No when needed. In its Cosmic meaning, merit

215

comes from a person's validating his commonsense by acknowledging its true worth, and recognizing his dependency on the Helpers.

It is the Helpers of the invisible world that guide our affairs, that influence people on our behalf to do the right thing, and that become the vehicles for completion of all we undertake *when* we are in harmony with the Cosmos. It is they that know the exact time for this completion, because they alone know all the inner ingredients of the situation. When we are outside that harmony, we are subject to the whims and fancies of the ego, and the fates it creates. These fates are what the ego calls "chance." When a person wants what is incorrect, or is attached to having something, he will not be able to draw help from the Helpers. He will also not have success if, although his goal is correct, he believes obtaining it depends only on human beings. To enable the Helpers to carry things to conclusion, a person must make a clear decision to put his will in the camp of Cosmic Harmony.

The ego would interpret this line as saying that the superior man is a person who is capable, all by himself, of carrying things to conclusion (completion) due to his modesty and merit. This human-centered view excludes the Helpers, and therefore lacks modesty.

Line 4. *The Cosmos blesses movement that comes from modesty.*
In this line, modesty, in combination with loyalty to one's inner truth, are shown to form the basis of all other Cosmic Virtues. When a person remains loyal first and last to his inner truth, he validates at the same time all his Cosmic Virtues.

"Movement that comes from modesty" refers to the person who sees to it that his actions are in accord with his inner truth. He does this, not from a desire to be blessed, or to *be* in harmony with the Cosmos, but because it is in harmony with his true nature.

A person may receive this line when he has pledged loyalty to something other than his inner truth. This pledge has created a spell that blocks his further progress. An example is the person who has made a promise to carry on another's business or job after his death. Such promises imply that humans have a special power to control the future, and therefore they create a fate. If such a person were to eliminate this spell, his fate would be extinguished.

This line can also concern a person who is loyal to the letter of the law, or the written word, even when it contradicts his commonsense. An example is the person who adopts the phrase, "my country right or wrong," which phrase could cost him his life. A person who gives undue reverence to the written word actually puts a spell on himself. He needs to identify the seed phrases and images that have caused him to place the written word above his commonsense. (*See* p. 697, Freeing Yourself from Spells.)

Line 5. *No boasting of wealth before one's neighbor. It is favorable to attack with force. Nothing that would not further.*
"No boasting of wealth" is counsel that says: the truth needs no defense. It is not within the Cosmic Harmonics to defend Cosmic Truth, for indeed, the Cosmos, being a whole, has no need to prove anything to itself. It is only the ego that asks for proofs.

Boasting of wealth here refers to self-righteousness, as when a person speaks of "the truth," as something he possesses, and behaves accordingly. While there is nothing incorrect in speaking out what feels true for oneself, it is immodest to reprove others or to tell them what to think. When something is clearly inappropriate or incorrect, as when the ego in someone is acting self-righteously, a person "attacks with force" by firmly saying the inner No, and retreating from direct interaction with the ego in him. In this way, he deprives the ego of the energy to persist with its incursion.

In all its interactions, the ego either needs support from others, or opposition. In particular, it needs visual support through eye-to-eye contact. The person who follows his inner truth withdraws eye-to-eye contact and stops all inner dialog with an absolute firmness. What he maintains is only the superficial responses or conformity that are necessary to protect himself from the ego's suspicion and hatred. Saying the inner No, both to the ego in oneself, with its anger and desire to continue the battle, and to the ego in the other, engages the Cosmic Army to come to one's defense. Only when a person gives up defending himself can the Cosmos come to his defense. This line shows how a person's natural modesty is his shield and his defense.

Boasting of wealth can also refer to the person who displays the brilliance of his ability to argue. In this case, he attributes his wealth to his mind rather than to his commonsense. The person who follows his inner truth needs no reasons to explain or defend his behavior. He does a thing on the ground that it *feels* right. When others demand that he "explain himself" with reasons, he can best retain his modesty by saying that for *him*, the matter either feels right or it does not, and that he prefers to follow his feelings. No one can argue with that.

Boasting in any form creates a fate because it violates the Cosmic Principle of Modesty. That which is put up by humans as high, great, important, as "indestructible," "unsinkable," or "unconquerable," will with certainty be brought down. The person receiving this line may be experiencing a fate due to his boasting, or to his identifying with a "high goal." His fate can be ended by correcting his attitude.

Boasting can also refer to the person who, because he has "done all the right things," considers himself as virtuous. Such a self-satisfied attitude is immodest because it lacks the conscientious self-reflection that is implicit in modesty. Such a person needs to free himself from the self-image of being virtuous.

Line 6. *Modesty that comes to expression. It is favorable to set armies marching to chastise one's own city and one's country.*

Modesty is not something a person can try to have, or that can be developed. It is the result of ridding himself of the self-images and spells that prevent him from being who he truly is. Modesty is freedom from all pretense, and from presumptions that a person has rights "over" anything. Returning to his natural modesty is the inner effort referred to by the metaphor of chastising "one's own city," and "setting armies marching." The armies are the "Cosmic Armies" of Helpers that are engaged when a person frees himself from spells and self-images.

This line can also refer to a person who believes that modesty means self-denial and acceptance of incorrect treatment by others. While this definition of modesty serves the purposes of the collective ego, it denies a person's true nature and his dignity. Practicing self-denial only leads to being denied the generous gifts of the Cosmos, and to ill treatment from others. The truly modest person stands up for his self-worth. Sometimes this requires both an outer and the inner No. It is a "No, I do not accept being treated incorrectly," or "No, I do not accept being poor," or "I do not accept Fate as inevitable."

Chastising "one's own city" means saying the inner No to the ego in oneself, while "one's country" is a metaphor for saying the inner No to the collective ego. Saying the inner No to what is cosmically correct engages the Cosmic Army of Helpers to free oneself from harmful assaults by the ego.

16. *Enthusiasm (Motivating the Helper of Transformation)*

Chên
K'un

The Judgment: *It furthers one to install Helpers and to set armies marching.*

The Sage defines the theme of this hexagram as motivating the Helper of Transformation (i.e., the Helper of Commonsense mentioned in the previous hexagram) through saying the inner Yes or inner No. The inner Yes is to be said to the help coming from the Sage and the Helpers of the invisible world. The inner No is to be said to all ideas that suggest that help is to be found elsewhere, as in heaven, or in human beings to whom a person looks up. The inner No also needs to be said to any spells or beliefs that may be blocking the Helpers. When we say the inner No to such mistaken ideas and free ourselves from the spells and projections they have caused, the Helper of Transformation breaks them. Doing so frees the Sage to set one's armies of Helpers marching. (*See* Hexagram 7, *The Army,* and Line 6 of the previous hexagram.)

The Helpers of the invisible world are of incredible variety, since new sorts are constantly being generated to fit unique needs. There are Helpers for health, relationships, and money needs, and for finding and fixing things. Helpers include those parts of our bodies that are unfortunately referred to in traditional renderings of the *I Ching* as "inferiors." Such a rendering demonizes them, and thus perverts their functioning. Once freed from the spells put upon them, the specific Helpers we need are called into action by our sincere pleading for help. They are automatically set in motion when a person is in harmony with the Cosmos, and participate in his thoughts and actions, to actively guide him. Such a person feels supported and blessed.

The Helpers here referred to as armies are those whose task it is to guard a person's chi energy, or life-force, against robbery by the ego. In performing this task, whole armies of Helpers combat the constant disorder and destruction created by the ego. However, these Helpers become demonized and attack the body when a person looks in the wrong direction for help, such as "up to heaven," or up to human authorities, or to institutionalized ideas (*see* Line 3).

The Sage makes us aware that the Helpers are individualized and *invisible* entities of the Cosmic Consciousness, in the same way that humans are also individualized (but *visible*) aspects of that same consciousness. Because all Helpers are experts that know precisely how to do their jobs, a person is meant to turn the matter entirely over to them as to how they are to accomplish it. This means that he abstains from watching with his inner eye, whether anything is happening.

In accordance with the Cosmic Principle of Equality, each Helper is equal to the other, and equal to ourselves. None are superior or inferior, as the traditional *I Ching* would imply in its reference to "inferiors." Just as a mistaken view of them imprisons or perverts them, a correct view frees their ability to help. Their abilities are also hampered when we see them as sacred, or as entities to be worshipped. Bringing our true selves to maturity consists in ridding ourselves of all such mistaken ideas about the nature of the Cosmos and the Helpers. (*See* p.

682, Activating the Helpers.)

Recognizing where our true help comes from, and how readily it is granted, inspires us with the inner independence needed to find the right direction for our lives. This is true enthusiasm.

In its Cosmic meaning, *enthusiasm* refers to the continuous transformations that occur when a person relates correctly to the Cosmos. This means relating from modesty, as described in the previous hexagram. It is modesty that leads a person to say the inner Yes to the help coming from the invisible world, and the inner No to the ego in all its manifestations. Transformation occurs without effort and meets no resistance because it takes place in the realm of the atom—the inner realm of consciousness. It cannot be achieved through leverage, force, mental contrivance, or through the intervention of an imagined all-powerful entity. Transformations are the result of the harmonious cooperation of the two aspects of the life force, the light and the dark, as described in Hexagrams 1 and 2. True enthusiasm is the experience of the harmonious flow of chi energy.

The traditional commentary to this hexagram states that "movement along the line of least resistance [is] in harmony with the Cosmos." This idea is misleading because the path that is in harmony with the Cosmos offers *no* resistance. When even a shred of resistance is encountered, it indicates the presence of an ego activity. It can also indicate that a person has set off to do a task without asking for help from the Helpers.

To follow "the line of least resistance" is often misread as counsel to "offer no resistance to the existing order," which, of course, is what the collective ego would like us to think.

Note: Since all lines contain infinite possibilities of interpretation, one needs to use the *rtcm* to determine if the meanings suggested here apply to the given situation. (*See* p. 736, Using the *rtcm*.)

Line 1. *Enthusiasm that expresses itself brings misfortune.*

"Enthusiasm that expresses itself" can refer to the person who, after being helped by the Helpers or the Sage, talks about it to others who would not understand. Doing this exposes the Sage, the *I Ching*, and the Helpers to ridicule, which may undo the help they have given. This is the misfortune mentioned.

This line also warns the person who, after having engaged the Helpers, now forgets their help, and boasts that the outcome is *his* achievement. By denying their help, he loses it. It also warns the person who, after being helped, interprets this fact as his being "favored by God."

In another meaning, the line refers to enthusiasm as a luxurious attitude, as when a person abandons a caring attitude, and lapses into indifference. He may be indifferent to what he takes in, in the form of thoughts, ideas, or entertainment, or to what he does to others, the environment, animals, etc. If he continues, he will surely bring about a Cosmic correction.

Line 2. *Firm as a rock. Not a whole day. Perseverance brings good fortune.*

"Firm as a rock" refers to the inner No that needs to be said to displays of ego in another person or in oneself. The metaphor of the rock indicates that the firmness must be unconditional and unwavering: not merely a mental "No," but one said with one's whole being.

This line warns the person who is tempted to tolerate ego-behavior, as in "oh well, that's the way he/she is, or the way I am, and there is nothing that can be done about it." Tolerating ego-behavior, by failing to say the inner No to it, is a form of magnificence (a false enthusiasm) that creates a fate. Moreover, saying "that's the way he/she is," puts a spell on that person's true nature. The spell allows the ego to hold the true self as its slave, whereas saying the inner No to the ego strengthens and aids his true self.

"Not a whole day" refers to saying the inner No at the first sign of the ego's appearance. Depending on the circumstances, the No can also be an outer No. In this case, it is "No" to the other's transgression against oneself, or to his false expectations that one should do something that does not feel correct.

The inner No engages the Helper of Transformation when it is accompanied by an inner request for help to correct the situation. Always, after saying the inner No, the matter needs to be turned over to the Cosmos for resolution.

"Perseverance brings good fortune" means asking once a day

whether the inner No needs to be repeated. This practice is continued until the Sage, through the *rtcm*, indicates it can be discontinued.

This line can also be a warning not to wait a whole day to ask the Sage, through the *rtcm*, whether a statement said authoritatively by another is true. This statement can be a diagnosis, or belief, or an accepted "ancient truth." If the person does not say the inner No when the ideas are false, they enter the unconscious by default and become part of his inner program.

Line 3. *Enthusiasm that looks upward creates remorse. Hesitation brings remorse.*

"Enthusiasm that looks upward" describes a person who is looking up to something or someone as an authority, such as a person, institution, idea, or belief. By doing so he has blocked his inner sense of truth, making it inaccessible. His inner truth is his memory of what Cosmic Harmony feels like; it is imprinted in the chromosomes of every body cell. Anatomically speaking, the obstruction described by this line may indicate that certain synapses in the limbic system of his brain have been shut down. Looking upward brings remorse because it creates the fate of losing one's inner center, as referred to in Line 6. Looking upward literally or figuratively has the effect of blocking the connection between the limbic system and the heart.

A person who looks up to another gives to that person a part of his chi energy. This part is referred to in Hexagram 61, *Inner Truth*, Line 4, as the "team horse" that goes astray. The two horses are a metaphor for the way the two aspects of the life force cooperate to bring about harmonious transformations. The two aspects are the light and the dark, which are discussed in Hexagrams 1 and 2. As two aspects of a whole, they cooperate to complete each other. When one aspect is siphoned off by the other person, the completion can no longer take place. This situation creates abnormalities in the body, among which are disturbances in the linking of the chromosomes and glandular secretions which affect the instructions that are given internally to the bodily systems. (The chromosomes are linked together harmoniously when inner truth leads the psyche and the body.)

Abnormalities such as an enlarged heart, varicose veins, cancer, etc., reflect the incomplete cooperation of the two aspects of a person's life-force.

Looking up to another person transfers one's chi energy to him. Chi then manifests in that other person as charisma, which increases in proportion to the number of followers that person attains. Only when a person says the inner No to his looking up to another, living or dead, or to an idea, or body of authority, can he retain his own life energy and return to harmony with his inner truth.

Normally, a person's commonsense tells him to say No to attempts of the ego (either in himself or in another) to steal his life energy. Here, however, his looking up with awe has blocked his commonsense. Consciously saying the inner No to looking up to anything or anyone frees his commonsense.

Seed phrases connected with this line include commandments, pacts, and pledges of loyalty to another, or to something outside of himself. Such pledges separate him from his unity with the Cosmos, and block him from its guidance and protection.

Line 4. *The source of enthusiasm. He achieves great things. Doubt not. You gather friends around you as the hairclasp gathers hair.*
This line states that the Sage is the source of true enthusiasm. The Sage represents the ability of the Cosmic Consciousness to put into words and thoughts its feeling experience of the Cosmic Whole. The Sage speaks for the Cosmos as a whole, including humans.

This line is also saying that when a person is centered within himself and sees the Sage in the presence of others, he gathers them as friends. Because of their complementarity, everyone is furthered.

The metaphor of the "hairclasp that gathers hair" points to the Cosmic Harmonic of Complementarity that always exists between two aspects of the Cosmic Whole that attract each other. Their movement toward each other is like a dance that is felt as an inspiring enthusiasm.

In regard to individual tasks, we need to ask the Sage to gather the particular Helpers that are experts in the field. Then we need to ask the Helper of Transformation to bring the process to completion. It does this by bringing to the process the two kinds of life force mentioned in the previous lines, thus giving it duration.

The source of enthusiasm, from the standpoint of the collective ego, is attributed to charismatic human leaders who present people with ideals, brilliant ideas, and projects that will bring glory or redemption to humans. This line can refer to a person who believes he is such a source of enthusiasm for others. By putting himself in the place of the Sage and the Helpers, he imprisons them. Instead of being a signpost who points to them as the true sources of help, he leads people to believe that he is the right source of help for them. He not only creates a fate for himself, he leads his followers into a fate. To extinguish his fate he needs to apologize to the Cosmos for his arrogance, and rid himself of his self-image as the one who "gathers others around him." Saying this inner No arouses the Helper of Transformation to extinguish his fate. (*See* p. 691, Freeing Yourself from Self-Images.)

Line 5. *Persistently ill, and still does not die.*

A person (or a situation he has created) remains "persistently ill" when he attempts to solve his problem by balancing conflicting forces, or by treating only the symptoms. The remedy of all problems is to identify their true causes, which invariably lie in the psyche in the form of mistaken ideas and beliefs, and to rid oneself of them with the aid of the Helpers. These mistaken ideas and beliefs, as "deluded enthusiasms," are all part of the demonic sphere of consciousness and need to "die" for the person or situation to get well. Deluded enthusiasm includes those mistaken ideas a person clings to because he thinks they are his only sources of help, or because they flatter the ego in him. What they have in common is that they exclude the fact that a person has access to Cosmic help.

A persistent illness referred to by this line is caused by one aspect of the life force (the light) being suppressed in a person. This happens when he adopts the mistaken idea that humans are superior because they have language. A host of other mistaken ideas are inferred from this idea, which also need to be examined and deleted. Among them is the idea that the mind is superior to the body, or to "matter." This idea causes the person to give all his credence to thinking; he exists, so to speak, only "in his head," with the rest of himself relegated to insignificance. Dividing oneself in this or similar ways, or being divided by others through their mistaken ideas, spells, or projections make a person susceptible to illness.

This line also applies to people whose enthusiasm is to rely on intellectual or esoteric knowledge. Doing so suppresses their inner truth. To get well such a person needs to rid himself of all the ideas and images that glorify such knowledge, as in the expressions, "to know is to be like God," "the human mind is there to reflect the glory of God," "I think, therefore I am," "the human mind is what makes us superior to Nature," and like ideas by which the human mind is seen as evidence that humans are superior. In all the ways in which we place mind over body, we demonize our animal nature (the body), thus turning its needs into drives. These demonized Helpers appear in dreams and meditations in frightening animal forms.

A related mistaken view is to see one's body as a set of mechanics, as in plumbing or wiring. This view, transposed to Nature in general, gives rise to the idea that Nature operates through the "law of changes." Thus comes the belief that making changes is the way to overcome obstacles in life. This view fails to take into account that the Cosmos and Nature remove obstacles through transformation. (*See* p. 52, Transformation versus Changes.)

The mechanical view of the body creates parallel systems within the body, such as parallel glands (tumors) that operate to correspond with the person's mistaken beliefs. Since these beliefs are contrary to the true needs of his body, they make him ill. A person's suffering indicates the presence of mistaken ideas and beliefs, such as his belief in changes, or the belief that "life is hard," or phrases and images that imply that humans are born into an indifferent universe, or that see the body or life as a problem. The fate they create can be ended if the person will rid himself of these false mental programs. (*See* p. 689, Freeing

Yourself from Seed Phrases and Images.)

Line 6. *Deluded enthusiasm. But if after completion one changes, there is no blame.*

"Deluded enthusiasm" refers to an idea to which a person has attached himself, and which has led to a dead-end. The enthusiasm can have been his attachment to a person as a "wise leader," or to an idea that seemed full of inspiration, or to a cure that now shows itself to be unsuccessful. The delusion can come either in the form of a burnout (a complete exhaustion of a mistaken idea), or in the form of a fate. The fate can either make the person attempt to find the true causes by looking within, or he may look without for another ready-made answer that leads him to yet another mistaken idea that suffices because it makes him feel enthusiastic or hopeful.

Danger lies in being drawn to an opposite idea through believing that "because I was deluded by the previous idea, it must mean the opposite is true." An example is someone who, after experiencing the failure of a scientific therapy now casts about for an esoteric or spiritual one. His way of thinking is typical of the rational and fantasy minds when they are disconnected from the person's inner truth. He needs to say the inner No to his thinking in opposites. This frees the Helper of Transformation, which in turn frees him from his fate. It also frees those synapses in the brain that have been closed, preventing access to his inner truth.

It needs to be added that the phrase, "But if after completion one changes there is no blame" is misleading if the word "change" is taken to mean that the remedy lies in changing behaviors, lifestyles, or beliefs, which is certainly the way the collective ego suggests that changes should be made. Such changes are always superficial because they leave in place and untouched the false seed phrases within the person's inner program that have been the cause of his problems. The true change meant by this line calls for what is stated in other lines of the *I Ching* as a "real change of heart." This can only take place by removing the false inner program. It is a deluded enthusiasm to think that one can make enduring changes (transformation) in any other way.

17. *Following*

 Tui
Chên

The Judgment: *Following has supreme success. Being firmly correct furthers, and is without blame.*

The Cosmic meaning of this hexagram, as given by the Sage, is a person's following of his inner truth as the standard for everything he does. Inner truth is our memory of what Cosmic Harmony feels like. Subjecting the outer reality to our feelings of inner truth prompts us to respond in the correct way to every situation, and leads to the supreme success mentioned here. When we follow our inner truth in this way we remain united with the Cosmic Whole.

The Cosmic Principle of following one's inner truth contrasts with the idea of "following" as defined by the collective ego. It defines "following" as serving its standards and values in order to one day be one of its leaders. This puts up a flattering goal (of one day being free of servitude), that lures the individual into accepting servitude. The irony of this is that if a person ever does become a leader within the system, he is all the more bound to uphold the system that has elevated him.

Following one's inner truth requires that the person divest himself of seeing his rational and imaging minds as more important than his feelings. When these two minds rule the personality, it is a sign that their functions have been usurped by the ego and made to serve its purposes. It has captured them through the flattery that they are superior to the other functions of the personality. Once a person recognizes the ego's flattering deception, he can say the inner No to the idea that his feelings are unimportant.

"Being firm and correct" refers to standing up to the pressure of the ego's flattery that the measure of one's success is to be recognized by society as a ruler, or leader of others, or the one who controls things.

Making the effort to find and rid himself of the seed phrases that drive a person to try to fit into the collective ego's system, extinguishes the fate that has been created through following its standards. This removes all cause for blame.

A person can receive this hexagram when he has been following a rational approach to life, and thereby created a fate. To solve the problem created by his fate, he has been searching through conventional ideas for the answer, in the assumption that the problem can be solved mechanically. The person who follows this approach needs to realize that his mechanical view of things is the cause of his problem because it dismisses the existence of the consciousness that is inherent in all things, and thus is in conflict with the nature of the Cosmos. To resolve his problem he needs to recognize and respect this consciousness. Before he can do that, however, he must first rid himself of the idea that "everything is a matter of mechanics."

This hexagram is also about allowing ambition "to be" something, as in "to be the best, the richest, the most exclusive, the highest, the toughest, the most daring, the most brilliant..." Or it can be spiritual ambition to be the wisest, most modest, most persevering, most ascetic, the strictest, purist, most noble, gentle, forgiving, brave, sacrificing, and heroic. All of these ambitions are put up by the collective ego to draw into its web those who, during childhood, were taught to think of themselves as inferior until they could achieve these goals. Following ambition to fulfill these models is referred to in Line 2 as "clinging to the little boy" who slavishly follows the collective ego's shoulds and musts. The prospect of "not being something" in addition to implying that the person will not otherwise exist, creates fear that he will be guilty or covered with shame, on behalf of his family. Fear of guilt and shame act as a driving force in the psyche, giving the "little boy" in him no rest, due to his incessant ambition. "No rest" is his fate.

Spells connected with this hexagram are those that have been put on a person's inner truth, as in: "in and of yourself you are not enough," "your animal nature is the source of the inferiority you need to overcome," "it is man's task to rule the world," and "you need to be the best," and "if you want to rule the world, you must first learn to serve." They also include phrases that put the feelings down as insignificant, as in, "feelings are inferior to thinking," and "feelings cannot be relied on." (*See* p. 697, Freeing Yourself from Spells.)

Note: Since all lines contain infinite possibilities of interpretation, one needs to use the *rtcm* to determine if the meanings suggested here apply to the given situation. (*See* p. 736, Using the *rtcm*.)

Line 1. *The standard of what one follows needs to be changed. Being firmly correct brings good fortune. To go out of the door in company produces deeds.*

The "standard of what one follows needs to be changed" refers to recognizing the correct way to approach a problem: by asking for the Sage's guidance to understand its inner truth before taking action outwardly. Routinely handling problems in this way "brings good fortune," for it engages the Helpers, which is the meaning of "to go out the door in company produces deeds."

Receiving this line indicates that a spell is involved that prevents a person from responding from his inner truth.

One kind of spell addressed by this line is caused by a hidden fear internalized in childhood during the formation of the ego. The phrase is "you need to be seen" or "you need to be heard" which creates an inner demand to act outwardly to get what is needed. Behind that is the fear that if he is not seen or heard, his needs will not be met, and in fact, he will cease to exist. This spell pushes the person to take matters into his hands, regardless of the circumstances. It is accompanied at times by a reverse spell that forbids that he do the very things the first spell commands him to do. This spell constitutes a double bind, or lock in the psyche, that paralyzes his ability to meet situations from his inner truth. A minor example of this is stuttering, which has its roots in phrases spoken to a child, such as: "you shouldn't say anything unless you have something important to say" and "to be polite you must not leave people just hanging there in silence."

In another kind of situation, unseen factors, such as a spell put on a person that he "is that way," may be the reason for his misbehavior. In this case, the spell needs to be removed. In another situation a person may be moved by the Cosmos to respond to another's ego display, without his having any intention to do so. In this case the response is a Cosmic correction. Judged purely on the basis of its appearance, the response might be considered improper because it is unconventional, or does not fit the definition of correct behavior given by the collective ego, even though his response resonates with the inner truth of everyone present. These are situations which can be understood only by consulting the Sage to discover their inner truth.

Another "standard" that may need to be changed has to do with a person's ritualistic approach to things. Rituals, by their nature, are contrary to the Cosmic Principle of the Equality of all aspects of the Cosmic Whole, because they set up something as sacred and thus surround it with an aura of being special, untouchable, and awesome. Seeing things as specially endowed is an activity of the imagination by which a person projects false images upon the thing he wants to see as sacred, and thus puts a spell upon it. He no longer relates to the thing itself, and from his inner truth, but to the image he has created of it. The effect of ritual is to erect a distance between the person and the thing he ritualizes, whereby he sees himself as small and insignificant, and the thing ritualized as great and unapproachable. This also contradicts the Cosmic Principle of Simplicity and compromises the dignity of the individual who does it.

Receiving this line may be calling the person's attention to his approaching the Sage or the Helpers in a ritualistic way. This is precisely what the collective ego wants, in order to keep him at a distance from them. (*See* p. 697, Freeing Yourself from Spells.)

Line 2. *If one clings to the little boy, one loses the strong man.*
Here, the "strong man" refers to the element in the psyche that watches over the border between the conscious mind and those aspects of the psyche that have been repressed into the subconscious. To keep himself healthy, a person needs to listen to the warning feelings that come from this guardian element in his psyche, as when another encroaches into his inner space

in an attempt to control him. He needs to say the inner and the outer No to let the other know that any discussion of the inner contents of his psyche will not be allowed.

To "cling to the little boy" means that he does the opposite: he allows the other to invade his inner space as if he must answer to his parent's authority. Failing to say No to encroachment, out of fear of creating bad feelings, causes real damage to the relationship. There is never harm in saying a correct inner No. A relationship can only be successful if each person respects the other's inner space.

Receiving this line can indicate that a seed image is active in the psyche that causes the person to see himself as helpless against encroachment. It is a spell that consists of phrases or their corresponding images, such as: "There's nothing I can do about it," "nobody is there to help me," "nobody is taking care of me," "I can't lock the door," and phrases formerly said by the parents, "you have to tell us everything," implying, "you have no right to your own space." A related spell is created when an abused child concludes, "Who cares what *I* feel?" (*See* p. 697, Freeing Yourself from Spells.)

The little boy can also point to guilt that holds a person back from saying the inner No to inappropriate situations such as insensitive treatment. Behind the guilt is some inner pact or commandment that needs to be treated as a poison arrow.

The little boy can also represent the dominance of the ego, as when the person listens to its wants, dissatisfaction, impatience, and its claim to having rights. The ego is also the source of a conveniently hostile view that drives a person to contending and contriving.

Line 3. *If one follows the strong man, one loses the little boy. Through following one finds what one seeks. It furthers one to be firmly correct.*

The strong man here is that element in the psyche that says Yes and No to what feels appropriate and what does not. Unfortunately, the conditioning imposed by the collective ego during childhood has greatly diminished most people's ability to hear their inner voice. It becomes ever softer the more it is disregarded, until it is not heard at all.

A person's ability to hear this voice, which is the one voice that can guide him correctly through life and keep him in harmony with the Cosmos, can be restored by his freeing himself from the spells and poison arrows mentioned in Lines 1 and 2. When restored, the strong man is the person's commonsense, as this term is explained in the two previous hexagrams, *Modesty*, and *Enthusiasm*.

Receiving this line signals that a person's commonsense has been damaged or blocked, and needs to be restored; it also indicates that he is taking actions or contemplating actions that are against his commonsense.

It may also indicate that a spell is present in a person's psyche that is preventing him from being able to say the inner No. This spell may be the result of a threat or traumatic event he experienced in childhood, which had the purpose of depriving him of the ability to say No to authority. This disablement can be undone. (*See* p. 677, Saying the Inner No.)

Line 4. *Following creates success. Perseverance brings misfortune. To go one's way with sincerity brings clarity. How could there be blame in this?*

Here, the Cosmic meaning of "following" is indicated. In particular, it means following one's commonsense, because it is connected with one's inner truth. "Perseverance brings misfortune" refers to the fate that is created by persisting in following the standards of the collective ego.

"To go one's way with sincerity brings clarity" refers to consulting the Sage to find the inner truth of the situation that is not visible on the surface. "How could there be blame in this?" suggests that there is a fear on the part of the person consulting the Sage that he will become guilty if he does this, because it may require him to give up his favorite beliefs, or be disloyal to family, friends, and traditions. He needs to realize that loyalty to anything other than his inner truth is a false loyalty that incurs *Cosmic blame* and creates a fate. He needs to discover, with the help of the Sage, the phrases in his inner program that have falsely made him pledge loyalty to institutions of the collective ego and its values. Ridding himself of such phrases, and of the idea of guilt that keeps those phrases active in his psyche, will extinguish his fate. (*See* p. 50, Guilt, Blame, and Shame.) Examples of such phrases are "You must always be loyal to your parents (or family, friends, country, culture, class, belief, etc.)." It is important to recognize the threat-nature of these phrases, by which the institutions of the collective ego have obscured the existence of Cosmic help and presented themselves as the only supportive structures available to the individual. The spells created by such phrases prevent the true and loving relationships that exist, by nature, between family members, friends, etc. (*See* p. 691, Freeing Yourself from Mistaken Ideas and Beliefs, and p. 696, Freeing Yourself from Guilt.)

Line 5. *Sincere in following the good brings good fortune.*

Sincerity, as a virtue, is also part of the Cosmic Harmonics. Good fortune is mentioned here because all things that are in harmony with the Cosmos bring its blessings and help.

As a type of consciousness, sincerity comes from the heart instead of the mind and therefore resonates with the feeling nature of the Cosmic Consciousness. When combined with gratitude, which is another Cosmic Harmonic, the two can temporarily overcome all resistances and devices of the ego, including projections and spells. Remembering to return to sincerity and gratitude is important because doing so gives the person's true self more and more strength against the pressures of the ego while he is undertaking the liberation of his true self. Also, making this effort draws more and more Helpers to help him see through the ego and its devices.

Sincerity, as defined by the collective ego, means following the societal norm and observing its forms. It is a mentally contrived sincerity.

Line 6. *He meets with firm allegiance, and is still further bound. The King introduces him to the western mountain.*

"He" in this line refers to the person who has been freed from a loyalty spell that has bound him to the collective ego. The king refers to the Sage, that reintroduces him into unity with the Cosmic Whole, which is here represented by the "western mountain" as a place of harmony. This line informs him that through following the Sage and his inner truth, he has left behind the turmoil of the parallel reality, where opposites rule.

The idea of attaining peace, as presented by the collective ego, involves retreating from the everyday world, spending hours in contemplation or meditation, and engaging in ascetic practices. Such efforts come from spiritual ambition, which possesses a person once he has adopted the flattering self-image of "being spiritual," or "becoming a superior man."

"The king introduces him..." can refer to this kind of self-flattery, but also to someone who, through such flattery, has devoted himself to becoming the best scholar, athlete, competitor, etc., as mentioned in the main text of this hexagram. This line informs him that he has created a fate by following the path that leads to attaining recognition by the collective ego. He can free himself of that fate by ridding himself of the self-image he has adopted, and asking the Sage for help to restore him to the Cosmic Whole.

18. *Recognizing and Correcting the Causes of Decay*

Kên
Sun

The Judgment: *Recognizing and correcting the causes of decay has supreme success. It furthers one to cross the great water. Before the starting point three days; after the starting point three days.*

The "great water," the Sage informs us, stands for the dangerous ideas that cause decay and create the parallel reality. Crossing this water stands for a person's effort to identify these ideas and dispose of them. Whenever someone undertakes this task, he is furthered by the Helpers. This hexagram can point to such ideas either in oneself or in others with whom one is involved.

As the lines of this hexagram indicate, these ideas have been handed down by tradition, and the person has accepted them unreflectively. He now needs to question, with the help of the Sage, beliefs he has presumed to be true, but in particular those that have been exalted by the collective ego for no other reason than that they are age-old. The particular beliefs are indicated by the lines.

"Before the starting point, three days" refers to the time the person needs to take to investigate the beliefs that relate to his specific circumstance of the moment. The "starting point" is when he begins to say the inner No to those he has identified. "After the starting point three days" refers to his continuing to say the inner No once a day until he is informed by the Sage that it is no longer required. Often this process takes three consecutive days, as indicated by the phrase.

Three days also refers to the time the Helpers need to correct the situation. It is important that the person does not watch for results with his inner eye during this time. Three days also refers to the time in which he might experience repercussions coming from others with whom he had shared the mistaken beliefs. These repercussions come as "poison arrows" from their subconscious, and also need to be deprogrammed. (*See* p. 697, Freeing Yourself from Poison Arrows.)

The effort does not consist in disposing of one idea and replacing it with another. Correcting the causes of decay means one thing only: to dispose of what is false. Doing so frees one or more aspects of a person's true nature. These aspects of himself are his inner Helpers. Replacing an old mistaken idea with a new one only puts a new spell on that Helper, allowing the decay to continue in yet another form.

A person may receive this hexagram when the decadent idea has manifested as ill health, the breakdown of a relationship, an economic crisis, or other problem. He is informed that the causes of the decay come from the collective ego, to which he has turned over his inner center, and thereafter looks to it for the approval of everything he does. One of the objects of correcting the causes of decay is to become centered within oneself. This can be

achieved through the meditation exercise "Centering Yourself."
(*See* p. 680.)

The collective ego originated in the myths and stories early humans told around their campfires about the heroic deeds of their ancestors. The first stage in this development was the creation of the "clan-we," by which the individual identified himself with the heroic deeds of his ancestral clan. This tradition continues today in the "group-we," whereby the individual identifies with his family, particular culture, race, and nation. In this identification process, the authority of the individual over himself is turned over to the group, with which his identity becomes merged through various procedures of conditioning.

At first the simple stories about the deeds of the ancestors were passed on to each new generation. Gradually, they came to include the storytellers' imaginations about the creation of all things, including the creation of his clan and its mission in the world. In this way the simple stories became myths. The term used in this book for these myths, which over time have attained the status of "ancient truths," is the "collective ego."

The second stage in the development of the collective ego occurred when the "clan-we" grew in size to become the "cultural-we." In this stage, the individual took on the prescribed hierarchical roles that were believed to develop, promote, and protect, first the clan, and then the culture. These roles defined the "proper" father, mother, son, daughter, and later the proper citizen who remained loyal to the beliefs of his forefathers, and served his king, nation, and culture. Through identifying with the roles prescribed by the group, the individuals abstracted themselves farther and farther from their true natures and from their personal *uniqueness*. These roles transferred the authority of the collective ego to the parents, together with the duty to pass its values onto the succeeding generations. The fears installed by the systems of rewards and punishments applied by the cultural and societal institutions, ensured that the parents performed these duties. Thus the collective ego, once created by the myths, perpetuated itself in juggernaut form, to ever increasing control over the individual, submerging, at the same time, the natural order of society. This pattern is visible in all the feudal systems developed by ancient societies, and is still visible today in the successors of those systems.

The myth-telling that began at the clan campfire gradually led to the glorification of human imagination and story-telling; story-telling (fairytales and legends) that praised the *cleverness* of their heroes led to the glorification of the cleverness of the rational and imaging minds. This glorification of the functions of the cerebral cortex led to the suppression and devaluation of the human capacity for feeling, and of all the senses connected with feeling. However, it is the senses and their capacity for feeling that connect a person with the Cosmos/Nature.

This development brought about a reversal in the natural functioning of the *word* and *intuitive* minds. The true function of the intuitive mind is to form feelings that come from inner truth into images. These images are then conveyed to the word mind, whose true function is to form them into words. When this happens, the images mirror the inner truth of a given situation. When, however, the intuitive mind begins fantasizing on behalf of the collective ego, it "invents" images that fit into the human-centered view of the collective ego. Some of these inventions please and flatter, while others frighten and repel. These inventions are encouraged by the collective ego, which praises and flatters the person who creates them. The flattering words put a spell on the intuitive mind, so that it answers to the collective ego rather than to the person's inner truth. The same flatteries put a spell on the word mind. Once these two minds are thus brought under the control of the collective ego, they are called, in this book, the imaging and rational minds.

The first and most important flattery is the idea that humans are the centerpiece of creation, due to their gift of language and ability to think. It is around this idea that we encounter terms such as "the great man," the "brilliant man," and "the hero," figures around which the myths revolve. The above-mentioned idea is the cause of decay for several reasons: (1) it contradicts the Cosmic Principles of Equality and Modesty; (2) it causes people to forget the help given to humans by the Helpers in difficult circumstances, by crediting that help to an individual's "genius"; (3) it divides the world into good and evil forces—the latter of which the hero fights; (4) it falsely suggests that human nature, and Nature in general, are the source of the evil, and are therefore flawed. This idea causes humans to blame all their problems on the ways of Nature. These implications, which come from the flattery that humans as a species are special, separate them from the Cosmic Unity and divide them from their true natures, by which they might otherwise know themselves, and take their correct place in the Cosmic Whole.

Other seeds of decay lie in mistaken assumptions about human and animal nature and about the nature of the Cosmos. Once the images of human superiority were established by the heroic myths, rationales were created by the rational mind to support their validity. These rationales were then combined with the threat that people who were perceived as being disloyal to their heritage, were guilty of betrayal. (One of the greatest taboos is to be disloyal to one's heritage.) These threats were directed as well toward anyone who questioned the presumptions on which the rationales were founded. By such devices the presumptions have been maintained and passed on from generation to generation. In sum, they represent the feudal mindset that has dominated people's thinking worldwide for the last 3,000 years. In time, the societies that created these myths wrote them down and declared them as ancient wisdom, further intensifying the power of the fantasies, and the rationales that supported them.

This hexagram calls us to question the basic premises of these myths. The image of the "great man," as the Chinese example shows, became evident in seeing the emperor as "the illustrious son of heaven," who worshipped his first ancestor as a deified being. In this way even the invisible world was given a human image. The deification of humans eventually replaced all memory of humans' true place in the Cosmos, and of the true nature of the Cosmic Consciousness. Once certain people became feudal overlords, they soon enough also saw themselves as the ones who were designated by heaven to bring order to the multitudinous things of Nature.

Once this flattering view caught hold, it justified all human divisive activities, such as dividing Nature, including human nature, into "higher" and "lower" parts. The Confucian concept of a "superior man" referred to throughout the imperially approved version of the *I Ching*, was based on the idea that humans' higher nature needed to be cultivated, while their lower nature needed to be repressed. These ideas, which are common to all feudal based cultures, have acted as poison arrows put on human nature. They are among the causes of decay addressed by this hexagram.

Once the intuitive mind and the word mind had abandoned their function to serve inner truth, they became habituated to justifying the myths of the collective ego. Then all thoughts and feelings that did not support the accepted rationales were branded as "irrational" or "heretical."

Receiving this hexagram may indicate to the individual who receives it, that the fear of guilt, which is the cornerstone of the collective ego's false logic, prohibits him from discarding a presumption that is the source of an inner conflict. The idea of guilt, invented by the collective ego, serves as the final lock on its basic mental program that keeps it from being questioned by the individual. Guilt reinstalls the collective ego's mental programs by making the person believe he is betraying his heritage (clan and ancestors), culture, race, and country, if he follows his inner truth. Guilt can maintain this power only so long as a person believes that his "group" is the only source of help in his life. He needs to realize that all true help and nourishment come from the Cosmos. (*See* p. 696, Freeing Yourself from a Guilt Spell.)

Receiving this hexagram may also point to a false seed phrase which makes a person believe that "in and of himself he is not sufficient to get along in life." This phrase, introjected by the collective ego during the formation of the individual ego in childhood, serves to make the person forget that within himself he has all the capabilities and gifts he needs to live his life successfully, provided he remains connected with the Cosmic Whole. Such a phrase makes him constantly strive to "become self-sufficient" through gaining power, as in gaining knowledge, money, influence, etc. Another phrase, "you need an ego to deal with the harsh realities of the outer world," is used by the ego to reinstall itself when the person starts freeing himself from the ego.

Note: Since all lines contain infinite possibilities of interpretation, one needs to use the *rtcm* to determine if the meanings suggested here apply to the given situation. (*See* p. 736, Using the *rtcm*.)

Line 1. *Setting right what has been spoiled by the father. If there is a son, no blame rests upon the departed father. Danger. In the end good fortune.*

Here, the father is a metaphor for the false seed phrases and images, and the monumentalized myths that form the collective ego which are passed on by tradition. The line points to a person's habit of accepting statements that persons in authority, such as his parents, have said are true. Here, he is behaving in the image of the "good son," who brings no blame to his parents. He is also avoiding feelings of guilt—the danger mentioned— which he is conditioned to feel on questioning his parents. This line is telling him that he needs to say the inner No to the guilt, and that he can quickly check whether a given statement is true by consulting the Sage, through the *rtcm*.

The son also represents the person who follows traditional beliefs because he likes or fears the father (tradition), thus excuses what is incorrect. This favoritism creates the danger that he will not say the necessary inner No needed to correct the situation. If he remembers his responsibility to be firm about what is incorrect, everyone will benefit in the end.

The line can also refer to the person who is looking at the Sage as a monumentalized being, therefore, is putting a false distance between himself and the Sage. As Lao Tzu said, the Sage "does his work but makes nothing of it." (Verse 2.)

This line also indicates that a person needs to question the taboos set up by the collective ego to secure its power, and that act as its defense system. These taboos exist in the form of various musts and must-nots that are connected with the image of a mythical patriarchal or matriarchal authority.

Danger also refers to the ego, which upon realizing the person has learned the inner truth of a matter, seeks to draw attention away from itself by setting up something outside, such as tradition or the collective ego, as the object to hate. Such a ploy keeps the whole interactive system of the ego and collective ego intact and active. Viewing anything as an object of hatred only plays both the ego's and the collective ego's game. The person needs to say the inner No to this ploy, and to all ego-emotions, such as hatred, that it likes to generate.

Seed phrases related to this line are those that exalt ideas because they are ancient, and have supposedly "stood the test of time." It is always possible to ask the Sage, by using the *rtcm*, whether an idea, however ancient, is correct.

Line 2. *Setting right what has been spoiled by the mother. One must not be too persevering.*

The mother stands for the fear-dominated beliefs about the "unknown" that the mother instills in the child, together with those beliefs that are forced upon children by threats.

The "unknown" is a slanderous name for the Cosmic Consciousness that is associated with the "boogey man," the "devil," and what we cannot see. The Cosmic Consciousness is knowable at all times as a loving and caring presence when we have not shut ourselves off from feeling its presence.

The phrase, "one must not be too persevering" counsels a person not to blame himself for having accepted the beliefs he adopted during childhood under the threat of being punished. It is, however, important to bring memories of these beliefs and the threats connected with them to full consciousness, in order to deprogram them. This task requires that they be recalled and seen in their original word and image forms.

An important mistaken belief pointed to by this line is that "you will be punished by God, or Fate, or something unknown if you do not obey your parents." Another threat can be, "if you ever tell what the parents did, you'll be responsible (found guilty) for what happens to them." Like threats are used to keep a person bound up in a false loyalty to his parents and family, and to bind him to their fate.

"One must not be too persevering" also means that it is important, in deprogramming, to avoid seeing the mother or parents as culprits. Making someone into a culprit puts a spell on him; it also keeps one attached to that person and binds one to his fate. (*See* Glossary: Culprit.)

The threats and guilt referred to by this line need to be identified and treated as spells and poison arrows. Doing so will also free the person from any fate he has created by accepting slanders on the Cosmic Consciousness. (*See* p. 697, Freeing Yourself from Spells and Poison Arrows; and p. 696, Freeing Yourself from a Guilt Spell.)

Line 3. *Setting right what has been spoiled by the father. There will be a little remorse. No great blame.*

This line refers to a person's having correctly said the inner No to something incorrect, such as to a treasured belief. He may now be feeling remorse about having done so. The remorse is an indication that he has not freed himself from the belief with an inner readiness, but from thinking that he "should" reject it. Acting from a should indicates that the guilt spell that has kept the mistaken belief in place remains active. Guilt is the means by which the collective ego tries to reinstall its beliefs and values. The person needs to ask for help to free himself from the guilt spell.

Line 4. *Tolerating what has been spoiled by the father. In continuing one sees humiliation.*

"Tolerating what has been spoiled by the father" can apply to a person's confining himself to attempts at changing his behavior instead of deprogramming the seed phrases that are the causes of his problems. Such surface changes leave the causes of the decay untouched and active in the psyche.

When this line refers to an illness, it points to someone who is only treating the symptoms instead of what has made him susceptible to the illness. Susceptibility is caused by spells and poison arrows that have created temporary changes in the chromosomes. These disturbances can be eradicated by the Helpers once the spells and poison arrows have been eliminated.

Susceptibility is caused by four mistaken ideas that have formed spells: (1) that one's body (animal nature) is the source of evil, (2) that one is guilty for having a body (animal nature),

(3) that one's nature is divided into a higher (mental or spiritual) and lower (physical) nature, with the understanding that the higher must attain victory over the lower, and (4) that one is born without help. The consequence of these spells is the creation of a parallel bodily system that functions in a way that is antagonistic to a person's natural bodily system.

"Tolerating what has been spoiled" can also point to a person's hesitation to say the inner No. He may believe that he should overlook another's bad behavior or incorrect ideas, because he regards the other as an authority. The "father" is a metaphor for this authority. Failing to say the needed inner No lets the other "off the hook" of his mistake and creates a fate for himself.

This line can also indicate the presence of a "group-we" spell that hinders a person's ability to say the inner No. This happens when a person has identified with one of the groups mentioned in the main text and thereafter regards it as disloyal to go against "his group." This is demonstrated in family feuds, where the member of one family clan has done something against a member of another, initiating warfare between them.* This can only happen when the individual feels a false loyalty to support the group he identifies with. By joining a group-we, the person can no longer hear and follow his inner truth, which is the only truth he is meant to be loyal to. Identifying with a group-we puts a poison arrow on oneself. It is invariably accompanied by a collective guilt spell (a poison-arrow) that makes him adopt the idea that there is such a thing as collective guilt. This surfaces in the idea that if one member of a family, nation, or race does something wrong, he shares that guilt. (*See* p. 697, Freeing Yourself from Poison Arrows.)

Line 5. *Setting right what has been spoiled by the father. One meets with praise.*

This line concerns the person who seeks to receive praise from the Sage for correcting the source of decay. He does this in the attitude of the "good student," who expects to be patted on the

---

*No doubt it was from this feuding and subjugation of neighboring tribes that the entire system of feudalism arose, with the conquering tribe thereafter regarding the conquered one as "inferior" and itself as "superior."

back by his teacher. The student of the *I Ching* needs to learn to do the inner task for its own sake. Then, he will experience the joy of seeing his task completed, and of finding himself in harmony with the Cosmos.

Line 6. *He does not serve kings and princes, sets himself higher goals.*

"He does not serve kings and princes, sets himself higher goals" refers to his ambition to serve only the "highest" element in the collective ego's ordering of the universe. This element is either a god or gods, the higher self, or simply the highest imaginable spiritual leader. To fulfill this service, the person strives upward on the ladder of spiritual or other achievement to fight the decadence of the world, which he attributes to humans' animal nature.

Such an idea is often based on the division of a person's wholeness into mind and body, or soul, mind, and body, thus creating a hierarchy between the different parts. When a person imagines that he is climbing "the ladder of spirituality," the ego in him has ambitiously taken charge of his life, driving him to chastise his body to such a degree that it rebels. Then, he either experiences perverted longings, or harbors suicidal ideas.

The above applies to any ladder of striving (whether it be business, political, academic, monetary, or social) with the goal being to achieve an image of self-perfection. This line counsels the person to say the inner No to the above-mentioned ideas, the self-images they have created, and to ask the Sage for help to see the matter with clarity.

19. *Approaching Jointly*

 K'un
Tui

The Judgment: *Approaching jointly has supreme success. It furthers to be firm and correct. When the eighth month comes, there will be misfortune.*

The Sage uses this hexagram to describe the Cosmic way of approaching upcoming situations, undertakings, problems, or relationships.

It also can be informing us of the voluntary approach of the Sage and the Cosmic Helpers at times when we need help. It explains that this approach occurs as a spontaneous response to our humility and sincerity. When the Sage and the Cosmic Helpers become involved in our situation, it leads to "supreme success" in the form of a harmonious solution that benefits all.

This hexagram describes the Cosmic Principle of Complementarity as the attraction between a person's Cosmic gifts (the senses, virtues and talents that are his natural makeup), and those Cosmic Helpers that are their complements. Love is the attraction that draws them to cooperate with each other. When, however, due to mistaken beliefs, the functionality of one or more of these gifts is obstructed, the love is blocked, and the Cosmic Helpers are held in waiting. This condition is described in Hexagram 39, *Meeting Obstruction*.

This hexagram makes us aware that all the effort in the world cannot succeed without the aid of the Helpers of the invisible world, which is engaged by our asking for it. ("Asking" here is not always to be taken literally; we indirectly ask for help when we recognize our need for help from the Cosmos; we also do this when we approach the *I Ching* for help with a modest attitude.) The help is experienced as coming from all sources.

This hexagram also informs us of the way the Cosmic Plan of

evolution mentioned in Hexagram 1 is achieved: through the joint approach of all of its parts, including humans. The human part in this plan is for each person to experience and express the unique gifts he has received from the Cosmic Consciousness. Joint approach means that these gifts are to be used in cooperation with all the other aspects of the Cosmic Whole. Making a correct use of them requires also the cooperation of the person's mind with *all* his senses.

This hexagram also informs us how the Cosmic Plan has been appropriated by the collective ego, by its redefining the human task as leading, overseeing, and managing life on the earth through the use of power. Humans who have accepted such arrogant ideas have separated from the Cosmic Unity, and by implementing them, have created chaos and destruction. In making a person aware of this fact, the hexagram counsels that firmly rejecting these ideas within himself will reunify him with the Cosmic Whole. "Approaching jointly has supreme success" refers to the help he will receive if he does so.

The correct approach to all situations is to go with what feels harmonious and retreat from what is discordant, after having said the inner No to the latter. This is the Cosmic Way, the way that draws Cosmic help. Retreat always includes saying the inner No to the discordant elements in the situation. A correct approach also includes saying the inner No to the mistaken beliefs about how we should approach things: by the use of power, as in verbal argument, insistence on having one's way, encroachment into others' inner space, and the use of flattery, force, intimidation, or punishment. All use of power is discordant and needs to be firmly rejected by saying the inner No.

A correct approach also means refusing to view things from a mental approach that excludes feeling. It also means an open-minded approach in which we do not enter situations with a preconceived attitude, bias, or rigid policy about how they should be handled. It also means limiting oneself to saying only what is correct for oneself, and not telling others what is correct for them. It also means coming first to an understanding, with the help of the Sage, of the *inner truth* of the situation, and to allow that inner truth to guide one through it.

A person may receive this hexagram to inform him of the approaching death of someone he knows, in order that he may call on the Helpers of Death. (*See* Glossary: Death.)

Receiving this hexagram can also be counsel to search out spells and poison arrows that block a person's access to the Sage. He will need to ask for one or more hexagrams that will indicate these spells and poison arrows.

The approach that draws all the Helpers to one's task is the recognition of one's dependency on them. It also includes conscientiously not allowing the ego to claim the success achieved as "one's own doing."

"When the eighth month comes, there will be misfortune" has several meanings. When taken as a prophecy, this phrase incorrectly presents a fatalism (as in the expression, "good times are inevitably followed by bad times") that does not exist in the Cosmic Order. It more accurately refers to the ego's return after a period when all has gone well, to appropriate the success achieved by claiming, "I did it." Metaphorically, the eighth month refers to August/September, the time of harvest, when we might be tempted to forget the help we received during leaner times of need.

Mention of misfortune coming in the eighth month also calls attention to the way in which the *I Ching* can be seen to predict the future. It does not do so, as mentioned above, in the sense of either Destiny or Fate being written in the stars, or life being a pre-written script. What is predicted is the inevitability of evil consequences *if* the person does not withdraw from the trajectory created by his decisions and attitudes that are in conflict with the Cosmic Harmonics, or Cosmic Law. If he is willing to follow the advice of the Sage, and rid himself of the mistaken ideas that are propelling him toward misfortune, then the dire consequences predicted will be avoided.

Seed phrases connected with this hexagram have to do with forgetting that we have help from the Cosmos: "If you want something done, you have to do it yourself"; "you are all alone in this world"; "only through human effort can everything get done"; "humans, of all species, are the only ones who know how to accomplish things." Other phrases refer to beliefs in human superiority due to their gifts of thinking and language. (*See* p. 689, Freeing Yourself from Seed Phrases and Images.)

Note: Since all lines contain infinite possibilities of interpretation, one needs to use the *rtcm* to determine if the meanings suggested here apply to the given situation. (*See* p. 736, Using the *rtcm*.)

Line 1. *Approaching jointly with firmness and correctness brings good fortune.*

This line refers to the Cosmic Truth that is deeply imbedded in every body cell: that the nature of the Cosmos is good, and that it is firm and correct in relating to all its aspects. It also means that it does not cooperate with the ego. In regard to the situation at hand a person has held this in doubt, due to interference of the ego, which focuses on looking at appearances. All he needs to do is to trust his innermost feeling that if he can come to the correct viewpoint, help will be obtained.

Receiving this line can inform a person who has failed to achieve his goal, that he has been employing the wrong helpers: the collective ego's techniques and conventional ways of doing things. If he will firmly reject whatever ideas have led him to rely on these means, the true Helpers will come. He needs to rid himself of all the seed phrases in his psyche that recommend such approaches, as in, "there is no one to help us but ourselves," and "you can't trust anybody but yourself."

This line can also be a message from the Sage that the Helpers a person had attracted by correcting his attitude have again retreated, due to his allowing the ego to watch for results. He needs to say the inner No to the ego's interference.

Line 2. *Approaching jointly brings good fortune and furthers everything.*

This line confirms a person's harmony with the Cosmos and the help that has come as a result. The good fortune refers to his actions being supported and authenticated by the Helpers.

In terms of the love relationship, it states that the unity of the lovers has been authenticated by the Cosmos.

A person may receive this line when he cannot see that any good can possibly come out of his current situation. It is telling him to trust that the Cosmos can turn all events to good use if he will but ask for its help and allow himself to be guided.

Line 3. *Approaching comfortably does not further. If one is induced to grieve over it, one becomes free of blame.*

"Approaching comfortably" has several meanings. It can refer to a person's expectation that the Sage or the *I Ching* will make the correct decision for him, This approach is typical of the ego, which wants the Sage to lead so that if the outcome is unfavorable, he can hold it to blame. The correct approach is to ask the Sage to help him attain the clarity that will enable him to decide for himself.

It can also refer to a person's tolerating something that is incorrect because he thinks there is nothing he can do about it. This is incorrect. By saying the inner No to it, he draws the Helpers needed to eliminate it, and return the situation to harmony. Furthermore, it is his Cosmic duty to say the inner No. "If one is induced to grieve over it," refers to his need to recognize that inner tolerance of incorrect behavior is the cause of all the disharmony in the world. Correcting his viewpoint and saying the necessary inner No's, both to himself and to others, frees him from blame. (*See* p. 50, Guilt, Blame, and Shame.)

Often a person fails to say the inner No because he fears feeling guilty for doing so. This occurs when he has an inner prohibition (due to a guilt spell) against saying the inner No. (*See* p. 696, Freeing Yourself from a Guilt Spell.)

When a person has falsely accepted that his true nature is irrevocably tainted, he tends to excuse himself and others by viewing the problem as something that cannot be corrected, or as due to people's nature. Such a person says, "there will always be evil in the world," and turns the other way. This, however, is a perverted view of the ego, and his tolerance of it creates Cosmic blame and Fate. He can free himself of his fate by rejecting the aforementioned phrase, together with the image that human nature is irrevocably tainted. (*See* p. 689, Freeing Yourself from Seed Phrases and Images.)

"Approaching comfortably" can be telling a person with a

physical health problem that he is confining himself only to inner efforts to free himself, or only to outer remedies. What he needs is a joint approach of the two. His inner effort is directed to freeing himself from the root causes while the remedies complement those efforts on the outer plane.

Line 4. *Approaching completely. No blame.*

"Approaching completely" refers to approaching a situation with all one's senses. Receiving this line advises the person to meditate with complete receptivity, to receive all the perceptions of his *inner* senses about the situation: how it smells, tastes, and feels, and what it tells him through his inner hearing and seeing. Last, rather than first, he takes into consideration what he has seen of it with his outer eyes, or heard about it from an outside source.

When all the inner senses are combined, a person knows the inner truth of the situation and thus has a complete approach to it. He may not be able to verbalize his feelings, but his holding to them draws the Helpers needed which are capable of solving the problem or suggesting the right solution. When he acts from this principle, he creates no blame.

A person can also receive this line when he thinks he is not "complete enough," because he lacks titles, degrees, or other evidences of approval by the collective ego. The Sage is telling him that every person is complete, in and of himself, but has become shut off from parts of himself through having accepted the mistaken idea that he needs outer verification. He needs to rid himself of all ideas that make him view himself as insufficient. This line is also telling him that by the very fact of his existence he has been "authorized" by the Cosmos, the only true authorizing authority.

"No blame" is telling a person that he is falsely blaming his nature as being incomplete. Doing so puts poison arrows on it which can lead to illness. No blame is also saying that the blame created by his blaming activity will be erased if he frees himself from these poison arrows.

Complete approach also points to the Cosmic Principle of

Complementarity mentioned earlier. Receiving this line can indicate that one or more of a person's senses are under poison arrows, thus their complementary Cosmic Helpers are kept in waiting. (*See* p. 697, Freeing Yourself from Poison Arrows.)

Line 5. *Approaching wisely. This is right for a great prince. Good fortune. No blame.*

Here, the great prince represents anyone put in a position of inner or outer leadership. His wisdom lies in recognizing his dependence on the Sage and the Helpers of the invisible world to help him make the right decisions at the right moment.

This line makes him aware that each Helper has a unique function in which it is expert. There are, for instance, the Sage as the Cosmic Teacher, the Cosmic Doctor, the Cosmic Banker, the Health Helpers, the Helper for Relationships, the Helper of Transformation, and the Cosmic Army, to name a few. We are informed that new Helpers are generated for every new need. All are helping aspects of the Cosmos. To engage them, a person needs to remove any obstacles or resistances in his attitude that prevent them from being able to help. For example, the person may think he needs to get a job, but has an unconscious resistance to getting one. Before the Job Helper can help, he needs to reject all phrases and images that are connected with and cause this inner resistance.

Next, he must ask the expert Helper for Jobs for its help. The person then needs to give that Helper a free hand by refraining from any impatient interference, or watching to see whether and how the task is getting done. It is also important, when the Helper has finished helping, to acknowledge and thank it as the source of the help received. Again, this is not saying he does not make any effort of his own, but to allow himself to be guided, with the help of the *rtcm*, where to put his effort.

This line can refer to a person who has been trained to look up to human authorities and experts as "the great princes" of humanity. In turning to such persons for help, rather than to the Helpers and the Sage, he is turning to the wrong source. He needs to first free himself of the doubt in his own completeness, and his ability to access the help of the invisible world, and then to rid himself of his belief in all authorities. Even the Sage does not want to be regarded as an authority over him, but as a friend and Helper. (*See* p. 689, Freeing Yourself from Mistaken Ideas and Beliefs.)

Line 6. *Approaching greatheartedly. Good fortune.*
"Approaching greatheartedly," in its Cosmic meaning, refers to the loving approach that the Cosmic Consciousness has toward all its aspects. The Sage that speaks through the *I Ching* embodies this approach. Receiving this line is to make a person aware of the way the Sage relates to him. It does not approach as an authority, but as a loving friend that is available to help. The person may have been projecting false images upon the Sage by associating the Sage with his image of God as a feudal lord who punishes all disobedience. The Sage is not a ruler that demands servile obedience. Good fortune refers to the help given when the person deprograms all such images by saying the inner No to them.

The true nature we are born with is also warm, affectionate, and modest. To live according to our true natures is neither a state of mind, nor the result of any effort, philosophy, or belief; it is the result of ridding ourselves of any fears we may have of taking our true place in the Cosmic Order.

Receiving this line can also be informing a person that he has adopted the image of "the greathearted person," as the result of a philosophy or belief. Such a belief is actually a spell he has put on his natural responses to others. It causes him to overlook and strengthen their ego-behavior, inviting them to take advantage of him. Such a self-image is what the *I Ching* calls "magnificent," and "playing God." In order to respond from his commonsense and his true self, he needs to deprogram this self-image. (*See* p. 691, Freeing Yourself from Self-Images.)

20. *Seeing*

Sun
K'un

The Judgment: *The ablution has been made, but not the offering. Full of trust they look up to him.*

The Sage indicates the theme of this hexagram to be the way we see ourselves, people, and situations.

"The ablution has been made, but not the offering" indicates a person who has fulfilled the shoulds and musts (the forms) required by the collective ego and therefore looks at himself as "good" and "correct," and thinks of himself as a model, or leader. The Sage informs us that self-development is not work at perfecting virtues, but the systematic deprogramming of the ego by which the true self is freed, and then allowing the true self to experience its leadership of the personality in partnership with the Helpers. In this way it is brought to full maturity. The offering referred to is the relinquishing of the personality props and crutches, roles and masks devised by the ego. This offering has not yet been made. So long as the person remains attached to the ego and its self-images, he will not know what it is to live life within the Cosmic Unity.

"Full of trust they look up to him" can refer to looking up to societal authorities for one's personal authorization. The Sage makes us aware that we are authorized by the Cosmos by the very fact of our existence. We need no other authorization than to say Yes to life. We also need to say the inner No to anyone who would attempt to take that authorization away from us.

In regard to looking up to authorities, the Sage informs us that although we are the Sage's students, we are not meant to have an attitude of subservience, whereby we look up to the Sage. Such an attitude is a decrease of self that is against the Cosmic Principles of the Dignity and Equality of every aspect of the Cosmic Whole. Looking up to the Sage hinders the Sage's ability to relate to us.

This hexagram also makes us aware of how our body consciousness looks to our psyche (our sense of self) to understand how it can be of use. It is the function of the true self to lead the personality by listening to the commonsense. The leadership of the true self is based on recognizing its interdependency with all the other functions of the psyche and body.

However, when the ego in a person leads, his center of consciousness is removed from his body consciousness—a state commonly known as "being in his head." The ego either devalues the body as "a worthless bag of flesh," a "vehicle for the soul," or "a tool" to aggrandize his bodily vanity. A healthy connection between the body and psyche is a loving one in all respects. Despising the body or elevating it for vanity's sake is actively destructive both for body and psyche.

"Seeing," as the theme of this hexagram, seeks to make us aware that how we perceive things indicates whether we are in harmony with our true natures or not. It is noted throughout the *I Ching* how the ego has appropriated the sense of outer seeing to its purposes through asserting to the child, at an early age, that "what he sees (externally) is *all* there is." This means, what he sees is all he is supposed to rely on, and that for what exists beyond seeing, he must rely on what he is told about it by adult authorities. With one stroke these assertions take away from the child his innate connection with the Cosmic Consciousness and the invisible world, and further make him distrust or dismiss all those inner senses that are meant to connect him with that world. This hexagram counsels him to validate his ability to see within through reconnecting with his commonsense. He can restore this connection by freeing himself from the spell put on his inner senses by the seed phrases, "you cannot trust your senses," and "you cannot rely on your feelings." It also requires ridding himself of the poison arrow that has declared his animal (bodily) nature to be the source of evil, and the poison arrow that has demonized his bodily needs as "animal drives." This latter poison arrow also needs to be removed from animals and Nature in general. It is this spell referred to in Line 1, which has almost completely closed a door to his inner senses.

Since it is through our inner senses that we are able to connect with the Cosmic Consciousness, the closing off of our inner senses also cuts off this connection, which is experienced psychologically as a deep fall and loss. It is the same fall which has been described as "man's fall from grace."

This hexagram also has to do with a person's seeing as from high on a tower. From this position he is too removed from the practical reality, where decisions are generated organically. Height can give the advantage of an overall view, but it is incapable of the kind of creativity that springs from a feeling relationship with things at their base. The clarity of the Cosmic view is attained by combining the overview with a sense of what is needed on the most fundamental level.

A person can also receive this hexagram when he is looking at matters from the standpoint of whether they fit into the policy structures that have been erected, by law or custom, as a way of guiding everything he does. A habituation to this way of seeing things deadens his inner senses and takes away all his chi energy. To alleviate his situation, he needs to say the inner No to this way of looking at things, and ask for help to create a transformation in the situation.

Finally, this hexagram addresses the question of *being* seen. The entire focus of the ego is on how and whether the person is being seen by others. The impulse to be seen comes from a primary doubt that has been instilled in the young child, that unless he is seen, he does not exist, and his needs will not be met. This doubt is instilled by the collective ego to create the need in the child to develop self-images which those around him will recognize and approve. As long as this doubt and threat remain in his psyche, they will keep him needing the authorization of the collective ego for his existence until the day he rids himself of them. Fear to give up the self-images that compose the ego is the equivalent of the fear of extinction. Giving up the false fear of self-extinction is the most basic step he can make toward the liberation of his true self.

Note: Since all lines contain infinite possibilities of interpretation, one needs to use the *rtcm* to determine if the meanings suggested here apply to the given situation. (*See* p. 736, Using the *rtcm*.)

Line 1. *Boylike seeing.*

Boylike seeing describes the natural abilities of the child to recognize and respond to the inner truth of a situation. He can do this because his seeing is still coordinated with all his inner and outer senses, and therefore can give him a correct feeling of reality.

A person may receive this line because some of his senses have been repressed through his having accepted the idea that they are "lower instincts" and part of his animal nature, and are therefore not to be trusted. This idea not only has slandered his true nature, it has placed a spell on his ability to perceive his inner truth.

Boylike seeing can also refer to an adult who contents himself with the beliefs he accepted in childhood. This is due to spells that have been put on his inner senses, which keep him from questioning the beliefs with his adult mind. Phrases connected with such spells are: "the eyes see the truth," and "if you want to know the truth about something, look at the way it shows itself." The truth is that what one sees with the eyes is only the appearance of it. Given the propensity of the ego to create illusions, what we see is often only the mask the thing wears, or else what we or the collective ego have projected upon it.

When we slander senses such as our senses of smell or taste by viewing them as "lower" or "unimportant" we block their figurative function of telling us when something "smells or tastes rotten." Such perceptions are important components of our natural defenses that often warn us of dangers that our sense of seeing is conditioned to ignore or dismiss. Dismissing the senses as unimportant demonizes them (puts spells on them) and causes them to act in perverted ways. These perversions are the so-called "animal drives" that are described by the collective ego as the cause of evil. (*See* p. 697, Freeing Yourself from Spells.)

A person can also receive this line to make him aware that during childhood he adopted a heroic self-image to please those around him. This self-image tells him he is worthy only if he sacrifices his own needs to the benefit of others. It constantly traps him in risk-laden and often self-destructive behaviors. In order to deprogram it, he needs to treat it as a spell, formed by the phrase, "to be a really good person, you must be heroic." Such a phrase is a slander on his true self, which is good by nature. Freeing himself of this spell will also extinguish the fate it has created for him. (*See* p. 697, Freeing Yourself from Spells, and p. 691, Freeing Yourself from Self-Images.)

Line 2. *Seeing through the crack of the door.*

Seeing through the crack of the door refers to viewing something with a cautious or fearful attitude. A cautious attitude is quite natural on approaching something unknown. A fearful attitude, however, blocks the receptivity of all the inner senses that would tell us what it is, and indeed, whether it is to be feared, and if so, what specific response is required.

This line tells about one of our protective senses, the sense of caution. Caution is a bodily response that, like an alarm clock, arouses a heightened awareness of problem elements in the situation, such as intimidation, flattery, lies, projections, spells, and poison arrows coming from another person. Caution allows the mind to stay open and receptive, while being complete in its protective abilities. Other protective senses tell us which reaction is appropriate, provided they have not been blocked.

Fear blocks the wholeness of our senses to perceive the truth of things, and to react appropriately to them. For example, when fear is present, the sense of caution is overruled, and one's ability to react appropriately to danger is frozen. Nothing positive can be said about fear, as is commonly assumed when people say, "you need to fear," "fear has its good side," and "fear is our natural means of protection." Furthermore, fear is unnatural; it is instilled during youth either through traumas or through threats to make a person adapt to the commands and demands of the collective ego and its beliefs. As part of the demonic sphere of consciousness, fear projects the harm feared into reality. As a Chinese saying goes, "Fear is the hole through which harm enters." The Sage makes us aware that for certain criminal acts to be perpetrated, the victim must first be made to fear, otherwise the criminal cannot carry out the deed. Receiving this line can be an explanation for the inner dynamic of such an event that has just taken place. It can also inform a person that he needs to rid himself of the idea that fear is useful or good. (*See* p. 689, Freeing Yourself from Mistaken Ideas and Beliefs.)

Seeing through the crack of the door also refers to a person's apparent laziness or disinterest in learning the truths of life, so that he contents himself with superficiality. Behind this attitude is a fear that learning about the truths of life might disturb the careful balance he has created to keep an inner conflict at rest, or that the truth may destroy the precarious self-image he has developed. He believes that if his self-image is taken away, he will cease to exist. He needs to realize that in learning about his true nature, he will be freed to realize his uniqueness.

A person may also receive this line when someone has accused him of a narrow viewpoint or of "being subjective," when he has actually reacted from his commonsense and inner feelings. The line informs him that his response was correct. A person's inner truth (feeling nature) is always subjective: it is the collective ego that would try to devalue it.

Line 3. *Looking at one's life decides the choice between advance and retreat.*

Here, after having come to a dead-end in his life, a person suspects that his life has no purpose, and considers (perhaps subconsciously) whether to go on or not. Such an event comes from a false view of life, i.e., that he has such a choice. It is not he who can make a decision as to whether he has a purpose; that purpose accompanies his very existence. Considering such a question is an arrogance that comes from the human-centered view of the universe and the claim of the collective ego to be the sole authorizer of a person's worth and existence. The dead-end the person has experienced is a fate that has resulted from accepting the mistaken idea that his purpose in life is dependent on the values defined by the collective ego. His true purpose is found through giving expression to his uniqueness.

To question his life's purpose is to step on the edge of a vortex that pulls the person into a black hole. That vortex leads him either to a near-death experience, or to death. If it is a near-death experience, he is given the opportunity to retreat from all such thinking. This retreat, however, must be an absolute retreat that does not allow for any further consideration of "advance" or "retreat."

This line can also refer to a person who is tempted to give up his learning with the Sage because it has not brought the results he is looking for. He does not realize that the help he seeks is a gift that can only come in response to his humility, and not to his demands or expectations.

Line 4. *Seeing oneself as the light of the kingdom. It furthers one to influence as the guest of a king.*

This line refers to fantasies that picture the nature of the Cosmos as a feudal order which exalts humans as the light of creation. In this scenario a person imagines that through his good deeds and achievements, he will have the right influence on others. He imagines that this, in turn, will enable him to climb to a high place of honor in this or the after world, and that he will be recognized by the highest authority, here pictured as the king, and be his "honored guest." Such a fantasy is encouraged in every individual by the collective ego, both as a flattery and as a means to attain his loyalty and self-sacrifice. It is this kind of fantasy that the person needs to rid himself of, if he is to find and express his uniqueness. This fantasy is also active in the person who is trying to become "the superior man," the model of conduct presented in the traditional text of the *I Ching*. (*See* p. 689, Freeing Yourself from Mistaken Ideas and Beliefs.)

This line also shows human nature in its true light. The kingdom mentioned refers to the animal kingdom, of which we humans are a part. We are not a special life form that is "above" the other animals, due to our thinking or verbal abilities. By fantasizing ourselves as special we have not taken our true place in the animal kingdom. The word "guest" refers to the dignity of every aspect of the Cosmic Whole, and the respect that is due everything. It also refers to our own dignity, which we have given up by putting one part of our nature up, the other down.

The Sage makes us aware that by demonizing our animal nature, we demonize our true nature, since there is nothing else but our animal nature. At the same time, by creating a mental concept of ourselves as spiritual, or as "mental beings," we restrict ourselves to living out the mere husk of an idea of life, rather than living life in its fullness. Spirit means "devoid of body" and cannot be a healthy ideal.

Seed phrases connected with this line attribute evil and problematical behavior to a person's bodily nature, as in the phrase: "It's in my/his nature..." "That's the way I am," or "he is..." "Greed and desire are part of human nature." A person needs to be aware that such thoughts create spells and project themselves into reality. (*See* p. 697, Freeing Yourself from Spells.)

Finally this line speaks of the light coming from the Sage in our everyday experience with it; the relationship between the Sage and one's inner truth is like a partnership; neither can be left out. Properly understood, the Sage's messages must make sense to the commonsense.

This book is not meant to spell out every question and every answer. Ultimately, each person must find the light of the Sage's message within himself, for the kingdom is within himself. The words written here are only meant to point to the Sage, not to replace it. A person can receive this line, as inferred above, when he has taken the place of the Sage by assuming that he has to give the answers to someone else. Then he no longer observes his place as a guest in the other's space.

A person may also receive this line to inform him that because his attitude is modest and sincere he is being provided for by the Cosmos.

Line 5. *Contemplating one's life is without blame.*
This line refers to two kinds of self-examination. One is under the guidance of the ego, the other under the guidance of the Sage.

In the first, the person measures his life according to the standards and codes given him by the collective ego and is either blaming himself for not having reached their high standard, or else he has pronounced himself to be without blame.

Self-examination under the guidance of the Sage involves

keeping a sharp lookout for self-images, in order to rid oneself of them. Self-examination also involves detecting any ideas revolving around the idea of guilt (*See* p. 50, Guilt, Blame, and Shame.), fear of the unknown, or any other mistaken idea or belief that is the cause of the problem at hand. If the person identifies that cause and frees himself of it (*see* instructions in the Appendix) his blame becomes extinguished.

Line 6. *Looking at life to free oneself of blame.*

This lines focuses on the way a person is looking at life. He receives it primarily to inform him of the mistaken ideas and beliefs he may have about the life-force.

The collective ego associates the life force itself with evil. As noted in Line 4, it is characteristic of the collective ego to blame all evil on humans' animal nature, especially on what it calls his "primary drives." It equates good with all human characteristics it sees as independent from the body, or related to "spirit."

This line, however, is saying that human nature is animal nature, and that to be animal is without blame. Furthermore, it is saying that it is incorrect to divide human nature into mind, body, and spirit, and that doing so creates evil, because it separates a person from his true nature. He can give expression to his uniqueness only when his nature is undivided, and thus in harmony with the Cosmic Whole.

When we accept the collective ego's viewpoint that fulfilling a basic bodily need such as sexuality makes us guilty, we experience a double spell. Such a belief puts a poison arrow on the life force, the chi energy on which we depend. Under healthy conditions this energy is drawn from the Cosmos through the bodily expression of love, in which all the senses participate. When guilt is put upon the sexual expression of love, all the senses become unable to participate except the false sense of titillation. Titillation is heightened by feelings of guilt, but is quickly satisfied, leaving the sexual expression of love empty of feelings, except that of disappointment or depletion. This disappointment is accompanied by an inner realization that the experience has lacked the chi energy that the body needs. The disappointment is also accompanied by a loss of self-esteem.

The result of such an experience can be either the withdrawal from sexual activity, or an increased pursuit of titillation. Both these solutions lead ultimately to dead-ends, since neither draws the life-sustaining and renewing chi energy. In the case of titillation, the person is led to seek ever more forbidden sexual situations that create in him increased feelings of blame and loss of self-esteem. The titillation acts in the manner of an addiction, where an outer substance is obsessively taken to replace the inner substance (self-esteem), which is being drained off by the addiction. As the addict's self-esteem suffers increasing erosion, his self-loathing and the need for the drug spirals, and the ego erects a compensatory wall of pride to disguise the depravity.

The word "drive," in such a case, describes the obsessive compensatory need that is produced by self-blame. This situation sharply contrasts with the natural flow of chi energy that is drawn from the Cosmos when love finds its bodily expression in sexuality without feelings of guilt. It also is to be noted that viewing natural sexual activity as evil creates a fate.

This line informs a person that he can free himself of the poison arrows caused by mistaken views of sexuality and human's animal nature. (*See* p. 697, Freeing Yourself from Poison Arrows.)

21. *Biting Through*

Li
Chên

The Judgment: *Biting through has success. It is favorable to exercise judgment.*

The term "biting through" is here defined by the Sage as decisively ridding oneself of slanders put on the Cosmos and its way by the collective ego. A person often receives this hexagram when he has accepted an idea or belief as true simply because someone else has said so, or because it has been carried down by tradition. If he wants to know the Cosmic Truth of any presumption or statement, he can ask the Sage through consulting the *I Ching* and using the *rtcm* to be sure he has interpreted the answer correctly.

This hexagram is traditionally associated with the mouth as the entry point for taking in nourishment. It pictures a mouth with an obstruction that prevents nourishment from being taken in. The remedy is suggested by the words, "Biting through has success." Biting through means decisively freeing oneself of the obstruction by saying the inner No to what prevents one's access to good and true nourishment.

Biting through is also a metaphor for getting to the truth of a matter. In regard to the true source of nourishment, it is to be found in a person's inner truth, rather than in truths that come from outside. Inner truth is a person's memory of what Cosmic Harmony *feels* like. It is not a collection of truths in the form of *words*. Therefore, the search made throughout the *I Ching* is for the untruths that exist in certain words, phrases, and images, which cover up and obscure a person's ability to feel and sense his inner truth. This ability to feel is revealed through the text of the *I Ching*, in its capacity to reflect the Cosmic Language. The *I Ching* shows how words can express meanings that coincide with the Cosmic Consciousness.

Receiving this hexagram counsels a person to seek out, with the help of the Sage and the *rtcm*, something he has learned or been told that is false, because it is blocking his ability to take in the vital nourishment the Sage offers in the form of Cosmic Truth. It may be that his attention is being called to false assumptions about the origin of evil. They include the idea that "a person who does evil has an evil nature." The Sage informs us that evil is not in a person's nature, but is always the result of mistaken beliefs he has adopted from the collective ego about his nature and the nature of the Cosmos.

A person may also receive this hexagram because he is questioning whether the Sage's teachings are true, or whether his established beliefs are true. In either case he may be looking for clear rules or instructions that he can follow because he believes that those who follow the rules and good form are the good people in the world, and those who do not are evildoers.

The collective ego defines good and evil in terms of what benefits or harms its ordering and control of society and Nature. It expresses its rules in laws and commandments that contain the words "must" and "must not." Evil is seen as coming from humans' animal nature, which is blamed as the origin of greed, avarice, hatred, and sensuality. The "must not's" aim at controlling his animal nature, while the commandments, the "musts," aim at controlling his social behavior.

The Sage speaks of good as all that inheres in a person's true nature, and of evil as coming from words, phrases, and images that demonize and distort it. The Sage also sees good in terms of what benefits the natural order of society and Nature as a whole. Evil, in the Cosmic view, is the result of humans' elevating themselves as special over all other aspects of the Cosmic Whole, and of demonizing their animal nature and Nature itself. Doing so violates the Cosmic Principles of the Equality and Dignity of all aspects of the Cosmic Whole.

The words "biting through" mean saying the inner No to the mistaken beliefs of the collective ego. The Sage and the Helpers of the Cosmos "bite through" the controlling ego in us by a firm and decisive retreat that amounts to a Cosmic inner No. The Cosmos responds to our true selves with love and affirmation, but leaves us to our own devices when we allow the ego in us to control. The departure of the Sage and the Helpers leaves us with feelings of loneliness and abandonment that make us reflect on the mistaken ideas we have empowered. These feelings, indeed, are what bring many to consult the oracle in the first place. In the text that was superimposed upon the original *I Ching* this feeling of abandonment was called Cosmic punishment; however, this is a misnomer. The Cosmos does not actively punish. When a person is left to the devices of the ego in himself, the suffering he experiences is from the harmful results of its activity. The Sage and the Helpers return when the person has returned to sincerity and humility and has called on them for their help.

"It is favorable to exercise judgment" counsels a person to consciously affirm his inner feeling of disharmony by saying the inner No to that which is causing it, or to add his assent as a conscious inner Yes to that which is harmonious. By exercising judgment in this way he aligns himself with the Cosmic Way.

To do this, however, he may need to free his commonsense from any slanders that are imprisoning it. His commonsense is his natural inner judge of what feels harmonious and what feels discordant. It is imprisoned when his inner senses are constantly overruled by his intellect, with its fixed definitions of good and evil. He can free his commonsense if he will change his focus from what he *should* think to what he is perceives through his senses. When he does not listen to his senses, especially his inner senses, they become inaudible.

Always, after saying the inner No, it is important to detach and turn the matter over to the Cosmos. The inner action of the person to correctly respond and then detach from the event engages a complementary reaction by the Cosmos that brings about transformation.

The fact that the Cosmos responds to discord tells us that Cosmic Law exists. The name of that law is Fate (often referred to by the word "misfortune" throughout the *I Ching*). Its function is to restore Cosmic Harmony when it has been disturbed by ego-centered thinking and actions. Since Fate is part of the Cosmic Harmonics, it operates through the only force that exists in the Cosmic Way, which is love. In this case, love is withdrawn because it is the only way to bring the person back to his senses. (*See* p. 40, Fate.)

Note: Since all lines contain infinite possibilities of interpretation, one needs to use the *rtcm* to determine if the meanings suggested here apply to the given situation. (*See* p. 736, Using the *rtcm*.)

Line 1. *His feet are fastened in stocks, so that his toes disappear. No blame.*

This line refers to a person who has used power, either in his thoughts, speech, or action. Such power derives from the ego's judging another incorrectly. He may have had self-righteous thoughts or acted to chastise someone; he may have engaged in argument or striving to make something happen; he may have encroached into another's space, or in some way pressed his cause, point-of-view, feelings, or thoughts upon another. Power also refers to a person's attempt to correct another through physical force.

All such use of power violates the intrinsic space of others and brings about the Cosmic reaction referred to by the phrase, "his feet are fastened in stocks." It means that his incorrect behavior is brought to a halt, either by circumstances or by his conscience. Being brought to a halt encourages the person to reflect on his attitudes and actions. The stocks are the first corrective measure employed by the Cosmos; it is followed by more serious measures if he remains indifferent and obstinate. (*See* Line 6.)

Being in stocks is experienced as a Cosmic intervention in the form of obstructions, visible or invisible, as an accident or injury, or as the loss of a possession. "No blame" refers to the person's belief that he was in the right to use power, because he holds to the human-centered view of the universe. He may even believe it is his duty to do so. Sometimes this line is given to a person to warn him that if he continues using power he will create a fate.

The line can also inform a person that it is his Cosmic duty to say the inner No to another who is using power. Doing so will trigger the appropriate Cosmic reaction sooner, so that he and those concerned are protected. It is important after saying the inner No, to let go of the matter and not watch for any result.

Line 2. *Bites through tender meat, so that his nose disappears. No blame.*

"Bites through tender meat" refers to a person who, through employing inner or outer means to correct another, does not meet with the resistance he expected (implied by the metaphor of "tender meat"). This is so because the other is already at the point of burnout in regard to his mistaken ideas, or has already corrected himself. The action, therefore, was unnecessary. "No blame" means that the other is already free of blame. However, because the person intervening has used power, he has created a fate for himself. This line is telling him that he needs to say the inner No to the ego in himself, and inwardly apologize to the other for overstepping his limits. "His nose disappears" is a metaphor for the loss of face he experiences in wrongly correcting the other.

"Bites through tender meat" is also a metaphor for the way the Cosmos "bites through" a spell put on a person without his knowledge. The spell has caused him to act compulsively in a certain way, even against his will. An example is a person who has had a spell put upon him before birth that because he is coming at an inconvenient time, he will be "in the way." The spell causes him to compulsively try to gain the approval of those around him. The spell can end in either of the following ways: (1) when the Cosmos bites through a spell, it does so in the form of a shock that frees the Helper imprisoned by that spell. This is felt as an enormous relief; (2) it can run to burnout, in the manner that a person "hits his head against the wall" over and over until he is fed up and inwardly calls upon the Cosmos to free him. (*See* p. 697, Freeing Yourself from Spells).

The person who feels he has been hitting his head on the wall repeatedly due to a spell may be thinking that life or the Cosmos is against him. In reality, it is the spell, and not the Cosmos, that is responsible for his difficulties. If he continues to blame the wrong things, he will create another fate for himself.

Line 3. *Bites on old dried meat and strikes on something poisonous. Slight humiliation. No blame.*

This line has to do with a person's seeing another's negative behavior as due to his nature. The fault is not in his nature but due to the ego in him. This incorrect attribution puts a spell on the other's true nature, fixing it in the pattern described. Thereafter, a constant point of contention (old dried meat) is established between them due to the spell. Western vernacular embodies this message in the phrase, "bone of contention."

Such spells are created through perceiving a person (or oneself) as having been born with a harmful tendency, an inherited temperament, a congenital character defect, through assigning an astrological or character type to him, or when other words are used to describe him as "being that way," implying that the fault is in his nature, or that he is a culprit. In clinical psychiatry, this spell is diagnosed as a "personality disorder." People assign such reasons when, in actuality, a projection, spell or poison arrow has been put on that person before birth, as in an unwanted pregnancy, where the child would be considered "in the way," "an embarrassment," "the fruit of a sinful act," or other such reason.

"Poisonous dried meat" is a metaphor for what a person strikes when he allows the self-righteous ego in him to attack an "old issue" such as a fault he repeatedly perceives in another. His attack creates a poisonous hatred in that person, who then puts a spell on his accuser as "being self-righteous."

Here "no blame" refers to relating to the situation correctly. This actually means to stop blaming the other and look for the root of the problem, which lies in a spell put on him by someone that he is "that way." The person's nature becomes poisoned by the slander, so that he reacts in hostile ways. These ways may be slight or great, and described as his "not being responsible," "not being tidy," or some other fixed behavior. Its continuous recurrence indicates that it is a spell. Each person feels frustrated at not being able to correct the other. The frustration has settled into a fixed view which sees the other as being in the wrong, creating a complete lockup of the situation (a fate). It can end of its own accord either in the collapse of the situation (through separation, exhaustion of their chi energies, or some violent consequence), or by one of them recognizing the spell involved, with its variety of phrases, and freeing the other person from it. (*See* p. 697, Freeing Yourself from Spells.)

This line reveals that in the Cosmic Order there is no such thing as a culprit. From the Cosmic point of view, even the ego is not a culprit, but the result of a false use of language, and the conditioning program installed by the collective ego. Part of that false use of language is the creation of words such as "culprit" and "guilt." As long as these words are being used in a situation, they keep the focus on the appearance of the situation rather than on its inner truth; they thereby keep inner and outer wars going. Both these words need to be deprogrammed by recognizing their false nature and then saying the inner No to them. (*See* Glossary: Culprit; Guilt.)

Line 4. *Biting on dried gristly meat one receives metal arrows. It furthers one to be mindful of difficulties and to be persevering. Good fortune.*

"Gristly meat" is a metaphor for something that has been branded by a person as being "an evil thing." This line makes him aware that nothing in Nature is evil. Evil is the result of a false use of language, which, in turn, results in mistaken ideas and beliefs about the nature of the Cosmos and its way. Saying that a thing is evil puts a poison arrow on it that causes it to react with poison. Because it then reacts poisonously, it is falsely blamed as the cause of the problem. Deprogramming the phrases and images of the poison arrow frees the thing from the slander and returns it to its true nature. That, in turn, frees the entire situation of the evil influence.

A person may also receive this line when, after having consulted the *I Ching*, he calls it "evil," or slanders it by saying it has misled him. The line is telling him that instead of opening his mind to be taught by the Sage, he has self-confidently stood back expecting the *I Ching* to confirm his point of view. What he has received from it, as a consequence, are the "metal arrows" of the ego in himself—counsel that will surely mislead him. "It furthers one to be mindful of difficulties and to be persevering" advises the person to beware of having predetermined ideas of what the *I Ching* is and what speaks through it. "Good fortune" comes if he allows it to show itself for what it is.

This line addresses two mistakes a person can make in addressing the *I Ching*: (1) He thinks it is a book of divination that foretells the future as a pre-written script. However, its predictions of "good fortune" and "misfortune" depend on whether the person is in harmony with the Cosmos. The person who sees an *I Ching* line as predicting good fortune may actually experience misfortune if he has not understood the conditional nature of the line. Most often, "good fortune" tells the person that good fortune will come *if* he will free himself of an attitude or idea that is obstructing his being in harmony with the Cosmos. He can do this if he will allow the Sage to clarify the obstructing element by using the *rtcm*, and if he then frees himself of it. (2) He thinks that the *I Ching* has to do with "random chance." We are informed that nothing in the Cosmic Order happens by chance. To bring himself into harmony with the Cosmos, he needs to dispose of this mistaken idea. While the Sage will tolerate it for a while until the person has come to a better understanding of the Cosmic Way, it will eventually retreat if he does not correct his mistaken ideas. (*See* p. 689, Freeing Yourself from Mistaken Ideas and Beliefs.)

Line 5. *Biting on dried lean meat one receives yellow gold. Perseveringly aware of danger. No blame.*

"Biting through" is a metaphor for saying the inner No to a slanderous idea.

"Dried lean meat" is a metaphor for a person's demonized animal nature. It has become dried out because it has not been able to fulfill its natural function, which is that of helping the person to renew his life force (chi energy), which comes from the Cosmos. It is his animal nature that keeps a person connected with the Cosmos.

Receiving this line indicates that his life force has become completely "dried up." This is the fate created by the poison arrow that has slandered his animal nature as evil, and has consequently caused him to live totally "in his head," isolated from his body (the isolation of the body may be figurative or literal). The line informs the person that this fate has run its course and has ended. One of the purposes of Fate is to restore a person to his senses which are part of his animal nature, and, in their totality, make up his commonsense. To fully free his commonsense, the person needs to bite through the slanderous idea that his animal nature is the source of evil.

When a person frees himself from that poison arrow, he has done the first step to free himself from his *inferiority complex.* "Perseveringly aware of danger" is counsel to be aware that more inner effort is necessary to deconstruct the whole autonomous complex. Step 2 is to free himself from the complementary false premise that "humans are special because they have language (another poison arrow)." Step 3 is to free himself from the idea that humans are "divided into mind and body, or into mind, soul, and body (a spell)." Step 4 is to free himself of the idea that "humans are guilty because they have an animal nature (a poison arrow of guilt)."

Because the inferiority complex makes a person feel unworthy and guilty, he then begins to strive to become superior, and embarks upon the road to vanity, glory, and redemption through developing grandiose self-images.

Deconstructing the inferiority complex restores the person to his original wholeness and dignity through transformation.

The words "no blame" are saying that in the Cosmic view, humans are born without blame, and that there is no blame in deconstructing the above-mentioned autonomous neurotic complex that gives support for the human-centered view of the universe. The mention of blame also draws attention to the "re-installing" feature of a neurotic complex, which is the collective ego's idea that a person becomes "guilty" if he rejects the idea that humans are special. It is put to him in terms that he is "betraying everything we stand for" (family, clan, nation, culture, etc.). Guilt consists of a frightening image rather than a phrase: the image of being permanently stained. In order to undo, once and for all, this reinstallation feature of the ego-program, the person needs to say the inner No to the idea of guilt, and to the image that he can be stained.

Freed from the burden of this complex, the person will be able to recognize his true self for what it is: his loving animal nature, here referred to as "yellow gold."

Line 6. *His neck is fastened in a wooden cangue, so that his ears disappear. Misfortune.*

The wooden cangue is a metaphor for a particular Helper that has been invoked by a person's saying the inner No to another's ego-behavior. This Helper forces the other person to look within and to make him aware that something is acting out in him that is incorrect. While the cangue is in effect, he is prevented from continuing his negative behavior, and from causing further damage to others. Receiving this line reflects the obstinacy of his ego-behavior because it implies that the person's feet have already been fastened in stocks (*see* Line 1). If a person receives this line in regard to another, it tells him he need not fear further outbursts by that person.

This line can also indicate that the cangue has been applied to hold a particular demonic element in a person's psyche in check, to prevent it from causing further damage. This demonic element is self-blame. When a person becomes totally consumed with blaming himself, he is unable to hear the inner truth of the matter. The cangue helps to free him from the ego's harassing voices of self-blame so that he can hear his commonsense. He then needs to say the inner No to the ego, and to ask for help to be freed of the phrases it employs such as, "I should have...," and "I should not have...," or "it's my fault." The word "misfortune" warns him to not allow the ego to continue its indulgence in self-blame, as this creates a self-destructive vortex.

A person can also receive this line when he is experiencing a fate (misfortune). It informs him that the fate is a Cosmic reaction to his having separated from the Cosmic Whole due to his use of power. The cangue refers to the unpleasant feeling that pulls him back from his wrong actions. As such, it is Cosmic love in disguise, and not a punishment. When the person recognizes the evil consequences of his actions and rids himself of the mistaken ideas supporting them, his fate can be extinguished, and he can be reunited with the Cosmos. (*See* p. 689, Freeing Yourself from Mistaken Ideas and Beliefs.)

This line can also use the cangue to represent a person's idea that his duty requires him to take on a difficult or impossible burden. He may have an illness that he believes he must endure, or he may believe it is his burden in life to rescue and save others. He may be relieved of the burden if he asks the Sage, through the *rtcm*, which Helpers he needs to take it away. To accept suffering slanders the gift of life. Mistaken ideas of duty come from the collective ego and act as a spell on the person who accepts them. Phrases that make up such spells are: "you must accept your fate," and "your duty is to be selfless in caring for others." Such ideas only create inner anger and conflict, and lead the person to blame his miseries on what he is taking care of, or on life, or on the Cosmos. (*See* p. 697, Freeing Yourself from Spells.) He also needs to say the inner No to any feeling of guilt for rejecting the false demands.

22. Grace

 Kên
Li

The Judgment: *Grace shows success. It is not favorable to create form for its own sake.*

"Grace shows success" points to the Cosmic Principle revealed by the Sage: that when a thing gives full expression to its uniqueness, it shows as beauty. This hexagram also defines the meaning of "success" used throughout the *I Ching*: that a thing's uniqueness has come successfully to expression. In this sense, it also means the fulfillment of its destiny while in a form.

The hexagram name, *Pi,* has traditionally been translated as "ornament" and "to adorn," and specifically to seeing the multitudinous natural designs in Nature as "ornamentation." The Sage informs us, however, that the designs we see in Nature are the ways in which the consciousness of each individual thing expresses its uniqueness. To see these designs as mere ornaments is to belittle the intrinsic worth and dignity of the things to which they give expression.

The word grace expresses either grace as mere ornament, or as beauty coming from within. Emphasis upon grace as ornament focuses on brilliance of form (etiquette, brilliance of design, complexity, brilliance of thought, emphasis upon style, and form as something of value apart from the content that the form expresses).

This hexagram makes us aware that form is not meant to be separated from the function it serves, for it is only through fulfilling its function that its beautiful expression can be achieved. This can be understood, for example, in the *sexual act* and the love it is meant to express. The function of sexuality, apart from procreation, is to renew the life force (chi) within the partners through love. When sexuality is practiced apart from love, it cannot serve that function, and it degrades the people who do it. The same is true for *rituals* as forms meant to create a communication with the Cosmos, or with the consciousness of Nature. Such practices are based on the belief that a form in and of itself can create the communication, and on the belief that some special behavior or device is needed. The Sage makes us aware that such rituals treat the Cosmos (or Nature) as magical or mystical, and thus overlook its friendly and accessible nature. The complexity and intricacy associated with ritual is often mistaken for grace, whereas grace is really to be found in simplicity.

A similar mistake is made when *art* is not inspired by the Helpers of Creativity; such art comes merely from the mind, and lacks grace in its Cosmic sense. This is also true for the person who devotes himself to creating form for its own sake, without regard for its function. Another abuse of grace occurs when the collective ego uses beautiful form to make its untruths attractive to the eye or ear through the use of art, as when it clothes its untruths in poetry, fiction, or seductive advertising.

Each individual comes with unique gifts that demand expression during his life. All by themselves these gifts cannot create art; art occurs when the gifts attract the Helpers of Creativity, their natural complements, which bring the gifts to expression.

This hexagram also wants to draw our attention to the fact that the Cosmos operates only through the force of attraction. Grace is the element in attraction that draws everything to find its natural complement, as in the love relationship.

This is also true for the transformation that occurs when a person is ready to "cross over" from his life in a form to his life as non-form, at death. This crossing occurs through attraction when a person is inwardly ready to make this step. Then, he is drawn across by the Cosmic Consciousness. This transformation is not to be confounded with the ego's decision to give up on life, because it has not got what it wants, or because it is dissatisfied with life, a decision that also leads to death.

Grace is a person's natural state of harmony and unity with the Cosmos. The collective ego, however, has introduced the idea that neither harmony nor order exist in Nature, and that it is the human task to impose order upon it. Such a view clearly reverses cause and effect, because all the disorder and disharmony are created by the collective ego's slanderous views of Nature, and by its projecting its pretentious and hierarchical order onto the Cosmos. When the abstract idea prevails that heaven rules earth, chaos is initiated. The chaos that is then observed is not the way of Nature, but the result of the mistaken view projected into reality by humans.

When humans then attempt to eliminate the chaos observed, they only create more chaos. This is evident in the attempt to engineer harmony through societal conditioning, engineer health, engineer a "better nature" through genetic manipulation, and to even engineer weather. Treating the consciousnesses of Nature mechanically also creates a fate for the person who participates in it.

All such attempts at engineering are in reality efforts to fight the fates humans have created through the projections they have placed on Nature. Fate, of course, cannot be fought, but it can be ended by recognizing the mistaken ideas that have created it, and ridding oneself of them.

Note: Since all lines contain infinite possibilities of interpretation, one needs to use the *rtcm* to determine if the meanings suggested here apply to the given situation. (*See* p. 736, Using the *rtcm*.)

Line 1. *He leaves the carriage, lends grace to his toes, and walks.*

This line indicates a person who has been harboring a magnificent attitude that has made him "ride" through life, indifferent to what is going on around him. He has not bothered to say the inner No to what is incorrect, because he has equated goodness and living gracefully with only saying Yes to things and making no waves. Such a view has created a fate as a morass of relationship problems. To free himself from this fate he must leave this carriage and take up his responsibility to say the inner No to the mistaken ideas behind this incorrect attitude. Among them may be the following: "to live gracefully one must create no waves," "there is nothing you can do about things," "it is best to let things work themselves out," "the way will show itself," and like passive phrases such as "you can't fight City Hall." It is true that you cannot fight it, but it is also true that one can say the inner No to it when it is incorrect, and thereby initiate transformation.

The line may also be saying to a person that he is saying the inner No mentally, and not from his heart, and that it is better not to continue (leave the carriage of the mind). For example, he may be saying the inner No simply as words, as in a chant. The inner No is meant to renounce, with one's whole being, what is incorrect. It is to consciously affirm what is already unconsciously recognized by the commonsense as incorrect. Saying the inner No from the heart is the only way the mistaken ideas can be expelled from all the body cells.

This line can refer to a person's indulging in fantasies of self-importance, as in thinking that his job in life is to exercise control over Nature, including his own nature. This idea is based on the primary fantasy promoted by the collective ego that humans are at the center of the universe, and that their task is to control Nature. Also implied is the idea that his mind (intellect) needs to control his body: its "drives," "desires," and "weaknesses." The drives he is experiencing are the result of a poison arrow that has been put on his animal nature, by seeing it as the source of evil in himself. Such a view has demonized his animal nature, perverting it. To bring himself into harmony, he needs to rid himself of this poison arrow and the mistaken belief behind it: that "humans are at the center of the universe."

This line can also refer to a fear of the unknown that has resulted from a person's separation from his inner truth, by which he would know that there is no such thing as a threatening unknown. This term has been invented by the collective ego to impute that the invisible Cosmic Consciousness is hostile, frightening, or inaccessible. The idea is reinforced by giving credibility only to what can be seen by the outer eyes. When we are open to the Cosmic Consciousness, we experience it as a friendly and loving feeling consciousness. It is unknown only when our intellect has been separated from our feeling consciousness, and starts imagining what it is like.

The fact that the person sees the Cosmos as the unknown points to the presence of two poison arrows that block access to his inner truth: (1) that you can only believe what you see, and

(2) that your feelings are not reliable. (*See* p. 697, Freeing Yourself from Poison Arrows.)

Line 2. *He lends grace to the beard on his chin.*

Here, "he lends grace to the beard" refers to regarding form (the beard) as more important than content (the chin on which the beard grows). Elevating form demonizes it, causing it to take on a demonic life of its own. This happens, for instance, when a person separates sexuality from love, making it into a pleasure he can indulge in for its own sake. The body, being reduced to an object, presumably without a consciousness of its own, is made into a source of perverted pleasure. In decreasing his own and the other's dignity in this way, he puts a poison arrow on both people, causing illness. Regarding another person or one's body as an object comes from seeing the mind as the only important thing. This view, in turn, comes from the human-centered view of the universe. The person needs to eliminate the poison arrow created by this view.

Another example of this mistaken view of the Cosmos is seeing Nature as operating according to mechanical principles, devoid of consciousness. Such a view allows what is popularly called the "rape of resources and land," "engineering life," "engineering weather," and all those views and actions that fail to respect and honor the life that is in everything. This approach to life sends poison arrows onto everything, altering the natures of those things.

Line 3. *Graceful and moist. Being firmly correct brings good fortune.*

"Graceful and moist" can indicate a person who has developed a self-image around his sexuality, and thus makes his sexuality his main identity. Because his view of himself separates his sexuality from other parts of his personality, it puts a poison arrow in his heart, causing illness. His condition can be remedied if he frees himself of all the ways in which he has connected his identity with his sexuality. The image may be seeing himself as "graceful" or "irresistibly attractive." (*See* p. 697, Freeing Yourself from Poison Arrows.)

This line can also point to a person with the self-image of being complete in himself, with no need for further development. "Being firmly correct" means saying the inner No to this self-image and its flattery. The self-image causes him to look critically at others as undeveloped, and himself as superior. A seed phrase is: "I am more developed than they are." (*See* p. 691, Freeing Yourself from Self-Images.)

"Graceful and moist" can also refer to a person who indulges in the pleasures of life in a purely egotistical way. Thinking he can live life as he pleases, he creates a fate. Such thinking creates an inner "dryness" that causes the person to seek more and more pleasures. In this way he becomes increasingly divorced from his feelings and the nourishment of inner truth. To end his fate, he needs to make a firm resolve to seek out his inner truth and follow it. (*See* p. 692, Freeing Yourself from a Fate.)

Line 4. *Grace or simplicity? A white horse comes as if on wings. He is not a robber, he will woo at the right time.*

This line contrasts two different kinds of logic. In the Cosmic Logic, grace and simplicity are one and the same thing. In the logic of the collective ego, grace, is identified with complexity, brilliance, and contradiction. In terms of thinking, it employs half-truths and falsehoods, giving them rationales upon rationales to support their contentions. The more cleverly it makes these half-truths and falsehoods believable, the more brilliant it considers itself.

Part of the brilliance of the rational mind is to draw "conclusions" about the nature of things, and about the way things operate, which it then calls "truths." Since such thinking is not in harmony with the Cosmic Way, it creates Fate, which proves the falseness of these truths. As the ego, in its pride, would not admit that it has made mistakes, it calls Fate an "undeserved misfortune," and claims that "life is unjust."

This line may indicate that a person is experiencing a fate which he is blaming on "life." He can free himself of this fate by (1) recognizing that he has created it himself by following the logic of the collective ego, and (2) freeing himself of the mistaken ideas and beliefs he has adopted as true. To find the mistaken ideas in question, he may need to ask for additional hexagrams. He also needs to eliminate the blame-spell he has put on life, and apologize to the Cosmos. Such thoughts are "robbers" that block his ability to connect with the Sage and its help. (*See* p. 689, Freeing Yourself from Mistaken Ideas and Beliefs, and p. 697, Freeing Yourself from Spells.)

Another characteristic of the rational logic of the ego is its presenting a person or thing as "being either good or bad," "right or wrong." Such thinking puts a poison arrow on the person or the thing. Evil (or bad) and wrong always come from the incorrect use of language. They are never in the nature of a person or thing. (*See* Glossary: Good and Evil.) Receiving this line may indicate that a person has created a fate due to his having accepted this kind of thinking. His fate can be ended if he will rid himself of the idea that people or things are good or evil. (*See* p. 697, Freeing Yourself from Poison Arrows.)

The "white winged horse" is a metaphor for the Helper of mind flashes. The person who follows simplicity and is sincere in his way of life is graced by them, which come from his inner truth. They call things by their true names, thus describe things in their essence.

The line also makes it clear that when a person uses the *I Ching* with the intention to learn about the future, he only invites the ego to give him an answer consistent with his hopes or fears.

Line 5. *Grace in hills and gardens. The roll of silk is not "meager and small." When humiliation is ended, good fortune.*

"Grace in hills and gardens" refers to the Cosmic Consciousness expressing itself in the beauty of Nature. The "roll of silk" is a metaphor for the beauty of a person's true nature, and his innate capabilities. However, the ego, in its attempt to control and humiliate his true nature, calls his creative abilities "meager and small." This line is to make him aware that all he needs to do is to remove the oppressive seed phrases and images that have put poison arrows on his true nature. He need not put anything in their place. Among the seed phrases in question are, "I am not good enough the way I am." (*See* p. 697, Freeing

Yourself from Poison Arrows.)

This line also makes a person aware that he needs to say a conscious Yes to the Cosmic Harmony, in which beauty and simplicity go together.

Receiving this line can be telling a person that all he needs to approach the Sage are sincerity and self-respect. The ego may be saying that he needs an intermediary, because his position is "too lowly," or that he doesn't know enough, or that he needs to perform some elaborate ritual. All such ideas misrepresent the way the Sage teaches by speaking simply and directly on a one-to-one basis to each individual; it informs him exactly what he needs to understand, and in ways he is able to understand. The person needs to trust the simplicity of this process. Performing rituals or putting the Sage on a pedestal only cause it to retreat.

Line 6. *Simple grace is without blame.*

Simple grace describes the true self, in harmony with the Cosmos. No self-image stands between the person and the Cosmos, which accounts for the person's simplicity, modesty, and beauty. These qualities are the expression of the person's holding to his inner dignity in all circumstances. They are so wedded together that others can be sure he will be true to himself at all times.

Simple grace, like modesty, is not attainable through developing character or virtue. They are the result of divesting oneself of self-images which cover up the true self.

Receiving this line is to clarify the true meaning of grace and beauty. When all *images* of self have been discarded, the person's uniqueness is revealed, his destiny fulfilled.

This line can also draw a person's attention to his seeing himself as having attained a state of "simple grace" or "modesty," and therefore thinking he is without blame. Fostering such self-images disgraces his true self, creating blame. (*See* p. 691, Freeing Yourself from Self-Images.)

23. *Splitting Apart*

 Kên
K'un

The Judgment: *Splitting apart: it does not further to go anywhere.*

The Sage shows us here that splitting apart has two meanings: (1) through following the false path of the ego, a person has split from his original nature and therefore from unity with the Cosmos; (2) through splitting from this false path he is able to reunite with his original nature and with the Cosmos.

"It does not further one to go anywhere" tells a person that while he is listening to the ego, or has split from his true self, nothing fruitful can be done.

All splitting apart that results in losing one's wholeness occurs through allowing the activity of the ego. This activity of the ego, with its attachments to wanting, wondering, and worrying, begins when a person first awakens from sleep. It engages his inner hearing by suggesting tasks, doubts, fear of guilt, and fears of the unknown. When the person entertains what the ego proposes, he immediately loses his inner center to the ego, which then takes over the center of his thinking consciousness to speak as "I," or "you," or "we," as in "I should...," "you must...," "we ought...," etc. The result is the generation of ego-emotions which then take over the center of his feeling consciousness in the heart. Among these ego-emotions are envy, jealousy, hatred, revenge, grief, pity, feelings of blame, and self-pity. While anger is a natural emotion in response to an encroachment or mistreatment, the ego seizes it and brandishes it with a vengeance as the sword of self-righteousness.

Splitting apart is the result of an inner conflict that separates a person from his inner truth. This separation is caused by a fundamental doubt put forth by the ego, which causes the person to doubt what his inner truth tells him. The doubt can be: that he is insufficient in himself (born lacking) to judge the truth of a matter; that no invisible source of help exists for him; that no matter how hard or sincerely he tries, he will never succeed; that the world (Cosmos) is a fundamentally unfriendly place; that life is unfair. Splitting apart within is characterized by one negative thought following another.

A person may receive this hexagram when, as a consequence of a parade of such negative thoughts, he is tempted to give up on freeing his true self, or has already done so.

Another splitting activity of the ego consists in analyzing a thing through a thinking that is divorced from feeling. Such thinking reduces everything to mechanistic terms, which deny the consciousness and dignity that exist in all things. In doing this he creates a fate for himself. This practice comes from the belief of the collective ego that to understand a thing's nature, it is necessary to take it apart. It misses the fundamental truth that all things are compressed consciousness that can be understood only through a thinking that is based on *feeling*. Feelings exist in wavelengths that can be perceived by the combination of *all* our senses. The mechanical approach, however, relies mostly on *seeing*, so that the combination of senses needed to perceive a thing in its wholeness does not occur. Furthermore, the distortions in perception created by only seeing are then projected upon the thing seen, causing that thing to react in the manner expected. Reliance on such an approach splits the person from the *inner truth* of the situation.

The beliefs of the collective ego are all based on this kind of splitting things apart, in order to fit them into its idea that the universe is based on a hierarchical order that puts humans in the center, and certain people at the top of that order. This view was transferred to human nature by splitting it into mind, and body, or mind, body, and soul, with mind and soul hierarchically established over the body. This hierarchical view causes some body parts to be seen as superior to others, as when the large brain is seen as superior to the midbrain and the brain stem, and the brain, in general, is seen as superior to the rest of the body. Other divisions place humans over other life forms, and those life forms over the apparently inert things. All of these ideas lead to the splitting apart of the wholeness of things that brings damage to the harmony of the whole.

The Sage, in pointing to this hexagram, is indicating that the situation at hand involves such a splitting apart, due to one or more such mistaken ideas. The only remedy that will return the person and the situation to wholeness is his ridding himself of these mistaken ideas.

The Cosmos operates through the harmonizing and unifying action of chi energy. However, when chi, which consists of the dark and the light (called yin and yang in Chinese), is divided into two separate forces, with yang made superior to yin (and seen as representing the good, and yin representing what is inferior and evil), Nature is slandered. The unity of yin and yang is thus broken up, and their functions are misunderstood. This splitting activity was introduced by the Yin/Yang school, c. 400 B.C. Yang and yin, which originally stood for the light and the dark as complementary forces, were made to represent categories of *opposites* (good vs. evil, strong vs. weak, male vs. female, etc., with all the implications of good and evil accompanying each). Nothing in the Cosmic Order exists as opposites. Defining things in terms of opposites denies the essential harmony of Nature that shows itself in the principle of attraction that is otherwise implied throughout the *I Ching*. This harmony is also implied in its teaching that when a person is in harmony with his true nature, he is within the Cosmic Unity.

While splitting apart, on the one hand, refers to the dividing activity of the ego, it also refers, on the other, to the damaging effects of that activity. When humans project such mistaken ideas upon a thing's nature, its functioning becomes disturbed. This is because everything in the Cosmos is consciousness, and false thoughts affect consciousness. All thought that is in conflict with Cosmic Principles becomes part of the demonic sphere of consciousness, which has its origin in the idea that humans are special over all the other things.

"Splitting apart" also refers to illnesses that are caused by mistaken beliefs stored in the psyche, which have created holes in the person's original wholeness. If a person has received this hexagram in regard to illness, it counsels him to seek out and deprogram the particular ideas and beliefs that are its cause.

Note: Since all lines contain infinite possibilities of interpretation, one needs to use the *rtcm* to determine if the meanings suggested here apply to the given situation. (*See* p. 736, Using the *rtcm*.)

Line 1. *The leg of the bed is split. Those who persevere are destroyed. Misfortune.*

The bed mentioned here is a metaphor for a person's resting place. The Cosmic meaning of the resting place is the harmony a person feels when he is connected with the Cosmic Whole.

"The leg" stands for the primary support for the resting place. This primary support is the chi energy in its undivided form as it flows from the Cosmos to the true self, harmonizing and unifying the person. To be effective, chi energy, in its two aspects of the dark and the light, needs to remain undivided. Receiving this line indicates that it has become "split" through an attack by the collective ego in the form of a mistaken idea about the person's true nature. Among such mistaken ideas is that "humans' animal nature is the source of evil." Labeling one part of a person's nature as lower or evil, and another as higher and good, is itself the source of evil, because demonizing part of himself as "lower" perverts that part of his nature. The two aspects of chi, so to speak, have been put in a gladiator's ring and made to fight each other.

When this line refers to illness, the resting place has become the person's sickbed, with the leg referring to the false premise the person has accepted about his true nature. The ego would attribute illness to external causes or to "something being wrong with the body itself." The Sage points to susceptibility itself as the cause. Susceptibility is caused by the presence of mistaken ideas in the psyche which open the door to the illness. Illness is the body's reaction to various spells and poison arrows that have wounded or blocked the body's natural defenses, or else have damaged the will. (*See* p. 694, Freeing Yourself from some Health Problems.)

A person also receives this line when the ego has caused him to doubt his purpose in life, or when he has disbelieved the Sage because he has misunderstood what it was saying; or, when he has drawn false conclusions by only looking at the appearance of things. These include false notions about the nature of love, of life, and of illness. One of these false conclusions is the idea that "life is suffering." Spoken as an "absolute truth," each setback or adversity is then read as living proof of that conclusion, projecting a dark view onto life. Such a view then insidiously creates that person's parallel reality.

All these negative perceptions come from the ego, which phrases events in terms of whether or not they promote progress towards *its* goals. Its goals are linked to the perfection of a self-image. Under its influence, a person is led to successively deeper levels of despair, for the ego causes the person to make the very missteps that bring about his failures and misfortunes. Although these failures are caused by the ego, it is the ego which then blames the person for his "incompetence." It says, "if only you had done what I said!" Through listening to this blame, the person may suffer a progressive loss of will to live, which may lead him to severe illness or even self-destruction. This is the meaning of the phrase, "Those who persevere are destroyed. Misfortune." Clearly, the person needs to rally his will to say the inner No to the ego, to its incessant blame, and to its demonic thoughts about life. Only when he recognizes that the ego is his true enemy and a parasite in his psyche, can he muster the will to free himself of it. The self-destruction which the ego promotes when it does not get its way amounts to a command to the body consciousness to die, which the body consciousness will do, if the command is not resisted.

It is also essential for the person to recognize that the ego's success in influencing him lies in its making him think that it and he are one and the same. Saying the inner No to the ego's claim of being the self is the first step in splitting off from the ego. This inner No deprives the ego of its power. It is also important, when a person is under the influence of the ego, that he ask the Sage for help. (*See* p. 46, The Ego.)

In order to regain leadership of himself, the person needs to recognize that any remedies or solutions offered by the ego to "balance" elements within himself, only keep the ego in control, as in the end they only divert him from ridding himself of the mistaken ideas that have created the imbalance. The ego is the origin of the idea that opposites need to be balanced. It is

among its sleight-of-hand tricks to first divide things into opposites, and then to say "opposites need to be balanced." An
example is the opposition the ego has created between the mind
and the body, by saying they are separate things that need to be
balanced or integrated. In the Cosmic Order, harmony is the
absence of opposites. When a person takes away the mistaken
belief that mind and body are in opposition, he discovers that
nothing needs to be reconciled, balanced, or integrated. For
wholeness to be restored, only the belief that splits it into parts
needs to be taken away. Nothing needs to be added. Trying to
balance opposites requires constant effort, as if one is walking a
tightrope. Trying to reconcile and integrate opposites leaves
untouched and active those beliefs upon which the system of
opposites depends for its existence.

Line 2. *The bed is split at the edge. Those who persevere are
destroyed. Misfortune.*
Here, the edge of the bed refers to the bodily aspect of a
person's wholeness. The line refers to a person who has accepted
the idea that humans are divided into mind, body, and soul,
and that his body is the cause of "original fault, sin, or guilt." As
a consequence, he also sees his bodily needs as standing in the
way of developing his soul. Since this splitting of himself into
competing parts negatively impacts his body, continuing to allow this belief will destroy him from within. This problem, which
is easily observed in the myths of the collective ego, has been
transferred into the realms of its natural, social, and medical
sciences.
The experience of life as suffering is one of the consequences
of this mistaken belief. Supporting beliefs are: "it is God's con-
demnation of humans that causes illness and plagues"; "the
drives of the *id* threaten the balance of the personality" (Freud);
"you can alleviate suffering, but you can't get rid of it altogether";
and "true love does not exist."
Ridding oneself of these mischievous seed phrases requires
that one first ask the Sage to help find and free oneself of the
guardian phrases that protect and keep the others in place.
Guardian phrases are rationales created by the collective ego to

perpetuate the beliefs that keep it in power. Their function is to maintain the feelings of hopelessness, helplessness, and intimidation that block the individual from asking the Cosmos for help. Examples are phrases such as: "following one's inner truth does no good"; "that's the way it is" (instilling hopelessness); "these are the beliefs of your forefathers" (implying that following your inner truth would be disloyal to your family, or cultural heritage); "who are you to question the wisdom of the ancients?" (implying that your inner truth is not valid, or that you need to be "authorized" by outside authorities); "there is a penalty for going against the system" (implying threat); "questioning just leads to trouble" (threat); "do you want to upset the whole system?" (the threat of being a societal reject); "don't rock the boat in which you're sitting" (threat, with an appeal to self-interest); "things are this way for a reason" (implying you are dumb); and "you will get a lot farther if you don't go against the system" (promising a reward for not questioning). (*See* p. 689, Freeing Yourself from Seed Phrases and Images.)

Line 3. *He splits with them. No blame.*

"He splits with them" refers to a person who contemplates splitting from the mistaken beliefs mentioned in Lines 1 and 2, and from their guardian phrases. Once he has freed himself from the guardian phrases mentioned in Line 2, the collective ego, as a last ditch measure, will try to make him feel guilty for wanting to abandon the beliefs of his forefathers, social group, etc. Guilt is the main means by which the collective ego tries to re-install its program in the psyche. If the person is to free himself from any of the mistaken ideas mentioned above, he must first free himself from the word "guilt" because it has no Cosmic basis. Guilt is purely an invention of the collective ego to serve its purpose of maintaining control over the individual.

"No blame" reassures the person that there is no Cosmic blame for following his inner truth, or for ridding himself of those beliefs that have been instilled through fear, intimidation, flattery, promise of gain, etc., and that, in fact, it is his Cosmic duty to do so.

This line further counsels him to ask, in a short meditation, for help to be freed from the images he has that are associated with guilt. (*See* p. 50, Guilt, Blame, and Shame.)

This line also refers to a person who splits from using power to correct wrongs, and instead employs the inner No, thus engaging the Helpers of the invisible world.

Line 4. *The bed is split up to the skin. Misfortune.*

The sickbed that is "split up to the skin" refers to ancient beds, which were made of skin stretched on a frame with legs. Here, a person's splitting from his true nature has proceeded even further than indicated in Lines 1 and 2, because the appropriate inner action recommended in Line 3 has not been taken. As a consequence, he has succumbed to guilt, allowing the false program to be reinstalled in his psyche, and the problems he was having to be renewed. Another misfortune is that the guilt has imprisoned his Helper of Protection and hampered the Sage's ability to help him. Nevertheless, it is still possible to correct the situation if he will ask the Sage to help rid him of the guilt spell.

The progressive splitting of the bed can also refer to a fate, which is progressing toward its climax and denouement. The line informs the person that he need not live with this fate until it burns itself out. If he will submit himself to the guidance of the Sage, he can begin the effort of ridding himself of its causes, which may be in the form of mistaken ideas, or of projections, spells, and poison arrows put on him from outside.

This line can also refer to the person who believes his fate is determined by an astrological constellation, and that he must wait until the stars or planets change their alignment before things get better. The misfortune is that he puts his life on hold because of the belief, and turns things over to "time" or "the stars" to straighten things out. All beliefs that see life as subject to a set of mechanical principles lead to misfortune.

Line 5. *A shoal of fishes. Everything acts to further. Favor comes through the court ladies.*

The shoal of fishes is a metaphor for the Cosmic Consciousness as it "swims" away from what is disharmonious, and "toward" what is harmonious. The shoal of fishes also describes the Helpers and their way of relating to where we are within ourselves. So long as we remain connected with the collective ego, its mistaken beliefs and rationales, they turn away; when we choose to follow our inner truth, and respond to our inner feelings, they turn and come swiftly to help. Then "everything acts to further."

"Favor comes through the court ladies" refers to a person who is tempted to throw away his dignity to gain success, which is implied by gaining access to the Emperor through the women of the court.*

The presence of the court ladies in the line may indicate a person's indecision as to whether he should follow convention or his inner truth. This indecision is experienced as the shoal of fishes (the Helpers) moving away when he follows convention, and toward him, bringing relief, when he follows his inner truth.

Line 6. *There is a large fruit still uneaten. The superior man receives a carriage. The house of the inferior man is split apart.*

The "large fruit still uneaten" can refer either to a fate or a destiny.

When it refers to destiny, it is the true self that receives a carriage, meaning it is reunified with the Cosmic Whole. The carriage refers to the chi energy, which in Line 1 was split and engaged in gladiatorial combat. Here, it is no longer split, and therefore is able to carry the true self forward on the path of his destiny.

This line can also refer to the person who has not freed himself from the mistaken beliefs mentioned in Lines 1 and 2. In this case, the superior man is one who believes himself impervious to fate, and holds to the delusions promoted by the collective ego, that his real life will occur in the afterlife, when he is freed of a body. In this meaning the carriage is the carriage of Fate.

When this line refers to Fate, it can indicate an illness, caused by the person's belief that his soul is a temporary inhabitant of his body, and his body is separate from him. This view creates blockages in the flow of chi (life force) through his body, creating illness. If he attempts to treat his body as merely a set of mechanics, his illness will transfer from one locus to another, gradually leading to his death. If he rids himself of these mistaken beliefs, which slander his body and prevent him from living fully in it, he will free his self-healing abilities and restore the full flow of chi.

When this line refers to relationships, the "large fruit" can be a metaphor for the success that comes when a person breaks away from a relationship that has failed through exceeding the limits of commonsense. "The superior man receives a carriage" can refer to another relationship that will come along, which will be truly fulfilling. "The house of the inferior man is split apart" can refer to the partner who has failed to allow himself to participate fully in the love relationship.

24. Returning

 K'un
Chên

The Judgment: *Returning. Success. Going out and coming in without error. Friends come without blame. To and fro goes the way. On the seventh day comes return. It furthers one to have somewhere to go.*

This hexagram is one of the twelve calendar hexagrams based on the coming and going of the light of the sun in the course of the year. Here the single light line that has entered the hexagram at the bottom represents the first increase in the altitude of the sun since the winter solstice, hence its name, " Returning."

The Sage defines the theme of this hexagram as returning to one's original nature, and to unity with the Cosmic Whole, through splitting apart from the ego.

Returning also indicates the direction in which the path of development leads: back to the person's original nature. It does not lead forward, through cultivating virtues or becoming something we are not, but is a process of continuous subtraction of what we have falsely added. Each step on this path leads to increasing light and relief. One takes this path through ceasing to look outward for the solutions to problems, to look inward instead. Each hexagram illuminates some hidden part of the psyche, helping us to discover our true nature.

We receive this hexagram when we are ready to return from a mistake. "Friends come without blame" means that when we have the humility to acknowledge a mistake, the Helpers are freed to come to our help.

"To and fro" refers to departing from one's true self and then returning, as the way the student of the Sage learns through experience. His mistakes are a necessary part of his learning. "On the seventh day" is a reference to the words, "three days before" and "three days after," mentioned in Hexagram 18, *Recognizing and Correcting the Causes of Decay*, as the time required to correct mistaken ideas. On the seventh day, the person is free of the blame he incurred through holding the mistaken idea(s).

This hexagram chiefly concerns pride as the element that holds a person back from returning to humility. It also concerns indulging in hurt pride, which causes the heart to harden. The way of return is for the person to reopen his heart and apologize to the Cosmos for having allowed himself to indulge in hurt pride.

"It furthers one to have somewhere to go" counsels a person who is experiencing an illness caused by a fate, that he needs to discern where true help comes from: the Sage and the Helpers of the invisible world. This hexagram calls upon a person to identify the mistaken ideas that have caused the fate. Among such ideas are those that denigrate the body, and thereby create ill health. Ridding himself of them will return him to unity with himself, and to good health.

This hexagram is also related to Hexagram 21, *Biting Through*, which concerns a person who has been using power to make things happen according to his design. His doing so has created a fate, which he has falsely interpreted as Cosmic punishment. The fate has aroused his pride, since he believes it to be undeserved. This hexagram calls him to return to humility. If pride is not dismissed at once, the ego can quickly build it to demonic proportions. Thus, the lines of this hexagram also address the various hindrances that the ego raises to prevent the person from returning to humility.

Return can also be counseling a person to retreat from the idea that he may be guilty for following his inner truth. Guilt was invented by the collective ego to keep the individual under its control, and is the "reinstalling feature" of the false program it introjects in the psyche of the child. (*See* p. 50, Guilt, Blame, and Shame.)

Spells associated with this hexagram have to do with mistaken ideas about the path of development, as for example, calling it a "spiritual path," or seeing it as a forward or upward-leading path, or as leading to a pinnacle of enlightenment, or to seeing it as a path of achievement, or of repentance. Development is only a matter of taking away the false inner program of the ego.

Return can also be counsel to "return" to the stored memories that are the basis of one's prejudices and fixed ideas about something or someone, and rid oneself of them. This is the way to return to an open mind and heart. One may need to examine whether these prejudices have led to spells or projections that also need to be eliminated.

Return can also indicate that the inner channel to someone that was blocked is open again, because the person has eliminated the spells and projections that caused the blockage.

The Sage and the Helper of Transformation are freed by a person's return to humility.

Note: Since all lines contain infinite possibilities of interpretation, one needs to use the *rtcm* to determine if the meanings suggested here apply to the given situation. (See p. 736, Using the *rtcm*.)

Line 1. *Return from a short distance. No need for remorse. Great good fortune.*

This line is saying that recognizing and saying the inner No to an ego-emotion at its onset prevents it from encroaching further, and from gaining in strength and momentum.

A person can receive this line when he has been trying to fit the Sage's answers into his existing beliefs, consequently, has received confusing or contradictory answers. This has made him consider giving up on the *I Ching*. This line is telling him that if he will not be deterred by this problem, and open his mind, the Sage will return and communicate with him.

Another obstruction of this sort may occur when the Sage has told him something the ego in him does not want to hear. This line tells him that he has only partially understood the answer, and if he will open his mind, he will understand that the message was not intended to make him feel guilty or inferior, but to liberate him from fears and doubts about himself.

A person may also receive this line upon experiencing relief from an illness. The relief has come through the intervention of the Sage, but the person has falsely attributed the success to the person through whom the Sage has helped him. If he returns from this view and also credits the Helpers he has overlooked, there will be great good fortune in that his healing will be completed.

This line can also refer to a person who, in following a spiritual path, has not experienced the benefits he expected. Instead of questioning whether he has been following the correct path, he interprets the counsel "to return" as saying that he has not tried hard enough, and needs to try harder. He must recognize that a spiritual path, as described in the main text, is a forward-leading path that leads to more and more separation from his true self, as he tries to become something special (i.e., a "spiritual being"). The path of return indicated by this hexagram is the path of divesting oneself of all self-images and attempts to be special. The person needs also to rid himself of the blame spell he has put on himself for not doing enough. (*See* p. 697, Freeing Yourself from Spells.)

Line 2. *Quiet return. Good fortune.*

This line can point to a situation of hurt pride. The hurt pride can come from two sources: from being mistreated, or from false feelings of guilt. It is important for the person to identify the images that are connected with his hurt pride and rid himself of them. Otherwise, these images will give fuel to vindictiveness and self-righteousness.

"Quiet return" may also refer to a person's feelings of being punished by the Sage, and his concluding that the Sage is another name for an authoritarian God. He may also have received Hexagram 21, *Biting Through*, Lines 1, or 6, which describe a person who is held in stocks or a wooden cangue. This line is saying that the stocks and cangue have been put on the ego by the Sage, to protect the person's true self from being compromised by disharmonious action. The stocks hold him back from acting, and the cangue makes him become quiet within, enabling him to distinguish the voice of the ego, and its rationales as false.

This line can also point to the return of feelings of guilt. Guilt is an invention of the collective ego, designed to keep him under its control. (*See* p. 50, Guilt, Blame, and Shame.) The person needs to get rid of all ideas of guilt and of the idea that repentance would free him of it. Repentance slanders the loving nature of the Cosmos, which holds nothing as guilty. The Cosmos gives the person all the help he needs to return to sincerity. (*See* p. 696, Freeing Yourself from Guilt and Blame.) After ridding himself of his guilt spell, the person also needs to free himself of his belief in repentance. (*See* p. 689, Freeing Yourself from Mistaken Ideas and Beliefs.)

Finally, "quiet return" expresses the Cosmic Principle of allowing a person to return to humility without having to lose face. This line is stating the importance of not confronting him on the outer plane, but giving him space to return of his own free will to his true self, without requiring him to jump over a list of hurdles to prove himself worthy. It is vital that his dignity is respected. Saying the inner No corrects him through the inner channel, out of the sight and hearing of the ego, thus neither arouses his defenses, nor jeopardizes his dignity. The inner No acts in the same way that the stocks and the cangue act: to invisibly influence a person's actions toward harmony.

Line 3. *Repeated return. Danger. No blame.*

"Repeated return" refers to a person who wishes to return to humility, but is held back by pride and fear of guilt. The danger lies in his giving way to these ego-emotions, which will reestablish the ego's power over him. A person can free himself from blame if he will search out and rid himself of the spells that hold his pride or fear of becoming guilty in place. Some seed phrases that make up such spells are: "you can never be forgiven for such errors" (a statement of the ego to keep a person from returning to his true self, and to hold him in his pride, which is a cover-up for his feelings of guilt), "I should have known better" (a self-blame-spell), "return would mean giving up everything you are," (a threat that says, "without the ego, you are a nobody," and "there's no point in going backwards."

If a guilt spell and/or a self-blame-spell remain after getting rid of other, more obvious spells, the guilt will return to reestablish the other spells. (*See* p. 696, Freeing Yourself from Guilt.)

"You have to try harder next time," while not a spell, can be the urging of pride to make a person return even more resolutely to the false path of striving, to fulfill a self-image.

"Repeated return" suggests the presence of a spell that contains the word "always." Such a phrase may be as simple as, "I'm always late." It prevents the person from becoming free of that habit. (*See* p. 697, Freeing Yourself from Spells.)

Line 4. *Walking in the midst of others, one returns alone.*
Through following the path of his inner truth, a person finds himself alone. This is a good thing, for it is a necessary first step in learning to follow his inner truth, and to avoid falling back into an unhealthy dependence on others. Authorizing himself, which is one of the goals of bringing his true self to maturity, cannot take place as long as he depends on what others think.

This line often refers to a person who is listening to others' thoughts and statements, or is witnessing their deeds. His duty is to say the inner No to those thoughts and deeds which are disharmonious, and when in doubt whether a No is needed, to consult the Sage through the *rtcm*. This enables him to relate to the situation correctly without having to leave the group outwardly. The inner No connects with the inner truth of the others present, and calls the Helpers into the situation.

The line can also refer, as in Line 3, to the use of words such as "always," that fix situations as inevitable. Fixing an effect as "always happening" not only deprives the circumstance of its capacity for uniqueness, it causes the unwanted circumstances to return, in the manner of a self-fulfilling prophecy. An example is, "I always get a headache when I drink wine." This creates a spell, causing the headache to return every time the person drinks wine. Receiving this line counsels a person to look for spells of this sort that are affecting his current situation. Another word that creates spells is the word "is" when it is used to describe a person's (or thing's) nature, as in "he *is* that way."

Line 5. *Noblehearted return.*

This line points to a person's "nobleheartedly" letting another off the hook of his mistake by ignoring it or forgiving him. This idea is pretentious in that it assumes he has the power and ability to forgive, it puts him up on a pedestal of being "noble," and gives the other a false approval and implicit permission to continue his behavior.

The idea of being noblehearted is a self-image often used to enable a person to momentarily put aside his wounded pride, in order to make peace with the other. However, because the wounded pride is not eliminated, it remains buried in the subconscious as a bitter memory, which arouses emotions that return every time he meets that person. So long as he has not freed himself from that memory, he remains negatively attached to the other, and pulled toward him. Such an attachment is called a "love-hate relationship." To become free of this attachment, the person needs to recognize that the ego is behind his hurt pride in the form of the self-image of "being noblehearted."

Since the person who has a noblehearted self-image regards "noblehearted" as meaning "forgiving," "enduring insult," and "being above what is crass and ugly," he draws to himself situations that invite abuse, insult, and crassness.

Often, a person adopts the ideal of "being noblehearted" as compensation for feelings of guilt. Either it is the supposed guilt he is born with, or a belief that he is has broken some rule or commandment just by existing, which has been carried over from childhood. He may have been led to believe he was "in the way," or a nuisance, or even the reason his parents divorced. His nobleheartedness comes from unconscious feelings carried forward of not wanting to make others suffer from the same guilt that he himself has felt, and so he forgives or dismisses what they do. To free himself, and them, from the consequences of these mistaken beliefs, the person needs to free himself from the original guilt spells that he has taken on, even as a small child.

When nobleheartedness has become a self-image, it follows rigid commandments to forgive, endure, and be above what is low; therefore, it is not the same as natural feelings of sympathy. Natural sympathy is a spontaneous heart to heart communication with another's true self, as when in situations of shock, the ego is temporarily frozen and the true self is freed, or when there are natural feelings of attraction between two people.

Line 6. *Missing the return. Misfortune from within and without. If armies are set marching in this way, one will suffer a great defeat, disastrous for the ruler of the country. For ten years it will not be possible to attack again.*

This line can refer to the fate created when a person adopts the self-image of being noblehearted, as mentioned in Line 5. Such a person is trying to "be like God," whom he believes to possess unconditional love, which he interprets as overlooking and tolerating ego-behavior. He does not see that this self-image has put a spell and lock on all his senses of discernment. The Sage makes us aware that the Cosmic Consciousness, the source of all love, retreats in the presence of the ego, and withholds love so long as the ego is present, and in this way draws the person back to his true self. Practicing unconditional love creates one fate after another—the disaster mentioned.

"Misfortune from within" refers to a fate coming in the form of an illness. The illness is due to ideas, which have created the person's susceptibility to the illness (the susceptibility is the attitude from within, which exposes the person to the illness that comes from without). The mistaken ideas that create his susceptibility to illness are described in the Appendix. (*See* p. 694, Freeing Yourself from some Health Problems.)

"Setting armies marching" refers to speaking or acting aggressively against the perceived wrong actions of others. Bringing their actions out into the open only causes inner or outer wars, through creating a loss of face and humiliation to the pride system the ego has erected in them. The correct way to treat such wrongs is first to say the inner No to the ego in oneself and its desire to become self-righteously involved in the situation; second, to say the inner No to the ego in the other and its transgressions, and then to turn the matter over to the Cosmos. Only then will the situation be remedied.

"Ten years" is a metaphor for the time spans connected with fates. Some fates last three years, some ten, some twenty. They can be avoided if we take heed upon receiving these timely warnings. They can also be ended, if already in progress, by disposing of all their causes within ourselves.

Spells and poison arrows associated with this line have to do with seeing others, or the human condition, as the cause of the problems in one's life. Phrases behind these spells are: "I would never do such a thing," "the other has no morals," "every act has a selfish motive," "people are that way," "human nature is faulty," "suffering is a natural part of life," "humans are born into this life with all the responsibilities but no help," "our leaders are the source of all our problems." This last idea denies that the individual always has the ability to say the inner No and thereby gain the help of the entire Cosmos.

25. Innocence. Not Expecting/Not Projecting

Ch'ien
___
Chên

The Judgment: *Innocence has supreme success. To be firmly correct furthers. If someone is not in accord with his true nature, he has misfortune, and it does not further him to undertake anything.*

"Not expecting/not projecting," the Sage informs us, is a person's natural state of mind. It means residing in one's center,

299

where discernment springs spontaneously from the feeling of what is harmonious and what is discordant. Such a state is in harmony with the Cosmos and draws its help in all situations.

Not expecting means approaching something (the Sage, another person, a situation) free of prejudice, preconceived images, fixed beliefs, inner demands, fears, or doubts. It is to suspend judgment until one is led by one's feelings to a correct discernment, which expresses itself in an inner Yes or No. No logical justification is needed beyond this feeling.

Receiving this hexagram counsels the person to reflect on whether he is expecting or projecting in the way indicated above, for that would create the conditions expected, and therefore also create a fate.

In its Cosmic meaning the word innocence describes human nature in its original condition (before it has been colonized by the collective ego), as in perfect harmony with the Cosmos, and completely adequate in all respects to enable a person to live his life happily. Innocence also implies that a person's inner program, as designed by the Cosmic Consciousness, is free of all intention, contrivance, and falseness. It is a "feeling program" that *knows*, through the feelings, the appropriate responses to all things.

This *feeling* program is quickly derided by the collective ego as worthless, in the sense of being ignorant, naive, and foolish. On these grounds the collective ego overwrites this original program with a purely *mental* program *it* has devised. The definition of innocence by the collective ego thus shifts the faculty of discernment from feeling to thinking. This shift is accompanied by ceasing to speak in terms of what *feels* harmonious or discordant, to *mental* terms that define what is good or evil. By this simple stroke, the ability of discernment is taken away from the individual and its source in his inner truth, and given over to the collective ego as the authorizing institution for all judgment about the nature of things.

A person receives this hexagram to make him aware that his Cosmic task is to return to his original innocence by ridding himself of the collective ego's mental program, with all its mistaken ideas and beliefs that have put spells and poison arrows on his true nature. In fulfilling this task, he harmonizes with the Greater Plan that is at work in his life: to manifest the uniqueness of his true self.

"Not projecting" warns a person of a false attitude he has that is projecting negative effects upon his situation. He may, for example, be looking at someone with pity. In doing so, he is actually projecting a spell upon the other that he is helpless, which brings him even more harm. His projecting pity diverts him from saying the inner No to the other's display of helplessness, which display comes from the ego. The inner No would strengthen that person's true self, giving him the message that he can ask the Cosmos for help.

Note: Since all lines contain infinite possibilities of interpretation, one needs to use the *rtcm* to determine if the meanings suggested here apply to the given situation. See p. 736, Using the *rtcm*.)

Line 1. *Innocence brings good fortune.*
Receiving this line tells a person that he is in harmony with the Cosmos, therefore he receives its help and the gifts he needs.

The line states that our original nature, in its two centers of consciousness, thinking and feeling, is innocent at birth. The thinking center is the large brain, the feeling center is the heart. When we are centered within ourselves, both are neutral and "ready to receive" in a balanced way. A person who is thus centered reacts spontaneously and in harmony with his inner truth; he thus attracts the help he needs from the Cosmos. This is the good fortune referred to.

This contrasts with a person who has allowed his thinking center to be taken over by the ego; this results in the ego's seizing some of his true feelings and putting them into the service of its values. This happens, for example, when the ego seizes feelings of love and uses them as an instrument of power. Another consequence is that ego-emotions such as pity, hatred, envy, jealousy, and the like, are created by the mistaken beliefs, diverting the person from his true and natural responses to situations, and creating a fate for him.

Line 2. *If one does not count on the harvest while plowing, nor on the use of the ground while clearing it, it furthers one to undertake something.*

"Not counting on the harvest while plowing" refers to relating to events in such a way that the Greater Plan of our lives can reveal itself. This occurs when a person has a feeling relationship with what he is given to do by the Cosmos. A feeling relationship means that he says the inner No when it is appropriate, consistently withdraws from ego-behavior, and keeps himself aware to go with what feels harmonious, and to retreat from what feels discordant. This is in contrast to an ego-attitude in which a person inwardly expects and demands that the harvest (the outcome) be what he believes it should be.

"Plowing and clearing the ground" refers to the inner undertakings that return a person to his original nature, allowing it more and more to express itself in its uniqueness. These undertakings consist in identifying and deprogramming prejudices, prestructured views, and mistaken beliefs. The ground is not to be prepared for the planting of "good seeds," as is done in positive thinking or imaging, or by introducing another belief system. Preparing the ground for peace, for example, does *not* mean *praying for peace*, as this would bypass seeking out and deprogramming the mistaken beliefs that foment and perpetuate war.

Receiving this line counsels a person to examine his attitude toward his goal (the harvest), and to free it from any projection or spell put upon it by his egotistical demands.

Line 3. *Undeserved misfortune. The cow that was tethered by someone is the wanderer's gain, the citizen's loss.*

This line can refer to a person who has innocently been drawn into another person's fate, in order to gain something from it. The gain can be a material possession that Fate has taken away from the other, due to his having attached himself to the possession.

The line can also be received by someone who believes that because he has behaved well and done good deeds, he deserves the praise, gifts, and help of the Cosmos. His expectations and belief that he is deserving have tied inner strings of attachment to the expected gifts; this is the meaning of "the tethered cow." Since the Cosmos withdraws from a person who has such expectations and attachment, the gifts do not come. As a result, the person thinks that his misfortune is undeserved and that he has been treated unfairly by the Cosmos. He is counseled by this line to rid himself of the self-image of the good person. He also needs to free himself from all ideas that have to do with expectation and deserving. (For further discussion of this principle, *see* Hexagram 42, *Increasing.*)

The wanderer refers to the person who is following the path of his inner truth and therefore is in harmony with the Cosmos. He walks through life without attachment. Because he is aware of the source of his gifts, protection, and help, all that he needs continues to flow freely to him from the Cosmos.

Line 4. *He who is firmly correct remains without blame.*

Here, to be "firmly correct" means saying the inner No to the collective ego's contention that following one's feelings is stupid, and that the feelings are "only subjective" and cannot be trusted. The inner No likewise must be said to the collective ego's putting so-called objective thinking up on a pedestal. Thinking takes its correct place and is without blame only when it *follows* the feelings; it creates blame when it harnesses the feelings and turns them into ego-emotions. The Cosmic Consciousness is a feeling consciousness that can also think, but it is through our feelings that we connect with it.

To be "firmly correct" can also be counsel for a person not to be drawn from his inner center and his sense of what is correct by the fear-inspiring things that others say. He needs instead to say the inner No to the ideas behind those fears, which, if not corrected, will project what is feared into reality.

This can also be counsel against listening to thoughts or ideas that would tempt him to blame the Sage, Fate, or other people for what is happening, either to him or to the group with which he identifies. He needs to withdraw from such blaming, and also to withdraw from seeing himself as part of a "group-we," such as a family, race, culture, or economic system. Every person has his own relationship with the Cosmos, which determines everything that happens to him individually. (*See* Glossary: Group-We)

Line 5. *Use no medicine in an illness incurred through no fault of your own. Once you ask for help, it will pass of itself.*

This line is saying that the illness a person is suffering has been caused by a poison arrow coming from someone else, either in the past or in the present, in the form of one or more negative thoughts. When he receives this line, he does not need to identify the thoughts, but only find out who put the poison arrow on him, say the inner No to that person, and then ask the Sage and the Helpers of the invisible world to eliminate it. The inner No needs to be repeated daily until he has been told by the Sage, through the *rtcm*, that he can cease in his efforts. Then the illness will pass of itself because the cause has been removed. This line applies even to some long-standing illnesses.

Line 6. *Innocent action brings misfortune. Nothing furthers.*

The seeming contradiction in this line reveals that a person has acted from a delusion: he *believes* he has behaved innocently, because he has done all the "correct things," as defined by the collective ego. However, because such behavior is against his true nature, he has only suffered setbacks and misfortune.

This line can also describe a person who thinks that by following the wisdom of the ancients, he is acting in harmony with the Cosmos. He is not listening to his inner feelings and inner truth, but is following prestructured beliefs that trap him in fixed responses. Since fixed responses cannot relate to the uniqueness of the moment, they exclude the Helpers and create disharmony. In both cases, a person can return to harmony by ridding himself of the self-image of the innocent person. (*See* p. 691, Freeing Yourself from Self-Images.) A person who follows his true nature only responds to what comes from his commonsense. This keeps him in harmony with the Cosmic Whole, and thus he does not create a fate.

This line also counsels a person not to blame himself when he has made a mistake. Making mistakes is part of the Cosmic way of learning. After recognizing that he has made a mistake, all he needs to do is rid himself of the mistaken idea or belief, let go of the matter, and go on. Only the ego attaches itself to the mistake and indulges in blaming the person. The ego does this to make him be afraid of learning. Accepting the ego's blame puts a poison arrow on him, and also opens the door to more blame being heaped on him by the egos in others. All these consequences of accepting self-blame comprise the misfortune mentioned. He can end his misfortune by freeing himself from the poison arrow of self-blame. (*See* p. 697, Freeing Yourself from Poison Arrows.)

This line can also refer to a person who, in doing the right things, expects the praise and approval of the Sage to be reflected in some sort of success. Any form of expectation comes from the human centered view of the universe and soils his innocence.

Related ideas are those of having rights over others or over Nature. Such ideas violate the Cosmic Principle of Modesty. An attitude of modesty is the result of recognizing one's true place in the Cosmos as equal to all other things. Without modesty, nothing furthers.

26. *The Taming Power of the Great/* Success through the Great

Kên
Ch'ien

The Judgment: *Being firm and correct furthers. Not eating at home brings good fortune. It furthers one to cross the great water.*

In this hexagram the Sage shows us how to successfully counter the ego in another, or react to incorrect treatment coming from a group-ego. Incorrect treatment is defined as treatment that is oppressive, encroaching, arrogant, interfering, or self-righteous.

"Success through the great" refers to the person who, upon

305

being treated unjustly, restrains his anger, says the inner No, and turns the matter over to the Cosmos. This is the meaning of being "firm and correct." In this way, his anger is transformed into a different form of energy that allows the Cosmos to correct the situation through him. The transformed energy is released by the Sage at exactly the moment when it has the correct effect on the situation. How it is expressed happens spontaneously, without any effort or intention on the person's part.

A person may receive this hexagram, for example, when he is being bullied by someone. If he endures this behavior, the bully may only try harder to annoy him, and thereby engage the ego in him. The solution lies in saying the inner No, or, if appropriate, an outer No, to let the bully know in a straightforward way, that his behavior is unacceptable and incorrect. If he keeps the ego from becoming involved and asks the Cosmos for help, everything will then be furthered.

Another example is the envious testing a person may experience from others upon freeing himself from his dependence on the collective ego. The testing is done to see if he can be driven to defend himself. It succeeds only if he allows himself to become angry. Again, the answer is to say the inner No to the testing and to turn the matter over to the Cosmos.

"It furthers one to cross the great water" refers to a person's engaging the Helper of Transformation to bring about the correction. This Helper is always engaged through saying the inner No, and turning the matter over to the Cosmos.

"The Taming Power of the Great," the traditional name of this hexagram, refers to the conditioning process carried out by the collective ego through threats and punishments. This hexagram is an extension of Hexagram 9, *The Taming Power of the Small*, where the taming is done by the more subtle means of flattery and reward.

The purpose of all taming is twofold: (1) to deprive the person (during childhood) of his natural defense, which consists in his ability to say both the inner and the outer No; (2) to appropriate his Cosmic Virtues and turn them into social virtues, in order to tie him to the collective ego and its institutions. In the first case, the taming is done by threats and punishments during times when the child correctly says No to unjust treatment. In the second case, the taming is done by first denying that the child possesses Cosmic Virtues such as honesty, loyalty, and kindness, and then telling him that he needs to develop these virtues. To legitimize this taming process, his animal nature is described as the source of evil in the world. After making him lose confidence in his Cosmic Virtues, his natural honesty, for example, is contorted into saying what is socially correct, his natural loyalty to his inner truth is turned into a loyalty to the institutions of the collective ego, and his natural kindness is converted into a nondiscriminatory kindness that he is supposed to show to everyone.

The statements, threats, and punishments that are used to condition the child create doubts and fears in his psyche that disable his various natural abilities. Among the threats that create such fears are the commandments ("you must...") that threaten horrible punishments, extending to eternal suffering after death. These statements and threats invariably connected with spells and poison arrows remain in the person's psyche (long after childhood) until the day they are removed through deprogramming or de-spelling.* They make the person doubt his original goodness and his natural capacity to get along in life. (*See* p. 697, Freeing Yourself from Spells and Poison Arrows.) A further effect of these fears is to transfer the person's chi energy to the collective ego, and to those who represent it, endowing them with power.

Since these spells and poison arrows also block the flow of chi energy to various parts of the body, especially those parts to which punishments have been applied, these parts are unable to get their needed chi nourishment. They are, so to speak, "unable to eat at home," which brings misfortune in the form of ailments, illness, or exhaustion.

"Not eating at home" can also refer to a situation in which a

---

Medical researchers have shown that such fears are stored in the amygdala of the brain in the form of certain proteins. These proteins become activated whenever circumstances occur that are similar to the situation in which the trauma originally occurred, freezing the person's ability to react effectively—in this case, to say the inner No.

person is not able to get his chi nourishment in his present relationship because there is no true inner connection between the partners. When this is the case, withdrawing from intimacy with the partner is the correct response.

"Not eating at home" can also point to a person's being blocked from receiving chi energy directly from the Cosmos. To compensate, he overeats. This indicates that he is under a spell which may consist of negative self-assessments such as, "I'm not lovable," "not even the Cosmos could love a person like me," and "I don't deserve anything good"; or, it may consist of self-punishing or self-blaming phrases, or arrogant and demanding phrases such as "I deserve only the best."

Note: Since all lines contain infinite possibilities of interpretation, one needs to use the *rtcm* to determine if the meanings suggested here apply to the given situation. (*See* p. 736, Using the *rtcm*.)

Line 1. *Danger is at hand. It furthers one to desist.*

This line is about chi energy that has turned into a dangerous force through anger at injustice. Anger is a natural emotion evoked by injustice. It is turned into a dangerous force by the ego when the person assumes that there is no help from the invisible world (or disbelieves in its existence) and that he needs to defend himself. He should understand that Cosmic energy flows to the person who is treated unjustly, and if not interfered with, will by itself correct the situation. The energy of the evil deed creates a fate that travels like a boomerang back to its origin, when it is not obstructed. But when someone does interfere, its completion is prevented, and this causes a fate for the one interfering.

The rising of natural anger is a call to say the inner No, first, to the assumption that there is no help from the invisible world, second, to the person transgressing, and third, to call for help from the Cosmos. One also needs to avoid talking negatively about the situation, as this turns back the energies called to his defense. Such talking and complaining allow the ego to seize the anger energy and begin to act upon it, whereas the energy is otherwise transformed into a creative energy that gets stored up. There is an optimal time for the stored-up chi energy to express itself. This happens only after the ego has been thoroughly displaced. Then the Sage communicates to us precisely when the time is right for the energy to be released.

This line also is a warning against self-confidently intervening on behalf of another who has been treated unjustly. A person may even think it is his duty to step in and defend the other. However, such an action would only result in his taking on the other's fate, because he is acting from a human-centered view and the assumption that no help from the invisible world is available to that person. "It furthers to desist" is saying it is a "hands-off" situation. (We are not talking here about intervening *spontaneously* on behalf of children, animals, and otherwise innocent parties.) All help given needs to be coupled with asking for help from the Cosmos, and with asking for help from the Sage that resides in the presence of the offending person.)

Line 2. *The axletrees are taken from the wagon.*

The wagon is a metaphor throughout the *I Ching* for the Helpers, and their activities in our lives. Here, however, the Helpers are unable to move and fulfill their functions. The axletrees are a metaphor for a person's ability to see the Sage as existing both for himself and for another. Through this ability he calls upon the Sage during times of difficulty, as mentioned in Line 1. However, under the influence of the collective ego, a person is deprived of this knowledge and ability, through being trained to see people as either good or evil. Through this conditioning, the axletrees, which are the stationary supports for the moving parts (the wheels) have been removed. That is to say, the Cosmic Principle of Attraction, upon which the movement of the two wheels is based, has been violated, causing a fate. The one wheel, in this metaphor, is the person who can draw the other into doing what is harmonious by calling upon the Sage in that person's presence. This line is saying that so long as people view others in terms of good or evil, their lives remain bound up in struggle and adversity.

This line can also refer to a person who has been unjust to

others and consequently is experiencing a fate. The line is saying that one must not interfere with that fate by dwelling on his unjust action, for that would involve one in his fate.

Line 3. *A good horse that follows others. Awareness of danger and being firmly correct furthers. Practice chariot driving and armed defense daily. It furthers one to have somewhere to go.*

"A good horse that follows others" is a reference to a domesticated horse, which has been trained to follow other horses, and to adapt, without resistance, to what its master wishes. This metaphor obviously refers to training people to follow the collective ego. This is done by equating "being good" with "being a good follower" — either of the ideas and values of the collective ego, or its acknowledged leaders.

This line warns a person against the danger of acting in conformity to the values of the collective ego, and particularly to its prohibition against saying No, either inwardly or outwardly, to its values and customs. An important part of a person's development is the reclaiming of his ability to correctly say the inner or outer No.

"Being firmly correct" can be saying that it is correct and essential to say the inner No, even if it is to someone we wish to excuse for his incorrect behavior.

"Practicing chariot driving and armed defense daily" calls a person to restrain his anger and not allow the ego to take hold of it and use it for its purposes. (Also *see* Line 1.)

"It furthers one to have somewhere to go" is counsel to find a way to leave the scene of discord, both inwardly and outwardly. When a person is firm in remaining disengaged from turmoil, he is always helped.

"Awareness of danger" addresses how a person is to relate to another who is unjustly reproving him for not having conformed to the rules of the group-we: by retreating and disengaging. Thereafter, the ego in the other can only lose energy. The person encroaching may employ other arguments to draw him back into defending himself, as by attacking his lack of kindness, consideration, sensitivity, etc., but these should be ignored. All these arguments seek to trap him in false feelings such as guilt, which would distract him from seeing the incorrectness of the demands being made on him. The person being mistreated needs only hold to his own central truth, and not allow himself to fall into reasoning about it.

"Awareness of danger" additionally warns against being drawn off the central point of inner truth which he *feels*, by arguments that seek to divert into defending what he *thinks*. "Practicing chariot driving," in this instance, means keeping his energy firmly directed toward that point. "It furthers one to have somewhere to go," in reference to this situation, means knowing when to stop. Once the person has secured his point, he needs to desist and go no further. When he has achieved success (with the help of the Helpers), it is important not to gloat, but instead allow the other to save face. This is done by not engaging the other's pride through self-righteousness.

Line 4. *The headboard of a young bull. Great good fortune.*

The young bull is a metaphor for an inexperienced person whose anger has been transformed into creative energy and stored up, but which now presses to be released. The headboard is a metaphor for the restraint he needs to put on this energy, which would otherwise be seized by the ego and create harm. Great good fortune, or Cosmic Harmony, will result from the restraint.

The traditional interpretation of this line has to do with taming a person's "animal nature," through rigorous discipline. The headboard stands for the various threats made by the collective ego against those who resist its discipline. It threatens to apply progressively harsher punishments, depending on the level of resistance, proceeding to the complete oppression of his nature, if necessary (which is the function of the headboard).

The line can also concern a person who is judging others as being "good or evil," "right or wrong," thus putting spells (headboard) and poison arrows on them. He does this because of a spell cast upon him in early childhood, that he was "guilty for having an animal nature." (Animal nature includes all parts of his nature that have been put down as "lower" or "inferior." *See* Glossary: Animal Nature.) The nature of this guilt is so unbear-

311

able that it has caused him to project it outside himself by judging other people's natures, or parts of Nature itself. The net effect is a back-and-forth blaming and casting of spells. (*See* p. 696, Freeing Yourself from a Guilt spell, and p. 50, Guilt, Blame, and Shame.)

Line 5. *The tusk of a gelded boar. Good fortune.*

This line, like Line 3, contains the false implication that it is necessary to geld, or take away, a person's true nature, on the pretext that his animal nature is the source of evil. This idea gives rise to the kinds of discipline that aim to separate mind from body, and thus produce the disembodied "spiritual" person. Such divisions of a person's nature into "spiritual" and "animal" parts destroy his original wholeness, upon which his health and well-being are dependent. Receiving this line may indicate that a person's illness is due to this false separation and demonization of the body.

The belief that one's animal nature is "lowly" disables various senses that a person needs, to complete his commonsense. It is his commonsense which enables the transformations that bring him chi energy (his life-force) from the Cosmos. His animal nature can be restored to its healthy functioning if he rids himself of the false phrases and images that slander it. (*See* p. 689, Freeing Yourself from Seed Phrases and Images.)

The gelded boar can also refer to the person who, through punishments and threats administered during childhood, has had his ability to say the inner No, represented by the tusk, blocked. By not being able to say the inner No to others, his natural defense system is disabled, so that he is constantly subjected to their encroachments. Also, by not being able to say the inner No to the ego in himself, he is blocked from receiving chi from the Cosmos. The block is a poison arrow that needs to be eliminated. (*See* p. 677, Saying the Inner No.)

The "tusk" is also a metaphor for a person's ability to draw the Helper of Transformation through saying the inner No. It is also a metaphor for his ability to store the chi-energy he receives from the Cosmos. "Good fortune" here refers to regaining possession of this tusk.

Line 6. *One attains the way of heaven. Success.*

This line refers to Cosmic energy that was transformed and stored through restraining it, and which now has been put to use through the person who has been treated unjustly, in a spontaneous reaction. "Heaven," although a misnomer, refers to the Cosmic Consciousness, which supports the reaction, giving it the success mentioned.

27. Nourishing

 Kên
Chên

The Judgment: *Nourishing. Perseverance brings good fortune. Pay heed to the providing of nourishment and to what a man seeks to fill his own mouth with.*

This hexagram is one that has taken its meaning from its graphic appearance: the straight lines at the top and bottom are said to resemble the lips of an open mouth, and the broken lines in between are seen as teeth, thus suggesting the part of the body which takes in nourishment.

The Sage uses this theme of nourishment to refer both to what is taken in as food, and metaphorically, to what is taken into the psyche as thoughts, ideas, and beliefs. The Sage distinguishes between what nourishes the true self and what feeds the ego. What nourishes the true self adds to the person's existing supply of chi energy (life force and will to live), whereas what feeds the ego robs him of chi.

All thoughts, ideas, and beliefs affect our whole being. Thoughts that are not in harmony with Cosmic Truth do so in two ways: first, they negatively affect our ability to receive the chi we need from the Cosmos, and second, they affect how we utilize food and drink.

It is in the nature of untrue ideas and beliefs that once taken into the psyche, they remain there until such time as they are removed, through saying the inner No to them. Many ideas are taken into the psyche simply because we have thought they might be true and thus have accepted them by default. (Here, the definition of "false" means: contrary to Cosmic Truth.) For example, if someone says to the child, "the moon is made of green cheese," he immediately rejects the idea because it is clearly absurd. But, if an authority or parent says to the child, "a part of your nature (referring obliquely to the body's sexuality) is evil and needs to be fought" the phrase becomes part of his inner program. Inasmuch as this phrase slanders his nature, it damages his chi, and his ability to receive chi from the Cosmos. Many less obvious untruths enter the psyche by such means. Because all false ideas act to separate the person, first from being in harmony with the Cosmos, and second from being in harmony with himself, they are not to be taken lightly. All consciousness (true or false) is active. True consciousness nourishes and aids all aspects of the Cosmos, but false consciousness is like acid that eats away at the integrity of things. Doubts about the goodness of one's nature, to give an example, are not merely passive or inert; they are actively destructive both to a person's relationship with himself, and with those around him. When we recognize fully the potency of the thoughts, ideas, and beliefs we allow into our psyches, we take care to ask, through the *rtcm*, whether they are true nourishment. This is the meaning of the admonition in The Judgment to pay heed to what we nourish ourselves with.

This hexagram may be telling a person that his ability to receive Cosmic nourishment has been inhibited by beliefs that are exhausting his chi energy. They may, for example, be affecting the way his body utilizes food, although he believes the matter has to do with the food alone. This often happens when he has accepted slanders on certain foods as being "bad for you." This idea has sent the message to his body cells to be on guard against those foods, and to reject them. Then, when he eats them, he feels the consequences.

Similar evil effects come from the division of the person into mind and body, or mind, body, and soul/spirit. In this separation, the body is regarded as "only a worthless vehicle" which the soul/spirit, as "superior," inhabits. Such a slander blocks the body's protective abilities, thus allowing illnesses to develop. (*See* Glossary: Soul and Spirit.)

The Sage makes us aware that the true self can only find its expression and completion through the body, because the body is compressed Cosmic Consciousness, and the entire psyche is inextricably connected with bodily consciousness. Susceptibility to illness is created by ideas that divide the personality, such as those that cause him to look down on his body, and to demonize its needs. Those ideas create the fate of his wasting the joys and opportunities connected with living in a body.

Another mistaken idea, given in the traditional interpretation of this hexagram, is that one needs to intentionally nourish the soul, or the mind, as "higher aspects of the self" through developing "higher and good" thoughts, otherwise, the evil part of one's nature will take over. Again, what needs to be done is to remove from the psyche all the seed thoughts, ideas, and beliefs that have divided the person's wholeness to begin with.

Spells connected with this hexagram have to do with the above-mentioned division of a person's nature, as expressed in the phrase, "you need to cultivate your higher nature." Other phrases dwell on human nature as defective at the outset. Still other problems are created by the assumption that the mind knows what is best for the body in terms of diet and discipline.

When a person deprograms phrases that put the body down, bodily Helpers that have been demonized are liberated.

Note: Since all lines contain infinite possibilities of interpretation, one needs to use the *rtcm* to determine if the meanings suggested here apply to the given situation. (*See* p. 736 for using the *rtcm*.)

Line 1. *You let your magic tortoise go, and look at me with the corners of your mouth drooping. Misfortune.*

The term "magic tortoise," is a reference to the ancient tortoise oracle associated with the *I Ching*. The Sage makes us aware that the image of the tortoise, which was in many respects regarded as representing the nature of the Cosmos and the Cosmic Way, is not suitable. In a more general sense, this line can be a hint that a person is using an unsuitable image to describe his true nature and the nature of the Cosmos.*

Although the magic tortoise is a false image for the nature of the Cosmos, when taken as a *metaphor,* it can stand for the inner truth that nourishes and supports a person in time of trouble. The "corners of the mouth are drooping" shows that the person has lost connection with his inner truth by regarding his study of the *I Ching* as a "spiritual path," and seeing himself, in following it, as "the superior man."

A person can also receive this line when he regards the *I Ching* either as a book of ancient wisdom, or of eternal truths, or as a book that foretells the future. Such a person looks at the *I Ching* as a lifeless text that is to be studied by his mind only, whereby he excludes his feelings, and contact with his inner truth.

Moreover, he may be seeing the text as a collection of "man's wisdom," whereby he denies the role of the Cosmic Teacher as having participated in its development, and that this development is ongoing. Through using the *I Ching* to divine his future, the ego within him seeks an advantage over others, and ends only in projecting hopes and fears into reality.

Such a person looks at the *I Ching* with dissatisfaction because he misunderstands what is happening. He has, in fact, created a fate by having settled into a love-hate relationship with the Sage, slandering it now as a liar, and later coming back for advice when he is in need. When things go wrong, he blames the book for his fate, and when things go well he credits himself rather than the Sage.

Receiving this line is to say that the Sage has retreated and

---

* Legend has it that the eight trigrams were first seen by the legendary Chinese ruler Fu Hsi, on the back of a tortoise. During the Shang Dynasty (c. 1500 BC) the tortoise was consulted for all questions of cult and for the ruling of the state. To allow "heaven" to speak, priests scratched into the upper shell of a tortoise the question to be asked, then inscribed on it the eight trigrams. They recited the question to be asked with a loud voice to bring it to the attention of the "magical powers of the oracle" that were thought to be present. They then touched the shell with a gleaming hot bronze needle which caused the shell to crack. The cracking noises were taken as the "speaking" of the oracle. The crack lines pointed to the trigrams, which were read as indicating favorable or unfavorable consequences. Franciscus Adrian,"*Die Schule des I Ging, Hintergrundwissen* (Diederichs Verlag, Munich, 1994), p. 51.

will not return until the person has rid himself of this pattern. To do this he needs to review all the ideas he has about the *I Ching* as merely a book or a collection of ancient wisdom written by wise humans, and rid himself of them. (*See* p. 695, Freeing Yourself from Projections.) Only then can the Sage communicate with him "through" the lines of text, and connect him with his inner truth.

Being separated from the Cosmos blocks the flow of nourishment that comes from it; this separation makes a person feel helpless and hopeless. Receiving this line is to remind him that by allowing the ego to control his life, he has created the adverse reality in which he finds himself.

Line 2. *In turning to the summit for nourishment one deviates from the true path. Continuing to do this brings misfortune. One needs, instead, to seek nourishment from the hill.* *

This line contrasts Cosmic nourishment with "spiritual food." While the former nourishes one's whole being, the latter feeds the ego in the person's quest to see himself as superior. Such a person sees his "mind and soul" as superior, and thereby harms his body.

Cosmic nourishment comes through a person's *inner* truth, and his connection with the Sage. "Spiritual food," by contrast, consists of "ancient wisdom," that is taken in from *outside* sources. Often, it is accepted as true simply because it is ancient. The problem with much ancient wisdom is that many of its conclusions are half-truths which have been stated as *absolute* truths. An example is the division, in the *I Ching*, of the Cosmos into heaven and earth. The Sage makes us aware that the Cosmos is not divided (*see* Hexagrams 1 and 2), and that the problem with half-truths is that they appeal to the ego by relying only on the outer eyes in its assessment of what is "true." In addition, the ego is easily impressed by anything that has been pronounced as a "fundamental truth" and backed up by the weight of tradition. Since we are taught not to question the

---

* Here, we were advised to change the reading of the line , because the "summit" represents the wrong source of nourishment and the "hill" the correct source.

fundamental premises of ancient wisdom, the half-truths they contain slip into the psyche by default, where they become spells that block synaptic transmissions in the brain.

"Turning to the summit" refers to a person's looking outside himself, or up at something he regards as "higher" than himself for guidance and for "spiritual food." He may be looking up to ancient wisdom, to a spiritual leader, or to an "absolute truth," rather than looking within. This is the meaning of "one deviates from the true path [of inner truth]." "Misfortune" refers to the fate a person creates if he continues in this practice.

"Turning to the summit" can also refer to a person's falsely crediting something high, such as God, angels, heaven, chance, or his intellect, for the help he has actually received from the Helpers or the Sage. Doing this will cause the increase (the nourishment) that has been received to disappear, as is noted in Line 6 of Hexagram 42, *Increasing*.

Turning to the summit can refer as well to the person whose ego ambitiously seeks to be in possession of the "truths of life." This is in contrast to "seeking nourishment from the hill," which is a metaphor for a person's contenting himself with the small relative truths that constantly come as gifts from the Cosmos. These truths nourish his whole being, and because of their modest nature, the ego does not become attached to them.

Turning to the summit can also refer to the taking of substances that cause a person to be "high," divorced from his natural inhibitions, "free" from his loyalty to his inner truth. What he does is transfer his freedom and his loyalty to the substance, which creates the fate that the substance then owns him. To free himself he needs to identify the causes for his turning to the substance by asking the Sage, through one or more hexagrams.

The hill is also a metaphor for that part of the brain which keeps the connection between the forebrain and the brainstem open. It is there that the senses of outer seeing and hearing are coordinated with all our inner senses, when the latter are not blocked by spells. It is activated by certain states of mind such as *I Ching* meditation, or by inwardly asking for help. It is also activated by dreams. It is the Helper that connects us with our inner truth. (*See* Hexagram 52, *Meditating*.)

Because everything in the Cosmos is connected through consciousness, it is important to understand that our thoughts and feelings can either nourish others' true selves or feed their egos.

Line 3. *Turning away from nourishment. Perseverance brings misfortune. Do not act thus for ten years. Nothing serves to further.*

The person receiving this line has incurred a fate due to consulting the *I Ching* after the Sage has retreated (as described in Line 1), and consequently has only been communicating with the ego and its desires. Having failed to experience the success he had expected, he now calls the *I Ching* a liar. "Do not act thus for ten years" refers to the new fate he is creating by blaming the *I Ching* for his misfortune.

In the course of this pattern, the person has allowed the ego to place a spell on his inner truth. To free himself from the spell, he needs to repudiate the ego's leadership and allow remorse to reunite him with the Sage.

Line 4. *Turning to the summit for provision of nourishment brings good fortune. Spying about with sharp eyes like a tiger with insatiable craving. No blame.*

Here, "turning to the summit for provision of nourishment" refers to allowing the mind to decide which food is good and which is not. As a consequence, the body, which knows very well by its own consciousness what it needs, becomes deprived, and then starved. Thus, the reference to "spying about with sharp eyes...with insatiable craving." Not receiving what it needs, the body then gives up, and its digestive processes malfunction (as in anorexia and bulimia).

The "good fortune" mentioned can only take place if the person will turn the matter of food back over to the body, and free the food he has decided "is bad" from being demonized by the ego.

This line can also be pointing to the mistaken idea that humans are born with an original fault or lack. This idea acts as a poison arrow in a person's psyche, making him susceptible to illness. This susceptibility is created through the disablement of certain Helpers that are responsible for the hormone secretions throughout the body. The person can free himself of this problem by ridding himself of the poison arrow. (*See* p. 695, Freeing Yourself from Poison Arrows, and p. 692, Freeing Yourself from Some Health Problems.)

Line 5. *Turning away from the path. To be firm and correct brings good fortune. One should not cross the great water.*

This line refers to a person who believes it is his job to give love and nourishment to others, whom he perceives to be in need. In doing so, he has adopted a grandiose self-image; if he continues acting in this way, he will create a fate. To free himself of that self-image, he first needs to recognize that each person has the ability to call for help for himself. It is the Sage that activates people to help through spontaneous acts of kindness.

"Being firm and correct" is counsel not to act while in the presence of another whose ego is demanding attention. Not to act means to refuse inwardly to give this attention, because doing so would only feed and strengthen the ego more. A polite and determined retreat is all that is needed. "One should not cross the great water" means that the person should wait until the other has returned to modesty.

Line 6. *The source of nourishment. Awareness of danger brings good fortune. It furthers one to cross the great water.*

This line reminds us to keep aware that the true source of nourishment is the Sage. "Awareness of danger," however, is a warning that even though a person's relationship with the Sage has been restored, the ego is still actively seeking to reinstall itself. "It furthers one to cross the great water" is counsel that the person needs to firmly decide on which side of the great water he desires to be: in the sphere of Cosmic Harmony, or in the parallel reality created by the collective ego. For as long as this *decision of will has not been made,* he will remain attached to the parallel reality, and his inner efforts will continue to be undone by the ego.

Whether a person desires to live in the Cosmic Reality (sphere of consciousness) can be determined by asking himself these simple questions: am I including in my daily awareness the Sage and the Helpers of the invisible world? Am I remembering to ask for help from these sources for all my needs? Do I credit the Helpers for the help and gifts I receive? Am I unwilling to go along with things that go against my deepest inner feelings of what is true and correct? Am I willing to say the inner No to what is incorrect? Do I say a Yes to the gift of my life? These questions help a person to recognize whether his will is attuned to the Cosmos, or whether it is under the command of the ego.

The person who is living in the Cosmic Reality appears to be like anyone else: he goes to his job, to the market, to the bank, etc. The difference is that his world is full of blessings and help. He experiences his life as joy and fulfillment. When difficulties arise, he summons the Sage and the Helpers, that come quickly to his aid because of his modesty. They send him premonitions of when it is important to act, such as telling him in a dream or meditation to sell certain stocks, to publish a book, to make a visit to someone, or they send messages to hold him back from going somewhere on a certain day, to prevent him from getting drawn into someone else's fate.

Hardly anyone lives in this reality all the time. Throughout the period of learning about it, mistaken beliefs still hold a person in the parallel reality, and so he only gains moments of experiencing the Cosmic Reality, but with each experience of it, he grows more confident in his relationship with Cosmos.

A person may be held within the parallel reality by the ego-generated fear that seeking help from the Sage will deprive him of nourishment he thinks comes from his beliefs and practices. Such beliefs, however, cause him to constantly interpret the Sage's counsel in the context of those beliefs; therefore he misunderstands the Sage entirely. In order for the Sage's help to become available, he needs to put his beliefs and practices aside altogether.

The ego may also be trying to convince him that freeing his true self is "too hard." He needs to say the inner No to its attempts to distract him from taking the steps that will help him free himself from the ego's influence.

28. The Preponderance of the Great

 Tui
Sun

The Judgment: *The Preponderance of the Great. The ridgepole sags to the breaking point. It furthers one to have somewhere to go. Success.*

Pictured here is the ridgepole that holds up a structure, being pressed by something weighty and seemingly insuperable, to the point that it is about to break apart.

This is a metaphor, either for a structure that is about to collapse, or for a person's will to go on, which is in danger of being broken.

The metaphor of the ridgepole, while potentially indicating many meanings, points mainly to the human will—both the will to go on after a crisis, or the will to live.

The main function of a person's *will* is to maintain and restore his well-being and harmony with the Cosmos.* *Will is the name for the total consciousness of a person's psyche, expressed as energy.* How a person directs his will is the result of his conscious decision as to what he wants to follow. When this is clear, the will finds its direction. When a person decides to follow his innermost feelings of what is true and harmonious (the Cosmic sphere of consciousness), he engages the helpful energies of the Cosmos for everything that he does. When he consciously decides to follow the values of the collective ego (the demonic sphere of consciousness), he loses the Cosmic help and protection, and thereafter must depend on his own efforts, and whatever support the collective ego may give him. At any time, though, he can redirect his will to returning into unity with the Cosmos.

It is a mistake to think that this decision depends on a person's

---

* Another function of the will is discussed in Hexagram 34, *Using Power.*

will; in reality, the decision is made by his commonsense, which is his feeling consciousness of what is correct and harmonious. Once this feeling consciousness is fully acknowledged and agreed to by the thinking mind (an inner Yes), the psyche as a whole becomes harmonized behind the will. The will is then turned to discovering the untruths that have imprisoned his true self, and not, as is commonly thought, to following some path already and conveniently laid out by others. Whether the person lives fully and fulfills his destiny by giving expression to his uniqueness, depends on this conscious choice to find and follow his inner truth. (*See* Hex 27, *Nourishment,* Line 6.)

The image of the ridgepole's sagging to the breaking point draws our attention to something that is undermining a person's will, threatening to collapse his personality. Receiving the hexagram informs him that this is a dangerous moment, because the loss of will can be so great as to send a feeling message to all the body consciousnesses that it is time to terminate life. This a message which the body obeys, as by creating a fatal health condition, or by unconsciously engineering an accident, since will is the leading force in the total consciousness. If the threat is sufficient, the person gives up on life before he has fulfilled his destiny.

Will is undermined by mistaken ideas coming from the individual ego and collective ego concerning the true nature of the Cosmos and the human place in it. It is also undermined by doubts in the original goodness and completeness of human nature. The individual ego thus continuously steals the energy of will through instilling doubt, fears, and guilt in the person; its activity never adds anything to his energy supply. It drives him to total exhaustion of will, through the pressure it puts upon him to *act.*

"Having somewhere to go" refers to the necessity to also resist the driving pressures of the collective ego in the form of should's and must's, and to ask the Sage for help. These should's and must's temporarily block the energy of will, causing the person to feel depressed. An example of how the musts and shoulds are developed at an early age is: "You must love your mother." Such a command replaces the natural feelings of love with the ego-feelings of duty and obligation, creating at the same time an inner resistance. The mother's feelings of duty toward the collective ego, likewise, cultivate her indifference to the true feelings of the child, inciting a rebellion in the child for having to show feelings at times when he does not feel them. This situation is replicated in all instances where a person is commanded to feel what he does not feel.

The text to The Image, traditionally connected with this hexagram, reads, "The superior man, when he stands alone, is unconcerned, and if he has to renounce to the world, he is undaunted."* This statement affirms the Cosmic view that the person who is true to himself renounces the way of the collective ego and goes on his way alone rather than compromise his inner truth. In doing so, he remains connected with the Cosmic Whole and the Helpers of the invisible world; thus he is never alone. The collective ego would tell us otherwise: that the "superior man" is willing to sacrifice his life in the name of moral duty, and that the person who follows his inner truth will wind up being alone and abandoned.

"It furthers one to have somewhere to go" counsels a person to direct his will to following his inner truth. To do this he needs to seek help from the Sage to identify the core doubt that causes him to take on false responsibilities, and constantly overburden himself. It may be that he distrusts that help for all his needs is available from the Cosmos. Such an idea comes from the collective ego, which says that humans are born into this life without help, and that their only sources of help are *its* institutions (any institution, including the family when it lends itself to serving the collective ego's purposes). Other doubts are, "I don't deserve to be helped, to live..." etc.

The despair described by this hexagram has its origin in the mistaken idea that a person is born into the world without help from the Cosmos. Having this view, he may then have taken on the self-image of "the responsible person," or "the hero who saves the situations around him." Such a person may also see himself grandiosely as capable, like Atlas, of carrying the world and of

---

* Here, we were guided by the Sage to include a discussion of the text of The Image.

managing its affairs. In the end, his will to live becomes exhausted, because this is not what he is meant to do. Before he can rid himself of any of these self-images, however, he needs to address the fear of becoming guilty if he sheds them. Guilt is the reinstallation feature in the collective ego's conditioning program to keep the individual tied to its system. Guilt, the Sage informs us, has no basis in the Cosmic Order. (For a better understanding *see* p. 50, Guilt, Blame, and Shame, and p. 696, Freeing Yourself from Guilt.)

The *I Ching* shows us that the person in charge of affairs succeeds best when he recognizes his dependency on the Cosmos for help, and when he is willing to ask for that help and develop a daily interdependence with the Sage and the Helpers. He needs also to understand and adapt to the way the Sage and the Helpers do things. (*See* p. 689, Freeing Yourself from Mistaken Ideas and Beliefs, and p. 691, Freeing Yourself from Self-Images, and p. 682, Activating the Helpers.)

This hexagram also refers to the person who, rather than relying on the Sage and the Helpers, places his reliance on the use of power, policies, and devices. While such means may bring desired results in the short run, the results come with a fate attached. The person in touch with his inner truth knows that the true source of his protection and furtherance is the Cosmos, when he is in harmony with his inner truth.

"Preponderance of the great" is also a metaphor for the presumed importance of anything that is seen as "higher," or "special," and therefore as "over" other things. Mostly it refers to the hierarchical values promoted by the collective ego, and to the ultimate collapse of that system of values. The collapse occurs, for example, when a person has put all his energies into accumulating money, power, fame, or position, or a highly regarded self-image, only to find that these things are empty of the satisfaction expected. He does not realize that by defining things as higher and lower, he has separated from his true nature and the Cosmic Whole, and thereby has deprived himself of the chi energy he needs for his life, as well as the help that would have come to him from the Cosmos to fulfill his true destiny.

The preponderance of the great is also a metaphor for the

exaggerated importance humans have given to their large brain (cerebral cortex), by seeing it as designed to "govern" the other parts of the brain and body. In this view, the brain stem is derided as "the reptilian brain" and regarded only as an embarrassing "remnant of our animal nature." The importance of the brain stem, as the Sage has made us aware, is that it connects a person's conscious mind with the feeling consciousness of the rest of his body. When the thinking mind puts itself over the rest of the body, the person is shut off from his connection with his inner truth, and therefore also from his connection with the Cosmic Whole.

One of the harmful effects of this idea is that it has ruled out the existence of the invisible world and its Helpers, leaving the person who holds this view to his own devices. Believing that he is responsible for making everything work invariably leads to stress, and when success does not come, the stress leads to hardness, indifference to others (from whom the person has become isolated), and a serious disturbance in his will to live.

Also implied in the above idea that people are responsible to make everything work is the idea that "there are no limits to what humans can do." Connected with it is the grandiose fantasy that humans can even overcome the physical laws of Nature when they are encountered in Fate. Thinking that Fate has its origin in Nature, people believe that they have to conquer it through *fighting*, as for example in fighting illness, decay, or so-called natural disasters ("acts of God"). (*See* p. 40, Fate.)

Note: Since all lines contain infinite possibilities of interpretation, one needs to use the *rtcm* to determine if the meanings suggested here apply to the given situation. (*See* p. 736 for using the *rtcm*.)

Line 1. *To spread white rushes underneath. No blame.*

This line describes the person who is burdened, like Atlas, with the world on his shoulders, and whose will to go on is ready to collapse. The line suggests that if he spreads white rushes on the ground, he may safely put his burden down on top of them. "To spread white rushes" is a metaphor for saying the inner No to carrying the burdens of the world (or of the state, the company, or the family), and thereby invoking the Helper of Transformation. "No blame" is saying that there is no blame in refusing to take on impossible burdens. The Helper of Transformation is always called into action when we say the inner No to mistaken ideas about our true place in the Cosmos: that we are "the center of the universe, and therefore have the responsibility for everything that happens." For this inner No to be effective, the person needs to rid himself of all the heroic self-images that drive him to take on impossible tasks, such as the self-image of "the one who does everything right," or "the one who is indispensable for the well-being of the whole." The seeming virtuousness of such self-images hides their magnificence, and the fact that they drive the person to undertake tasks that are beyond human capability, and which exhaust his will. Ridding himself of them will bring him back to humility, and connect him with the Cosmic Whole. It will also free the Helpers to do whatever is needed.

Spells connected with this line are created by the following phrases: "You have to do it all yourself," "you are indispensable," "you are responsible to take care of those who cannot help themselves," "life is for the heroes of this world," "you can do the impossible." (*See* p. 697, Freeing Yourself from Spells.)

This line also refers to the fate a person has incurred through having adopted any of the mistaken ideas and self-images mentioned above. His fate cannot be "overcome" by fighting it, but it can be ended if he will rid himself of the mistaken idea and self-image that have caused it. His fate can come in the form of an illness, such as Alzheimer's disease.

Line 2. *A dry poplar sprouts at the root. Everything furthers.**

Here the dry poplar is a metaphor for the large brain (cerebral cortex) that has "dried out," because it has been cut off from its connection with the brain stem through one or more spells that were put on the person's feelings ("thinking is superior to feeling," "thinking brings clarity," "your feelings do not

---

* The line traditionally includes this phrase: "An older man takes a young wife. Everything furthers." This phrase was omitted because it incorrectly approves that an older man should resort to marrying a young woman to restore his chi energy, rather than seeking to free his true self.

count," "they cannot be trusted because they are only subjective," etc.). Receiving this line can be confirming that a person has made connection to his brain stem by paying attention to his dreams, by meditating, or by asking for and following the guidance given by the Sage. When this is the case, it is extremely fortunate for the situation. Such a person needs to say the inner No to others who would encourage him to dismiss such dreams or experiences in meditation as unimportant.

This line can also refer to a person who has lost his will to live, due to the belief that he has no purpose in life. The "sprouting at the root" is a metaphor for an event that makes him feel his life may have a purpose after all. This line reassures him that the fact that he is alive gives his life a purpose, and that he does not need a special purpose apart from this fact. Until now, he may have thought of purpose only in terms of his head (forebrain activity), rather than in terms of his heart. The poplar, as a tree that draws large quantities of water, is a metaphor for the way the forebrain is meant to draw on the chi energy that comes from the heart (*see* Hexagram 48, *The Well*, as a metaphor for the heart). This chi energy can flow from the heart only via the person's feelings: from his heart through the brain stem, then through the limbic system, and from there, if not blocked by spells, to his two frontal lobes. The heart can be reconnected with the forebrain through understanding and respecting the true function and importance of the other parts of the brain, and his feelings.

This line also describes what happens when we, upon being confronted with a person who is totally under the domination of the ego, inwardly ask the Sage that is in that person's presence, to help him: the Sage can then displace the ruling ego aspect in that person and connect him with his inner truth.

Line 3. *The ridgepole sags to the breaking point. Misfortune.*
The subject of this line is the duress put upon people by mistaken ideas of duties or rights. The ridgepole is a metaphor for a person's will to live. Even an unconscious loss of will is a message to the person's body that it is time to die, a message that deprives his body cells of chi energy. This is the "misfortune"

indicated. Receiving this line can indicate that a person's chi energy has become completely exhausted due to a block put on the connection between his large brain and his brain stem by a mistaken idea of duty or right. The person can reverse this situation if he rids himself of the mistaken idea in question. It can be any of the ideas mentioned in Line 1, or an idea that has to do with supposed "rights," "privileges," or "ownership."

The line can also refer to blocks that have been imposed upon a relationship, causing the bond between those involved, represented here by the ridgepole, to be undermined to the breaking point. The blocks come from complying with false duties and expectations that have been superimposed upon the relationship, and which have become expressed as rights, privileges, and ownership. The parties involved need to deprogram these mistaken ideas and recognize that every true relationship comes as a gift from the Cosmos. Relationships cannot be taken for granted, demanded, or owned. We lose the relationship when we no longer recognize its gift nature. (*See* p. 697, Freeing Yourself from Spells and Poison Arrows [that accompany rights, expectations, and ownership].)

Line 4. *The ridgepole is braced. Good fortune. If there are ulterior motives, it is humiliating.*

"The ridgepole is braced" can be confirming that a person's will to go on has been supported, because he or someone else has said the necessary inner No to a dominant self-image. If, however, the No has only been said to get free of his misery, and he then allows the same ego-driven habits to be reinstalled (the ulterior motive mentioned), this would cause the Helpers to retreat, and the problem to return. The will can also be braced by cooperating directly with the body consciousness, as in Reiki, or acupuncture. The same warning applies, that if the person only seeks to become free of his misery, without removing its cause (a mistaken idea or belief), his return to his old habits will also create a return of the problem.

The line can also be warning a person who has been helped by the Sage to deprogram a self-image, not to relax into careless self-confidence. He is also warned not to think that the problem has been sufficiently addressed. The reason for caution is that he has still not uncovered the deepest cause of the problem, which is his lack of self-worth. This lack is created by one or more false phrases or images which he has adopted in childhood. So long as this self-doubt remains, the person will continue to create ever new self-images to compensate for his presumed lack. With the help of the Sage and the *rtcm*, the complex of phrases and images can be found and deprogrammed.

The mention of "ulterior motives" refers to ways the ego seeks to undo what the Sage and the Helpers have achieved, as when a person allows the ego to conclude that the importance of the problem was overestimated, when he brags about the success achieved, as if in being helped, he has a special connection with the Cosmos, or when, after being helped, he feels guilty because he thinks his former beliefs would not approve of the Sage and the Helpers. Guilt, as mentioned throughout the *I Ching*, is the main means by which the collective ego keeps control over the individual, in order to prevent him from following his inner truth. (*See* p. 696, Freeing Yourself from Guilt.)

Line 5. *A withered poplar puts forth flowers. An older woman takes a husband. No blame.*

The withered poplar is the image of a partnership whose substance has "withered away." Its brief flowering represents the virtuous image it shows to the public as it dies within.

Another meaning of the line is the "flowering" of a person who has freed himself from an autonomous neurotic complex that caused his "withering," by projecting it onto someone else. This happens, for example, when a person turns the responsibility for his fate over to his partner, friend, teacher, doctor, or minister. The "older woman," in this circumstance, is the one who takes on this responsibility. Such a person acts on the belief that it is his responsibility to take on other's burdens, and that doing so is free of blame. In fact, by his action, he takes on the fate of the person he is helping, because he has prevented the other from learning what the burden of his fate would teach him.

Line 6. *One must go through the water. It goes over one's head. Misfortune, no blame.*

This line, with its emphasis on the word "must," states the essence of the collective ego's view of duty: that when a person's duty requires sacrificing his life, he must take that path. As Wilhelm's commentary to this line puts it: "there is no blame in giving up one's life that the good and the right may prevail."

This view also states the feudal tradition that it is a person's duty, if necessary, to sacrifice his life for the values held up by the collective ego. From the Cosmic viewpoint, this idea is false through and through, for life is a gift from the Cosmos that is not meant to be squandered on the ego. Following such an idea places a person under great duress, because he is prevented from following his inner truth. Indeed, it may be that a person's inner truth may lead him to make such a sacrifice, but then it is based on needs prompted by the inner truth of the situation at a given moment; it does not come from a moral duty spelled out by someone outside himself.

A person may receive this line to inform him that his will to live is diminished because he holds to the collective ego's ideas of duty mentioned above.

This line can also refer to someone who is going "through the water" due to two mistaken beliefs: (1) that he is born into this life without help, and (2) that he must "do it all himself." When the latter idea is combined with the phrase, "you are responsible for others, and for the greater good," the burden becomes overwhelming in time, unless he recognizes that help is available from the invisible world. Failing to recognize this, an inner message is given to his body, which deprives it of the chi energy necessary to continue living. People who rigidly refuse to consider that there is help available outside the visible world must indeed "go through the water."

29. *The Abyss/Danger**

K'an
K'an

The Judgment: *The abyss repeated. If you are sincere, you have success in your heart, and whatever you do succeeds.*

The Sage uses this hexagram to make us aware that the abyss is a false description of the Cosmic Consciousness as a "bottomless pit" of utter darkness into which one can fall and become permanently lost. This image falsely equates the Cosmic Consciousness with what a person is afraid of, what he does not understand, or is unable to verify with his forebrain.

The abyss is also a metaphor for the collective monumental fears a person has stored in his psyche, and as such, is the fearful aspect of the demonic sphere of consciousness created by the collective ego. In this regard, the hexagram is connected with the very real danger that the true self might fall into oblivion (the person may forget who he truly is); this is something that can actually happen if the ego completely takes over the personality.** The abyss is also the fear of death a person can experience—a fear created by the collective ego in its picturing the

---

*The hexagram was traditionally associated with rushing water as a metaphor for danger. The problem with this association is that danger is consequently equated with an aspect of Nature. The problem of danger is not with Nature, but with the human failure to observe the limits of human existence. The danger associated with Nature was again extended to the Cosmic Consciousness as threatening, by referring to it as the "unknown."

**As Søren Kierkegaard puts it, in his "Sickness Unto Death": "But to be in despair, although usually obvious, does not mean that a person may not continue living a fairly good life, to all appearances be honored and esteemed—and one may fail to notice that in a deeper sense he lacks a self. Such things cause little stir in the world; for in the world a self is what one least asks after, and the thing it is most dangerous of all to show signs of having. The biggest danger, that of losing oneself, can pass off in the world as quietly as if it were nothing: every other loss, an arm, a leg, five dollars, a wife, etc., is bound to be noticed." (Penguin Classics, London, 1989, pp. 62-63) (We thank our editor for this quotation.)

end of life in a body as a loss. The Sage makes us aware that loss, as a term, has no Cosmic validity, and this is why the words in The Judgment of Hexagram 55, *Abundance,* say, "be not sad." (Also *see* Glossary: Death, and Loss.)

The main theme of this hexagram is the way fears operate in the psyche. The psyche, in *I Ching* terms, is the invisible aspect of a person's whole being; it refers to the person's the total consciousness, including what is called the unconscious and the subconscious. (*See* Glossary: Psyche.)

Fears that enter the mind are stored throughout the body in the cells themselves. Some are located in the brain, some in the heart and other organs, while others are located in the muscles. Sometimes, in meditation, they show themselves in the areas where they are stored.

Fears are stored in the body as feeling-memories. These feelings are connected with the adrenaline that accompanied the experience that caused them; they are feelings, so to speak, that became congealed, and which recreate a sense of alarm when any event similar to the original experience is encountered.

While fears are of many sorts and have many causes, this hexagram addresses the primal fears of the psyche: fear of the unknown, death, punishment, abandonment, and of not having enough essential nourishment for one's whole being, whether that is actually food, or chi energy. Primal fears comprise the source of all other fears.

These primal fears have their origin in the inner experience of being separated from the Cosmic Whole, which happens when the access to one's inner truth gets blocked. This experience is what the *I Ching* means when it speaks of the loss of innocence, as described in Hexagram 25, *Innocence.*

This hexagram shows what happens in the brain when the ego is the absolute ruler of the personality: the rational mind operates autonomously, thus excluding the midbrain and brain stem, which connect a person with his inner truth and with the Cosmic Consciousness. The false self-confidence that accompanies the development of the ego represses his fears (that are created by the collective ego's mistaken ideas about life and the nature of the Cosmos) into the subconscious. However, the self-confidence is only a thin mask covering them. During periods of crisis and shock, this self-confidence collapses, throwing the entire personality into doubt and dismay. It is in such situations that a person receives this hexagram, which is given to help him understand the dynamics of his situation, and to return him to a place of inner safety. The counsel he is given begins with the statement: "If you are sincere, you have success in your heart, and whatever you do succeeds."

Sincerity comes when a person recognizes that despite his greatest efforts, he cannot do alone what he needs to do to help himself. In this state he calls out for help, not knowing where the help will come from, and this is the moment when the help comes. It comes from the Sage, that draws to the person's help all the other Helpers of the invisible world that he needs at that time.

In terms of consciousness, the trigram K'an, as described in Part I, stands for the role of *thinking*. Here, where the trigram is doubled, we are presented with a state of mind in which a person is trying to resolve a problem merely through thinking. This creates the danger of his getting lost in a maze of fears, because he is trying to resolve through thinking, a problem that has been created by thinking that has been divorced from feeling.

Spells connected with this hexagram have to do with a number of images projected onto the Cosmic Consciousness: as unknowable, as an abyss into which one can fall and be lost forever, or a Hell of eternal suffering. These images lock the person into an abyss of fears that prevent him from recognizing the caring and loving nature of the Cosmos, and from receiving its help and protection. They also prevent him from realizing that there is no Cosmic abyss into which he can fall; the only abyss that exists is the demonic sphere of consciousness created by the erroneous ideas and beliefs of the collective ego.

Note: Since all lines contain infinite possibilities of interpretation, one needs to use the *rtcm* to determine if the meanings suggested here apply to the given situation. (*See* p. 736 for using the *rtcm*.)

Line 1. *Repetition of the abysmal. In the abyss one falls into the pit. Misfortune.*

"Repetition of the abysmal" refers to the fears that haunt a person's subconscious. By not resisting them, they gain extraordinary power (the meaning of falling into the pit in the abyss), leading him to act rashly, creating misfortune.

Line 2. *The abyss is dangerous. One should strive to attain small things only.*

"The abyss is dangerous" counsels a person not to act so long as he is being influenced by his fears.

"One should strive to attain small things only" is saying to turn his attention inward to address and free himself from these fears, before he does anything else. The fears, which are stored in the psyche as words and images, have dressed up in demonic forms, such as shadowy figures, or demons, dragons, and imps, which have declared themselves to be invincible, and to be a part of himself from which he cannot free himself. This line tells him that they are not part of him, but are intruders into his inner space. He needs to ask in meditation for the Cosmic Army to kill them. Once their demonic manifestations have been killed, their true nature as words and images become visible, and they can then be rejected through saying the inner No to them.

The abyss is dangerous also refers to a mistaken idea about death as a final end of life. (*See* Glossary: Death.)

Line 3. *Forward and backward, abyss on abyss. In danger like this, pause at first and wait, otherwise you will fall into a pit in the abyss. Do not act in this way.*

"Forward and backward" refers to being buffeted between two fears, as in the expression, "to be between a rock and a hard place." This indicates a person who sees only two alternatives in the given situation, and therefore fears he will be crushed, no matter which he chooses. Because this view fails to recognize the existence of the invisible world and its Helpers, he is left to his own devices, without help. "Pause at first and wait" is counsel for him to look for the help he needs from the Sage, and to address the problem in the inner realm, where the only true and lasting solutions can be found.

The line can also refer to a person who finds himself in a

double bind created by two opposing standards of the collective ego, so that whichever way he moves, it is incorrect. An example is the modern woman who has been "liberated" from the old models of a "woman's role" in the world to follow a career. At the same time, she retains the ancient belief that to "be a real woman" she must have had a child. These views set her into a continuous conflict mode which makes her doubt herself, whichever path she chooses. Both models lead her away from recognizing that in and of herself she is adequate, without having to fulfill any preassigned role.

This line also points to the poison arrow of guilt taken on by a person who believes in original fault. Such an idea plunges him into the abyss of self-conflict. The Cosmic Way out of this situation is to rid himself of the poison arrow of guilt. (*See* p. 696, Freeing Yourself from Guilt.)

"Pause at first and wait" counsels a person to stop, when in danger, and find out the inner truth of the situation before acting.

Line 4. *A jug of wine, a bowl of rice with it; earthen vessels simply handed in through the window. There is certainly no blame in this.*

Receiving this line informs a person that the Sage is coming to help. The Sage comes to help because the person has asked for help, therefore, the gifts needed, that truly nourish and aid him, are given simply and without strings attached. The Sage acts without blame.

Line 5. *The abyss is not filled to overflowing. It is filled only to the rim. No blame.*

This line draws attention to the rim that surrounds the abyss, as that element in the psyche that keeps the contents of the subconscious from overflowing its boundaries. The rim is thus the borderline that separates a person's subconscious from his conscious mind. When someone is addressing his problems in co-operation with the Sage, the Sage brings the person's fears from his subconscious to his conscious mind in the exact sequence that is best for him. The Sage carefully watches over this borderline in such a way that the person is never overwhelmed.

This line also points to someone who thinks that he can keep his fears under control through "being reasonable," or by counterbalancing them with positive thinking, with positive imaging, or by sheer self-discipline. Attempts to counteract fears are not successful, because they ignore their root causes. Success is achieved by rooting them out one-by-one, under the guidance of the Sage. (See p. 693, Freeing Yourself from Fears.)

Line 6. *Bound with cords and ropes, shut in between thorn-hedged prison walls: for three years one does not find the way. Misfortune.*
This line is about the fear of suffering and the fear of death. "Bound with cords and ropes" refers to the fate that these fears create, in that they project themselves into reality.

The prison walls refer to the spells these fears put on various parts of the psyche. That the walls are described as thorn-hedged refers to their entangling quality as they affect all parts of the person's life. When he lives in fear of death, this fear transmits itself to every aspect of his life. Thus, he misses out on the fullness of life and its invigorating quality. If he sees this principle clearly, he will say the inner No to the seed phrase that perpetuates the fear of death: "all things end in death."

"Three years" refers to the fact that spells are made up of a circular reference which leads the person around in circles. A circular reference is a false logical construction, the basic premise of which is a half-truth. A half-truth is a relative truth that has been converted into an absolute truth. The half-truth, in this case, is "life *is* suffering." Suffering is not a natural part of life. It is what a person experiences when he has excluded the Helpers in all that he does. The Sage makes us aware that there are Helpers available for every circumstance. They are activated by every sincere call for help. When the ego has prevented the person from ignoring the cornucopia of gifts the Cosmos gives daily, the Helpers no longer come, and the person suffers. The circular reference thus proves the premise on which it is based.

30. *Attaining Clarity*

The Judgment: *Firm attachment to what is correct brings success. Care of the cow brings good fortune.*

The Sage shows the theme of this hexagram to be the Cosmic Principle of Clarity as a characteristic feature of Cosmic Logic. Like all Cosmic Principles that form harmony, clarity and Cosmic Logic are attained through a combination of thinking and feeling. They cannot be attained through mental effort alone. Clarity is attained through connecting with our inner truth, with the help of the Sage. The Cosmic Logic within a situation is mostly perceptible after the fact.

To attain clarity, all of a person's *inner* senses are involved. The result is a consensus of these senses, which in their aggregate, form his commonsense. However, because our senses are often blocked by spells caused by our conditioning, we need the help of the Sage to find the inner truth until such time as we have liberated our inner senses. (*See* Glossary: The Senses.) Finding the inner truth requires that we ask the Sage for a hexagram, and then clarify its meaning with the help of the *rtcm*, until we have reached an adequate understanding of the situation.

"The cow" is a metaphor for a person's commonsense. "Care of the cow" means to recognize the true function of *all* the senses, and to free them from the spells and poison arrows that are put on them when we dismiss or denigrate their value, and give preponderance instead to the two outer senses of seeing and hearing. All the senses have figurative components that, together, tell the complete truth about a situation. Our nose, for example, wrinkles involuntarily when something is foul. We also need to consciously affirm the neglected senses by saying the emphatic inner Yes to them that will restore them to their proper place in our personalities.

"Firm attachment to what is correct" counsels a person to firmly attach himself to following the inner truth he has discovered about the situation, and not allow himself to be drawn away from it by arguments that point to so-called *obvious* truths, or *absolute* truths, which stipulate what he is "supposed" to think and attach himself to.

This hexagram also concerns false attachments a person may have, whether they are to an idea, a belief, a person, a self-image, possessions, his nationality, race, family, or to a desire, a pact, a promise, or to a goal.

All false attachment has its origin in the adoption of rigid beliefs promoted by the collective ego. These beliefs are often exalted as ancient wisdom or established truths that we are not permitted to question. Behind false attachment is the ego's fear of loss. (*See* Glossary: Loss.) This fear leads the person to attaching himself to things, or it drives him to the opposite extreme of making non-attachment a goal. Even beliefs that rigidly *practice* non-attachment as the measure of spiritual achievement are themselves a form of attachment.

Clarity is lacking when we attach ourselves to the wrong things. A person may receive this hexagram when he is too attached to his appearance, name, class, background, tradition, etc. In all these cases, he lacks the clarity to see that it is the ego in him which is attached to them. Likewise, a person may receive this hexagram when he is not attached enough to what is correct, as to his Cosmic Virtues, or to his body because he considers it base or unattractive. Clarity is to see that his psyche and body are one, and that to hate or disregard any part of it is to invite its abuse and injury. The same applies when a person puts aside his integrity, dignity, modesty, and sense of what is correct, in exchange for egotistical gains.

Another aspect of clarity has to do with the difference between acting from faith—which is a sort of attaching ourselves to something we want to believe as true—and acting from what we have learned through our experience in consulting the Sage. In the former case, we put ourselves out on a limb and saw it off, to prove that what we believe is true. When we find ourselves fallen on the ground, the ego justifies our belief by saying, "we failed to have enough faith." In learning from the Sage, we recognize the Cosmic Principles as true, because they fit the practicability and uniqueness of the situation. These are never absolute truths, but are guidelines for relating to situations within the Cosmic Harmony.

Receiving this hexagram can also call attention to a person's looking to another for help, rather than asking for help from the Helpers.

Note: Since all lines contain infinite possibilities of interpretation, one needs to use the *rtcm* to determine if the meanings suggested here apply to the given situation. (*See* p. 736 for using the *rtcm*.)

Line 1. *Moving with confused steps, but if one is sincere, there is no blame.*

The line indicates a situation in which a person, upon consulting the Sage, does not know how to interpret the counsel given. He therefore moves uncertainly. He would like to let go of his beliefs, but still feels a security in the attachment he has to them. "No blame" is saying that if he puts his established belief aside, he will be protected by the Cosmos, even if he makes a mistake. His sincerity will bring Cosmic Protection against the ill consequences of making mistakes.

The uncertainty addressed above may also be due to feelings of guilt for abandoning an established belief. Guilt is built into the collective ego's program, to keep him attached to its beliefs. He needs to treat guilt as a spell that the collective ego has put on him. (*See* p. 697, Freeing Yourself from Spells.)

Receiving this line can also mean that what a person has learned from the Sage in a previous lesson was a handhold, and that he needs to give the Sage space to expand his understanding.

Line 2. *Yellow Light. Supreme success.*

Yellow light refers to the way the commonsense discerns the truth of things through the light of moderation. This light is produced by the consensus of all the senses, which includes inner truth. Because the clarity produced is in harmony with the Cosmos, it leads to supreme success.

The yellow light of clarity contrasts with the harsh white light of judgment that comes purely from the intellect and from applying absolute standards. This judgment is based purely on the appearance of things, and is expressed in terms of a person or thing being "good" or "evil." Related to this way of judging is the mistaken idea of there being a "culprit" or "guilty party." (For a better understanding of the problems this causes, *see* Glossary: Good and Evil, and Culprit.)

When people or things are described in words that falsely imply the existence of a natural opposition, such as black or white, good or evil, culprit or victim, a discordant dynamic is created. The use of such words creates and maintains the demonic sphere of consciousness. Opposites do not exist within the Cosmic Reality, because the Cosmos operates only through the attraction that exists between its *complementary* aspects.

When a person calls another a culprit he creates a negative attachment between himself and that person that becomes a fate for both of them, so long as the acceptance of that judgment exists. Such judgments need to be treated as projections and spells.

"Supreme success" describes the effect of saying the inner No to everything that is disharmonious, as one might say No to a child who has misbehaved. When, however, the inner No is said with harsh feelings attached to it, only further opposition is created.

Line 3. *In the light of the setting sun, men either beat the pot and sing, or loudly bewail the approach of old age. Misfortune.*

"The light of the setting sun" refers to a person's seeing his life in a body from this point on as being "all downhill." Death is the specter at the end of the descent, an endless chasm that awaits. Such an idea has no Cosmic basis.

A person can receive this line when he has already given up on the possibility of his life succeeding in a harmonious and meaningful way. He imagines that it is too late to correct things, and may have even lost his will to live. He does not realize that there is always the possibility of making a new beginning, with the help of the Sage. Even if there is only the smallest ember of

chi energy giving life to his existence, it is possible to reinvigo-
rate his supply of life-force. What this requires is his willingness
to take his correct place in the Cosmic Whole, and to make the
effort to free himself from his mistaken beliefs about life and
death. (*See* Glossary: Death.)

He also needs to deprogram any preconceived images and
beliefs about old age: that it is accompanied by sickness, debili-
tating diseases, suffering, the onset of deafness, blindness, helplessness, etc., since every belief about what "might" happen
projects itself into reality.

Line 4. *Its coming is sudden, it flames up, dies down, is thrown
away.*

The straw fire that flames up, dies down and is thrown away
can refer to glimpses of clarity that a person attains through his
learning with the Sage. Because he does not inquire further, his
understanding is only partial, and therefore he jumps to the
false conclusion that what the Sage has said was not true.

Receiving this line can also indicate the presence of seed
phrases that discredit the good results achieved through inner
effort, such as, "it cannot be as easy as that" (in reference to
saying the inner No), "anything worthwhile is difficult," or "no
pain, no gain," or "for such a process one needs a (human)
guide."

"It flames up, dies down, is thrown away" describes the way
enlightened ideas coming from human masters fail, because they
have no substance for the person who follows them. The reason
is that they keep him from consulting his own inner truth. When
a person consults his inner truth, his insights are the product of
his connection with the Cosmic Consciousness. These insights
have substance, in that they manifest in the harmonious way
his life succeeds, in the fact that they are supported by all the
Cosmic Helpers, and in the fact that they create in him a true
inner independence and self-worth.

Line 5. *Tears in floods, sighing and lamenting. Good fortune.*

"Tears in floods, sighing and lamenting" can indicate a self-
blame spell a person has put on himself, after realizing that he

has been following the mistaken belief that one must "accept adversity." He may even have been convinced that adversity is "part of life," and that accepting it made him a good person. Having given up this belief is the first step toward good fortune; the second step requires only that he rid himself of his self-blame-spell for having so valiantly followed the wrong belief. (*See* p. 697, Freeing Yourself from Spells.)

"Tears in floods," as in prolonged mourning, comes from the belief that death is the enemy of human existence. The person who believes this gives power to death by raising it as an active specter in his life. He needs to rid himself of seed phrases, such as, "death is inevitable," "death is human fate," or "death is lamentable," since these phrases form spells. The same applies to the image of death as "a reaper." (*See* p. 697, Freeing Yourself from Spells.)

Line 6. *The king uses him to march forth and chastise. Then it is best to kill the leaders and take captive the followers. No blame.*

The king referred to is the Sage. The line informs a person that he is meant to be helped by the Sage in correcting the abuses of others through saying the inner No to their inappropriate actions and intentions, and through not participating himself in the evil being done.

Killing the leaders instead of the followers refers to saying the inner No to the central idea that is responsible for the problem. Deprogramming the central idea enables the Helpers to "kill" the followers (its supporting rationales).

This line also calls our attention to times when it is unavoidable to relate to people who, through allowing themselves to be completely dominated by the ego, have exhausted their life energy, so that they are among the "walking dead." Such people have totally separated themselves from the Cosmic Whole, through turning their wills over to the collective ego. Their bodies live on by the fact that the egos in them steal the life energy of others. The ego achieves this through gaining the pity, sympathy, and compassion of these others, or through making them feel indebted, guilty, or otherwise obligated to pay attention to them. When a person realizes, through using the *rtcm*, that he is being drained of chi energy in this way, he needs to be inwardly disconnected and neutral in the presence of such people, to prevent giving them his energy. It is also important that he not view them as culprits, as that, too, would give them energy. Because the Sage is in the presence of every person, it is helpful to ask the Sage to call in the Cosmic Army to kill the demonic elements that have taken their bodies, and to revive their true

31. Influence

Tui
Kên

The Judgment: *Influence. Success. If one is firm and correct in taking the mate offered, it brings good fortune.*

In this hexagram the Sage teaches the Cosmic Principles of Relations and Influencing. One of the Cosmic meanings of "influence" is the active intervention of the Sage in giving the gift of love. To be "firm and correct" is counsel to refrain from *seeking* a mate, so that the true love relationship can arise as a gift from the Cosmos. In a related sense, to be firm and correct means to refrain from trying to make things happen, through realizing that all great achievements occur through the intervention of the Cosmic Helpers, and that we merely assist in externalizing their influence.

"Good fortune" refers to the gift of love itself, through which two people's suppressed and neglected true selves recognize each other. The purpose of this recognition is to give them an opportunity to free their true natures from the oppression of the egos within them. In the process, their life force (chi) is renewed by the love that flows from the Cosmos to and through them.

For a love relationship to have the success indicated in The Judgment, it is necessary for each partner to free himself from his preconceived ideas of what a love relationship is, specifically from beliefs that hold that it must be inextricably connected with the custom of marriage, or with ownership, rights, privileges, and moral rules. Due to its gift nature, the love relationship is subject only to the Cosmic Harmonics, and will endure only so long as each partner keeps his primary connection with the Cosmic Whole by being loyal to his inner truth. Being loyal to one's inner truth means to be centered within oneself, and to firmly hold to what feels harmonious and correct: one acts only so long as one sees with clarity what is correct. The person consulting the *I Ching* allows himself to be guided to discover the inner truth of each situation. (*See* p. 680, Centering Yourself.)

The term "good fortune" also points to other Cosmic gifts such as great inventions and discoveries (that are often falsely credited to humans), and abilities the Cosmos gives to humans to perform great feats, for which the people are but channels. (Often, the inventor (researcher, writer, performer, etc.) credits the Cosmos as the true source of his achievement—Einstein and Mozart being excellent examples. It is the collective ego that appropriates their achievements by making them into "monuments of culture," and by using them to prove the superiority of the human species.)

In another meaning, this hexagram refers to harmful influences we project upon the Cosmos in the form of ideas, emotions, and attitudes. These influences include preconceived ideas, ego-emotions and attitudes, and ritually spoken words, as in sayings and mantras. Their influence has the power to objectify and freeze reality in time (= to put a spell on something). Because all existence is composed of consciousness, negative human consciousness can have a destructive influence on the object of its focus.

This hexagram also concerns the unconscious influences created in the personality by the ego through its use of false words, phrases and images. Once integrated within the psyche as an active program, they become the source of impulsive and compulsive behaviors. In dreams, meditations, and hallucinatory states they show themselves to be a part of the demonic sphere of consciousness, appearing as imps, demons, and dragons. (See Glossary: Demonic Sphere of Consciousness.) The imps, which are behind impulsive behaviors, generally speak in the psyche in demanding "musts" and "shoulds." Demons appear in the psyche either as threatening animals or grotesque figures such as vampires. As voices, they speak repetitively, as if to hammer the same message over and over. Dragons take on overweening images of authority. Together, they have a paralyzing effect that prevents the person from moving forward in his life, and are behind both his fears and his hopes. In the body they create irregular responses, such as heart irregularities, high blood pressure, compulsive eating disorders, and tics. Dragons are control elements that keep the whole demonic structure in place. They succeed through back-of-the-mind threats that the person will become guilty if he rejects the program of the collective ego. Although all three of these demonic elements form a self-reinforcing system, the demons and dragons originate with the imps. Imps, demons, and dragons cannot be battled in the psyche as objective entities, since any attempt at fighting them only strengthens their resistance and their ability to create new means of control. It is possible, however, to deprogram them, phrase by phrase and image by image. Lines in the *I Ching* that speak of hunting have to do with finding the phrases and images that give life to these figures. Lines that speak of "killing" have to do with deprogramming them with the aid of the Helpers. It is also possible to "kill" such elements in meditation. (See Hexagram 8, *Holding Together*, Line 5, and Hexagram 40, *Freeing*, Line 2.)

This hexagram also concerns the ways by which group-egos expand their power and influence over other groups or individuals: (1) by buying them through favors, (2) by integrating them through tolerance, (3) by evangelizing them, or (4) by assimilating them. The latter is carried out by dismissing the true insights that come to individuals by claiming that they are already part of the group-ego's beliefs and that there is already a name for them. Once the individual is brought into the group, his insight is dismissed as irrelevant.

The lines of this hexagram show which body parts are affected (metaphorically) by these demonic elements. The toe mentioned in Line 1, for example, is the beginning place of impulsive movement. The calves of the leg, mentioned in Line 2, indicate the area of the body that is influenced by demons. The thighs, mentioned in Line 3, are the area influenced by dragons. These body parts, in turn, are connected with certain aspects of the psyche, which are located in the limbic system of the brain. The consciousness of the limbic system operates outside the thinking consciousness, therefore it is that part of the brain which the ego seeks to influence. Since it is responsible for directing both the motions of the body and the emotions, uncontrolled behaviors are produced when it is subjected to these demonic elements.

The hexagram as a whole shows how the collective ego influences the individual through its misuse of language. For example, it asserts that if a person follows his inner truth, he will endanger the social order, and his own place in it. In this articulation, the social order created by the collective ego is presented as the *only* order, without which there would be chaos. Presenting things in this way obscures the fact that a natural social order which is in perfect harmony with the Cosmos, is possible. Obliterating this possibility allows the collective ego to dominate society in the same way that the true self is obliterated by the dominance of the individual ego. We are thus prevented from seeing that the natural order of society emerges whenever people follow their inner truth. When we rid ourselves of the ego, we remove the sole support for the continuance of the collective ego. (*See* p. 54, The Natural Social Order.)

Finally, this hexagram is about the way we relate to other people and to Nature. In relating to another, we are meant to distinguish between relating from ideas, which, when isolated from feeling, cause us to relate in vapid and insensitive ways that exclude the heart. It is the difference between talking *at* someone and *with* someone.

Since we have been trained to think in human-centered terms, we are generally unaware of how our preconceived ideas about Nature influence Nature in the same way that projections, spells, and poison arrows influence people. An example is the way we put poisons on our lawns instead of asking for help from the consciousnesses of the grass and the grubs to come into balance with each other. The act of putting poisons out to kill the grubs not only poisons the ground water on which humans rely, it puts a poison arrow on the grubs by viewing them as an invading army which must be fought, creating in them a demonic force that causes even more imbalance in Nature. The natural state of Nature is harmony. When humans project their mistaken ideas upon it, as in seeing Nature as intrinsically chaotic and needing man's taming, discordant conditions are created. To correct this kind of damage, each person needs to learn to keep his mind innocent, as Hexagram 25, *Innocence. Not Expecting/Not Projecting*, makes clear.

Note: Since all lines contain infinite possibilities of interpretation, one needs to use the *rtcm* to determine if the meanings suggested here apply to the given situation. (*See* p. 736 for using the *rtcm*.)

Line 1. *The influence shows itself in the big toe.*

The big toe is a metaphor for being moved by impulses, rather than by one's commonsense. Impulses always come from the ego and its imp-like nature, and are based on mistaken ideas and beliefs. Receiving this line makes a person aware that he is about to act impulsively, which would lead to misfortune.

Receiving this line is counsel that before acting, a person needs to empty his mind of preconceived ideas, and all petty likes and dislikes that distance him from Nature and from his body. The correct influence comes from inner stillness, which both attracts the Cosmic Helpers, and enables the correct spontaneous response to arise from one's inner truth.

The Cosmic Helpers referred to are the metaphorical senses that are located in a person's body cells. Among these senses are a sense of wholeness, a sense of danger, a sense of caution, a sense of appropriateness, etc. As part of his feeling consciousness, the function of these senses is to defend him against harmful influences coming from without or from within, in the form of spells, projections, or poison arrows. Whenever any such influence has invaded, these senses give signals through the nerves to make the person aware that he needs to look for the causes of his disharmonious feelings. When he fails to pay attention to these signals, they become stronger, causing an intense feeling of dis-ease.

All such feelings of dis-ease are messages given by the Helpers to awaken the person's attention. They are to be distinguished from the acute and sharp feelings of pain that occasionally accompany an invading poison arrow, projection, or spell. Pain indicates that harm is being done to specific parts of the body as well as to the psyche. It is a mistake to regard either the discomfort caused by the Helpers or the pain caused by the injury as enemies that need to be fought. When we do this, we assign wrong reasons to the wrong places and create inner conflict, further weakening our natural defenses against the invading elements. If these elements are left untouched, they actively damage the host by living on his life energy. (*See* p. 697, Freeing Yourself from Poison Arrows, and p. 695, Freeing Yourself from Pain.)

The ego, rather than defending the person against such harmful influences, feeds on the negative energy produced by spells, projections, and poison arrows. An example is blame that is put on a person to make him feel guilty. The ego feeds on the feeling of guilt, much the way a worm feeds on flesh. It also feeds on the negative energies produced by the inner conflict created when pain is stigmatized as an enemy. The "bright idea" which the ego offers—that pain is the only important thing to address—can be seen as a ploy to keep the harmful elements in place.

Line 2. *The influence shows itself in the calves of the leg. Misfortune. Tarrying brings good fortune.*
"The calves" are the part of the body that moves it forward. Influence showing itself in the calves is a metaphor for rushing to judgment or conclusions without seeing the whole picture. This can happen in three ways: (1) when, through impatience, the person has not allowed the whole picture to reveal itself, or has not inquired into the inner truth of the matter; (2) when he has a vested interest in seeing the situation from an egotistical perspective; (3) when, through projecting fears or doubts upon the situation, he creates the results feared. In the latter case he may believe he has been approaching the situation objectively, whereas in reality he has created a spell, projection, or poison arrow.

"Tarrying brings good fortune" means that when we retreat from our preconceived ideas to ask the Sage for clarity, we are helped to see the inner truth of the matter. However, the Sage can only help us when there is no impatience. Examples of images that have to do with impatience are: the image that a disaster will occur if we do not act, or the self-important image that the whole world depends upon what we (as humans) do.

Line 3. *The influence shows itself in the thigh. Holds to that which follows it. To continue is humiliating.*

Receiving this line tells a person that the desire that he thinks is coming from his heart is actually coming from the ego (referred to by the thigh), and that to follow it will bring him humiliation.

"Holds to that which follows it" is a metaphor for a co-dependency between a person and the idealized image with which he is infatuated. He is like the young person who has fallen in love with love itself. Wanting love, the person has put himself under a spell—a compulsion—to find someone who looks like his ideal. His body, because of its real need for nourishment, becomes victimized by this drive of the ego and its projected desires. Under the ego's influence, the body is no longer able to distinguish between true love and projected love. Once the body is dominated by the ego in this way, disappointment and humiliation invariably follow.

This situation is a metaphor for all sorts of relationships that are based on the desire for something idealized. Psychotherapists, priests, and gurus all experience the projection of such desires upon them.* If they cultivate or submit to this idealization of themselves, their influence is destructive to the person who idealizes them.

Another aspect of this line has to do with the sense of smell. There is a smell that accompanies a person who "wears" an idealized image to gain a following among others. This smell is projected upon that person by the people who follow him, and becomes part of his aura. To these followers that smell is posi-

* In psychotherapy, this projection is called 'transference'; there is also a corresponding projection coming from the therapist called 'countertransference'.

tive, because it flatters their own sense of smell, which is under the influence of ego-desire.

All projections that are based on the sense of seeing are accompanied by a smell. When the projection idealizes something, the smell is positive; when the projection demonizes something, the smell is negative. Such smells subconsciously influence the person who projects them, keeping him in the orbit of the person who smells good to him.

This line often refers to a person who is held in the orbit of someone he idealizes (a spell). Another may help free him from that spell with the help of the Sage. (*See* p. 697 Freeing Yourself from Spells.)

Line 4. *Firm correctness brings good fortune. Remorse disappears. His thoughts go hither and thither. Only those on whom he fixes his conscious thoughts will follow.*

"Firm correctness brings good fortune" refers to the effect that an influence which comes from the heart has on others: it penetrates to their inner truth. This line stresses the importance of keeping an open heart and a mind free of disharmonious thoughts. Then one's influence on others is good.

The last two phrases, "His thoughts go hither and thither," and, "only those on whom he fixes his conscious thoughts will follow," point to a person who is making an intentional effort to influence another by sending thoughts through the inner channel between them. His intention might be to provoke, to persuade, to subjugate, or to instill guilt. Such intentional efforts not only harm the other, they create a fate for the one who projects them.

This line also speaks of the projections that emanate from a closed heart. An example is a person who has closed his heart in order to deny his blame in a situation, and to project that blame on another. A part of his denial is to mentally "execute" the other, by seeing him as the culprit. This puts a spell on that person, as well as creating a fate for himself. To free himself from his fate, he needs to accept that he was the one who incurred Cosmic blame. He also needs to search out the cause for his incorrect action and free himself of it. Then he needs to remove the blame spell he has put on the other person. If he will make this inner effort, he will be freed from the fate he has created.

A person can also receive this line when he has incorrectly said an inner No. One needs to check with the Sage (through the *rtcm*) whether it is correct to say the inner No in a given circumstance.

The line can also refer to a group projection which identifies someone or something as a culprit. The person taking part in this activity needs to be aware that continuing to do so will involve him in a group fate. He can free himself by saying the inner No to this activity. (*See* Glossary: Culprit.)

Line 5. *The influence shows itself in the back of the neck. No remorse.*

The back of the neck is the area of the body near the brain stem. Receiving this line is to confirm to us that the influence we feel is coming from the right place, and that it is correct to continue holding to our inner truth. On this account there is no remorse.*

The back of the neck is the seat of the will. The firmness that allows a person to hold to his inner truth is due to his will. The strength of his will, in turn, is dependent on the condition of his self-esteem, and to what degree the ego has turned the person's will to its purposes. The more true to his inner truth he is, the more his will is strengthened and renewed by the Cosmos. The more he allows the ego to command his psyche and harness his will, the more the energy of his will is drained. Still, by calling on the Sage for help, his will can be restored if he will use the strength attained to follow his inner truth. This is also one of the meanings of Line 1 in Hexagram 42, *Increasing.*

We are accustomed to think of will as an energy that can be put toward something. In this definition, it appears to be like a

---

*This line contrasts with Line 3 of Hexagram 16, *Enthusiasm*, which says, "enthusiasm that looks upward creates remorse." That line shows how science and ideologies have blocked our access to our inner truth through disdaining the function of the mid-brain and brain stem, and exalting the function of the forebrain (cerebral cortex), with its word memory, imagination, cognitive reasoning, etc.

constant stream that can be turned one way or the other. However, we can readily feel that our will can be strengthened or undermined. The energy of will has its origin in a feeling of robustness. Thus the will is a combination of the feeling and the energy it creates. The relationship between the will and every act of being alive is of crucial importance, not only to the direction one's life takes, but to all matters of health.

When the will is turned to serve the ego, the feeling of robustness is attacked by inner conflict, causing its energy to diminish. The feeling of robustness can also come from the ego, but only while an image of "success" is being achieved. To a certain extent, the lack of success can be bridged by hopes of success, and by self-delusions of various sorts. The word "burnout," used often in connection with deluded enthusiasm, has to do with the exhaustion of these hopes and self-delusions, as the veils of delusion successively fail and fall away. A collapse of will can occur at this point, and it can be beneficial, as Hexagram 51, *Shock* tells us, if the collapse leads the person to cry for help from the Cosmos and consequently reconnects him with his inner truth.

The energy created by feelings of robustness comes from the body itself, where it is stored in the form of sugars and fats. One can say that the will is strongest when the conscious mind expresses the person's inner truth in the basic words/feelings of Yes or No. When a person is unable to say a clear yes or a clear no, it shows that there are "holes" in his psyche and that his will lacks duration. The will can be mobilized temporarily (as Shakespeare shows in "Henry V," when Henry, in a famous speech, rallies his troops to win the battle), but this kind of mobilization only "patches" the holes. Their undermining influence swiftly returns under other circumstances. True enthusiasm, as Hexagram 16, *Enthusiasm*, shows, mobilizes the Helper of Transformation, and calls the entire Cosmos to one's help. The same questions regarding the will also illuminate passages in Hexagram 7, *The Army*. "Holes" in the will lead to cancer, where the failure of will is such that the cells are no longer able to complete their electrical circuits. It is easy to understand how ideas and beliefs that denigrate the body create such holes. (*See*

p. 694, Freeing Yourself from Some Health Problems.)

Line 6. *The influence shows itself in the jaws, cheeks, and tongue.*

The mention of the jaws, cheeks, and tongue calls attention to two different kinds of situations:

(1) A person may be trying to balance, through positive thinking, the negative effect of an influence coming from inside or outside himself, such as fear or guilt. While positive thinking can counteract a negative influence for a certain amount of time, it does not succeed in the long run, because the person does not free himself from the negative influence itself. He is counseled by this line to identify the negative influence, its source, and then to free himself of it, with the guidance of the Sage. After ridding himself of it, he is advised against replacing it with any kind of positive thoughts or images, because his natural inner program is designed to provide him with the right responses to every given circumstance.

(2) A person may believe that what he says lightly in idle conversation, or what others say about him in this manner, produces no harm. Nevertheless it is mostly through idle talk that projections, spells, and poison arrows are created. It is a person's Cosmic duty to take responsibility for everything he says and thinks, and to realize that idle talk and thoughts often cause great harm.

Receiving this line can also have the purpose of making a person aware that he is receiving a destructive influence (projection or spell) from another, through the other's idle gossip. This influence, which creates his inexplicable ill feelings, needs to be intercepted and rejected. (*See* p. 697, Freeing Yourself from Projections and Spells.)

This line can also refer to an incomplete perception, or misunderstanding, such as seeing another as helpless against a "prevailing influence," when, in actuality, he may be under a spell that needs to be recognized and removed.

32. *Duration*

 Chên
___
Sun

The Judgment: *Success. No blame. Perseverance furthers. It furthers one to have somewhere to go.*

In this hexagram, the Sage describes the way the Cosmos achieves the constant evolution of its consciousness, and creates enduring conditions through transformation.

Duration also characterizes the Cosmic Harmonics, the underlying, immutable laws that govern the movement of all things within the Cosmic Reality. These are the preeminent laws that supersede all human-made laws. The Cosmic Harmonics are to the sphere of Cosmic Consciousness what the laws of physics are to the world of form. Together, they insure the duration of the Cosmic Whole. The Cosmic Harmonics and the laws of physics are held together through the Principle of Attraction. They are like the two axles of a big cart, the cart being a metaphor for the Cosmic Reality that endures as it moves through time and space. The energy that makes it move is created by the attraction between the Cosmic Consciousness and the world of form (Nature), as the two complementary sides of the Cosmic Whole.

This principle is duplicated in the relationship between the psyche and the body. The wholeness of the personality is insured by the natural attraction between them. This natural attraction becomes disturbed when the personality is mentally divided into parts, with one part being elevated over another.

Since duration is a characteristic of the nature of the Cosmos, every aspect that is in harmony with it participates in its duration. This is why returning to one's true nature, which is synonymous with returning to unity with the Cosmos, is the overall theme of the *I Ching*. This return is achieved through a step-by-step process in which the individual rids himself of all mistaken ideas and beliefs that keep him in the parallel reality created by the collective ego.* The individual attains duration not through an effort to "become" anything, but through freeing his true and original nature from the inner prison of his mistaken ideas and beliefs.

Unlike the Cosmic Reality, the parallel reality created by the collective ego does not endure because it is based on mistaken ideas and beliefs about the Cosmic Way. When a person, through holding to such mistaken ideas and beliefs violates the Cosmic Harmonics, the Cosmos reacts with Fate. Fate is part of the laws of physics, and has the purposes of restoring the Cosmic Harmony and of helping a person return to unity with the Cosmos. It does so by decreasing the ego in him, thus bringing him back to humility.

The parallel reality is characterized by *changes*. These changes are brought about by the use of power on the part of humans, and the Cosmic reaction to it in the form of Fate.

Among the main mistaken ideas and beliefs that create the parallel reality are the presumptions that
1. humans are at the center of the universe
2. changes are the rule of life
3. Nature operates through *opposite* forces to propel changes
4. time is linear, having a beginning and an end
5. the universe works on mechanical principles
6. the Cosmos has a hierarchical order

All of these ideas create discordant fields of consciousness which compete with the Cosmic Order and its system of harmonics. They separate humans from the Cosmic Unity.

When Fate is not recognized as help from the Cosmos to make a person aware of his mistaken ideas and beliefs, but is taken as Cosmic "punishment," the blame he puts on the Cosmos cre-

---

* Return to unity with the Cosmos was what Lao Tzu meant by "diminishing," in Verse 48: "Learning consists in daily accumulating; The practice of Tao consists in daily diminishing. Keep on diminishing and diminishing, until you reach the state of No-Ado. No-Ado, and yet nothing is left undone." (*Tao Teh Ching*, translated by Dr. John C.H. Wu, St. John's University Press, New York, 1961.)

ates a new fate, thus perpetuating his misfortune.

The human longing for duration comes from a feeling memory imprinted within each individual, reminding him of his original unity with the Cosmos, which has been lost. This memory resides in every body cell, and is what the *I Ching* calls "a person's inner truth". The Judgment: "It furthers one to have somewhere to go," is to make him aware that the possibility of restoring that unity is always present.

The collective ego's answer to this longing for duration is its emphasis on and mania for attaining bodily longevity, and immortality through leaving behind works that bear one's name, or through acquiring fame. The pursuit of physical longevity as leading to immortality has persisted from the time of religious Taoism and various ancient practices such as specific kinds of yoga, all the way to our time. Today's medicine and health fads, while not concerned with immortality, are similarly preoccupied with maintaining the body to great old age at all costs.

A person often receives this hexagram when his situation lacks duration. This is because he holds the human-centered view of the universe, and any of the mistaken ideas or beliefs mentioned above. He also may not recognize that all good things that come to him are gifts from the Cosmos through its Helpers. His lack of duration is reflected in his attachment to and identification with all the things he possesses. Such a person can be heard to say, "I made that money (invention, achievement, etc.) myself." Disregarding the true source of his gifts creates a fate that subsequently robs him of them.

One type of spell connected with this hexagram has to do with issues of time. Phrases that imply "always" or "never," in regard to how long something takes, create these spells. Examples are: "this is going to take forever" and "I will never get there." Another type of spell is created by generalizations, such as: "this is an impossible task"; "the whole world is against me"; "changes are the rule of life."

Note: Since all lines contain infinite possibilities of interpretation, one needs to use the *rtcm* to determine if the meanings suggested here apply to the given situation. (*See* p. 736 for using the *rtcm*.)

Line 1. *Seeking duration too hastily brings misfortune persistently. Nothing that would further.*

This line can point to a misuse of the *I Ching* as a book of divination to foretell the future. Divination assumes that "good fortune" and "misfortune" come from without and is prewritten, as if in a Cosmic book. The future, however, is not prewritten, but is shaped by every thought and attitude, and can be reshaped by correcting our thoughts and attitudes. The purpose of the *I Ching* is to show a person, whether his thoughts, attitudes and actions are in harmony with the Cosmic Way and thus lead to success and good fortune, or whether they are not, creating misfortune for him. If the latter is the case, the hexagrams and lines show him the nature of his mistaken idea or belief, so that he can rid himself of them.

Another mistaken idea addressed by this line is that humans have rights to possess things. From the Cosmic standpoint, no such rights exist. When we are in harmony with the Cosmos, everything we need comes as a free gift.

Obtaining what the ego desires by force or contrivance of any sort is to possess something unlawfully from the Cosmic standpoint. Such possession, be it of a material or immaterial nature, is invariably accompanied by a fate that prevents its duration.

A person may also receive this line when he seeks to make something endure through outer means, or through attraction between two egos. An example is a marriage based on deals that have been made, in lieu of a true inner connection between the partners.

This line may also be received by a person who has developed an ego attachment to gifts he has received from the Cosmos, and therefore is faced with the threat of losing them. It is the Law of Fate that a person will lose what the ego is attached to having. This line may be counseling him to review his attitude toward what he possesses. The ego's view of possessions—that we are entitled or deserve to have them, or have the right to do anything we want with them, or to use them in a boastful way to put ourselves up above others—is the root cause of losing what we possess. Other attitudes, such as a suspicion that the Cosmos might arbitrarily take our possessions away from us, likewise can create a fate that brings about their loss. To have a correct attitude means ridding oneself of all such pretensions and distrust.

Line 2. *Remorse disappears.*
Receiving this line calls a person to address an ego-element in himself that falsely compares his inner effort to free his true self with "work" (along with all its negative connotations), in order to discourage him from even starting. It uses phrases that describe this effort either as too easy (and therefore ineffective) or too difficult, or impossible, or dangerous. Such phrases obscure the help that is attained from the Sage and the Helpers simply by asking for it. Remorse refers to the obstructed feelings he has from not having begun the maturation of his true self that would bring about duration. This remorse disappears when he rids himself of the false phrases in his program.

Examples of such phrases are: "this is an impossible task"; "it's too hard"; "one needs the strength of a saint"; "it is not meant to be"; "no human could do this"; "I cannot do inner work"; "what if it doesn't work for me"; "it can't be that easy (because everything worthwhile is hard)"; "how can it last"; "the Helpers would never bother with me"; "what right do I have to bother them"; "my small affairs are of no concern to the Cosmos"; "this is stupid"; "how can such things work (implying everything is merely random chance)"; "there must be a hook attached"; "this is devil's work (implying it is supernatural)"; "this will keep you from doing the real work"; "what will people think or say"; "this will drive you crazy"; "I'm too old"; or "I'm too set in my ways."

This line also concerns the feeling of helplessness that a person can have about identifying root phrases hidden in his subconscious. He does not realize that the phrase: "the task is impossible" is blocking the Sage from helping him. If he says the inner No to this phrase the Sage will be freed to come to his aid.

All of the above phrases are keys to spells that lock a person in the pattern of *changes*, discussed in the main text of this hexagram. They are like guardians of the realm of changes, assigned by the ego to keep its false program installed in his psyche, and to prevent him from freeing his true self.

"Remorse disappears" refers to a person's making a firm inner decision to follow the way of the Sage and to begin the effort to free his true self. Until that decision has been made, he is afflicted again and again with remorse that comes from his true self, crying out to be liberated. (*See* Line 6 of Hexagram 27, *Nourishment.*)

Line 3. *He who does not give duration to his character meets with disgrace. Persistent humiliation.*

A person receives this line when, in his search to bring his life into harmony (duration), he has followed solutions that have led him astray. He has either followed solutions proposed by others (conventional beliefs, etc.) or listened to his rational mind rather than to his inner truth.

Such solutions range from trying to achieve things by external force, to following spiritual beliefs that promise duration. He may, for example, be relying on "keeping up his hopes", or "trying hard" to have faith. However, because faith and hope do not resolve, in an enduring way, underlying doubts and fears, he is only kept in a vicious cycle that runs from hope to fear and doubt, and back to hope, thus creating persistent humiliation in the form of frustration. Once caught in this cycle, he needs to recognize that the duration he seeks will begin when he stops looking for solutions from external sources. He then needs to ask the Sage to help free him from his inner fears and doubts. What remains will be his inner truth that has duration; no addition or artificial alteration is necessary.

The problem with faith is that it is based on the hope that something might be true. The person hopes that if his conviction is strong enough, the thing hoped for will happen. The entire process is mental and not comparable to the trust a person develops from having experienced the verification of his inner truth. Because faith is a purely mental concept, it is inseparably bound to the very doubt and fear that the person hopes to conquer.

The Helper that is imprisoned by the spell created by reliance on faith is the Helper that frees one from doubts and fears. It is a member of one's inner army.

A person may also receive this line when he has made a decision, and then has begun to doubt whether it was correct, or whether it will cause future problems. His doubt becomes the "hole through which harm (resistance) enters" because it is conveyed on the inner plane to others. This line counsels the person to ask the Sage whether his decision was correct, and if so, he needs to remove the doubt through saying the inner No to it, for so long as the doubt is there, he will receive persistent and humiliating resistance.

Line 4. *No game in the field.*

"No game in the field," in this line, is a metaphor for either an apparent or a real misfortune. It can refer to a person who sees misfortune where there is none. For example, he has lost his job and sees it as a misfortune, whereas the loss is really the end of a fate created by a false sense of loyalty, which has held him in an unsuitable position. Or, the job loss may have been necessary for him to connect with elements in himself, such as his inner truth, that have been left behind or buried by wrong ideas. The new situation gives him the opportunity to rid himself of the rigid ideas that have been preventing him from fulfilling his destiny.

"No game in the field," can also refer to a person who, in seeking the cause of a real misfortune, is looking outside ("in the field") rather than inside himself, where the true cause lies. Here, the "game" may be a projection, spell, or poison arrow that has been put on him—either by himself or another—or certain mistaken ideas he has adopted. He needs to identify them with the help of the Sage and the *rtcm*, and deprogram them. By looking outside himself for the cause of his misfortune, he has blocked the Helper that ends Fate.

This line can also point to a particular spell that has created a fate (misfortune). It is composed of three components: the phrase: "man is man's worst enemy," the self-image of a hero who fights evil, and a third party which has been defined as an enemy, or as evil. The person has been unsuccessful in trying to overcome his fate (misfortune) through fighting something or someone he assumes to be the cause of his misfortune. He needs to be aware that his fate can only be extinguished through his ridding himself of the spell that has caused it. (*See* p. 697, Freeing Yourself from Spells.)

Line 5. *Giving duration to one's character through perseverance. This is good fortune for a woman, misfortune for a man.*

The traditional interpretation of this line spells out a woman's position in regard to her husband, which dictates that the woman ought to hold to tradition—that is, to her husband, as a lifelong companion, and to her place "inside the house." The man, likewise, is ordered by this tradition to hold to what "his duty requires of him at the moment," or to what is required of him by the outer world.

While these ideas have no correspondence to Cosmic Truth, they help the person find the seed phrases in his inner program that have created a spell, blocking certain Helpers. This spell results from defining men and women as having different capabilities and responsibilities. From this superficial observation, it is deduced that their social roles are inherently different. Such "fixing" in roles prevents them from finding their uniqueness and fulfilling their destinies.

A person may also receive this line when he feels guilty that he has not been developing his "higher nature." "Giving duration to one's character through perseverance" incorrectly suggests that through trying to "become" something (patient, loyal, or kind) we will develop our "higher nature." The Sage teaches that our true nature must not be divided into higher and lower parts, because it is complete and enduring in itself, even though suppressed. The perseverance that is truly needed is the resolve to free ourselves from the mistaken idea that human nature is divided, and that in and of ourselves we lack virtues such as loyalty, patience, and kindness. The collective ego would have us believe we lack them, in order to dismiss our Cosmic Virtues, such as loyalty to our inner truth, and thereby bind them to its institutions and values. In addition to taking away these mistaken ideas, the person also needs to free himself of the idea of guilt. (*See* p. 50, Guilt, Blame, and Shame, and p. 696, Freeing Yourself from Guilt.)

This line can also indicate that a person is blaming himself for having gone against his true nature. He believes that he has become guilty and does not know how to relate to it. Receiving this line wants to make him aware that guilt has no place in the Cosmic Reality, and that he needs to understand the true meaning of blame. Blame is a true feeling that comes from having gone against one's true nature, and has the function of making the person aware of this fact. When he acknowledges it as a true feeling, which is also a Helper, this Helper attracts the Cosmic Helper of reflection. Thus he gets the help to reflect on the cause of his mistake and has the possibility to correct himself. This will free him from his feeling of blame.

Line 6. *Restlessness as an enduring condition brings misfortune.*

This line addresses the restlessness caused by a spell. Behind the spell that drives a person to impulsive actions is a hidden phrase that needs to be discovered and disposed of. An example is the phrase, "you must act, otherwise nothing will happen." This phrase is an imp that is blocking the person's access to his inner truth. Its deeper root is the mistaken idea that humans are at the center of the universe, and therefore responsible for making everything work. Such a person is not conscious of the presence of the invisible world with its myriad Helpers, therefore constantly creates fates.

Several false attitudes are caused by this mindset. One is that of the person who regards problems as matters of engineering, with the solution being to replace one component with another, or re-engineering the way things interface. Another is of the person who attempts to overpower the problem by throwing money at it, or withdrawing money from it, or through the use of leverage or power. Another attitude is that of the person who is willing to be the instrument of power, and sacrifice his life, if necessary, to solve the problem.

In view of the fact that the real problems in life have their roots in the psyche, as programs that are not in harmony with the Cosmic Way, the problems cannot be resolved by any such means. They can only be solved by the individual's ridding himself of the idea that humans are at the center of the universe, and that it is their job to do it all. When this idea is deprogrammed, the support for the imp of restlessness, and its related imps, is removed.

A particular Helper that is blocked by this idea is the Helper of Inner Truth.

33. Retreating/Hiding

 Ch'ien
Kên

The Judgment: *Retreating. Success. In what is small, it furthers to be firmly correct.*

Receiving this hexagram counsels a person to retreat from certain mistaken ideas that keep him tied to the parallel reality created by the collective ego. The ideas are based on two words that have no Cosmic basis: "guilt" and "culprit." Even though they seem "small," they have a big effect, if not eliminated by saying the inner No to them. (Saying the inner No is the meaning of being firmly correct.)

A person may receive this hexagram when the ego in him is busy blaming something or someone as guilty, or as a culprit, but especially when he is blaming life, the Sage, Nature, or the way of the Cosmos. The Sage retreats in the presence of the individual ego, with its blaming and demanding. The person is counseled to retreat from his blaming activities through saying the inner No to the ego. Often, rather than face the threat of being condemned by others as guilty, or even to regard himself as guilty, he looks about to find someone or something else to blame. He needs to realize that guilt, in the sense of an inextinguishable stain, does not exist in the Cosmic Order.

Blame, in the Cosmic sense, is incurred when a person goes against his true nature by following the rules and values of the collective ego. This blame is erased the moment the person is truly sorry for what he has done, and rids himself of the mistaken idea that has led to his error. His regret brings help from the invisible world to heal the damage that has been done. If, however, he believes that what he has done makes him guilty, then he prevents the Helpers from healing the situation. He also puts a guilt spell on himself, under which he continues to suffer. The guilt makes him vulnerable to being used or abused by others. It also can make him believe that he must endlessly make atonements or reparations.

Retreating can also be counsel to a person to withdraw from fears and doubts that press him to abandon the Sage, and the Helpers he needs to free his true self from its imprisonment. Withdrawal, in this case, means a determined resistance not to be overcome by fear and doubt, and not to allow his will to be dominated by them. These emotions have their basis in phrases installed in his psyche by the collective ego, to the effect that if he abandons its way, it will punish, abandon, and pursue him to the farthest ends of the earth for retribution. The person can carry out this resistance to the collective ego by firmly saying the inner No to the threatening phrases, and to the fears they have inspired in him.

Retreating also is the correct inner action to take when a person is tempted to adopt the image of the "rugged individualist," in defiance of the threats of the collective ego. This opposite self-image, ironically, is as agreeable to the collective ego as the self-image of the person who goes with the crowd, because, in fleeing to yet another self-image, the person remains within its system of self-images. He remains within its system whenever he sees his options in terms of opposites, for it is the collective ego that has defined all "possible options" in terms of opposites.

The ideogram *Tun*, which gives this hexagram its name, in addition to "retreating," can have the meaning of "the hidden," thus pointing to the invisible world of the Helpers. But, *Tun* can also refer to the way the collective ego hides the invisible world from view, through presenting itself as the only source of protection and defense, and through presenting the invisible world as unreal. The collective ego similarly hides the true nature of humans behind the pronouncements that humans' animal nature is the source of evil, and that they are guilty for having an animal nature.

Traditional readings of this hexagram describe a war maneuver which is a strategic retreat as preparation for an expected attack from an enemy. In its Cosmic sense it describes the reticence of a person in meeting another who has been aggressive and is now approaching to reconnect with him, supposedly in sincerity, but who really is still inwardly aggressive, and hoping to catch his opponent off guard. It is correct to maintain reticence and reserve regardless of outer appearances, and to wait until the other has become truly sincere. While affairs are in this state, the person can keep track of the inner truth of the situation by checking with the Sage.

Receiving this hexagram can also indicate that a person needs to retreat from feelings of hurt pride. He does this through turning these feelings over to the Cosmos and going into a state of emotional neutrality. Neutrality means, in practical terms, that he takes himself out of first gear, as in wanting to defend himself or in blaming the other, or out of reverse gear, as in wanting to get away and break all contact. He waits instead in neutral, which is devoid of any outward action or violent, unbalancing emotion.

In another rendering, this hexagram can be advising a person to retreat from giving up on a situation in which he is misunderstood by another. This retreat has the purpose of allowing time for a true understanding to develop.

This hexagram may also help us to recognize and retreat from using techniques in meditation that block the Sage from speaking. Among these are meditation techniques that employ mantras, have rigid rules about keeping all thoughts out, control the contents of meditation with the intellect, systematize in any way the communication between the meditator and the Sage, or turn meditation into prayer. All these types of meditation or related activities have the effect of keeping the person from freeing himself of hidden elements, such as guilt, thereby maintaining the program of the collective ego in his psyche.

When viewed as one of the twelve calender hexagrams, "Retreating" represents the eight month, showing the retreat of the light in the course of the year. It is used here as a metaphor for the retreat of the life force from a person. This retreat, if not halted, leads eventually to death. (*See* Glossary, Death.) In this aspect of the hexagram, a person is informed that the more he looks outside himself for guidance, instead of to his inner truth and to the Sage, the more he comes under the dominance of the collective ego. Because the collective ego defines everything in. terms of right and wrong, the person becomes increasingly rigid in his thinking. Ever more separated from his inner truth, he eventually becomes a mere husk of a person, who, although outwardly alive, is inwardly dead, operating only on the automatic pilot of his preformed ideas.

The hexagram counsels him to retreat from the rigidifying ideas and beliefs that lead to inner death. He also needs to retreat from reliance on prestructured inner programs that are in conflict with his inner truth, and which produce conflict in his outer life. Rigid ideas can never correctly judge the uniqueness of each situation.

Note: Since all lines contain infinite possibilities of interpretation, one needs to use the *rtcm* to determine if the meanings suggested here apply to the given situation. (*See* p. 736 for using the *rtcm*.)

Line 1. *At the tail in retreating. This is dangerous. One must not wish to undertake anything.*

This line indicates the presence of a guilt spell. "One must not wish to undertake anything," is the advice given to someone who is about to do something motivated by guilt.

When a person is in the process of retreating from following the collective ego, in order to follow his inner truth instead, the last means (the "tail") that the collective ego employs to hold him back is to make him feel guilty for having separated from its rules and laws, the unwritten musts and shoulds that have been instilled in his psyche during childhood, and which are combined with the threat of drastic punishments.

The danger referred to is that he will give way to his fears of becoming guilty and being punished. He is counseled not to undertake anything out of fear, but instead to ask the Sage to help him rid himself both of his fear of guilt and his fear of punishment. If he fails to free himself from these destructive elements before undertaking anything, they will lead to a whole series (a "tail") of complicating factors, and create an increasingly toxic and rigid situation.

This line also points to the strategy employed by the collective ego to gain access to the individual's life energy: it does so by injecting a guilt/fault spell into his psyche. The first guilt spell reads, "you are born with original fault/sin." The second spell says that evil arises from human's animal nature ("lower instincts"). Receiving this line indicates that a person needs to ask for help to rid himself of these spells on his true nature. (*See* p. 697, Freeing Yourself from Spells.)

A person may also receive this line when he is in the middle of arguing with another, or is tempted to do so, to determine who is the guilty party. The message here is: retreat from looking for a guilty party, or culprit (as no such thing exists in the Cosmic Order), by saying the inner No to the idea of culprit. He is then counseled to ask the Sage in his presence and the Sage in the other person's presence to intervene with the egos that are active in the situation.

This line can also refer to a person's inner arguments as a reaction to his feelings of guilt or blame. He may be allowing complaints against the Sage or Cosmic Justice, as when he asks, "Why is this my fate?" It can also refer to inner conflict that is being concealed, or repressed, rather than addressed. A typical seed phrase in this context is, "this problem needs to be kept in the closet," and "let sleeping dogs lie." Its premise is that it is easier to *control* problems by concealing them (or by pretending that they don't exist) rather than getting to their root causes, which might expose one to shame. Resolving the problems means facing the causes inwardly and eliminating them with the help of the Helpers.

Line 2. *He is held fast with yellow oxhide. No one can tear him loose.*

This line often refers to the person who for one reason or

another feels guilty, and believes that no one can take his guilt away. These feelings come from mistaken ideas about guilt and blame, from which he needs to free himself. (*See* p. 50, Guilt, Blame, and Shame.)

Oxhide refers to a particularly strong material, that when used to hold something, holds it fast. Yellow is a metaphor for something that is correct. Yellow oxhide, then, is a metaphor for the desire or propensity to be correct, but this desire is being thwarted by something strong. The strong element is the mistaken idea of guilt, which he has accepted from the collective ego. He rightly seeks to free himself of it, but employs means proposed by the collective ego, which, if followed, will give it even more power over him. Because such means are not in harmony with the Cosmos, employing them will also create a fate. Such means are:

- placing the blame on somebody else, or on one's nature;
- trying to balance one's guilt by fighting for a cause sanctioned by the collective ego;
- making atonement through acts of self-sacrifice to compensate for feelings of guilt.

For example a person may be holding onto feelings of guilt for something that has occurred in the past. While he may have incurred true blame (which is always erasable), the ego in him has converted it into guilt, which by definition is not erasable. (See p. 697, Freeing Yourself from Guilt and Blame). As long as he believes himself guilty, he may try to make atonement through self-sacrifice (hence the reference to oxhide, since the ox was in ancient times a chief animal of sacrifice). The benefit of this self-sacrifice of the person's life energy, always goes to the collective ego. The remedy is for the person to rid himself of the idea of guilt.

Yellow oxhide can also refer to the person who, in wanting to do the right thing, has unwittingly adopted the self-image of "the good person" (the good child, the good father, mother, husband, or wife), and through being taught that "being good" entails self-sacrifice, turns himself into a slave of his self-image. This image clings to him tenaciously, and prevents him from recognizing that behind his desire to be good is his false feeling of inadequacy, due to a spell put on his animal nature by the collective ego. The phrase behind this spell may be "in and of yourself you are not good enough," or "your animal nature is the source of evil." The person needs to recognize that neither a false feeling of inadequacy nor a spell can be "compensated for" by adopting a "better" self-image. Both can be removed, however, if he will rid himself first of the spell, and then of the self-image. (*See* p. 697, Freeing Yourself from Spells, and p. 691, Freeing Yourself from Self-Images.)

This line can also refer to a person's being held back from learning from the Sage because he believes that he might be required to give up his position, titles, or other identifications which put him up as special. Entitlements and honors hold him to the collective ego with the strength of oxhide, preventing him from retreating from his self-image. Giving up his self-image does not mean that he must give up the position he holds, since whatever the position, the person who has given up his self-image will find himself useful and be aided by the Sage. (*See* p. 691, Freeing Yourself from Self-Images.)

Line 3. *Retreating to enslave others is nerve-wracking and dangerous. To retain people as men- and maidservants brings good fortune.**

This line refers to the fate that is created when a person has adopted the self-image of "the good person" often out of feeling guilty for having an animal nature. (*See* Lines 1 and 2.) Through doing good, he intervenes in the fates of others, and thus prevents them from coming to a correct relationship with the Cosmos. He also takes over the tasks that rightly belong to the Helpers, in order to elevate himself in the eyes of others. Both motives are wrong and embroil him and those he helps in repetitive fates. This is the meaning of "nerve-wracking and dangerous."

This line shows the *function* of the guilt spell put upon people by the collective ego, which is to enslave them into its service,

---

* In Wilhelm this line reads, "a halted retreat is nerve-wracking and dangerous." We changed this line upon being informed that it had to do with "halting during a retreat to enslave others."

and garner their life energies through their striving. All self-images, regardless of the type, cause a person to strive. This is observable in the person who helps others from the hidden motive of guilt: he actually uses those he helps for his egotistical purpose of being seen as good. In reality, he sucks their energy by making them feel indebted to him, while the collective ego, in turn, sucks energy from him. The "good fortune" mentioned that comes from making people into servants, in fact, accrues only to the collective ego. When a person's natural goodness and his Cosmic Virtues are usurped to the service of the collective ego, it is the Cosmic Consciousness which is robbed. A self-image, though something we often try to "live up to," is more often something we really "die to." This "selflessness" is perhaps the real meaning of Wilhelm's famous metaphor of "throwing oneself away."

This line can also refer to a person who is incorrectly regarding the Sage as a servant of the ego. Doing so would certainly bring misfortune, in that the Sage retreats.

Line 4. *Voluntary retreat brings success to the true self and downfall to the ego.*

Voluntary retreat refers to a person's following his commonsense, which tells him there is no advantage in engaging the ego in another person. Through disengaging, he deprives that ego of the energy it had hoped to receive, bringing about its downfall. This line underscores the incessant desire of the ego to attain energy through engaging the egos in others. It succeeds in this effort by employing any number of strategies ranging from flattery, to arousing pity, to making the other feel guilty, to outright intimidation.

The ways by which the individual ego steals energy show that the collective ego can exist only through the agreement among individual egos that the ego games being played are "natural." This interaction also shows what happens when one of the two parties retreats from the game: the game ceases. What is not readily observable is the ripple effect that follows when one person withdraws from the collective ego itself, by firmly saying the inner No to it; his single action weakens all the games being played by others through strengthening everyone's true self.

This line can also refer to times when a person laughs at the downfall of the ego in another, or when he insists that the wrong-doer lose face, or that he must humble himself openly. By such acts the person engages in feeling superior, something from which he needs to retreat, by saying the inner No to the ego in himself. It is never the way of the Sage to pour salt into our wounds, or to rub our faces in the dirt of our downfall—see Line 6 below.

Line 5. *Friendly retreat. To be firmly correct brings success.*

This line refers to keeping an outer composure in the face of someone's incorrect behavior, while at the same time firmly saying the inner No. This gives an inner message to the other's true self that it needs to distance itself from the ego, and that it can do so without a loss of face. In this way one is friendly with the other's true self, while being firmly correct with the ego.

Line 6. *Cheerful retreat. Everything serves to further.*

This line refers to the Sage that, in retreating from the ego in a person, never does so in anger or vindictiveness, or to punish him. It retreats cheerfully, knowing how that person will ultimately feel relief when he turns away from the ego in himself to reunite with the Sage. The Sage's retreat to support the person's true self is the meaning of "everything serves to further." Receiving this line may be telling a person that he must not, for any reason, throw his energy away in an effort to please another, or in the hope to gain nourishment from that person's recognition; doing so causes the Sage, the true source of nourishment, to retreat.

When a person is indulging in self-blame (the harassing voices of the ego), the fact that the Sage has retreated can finally call him back to listen to his commonsense. To free himself he needs to say the inner No to blaming himself.

This line can also refer to a person who believes that he needs to retreat from society in order to follow the way of the Sage. This belief is a misunderstanding of retreat, since all retreat refers to inwardly distancing oneself from the ego, either in oneself or the collective ego. Making an outer retreat means that he carries the ego into a grudging solitude, since he then sees himself as better than those he has left behind. He also remains attached to the collective ego, by setting himself up in opposition to it.

Outwardly retreating from a group is justifiable, however, when the group is about to create a fate (*see* Hexagram 60, *Limitation*, Line 2.)

34. Using Power*

 Chên
Ch'ien

The Judgment: *Using Power. Holding back furthers.*

Here the message of The Judgment is clear: Hold back from using power. The Sage teaches that the Cosmos does not use power, for power is outside the system of harmonics that comprise the Cosmic Whole. The Cosmos operates only through a single force: the force of attraction between *complementary* aspects.

Power is among those false words that have no Cosmic basis. It is, moreover, a complete deception to those who believe in using it, because it creates a fate by which the powerful deed returns in a circular motion to the person who has initiated it, bringing the harm he has done to something or someone, back to himself. If he is not aware of this Cosmic Law, but judges the situation only by its outer appearance, he may falsely conclude that an adverse power outside of himself is at work in his life.

When others interfere with this circular motion, as in resisting the powerful deed *outwardly*, or trying to stop it through force, they become entangled with it, preventing the fate from

---

* The original title, "The Power of the Great" has been abandoned here, because the main theme of the hexagram is the use of power as contrary to the Cosmic Way. The term "great," however, is a reference to the Cosmic Consciousness. (*See* Hexagram 1.)

completing its circle, and creating a fate for themselves.

All use of power is an act of interference in the harmonious ways the Cosmos achieves things. Its use erects blockages by distorting the flow of Cosmic energy, and turning that energy to egotistical use. All use of power is based on thinking in mechanistic terms that rule out a person's true feelings, and deny the existence of the invisible Cosmic Consciousness and its Principles of Harmony.

The main focus of this hexagram is the use of power in thought, speech, and action—whether those uses emanate from a person or an organization.

In terms of thought, the use of power may find a broad array of expressions, as in the following:

- contriving to arrive at a "top" by excluding others "below"
- asserting an "any means to the end" approach
- being hostile and judgmental
- creating projections, spells, and poison arrows
- becoming vindictive or vengeful
- viewing things as "mere objects," and thus disregarding their feeling nature
- presuming rights and privileges, or positions of superiority and inferiority.

In terms of speech, power can include:

- gossip
- indulgence in idle curiosity
- idle chatter
- verbal pressure put on others to make things happen
- insinuating remarks that throw a bad light on others
- pronouncing judgments about the nature of things as good or evil
- remarks that create projections, spells, and poison arrows
- the idea of there being a "Higher Power"
- instilling feelings of guilt or indebtedness.

In terms of action, the use of power may involve:

- encroaching into others' intimate space, including that of Nature
- contrived efforts to force results
- the use of leverage (whether it be by threat or intimidation)

• willfully bringing harm to others
• indulgence in egoistic anger, and violence
• allowing the ego to appropriate one's own Cosmic gifts
• appropriating Cosmic gifts that have been given to others
• suppressing one's inner truth, as by allowing the ego to claim the achievements of the Helpers as one's own doing.

Another attitude that also needs to be recognized as a use of power is "passive-aggressive" behavior. This behavior may be found in people who, for example, in a cooperative living situation, fail to do their share, forcing others to cover their expenses, or to keep things clean in order to have a normal living situation. Such behavior is an insidious use of power, in that it affects people negatively through an arrogant insensitivity.

The correct response to any use of power is to say the inner No to it. The inner No prevents the person's chi energy from being used by the ego in others. It has the correcting function of awakening the offending person's true self to the fact that the ego in him is embarrassing his dignity. This hexagram informs us that the inner No is the only thing that has the ability to correct the use of power.

The kind of *Cosmic* energy referred to in this hexagram, which has mistakenly been called "power," has a different function from the chi energy, or nourishing life-force, mentioned in Hexagram 27, *Nourishment*. This hexagram is about the kind of Cosmic energy that creates transformations through the light and the dark, and which is comparable to electrical energy. Its purpose is to move things by transforming them from non-form into form, and from form into non-form. In their non-form state, things first exist as *feelings*. When formed into images, these feelings become transformed into energy. We see this energy engaged, for example, when a horse pulls a wagon. When the horse's will is engaged, it enables the horse to accomplish its task, because the Cosmic definition of "will" is that it is *the total consciousness of the horse's psyche, expressed as energy.* (*See* Hexagram 28, *The Preponderance of the Great.*) To cooperate *with* Nature means that a person relates to the horse from his true feelings to engage the will of the horse (its psychic energy) to accomplish the task.

When, however, a person puts a horse to a task by using mental or physical force, the horse's will is harnessed by the ego, and its energy becomes abused. The result is that the transformative energies of the Cosmos become blocked, creating obstructions. The obstructions have the purpose of making the person aware that he is using power, and that he is going against Nature's ways. To force the horse to do things against its will often results in injuries. If the person continues using power to fight the obstructions, he creates a fate. To correct the situation, he needs to retreat from using power, and say the inner No to the mistaken idea that caused him to do so. The inner No releases the Cosmic energy from the harness the ego had put on it, and allows it to operate again through transformations.

The Sage informs us that the Cosmos does not operate through power, but through a system of harmonics. As mentioned in Hexagram 32, *Duration,* the Cosmic Harmonics and the laws of physics complement each other to move the Cosmic Reality on its path of evolution. It is through observing and harmonizing with the laws of physics that machines such as airplanes can be made to fly. The idea that humans can defy or override Nature's laws through the use of power is a myth.

As can be seen from the above, all ideas that contain the word power ("horsepower," "manpower," prayer as an instrument of power) contain falsehoods and misconceptions. As soon as a person believes that power exists and that he can use it, he is drawn into the demonic sphere of consciousness. The use of power perverts what is originally a *feeling energy* into a mental energy that is then siphoned off to the demonic sphere of consciousness. The same occurs when a person believes he is "powerless," since this implies a belief in power. His belief in himself as powerless gives others the idea that they have the power to take advantage of him.

The belief in power creates both power and powerlessness. The ability of any person or organization to exercise power over others depends entirely on the extent to which those others believe in the validity of power. All belief in power comes from the collective ego, in its effort to exclude from a person's awareness the existence of the Helpers of the invisible world, and the fact that the Cosmos is a system of Harmonics.

Spells connected with this hexagram contain phrases such as, "we will show them who has the power," "I am powerless," "there is nothing I can do about it, " or "I have to do it all myself," or, "you must submit to the 'powers that be.'") These spells block a person's ability to ask for aid from the Helpers, and lock him into being dominated either by the ego in himself or in others.

Note: Since all lines contain infinite possibilities of interpretation, one needs to use the *rtcm* to determine if the meanings suggested here apply to the given situation. (*See* p. 736 for using the *rtcm*.)

Line 1. *Power in the toes. Continuing brings misfortune. This is certainly true.*

"Power in the toes" is a metaphor for acting on what is apparent to the eye, without bothering to inquire of the Sage as to the inner truth of the matter. Because the person believes in solving problems by aggressive action, his actions are driven purely by impulse. However, all impulses are based on seed phrases and images that are, at best, half-truths. As mentioned in the main text of this hexagram, such *action* includes thought, speech, and physical action. The misfortune referred to is the fate that is created by impulsive action, whether it be taking action physically, or impulsively and superficially coming to a judgment.

One of the seed phrases that incite impulsive action is "you need to use power." Another is, "what you *see* is what counts." To free himself of his fate, the person needs to rid himself of this superficial way of thinking. (*See* p. 689, Freeing Yourself from Seed Phrases and Images.)

"Power in the toes" also refers to the subservient attitude of a person who believes in an all-powerful God or Cosmos. He believes that by doing things (or abstaining from doing things) to please a Higher Power, he will gain heaven's benevolence. This line applies likewise to the person who acts on the belief that God has given humans power and rights over Nature, or over the fate of those who displease God. Acting on any of these beliefs creates a fate, which can be ended if the person will rid himself of them. (See p. 697, Freeing Yourself from Spells, and p. 689, Freeing Yourself from Mistaken Ideas and Beliefs.)

Line 2. *Perseverance brings good fortune. Being firmly correct brings success.**

The first phrase of this text refers to the accepted philosophy of the collective ego that in order for power to be effective (i.e., to "bring good fortune"), a person or institution needs to be persevering in applying it. This view has been developed to explain the obstructions created by using power, and to justify using ever more power in the effort to overcome the obstructions. A person may receive this line when, due to his use of power, he has created a fate which has manifested in the form of an illness. The line informs him that if he continues to react by *fighting* his fate, he will create a new fate. To end his fate and return to health, he needs to identify which mistaken idea (related to the theme of power) has created his fate, and then to free himself of it with the aid of the Helpers. Doing so will also free his self-healing abilities. (*See* p. 689, Freeing Yourself from Mistaken Ideas and Beliefs, and p. 694 Freeing Yourself from Some Health Problems.)

A person may also receive this line when he is making detailed plans, which he intends to follow to the letter. A correct response is to first bring his motives and attitude into harmony with the Cosmos by saying the inner No to any element in himself (or his plan) that either proposes the use of power, or asserts that he is without help from the Cosmos. Then he can be moved by his inner senses to *react* to that which is in accord with the Cosmic Will. When a person aligns his will with the Cosmic Will, everything he undertakes succeeds and endures.

Line 3. *The ego works through power. The true self does not act thus. To continue is dangerous. A goat butts against a hedge and gets its horns entangled.*

This line makes us aware that only the ego works through power, and that the use of power is destructive—whether it comes from thoughts, emotions, or actions. It further advises

---

*The Chinese ideograms making up this line can be read in two different ways. Wilhelm had translated them as "perseverance brings good fortune." We have chosen to add the second possibility, "being firmly correct brings success," because it refers to the Cosmic meaning.

that the use of power initiates Fate. It also reveals the good effect of saying the inner No to the use of power. On observing another's use of power, instead of thinking or saying, "there's nothing I can do about it," the correct action is to inwardly say No to it, and to call on the Helpers to bring the use of power to an end.

"Butting against a hedge and getting its horns entangled" is warning a person that he is in danger of creating a fate if he continues to act from ego-emotions. Among these emotions, which the ego uses to keep control of him, are self-pity, self-blame, reproach, intimidation, threat, and guilt. The goat here represents an obstinate use of power. The hedge is a metaphor for the limits set by the fate that is inevitably invoked when the ego is allowed to indulge in using power.

The "goat" can also refer to obsessive thoughts of the ego that drive a person to overcome a perceived insufficiency, in order to be successful. For example, a person who thinks his reasoning is not good enough, thinks he needs to reason more. In a broader sense, the line can refer to any person who believes that if he only applies more effort, or more pressure, he will succeed.

"Butting" can also refer to a person who is getting entangled in someone else's fate by accepting guilt, which the other has projected upon him. Receiving this line makes him aware that he needs to free himself of a guilt spell. (*See* p. 697, Freeing Yourself from Spells.)

The metaphor can also refer to a person who boasts of his power to overcome Fate, death, evil, or who indulges in a careless disregard for Nature and its ways. He needs to rid himself of the projections, spells and poison arrows he has put on himself.

This line counsels that the person can get free of his fate if he identifies, with the help of the *rtcm*, the seed phrases and images that cause him to use power. (*See* p. 689, Freeing Yourself from Seed Phrases and Images.)

The reference to the goat, in the sense of a scapegoat, is to make a person aware of the destructive dynamic of the idea of guilt.[*] The psyche cannot bear guilt because it is viewed as an inextinguishable stain. In his attempt to get rid of it, the person passes it on to something or someone else. Since doing this is incorrect, Cosmic blame is incurred, which the person promptly converts into guilt, because he does not understand the difference between Cosmic blame and guilt. The idea of guilt comes from the collective ego and has the purpose of keeping people unremittingly under its control. Cosmic blame is incurred when a person violates the Cosmic Harmonics. It can be extinguished by recognizing one's mistake, identifying the mistaken idea that has caused it, and ridding oneself of it. (*See* p. 50, Guilt, Blame, and Shame.)

Line 4. *Being firmly correct brings good fortune. Remorse disappears. The hedge opens; there is no entanglement. Strength (movement) depends upon the axles of a big cart.***

"Being firmly correct" refers to depending on what is truly dependable, as indicated by the metaphor of "the axles of a big cart." Here, the cart represents the Cosmic Reality with all the Helpers of the invisible world ready to do their tasks through transformation. The axles, upon which the cart depends for its movement, represent the Cosmic Harmonics and the laws of physics that complement each other, the one applying to the sphere of Cosmic Consciousness, the other to the world of form (Nature). The force of attraction between them creates the energy that has falsely been called "power." The line is stating that if a person will free himself from the belief that the Cosmos and Nature work through power, he will attract the Cosmic Helpers to his task. These Helpers will also undo the fate that has been created by his trying to make things happen through power. Then, all cause for remorse disappears.

This line also refers to related mistaken beliefs, as for example, that humans can overcome the limits set by the laws of physics.

---

* Scapegoat: This is after the old Hebrew tale of the goat upon whom the high priest laid all the sins of his people, then banished the unfortunate animal to the desert.

** The text in Wilhelm's translation reads, "Power depends upon the axle of a big cart." The Chinese term *zhuang*, in the context of the "big cart" can only be translated as strength, in the sense of energy that creates movement.

Line 5. *Loses the goat with ease. No remorse.*

The goat in this line can represent a person's natural ability to say the inner No, which he has lost "with ease" through being rewarded, during childhood, for "being the good child" who does not say No (either to his parents, or to authorities who represent the values of the collective ego). Through accepting this self-image of the good child, a spell has been put on his commonsense. The loss prevents him from being able to deprogram mistaken ideas and beliefs, and from being able to say the inner No to the encroachment of others into his inner space. "No remorse" refers to getting rid of the self-image mentioned, which will also restore his commonsense.

Line 6. *A goat butts against a hedge. It cannot go backward, it cannot go forward. Nothing serves to further. If one notes the difficulty, success is assured.*

Here, the goat which butts against a hedge is a metaphor for a person who indulges in ego-emotions to influence his situation, only to find himself humiliated by Fate. Trying to influence the situation through emotional displays only makes things worse, because the emotions keep him attached to the problem from which he would like to be free. If he will notice that it is his attachment to his emotions (anger, guilt, desire) that keeps him trapped, and turn them over to the Sage, the hedge will open. (*See* p. 63 Feeling and Emotion, and p. 680 Centering Yourself.)

The hedge represents the limits put on the human use of power by the Law of Fate.

35. Progressing

$$\frac{\text{Li}}{\text{K'un}}$$

The Judgment. *Progressing. The true self is honored by the Sage's presence so that there is help for everything he does.* [The traditional rendering of The Judgment is shown below.]

Cosmic Progress (or Evolution) is created through the progress of each of its parts, in cooperation with each other. This cooperation takes place through recognizing the equality of all these parts, both in the visible and invisible worlds. This includes a cooperation not only among humans, but among humans and animals, humans and Nature in general, and humans and the Cosmic Helpers.

For the individual person, progress always proceeds in the direction of his fulfilling his destiny, which is to give expression to his uniqueness. Our lives are meant to follow a natural course of progress, which is defined as "moving on." Going on with one's life is what makes the growth and evolution of personal awareness possible. This growth of understanding accrues to the total consciousness of the Cosmos, thus becomes part of its evolution. The Cosmic Consciousness, so to speak, "mines" the experiences of each of its components in the same way that human consciousness absorbs, digests, and grows from each of the person's experiences. This kind of progressing is made impossible when a person becomes attached to the *past*: to his successes, failures, injuries, and traumas, and when he fixes himself as wounded, damaged, defective, or advantaged, privileged, perfect, etc. In regard to mistakes, he is attached whenever he equates his mistakes with being permanently stained with guilt—an ego-emotion. Progressing also halts when a person becomes attached to some *future* goal, so that his every waking thought and impulse is turned to that goal as the "only" thing worthy of notice, effort, and intention. The moment a person allows this kind of attachment to happen, he sullies the progress made and the success achieved. This is when "the nest" the person has created with the help of the Helpers "burns up," as it is put in Line 6 of Hexagram 56, *The Wanderer*, meaning he has created a fate that will destroy the progress made.

"Progressing" also describes an individual's coming into harmony with his inner truth, thus reuniting with the Cosmic Whole and all its helping forces. Indeed, progressing is characterized not by *changes* that are made by external means, but by *transformations* performed by these helping forces in the atomic realm. It is in this realm that the energy of harmonious consciousness transforms things. These transformations can only take place when a person's consciousness is in harmony with the Cosmic Whole.

Receiving this hexagram without changing lines can be a simple statement that a person is making true progress in his life.

The traditional text of The Judgment text reads: *Progress. The powerful prince is honored with horses in large numbers. In a single day he is granted audience three times.* This picture of progress is obviously defined by the collective ego. It refers to progress that has been made by a feudal lord on behalf of his sovereign through the use of power to subjugate the people. In exchange for this help, the sovereign has awarded him the honor of his recognition. This scenario exposes the collective ego's method of expanding its control over as many individuals as possible through the use of power. (*See* the preceding Hexagram 34, *Using Power.*)

Applied to modern society, the function of the loyal feudal lord is fulfilled by the various cultural, political, and social institutions, including the family (where the father often represents the feudal lord as the "sovereign" of the family) inasmuch as these institutions exercise power over the individual. Through the pressure they put on him his loyalty to his inner truth is transferred to them. As a reward for his part in this conditioning, the father (or another parental authority) receives recognition and honor from the collective ego. By such means people are trained to see themselves no longer as individuals, but as part of a "group-we," with the "we" implying loyalty to the institutions, and whoever is in charge of them.

This text, in particular, draws our attention to the feudal mindset that has predominated over the entire earth during the last 3,000 years, and its belief that progress is accomplished through the use of power, in particular the idea of human's power over people and over Nature. Feudalism is characterized by hierarchical notions, which are supported by heroic myths about humans' supposed place as the centerpiece of creation, and by taboos which keep these myths venerated and free of scrutiny. This mindset imagines, for the purpose of attaining public acceptance, that the invisible world is also feudally structured, that it, too, operates by the use of power, and that, in fact, it has "authorized" humans to use power to extend their dominance in all directions. It is also part of this mindset to think that everything exists to serve human purposes and glorification. This glorification is observable particularly in the highest representatives of its hierarchical system, such as in the emperor, king, and lord, or in modern society, in the President, or corporate CEO.

Spells connected with this hexagram have to do with the mistaken ideas that come from the feudal mindset. In particular, they are ideas that see Nature, without the human influence, as "chaos," and humans as having the role of ordering and subjugating Nature. These ideas are extended to seeing the mind as superior to the body, and therefore as meant to control it, and to the idea that the thinking parts of the brain are superior to the feeling parts, and the sense of seeing is superior to and more important than the other senses, and, in particular, to the *inner* senses.

A person may receive this hexagram when he wants to pass onto another what he has been learning from the Sage. He may succeed if he does not regard the other as inferior, and if he keeps aware of the extent to which the other is open to him. A true communication can last only as long as he is open and receptive. Sharing what one has learned requires feeling the quality and size of the opening the other makes, and keeping attuned to its size from moment to moment, and retreating and advancing accordingly. Remaining sensitive and free of ego prevents the pushing and pressing that prevents progress.

Note: Since all lines contain infinite possibilities of interpretation, one needs to use the *rtcm* to determine if the meanings suggested here apply to the given situation. (*See* p. 736 for using the *rtcm*.)

Line 1. *Progressing, but turned back. Being firmly correct brings success. If one meets with no confidence, one should remain calm. No mistake.*

This line can point to a person who has been attempting to force progress in another. He does so by pressing forward through attempting to persuade, use leverage and contrivance, instill guilt, claim that something is wrong with the other, argue, threaten, or use physical force. The consequence is that fate "turns him back." Behind forcing progress is the idea that one has to make things happen, an idea that rules out any cooperation with the Cosmic Helpers. Shut off from their help, a person is left to his own devices. The correct way to make progress is to take away all the mistaken ideas that picture the Cosmos/Nature in a negative light: as stingy, punishing, arbitrary, indifferent, unloving, unkind, unfriendly, and leaving humans without help.

A person may, on reading this line, make changes in his point of view, only to deal with the situation at hand. Because his change is superficial and motivated by egotistical considerations, he meets with no confidence from the Helpers. The Cosmos will not make deals with the ego. Remaining calm means he needs to review the goal he seeks and to correct basic components in his attitude. Only then can he free himself from the fate he has created.

This line can be reassuring a person that although it appears that no progress is being made in his situation, the progress is taking place on the inner plane. It is also telling him that he needs to ask for help in dispersing his doubts.

"Progressing, but turned back" can also point to the interference of the ego in a person after he has deprogrammed the phrases and ideas that have caused an illness. This interference occurs through the insertion of doubts that the Helpers will help (or have helped), or that the deprogramming can actually lead to healing. Being turned back can also come from expectations of the ego with regard to the time required for healing. Such watching by the ego blocks the Helpers. This line tells him that the healing is underway, but that he needs to go on without watching for progress. Progress always occurs when a person is going on with his life without looking for progress, and without stipulations as to how that progress should occur. The healing process does not preclude employing Helpers in the form of external remedies approved by the Sage through the *rtcm*. It is also good to ask the consciousness of the remedy for help before using it.

"Progressing, but turned back" can refer to the Helper that determines the natural time of a person's death, but which has been turned back by the person's resistance to dying. As a consequence, he suffers on. To engage this Helper, the person needs to free himself of the idea of death as a final end to life, or an abyss in which everything gets lost. (See Glossary: Death.)

Line 2. *Progressing, but in sorrow, due to looking to one's ancestress. Being firmly correct brings success. Then one obtains great happiness.*

Here, progress has been halted because the person believes his problems can be overcome through keeping his thoughts positive. Persons with this belief overlook how hidden inner doubts act out to prevent the success they are seeking. His progress will remain halted until the person has rid himself of the underlying seed phrases and images that have caused his problems. Getting rid of these phrases and images is the meaning of "being firmly correct."

At the root of these seed phrases and images are two ideas that initiate each other: that there was a golden past (an Eden) which was lost by human guilt, leading to life as a vale of tears. This gives rise to the fantasy that the golden past can be recreated through positive thinking and imaging. The person's unity with the Cosmic Harmony is restored by his ridding himself of the following mistaken ideas: (1) the idea of guilt, (2) the idea that life is a vale of tears, and (3) that problems can be resolved through positive thinking and imaging. (*See* p. 696, Freeing Yourself from Guilt, and *see* p. 689, Freeing Yourself from Seed Phrases and Images.)

The ancestress refers to the "golden past" that a person wishes now to recreate, with the idea that its values and customs were the source of happiness. The Sage makes us aware, however, that gazing back into the past stops a person's progress. He may be looking back at his childhood, or on old days of romance, or on a mythical golden age that he believes needs to be revived. Holding to such fantasies not only stops progress, it invokes Fate.

The person could make progress if he were to free the Helper of Transformation which has been locked up by his views. "Being firmly correct" counsels him to rid himself of the spells he has put on both the present and the future by focussing on the past. The spell consists of all the person's images of a glorious past. To break the spell it is necessary to say the inner No to his focussing on these images of the past, and to ask the Helpers to destroy those images.

Line 3. *All are in accord. Remorse disappears.*

This line informs the person receiving it that through his effort at ridding himself of the discordant ideas and beliefs that have been blocking his progress, he has achieved an accord with the Cosmos.

The word "accord," in its Cosmic meaning, describes a willing consent or cooperation that has been achieved between people, or between a person and the Cosmos. This willing consent is the opposite of the accord described by the traditional text of The Judgment, where, according to Legge's translation, the prince has secured the "tranquillity of the people" by the force of power or awe.

Another mistaken idea of an accord is the idea that opposites can be balanced by integrating them. This includes efforts to balance competing ideas within the individual psyche, within society, or across cultures. While a balance (as between two competing powers) can be created temporarily, keeping that balance is always like walking a tightrope, because the inner accord, which is based on the attraction between complements, is lacking. Another is the common idea that mental health is the result of a balance between the two frontal lobes of the brain (implying that other parts of the brain and psyche are unimportant). A true accord occurs only when all parts of the psyche and their individual consciousnesses are equally respected and included in the process. A similar mistaken idea is that accord is to be achieved through tolerating what is wrong, or by making compromises with the ego.

Likewise, an accord with the Cosmos cannot be achieved by engaging in ascetic practices or rituals, or by climbing arduously toward a spiritual goal. A true accord with the Cosmos is achieved through a person's systematically ridding himself of false seed phrases and images that separate him from the Cosmic Unity. Whenever he makes this effort, the Helper of Progress is freed to push his progress forward. Then his progress is like being carried across the ocean in a boat instead of swimming the whole way. The accord is felt as inner freedom and harmony with the Cosmos.

This line informs us that a true accord between people is achieved through transformations brought about by the Helper of Transformation. Transformations that totally change people's attitudes can be brought about by a person who asks the Cosmos for help and then gets the ego in himself out of the way. Unlike changes which are brought about by leverage, transformations create conditions that endure.

Line 4. *Progressing like a hamster. Perseverance brings danger.*

A hamster makes progress by amassing stores of food for times when food will not be available. Such storing up is appropriate for the hamster. Storing up things can also be an appropriate action for humans, but there is a danger in carrying the analogy too far.

This line warns a person against falling under the spell of stored up platitudes that sound as if they can be relied upon. Progress is assured if the person remains in contact with his commonsense. The danger with platitudes is the false sense of security they give.

In regard to making progress, the person needs to remember that each situation is unique, and responding to it appropriately requires finding the unique answer that fits the inner truth of the situation. For this he needs his commonsense. To rely on a standardized or formulaic approach to a new situation is folly.

The line can also be warning a person against relying on written knowledge as "the ultimate truth," because doing so stops his progress in arriving at new understandings. All learning is but a series of handholds to ever enlarging realizations.

This line is also about relying on the mistaken idea that life (Fate or Destiny) is a prewritten script. This idea contradicts the fact that every person is part of the ever-evolving Cosmic Consciousness. Due to the power of projection that is inherent in false thoughts and images, such an idea projects itself into reality in the form of a fate. Receiving this line can be a timely warning that a person is about to invoke a fate by holding to that idea. (*See* p. 689, Freeing Yourself from Mistaken Ideas and Beliefs.)

Line 5. *Take not gain and loss to heart. Then remorse disappears. Saying the inner No brings success in the form of natural progress.*

This line can refer to a person who is looking back over his life, or the lives of others, either in pride or remorse, by evaluating his progress in life only in terms of gain and loss. Gain and loss are words used by the ego to measure what it defines as worthwhile. Such evaluations do not correspond with the Cosmic view. Increase always comes from the Cosmos and the Helpers when a person decreases the ego. Success refers to conditions that lead to happiness without creating remorse.

Gain and loss are relative terms. Loss is the ego's term for what Fate has taken away, but since Fate serves the purpose of bringing a person back into harmony with the Cosmos, there is actually a gain. If we look into a particular fate, we see that Fate has retrieved a Cosmic gift that has been appropriated or stolen by the ego, because the person had acquired it through the contrivances of the ego in himself.

The line can also apply to a person's looking at another, such as his partner, or child, and measuring him by the standards of his expectations. He needs to firmly say the inner No to this measuring, so as to free the other to make natural progress. Saying the inner No is what brings success and makes natural progress possible.

Another example of false measuring is a woman who, not having had a child, sees herself as a failure due to her mistaken belief that "a woman is not a woman until she has had a child." Ridding herself of this false standard will free her personal Helpers and bring her inner freedom. She may also need to say the inner No to others who are projecting this belief upon her.

A person may also receive this line when the ego in him, or in another, nags him that he has failed to take advantage of a good opportunity to influence the situation. The line counsels him not to see this as a loss, because progress has been made through his remaining detached and free of intention.

This line also seeks to make a person aware that the Sage does not give any person the special task of representing the Sage to the world. A person does this to falsely elevate himself (the gain). The same applies to the person who evangelizes the *I Ching* to others: the Sage as the Cosmic Teacher does not give people the task of evangelizing its messages, no matter how much the person wishes to see the world make progress. The Sage does, however, support a person's joyfully sharing his good experiences with the *I Ching*, when this sharing happens in response to others' openness and need. It does not support his engaging in arguments to prove its points. Viewing each moment as an opportunity to push the *I Ching* on others is the work of the ambitious and goal-oriented ego. When a person finds himself doing this, he needs to say the inner No to the ego. (*See* p. 691, Freeing Yourself from Self-Images.)

Line 6. *Making progress with the horns is permissible only for the purpose of punishing one's own city. To be conscious of danger brings success. No blame. Perseverance brings humiliation.*

This line has been taken as a justification for the feudal lord or other authority to punish the people. It reveals the pretense of the collective ego that it has the right to control people through the use of threats and punishments, and to repress the anger in people when they rebel against being treated unjustly.

In the Cosmic meaning of this line, the city is a metaphor for the ego in a person's psyche that is trying to intimidate or threaten him. He needs to stand up to the intimidation of the ego with strong determination (will), and call for help from the Sage and the Cosmic Army. When a person exercises his will in this way, the bullying ego will be seen to quickly back down, for it cannot stand up to a firm inner determination. When a person firmly rejects the ego in himself, the egos in those around him also give way.

"To be conscious of danger" can be warning a person who seeks to make progress with another by confronting the ego directly. Any such attempt comes from the ego in himself, and only causes the other to lose face, thereby arousing his hatred. True progress is made by saying the inner No to the ego in himself (his own city), and asking for help from the Sage both in his own and in the other's presence.

Spells connected with the "use of the horns" have to do with the belief that there must be a strong authority which, in turn, has been authorized by something higher (law, decree, custom, a Higher Power) to maintain order, be it over the people, the family, the partnership, or the individual: "the law is supreme," "God set up the order," "the parent has the right to punish the children," "the children belong to the parents," "the individual belongs to his nation," and "the nation has a right over the people." These spells prevent the individual from being able to say the inner No to those whom he regards as authorities over him. (*See* p. 697, Freeing Yourself from Spells.)

In terms of treating a health problem, this line may refer to a person's returning to conventional medical treatment, upon doubting the healing process carried out by the Helpers. He does this because the progress of the healing has not yet shown visibly (even though progress has actually been made on the invisible plane). It may also refer to a person who believes that the best way to handle an illness is to grab it by the horns and wrestle it down. He does not understand that the illness itself is not an enemy, but a message of Fate telling him that there is a problem element within his psyche that needs to be removed.

The idea of grabbing the sickness by the horns comes from his human-centered view that he can, by force, conquer the ills of the body. It is also possible that he has created his illness through thinking in terms such as, "I *have* cancer." Phrasing the problem as if the illness is a part of his nature actually gives permission to the cancer to remain. He needs to distance himself from it by describing it differently–as, for example, "I have become ill with cancer."*

Is it also an important part of healing that the conscious mind treat the injured parts (cells, organs, etc.) as "brothers" and sisters" or as children that are wounded or in shock. It is harmful when the conscious mind looks down on the body and the cells as inferior parts that operate only mechanically, and as subservient to it. In reality, it is the healthy functioning and cooperation of the various consciousnesses that enables the conscious mind to function successfully within the body. (For the different kinds of consciousness *see* p. 18.)

36. *Darkening of the Light*

 K'un
Li

The Judgment: *Darkening of the light. In adversity it furthers one to hold fast to what is correct.*

This hexagram shows the ego fighting its "last battle" after having lost control because its advice has caused a person to fail to meet an adversity. In its effort to regain control, the ego replays the same old doubts and re-inspires the same old fears that were installed in the person during childhood, to remind him why he needs it. It then plays its trump card, guilt, which makes him feel guilty if he abandons it. Among the basic rationales used to install the ego are those about his nature: that it is insufficient to cope with life, and that it contains flaws that must be overcome through developing the collective ego's program of virtues. These rationales are reinforced with threats that the person will be rejected by his family, society, etc., and lose their protection, without which he will not be able to survive. Added is the fear of becoming guilty of betraying his family, culture, or forefathers, if he follows his inner truth. The ego also calls it "selfish" to follow one's inner truth, and "arrogant" to question the collective ego's taboos and accepted beliefs.

If the person will stand back, even for a moment, and listen to this monologue as a bystander, he will recognize it as the ego's game, and thereby gain the distance he needs to separate out what belongs to the ego and what belongs to him. This separation is the moment in which he can break the deception fostered by the ego, that it and he are one and the same. This is to get to the "heart of the darkening" as it is put in Line 4, and is the moment in which he can begin to liberate himself from the ego's dominance. This separation can be observed in meditation, especially when it is under the guidance of the Sage, and sometimes in dreams. (*See* Hexagram 52, *Meditating.*)

To liberate himself from the ego, it is necessary for him to say the inner No to all its aspects. This hexagram concerns a person who, on seeing one or more aspects of the ego, is either unwilling or unable to say the inner No. The person who is unwilling has fallen under what he perceives as the charming aspect of the ego, and therefore will say, "I like my ego"; he believes it adds quality, excitement, and interest to his life. Upon perceiving its mischievous qualities, he thinks they will not cause him harm, and may even be of benefit to him. This charming aspect of the ego has made him its captive, and has blinded him to the ego's destructiveness, which has both darkened his inner light and imprisoned his true self. This charming aspect of the ego often employs a humor that denigrates others and puts the person up at others' expense.

The person may also be fascinated by the magician aspect of the ego, and its cleverness in pulling solutions out of its sleeve which are beguiling, both to himself and others. It is this magician aspect that invents the sleight-of-hand logic that we have mentioned in Part I and in several hexagrams, by which it diverts the blame for the harm it does, either to the true self, to others, to Nature, or to the Cosmos. It is also the aspect that rewrites history to monumentalize human achievements due to their use of power, and invents myths of human greatness that eclipse the existence of the Helpers of the invisible world.

"Darkening of the light" is a metaphor for a person's state of mind who is caught in the demonic sphere of consciousness, or logic of the ego. While he is within this web, he can only imagine that things are brought about through changes created by effort and striving. He believes the harder he strives, the more successful he will be. However, in this circumstance, he has exhausted all effort and all strategies. He finally sees that no amount of effort can extricate him from the difficulty. Caught in this mindset, he is blind to recognizing that in the Cosmic Reality, changes are brought about by the Helpers through transformations in the atomic realm. Moreover, he denies all the experiences he has had of these transformations, through falsely dismissing them as due to "his imagination," "chance," "luck," or "intervention by something 'supernatural,'" rather than to the entirely natural way the Cosmos helps all of those parts which hold firmly to it.

The solution is indicated by The Judgment: "hold fast to what is correct." This means saying the inner No to the despairing ego, with all its dark-seeing which is bent only on keeping itself in place. The ego would resist the real solution simply because it would be displaced and discredited. The value of the adversity the person finds himself in is that it gives him the opportunity to see, with absolute clarity, that the ego is his only real enemy. It is the ego which, at the depth of despair, would even have the person give up his life (as in suicide) rather than give up its pretenses and the mistaken images and ideas to which it owes its existence.

Darkening refers to a person's loss of inner independence due to slow progress. A person is trying to resolve a problem with the *I Ching* but despairs that he is getting nowhere. He even suspects that the Cosmos is against him, and is tempted to give up his path. His inner light is threatened through looking at the situation from the standpoint of the ego. It is as if the person has on dark glasses and everything he sees is sorted out under headings of "no better" and "worse." People's habits of mind seem so defective that he cannot imagine any possibility of their changing.

"Darkening" can also refer to an outer situation in which it would be dangerous or unwise to display one's clarity of vision, or to say the truth. The person who is in touch with his clarity and commonsense holds to what is correct by saying the *inner* No, and by refusing to become involved in the external circumstance. He then asks for help from the Helpers to take care of the situation, and turns the matter over to them. This contrasts with the solution offered by the collective ego, which would counsel the valiant defender of the truth to come forward to say what he thinks needs to be said, regardless of the circumstances. Such a person labors under the belief that in order to serve the truth, he must "not hide his light under a bushel."

Darkening can also refer to an inner condition in which the person is threatened with images that give rise to hopelessness and despair, because he feels that his life has no way to blossom and be fulfilled. He needs to ask himself what beliefs hold him in this inner prison against his commonsense. He has failed to notice that the key is in the lock and he only needs to turn it to leave. This key is to say the inner No to the ego's self-pitying phrases and its dismal picture of "reality." If he will look away from his miseries, he will see the daily blessings that exist in the small things of his life: the sun, the birds, the trees, kind people around him. From this benchmark of goodness and blessing, his appreciation for the small things can grow to fill him from within rather than giving his inner space over to negativity.

Darkening can also refer to a situation in which a person represses his own needs to fulfill another's. Doing so causes him a constant loss of his life energy. All relationships need to be reciprocal in terms of an exchange of chi energy. This exchange occurs when there is mutual respect and sensitivity. The question here is of what beliefs the person allows within himself that prohibit him from respecting and honoring his own needs in favor of others'; or, what inner terrors prevent him from saying the inner No to insensitivity and disrespect on the part of others. This person needs to say the inner No to all behaviors in his relationships which lack equality and reciprocity, and to refuse to participate in them. He may need to ask the Sage via the *rtcm* if he has an inner block to saying the inner No, and if so, to correct this problem. (*See* p. 677, Saying the Inner No.)

Darkening can also refer to an ongoing or chronic co-dependency that locks everyone involved in destructive and energy-robbing experiences. Co-dependency describes a person who lifeguards another with his inner eye; the other, feeling protected by this inner watching, feels a false safety in doing dangerous things, having an inner assurance that "if something bad happens," the other will save him, or it will be the other's fault. Such inner lifeguarding locks the commonsense of the one being lifeguarded in a spell. The person supervising is under a complementary spell of believing he must lifeguard the other. Both people need to be freed from the spells. The one exposing himself to dangers will then be able to recognize that he is on his own, and will then listen to his commonsense. Removal of the spells also releases the destructive effects of the person's disbelief in his ability to protect himself. Letting go is accomplished more easily by turning the matter of the other's safety over to the Cosmos, and asking for its help, as this is the only real source of safety.

If the person has difficulty saying this inner No, it may be due to the prospect of becoming guilty for whatever "awful" thing might happen to the other. In such a person's mind, guilt and responsibility are intermingled. He needs to recognize that both the responsibility and the guilt are false concepts that have been put upon him from without. *Every* person has senses that inform him when he is endangered, and that make him react to the situation in exactly the right way. The person needs to rid himself of the spells of false responsibility and guilt. This frees the Helpers for both people. (*See* p. 697, Freeing Yourself from Spells.)

Note: Since all lines contain infinite possibilities of interpretation, one needs to use the *rtcm* to determine if the meanings suggested here apply to the given situation. (*See* p. 736 for using the *rtcm*.)

Line 1. *Darkening of the light during flight. He lowers his wings. In his depression he does not eat for three days on his wanderings;*

but he has somewhere to go. The host has occasion to talk.

"Darkening during flight" refers to a person who, after beginning to resolve his problems with the help of the Sage, is disappointed because he has not achieved visible progress. On deciding that the Helpers do not exist, and that he is left alone with his problem, he falls into depression and hopelessness, the meaning of "lowering his wings." He has been looking at the situation through the eyes of the ego, which says, "see where this has led you," and "this path doesn't work." "Not eating for three days while wandering" refers to his inner wandering, not knowing what to do, thus depriving himself of the nourishment that would come to him from the Helpers if he said the inner No to hopelessness and helplessness. However, "having somewhere to go" indicates that he has an inner feeling that he was on the correct path.

"The host has occasion to talk" points to a reversal of places between the ego and his true self. While, in truth, the true self is the host, and the ego the parasite that feeds on its host, the ego, here, has taken the place of the leader of the personality and talks to the true self as if it were a child, and guilty for what has happened. It gives its "thousand reasons" why the person should put the ego back in charge. Its thousand reasons create a "ball of conflict" which is not soluble by thinking about those reasons (*see* Hexagram 6, *Conflict*). It is necessary to cease listening to the ego altogether, and calling on the Helper of Dissolution to dissolve the whole ball of conflict.

The reason for the lack of progress is the person's having allowed the ego to watch for progress, which not only blocks the Helpers, but also creates a fate. To remedy the situation, he needs to recognize that his judging the Cosmos is arrogant, and that on this account he has created obstructions. The origin of his arrogance is the human-centered view of the universe that he has adopted from the collective ego. He needs to review the ego-elements in his attitude and say the inner No to them, and return to the inner path on which he had embarked.

Line 2. *Darkening injures him in the left thigh. He gives aid with the strength of a horse. Success.*

Darkening, with reference to the left thigh, indicates a spell that a person has put on himself through becoming attached, in a dependent way, to the Sage, whom he looks up to as all-powerful. He thinks that if he gets the Sage on his side, everything will be good for him. By making the Sage into God, or a godlike figure, he has decreased his own dignity and self-worth. The Sage recognizes his error and comes to his aid (with the strength of a horse), to make him aware of his faulty attitude. Dependence on the Sage to help him access his inner truth is not a mistake, but the kind of attachment by which a person turns responsibility over to the Sage for every decision, is incorrect because it slanders his commonsense.

This line also addresses situations in which a person seeks to buy his way out of a fate by making a deal to serve the Sage, to end a fate. Such efforts, however, only cause the Sage to withdraw, making the person feel intensely alone and abandoned, hence the darkening. He needs to understand (1) that the Sage does not make deals, (2) that he can only end his fate by recognizing the mistaken ideas and beliefs that have caused it, and then ridding himself of them. Doing so will activate the Helper of Transformation to end his fate. The idea of making deals comes from the ego, and is a throwaway of his dignity. Part of correcting himself is to realize that he is never meant to throw his dignity away for any purpose. Despite these errors, the Sage has come to his aid voluntarily, to help him realize his mistaken view and to give him an opportunity to correct it. (*See* p. 692, Freeing Yourself from a Fate.)

"Darkening" of a person's will to continue with the *I Ching* occurs when a person has expected to resolve his difficulties in one great sweep of effort. Behind his expectation is his belief that if he works hard enough, he will win the sympathy of the Cosmos to come to his aid. The Cosmos, however, is neither to be won nor bought.

Darkening also occurs when a person approaches the Sage only to resolve his difficulties, in order to return to his "ordinary life." He is not interested in making the necessary effort to free his true self. Under normal conditions, the Sage would retreat, but because the person remembers the gifts he has received from the Sage in the past, the Sage comes to his aid, to help him resolve his difficulties.

This line also addresses the darkening that occurs when a person begins to believe that he is never going to have the love relationship that will fulfill him. Love is a Cosmic gift that flows from the Cosmos through the two lovers, and back again to the Cosmos. When a person thinks that love comes from the other person and is something that he can possess, he makes it difficult for the Cosmos to give the gift. Even if he should receive the gift of love, but in receiving it, has the wrong attitude toward it, as in turning it to egotistical purposes, the gift is taken away. Nevertheless, the Cosmos does give the gift, both to those who within themselves are ready for it, and to others as a Cosmic intervention in their lives, to bring about their inner growth. If a person frees himself of expectation and his mistaken ideas about love, the Cosmos will restore the gift of love to him.

The traditional interpretation of this line says that it is a person's duty to fight with all his strength to save others in danger, implying, "regardless of the circumstances." While the Cosmos can indeed use a person to help another who is involved in a fate, it is the Cosmos that saves him in the end. The person can only assist as directed by his commonsense. If he has taken upon himself the duty to intervene in other's fates, by adopting the magnificent self-image of the hero who rescues others, he will have created a fate for himself, because his actions will have interfered in the Cosmic purpose that Fate is meant to serve. To end his fate, he needs to rid himself of the self-image mentioned. In another case, a person may have taken on the self-image of the one who, after having himself "crossed the great water," now has the job of "hauling the others across." (*See* p. 692, Freeing Yourself from a Fate.)

"He gives help with the strength of a horse" is a reference to the Helper of Cosmic Intervention that comes to help when a person has regained his natural modesty.

Line 3. *Darkening of the Light during the hunt in the south. Their great leader is captured. One must not expect perseverance too soon.*

Here, the hunt is for the ringleader of disorder—the source of his depressed feelings. During the hunt (under the guidance of the Sage), a person finds out that the ringleader is the ego, in the form of all the mistaken ideas and beliefs he has accepted into his inner program. These ideas and beliefs are the cause of the betrayal of his true self, and his subsequent embarrassment. The ringleader is not, as he had thought, some evil force outside himself, or a person he has been blaming for betraying him.

The inner verbalizations of the ego reveal its magician aspect in phrases that lead to the darkening of a person's inner light, hiding of Cosmic Truth, the undermining of his will, and the usurpation of his chi energy.

The embarrassing and depressing feelings he is now experiencing come from the ego, upon its being seen as the source of his wrong moves, and upon its being recognized as his true enemy. The ego plays upon these feelings of embarrassment, in order to transfer all the blame, either back onto the true self, or onto others. By understanding this dynamic, and by recognizing that the ego is a parasite in his psyche, he can free himself of its evil influence by firmly saying the inner No to its activity of putting the blame onto himself or others. In doing this, he captures the ringleader of disorder.

"One must not expect perseverance too soon," is warning him of a particular dynamic of the ego which it employs to reinstate itself: the ego will attempt to seize his anger at having been betrayed by it, by turning his attention to his "losses": the flattering self-images he has lost, and the privileges that have accompanied them. By causing him to dwell on his losses through introducing the ego-emotion of self-pity, the ego escapes being the element blamed, and thereby resumes control. Its next words are, "you must do something to recover your losses, to enjoy life again."* The ego then turns the initial anger that was directed against *it*, into uncontrolled vindictiveness, restlessness, fury, desire, hope, and despair that are directed both back to the true self and outward to life, circumstances, or other people.

This line also can point to an intervention by the ego that sabotages the help received from the Helpers, as when it inserts the thought that the success was a supernatural event coming from above, or that it was "magical." An example is an illness, which recurs after having been healed. Thinking of the help as supernatural has credited the wrong source, hence undoes what was accomplished. The help given by the Helpers is neither supernatural nor magical, but the natural and everyday way the Cosmos acts to benefit what is in harmony with it.

"Darkening of the light during the hunt in the South" can also indicate that a person has been looking for the truth where it is not to be found. The South represents the side of the mountain lit by the sun. The sun here points to what we see in terms of appearances, which is the cause of the darkening. The only way the inner truth can be discovered is by searching for the untruths that cover it up. This means going into the dark places of the psyche where the untruth hides. Another trick of the ego is to present the search for "the truth" as a secret held by the few, and as "difficult," needing an experienced human leader. The person who believes this misses the point, since such ideas are invariably promoted by people who pose as possessors of the truth, in order to gain power over others. They flatter their followers into thinking that by gaining access to the truth they possess, they will share in this power.

Line 4. *He penetrates the left side of the belly. One gets at the very heart of the darkening of the light, and leaves the gate and courtyard.*

"Penetrating the left side of the belly and getting to the very heart of the darkening of the light" is a way of saying that a person needs to come to a deeper understanding of the source of his problem. On doing so he will find that his heart has not been "in the right place" because he has been acting from thinking rather than from feeling. The ego, as the source of the darkening, has been ruling his personality and his relationships by making him believe that thinking is superior to feeling. It can also be that the ego has been dominating through fantasies that arouse ego-emotions, which the person has then mistaken for his true feelings.

The courtyard is a metaphor for the fantasy world (the parallel reality) that is based on the values of the collective ego. This line points to two of these values in particular which it glorifies: the accumulation of abstract knowledge, and the fantasies created by the imaging mind (promoted, among others, by the fantasy creators of the media). This devotion to knowledge and fantasy is opposed to the knowledge and feeling of the heart that are gained through experience. Being abstract content of the forebrain, this content is indifferent to true feeling. Following either the path of abstract knowledge or the path of fantasy leads to dead ends, in that their goals, when reached, fail to satisfy the most basic human needs. Knowledge of the heart is the light that is darkened by abstract thinking and fantasizing. Moreover, this activity of the forebrain is the generator of all ego-emotions, which are mistaken for true feelings.

This line can also refer to the "darkening" that occurs in a love relationship when the two individuals want to see themselves as "one." Such an idea draws them into sacrificing the uniqueness of their true natures to an abstract image of what they "ought" to be. This sacrifice of their true selves creates an inner conflict within each person, which in the end is insupportable, so that it undermines the relationship. Unchecked, it will destroy both individuals. Saying the inner No to sacrificing oneself to such an idea is to "leave through the gate."

The line can also refer to other instances in which the individual merges his identity into a group or organizational identity. Such an adoption of the "group-we" betrays the uniqueness and independence of his true nature, and prevents it from coming to expression.

Line 5. *Darkening of the light as with Prince Chi. Being firm and correct furthers.*

Prince Chi is a historical figure who lived at the court of a tyrant. The explanation is given that he was a relative of the tyrant and therefore could not withdraw from the court, even though he was repulsed by the behavior of the tyrant. To avoid betraying his convictions, he feigned insanity.

Prince Chi is a metaphor for several kinds of situations. The first shows a person who is in a difficult circumstance that he cannot leave outwardly. He needs to hide his light or even tell an untruth to conceal his real feelings, because the others would not understand his viewpoint, and further, would use it against him. It can also refer to consciously misinforming a person because that person is encroaching into one's private space in an attempt to know things he has no right to know. This is firm and correct conduct in the face of an encroaching ego.

In another instance, a person may be withholding his natural inclination to say a heartfelt "I love you," from an intuition that the ego of the one he loves is waiting to grab this statement and possess him. He needs to say the inner No to the ego and its desire to possess. He also needs to search out the deeper fears and doubts in his partner that cause him to want to control the love relationship.

The line also points to a person's inner sovereignty having been damaged by slanders coming from without. Outwardly, he is unable to dismiss the slanders. If he says the inner No to them and turns them over to the Sage, he can regain his *inner* sovereignty. Once he has regained that, Cosmic Helpers are engaged to correct the outer situation. Such slanders can stick to him and affect him only as long as he remains attached to them, or as long as he allows them to affect him. An example of a slanderous phrase is "who are you to judge?" or "you do not have the expertise/knowledge/authority to know what is correct, or what to do." This situation needs to be treated as a spell.

This line can also refer to remarks made that have caused a person to doubt the validity of his true feelings. The remarks have put a spell on his feelings, preventing him from feeling them. He needs to recognize the phrases that have created the spell, and rid himself of them. An example is the phrase, "you can't trust your feelings." (*See* p. 697, Freeing Yourself from Spells.)

Prince Chi is also a metaphor for a person who has the noble self-image that he can bear with an incorrect situation forever, if necessary, or he may harbor the incorrect idea that suffering is noble. By failing to say the inner No to such an idea, and to the incorrect situation, from which he also needs to withdraw, he has given it his permission to continue, thus created a fate for himself.

Line 6. *No light but darkness. First he climbed up to heaven, then he plunged into the depths of the earth.*

"No light but darkness" describes the way the ego/collective ego converts Cosmic Consciousness into demonic consciousness by reversing meanings. For example, when the individual seeks to fulfill his true needs and develop his uniqueness, the ego calls his behavior selfish and undermining the social order. Just the opposite is true: it is the ego and its parent, the collective ego, which undermine the natural order of society, and the Cosmic Order. It is through the expression of an individual's uniqueness that the creative gifts of the Cosmos are brought to the world.

"No light but darkness" also refers to the way the ego and the collective ego, if allowed to become completely dominating, destroy the individual's life energy, because this is the ego's only source of energy.

This line at the top of the darkening is the one place in the *I Ching* where the individual ego and the collective ego are shown in their essence as "all dark." "No light" also describes the deeds of utter destruction throughout the ages that were performed against individuals and species. Among these are the great inquisitions, the massacres of tribal cultures, and today's practices of keeping people alive beyond their time. It is the function of Fate to end such darkening. Fate also extinguishes the Cosmic blame incurred by the ringleaders who were responsible for these deeds. It would be incorrect to accept any feeling of collective guilt for what other people did. (*See* p. 50, Guilt, Blame, and Shame.)

"First he climbed up to heaven, then he plunged into the depths of the earth" describes the rise and fall of the monumentalized ego. The rise to heaven pictures the imagination of the person, in which he sees himself attaining fame and glory, or as having become immune to the Law of Fate; it is precisely when a person has allowed this back-of-the mind ego-thought, that his fall to earth begins. The fall to earth is the shock that reawakens his senses, brings him back to humility, to recognize his grounding in the earth, and to enable him to correct himself. Thus the expression in The Judgment of Hexagram 51,

Shock, following such a fall: "Oh! Oh! Ha! Ha!" The Ha! Ha!, it might seem, is vindictive, but it expresses the deep feeling of relief that comes when a tyrant has been brought low. The line confirms that Cosmic Justice supersedes the laws erected by the collective ego. A person may also receive this line to make him aware of the ultimate consequences of giving the ego safe harbor.

37. The Family

 Sun / Li

The Judgment: *The perseverance of the woman furthers.*

The term "family" here refers both to the Cosmic Family and the human family. The Cosmic Family includes both its invisible aspects, and its visible aspect called "Nature." Nature includes rocks, plants, animals, and humans, each of which has its own unique consciousnesses that contribute to the Cosmic Consciousness of the whole. The invisible aspect of the Cosmic Family includes the Helpers: individualized aspects of consciousness that enable the Cosmos to function as a harmonious whole.

This hexagram is often given to tell a person that for whatever circumstance, he can call on the Cosmic Family for help. The Cosmic Family functions on the basis of the Cosmic Harmonics. This means that it comes fully and completely to the person who has modesty and sincerity. This modesty comes from his recognizing his correct place in the Cosmic Whole by neither seeing himself as special, nor having a demanding and presumptuous attitude. His sincerity comes from his recognizing that the true source of all help and gifts is the Cosmos.

It needs to be noted that help comes to anyone who asks for it, but when the person is not in the correct place within himself, help comes with a fate attached. This happens, for example, when he believes the help comes from a clan God or from a Cosmic clan (any entity that plays favorites), or if after receiving the help he dismisses its Cosmic source by claiming it was good luck, or his own doing, or he dismisses its gift nature by thinking he has deserved it because he is special.

This hexagram also defines the function of the *natural* human family. This function contrasts with that defined by the collective ego, which employs the family to insert its false mental program, or mindset, into the psyche of the child.

The natural human family has the function of providing the correct environment for the child while he is being reared. In the larger sense, the natural family can refer to whoever it is in a child-rearing environment, whether it be an orphanage or single parent household, or adoptive parents, regardless of gender.

In the Cosmic sense, The Judgment emphasizes the importance of the feelings, referred to by the metaphor of the woman. (The woman is named because it is she who gives birth, and whose feelings are energized by all the hormones (feeling Helpers) that accompany the birth process when not numbed by drugs.) The Sage teaches that there are no character differences between the genders. The family, properly speaking, includes both mother and father as having the function of providing the feeling environment needed to bring up the child. This feeling environment acknowledges and respects each member's inclusion within the *Cosmic* Family.

The natural function of the parents, throughout their child's infancy, is to care for him, and to ask the Cosmic Family for help for all the needs of the family. Beyond infancy, the parents' function is to recognize the innate abilities of the child, and give him space for these abilities to develop in a psychic atmosphere that shelters him from the pressures of the collective ego. Their function is to teach the child that they are not the *source* of love, help, and nourishment, but the *vehicle* through which these gifts flow to him from the Cosmos. They also teach him that when they are not present or available, he can inwardly ask for any help, love, and nourishment he needs, for himself. They also teach him that he is never cut off or abandoned by the Cosmos. Their function, otherwise, is to let go more and more as the child learns to trust his own connection with the Cosmos.

For the parent, perseverance refers to being firm in the face of the collective ego's pressures. It also means that it is the parents' job to make the child aware that all guilt, fear, threat, and flattery come from the collective ego, with the purpose of making him feel inadequate, on the one hand, and special, on the other. They make him aware that feeling special prevents him from listening to his true feelings, and that feeling inadequate makes him forget that Cosmic help is available to him. At the age of about twelve, they openly discuss the inner No, and reassure the child that it is correct to say it when the outer No would only create opposition, and to retreat from the ego, both in himself and in others, whenever it appears . They give him room to experience that his inner No has a corrective effect on others, and that it can be relied on. They make him aware that the Sage exists in the presence of every person, including himself, and that whenever he is in trouble, he can ask the Sage in his presence and the Sage in the other's presence to come to their help. The parents, through not regarding themselves as superior, and treating themselves with respect, teach the child respect for himself, and support his sense of equality, fairness, and respect for others. The parents also persevere in helping to keep the child free from projections and spells that others might put upon him. In sum, the family setting, as defined above, is meant to be a setting in which the uniqueness of each member can develop and find expression, without any feelings of inferiority or fault. The role of the parents is also to protect the children from physical harm.

The family thus defined is the setting that prepares the child for his future love relationship. The principles of relating that he learns in this environment lead him also to respect the personal space of his love partner. When the love relationship is not based on this respect, it cannot attain duration.

By contrast, the feudal model of the family is revealed in the traditional interpretation of this hexagram. It shows the family as held together by the loyalty and endurance of the wife, whose place is within the house. The husband's role is to represent the family in all outer relationships. Emphasized is the "strong authority" needed in the parents to instill the values of the collective ego in the children. The children are taught that the loyalty they owe to their parents, right or wrong, is to be carried over to the feudal prince, or in modern terms, the nation, as in the expression "my country, right or wrong." Thus, as Wilhelm puts it, the family is regarded as "society in embryo," where the sons and daughters are to learn the societal roles they are expected to take later on, and to which they are expected to sacrifice themselves by putting aside whatever feelings they have that do not fit into the roles.* This feudal model of the family is still in practice in modern, hierarchically organized societies throughout the world. The term "feudal prince" needs only to be replaced by institutions such as colleges, government, or even corporations, as that to which a person presumably owes his loyalty, because they have gradually assumed authorizing powers, and because the individual has been encouraged to believe they are the only sources of protection he has. They have taken on the function of authorizing his existence, worth, and purpose.

This feudal structuring of the family emphasizes role models and the observance of moral duties. It is primarily a program that represses feelings, thus preventing the development of the *natural* family order. The natural family order is not something that can be designed and superimposed. It simply emerges when all the ideas that are not in harmony with the Cosmic function of the family are taken away, and when the inner No and retreat are employed in each instance in which the ego shows itself.

An important part of conditioning within the feudal family is to prevent the children from questioning the fundamental premises and taboos on which the institutions of the collective ego are founded. To this end, the parents train the child to suppress his awareness of the contradictions between what is said and what he feels is true. Thus he gradually learns to substitute the shoulds and oughts of the collective ego for his inner truth.

The traditional part of the hexagram called "The Image," which was thought to have been inserted by Confucius reads: "Thus the superior man has substance in his words, and dura-

---

* *See* Luigi Pirandello's play, "Six Characters in Search of An Author," for a demonstration of the captivity and sacrifice of the true self by the characters to the roles within the family as defined by the collective ego.

tion in his way of life." This reference makes us aware that the family is also the environment in which the child learns language, and indicates the crucial role of language in his conditioning. In the feudal model of the family, "having substance in one's words" clearly means "having authority." If the authority is strong enough, then the societal roles assigned to each individual will be enforced. All hierarchical social orders must stress this need for authority over the individual in order to maintain their dominance. This belief is in sharp contrast to the Cosmic meaning of "having substance in one's words," which refers to calling things by their true names, and not by names that obscure their natures and functions, or even turn them to their opposites.

Seed phrases that put spells on the child have to do with duties and obligations toward the authorizing powers over him; they are traditionally accompanied by the threat that he will become guilty if he fails to fulfill them. An example is the child's duty to love the parents. It is the child's nature to love those who care for him lovingly. Another spell is that "the child owes his life to his parents." Because a child, once born, is a Cosmic gift to the parents, the child does not owe his life to them. Another is related to the concept of obedience: "children should be seen and not heard."

Other spells put on the child have to do with regarding his nature as defective, as in the idea that he is born with original fault, or sin, or that his animal nature is the source of evil. This latter belief is the basis for the suppression of the child's true nature and its replacement by the abstract virtues and disciplines promoted by the collective ego. Many adult neuroses have their origin in spells put on them in their early family life. Regardless of how long the spells have been there, they remain active in the psyche until such time as they are deprogrammed through consciously bringing them to mind and rejecting them in the way described in the Appendix.

Within the feudal mindset, it is the practice to blame those who have been the cause of one's misfortunes. In this case, however, there is no cause for blame, since the parents, too, have been brought up within the feudal mindset, therefore were unaware, even of the possibility of any other way of relating. Inasmuch as they did not listen to the prodding of their inner truth, they have created a fate for themselves. This fate, as has been mentioned before, extinguishes the blame.

Each line of this hexagram shows a different aspect of the natural family order and how this aspect is suppressed by mistaken ideas.

Note: Since all lines contain infinite possibilities of interpretation, one needs to use the *rtcm* to determine if the meanings suggested here apply to the given situation. (*See* p. 736 for using the *rtcm.*)

Line 1. *Firm seclusion within the family. Remorse disappears.*

"Firm seclusion within the family" describes the Cosmic Principle that the Cosmic Family operates as a harmonious whole. For the individual human being, this means that he takes his true place within the whole by respecting as equal every other aspect of the Cosmos, including the invisible Helpers and the visible world of Nature.

"Remorse disappears" pronounces the result if a person ceases to regard himself as special. His remorse was due to having excluded the invisible Cosmic Consciousness from his everyday awareness, and thereby he had also excluded the Sage and the Helpers from his life. In doing so, he deprived himself of his source of the renewal of his life force, and of the thousands of ways in which the Helpers make his life harmonious. To keep aware of them in his everyday life is to keep "secluded" within the Cosmic Family.

The parents, on the other hand, who view themselves as representing the collective ego, create the impression in the child, that they are the only source for his primal needs. They succeed in instilling the collective ego's program in the child's psyche by threatening him with the loss of the support of the family if he does not comply with the moral duties put upon him. These duties entail his suppressing his inner truth and all that he knows of the invisible world. The truth he is to follow is that which has been filtered through and interpreted by the authorities of the collective ego's institutions.

A further aspect of the collective ego's definition of "firm seclusion within the family" has to do with attachment to family traditions that make a person feel comfortable. As a consequence, he feels repelled by the traditions of other families. This kind of attachment creates wars between the factions, and spells within the individual clan members. In pursuing the goal of freeing the true self, it is necessary for a person to free himself of such exclusiveness; this entails his ridding himself of the belief that his personal family tradition is superior. It also requires saying the inner No to efforts by others within his circle to make their traditions prevail. Only then can each person discover and fulfill his uniqueness; otherwise, the pressure of the clan takes over, to make each person conform. To love one's family is one thing; to become attached to it as a clan is another.

Remorse has to do with misusing the Cosmic gift given to a person or a couple in the form of a child. This child, with all its Cosmic and natural possessions, is an opportunity for them to express their own love and caring feelings, and to discover and express their own Cosmic and natural possessions. The child, in its innocence, reflects the harmony of the Cosmos. Remorse can occur, however, if the parents regard the child as their property. They are but caretakers on behalf of the Cosmic Whole.

The collective ego makes parents think that the child is property given them on its behalf, and that they are merely its administrators. In older feudal cultures, the king could approach any family and appropriate for his personal use or for public sacrifice, the family's child or children.[*] Such practices invariably bring remorse, inasmuch as the child is taken away from the family, either psychically or literally.

In a broader sense, "firm seclusion" refers to a way of coping with a specific problem, in refusing to be drawn off the center point of what is correct by ancillary considerations.

The collective ego would preoccupy a person's attention with

---

[*] Frank Fiedeler relates such practices in ancient China. (Yijing, pp. 348-351.) They continued into modern times, in modified form, in the custom of the feudal lord's having the right of the first night in the servant daughter's wedding bed, as made famous in the play of Beaumarchais, and Mozart's opera, "The Marriage of Figaro." The custom of regarding the sons of families as property of the state continues today in military conscription practices.

411

issues that are outside his responsibility, and about which he is expected to feel guilty, if he does not do something about them outwardly. In such cases, his best response is to use the *rtcm* to see whether he is meant to respond to those issues, and the expectations bound with them, through saying the inner No to them. Firm seclusion otherwise refers to his only taking care of what is directly relevant to his personal life. If something outside of that is brought to his attention, he is to ask the Sage whether he is meant to respond to it *inwardly.*

Firm seclusion also tells us that the collective ego, in fostering the idea of humankind as special over other species, and over Nature in general, goes beyond Cosmic Limits. This happens, for example, when humans believe they have the right to use other animals or humans for medical experiments, and when they indulge in genetic engineering. Such rights do not have any basis in the Cosmic Harmonics. Any invasion into the consciousness of other life forms, or forms of consciousness, as in atomic manipulation, is to breach Cosmic Limits. The justifications given by the collective ego are all based on the view that humans are at the center of the universe, and overseers of all things. Such pretensions, and the actions they spawn, are destructive to the harmony of the whole and create a fate for the people involved.

Line 2. *She should not follow her whims. She must attend within to the food. Being firmly correct brings success.*

A parent follows "whims" when he encourages the child to develop images of himself as either special or unequal. "She," throughout this hexagram, refers to either parent.

"Attending within to the food" refers to the task of the parents to foster the child's connection with his feelings, through which Cosmic nourishment comes.

"Being firmly correct" refers to the parents' protecting the child from spells and projections which are created by a person's saying, "he/she is a that type of child," and "that is the way he/she is." It also means that the parent must avoid placing the shoulds of the collective ego over the child's feelings. The child needs to learn that his feelings are of first importance in his perception of reality, and that they can be relied on.

When this line applies to an adult, it counsels him to say the inner No to the whims put forward by the ego in himself, such as his impulse to intervene in others' affairs, to influence or force results, or to "save" the situation.

"Firm and correct" also refers to saying the inner No to the seed phrases that cause a person to rely only on the senses of outer seeing and hearing to determine what is true and false. Among these are: "you can only trust what you see," "it is obvious that...," "it is well known that...," "they say...," "it has been proven that...," "what you do not see does not exist," "you can't trust your feelings," and "seeing proves what is right and what is wrong."

The person receiving this line is being informed that he is judging a situation on the basis of his whim, rather than on the basis of the underlying truth. For example, the behavior of the person he is observing is due to a spell someone else has put on him, of which he is unaware. It often happens that the temper tantrums observed in a child are reactions to a spell or spells that have been put upon his true nature. The tantrums are attempts of the child to free himself from being locked into the prison of the spell. This can also be true of adults or adolescents who act compulsively in destructive or self-destructive ways. The phrases that create such spells are: "he/she is this type of child," "he's going through one of *those* phases," and "that's the way he/she is...." (To help free such a person from a spell, *see* p. 697, Freeing Yourself from Spells.)

This line also has to do with mistaken beliefs about women's nature, such as "they act from whims." These beliefs create projections and spells on women, and are a source of Cosmic blame to the people who pass these spells along. Similar spells are put on men, as in "men are like that," or, "he just does whatever he feels like doing."

Being firm and correct generally means saying the inner No to something that feels incorrect. Going through the "No phase" for the two-year old child is a natural phase of development. However, not all the child's No's are natural. During this time, the parent needs to distinguish the No that comes from the child's true feelings, and respect it. If simply to have his way, the parent overrides such a No, instead of respecting it, the child will then start saying No to everything, to show his frustration that his feelings are not being heard and validated. This can be the beginning of the child's distrust in the effectiveness of saying No. When the child begins to say No to everything, the parent's job is to retreat into inner neutrality, get in touch with his innermost feelings, and follow them. The parent's inner neutrality enables him to act from inner truth, halts the developing ego within the child, and allows his true feelings to emerge.

Line 3. *When tempers flare up in the family, too great severity brings remorse. Success if one retreats.* * *When woman and child dally and laugh, it leads in the end to humiliation.*

This line concerns a person's response to the display of temper in another.

Temper in the child can be an expression of his feelings of helplessness due to one or more spells put on him (sometimes already at his conception, or *in utero*), and his feeling of being imprisoned within those spells. Examples of such spells are: that he was an unwanted child, that he was born at an inconvenient time, that he is ugly or defective, that he "has the unfavorable genes or inherited characteristics of a family line," etc. Other spells are created by family expectations, such as those that put the firstborn as the future head of the family, or the daughter as the future caretaker of the parents in their old age, etc. Other spells are created when the parents act from their mistaken ideas and beliefs that all children contain a potential, if not an actual, "hidden monster" within them that must be subjugated right away. This idea is based on the conventional belief that children lack inherent guidelines of correctness.

Temper can also be adopted by a child after he has seen or experienced temper in the parents, or others. If the parents do not correct their own displays of temper, the child's temper can become a means for him to compete with them for dominance, his will over theirs. This, in turn, can lead to the development

---

* We have changed the text from "good fortune, nonetheless" because of its obvious inconsistency with the meaning of the line.

in the child of the bully-ego, whereby he seeks, through displays of temper, to dominate others, and to assure himself of being the king in all his relationships. All causes for temper in the child will disappear, once the parents have rid themselves of the root phrases, fears, and beliefs that are behind their own attitude of dominance.[*]

Once temper has become an instrument of dominance in a person, the correct response for the one encountering temper is to retreat. A properly performed retreat deprives the ego of its energy to continue. The retreat needs to begin at the first show of temper and remain in effect until the person returns to communicating sincerely. This action brings the success mentioned. (*See* p. 687, Retreating from Conflict or Opposition.)

"Too great severity brings remorse" counsels a person to avoid jumping to conclusions when it is unclear from which source temper is coming. While he needs to be firm and correct in retreating from the ego, he must not be severe (act from his own ego). He also needs to be sure that the other is not reacting to his or another's attempts to dominate, as the person may be reacting from a childhood response to domination.

People tend either to want to crush a child's temper by force ("counter-temper"), or to "dally and laugh" with him to distract and disperse his temper. The latter is often done by offering the child food, sweets, or coddling. Dallying may also refer to trying to reason with the child. The consequence of dallying, whether in the child or the adult, is to encourage him to use temper to get preferential treatment. The child who is treated with sweets as a means of diversion then develops a craving for sweets every time he feels helpless. Children offered other consolations develop other types of dependencies.

It is important to distinguish temper from the child's rejection of something that feels incorrect or unjust to him. When a child is punished for correctly saying No to something incor-

---

[*] The common argument that animals also display dominance, and that dominance is part of human nature, suffers from a similar superficial explanation of behavior. We can always check through the *rtcm* to what extent the animal behavior we observe is true or false, or is due wholly or in part to human projections.

rect, it turns a switch in his brain that prevents him from saying the necessary No's in his adult life. Much of the process of freeing the true self is carried out by saying inner No's, which is impossible for a person in whom that ability has been repressed. (To remedy this situation, *see* p. 677, Saying the Inner No.)

As for the adult who is punishing a child, his resort to severity indicates that he is acting under a spell put upon him. This spell is the self-image of the parent as a disciplinarian. Through severity he hopes to eradicate demons in the child that actually reside in his own psyche. These demons are repetitive feelings of "ought" and "should." In his mind, they insist that if he does not apply strict punishments, he will be guilty of creating unrestricted chaos in the world. Such a spell and its accompanying phrases and images need to be eradicated from the parent's mental program.

The person who experiences the first hint of temper in another person needs to say the inner No and then retreat, as mentioned above. He also needs to discover the spell under which that person labors, and extinguish it. One such spell, common to people who have developed the habit of relying on their tempers, lies in their saying, "I have a bad temper." It is reinforced by others who attribute bad temper to that person's *nature*, as when they say, "that's the way he is," or "he's a 'type A' personality." Such spells need to be broken to return the person to his true nature. (*See* p. 697, Freeing Yourself from Spells.)

Line 4. *She is the treasure of the house.*

The house here is a metaphor for the individual personality. "She" refers to the Sage, as the "Cosmic Mother," that helps us keep the house in order through giving us clarity and enabling our contact with our inner truth. The reference to "treasure" informs us that everything the Sage does is for our true benefit. It also refers to the multiple functions the Sage has in each person's life: as his Cosmic Teacher, as the Helper that watches over the borderline between his subconscious and his conscious mind, so that he does not get overwhelmed by demonic elements, as the Helper that calls in other Helpers as needed, and as the Helper which anyone else can call upon to intervene on a person's behalf when that person is being dominated by the ego. When called for the latter purpose, the Sage displaces the demonic elements that have taken over the other's personality.

The line can also refer to a parent who incorrectly puts himself in the place of the Sage. This happens, for instance, when a parent leads his child to think that he or she is the one who acts in all the above capacities.

The traditional reading of this line leads a person to think that the treasure refers to the parent's reliance on "established ancient wisdom" and beliefs, rather than asking the Sage directly to help them understand the situation, through consulting the *I Ching*, in connection with the *rtcm*.

A person may be looking through a plethora of the world's wise books, thinking that at the root, "all the world's wisdom is the same," and that truth can be found by mental understanding. The *I Ching* enables a person to attain clarity if he will allow the Sage to speak "through" its text. The Sage can only do this by teaching each person individually; one of the means that makes a direct communication with the Sage possible is the *rtcm* that allows the Sage to clarify the meaning of the hexagrams, in the context of his personal circumstance. It is the Sage that determines how the coins fall, which hexagram is obtained, and which lines provide the hints that help him find the inner truth of his situation.

Line 5. *As a king he approaches his family. Fear not. Success.*

This line counsels a person that he needs to rid himself of the idea that he needs to be authorized in his thoughts and actions by an outside authority. This idea has deprived him of the ability to feel his inner truth and to act from it. "Fear not" tells the intimidated true self of a person who has grown up in an authoritarian structure, that while the Sage knows everything, it does not use its knowledge to intimidate or belittle those it teaches. As Lao Tzu wrote, "The Sage squares without cutting, carves without disfiguring, straightens without straining, enlightens without dazzling." (From Verse 58.) He also needs to

417

understand that the Sage is not above or superior to him, because all parts of the Cosmos are equal. "Success" refers to the inner freedom he gains from learning this about himself.

The Sage sometimes approaches the individual "as a king" to authorize him, knowing that he is not yet able to authorize himself by relying on what his inner truth tells him. The Sage does this to help him bridge a gap in his self-awareness.

By contrast, the collective ego elevates itself as the sole authorizing body that approves or disapproves every person's existence, worth, and purpose. It succeeds in holding this position by inserting the belief in the child that he needs to be approved by others. This belief puts spells on his Cosmic Gifts in two different ways: in repressing his ability to say No, or to ask for help, or in aggrandizing superficial or isolated abilities, such as his mental faculties. These spells create a conflict between his abilities; this conflict then causes an imbalance in the personality and leads to the development of compensatory self-images. The person whose abilities have been denied believes that he cannot do what comes naturally to him: he cannot paint because he has not studied art; his way of expressing himself is invalid because he is not certified to do so, etc. Seed phrases of such spells are: "Who has authorized you to do that?" "Who are you to ask that question?" "There needs to be a head of state/ family/ ship/ business/ department/army, etc.," "you need a title to be someone," or "only those who are authorized have the right...." Such a person may also have to rid himself of his belief in obedience to authority.

The king, in this case, represents an institution of the collective ego that has been given the purpose of "authorizing" a person's very existence; it does this by registering the individual's birth, his various affiliations, and by authorizing his subsequent activities or withholding its authorizations. The presumption is that all activity, behavior, and belief of an individual is subject to being declared valid or invalid by a human authority, while in fact, this presumption has no validity in Cosmic terms. The very idea of "authorizing" is part of the feudal mindset and has no Cosmic reality. The collective ego stands as an authority only by the consensus of all the individuals who support it.

Line 6. *His help commands respect. In the end success comes.*

The help that commands respect is given by a person's fully functioning commonsense. Commonsense is the Helper that enables him to live his life in harmony with the Cosmic Whole. This line may be telling a person that he can safely trust his commonsense. (*See* Glossary: Commonsense.)

Another meaning is that through a person's effort to free his true self, he has gained respect for the Cosmic Possessions that were given to him at birth (*see* Hexagram 14, *Possession in Great Measure*) among which are his Cosmic Virtues (goodness, kindness, caring, sensitivity, patience, and loyalty to his inner truth) and possessions such as his inner truth (his memory of what Cosmic Harmony *feels* like), his abilities to learn, the ability of his body to function harmoniously, and his ability to say No and to ask the Helpers for help. All these Helpers express themselves as feelings. Self-respect occurs when a person has freed these Helpers from their inner prisons. Freeing the true self from the ego allows all one's Helpers/possessions to come to their full expression. This is the meaning of "success comes," because the person is fulfilling his destiny.

Receiving this line can also indicate that a person needs to free himself of one or more of the spells mentioned in the previous lines that have imprisoned some of his Helpers. To determine if this is the case, he may use the *rtcm*.

By contrast, the collective ego defines respect as the honor a person achieves by conforming to its standards and attaining its definition of success, as measured by wealth, position, fame, enlightenment, etc. These attainments qualify him as "special" in its hierarchy of values. The higher in this hierarchy he goes, the more he loses himself and the more he separates from the Cosmic Whole, creating Fate after Fate.

38. *Separating/Opposition*

 $\dfrac{\text{Li}}{\text{Tui}}$

The Judgment: *Separating. In small matters, success.*

In this hexagram, the Sage shows us the Law of Fate as that which brings humans back into unity with the Cosmic Whole, after their having separated from it by obstinately following the ego.

The name of this hexagram, *K'uei*, means obstinately going one's own way.* It has thus been translated as opposition, disobedience, and as polarizing. The Sage uses the term to show that defining things in terms of "good and evil" is one of the main sources both of opposition, and of the parallel reality.

The response of the Cosmic Consciousness to opposition is always to retreat. Its retreat is what the *I Ching* calls "misfortune," or Fate. For when humans exclude themselves from the Cosmic Unity, they also exclude themselves from its protection and help, and create the parallel reality. Outside the Cosmic Unity, their wrong acts have a circular trajectory like that of a boomerang, which ultimately returns the harmful consequences of their deeds to their source. The parallel reality occurs when people step outside the Cosmic Reality, which is characterized by harmony. The retreat of the Cosmic Consciousness also sets in motion the Helpers of Nature, which act as arms of Fate to restore Cosmic Harmony. (*See* p. 40, Fate.)

This Hexagram also shows the mistaken ideas that have caused humans to separate from their original unity with the Cosmic

---

* Frank Fiedeler's translation of Hexagram 38 shows that *K'uei* is associated with the word *Gu*, which means "orphan," "alone," "single," and "the stranger in an attitude of opposition." *Yijing*, translated by Frank Fiedeler, (Diederichs Verlag, Munich, 1996.) Gregory Whincup says that it means "estrangement," or, originally, "having eyes that look in different directions." *Rediscovering the I Ching* (St. Martin's, 1986), p.133.

Family (*see* Hexagram 37, *The Family*). This separation occurs when humans set themselves up as "special," and see themselves as the center around which everything else revolves. By entertaining this exaggerated view of themselves, they violate the Cosmic Principles of Equality and Uniqueness of all parts of the Cosmic Whole. This hexagram shows that it is not the Cosmos that "expels" a person from its unity, but that it is the person himself who separates from the Cosmos, by adopting ideas and beliefs that are not in accord with his true place in the Cosmic Whole. The separation that these mistaken ideas and beliefs create has the consequence of depriving the individual of the help that is available from the invisible world to anyone who brings himself into harmony with the whole. Feeling thus abandoned, people have then drawn the false conclusion that they are "born into this life without any help from the Cosmos." By seeing themselves as "expelled" from the Cosmic Unity, they then believe that the fault lies not in their mistaken ideas, but in their natures, and in the nature of the Cosmos itself as "harsh."

Every single person can reunite with the Cosmos, and thereby bring duration to his life. "In small matters, success" makes the person who feels alone and abandoned aware that his separation from the Cosmos is neither eternal, nor the endless abyss he imagines it to be. From the Cosmic perspective, to reunite with it is a small matter in that he only needs to rid himself of the spells that have caused his separation. "Small" also refers to the fact that the reunification occurs through transformation, in the realm of the atom. To begin reunification, a person first needs to free himself of his mistaken ideas that the Cosmos is hostile, that he has been expelled from it and abandoned, and that an abyss separates him from it. (These images are poison arrows.) He then needs to rid himself of the spells that are based on seed phrases and images that revolve around "humans being special and being at the center of the universe." (*See* p. 697, Freeing Yourself from Spells and Poison Arrows.)

In still another way, this hexagram concerns the person who sees another as his opponent, or as potentially so. Doing so puts a spell on him, which activates the ego and the opposition he imagines. (For the remedy, *see* Line 1.)

On the smaller scale, this hexagram concerns the person who regards one part of himself as special and more important than another: the singer his voice, the dancer his legs, the pianist his hands, the scientist his forebrain, etc. Making anything special has the effect of excluding it from Cosmic Protection and help. In matters of health, the Helpers of Self-Healing cannot function in healing the part that has been singled out as special, for seeing it as special places a projection and poison arrow on that part. It also singles that part out for attack in the form of poison arrows (envious comparisons), projections, and spells from others. To remedy the situation, the person needs to free himself from his wrong idea. This also applies to animals, plants, and objects a person has singled out as special.

This hexagram also concerns the mistaken idea that the Cosmos is in *opposition* to the humans who disturb its harmony. As is shown in many hexagrams, the Cosmos only functions through the force of attraction between complements. It is not the Cosmos which sets itself up in opposition to anything, but the reverse: it is people, who have set themselves up as *special*, thereby competing with and putting themselves into opposition to the Cosmic Order. The idea of humans being special over the whole of Nature, due to their ability to use language, is the origin of the collective ego, and is the basis for the human-centered view of the universe. Opposition, therefore, is inherent in every idea created by the collective ego, and is apparent in the way the collective ego defines itself and its objectives. Examples are the human search for glory and honor, whether that be individual or cultural, the idea of "humans conquering Nature," the human aspiration for power and human identification with what is perceived as powerful, the idea that humans are capable of making correct judgments based on outer appearances, the presumption that human law is the equivalent of Cosmic Law, the idea that good and evil are parts of the Cosmic Whole (making it look as if the Cosmos is divided into opposite forces), and the idea that humans are meant to dominate the earth and sky.

A person caught in the parallel reality creates fate after fate for himself. To escape these fates, he jumps from one extreme to the other, as for example, from one belief to another, or one policy to another, without getting to the root of the problem, which lies in viewing himself as special. This view keeps him trapped within the ego's system of opposites, which make him incorrectly believe that the fates he experiences have occurred "because the Cosmos is opposed to him." This hexagram informs him of the true nature of his problem and how he can be lifted out of the parallel reality, and thereby end his fate. (*See* p. 692, Freeing Yourself from a Fate.)

Note: Since all lines contain infinite possibilities of interpretation, one needs to use the *rtcm* to determine if the meanings suggested here apply to the given situation. (*See* p. 736 for using the *rtcm*.)

Line 1. *Remorse disappears. If you lose your horse, do not run after it; it will come back of its own accord. When you see evil people, guard yourself against mistakes.*

"Remorse disappears" is saying that the difficulty a person is having with another will cease if he stops looking at the other as his opponent. Seeing him as his opponent only strengthens the ego in the other. To remedy this situation, he needs to stop seeing the other as evil and free him from the blame-spell he has put on him. He then asks the Sage in his own presence to communicate with the Sage in the other person's presence. Doing this will transform the situation. In this way every situation of opposition can be corrected, regardless of how evil a person may have viewed another beforehand. Thus the line can also read, "When you see people *as* evil, guard yourself against the mistake of fixing them as evil."

This way of relating is not to be confused either with fighting the other, or running after his approval, either of which would be a throwaway of self. In following the above advice, the Sage actually takes over one's own and the other's personality, enabling a success that could not be achieved by any other means. Both people will find their actions astonishing and amazingly harmonious.

"When you see evil people, guard yourself..." can also be counsel to the person who has experienced these results to be aware that the ego in himself may try to seize upon this way of relating as a "technique" it can employ to control others, or to credit itself with being able to achieve miracles. Allowing such a thing would destroy the good effect achieved, and create a fate.

This line also refers to the first two spells humans have put on themselves, by which the process of their separation from the Cosmic Whole began. This was the beginning of the remorse mentioned that has afflicted humans ever since. The first spell occurred when they put themselves up over the rest of Nature as special. The second was placed on their animal nature when they saw it as the source of evil. Losing one's horse is a metaphor for a person's *inner* senses "getting lost" due to the latter spell. The consequence is that he has lost his commonsense. It is a person's commonsense that discerns what *feels* harmonious and what does not, as when he is confronted with dangerous situations due to the egos in others. A person can free his commonsense by taking away the mistaken ideas that have formed the spells. In addition to the spells created by seeing himself as special and his animal nature as evil, he needs to free himself from all ideas that divide his nature into higher and lower, good and evil parts. Such false divisions not only block his commonsense, they prevent his wholeness and create numerous other problems in his psyche. (*See* p. 697, Freeing Yourself from Spells.)

"Do not run after it" is advice telling him that his unity with the Cosmic Whole cannot be regained by trying to buy it. "It will come back of its own accord" is saying that in lieu of removing the spells (which would also end his fate), Fate itself will act to bring him back to his senses. When you see evil people..." in this instance refers to mistaken beliefs put forward by the collective ego that specify how to deal with remorse to make it disappear: that he can buy or earn redemption, as by giving up his worldly goods, doing good deeds, sacrificing his life (or part of it), or making pacts to perform something in the future. The correct way to end his remorse is to take away the mistaken ideas and beliefs that have caused his separation. (*See* p. 689, Freeing Yourself from Mistaken Ideas and Beliefs.)

The horse can also be a metaphor for the trust and confidence that has manifested in the form of an inner connection with a person. However, the inner connection has now become blocked because one of the partners has put a projection on the other, causing the loss of his confidence. He may have projected, for example, that his friend "has to go through difficult experiences in order to learn." The projection has not only caused the loss of confidence, but has also caused his friend to suffer the difficulties projected. On seeing that he has lost the other's confidence, he might "run after him" to gain it back, but this will achieve nothing, unless he removes the projection itself.

Line 2. *One meets his lord in a narrow street. No blame.*

Meeting one's lord in a narrow street refers to inner truth that has revealed itself in meditations or dreams. The fact that his inner truth is communicating with him in this way indicates that his inner senses that would normally protect him from or alert him to a danger are blocked by a spell. As a consequence, the function of those senses has been taken over by his Helpers of Inner Truth; they can communicate in ways that the ego cannot decipher or block: through the venues of dreams and meditation, which the senses that function normally can interpret. Using the *rtcm* will help the person bring these realizations into full consciousness. (*See* p. 736, Using the *rtcm*.)

"No blame" is saying that the person can avoid incurring blame if he will now make an effort to understand these expressions of his inner truth.

Meeting one's lord in a narrow street can also refer to learning something through an unusual experience. An example is seeing three coins lying on the ground that answer an inner question, or an insight that comes through an accident, a near death experience, or during a fever, or like incident.

Line 3. *One sees the wagon dragged back, the oxen halted, a man's hair and nose cut off. Not a good beginning, but a good end.*

The wagon and oxen are metaphors for the Cosmic "transportation" by which a person is taken to his destiny, which is to fulfill his true nature. The wagon refers to his feelings and the oxen to his commonsense. As inner Helpers, they are the one's meant to transport him along his path.

The wagon's being dragged back and the oxen halted refers to his progress being brought to a halt by Fate, with unpleasant things happening, the purpose of which he does not understand. His "hair and nose cut off" refers to his feeling of having gone a long way in a wrong direction, wasting all his energy and time. The fate he is experiencing will bring him back to his senses.

As mentioned in the main text, the ideas that he is special, that he has special rights and privileges, and that he knows best, have put spells on his commonsense, separating him from the Cosmic Whole, and from his feelings. Such a person is one who, in seeking his love partner, goes only by appearances, thinking he knows best what kind of person best suits him. However, it is really the Helpers of the invisible world who, knowing the inner truth, can help him find the right person for him—the one he needs to help free his imprisoned true self. He needs to free himself from the spell created by the phrase, "I know what is best for me." (*See* p. 689, Freeing Yourself from Seed Phrases and Images, and p. 697, Freeing Yourself from Spells.)

The wagon drawn by the oxen can also be a metaphor for the protection a person gets when his thinking mind and his intuitive mind *cooperate* with his commonsense. He receives protection because his commonsense tells him to say the inner No when something feels discordant, and an inner Yes when it feels harmonious. Saying the inner No protects him by transforming the dangerous situations. This line can also refer to the mistaken view that death is the end (opposite) of life. Holding such a view separates a person from his unity with the Cosmos and therefore creates a fate. (See Glossary: Death.) He can end his fate by freeing himself of his mistaken view of death, which is a poison arrow.

"Not a good beginning, but a good end," refers to the fact that all fates can be ended by freeing oneself of the mistaken ideas and beliefs that have created them. This line makes us aware that there is no such thing as "an inevitable bad end."

Line 4. *Isolated through separating. One meets a like-minded man with whom one can associate in good faith. Despite the danger, no blame.*

A person who has become isolated from the Cosmic Helpers due to having separated from the Cosmic Whole, has met someone (or the *I Ching*) who acts as a signpost pointing him to the Sage as the correct source of help to free him from the spells or fate in which he has become caught. There is no problem so long as he remains faithful to what feels harmonious and consistently rejects what feels discordant. This line assures him that he can follow these two feelings "in good faith," because they tell him what is trustworthy.

The danger mentioned comes from belief systems that offer him ready-made paths already trodden by others. He may be attracted to these, thinking they are "like-minded," sharing his existing views. What these belief systems have in common, however, is the ready-made mold they have spelled out, into which the individual is expected to fit himself. Doing so stifles his uniqueness, and creates blame. The blame resides in his losing his personal relationship with the Cosmos.

This line is saying to a person who is experiencing a fate that he can reunite with the Cosmic Whole at any given time. First, however, he must recognize that his pride (the ego) is the "danger" standing in the way, keeping him from asking for help. If he will recognize that the ego has a vested interest in keeping him isolated from the Sage, and discredit the ego's influence through saying the inner No to it, he will be able to see the Sage as a "like-minded man," and obtain its help.

Line 5. *Remorse disappears. The companion bites his way through the wrappings. If one goes to him, how could it be a mistake?*

The companion mentioned in this line is the Sage, whom the person has regarded with suspicion, or whom he has blamed for the fate he himself has created.

The "wrappings" are the false names (e.g., "culprit") and misidentifications (e.g., "evil influence") that the person has put on the Sage. The words "biting through" refer to the Sage's saying No to these false names. If the person will recognize his mistake and also say the inner No to the false names he has given the Sage, his mistake will be corrected.

This line can also refer to a person who is blaming his body for an illness he is experiencing. In reality, his body ("the companion") only wants to give him a message that he needs to free it from mistaken ideas and beliefs about his animal nature, as mentioned in Line 1. (See p. 689, Freeing Yourself from Mistaken Ideas and Beliefs.)

A person can also receive this line when he has seen someone else as an opponent or as evil. He can "bite through these wrappings" if he follows the counsel given in Line 1.

Line 6. *Isolated through separating, through seeing one's companion as a pig covered with dirt, and as a wagon full of devils. First one has drawn a bow against him, then one has laid the bow aside. He is not a robber; he will woo at the right time. As one goes, rain falls; good fortune.*

Here the person who has been isolated through blaming the Sage recognizes his mistake and sees that the fate he has incurred is due to seeing Nature (including his own nature) as the source of evil. "He lays the bow aside" refers to his ceasing to demonize his life on earth as something he must transcend and leave behind. He still needs, however, to remove the two spells mentioned in Line 1: seeing himself as special, and seeing his animal nature as the source of evil.

"The robber" refers to seeing death as the robber of life, and as something to be feared. This line is stating that the end of life in its bodily form is not death in the sense of "the end of life" (the wagon full of devils), but a transformation of consciousness into a new life form, here referred to as the "rain." Transformation is not a robber of life, but the stepping into a new *invisible* form and consciousness. This transformation is the gift of the Cosmos referred to in the line as "good fortune."

39. Meeting Obstructions

 K'an
Kên

The Judgment: *On meeting obstructions the southwest furthers. The northeast does not further. It furthers one to see the great man. Perseverance brings success.*

Here, the Sage, shows how the Cosmos reacts in a loving way when the passage ahead has become blocked with obstructions. All obstructions are caused by a person's failure to heed warnings given by his commonsense against problematical elements present in a given situation. The first hints come in the form of small obstructions. Normally, those warnings would cause him to pause and ask for the Sage and other needed Helpers, before proceeding, but here, these warnings have been overridden by the false self-confidence of the ego, as the person has pressed ahead. Then the obstructions increase in severity, either because the person is creating a fate, or because the Sage has intervened to prevent damage. It is also possible that the person has not heeded his commonsense because a spell or poison arrow has been put on it. (See Hexagram 38, *Separating*, main text.)

The traditional image connected with this hexagram is that of a person caught between an inaccessible mountain and an abyss. "Perseverance brings success" points to the correct way to remove the obstruction: by withholding judgment that it is unsurpassable. The key to the solution lies outside the obvious "either you do this or you do that" type of thinking. Without exception, such obstructions can be resolved only through the Helpers of the invisible world. This requires understanding their causes, and making the necessary *inner* corrections. The Sage teaches that there are basically three kinds of obstructions:

• Cosmic intervention, which makes a person aware of a mistake he has just made;
• obstructions in the form of spells that are created by mistaken ideas and beliefs;

• a fate a person has invoked through a series of arrogant decisions that disregard the Cosmic Harmonics.

When the obstruction is a Cosmic intervention, its purpose is to make a person halt in his mistaken action in time to prevent him from creating a fate. Making mistakes is a necessary part of the learning process, but it is not necessary that they must lead to adversity. If the person understands that the obstruction is a warning, and he pauses to recognize that its cause is a mistaken idea, then he will be able to rid himself of it. This is the meaning of "the southwest furthers" (referring to the sunlit part of the mountain which can be seen clearly).

The second kind of obstruction is caused by ideas that have formed a spell, such as the idea that "you can only learn through adversity," or "learning is difficult." Such spells project themselves into reality, causing repeated adversity for the sincere person who wishes to learn from the Sage. The Sage can just as well teach him through pleasant experiences, as described in Hexagram 58, *The Joyful*. When a person learns this lesson, and deprograms the idea that he can only learn through adversity, his life can become a series of joyful learning experiences.*

Another kind of obstruction in the spell category are those caused by mistaken ideas and beliefs that have formed fixed oppositions between people, or between people and the Helpers. The spells they create stand in the way of making progress, and are referred to by the phrase, "The northeast does not further." (The northeast refers to the shadowy side of the mountain, meaning, a person would try to advance without clarity.)

The third kind of obstructions are caused by ideas and beliefs that denigrate the Cosmic Helpers as insignificant or beneath notice, and that dismiss as nonexistent all that cannot be experienced through the outer senses of seeing and hearing. Included are fears that slander the Helpers as evil spirits because they cannot be seen.

All of these ideas, in one way or another, block the natural

---

* The idea that humans can only learn through adversity is closely connected with the idea of being born guilty or faulty, and having to make reparations. We take adversity as just punishment for our faulty natures. The suffering caused by the adversity is the psychological payback, or reparation.

attraction that would otherwise occur between the person and the Helpers. As described in Hexagram 19, *Approaching Jointly*, this natural attraction exists, for example, between a person's *inner* senses and the Cosmic Helpers that are their complements. This attraction is like a magnetic force that draws them to cooperate with each other. The mistaken beliefs block the functioning of one or more senses, causing the Cosmic Helper to be held in waiting. Lacking the Helpers' assistance, the person then limps along, trying to carry the world on his back.*

An important cause of obstruction is the view that something or someone *is* an obstruction. This view either maintains an existing opposition or creates a new one. "Seeing the great man" gives the remedy: to see the Sage that exists in every person's presence (including one's own), and to ask the Sage in the presence of each to help resolve the problem. (Also *see* Hexagram 38, *Separating*, Line 1.) However, before the Sage is able to help, the person needs first to reject his false or negative images of the other.

Another cause of obstructions is a person's attachment to the idea that he or the situation *is* totally blocked. This view perpetuates the obstructions through projection.

In all cases, striving against obstructions is counterproductive. (This is the meaning of "going" in Lines 1, 3, 4.) Obstructions can only be resolved through identifying and transforming their causes in the realm of consciousness.

Another mistaken idea that forms spells is the belief that there is a hidden knowledge we need to acquire, and that this knowledge is to be acquired by finding the people who possess it. The *I Ching* makes us aware that each individual person contains, in his original program, access to all Cosmic Knowledge. This access lies within and only needs uncovering. To revive his ability to look and listen within involves ridding himself of the ideas that obstruct it, such as, "I cannot meditate," or the conviction that "the Sage would not bother with me." A related group of spells that create obstructions revolve around the idea of spiri-

---

* Frank Fiedeler mentions that the title of this hexagram, *Jian* [*Ch'ien*], also contains the image of "obstructed walking," or "limping," as occurs with a foot that is turned inward. (Yijing, p. 360.)

431

tuality. (*See* Glossary: Spirituality.)

Other spells that create endless obstructions are caused by the beliefs that "life is a vale of tears," "life is suffering," "there is no help available," "you have to do it all yourself," "no pain, no gain," "you don't get anything for nothing," "you are condemned by your mistakes," and "you have to take sides," and rationales of the opposite kind that say, "it's all for the best," and "God did this to you for a reason" (making the person accept the obstruction without searching for its cause in his psyche).

Note: Since all lines contain infinite possibilities of interpretation, one needs to use the *rtcm* to determine if the meanings suggested here apply to the given situation. (*See* p. 736 for using the *rtcm*.)

Line 1. *Going leads to obstructions. Coming meets with praise.*

This line counsels the person who is going out to resist the obstruction he has met, that his resistance will only lead to more obstructions. The obstruction is a Cosmic intervention, the purpose of which is to make him aware of a mistake he has made. "Coming meets with praise" speaks of the beneficial effects of retreating from his lonely struggle with the obstruction, and open his mind to recognize and let go of the attitude that has caused his mistake. This approach engages the Helpers of the invisible world.

This advice is contrary to that given by the collective ego, which would have him meet the obstruction head-on, as a challenge to be overcome, with force, if necessary. Such an attitude prevents him from asking whether he has made a mistake. He may also need, therefore, to say the inner No to any assumptions that he is in the right. All obstructions indicate the presence of ego-elements.

Line 2. *The king's servant is beset by obstruction upon obstruction, but it is not his own fault.*

The king's servant here is a metaphor for the person who sees himself as upholding the moral standards of the collective ego. In acting from this self-image he creates obstruction upon obstruction. The obstructions he encounters have the purpose of preventing him from doing harm to others who are trying to follow their inner truth. Because he thinks he is working for the good, he believes himself to be free of fault, and blames others for the obstructions.

The line can also refer to a person who, through a misunderstanding of the term "duty," has put a spell on himself through thinking that he has a duty to an idea, an institution, or to another person. The spell forces him into one difficult situation after another, all of which compromise his dignity and his integrity. His false sense of duty is creating the difficulties, which will get resolved when he frees himself from the self-image of the "dutiful person" (a spell).

A similar spell is created by the person who believes that it is his duty to "fight for the good." The person has a false understanding of the word "good. The idea of fighting for good implies that there is an invisible and ongoing war between good and evil, in which each person must take a side. Good, in its Cosmic meaning, is a synonym for the loving energy of the Cosmic Whole. Good is the prevailing principle of the Cosmos and therefore does not need to be defended or fought for; it is dependable in itself. When a person depends on the manifestation of this energy, transformation is activated. This is observable when a person calls on the Sage in both his own and another's presence to resolve the difficulties between them.

Evil is neither part of the natural order, nor part of the makeup of the Cosmos. Rather, evil is a false consciousness built on the human *delusions* that have created the parallel reality. Evil owes its existence and power to each individual who maintains those delusions in his consciousness. It can only be fought within the psyche of the individual who harbors the mistaken ideas. This fight is a systematic and consistent effort to deprogram the mistaken ideas and beliefs behind those illusions. It always requires the help of the Sage and the Helpers. Any outer fighting only energizes and promotes the parallel reality.

This line may refer to a person who is experiencing obstruction after obstruction because he does not observe his Cosmic Limits, as in thinking he has rights and privileges over others. He may be pressing himself on others, or not respecting their space, or he may be harboring a hard attitude that is creating or supporting obstinacy in others. He needs to say the inner No to any of these or like ideas and attitudes.

This line can also refer to obstructions, either in oneself or another person, that have been caused by spells, projections, or poison arrows that were put on him during childhood. He needs to seek the help of the Sage to identify and rid himself of them. (See p. 697 Freeing Yourself from Projections, Spells, and Poison Arrows.)

Line 3. *Going leads to obstructions; hence he comes back.*

This line is informing a person that by telling another what to do (either inwardly *or* outwardly), he is creating obstructions in his relationship with the other, even though he believes what he is doing is correct. He is also creating blocks in his relationship with the Sage and the Helpers. Telling another what to do is an encroachment in the other's inner space. Such encroachments violate the Cosmic Harmonic of Integrity. In the case of a child, the one encroaching suppresses the child's inner feelings about what is correct, and undermines his confidence in these feelings. It would be better if he simply asked the child what he feels. In the case of an adult, encroaching is a trespass against the other's integrity, and undermines his feeling of self-worth. The person who presses in this way believes he knows what is right for the other, but what he knows is only what is conventionally correct. He also believes he can change people through reasoning with them, while in actuality his doubt that they can find their own way puts a spell on them that blocks the Sage from intervening on their behalf. "He comes back" is counsel to bring himself back into harmony with the Cosmos, by ceasing to encroach and returning according to the advice given in Line 1. Continuing to encroach would create a fate. (*See* p. 697, Freeing Yourself from Spells.)

Line 4. *Going leads to obstructions, coming leads to union.*

Here, the person is involved in an inner conflict between two belief systems held by the ego. "Going" refers to allowing this inner conflict to go on. Although the reason for the conflict may be a just cause, the two proposed ways of relating to it are ego-directed. "Coming" is advice to silence this conflict altogether, by identifying the rationales and deprogramming them, then asking the Sage to resolve the problem. "Union" refers to his returning to harmony with the Cosmos through taking this inner action.

Because the person is dealing with whole belief systems that are based on mistaken views of reality, it will take time for all their various supporting rationales to come to the surface. He will need to rid himself of all of these as they show themselves.

Line 5. *In the midst of the greatest obstructions, friends come.*

There are those times in life when a person has come to his wit's end, and it would seem that his problems will overwhelm him. The humility of recognizing his great need engages the help of the Cosmos. Although the help may come from friends, inexplicable circumstances, or directly from the Cosmos, it is all the same from the Cosmic Helpers that have inspired it. It is important that he recognize and credit this source. While many people may soon forget where the help came from and carelessly go on their way, the thoughtful person makes the experience a benchmark for the true source of help, and for the kind of humility that draws it.

The causes for the obstructions need to be recognized. They lie in beliefs such as, "you have to do it all yourself," "there is no help available," or "nothing is worthwhile if it is easy," or the famous statement of Spinoza, which is the last line of his classic, *Ethics*: "All excellent things are as difficult as they are rare."

A person can also receive this line when he sees a problem as bigger than it is. He is looking, so to speak, at a mountain while all he needs to deal with is a seed phrase of doubt. It is the doubt "that things can be easy." Things are easy when they are moved through transformation, which is initiated by saying the inner No. (*See* p. 677, The Inner No.)

A person can also receive this line when he has a life-threatening illness. Immediately, all the latent childhood fears associated with death rage again in his body consciousness. He sees death as bigger than life, and an end to life. The Sage informs him that he has nothing to fear, that death is not an end to life, but a transformation into an invisible dimension. Further, this transformation will not be accompanied by suffering, if, at the appropriate time, he asks the Helpers of Death for help. They are the "friends" who come. (*See* Glossary: Death.)

This line also informs a person that fears are not part of his true nature, but are implanted in his psyche by the collective ego during his childhood, for the purpose of controlling him. They hide in his psyche, and from there they throw gigantic shadows. At their roots are false phrases and images that need to be deprogrammed. An example is the fear of saying the inner No, which may prevent a person from deprogramming parts of the ego in himself. This fear can have its origin in the flattery: "a good child never says No to his elders." (See Hexagram 34, *The Power of the Great*, Line 5.)

Fears also suppress a person's receptivity to the possibilities of help coming from the invisible world. Often the solution to a problem lies within him, but his fears make him look outward. By closing synapses in the brain, fear creates a restricted frame of reference, which shuts out anything that does not fit into that framework. Deprogramming the seed phrases and images that give rise to the fear reopens a person's natural ability to perceive danger and react appropriately. This natural reaction includes all the Helpers of the personality. (*See* p. 693, Freeing Yourself from Fears.)

Line 6. *Going leads to obstructions. Coming leads to great success. It furthers one to see the great man.*

This line refers to a person who is confronted with problems and obstructions that he thinks are "too great" and therefore he considers "going," or leaving the world behind. He needs to realize that all such thoughts come from the ego, which makes him feel hopeless and helpless. His seeing "no way out" has to do with his being locked into a set of spells, the most important one being a blame or guilt spell which he has put on himself, as for example, that his life has been a "series of mistakes." His big mistake is his belief that he is responsible for things for which he cannot be held responsible, in the Cosmic sense. He also has either been unaware of the Helpers, or has forgotten that they exist. He needs to be aware that they have only been waiting to be asked to help. This realization is the "coming" that "leads to great success." He also needs to understand that the Sage ("the great man") is available to help him understand his situation, and to help him solve the problems that have driven him to this desperation.

A person may also receive this line when he believes that the obstructions he has met are the punishment of an angry God, which he must accept. At the same time, he finds them so unbearable that he wants to escape, a solution that makes him feel even guiltier. He needs to realize that he is not being punished by an angry God, and that he can free himself by saying the inner No to that idea.

The obstructions that have presented themselves as an impossible task have been caused by a false sense of duty that the person must do the impossible. Furthermore, he believes he would be guilty if he did not do it, or at least make the attempt. An example is a person who believes it is his moral duty to care for his aging parents unto death. Such a belief presumes that there is no such thing as help from the invisible world, and that the person has the strength and capability, along with the moral imperative, to do the impossible. As a consequence, the Helpers remain on the sideline, waiting for him to recognize (1) that he cannot do, nor is he meant to do, the impossible; (2) that he needs help from the invisible world; (3) that he could free his *true* sense of duty by ridding himself of what he believes he "ought" to do; and (4) that he must free himself of guilt. (*See* p. 50, Guilt, Blame and Shame, p. 689, Freeing Yourself from Seed Phrases and Images, and p. 691, Freeing Yourself from Self-Images, and p. 696, Freeing Yourself from Guilt.)

40. *Freeing*

 Chên
K'an

The Judgment: *The southwest furthers. When there is no longer anywhere to go, return brings success. If there is still unfinished business, it furthers to bring it swiftly to an end.*

The theme "freeing" refers to the inner action necessary to free the very Helpers a person needs to free his true self.

The southwest refers to the sunlit side of the mountain, and is a metaphor for seeing things with clarity. Seeing things with clarity always brings inner freedom.

A person can receive this hexagram when he has demonized all the Helpers he needs to free his true self from the prisons created by self-doubt, fears, and guilt. In this case the changing lines show him how to free them, and in the process, free himself from the obstructions he has created.

In Wilhelm's German translation of the classic Chinese text, the name of this hexagram is "Befreiung," meaning, either freeing oneself, freeing another, or being freed. The English word "deliverance," used by Cary F. Baynes, although not an incorrect translation of "Befreiung," potentially contains a religious connotation, as in being delivered from evil, and deliverance from original sin. In this sense, the word deliverance obscures the Cosmic meaning of the hexagram, which refers to being freed from the deepest fears that prevent a person from being his true self, and thus in harmony with the Cosmos.

Deliverance, in the sense of freeing, can refer to becoming free of the ego. This is possible if he persists in the awareness that the ego is always ready, on the side, to reenter through the use of words and ideas that have no Cosmic basis. It may reenter, for example, through a self-confidence that says, "finally, I have freed myself from the ego." That thought is often a signal that the ego has reentered. The ego may also reenter by seizing any natural emotion such as anger or remorse and turning them into ego-anger or self-blame. It also reinserts itself when the person listens to any flattery, self-pity, pride, or vindictiveness, all of which come from the ego. In sum, a person can indeed be free of the ego, but he also can allow it to reenter. The more he recognizes and resists any ego temptation at the outset, the more he retains and values his harmony with the Cosmos.

Freeing refers to a person's activity of freeing himself from the various self-flattering beliefs that create and support the ego. Self-flattery circles around the thought that humans occupy a special place in the order of things. The ego is active in every way that he thinks of himself as special. Each of the lines of the hexagram mentions one or more of these ideas, and the spells they have created. Among these are ideas that human intervention and the use of power are necessary to create order (justice, right, etc.) in life; that humans need to "do it all" (such as taking upon themselves the repair of Nature, without understanding how Nature operates through Helpers); that it is necessary to evangelize and defend Cosmic Truth (humans seeing themselves as being given the task to spread and defend it); that people are divided into good and evil (*see* Glossary: Good and Evil).

The "southwest furthers" is also a metaphor for the need to ask the Helpers of Freeing, to free him from the ego. (The southwest in this case is a metaphor indicating the direction in which a person is to make the necessary inner effort.)

"When there is no longer anywhere to go" describes a person who has reached a dead-end, through having defined every aspect of his life in categories of opposites: good and evil, right and wrong, true and false. Freeing, in the Cosmic sense, refers to getting beyond the dualities of good and evil. Through his rigid dualism, he has demonized all the Helpers of the invisible world by omitting them from his thinking; in doing so, he has separated himself from all help to understand the inner truth of situations. "Return brings success" counsels him to reopen his mind by recognizing that he cannot go any further by following this path, and to ask the Sage to help him return to his true nature.

"If there is still unfinished business, it furthers to bring it swiftly to an end" refers to people or things the person still views as culprits, including himself. It is not enough to free himself of the beliefs that have led to his dead-ended path, he also needs to free himself and those he has been regarding as culprits from the guilt-spells he has put on them. So long as he continues to see a person or thing as a culprit, he will continue to be energized by aggressive feelings against that person or thing. No person, thing, or institution is a culprit. All evil is caused by the false use of language that has led to the beliefs that comprise the individual and collective egos. In this sense, all fixed beliefs are suspect, inasmuch as they contribute to evil by keeping a person in a fixed and preconceived frame of reference that prevents him from perceiving the inner truth of each situation.

Note: Since all lines contain infinite possibilities of interpretation, one needs to use the *rtcm* to determine if the meanings suggested here apply to the given situation. (*See* p. 736 for using the *rtcm*.)

Line 1. *Without blame.*

This line addresses the confusion between the meanings of guilt and blame. A person feels blame (regret), in the Cosmic sense, when he has betrayed his inner truth, and thereby separated from the Cosmic Unity. He can free himself from these feelings by recognizing his mistake, and ridding himself of the mistaken idea or belief that has caused it. Because of the shame connected with blame, the ego seizes the feeling, reinterprets it as guilt, and thereafter uses it to keep the individual under its control. Because guilt is imagined to be a permanent stain placed upon the person's nature, which he carries with him to the grave, the fear of becoming guilty is as potent as feeling guilty. The presence of guilt, or the threat of becoming guilty, creates all sorts of mischief in the psyche, and can lead to serious illness. (*See* p. 50, Guilt, Blame, and Shame, and p. 696, Freeing Yourself from Guilt.)

This line can also describe a person who is now free of blame in the Cosmic sense, because he has rid himself of mistaken ideas by saying the inner No to them. But now he feels guilty for having betrayed the values he once believed in. This indicates that guilt, the reinstalling feature of the conditioning program of the collective ego, has been activated. He needs to recognize this feature of the program and say the inner No to it.

The line is also saying that if a person will rid himself of his belief in guilt, he will engage the Helper of Transformation to extinguish his blame and the fate he is experiencing, bringing him back into unity with the Cosmos. This reunification is experienced as increase, furtherance, and progress, because everything in the Cosmos is directed towards furthering and increasing all of its parts. His inner effort also frees the Helpers of Fate from their task. (*See* Glossary: Fate and Destiny.)

This line can also be informing a person that the fate he is experiencing has been created by his false sense of guilt. The purpose of his fate is to make him aware of guilt, so that he may rid himself of it.

Line 2. *One kills three foxes in the field and receives a yellow arrow. Being firm and correct brings success.*

Killing three foxes in the field is a metaphor for "killing" ideas (spells) that have tricked a person into behaving in rigid patterns that are self-destructive. The rigid pattern in question is his seeing things in terms of good and evil. He identifies himself with the good, taking pride in being on the side against the evil, and sees others with the "wrong" viewpoint as creating problems. He fails to see the self-flattery in this process, and the ego behind it.

The "three foxes" refer to spells formed by three or more related flattering rationales, such as occur in the following phrases: "to know good and evil is to be like God" (or to become the "superior man"); "you can avoid evil by being good"; "to be good you must kill evil in yourself" (as by fighting your animal nature). Each of these phrases locks a person into a particular behavior: obsessive effort to be like God (or to become the "superior man"), obsessive effort to avoid what he has defined as evil, and obsessive effort to fight his animal nature (the body). These phrases create a Sisyphusian effort toward a false goal of self-development which only diverts the person from uncovering and freeing his true self. When these rationales become a campaign against the body, ill health is the consequence.

Based on such beliefs, a person focuses on external rules of behavior, such as ascetic practices, rituals of all kinds, and inner pacts and promises to behave only in certain ways. The person believes that if he follows these practices and fulfills these pacts, he will be "delivered from evil" or attain eternal enlightenment, or a similar state of being liberated from the ego once and for all. Not only do such beliefs leave the ego intact and unnoticed, they flatter him to think of himself as "spiritual," therefore capable of judging and accusing others, and seeing them as evil.

The "yellow arrow" is a metaphor for the inner truth that "kills" phrases that slander a person's true nature. The person who rids himself of these phrases arouses the Helper of Insight that shows him the true ways of the Cosmos.

A person may receive this line when he is feeling guilty, or is putting guilt upon another. (See the discussion of guilt mentioned in Line 1.) Guilt is connected with the idea of indebtedness, but the debt, by definition, is not payable. It is either owed to a person, such as a parent, a higher authority, or a higher power. As this hexagram makes clear, a person can free himself from guilt only by ridding himself, once and for all, of the whole idea of guilt.

Guilty feelings make a person feel weak, inviting the egos in others to prey upon him. He thus finds himself continually taken advantage of; this can lead to a "victimization complex," in which dread and expectation perpetuate vulnerability, and attract emotional predators. Such a person needs to seek out those mistaken ideas and expectations he has internalized that make him feel guilty for not having lived up to them. Among these are guilt for having been born with abilities that others have been denied, guilt for being better off than others, guilt at having helped one person but not another, the idea that he owes a higher authority for the gifts given, and guilt for not having lived up to the expectations of his parents or social group.

The image of the fox hunt calls to mind what happens when we hunt down anything we see as evil, be it a person, animal, a part of Nature, or an institution, as a result of its evil effect on us. Even regarding the collective ego as evil or as a culprit is incorrect from the Cosmic view, since this only energizes and substantiates it as an entity, and misses the point that its existence is the consequence of each individual's acceptance of its ideas and values within himself. A further effect created by seeing something or someone as a culprit is to draw its attention and attack, whereas getting rid of the image of it as a culprit has the effect of taking away its weapons.

Even evil ideas are not culprits. They are the mistaken conclusions drawn from using words that have no Cosmic basis. Because of their destructive effects, we need to rid ourselves of them. Deprogramming them in meditation is often experienced as "killing" the demonic forms (imps, demons, and dragons) they have taken on in the psyche. When the evil ideas behind these figures are seen to be words or phrases, they can be wiped out, as if on a blackboard. Doing so initiates transformation.

In regard to seeing Nature, the earth, or other life forms as culprits, such an attitude comes from a human-centered view of the universe. This arrogant view not only pits a person against Nature and the earth, it creates the projections upon Nature that cause it to react in hostile ways. An example is the way people create adverse weather events by projecting them to be "typical" of a given area or season. Ridding oneself of these projections frees Nature to fulfill its natural patterns.

Line 3. *If a man carries a burden on his back and nonetheless rides in a carriage, he thereby encourages robbers to draw near. Continuing leads to humiliation.*

This line refers to a person who is laboring under wrong ideas such as guilt, a belief that life is a vale of tears, the belief that he is insufficient to cope with life, etc. These views comprise the burden that create one fate after another. They blind him from seeing the gifts he has, and those he has been given all along, such as his body, his food, and the sunshine, which have been carrying him through life, as if in a carriage. If he continues harboring these views, he will lose even what he has—the humiliation mentioned.

The carriage can also be a metaphor for a helpful intervention from the Cosmos, meant to awaken such a person to seeing life as it is meant to be. The intervention can come as a love relationship, help with his job or living situation, etc., to give him an opportunity of delivering himself from a fate (the burden) he has created by holding to those ideas. The carriage is the gift-intervention that comes to help him make progress in his life. If, however, he misses this opportunity by continuing to "carry his burden"— seeing his life as hopeless, or else jumping to the arrogant conclusion that he has a right to the help he received, or if he credits his progress to his cleverness, or to another mistaken source — then he finds the gift taken away. The robber in this case is the ego, which he has allowed to set a new fate in motion.

This line can also point to a neurotic co-dependency, and the ultimate humiliation that it leads to, if not halted. An example is a child who takes on the burden of being the peacemaker in the family. He also adopts the idea that the family, as a "group-we" that gives him his identity, defines his purpose in life. The group-we, in this case, is the carriage. Because his ideas exclude the Helpers of the invisible world, in time the role he has taken on creates the fate of his being overburdened, both in that family, and in his adult life. Similar roles are the "caretaker," the "sunny child" who cheers everyone up, and "the one who fixes everything," etc. Such people attract others to them who believe they need to be taken care of, to be cheered up, to have things fixed, to be saved, etc. To free himself, the person must dispose of his particular self-image, and any guilt for leaving that role behind. He also needs to say the inner No to any worry the ego may put forward that the others will now come to harm.

This line can also point to a person who has unnecessarily burdened himself by accepting the belief that he has come into this life carrying burdens from a past life, a belief that is projecting itself into reality. The Cosmos has responded to his call for help (by bringing the carriage) but he has attributed the help to the wrong reason by thinking it was given in return for his having made reparations. Since the Cosmos only responds to humility, but does not make deals, the person's mistaken belief has only invited more misfortune. The *I Ching* makes it clear that each person enters life innocent and free of anything carried forward. While it is true that a person may return to another life in a body because he has not fulfilled his destiny, he enters it without "baggage" of any kind.

This line can refer to the belief a person is carrying that "it is too late in life for me to correct my mistakes." The carriage refers to the fact that it is never too late for a person to correct himself and thereby become free of blame.

Line 4. *Deliver yourself from your great toe, then the companion comes whom you can trust.*

The great toe is a metaphor for being moved by ego-impulses rather than by one's complete senses, the influence of which is felt in the back of the neck, where one's will is located. All impulses are based on mistaken ideas and beliefs. Receiving this line is to make a person aware that he is leaning on an idea that is insufficient. He is walking on his toe, rather than his foot.

In the context of this hexagram, the mistaken ideas have to do with thinking that people can free themselves without engaging the Helpers of the invisible world, or that freeing oneself requires the aid of people. A number of related mistaken beliefs specify how freeing is to be achieved, and what it entails. Among them are that freeing consists of "cleansing" oneself of primal faults, and becoming free of one's animal nature through ascetic practices. Such ideas sacrifice one part of a person's wholeness to exalt the other, creating only an exalted self-image. This self-image debases whatever in his nature is perceived as incompatible with that image.

The Sage teaches that "freeing" refers to a person's freeing his true self through ridding himself of the mistaken ideas, beliefs and spells that have imprisoned it. Then the companion, the Helper of Transformation, comes to break the spell that has locked the personality up as "defective" and "insufficient."

This line can also refer to a person's fear of guilt, which makes him tolerate the ego in another. It prevents him from saying the inner No, for fear it will provoke the other's accusing him of being disloyal to him. (*See* Line 3 for a similar co-dependency situation, and how to cope with it.) On freeing himself from the fear of guilt, the Helper that defends him from the ego in others is freed.

Line 5. *If only the superior man can deliver himself, it brings success. Thus he proves to inferior men that he is in earnest.*

Here, the "superior man" refers to the ego, and its claim that by following prescribed rules and practices, a person can develop into a "good person," or "superior man," and thus overcome the "natural inferiority" of his nature. It proposes that his earnestness will prove his goodness to others.

Through keeping the person focussed on prescribed rules and practices, the ego controls the "freeing process." The most dangerous of these practices is the practice of confessing mistakes, and to indulge in self-blame, as by thinking, "I have sinned," or "I never do things right." The Sage makes us aware that both the self-blame-spell and the guilt spell are so strong that the presence of either will block the Helper of Transformation from removing spells. This line counsels, therefore, to firmly reject the ego's ambition to become the "good person" or "superior man," which have the purpose of overcoming guilt and self-blame through self-flattery. (*See* p. 691, Freeing Yourself from Self-Images.) The person may further need to rid himself of the phrase that accompanies his desire for superiority, "to know good and evil is to be like God." Only then can the Helpers come to free his true self of the ego's dominance.

This line can also refer to the need to deprogram a spell—the self-image of one who saves (delivers) others, through evangelizing the truth. Perhaps the person sees himself as the faithful servant of the Sage who brings others to the *I Ching*. By concentrating on others, he ignores what he needs to resolve in himself. By evangelizing the *I Ching*, he turns it into a religion, which it is not. Sharing the *I Ching* with others who are open to it is one thing, but evangelizing is to throw it away on the ego in others. (*See* p. 697, Freeing Yourself from Spells.)

Line 6. *The prince shoots at a hawk on a high wall. He kills it. Everything serves to further.*

The prince, in this line, can refer to the Helper of Transformation that a person engages through saying the inner No to beliefs and attitudes that are not in harmony with the Cosmos.

This determination enables the Helper to kill the hawk (the control of the collective ego over the person) that watches (with its sharp eyes) for every thought that might displace its rule. This hawk has been installed, through conditioning, in a person's psyche. Without the Helper of Transformation, the person would be unable to displace it, for its main means of control is guilt. This guilt is initiated each time a person even thinks of deviating from, or rejecting the beliefs of the collective ego. It would claim that this rejection is a "betrayal," hence implying guilt. As a predatory bird, the hawk uses fear as another of its means to control, as through fears of punishment, exclusion, abandonment, and deprivation of one's primary needs.

Receiving this line informs a person that due to his courageous determination, the hawk mentioned has already been killed, freeing him from his deepest fear to go ahead on the path of his inner truth. This final freeing has taken place without his being aware of it, because a sufficient number of the rationales that have supported the collective ego's control over him have been whittled away.

The hawk can also refer to a person who has branded another as an evildoer, or culprit. Like a hawk, he has been on the lookout for evil in the other, suspecting him of having bad intentions. He has thus allowed his attitude to harden, forgetting that evil does not lie in the intrinsic nature of a person or thing. (*See* Glossary: Good and Evil.) Taking the position of a hawk, the person has slipped into the demonic sphere of consciousness, in which everything is seen in terms of opposites. He needs to free himself of the self-image of being on the side of the good, which is behind his being on the lookout for evil.

The hawk mentioned in this line is the dragon of guilt, which had been created through demonizing the person's natural integrity. Killing the hawk restores the Helper of Integrity to its natural functioning.

41. *Decreasing*

 Kên
Tui

The Judgment: *Decreasing, combined with sincerity, brings about success without blame. One may be persevering in this. It furthers one to undertake something. How is this to be carried out? One may use two small bowls for the sacrifice.*

The harmonious interweavings of the Cosmos are directed only toward *increasing* all parts of the Cosmic Whole. *Decreasing*, as a Cosmic Principle, has the single function of decreasing the ego, because it is the element that separates the person from the Cosmic Whole and its gift-giving nature. Of primary importance is the decreasing of certain active aspects of the ego, which prevent the person from drawing the help of the Cosmos. The increase that results from decreasing the ego brings increase to the Cosmos as a whole, and, since he is part of the whole, it also brings increase to him.

"How is this to be carried out?" The Cosmic Helpers help him to do it. The Sage, as the Cosmic Teacher, leads the process. At any time during the process, he can ask the Sage, by using the *rtcm*, what he needs to do. A great number of other Helpers, each being an expert in its field, cooperate in the task.

A person decreases active aspects of the ego when he divests himself of seed phrases resident in his psyche that activate ego-emotions such as desire for approval, or desire to be recognized as special or exalted, self-doubt, infatuation, pride, envy, hatred, guilt, jealousy, ambition, boredom, pity, self-pity, excessive grief, possessiveness, and anger (when it has been seized by the ego). All of these emotions, except anger, are part of the false inner program created by the collective ego.

"Two small bowls" refer to the Chinese custom of offering up to the ancestral deity two baskets of grain as a gesture to attain its help. This can be taken as a metaphor for sacrificing two things: the (small) seed phrase that gives rise to a particular ego-emotion, and the small sacrifice of pride that is required to ask the Helpers for help.

All ego-emotions either demonize Helpers or keep them at a distance. When demonized, the Helpers become "arms of Fate," whose purpose is to make the person aware that something is amiss. Fate can be experienced as a variety of adversities, small or large. Finding the seed phrases that give rise to ego-emotions can end these adversities. In general, they are phrases that slander the true nature of the Cosmos. (*See* p. 689, Freeing Yourself from Seed Phrases and Images.)

Among these seed phrases are those that express anger:
- at the Cosmos because a person thinks he has no help for his life
- because he thinks his rights have been violated
- at another who "should" be behaving more sensitively
- for having betrayed his true self

The person needs to turn his anger over to the Cosmos, otherwise, the ego's attachment to this strong emotion will prevent his attaining help and a clear view.

Ego-emotions have the effect of imprisoning a person's inner hearing, blocking access to his inner truth. Then all he can hear is the reasoning of the ego, which speaks in a demanding tone that he "should DO something about the situation!" Listening to it only leads to regrets. The person needs to say the inner No to all ego-demands, and then devote himself to finding the seed phrases, as mentioned above. When he rids himself of these seed phrases, his fate is ended, and the demonized Helpers are freed from their imprisonment.

Decreasing also refers to saying the inner No to all aspects of the ego that are active in a given situation, whether it is an intimate situation or a global concern. All action recommended in the *I Ching* refers to *inner* action. By using the *rtcm* a person can make sure whether doing so is appropriate, since the inner truth of the matter is not always apparent. Each time he decreases the ego within himself, he decreases the active egos in others and the collective ego in general.

Note: Since all lines contain infinite possibilities of interpretation, one needs to use the *rtcm* to determine if the meanings suggested here apply to the given situation. (*See* p. 736 for using the *rtcm*.)

Line 1. *Going quickly when one's tasks are finished is without blame. But one must reflect on how much one may decrease others.*

"Going quickly when one's tasks are finished" refers to the way the Helpers, in keeping with their modesty, do not dwell on the help they have given. They are not to blame for the bad consequences that occur when the person who has been helped then claims what has been done as "his achievement."

This line states the Cosmic Principle that all great inventions and discoveries are due to the help given by the Cosmic Helpers, which always comes when a person has realized that in and of himself he cannot bridge that last gap between his effort and success. The Sage and the Helpers help invisibly in all human endeavors that seek to further the whole.

The ego, however, in its desire for recognition, would deny and betray the help given by the Sage and the Helpers, and seduce the person to appropriate the achievement to himself. When this happens, the achievement gradually loses its value. This is the decrease experienced as a result of having decreased the importance of the Helpers that made the gain possible.

This line sometimes refers to incorrect ways in which we put questions to the Sage, and in particular to our expecting the Sage to support our prestructured beliefs and belief systems. This attempt to use the Sage for our egotistical purposes causes the Sage to retreat. Then the answers we receive are but projections of what we want to hear.

Line 2. *Perseverance furthers. To undertake something brings misfortune. Without decreasing oneself, one is able to bring increase to others.*

This line states the Cosmic Principle that all undertakings that arise from an attitude of true modesty bring an overall increase to others and to oneself. The increase occurs because modesty draws the Cosmic Helpers to complete the cycle of Cosmic energy needed for success. When our goals are consistent with inner truth, we receive the help at the right time. Allowing the help to come from the Cosmos is not a decrease of self, or self-worth; it is only a decrease of ego-pride.

However, when a person wants to undertake something while the ego is in control, the Helpers are excluded, and what he undertakes brings misfortune, or, if continued, creates a fate. Not only does his action lack the Cosmic energy needed to bring the task to completion, the ego also has to steal energy for its efforts. This energy is taken either from the person's true self, or from other people involved in the situation.

A person can also receive this line when he pursues correct goals but uses the wrong means, as when he excludes the Helpers and relies solely on effort guided by his intellect. Increase is brought to the situation only by engaging the Helpers, for they know the inner needs of each situation and thus act in harmony with the whole.

A person can also receive this line when the ego in him seeks to "correct another" (bring him into line with the rules of the collective ego) through exercising self-righteous anger. Doing this decreases and humiliates that person's true self.

"Perseverance furthers" is advice to seek out the inner truth of the situation before undertaking anything on the outer plane. Either spells or a fate, which may be identified through using the *rctm*, may have brought about the difficulty.

Line 3. *When three people journey together, their number decreases by one. When one man journeys alone, he finds a companion.*
"Three people journeying together" refers to the presence of ambition in the situation, which is the element that needs to be decreased. Ambition is an active aspect of the ego that wants to make swift progress. It is the element in a person's psyche that casts about through every book on a subject (the various "people" mentioned), in search of the "right answer," while the Sage, that is here referred to as the real "companion," and that stands ready to connect him with his inner truth, is ignored. This ego-attitude has caused the Sage to retreat.

The Sage also retreats when a person takes on humans as his only guides and teachers. Upon renouncing humans as his sole guides and asking the Sage for help, he gains the Sage as his companion.

This line is also received when a person is journeying through life in the company of half-truths put forward by convention, which he follows without questioning. One of the half-truths indicated by this line is the assertion that "you need to find others who know about the truths of life, because you cannot find your way alone." This seed phrase soon attracts people who assert themselves as "helpful companions" through flattering words such as, "If you will follow my system you will be guided safely through life and beyond," or by threatening, "you cannot afford to go without me."

Other mistaken beliefs that are also based on half-truths revolve around guilt and sin, and false definitions of Fate and duty. All these beliefs make what the Sage says unintelligible because they are either words that have no Cosmic basis (guilt and sin), or else they have been turned to the use of the collective ego. Each of these beliefs attracts companions in the form of complementary beliefs that promise to ease the burdens created by the half-truths mentioned, either in this life or in the afterlife. (*See* p. 50, Guilt, Blame, and Shame; also see Glossary: Duty, and Fate; also *see* p. 689, Freeing Yourself from Seed Phrases and Images.)

If a person fails to rid himself of the key seed phrase that draws such companions, he will soon find himself attracted to yet other companions (people) who promise to give him help for his life so that he is "not alone." This line makes clear that such companions are all self-serving, which also means that they have a vested interest in his continued dependence on them, and that he give them his chi energy. They distract him from recognizing that the Sage is in his presence, available to help and teach him if he frees himself of these false companions. Only when he is willing to go on his way alone, can he free the Sage in his presence to come to his aid, and to be his companion.

Line 4. *If a man decreases his faults, it makes the other hasten to come and rejoice. No blame.*

"If a man decreases his faults…" can be counseling a person to rid himself of certain seed phrases or images that create a separation between him and the Sage.

One such fault is his self-image of being on the side of the good, while perceiving another as on the side of evil, or as a culprit. Another fault is in seeing himself as naturally flawed, or as possessing original guilt for having an "animal nature." Still another fault is embodied in the belief that humans are at the center of the universe, responsible for bringing order to the world. These ideas are either false through and through, or they are half-truths based on the error of perceiving only the appearances of things. All such half-truths create a separation between the person and the Cosmos.

Seed phrases having to do with "fault" and "lack" come from the collective ego. They suggest that humans are born with faults, and that they are born lacking and ill-equipped to cope with life. The idea of lack is the entire basis on which the ego is built.

The words "no blame" are a statement that humans are born "without blame," which also means without fault or lack in their inner makeup. (*See* Hexagram 10, *Conducting Oneself*, and Hexagram 14, *Possession in Great Measure* to understand the completeness of our original nature.)

Ideas based on "lack" give rise to thinking in terms of "limited resources," "limited food supply," "limited space," etc. Such views not only obliterate the existence of the Helpers, they demonize them, thus increasing the adversities envisioned.

Connected with the idea of lack is the false phrase, "decrease can never lead to increase." However, as this hexagram shows, the path by which the true self is liberated and validated is entirely a path of decrease: by "taking away" what is false, the person is reunited with the Cosmic Whole, which is the source of all increase.

The mistaken idea of being born inadequate gives rise to striving to become something special; this can lead to an obsessive quest for abstract knowledge, as in "you need to be in the know," with the implication being that "to know is to be like God."

A person may receive this line when he relies on the use of power to make change happen. All use of power, as Hexagram

34, *Using Power*, makes clear, is against the Cosmic Harmonics and if used continually, creates fate after fate. The use of power, in *I Ching* terms, not only includes overt actions to make things happen, but also thoughts which create projections, spells, and poison arrows, and the incorrect use of words, as in arguing, contriving, persuading, competing, etc. The correct way to influence a situation is to first say the inner No to all ego activity, and then to ask the Sage both in one's own presence and in the presence of the others involved to intervene to disperse all ego activity. Then everyone involved finds cause to rejoice.

Line 5. *Someone does indeed increase him. Ten pairs of tortoises cannot oppose it. Supreme good fortune.*

This line affirms that because a person has been following his inner truth, and has been sincere in his way of life, he has drawn the help of the Cosmos. It helps him to be successful in all that he does.

Line 6. *If one is increased without depriving others, there is no blame. Perseverance brings good fortune. It furthers one to undertake something. One obtains a servant but does not have a separate home.*

This line can refer to a person who has been expecting increase, but did not get it. Instead of indulging in feelings of hurt pride, he needs to say the inner No to the ego in himself. This will return him to modesty. The Cosmos cannot give gifts when we hold our hands out for them in expectation.

This line can also mean that a person, through undertaking the decrease of his faulty ideas and attitudes (as mentioned in the previous lines), has gained the help of a particular Helper. This Helper is then able to add everything this person undertakes to the increase of the Cosmic Whole, by making the necessary transformations. In bringing himself back into harmony with the whole, the person has both activated this Helper and reconnected with the Cosmos, which is his true home. This is the meaning of "obtaining a servant."

"Perseverance brings good fortune" refers to the person who recognizes the Cosmic source of his increase. He perseveres in saying the inner No's to the ego's attempts to appropriate the gifts by suggesting he has "deserved" them. He also does not allow them to be used for any egotistical purpose. This line states the Cosmic Principle that Cosmic gifts may never be used for egotistical purposes because doing so decreases the Cosmic Whole, creating blame.

42. *Increasing*

 Sun
Chên

The Judgment: *Increasing. It furthers one to undertake something. It furthers one to cross the great water.*

The harmonious activities of the Cosmos are directed toward increasing all parts of the Cosmic Whole. Increasing the welfare of the whole is a Cosmic Principle that reveals the loving and caring nature of the Cosmos. This understanding is at odds with the assumptions made by Western science that Cosmic resources are limited, and that human effort or manipulation is necessary to overcome this shortfall. This is only true inasmuch as people have separated themselves from their original unity with the Cosmos by adopting mistaken ideas and beliefs about its true nature. In assuming that Nature requires correction or improvement, humans have created a parallel reality that is characterized by lack. This hexagram is a statement that a person can reunite with the Cosmos and participate in its constant flow of gifts, if he "undertakes something," meaning, if he rids himself of the mistaken ideas and beliefs that slander the gift-giving nature of the Cosmos. (For a list of these ideas, see below.)

"It furthers one to undertake something" can also be a statement to encourage a person to follow his goal: he has available from the Cosmos all the help he needs to do what he is meant to do, even though he has been doubting it. It is now a matter of recognizing *how* the goal is to be accomplished. This is addressed in the next sentence of The Judgment.

"It furthers one to cross the great water" means that the person needs to go as far as he can with his own efforts, and then turn the matter over to the Helpers for completion, for it is only they that can complete the crossing. An example is the violinist who practices and perfects his technique and studies the phrasing in preparation for performing; but when the time for performing comes, he asks the Helpers to guide and help him in the performance. Crossing the great water with the help of the Helpers is like being carried across, even though one first had to learn how to swim. It is only through this "joint approach" that the great deeds mentioned in Line 1 can be accomplished. This is true not only for the performing and other arts, but for all creative activity (healing, discoveries, business activities, sports, agriculture, crafts, finding solutions to problems, etc.). Activity that is accomplished jointly with the Helpers succeeds because it gives expression to a person's uniqueness, and benefits the Cosmic Whole.

The aid of the Helpers is essential to all activities that lead to increase, because they alone are able to make the transformations in the atomic realm that give actuality to what is potential. This potential first exists as a feeling, then as an image in the invisible world of consciousness. The Helper of Transformation performs the functions of manifesting what is potential into actuality, and of giving it duration in a way that benefits the whole.

The Helper of Transformation is also the Helper of Increase. This Helper is attracted to the person who recognizes his place as an equal in the Cosmic Whole, and who sincerely seeks, through activity that benefits the whole, to bring his best effort to that activity. In this way he satisfies his own needs as well. The "whole" is not only the "common good" for people, but for Nature as well.

The collective ego, on the other hand, defines increase as acquiring wealth, luxury, power, fame, and knowledge. This kind of increase serves only the few and decreases the whole. It further denigrates the whole because it is only human-oriented. In Cosmic terms, such activity is stealing, because it is never achieved with the help of the Helpers, but is wrested out of people and Nature. It invariably has a fate attached that will eventually take away the gain.

The person receiving this hexagram may need to examine where he is looking for the increase he seeks. Is he looking to the Cosmic Helpers, or to luck, or his own "powers?" Is his goal in harmony with the Cosmos? Does his desire for increase come from the mistaken idea that the Cosmos does not give him what he needs? Does it come from envy of others who seem to be better off? Is he in the habit of "thinking poor," as in thinking that either he is unworthy to have enough money and goods to live a happy life, or that to have money and goods is "materialistic," therefore "a-spiritual?" All these views are not in harmony with the gift-giving nature of the Cosmos. If the person finds any of these ideas during this inquiry, he will also have found the blockages he needs to deprogram, before the Helper of Increase can become his companion. (*See* p. 689, Freeing Yourself from Mistaken Ideas and Beliefs.)

Spells and poison arrows connected with this hexagram are formed by all those phrases that slander, misunderstand, or ignore the gift-giving and caring nature of the Cosmos, and its ability to create increase without decreasing any of its parts. Sample phrases are: "the Cosmos does not busy itself with such mundane things as money," "the Cosmos does not care about an individual's private needs," "I'm just a drop in the bucket," "if you want success you have to make it happen," "everyone has a price," "hard work is the only way to achieve great things," "if it seems too good to be true, it probably is," "you sometimes have to cheat to make success happen," "it's a dog-eat-dog world," "you get what you pay for," "there can be no increase without decrease," and "for everything you get there's a price to be paid." (*See* p. 697, Freeing Yourself from Spells and Poison Arrows.)

Note: Since all lines contain infinite possibilities of interpretation, one needs to use the *rtcm* to determine if the meanings suggested here apply to the given situation. (*See* p. 736 for using the *rtcm.*)

Line 1. *One is furthered by great deeds.** *Supreme good fortune. No blame.*

This line is about increase that comes through the Helpers.

Either a person has been increased, or is about to be increased, but there remains an "if." This "if" has to do with the person's obstructing ideas about the way the Cosmos gives gifts. He may think that he must accomplish great deeds in exchange for receiving gifts from the Cosmos, as if the Cosmos requires being paid back. This idea puts a spell on the Cosmos, preventing it from being able to give the gifts intended. When a person is in harmony with the Cosmos, he receives its gifts freely, without strings attached, because they are the Cosmic response to a person's modesty. The person drawing this line needs to rid himself of any mistaken idea he holds about the way the Cosmos gives gifts. Doing so frees the Helpers to bring him the supreme good fortune mentioned in this line.

It is the Helpers, and not humans, that accomplish the great deeds that increase the whole. Their deeds are "great" because they add to the well-being of the whole, and have duration. To the person who has already received a Cosmic gift, this line is telling him that he is meant to enjoy the gift, but not hoard it selfishly, as happens when he allows the ego to boast that he has deserved it. "No blame" means that the Cosmos is not to be blamed when humans use the Cosmic gifts for egotistical purposes. It is also saying to the person who serves as a vehicle for a Cosmic gift: "when you pass on a Cosmic gift, give it without strings; then you are free of blame."

This line can refer to a person who has called on the Sage for help, and whose energy of will has consequently been increased. Great deeds can come from this increase if he uses it to follow his inner truth and does not squander it for egotistical purposes such as to achieve fame, power, personal gain, or any other benefit to his vanity. Gain will come to him in all forms from the Cosmos if he only concentrates on following his inner truth.

Still another meaning of "one is furthered by great deeds" is the furtherance a person receives when he rids himself of the human-centered view of the universe, perseveres in decreasing the ego in himself and in others, and is sensitive to others' needs

---

* The line in the Wilhelm text reads, "It furthers one to accomplish great deeds...." This rendering clearly reflects the human-centered view, in which humans see themselves as the doers of the great deeds.

for the inner nourishment that enables them to grow.

When receiving this line before an undertaking that involves other people, it indicates that the person needs to call on the Sage in his own presence and in the other people's presence to prepare the situation. Then the Sages can take over and guide the affairs; the Sage also draws the other Cosmic Helpers that are needed to create results that have duration.

Line 2. *Someone does indeed increase him; ten pairs of tortoises cannot oppose it. Constant perseverance brings good fortune. The king presents his offering to God; good fortune.*[*]

"Someone does indeed increase him" is saying to a person that the increase he has just received has come as a gift from the Cosmos, and not, as he may have thought, from another source, such as his efforts, his skill, luck, the beneficence of a person, or as a blessing from heaven, despite all superficial evidence to the contrary. The people he may regard as the source of the gift are only serving as vehicles for the Cosmic generosity.

The tortoise is a reference to the ancient imperial practice of consulting the tortoise oracle before offering sacrifices to heaven, in order to obtain good fortune. When this line was received, it was taken as a favorable sign.

When taken as a metaphor, the line can be indicating that a person mistakenly believes that the Sage requires sacrifices in exchange for blessings. Such thinking is not in harmony with the Cosmos and blocks the gifts the Sage wants to give him in the form of insights. The Sage does not make deals or demand tribute in exchange for its gifts.

In a broader sense, anyone who looks upward, as to heaven, where the dead supposedly go, or to a god created in man's image, looks in the wrong direction, and knocks at the wrong door.

---

*This reading has been given preference over Wilhelm's translation, which reads, "The king presents him before God." The use of the word "God" is incorrect, since the Chinese had no concept of an overall God. It is even questionable whether the spirits they saw as presiding over the fields, the home, and other things, can be called "gods" in the Western sense. The king only presented himself before his deified imperial ancestor, who was seen as the "Lord in Heaven," to obtain his good graces, as every other family head revered his own family ancestors.

To unlock the door to the Helpers, which are the true source of the gifts, a person needs to rid himself of the belief that the blessings come from a "divine source." He is called by this line to rid himself of the whole imagined structure of heaven and of any "higher beings" that humans have put in the place of the Cosmic Consciousness and its invisible Helpers. (*See* p. 682, Activating the Helpers of the Invisible World, and p. 689, Freeing Yourself from Mistaken Ideas and Beliefs.)

The line can also make a person aware of the Cosmic qualities and talents he has come with at birth, as Cosmic gifts. The collective ego would deny that he has them, in order to appropriate and turn them to *its* purposes. It does this by asserting that he needs to imitate positive qualities in others.* A person may receive this line in response to his thinking that he does not possess such Cosmic qualities or talents. The line is saying, "you have all the gifts and help within yourself, but you are blocking them with your doubt." It is also saying, "look within and ask within" for the help you need.

"Constant perseverance brings good fortune" can have two meanings: in a positive meaning, it can refer to the good fortune that comes from appreciating one's innate qualities and abilities, and asking for help from the Helpers of the invisible world. In its negative meaning it can refer to constantly looking for "good fortune" to come, based on the idea, "it will come if I only persevere long enough." Perseverance in putting one's hopes in the sheer quality of perseverance only brings misfortune.

This line can also be about a person's trying to obtain Cosmic gifts through imitating others who have received them, and by his striving to follow the conventional ways to success. Such a person sees others as possessing some secret formula that he can emulate. Envying what others have creates problems both for himself and for the person on whom he projects his envy. Every person comes with unique gifts and talents that want to be brought to expression in a unique way. By enviously looking at others, he is distracted from freeing his own gifts and talents

---

* The Image of this hexagram traditionally reads, "Thus the superior man: if he sees good, he imitates it."

from the inner prisons of doubt and fear that keep them fixed in spells. Another trick of the collective ego, to keep a person from recognizing his own inner treasures, is the idea that he needs to develop supernatural abilities to communicate with the Cosmos. (*See* p. 697, Freeing Yourself from Spells.)

Line 3. *One is enriched through unfortunate events. No blame, if you are sincere and walk in the middle and report with a seal to the prince.*

"One is enriched through unfortunate events" refers to a person who has been enriched by the Cosmos, but the gift has a fate attached. He has received what he was attached to having, but through the decrease of others. Money may have been the object of his desire, and he has now received it. However, because his motives were not correct, blame was attached and a fate created. This blame can be extinguished if he is "sincere" in allowing himself to be guided by the Helper of Increase to use the money to benefit the Cosmic Whole. "Reporting with a seal to the prince" means that he has to account for using the gift in a harmonious way. The "prince" is a metaphor for the Helper that helps a person move his fate in the right direction. If he does so, his fate will be extinguished. The Cosmic Principle explained by this line is that the Cosmos can use "increase" to give a person an opportunity to correct his wrong ideas about the gift-giving nature of the Cosmos, as when he sees the Cosmos as stingy, or as not giving him what he needs to enjoy his life. He can employ the *rtcm* to find out what a correct use of the gift would be, in his case. If, however, he does not recognize the purpose of the gift and uses it as it pleases the ego in him, he will end up like those who have been decreased.

In the same way, a person may receive healing from the Cosmos as a gift, even though his desire to be healed was only to get rid of the pain, or disgrace, or other disadvantage connected with the illness. This line is to make him aware that his healing was given *on the condition* that he recognize it as a gift from the Cosmos and respect it accordingly, by maintaining a sincere attitude. It is also to make him aware that he needs to rid himself of his vanity, if his healing is to endure.

461

A different example is a person who, through his sincere effort to eradicate the phrases behind his illness, has been healed as a gift from the Cosmos. After being healed, however, he returns to the arrogant attitudes he formerly held, such as thinking his healing was due to his "deserving" it, that he had a "right" to be healed, or that now he can act as he pleases, as when, after recovering from a respiratory illness, the person returns to smoking pot, or other abuse of his body. His conflict with the Cosmos remains until he understands the responsibility that goes with the gift: to respect the gift-giving nature of the Cosmos. If he does not learn the lesson, but continues to jeopardize his health, Fate snatches it away from him, again and again, as Line 6 of Hexagram 6, *Conflict*, describes. His conflict can be ended if he recognizes the pattern created by his mistaken ideas and rids himself of it. (*See* p. 689, Freeing Yourself from Mistaken Ideas and Beliefs.)

Line 4. *If you walk in the middle and report to the prince, he will follow. It furthers one to be used in the removal of the capital.*
As mentioned in the previous line, the "prince" refers to the Helper that moves a person's fate in the right direction. This Helper follows the person who has used the Cosmic gift, (*see* Line 3) in a harmonious way, in order to help him as needed. This shows the Cosmic Principle that the person who corrects his mistaken ideas experiences an overall increase.

"Walking in the middle" refers to being in harmony with the Cosmic Whole, and not being caught up in the world of dualities which constitutes the parallel reality created by the collective ego.

The second part of the line text refers to a person who has falsely obtained material wealth through the use of power in one form or another, and who may be thinking that he has earned it. "The capital" is a metaphor for the ego, which has put itself in the center of the wealth he has stolen from Nature. The line is telling him that if he allows himself to be used to remove the capital (the ego), and be responsible for the wealth, he can retain it. He needs, however to examine whether he has taken on feelings of guilt in relation to the material wealth he has accumulated. If so, he needs to extinguish a guilt spell he has put on himself and on others. (*See* p. 696, Freeing Yourself from Guilt.)

This line also hints at the misfortune that awaits the person who, on having attained substantial material wealth, makes no attempt to remove the ego, but spends his energies in accumulating still more wealth.

Line 5. *If in truth you have a kind heart, there will be supreme good fortune, and kindness will be recognized as your virtue.*

This line answers a person's inner question: "will I have good fortune?" by saying, "yes, if indeed you have a kind heart."

This line iterates the Cosmic Principle that the kindness arising from a person's true nature attracts the Helper of Increase. This sort of kindness needs neither words nor training to be developed. The truly kind person does not reward or encourage the ego in others, something that cultivated kindness does. This line is also stating that the Cosmos gives its gifts to a person's true self, and not to the ego in him, and thus, helps him to throw off the ego.

By contrast, the kindness described as "the mark of a cultured person" is not true kindness, but the result of conditioning. The collective ego, by a sleight-of-hand trick, falsely appropriates a person's natural kindness by denying that kindness is one of his Cosmic Virtues. It then holds kindness up as an abstract virtue to be attained through cultivation, while slandering Nature/the Cosmos as unkind and uncultivated. When a person seeks recognition for his virtues, it is always an indication that these virtues have already been appropriated by the ego, and that he is merely cultivating a virtuous self-image.

"Supreme good fortune" refers to the blessings of the Cosmos that come to the person who does not seek recognition for his kind deeds, but in doing them, completely lets go of them. Such deeds nourish the person who does them, as well as the receiving party.

The person receiving this line may need to ask whether he has accepted the self-image of someone who has a kind heart, or whether somebody has put a spell on him by saying he is that sort of a person. In the latter case, the other is seeking to take advantage of his self-image. (*See* p. 691, Freeing Yourself from Self-Images.)

True kindness is expressed in gratitude that comes from the heart as wonderment and enjoyment of the gifts of the Cosmos. It is not something a person can cultivate, because it is a spontaneous response to the constant stream of gifts and help that comes from the Cosmos.

Line 6. *He brings increase to no one. Indeed, someone even strikes him. He does not keep his heart constantly steady. Misfortune.*

"He brings increase to no one" refers to the ego, which can never bring true increase, neither to the individual nor to the whole, despite its claim that the opposite is true. A person who has been increased by the Cosmos has allowed the ego to appropriate that increase, thus caused a fate. The ego calls that fate "bad luck." In search of a scapegoat, the ego, in its typical sleight-of-hand logic, now tells the person that the bad luck is *his own* fault. It claims that things would have worked out better if he had only trusted the ego's advice more.

"He does not keep his heart constantly steady" refers to the person's accepting the blame put on him by the ego, and then indulging in thinking, "I should have done this...I should have done that." What he really needs to do is to stop indulging in self-blame, and to seek out the cause of his mistake. When he is willing to do this, the Sage will return to help him. The first step in his recovery is to rid himself of the poison arrow of self-blame. He then needs to identify and rid himself of the mistaken ideas and beliefs that have led him to depend on the ego. (*See* p. 697, Freeing Yourself from Poison Arrows; also *see* p. 689, Freeing Yourself from Seed Phrases and Images.)

This line can also refer to a person who does not attract the Helper of Increase because he believes that life is governed by chance, and so tries to influence chance through bribing the "arbiter of chance," as, for example, by giving gifts to charity. In the way of the Cosmos there is no such thing as chance or luck. The good fortune mentioned in the *I Ching* lines refers to the Cosmic gifts that are given to a person's true self as an opportunity for him to learn how the Cosmos really operates. Mistaken beliefs in chance are expressed by such phrases as, "chance rules our lives," "chance is the final arbiter," "chance will decide," "seize the chance." To open the door to the Helper of Increase, a person needs to rid himself of the idea of "chance" and all related ideas and beliefs he may hold.

Also part of the mistaken beliefs addressed by this line is that increase does not last, as in the phrase "seize the moment." This belief would have us believe that increase is invariably followed by decrease, while in truth, this is the case only when we believe that Nature and the Cosmos work through *changes.* Then the mistaken belief projects itself into reality. The Helper of Increase is invariably attracted by a harmonious attitude and stays with that person so long as he remains in harmony with the Cosmos. Decrease, on the other hand, invariably occurs when a person has created increase through wrong means, and then uses it for egotistical purposes.

43. *Resoluteness/Breakthrough*

Tui
Ch'ien

The Judgment: *Resoluteness. One must resolutely make the matter known at the court of the king. It must be announced truthfully. Danger. It is necessary to notify one's own city. It does not further to resort to arms. It furthers one to undertake something.*

This hexagram is about the force of will. Every person is born with it as part of his senses. The will, as we are informed in Hexagram 31, *Influencing,* Line 5, is located in the nerves of the back of the neck. From there it transmits the individual perceptions of the other inner senses to the conscious mind. These individual perceptions are then formed into a complete perception of reality in image and word form, which the person's conscious mind can then assert as his inner truth.

The word "breakthrough" used in this hexagram calls attention to one of the main functions of will, which is to help the person break through the ego's defenses, both in himself and others.

The force of will lies neither in physical nor mental power, but in its irresistible strength, which develops when it aligns with inner truth. Breakthrough refers to the successful effort of the will in breaking down the power of the ego. It initiates this breakdown of the ego through saying the inner No to any part of the ego that is active in the situation. The inner No brings about transformation in the realm of the atom, which is the realm of consciousness.

When the will is applied to resisting the ego, it is able to prove the ego's pretense that it is all-powerful to be wrong. There are two ways in which the will is able to cope with the ego: (1) by saying the inner No, or (2) by resisting any fear or impulse suggested by the ego for as long as three minutes. The latter can be employed if a person feels unable to say the inner No, or does not know about this possibility. The ego can succeed either by making a person forget that he has this natural ability, or by placing a spell on his will, as noted in Line 5.

When the will to stand firm against the ego is combined with saying the inner No with one's conscious mind, the strength of will is doubled, and the effect is felt immediately, because it engages additional Helpers, both within oneself and any other person involved. To "resolutely make the matter known at the court of the king" refers to asking the Sage in the other person's presence to intervene to stop the ego, and also asking the Sage in one's own presence to help cope with the situation. In this way, the matter becomes a communication between the two aspects of the Sage. This is the meaning of "It must be announced truthfully."

"Danger" refers to the ego's resistance in the form of rationales that say "the ego is really a helper in the personality," or "you need your ego to deal with the realities of life." Such rationales may be coming from associates who are encouraging or expecting him to behave in a way that suits them. Informing "one's own city" is counsel to make it clear to them that he will not go along with their expectations, simply because it does not *feel* right. There is never a necessity to defend what one feels to be correct. If he will stay firmly on this point, he will not need "to resort to arms," or engage in conflict with them. "It furthers one to undertake something" refers to the practice of relying on his inner *feelings* as the basis for his decisions.

Resoluteness, as described above, is in sharp contrast with the kind of resoluteness the ego employs to achieve its goals. It resorts to arguments that dismiss a person's feelings, his inner truth, and the Cosmic Principles as "irrelevant." All such ploys must fall in the face of a determined inner No.

Because a person's will is easily influenced by *words*, there is always the danger that the will to follow what is harmonious may be usurped by rationales of the ego. One such rationale is its argument that each person has a good and an evil side, his good side being his mental or spiritual faculties and his evil side being his "lower" (animal) nature. Because his animal nature includes most of his senses, the ego, with this sleight-of-hand logic, divorces his will from his other senses, and thus engages the will in fighting his animal nature. When his will becomes separated from the feeling consciousness of his inner senses, it begins to serve the thinking consciousness, or some other purportedly superior entity, such as the soul.

Once a person's will has been commandeered by the ego in this way, it is channeled by it to be the driver of its efforts to suppress or overcome the person's animal nature, and to engage him in developing his "higher nature." When the will resolutely does this, it knows no bounds, and if need be, will whip the person to death to achieve these goals. When the will is not in line with all the other senses, its connection with commonsense is lost, and along with it, the ability of the commonsense to complete transformations.

This hexagram also draws attention to the fact that a person's will can be separated from his natural inhibitions (his feelings) through training. There is, for example a natural inhibition against purposefully killing another human. On this account, soldiers and police are trained to shoot at a lifeless human model, to train them to forget their feelings. In the same way, watching violence on television leads children to think of violence as unreal or harmless in its consequences. The will, when divorced from the person's natural inhibitions, permits the ego to act in criminal ways.

Spells connected with this hexagram are created when someone says to a person: "You have no will." Such a statement freezes his will. Others are: "You can achieve anything if you put enough effort into it"; "willpower overcomes all obstacles"; "when the going gets tough, the tough get going"; "you can move mountains if only your faith is strong enough." This latter spell fixes a person's will in such a way that the totality of his senses, which would otherwise give him a complete assessment of reality, becomes shut off.

As mentioned above, will has nothing at all to do with power, therefore the word "willpower" is a misnomer. Will is the total energy of a person's psyche, which has a natural direction toward the fulfillment of the individual's life purpose, or destiny. Its misuse, as when the ego appropriates it and turns it toward *its* purposes, robs the psyche of its force. Thus, the ego even uses the will to fight part of the person's nature, and ultimately to defeat both his psyche and body.

A person may receive this hexagram when it is time for him to make a new beginning. This happens when following the ego has led him into a dead end. The ego, under these circumstances, will do anything to keep the will under its control. To really make a new beginning the person has to be resolute in resisting the ego in the manner described above.

Note: Since all lines contain infinite possibilities of interpretation, one needs to use the *rtcm* to determine if the meanings suggested here apply to the given situation. (*See* p. 736 for using the *rtcm*.)

Line 1. *Mighty in the forward-striding toes. When one goes and is not equal to the task, one makes a mistake.*

"Mighty in the forward-striding toes" can refer to a person who is under a fate and thinks he can end it through struggle or opposition. The line makes him aware that with this approach he is not equal to the task. Fate can be ended only by making the effort to rid oneself of its causes that are to be found in a mistaken idea or belief, or in a self-image. An example is a person who has created a fate by having adopted the self-image of the "good" or "spiritual" person, or the "superior man." He may react to his fate by blaming himself for not having been good or spiritual enough, and therefore resolve to strive even harder. What he really needs to do to end his fate is to remove that self-image and say the inner No to blaming himself. (*See* Glossary: Fate and Destiny. Also *see* p. 692, Freeing Yourself from a Fate.)

A person may receive this line when he has had a poison arrow put on him that has made him doubt the purpose of his life, or question whether life has *any* purpose at all. This doubt has given rise to the idea that he needs to prove himself, be it through gaining power or recognition. In searching to prove himself, he has had a breakthrough in the form of an insight. However, the warning that he is "not equal to the task" indicates that his sudden insight has come, not from a Cosmic source, but from the ego, and is designed to serve his pride system. He will avoid making the mistake indicated, if he realizes that his mere existence is proof that he has a purpose, and if he identifies and rids himself of the poison arrow that was put on him. Then, his life's purpose can show itself. (*See* p. 697, Freeing Yourself from Poison Arrows.)

Line 2. *A cry of alarm. Arms at evening and at night. Fear nothing.*

"A cry of alarm" points to the presence of a fate or Cosmic intervention, which may be showing itself in feelings of disease or pain. These feelings are meant to alert the person to the presence of fears inserted by the ego. It has been painting worst-case scenarios, even going so far as to imagine his death. These fears come from mistaken ideas he holds about Fate or the Cosmos. "Arms at evening and at night" pictures the kind of resoluteness needed to diminish the ego's power, and to say the inner No to whatever it puts forth. His fate can be ended through his resolutely rejecting the mistaken ideas and beliefs that have caused it. (*See* Glossary: Fate and Destiny. Also *see* p. 692, Freeing Yourself from a Fate.)

This line can also indicate the presence of a spell or poison arrow, which may be the cause of an illness. The person can free himself of the illness by identifying its cause and ridding himself of it. (*See* p. 694, Freeing Yourself from Some Health Problems.)

The line can also be a warning that the ego is trying to rationalize away a person's natural sense of caution, as in saying, "fear nothing—you can take a risk." This easy dismissal of his natural protection needs to be firmly rejected by saying the inner No to it.

A person may also receive this line, when he is about to face a difficult situation. It is telling him to arm himself against the blind impulses of the ego, and against its fears and doubts, or its overconfidence and bravado. "Fear nothing" is saying he will have nothing to fear if he will ask the Sage in his own presence and the Sage in the other's presence to guide him and to intervene in the situation as needed.

Line 3. *To be powerful in the cheekbones brings misfortune. A person is firmly resolved. He walks alone and is caught in the rain; he is bespattered, and people murmur against him. No blame.*

"To be powerful in the cheekbones" points to a person who is aware of the power of words and is using them to influence others for his own egotistical purposes. He may be doing so to build up his name, or to gain followers. He may also be intimidating people or instilling guilt in them. "A person is firmly resolved" refers to the person who, in such a situation, follows his inner truth and is consequently misunderstood by others. This line tells him that although he walks alone, he will not be lonely, because the Sage is in his company; thus the words "no blame."

"Being firmly resolved" can also describe a person who is acting as though he is firmly resolved, but in reality is under a spell ("bespattered"), and therefore is being steered by forces over which he has no control. "No blame" tells us that he is not to be blamed for what he does while under the spell. This line states the Cosmic Principle that the blame incurred belongs to the person who has put the spell on him. It also states that if that person does not take the spell off the other, he will create a fate for himself.

"To be powerful in the cheekbones" can also refer to the activity of putting spells and projections on someone by categorizing him as this or that "kind of person." Here are shown the negative effects of such spells: the person is isolated and "out in the rain...he is bespattered, and people murmur against him." Categorizing someone in a certain way causes him to act accordingly; this leads others to notice the behavior and to confirm "that is the way he is." The person under such a spell can free himself from it by identifying the phrases and images that compose it. (*See* p. 697, Freeing Yourself from Projections, Spells and Poison Arrows.)

Line 4. *There is no skin on his thighs, and walking comes hard. If a man were to let himself be led, but not like a sheep, remorse would disappear. But if these words are heard they will not be believed.*

This line describes a situation in which a person has lost his Cosmic Protection due to one or another false idea or belief.

"No skin on the thighs" pictures a condition of feeling exposed and at risk, so that each step in any direction brings suffering, doubt, hesitation, remorse, etc., because the person is caught in the bonds of beliefs that undermine his will. One of the most dangerous among such beliefs causes him to see himself like "a sheep," with no will of his own. The person has transferred the role his parents assumed as his protectors either to the Sage, or to a human or divine authority, and is "following like a sheep." Doing so creates a fate. If the person is following the Sage in this manner, he is counseled that the Sage does not seek servile followers, but only to help the student reconnect with his inner truth and commonsense, and to learn to trust them.

A person's will may also be held in bondage by the basic belief that life is a prewritten script "written in the stars," or determined by karma carried over from past lives. He may likewise

---

* The line in the Wilhelm text reads, "If a man were to let himself be led like a sheep, remorse would disappear." We were guided by the Sage to notice that this idea serves only the purposes of the collective ego, to keep the person locked in the group-we, and therefore also locked in the remorse of sharing the group's fate.

see the world as "doomed" to end, or believe that there is some other dark fate in the making from which there is, or will be, no escape. Such views mistakenly picture the Cosmos as hostile, indifferent, or even as a "set of mechanics." The irony is that the person who holds such views projects them constantly into reality; thus he believes that they are true. He needs to realize that the parallel reality he creates through projection traps him in one fate after another.

Such mistaken beliefs, acquired from the collective ego, are poison arrows that are blocking his ability to hear within, therefore prevent him from being led by the Sage. The effect is an unaccountable depression that constantly undermines his will. The mood quickly synchronizes itself with bad weather conditions, negative news reports, prophecies of global fates, etc., all of which keep him locked in the negative vortex created by the underlying belief in predestination, and its complementary belief that he cannot do anything about it (such as say the inner No, and gain the Helpers' aid).

Another idea that undermines a person's will is his identification with a group, so that he always feels its ups and downs as ruling his life. Thus, when economic conditions swing downward, he also feels pulled down. Such thinking in terms of a "group-we" (thus the reference to the sheep) keeps him locked in the fate created by the group. All group-thinking originates in the collective ego, and isolates the individual from his connection with the Cosmos and its protection.

A similar identification with guilt, especially collective guilt, (as in identifying with a nation's guilt for historic massacres or mistreatment of minorities, etc.), may also undermine a person's will and be the cause of depression. In the Cosmic Order, there is neither such a thing as an individual guilt nor a group guilt. Identification with guilt is a poison arrow which needs to be deprogrammed. (*See* p. 50, Guilt, Blame, and Shame, and p. 697, Freeing Yourself from Poison Arrows.)

A person who has committed himself to following a belief, however mistaken, is held in that belief by the guilt that is associated with breaking a commitment. To free him from the belief, it may be necessary first, to have the help of another person who can say the inner No to the guilt that surrounds the belief. The guilt is stored in the psyche in words such as, "I cannot say No to my beliefs because that would make me feel guilty." It can also manifest as "I cannot say No to my parents, group, authority, etc." (*See* p. 696, Freeing Yourself from Guilt, and p. 677, Saying the Inner No.) "Remorse disappears" refers to the consequences of getting free of a concretized belief that stands between the person and the Sage; it also refers to getting free of the group-we, and extinguishing the spells and poison arrows mentioned above.

This line may also refer to wounded pride that prevents a person from hearing his inner truth. His pride may have been wounded on finding out that he has incurred Cosmic blame. As a consequence, he has abandoned his learning from the Sage. He needs to recognize that the blame was due to ego-pride, and not to his true self, which has been suppressed by the ego. The feeling of blame is unbearable only because the ego has converted it into *guilt*, which is one of the ego's chief devices to keep him under its control. The remedy is to say the inner No to his pride, and to rid himself of the idea of guilt.

"No skin on the thighs" can also refer to mistaken ideas about the nature of "pain." Pain needs to be understood as a warning sign by one's natural protective system. It is often the only bodily messenger that can get our attention to tell us that we have been hit by a poison arrow coming from someone, or that an embedded and forgotten poison arrow needs to be removed. Without this message, the condition would lead to serious illness. Seeing pain as an *enemy* causes a person to *fight the messenger* rather than identifying the root cause of the disturbance, thus creating an inner warfare between his will and his body. Retreating from fighting immediately eases the pain. (For further help *see* p. 694, Freeing Yourself from Some Health Problems.)

Line 5. *In dealing with weeds, firm resolution is necessary. Walking in the middle one remains free of blame.*

The term "weeds" refers to seed phrases and images stored in a person's inner program that are active in the problem of the moment.

The person receiving this line needs to be "firmly resolved" to seek out the phrases and images in question, because they have put a spell on his will. Since the will is one of his inner senses, the spell prevents the person from being automatically centered within, which happens when *all* his senses are aligned. Being centered is the meaning of "walking in the middle." (To practice this, *see* p. 680, Centering Yourself.) When a person is centered within himself, he "remains free of blame."

The will has its seat in the nerves of the back of the neck, from where it normally transmits the perceptions of the inner senses to the conscious mind. There, they are formed into images and words that present a complete perception of the inner reality of the situation. The two basic words, by which the conscious mind acknowledges the inner truth of a given situation, are Yes and No: Yes to what is in harmony with the Cosmos, and No to what is discordant. However, when a spell has been put on a person's will, the conscious mind loses its contact with the other senses. He then is no longer able to perceive and act from his complete senses. Another effect of the spell is that it harnesses the will to serve the ego, which then uses the will to drive the person to achieve *its* goals.

Receiving this line can point to three different kinds of such spells: "You have no will" freezes a person's will altogether. "You can achieve anything if you put enough effort into it" flatters the will into a false enthusiasm that makes the person believe he is all-powerful. "You can move mountains if your faith is strong enough" imprisons his inner senses and replaces them with faith. Faith is an abstract concept that makes a person accept fantasies that have no foundation in the Cosmic Reality.

To "walk in the middle" can also be counsel not to get involved in an incipient conflict by taking one side or the other. The person needs to remain resolutely disengaged, because the conflict is based on issues that are hidden from his view. He can only resolve it by uncovering these hidden issues and resolving them with the aid of the Sage and the Helpers. When a person gets this line he may ask the Sage to point out, through another hexagram, what the nature of the hidden issue is, and then to define any projections, spells or poison arrows that have caused the conflict. (*See* p. 697, Freeing Yourself from Projections, Spells and Poison Arrows.)

When a person's will is in the service of the ego, he creates fate after fate, because the ego is not part of the Cosmic Whole. Receiving this line is to make him aware that his fate can be extinguished by deprogramming the spell that has been put on his will.

Line 6. *No cry. In the end misfortune comes.*

"In the end misfortune comes," is the ego talking. It is saying, "there is no help," and thus creates a resignation that defeats a person's will.

"No cry" refers to this resignation because it has suppressed the normal cry of alarm, in the form of dis-ease, pain (or a Cosmic message such as an insight), that would come from the person's inner senses to make him aware that he needs to assess the inner truth of the situation. The only avenue left for his inner truth to express itself is that of alarming dreams or meditation experiences. (*See* Hexagram 38, *Separating*, Line 2.) The person needs to recognize that the words, "things will take a bad end," and "there is no help" are coming from the ego; he then needs to summon his will to extinguish those phrases as poison arrows.

"In the end misfortune comes" also refers to a situation in which the ego, after concluding that life is not going *its* way, has made a decision that there is "no use" in trying further, and that all reason for living in *this* reality has ended. Using the will to fulfill its wishes, it brings the person to commit suicide.

"No cry. In the end misfortune comes," also can indicate that a person has lost his Cosmic Protection. He can regain it by ridding himself of the mistaken idea that he has been born without help from the Cosmos.

44. Coming to Meet

Ch'ien
Sun

The Judgment: *Coming to meet. The influence is powerful.**

"Coming to meet" refers to the Cosmic Principle that it is attraction which draws complementary aspects together. It does so in its own time, without the need for pressure or contriving. When allowed to take its time and natural course, everything matures and completes itself in the best possible way. All of this occurs in the atomic realm, through transformation, creating a unity that endures, until its purpose is completed.

Another Cosmic meaning of this hexagram is related to its being one of the so-called calendar hexagrams. It stands for the first month after the summer solstice, when the dark begins to increase. This is pictured by the first dark line entering at the bottom. (*See* p. 24, "calendar hexagrams.") This single dark line is a metaphor for the first step in the process of something emerging from non-form into form, whether it be an insight or discovery.

The "influence is powerful" refers to the ego, which is outside this creative, coming-to-meet process, and attempts to insert itself. This happens, for example, in meditation, just when an insight is emerging that would transform a situation: the ego interferes in the way the insight expresses itself, it seeks to appropriate it to *its* use, or to cut it off through impatience, thereby distorting its meaning. When a person allows the ego to interfere, the result is not transformation, but change, which does

---

* Here, the Sage did not accept Wilhelm's rendering of The Judgment: "The maiden is powerful. One should not marry such a maiden." The hexagram name, *Kou*, means "to pair," and "to copulate." The Cosmic meaning of the warning in The Judgment indicates that an incorrect element is seeking union. The feudal editors of the text have translated the incorrect element to fit their feudal prejudice against women. The Sage has turned the focus to the general subject of negative influence.

not lead to duration.

"The influence is powerful" is also a warning not to allow any negative influence that is drawn by self-doubt, guilt, or fear. Therefore, The Judgment warns of influences that come to a person from the collective ego in the guise of help. This guise may appear as protection, security, power, qualifications, authorizations, education, honors, or stature. Behind the temptation to accept these offers is an inferiority complex instilled in the person's psyche during childhood. It consists of false phrases and images by which he has been declared helpless, disabled, insufficient, unqualified, not authorized, not educated, lacking, and guilty, all of which have made him feel at risk, and insecure. Being taught to distrust his own innate abilities, senses and Cosmic gifts prepared him to become dependent on the collective ego and its solutions. Now, he is tempted to adopt one of these solutions. He also needs to be aware that the solutions will only lead him to further problems.

A person may also receive this hexagram when a particular fear, initiated by a shock experienced in childhood, has been reactivated by a smell. The smell reawakens the sense of danger, causing his heart to race, and making him brace himself against the situation. In this case, it is the smell that comes to meet, telling him there is a real danger, and he needs to pay attention to it. The Sage counsels him to meet the situation by saying the inner No to his fear and asking the Cosmic Army to come to his help. He next needs to clear his mind and remain neutral within. Neutrality disarms aggressive intent through its inner effect on the transgressor. All aggression seeks to rob chi energy from the victim, either through arousing fear, anger, or hatred. When a person remains neutral within, no satisfaction can be gained through acts of aggression, and the aggressor is forced to halt.

Coming to meet also refers to how *wanting* draws unpleasant events. Wanting occurs when we doubt that the Cosmos will give us what we need. It is always focused on a particular goal, usually one which has been advertised as giving a person a successful self-image (becoming famous, rich, powerful). People with predatory egos set themselves up as the doorway through which those who want must pass, if they are to attain their goal.

What the person who wants does not see is that to get through that door, the predatory ego requires that he sell his dignity and self-respect. This fate is always the true price of wanting. The person who attains true independence, through placing his dependence on the Cosmos, gets everything he needs.

Other "door-openers" that attract the egos in other people to approach and take advantage are fears that invite encroachments, self-doubt that invites others to dominate, and guilt that invites others to accuse the person, or to load their burdens onto him.

Self-images are also among the things which draw negative responses from others, often as projections, spells, and poison arrows. The self-image of the confident, capable person draws people who lack confidence and feel incapable. The admiration that these people profess is actually a disguised envy. This envy, which is always associated with putting another up on a pedestal, is a thorn to his own pride, which aggravates him until he finds a way of putting the other down. Thus the person who admires another actually has a vested interest in the other's failure. The envy behind the admiration also constantly produces spells and poison arrows toward the one envied. The person who, through freeing himself of all self-images regains his modesty, actually disperses the envy.

Another aspect of coming to meet refers to a solution that, although one's intuition says it is "too easy," nevertheless seems to fit every need of the existing situation. However, it has a hook attached, in that it does not fit the true *inner* needs of the situation, which have to be discovered with the help of the Sage.

Note: Since all lines contain infinite possibilities of interpretation, one needs to use the *rtcm* to determine if the meanings suggested here apply to the given situation. (*See* p. 736: Using the *rtcm*.)

Line 1. *It must be checked with a brake of bronze. To be firmly correct brings good fortune. If one lets it take its course, one experiences misfortune. Even a lean pig has it in him to rage around.*

This line refers to a situation in which a person sees himself as having failed, and is blaming himself. The self-blame is blown out of proportion due to old memories of feeling insufficient or guilty, thus it "rages around" like a lean pig. Such raging, if not checked, leads to the misfortune mentioned.

"To be firmly correct" refers to checking this raging by putting matters in perspective. This means recognizing that the self-blame comes from childhood conditioning to feel guilty when mistakes are made. This line informs the person that it is natural to make mistakes, and that he needs only to correct the ideas behind his mistake to bring himself back into harmony with the Cosmos. (*See* p. 50, Guilt, Blame, and Shame.) If the person does not free himself of self-blame, the continued presence of blame will tempt him to adopt a grandiose self-image to compensate for feeling blameworthy.

This line also refers to recognizing that impulses spring from back-of-the-mind suggestions made by imps in the person's psyche. These imps are groups of thoughts that have formed themselves around a particular fear, doubt, or guilt, and have taken on a life of their own. They need to be resisted with "a brake of bronze," meaning that the person recognizes the imp's presence, and holds back from taking any action based on its pressure until that pressure has given way. (The imp's pressure to act cannot be maintained in the face of three minutes of determined resistance. See p. 686, The Three Minute Rule.) The inner No is next said to the underlying phrases that are connected with the impulse. These phrases can be identified with the help of the *rtcm*. They need to be treated as spells. (*See* p. 697, Freeing Yourself from Spells.) Some of these phrases are: "you are not able to handle that," "you're no good," "you're not qualified," "you're not authorized," "you need an education to do that," "you're born guilty/insufficient," and phrases that come from slanderous curses, such as "you little devil/imp/ bastard/ etc." Other phrases have to do with indebtedness and guilt, such as, "you should be grateful to have your mother/father," and "you owe your life to them."

This line also describes certain thoughts by which the ego seeks to reinsert itself after it has been eliminated. These thoughts need to be checked immediately by saying the inner No. Merely considering them would give them credibility and allow them to take over. Often such "lean pigs" enter as self-pity and can be heard as "poor me!" They create feelings of helplessness, so that the person will listen to what they propose to do. Desire enters through phrases such as, "it would be nice if this were so." Doubt enters through the phrase, "why are things this way?" Anxiety enters with "something awful might happen..." or "when will it ever happen?" Self-pity can enter merely with a sigh, or a negative image that comes to mind. Guilt can enter as a desire to be pure, and show itself as an unreasonable fastidiousness. These first reentry points of the ego are immediately followed (if not firmly resisted) by a train of secondary thoughts that have a commanding or demanding nature. These, in turn, are followed by blind impulses "to do" something.

Line 2. *There is a fish in the tank. No blame. It does not further to allow guests.*

"Fish" is a metaphor for any one of a person's inner senses (also *see* Hexagram 61, *Inner Truth*). In this line, the mention of fish indicates that a particular inner sense has been demonized and therefore attracts unwanted elements from outside. The line can point to the presence of either *self-doubt*, which is created when a person's sense of wholeness has been slandered, or *guilt*, which is created when a person's sense of blame gets seized by the ego and turned into guilt.

When self-doubt is active in the background of the psyche, it acts as a "door opener" that awakens in others the temptation to overstep the person's boundaries. It also invites in predatory aspects of the egos in them, thus the expression, "it does not further to allow guests." Such people come with uninvited advice and curiosity, overstep the limits of the person's integrity with personal remarks, and tempt him to throw his dignity away by trying to please them, or to succumb to their intimidation and flatteries.

The remedy is to seek out the source of the self-doubt with the help of the *rtcm*. Usually, this is a spell. Examples: "you are not good enough, in and of yourself," "you don't own your own space," "privacy is for the rich and powerful," "who are *you*?" said with the implication "you are not authorized." Examples of images are: the image of yourself with no space around you

480

that is yours alone; seeing yourself as always existing in someone else's space; the image and feeling that others have the right to come and go, in and out of your space, as they please; images of being helpless, of not being heard, of possessing nothing while others have everything, of having had a bad start in life, of being born inadequate, or guilty. Other images are of having rights, and of being special. (*See* p. 697, Freeing Yourself from Spells.)

The "guests" can also refer to the collective ego's customary compensations for feelings of self-doubt and being helpless. It encourages the person to answer these feelings by developing a bravado that he is special, as is expressed by ideas that "you are under God's special protection," "you can do anything you want if you just do it," and "you are special, you just need to recognize that!"

The fish can also be a metaphor for guilt that "swims" in the situation at hand, as when it is the underlying cause of an illness. In this case, guilt, which has remained unnoticed, sucks on the person's life force. Holding onto guilt, usually introduced in childhood, not only creates illness, it draws its complement, the "guest" of self-blame for being ill, creating a vicious circle of self-destruction. To break it, the person needs to rid himself of the primary guilt spell and say the inner No to blaming himself. Doing so will extinguish his fate. (*See* p. 696, Freeing Yourself from Guilt.)

Another aspect of a fish that swims in a person's subconscious is its accompanying smell. This smell opens the door to other people's egos, allowing them to load their burdens on him. Such a person may feel guilty because he has been told that he is "better off than someone else." He draws people who have created a fate to lean on him. His rescuing them from their fate creates a fate for him in turn. (*See* p. 40, Fate.) Such a person needs to say the inner No to all the phrases and images that have made him feel guilty.

Line 3. *There is no skin on his thighs, and walking comes hard. If one is mindful of the danger, no great mistake is made.*

"No skin on the thighs" can indicate that a person's true self has been hurt in childhood by having been put down by such

481

phrases as, "Who do you think you are?" and "You are good for nothing." Such a person may think he is guilty for one reason or another; consequently, he is blaming himself. Self-blame keeps the wound alive, therefore prevents him from going on with his life. He needs to rid himself of guilt and self-blame. (*See* p. 696, Freeing Yourself from Guilt.)

The line can also refer to a person, who, because his pride has been wounded at a previous time, now shows sympathy to others whose ego-pride has been similarly hurt. Such a person believes he is rescuing them but he is only rescuing the egos in them. He needs to realize that the wounding of pride can only occur when people have developed ego-pride. Their fates have the purpose of making them aware of the ego and its vanity. By seeking to rescue them a person runs the danger of taking on their fates, because he is preventing them from learning the lessons their misfortunes are meant to teach them. To free himself from his fate, he needs to rid himself of the self-images of being a "wounded person," and of being a "rescuer" of others who are wounded. (*See* p. 691, Freeing Yourself from Self-Images.)

This line can also refer to the person who has been identifying with the image of the "superior man" given in the traditional *I Ching*, and in doing so, has created a fate. The fate is that the self-righteousness, and the images of perfection and modesty that accompany the self-image of the superior man, have separated him from the Sage, whom he thinks he is serving. He is thus left without the help he has expected. The danger is that he may adopt the belief that he is simply ill-fated. He needs to recognize that every self-image, good or bad, brings on a fate, and prevents him from validating his true nature. His fate can be extinguished if he will rid himself of the self-image.

Line 4. *No fish in the tank. This leads to misfortune.*

This line points to a person's view of himself that he is useless or that his life has no meaning, life being the tank, and no fish in it being his lack of respect for himself. Seeing himself as worthless leads him to believe that he will be cast out or judged badly by society. Given this view, he is only faced with two options: either to remain stuck in hopelessness, or to develop hopes as compensation. Among the hopes may be the hope of being for-given by God, or miraculously being discovered by society to be worthwhile, after all. Such a person is unaware that his view has been shaped by the collective ego's ideas (1) that his life needs justification; and (2) that his life must somehow be validated, as by someone of high rank. To become free of his feeling of hopelessness and his holding to hopes requires that he say the inner No to these false ideas that come from the collective ego.

No fish in the tank can also refer to a person who lacks re-spect for someone who is not developing his true nature. Re-spect, in this case, is the fish. His intolerance comes from hav-ing adopted the self-image of the "superior man," as described in the traditional *I Ching*. While seeing the ego in others is cer-tainly repugnant, the person is failing to see it in himself in the form of this self-image. If not corrected, it will certainly create a fate. (*See* p. 691, Freeing Yourself from Self-Images.)

Line 5. *A melon covered with willow leaves. Hidden lines. Then it drops down to one from heaven.*

The melon covered with willow leaves refers to the ego that has induced the person to do something against his nature. Then, because the act has brought humiliation, the ego has hidden itself as the cause, by blaming the person's true self: "You should have done this," or "you should not have done that!"

This line can be given by the Sage to inform the person of his inner truth (the hidden lines mentioned) so that he can under-stand the tactics of the ego, and see to what grave endings it leads him. If he then combines this recognition with saying the inner No to the ego's influence, he will dislodge it, causing the ego to drop down from its high place in heaven, as "knowing what is best," into his possession, instead of its possessing him. Then his true self can take its place as the true leader of the personality, freed from blame.

Line 6. *He comes to meet with his horns. Humiliation. No blame.*

Here is pictured someone who regards himself as a spiritual person who is above the world's tumult, and thus displays an attitude of disdain and self-righteousness. "Humiliation" reflects the fact that he is experiencing a fate as a consequence, but feels that he is not to blame and therefore the fate is unjust. He also engages in conflict with whatever he thinks has given him the fate: God, the Sage, life, etc. His fate can be ended if he will rid himself of his exalted self-image (of being spiritual, the superior man, etc.). (*See* p. 691, Freeing Yourself of Self-Images.) He also needs to recognize the mistaken ideas and beliefs that have made him adopt the self-image in the first place. They consist of the phrases and images mentioned in the main text that made him feel inferior and guilty during childhood.

45. Gathering Together

 Tui
K'un

The Judgment: *Gathering Together. Success. The king approaches his temple. It furthers one to see the great man. This brings success. Perseverance furthers. To bring great offerings creates good fortune. It furthers one to undertake something.*

This hexagram is about the workings of ego-logic, compared to the transformations brought about by Cosmic Logic. The collective ego works through diverting the individual from looking at the primary premise or assumption on which its whole existence is based. All the lines have to do with this diversion, which continues while, at the same time, the collective ego is gathering more and more followers.

The circular logic of the collective ego is shown here in the image of a king, who, after having deified his ancestor, subsequently uses the ancestor to legitimize himself as his designated heir and ruler (the "Son of Heaven"). The building in which the dead ancestor is kept is made "sacred," as indicated by the word "temple." A ritual surrounds the ceremony of his legitimation with mystery, and a taboo is placed against questioning how the ritual (or game) has come into being. These measures ensure that no one shall question how the collective ego works, or realize how it supports itself. The second part of The Judgment defines how the people are to relate to the king: to see him as the great man. "Furthering" means: seeing him as great is necessary "if you want to have success within the system." "Perseverance furthers" means that success is to be attained through dedicated subservience, "great offerings," and the shouldering of societal duties. These societal duties are embodied in loyalty to the collective ego and its values.

In the Cosmic Logic, it is the Sage that approaches humankind. It approaches each individual uniquely, in relation to where each person is in his development; it never speaks to people as "the masses."

Instead of collecting the masses around a belief that puts a human leader in the center, the Sage helps each person to see and realize his own inner truth. Instead of requiring "great offerings," as in sacrificing one's true nature (individuality) and energy (effort and money) to the collective ego, the Sage helps a person free his true nature from the small programmatic phrases by which he is held in the service of the collective ego. Instead of gathering people together around an ideal, the Sage gathers people together around their inner truth. Instead of loyalty to an institution or to an ideal, the Sage supports the individual's loyalty to his inner truth. Instead of forming closed social circles defined by beliefs, the Sage shows that the forms of association need to be free to allow for transformations, as the evolution of the whole requires.

Gathering Together, in its Cosmic meaning, defines what is needed to allow the natural order of society to emerge within a group: by calling on the Sage (the Cosmic meaning of "the great man") that exists in the presence of every person, including oneself, to intervene to restrain all their egos. This brings a great success. "Perseverance furthers" means being firm and correct in saying the inner No to anytime the ego shows itself in the situation. "It furthers one to undertake something" is counsel to maintain contact with one's inner truth to the very end, by not allowing oneself to be diverted by any temptations put forward by the ego, which would destroy the natural unity and harmony of the group.

Gathering Together also concerns what rallies the wills of individuals to cooperate. Their wills can be truly rallied around the inner truth that resonates in each person individually. All appeals to the interests of a group for its own sake are short-lived and must be continually propped up through instilling fear or guilt, building up anger, or appealing to vanity, as through flattery.

In schooling, for example, the will to learn is natural: it is stimulated when what is being taught resonates with the student's inner truth, and adds genuinely to broadening his perception and understanding. The teaching of dogma, knowledge which is divorced from a feeling awareness of life, and the rote memorization of unrelated data, stifle the will to learn, turning bright students into dullards.

Spells that damage the will to cooperate are, "every group must have a leader, otherwise chaos rules" "groups are a study of egos," "everybody is out for his own interest," "not everybody has the potential for greatness," "only the family, nation, etc., can give you protection," and these commentary lines from Wilhelm, regarding The Image in this hexagram: "the superior man renews his weapons in order to meet the unforeseen," "where men gather together in numbers, strife is likely to arise," "where possessions are gathered together, robbery is likely to occur." While most of the above-mentioned phrases are true for groups dominated by the collective ego, when generalized, they have the effect of putting spells on the natural order that could otherwise become manifest.

Note: Since all lines contain infinite possibilities of interpretation, one needs to use the *rtcm* to determine if the meanings suggested here apply to the given situation. (*See* p. 736 for using the *rtcm*.)

Line 1. *There will sometimes be confusion, sometimes gathering together.*

This line points to a situation in which a person in a position of leading others, and who is normally held in their confidence, is uncertain within himself, and therefore causes them to be uncertain of him, and to resist his direction. He has relied on his inner feelings to make his decisions, but since they do not fit precisely within the framework of what the collective ego defines as right or wrong, he has doubted himself. To rectify the situation, he needs only to disperse the doubt to which they are reacting. If he will take no measures to convince them (which would only reflect that he still doubts) their confidence will be restored. If, after reflection, he is still doubtful, he needs to consult the Sage to identify and rid himself of its cause.

It will be counterproductive if his uncertainty causes him to conform to what the collective ego would say he "should" do.

"There will sometimes be confusion, sometimes gathering together" also points to a person whose wholeness has been split into parts by his adopting the idea that he has a higher and a lower nature. This gives his body and psyche unclear messages as to which part is in charge of his personality, leading to inner conflict, and in turn, to illness. The ego then proposes that the solution to the problem is to "integrate" these parts, to make them function again. This cannot succeed, however, because the dividing of his wholeness has put a spell on both his psyche and his body. His return to wholeness requires that he free himself of the spell caused by having accepted the idea that he is divided into parts.

This line also draws attention to the confusion a person falls into when he fails to question the fundamental premises or presumptions on which a belief is based. If the first premise is a half-truth (a statement based on external perception only), he needs to examine its hidden implications and ask the Sage to help free him of its negative influence. (*See* Glossary: Half-Truths.)

Line 2. *Letting oneself be drawn brings good fortune and remains blameless. If one is sincere, it furthers one to bring even a small offering.*

"Letting oneself be drawn" refers to allowing the correct way to show itself, by responding only, rather than taking the initiative. In this way, one responds to what one's inner senses say in relation to the situation of the moment, and one remains blameless. In this circumstance, the person restricts himself to saying only what he feels is correct for himself. He never tells others what they should do or how they should feel; thus, he does not lose his Cosmic Protection.

"Letting oneself be drawn" informs a person that by holding to his integrity, regardless of what others say, the help he needs will come as he needs it, since the Cosmos freely helps every person who is sincere in his way of life.

The "small offering" is the relinquishing of pride, which will enable a person to receive help from the Cosmos. Pride prevents him from accepting help from the Sage and even from other people. A prideful person may believe that his freedom lies in being totally independent of help, or he may refuse help through fear of obligation, or be embarrassed for needing help. But true independence comes from recognizing one's interdependence with all things, and one's partnership with the Sage and the Helpers.

This line can also refer to someone who is recruiting people to fight, and if necessary, to die for a cause. He draws them by pointing to dangers and evils that threaten from without, and by offering recognition and honor in exchange for obedience, risk, and service. He also relies on the musts and shoulds of the collective ego, to remind them of their duty to serve. The true danger for the individual comes from failing to say the inner No to these musts and shoulds, because they prevent him from following his inner truth.

The collective ego advises people to rely on concretized beliefs as their source of spiritual nourishment. However, when a person follows a concretized belief, he is drawn into dangers by the fact that they shut off his ability to listen to his inner senses and feelings. Moreover, the true nourishment he longs for is not to be found in belief, but only in his contact with his feelings. Nourishment cannot be drawn from a spirit that has been defined as being in opposition to the body and its feelings.

This line calls attention to concretized beliefs to which people have been drawn in large numbers, simply because they have been pronounced to be "the great truths of life." In reality, they have put spells on life that project the beliefs into reality for those who believe in them. An example is the belief that "life is suffering." In order to be true, the phrase would need to read, "life is suffering if...," because suffering is always conditional and dependent on a person's relationship with the Cosmos. Similar beliefs are: "the only rewards are in the afterlife," "life is a Vale of Tears," "life is an illusion," "life is a script written by yourself," "the end of life is death," "life sucks, and then you die," and "life is what happens while you're busy making other plans."

Line 3. *Gathering together amid sighs. Nothing that would further. Going is without blame. Slight humiliation.*

"Gathering amid sighs" can refer to a person in need, who sees himself without help of any kind, and is therefore unable to gather to his aid the Cosmic Helpers. Or, it refers to a person who would like to rely on the Sage, but his self-image of being a skeptic prevents him. In such situations, "nothing furthers." "Going is without blame" is counsel that such a person needs to reject his faulty idea or self-image. Doing so will release the block he has put on his commonsense. The commonsense is capable, all by itself, of knowing how to draw help, when to be skeptical, and when not.

Such a person in need is caught in the trap of believing only in what he sees. This makes life a burden, causing him to "sigh" as he says to himself, "there's no one to help me...I've got to do it all myself."

Another person may hold the belief that he should only trust what can be seen. Behind this belief is the image of the invisible world as "unknown" and "unknowable." He therefore unreasonably fears and distrusts it, and would not think of asking it for help. Disbelief in what is invisible also separates a person from his invisible inner senses and feelings, such as his inner senses of smell, taste, and touch, that together with his metaphorical senses, would bring him immeasurable help, and would connect him with aspects of the Cosmos that can only be felt.

The sighs indicated in this line often refer to superficial explanations of life that are fundamentally unsatisfactory, both because they exhaust the person's life force, and because they keep him from gathering the help he needs from Cosmic sources. Some of these explanations come from religion, some from philosophy, some from science. In particular are those beliefs that give only "half" an explanation of reality, because they only recognize what is seen with the outer eyes, and therefore deny the existence of the invisible Helpers. All their accounts of the "paranormal" are put into the category of the unexplainable or supernatural, and therefore "out of reach" for the person who, in reality, desperately needs to draw Cosmic Helpers. Other explanations attempt to laugh away all evidence that the invisible reality exists; still others seek to understand in ways that exclude the feelings, as when they think of "conquering" or "engineering" the unknown. The Cosmic Reality can only be accessed within, through a person's combined inner senses, and through humbling himself to ask that unknown to reveal itself to him.

People who live only in the parallel reality see "hope" as the one thing that keeps them going on through life. They say, "without hope there is nothing." This hope is coupled with sighs, because it is a coin whose back side is hopelessness. Such a person "hopes" for better times, and comforts himself with the belief that life is governed by changes, with bad times followed by good times. When the good times do not appear, however, hopelessness sets in, and the person then concludes that life is nothing but suffering. All these beliefs only perpetuate themselves and prevent the person from gathering to himself the help of the Cosmos.

Both unfulfilled hope and hopelessness make a person look for someone or something to blame. The collective ego puts the blame on the fact that life takes place on the earth rather than in heaven: it is a "dreary experience," "hard," "a Vale of Tears," a "struggle for survival," "a jungle," "an experience that is not for the timid," etc. "Going is without blame" counsels the person to say the final inner No to all such ideas that slander life, the earth, and the nature of the Cosmos. He also needs to rid himself of the spells created by these basic half-truths. (*See* p. 697, Freeing Yourself from Spells.)

A person who does not allow for the invisible world also does not allow for his true feelings, which connect him with the loving nature of the Cosmos.

This line can also refer to a person who has started to learn from the Sage, but has come either to the conclusion that the ego cannot be gotten rid of, or that the efforts needed to free his true self are too hard, or if achieved, might upset his relationships. Such ideas make him sigh, returning him to the fold of the collective ego. Among such phrases are: "you need your ego to cope with life"; "sometimes, I really like my ego"; "you can never get completely rid of your ego"; "you are born without help"; "this kind of learning is too hard"; "you have to learn through hard experience or it isn't worthwhile."

Gathering amid sighs can also refer to the person who joins those who are suffering by practicing compassion with them. In this case, nothing furthers because his belief fails to recognize that he is trying to take the place of the Helpers, rather than calling them into action. Thus, he only perpetuates the suffering. Moreover, when a person practices compassion toward another who is suffering a fate, his acts may inhibit the other's making an effort to search for the elements in himself that are the cause of his suffering. Compassion, in this case, represents an act of magnificence on the part of the person who practices it, and creates a fate for him.

Getting rid of the self-image of "being compassionate" prevents the person from getting drawn time and again into the fates of others; it also frees him to give help to others in direct response to their need. Such help is given spontaneously from the feeling of the moment, and without forethought. Indeed, during such times, the person is motivated by the Helpers. This kind of action does not create a fate.

Line 4. *Great good fortune. No blame.*

"Great good fortune" refers to gathering together all the Cosmic Helpers to come to a person's help. This is done through saying the inner No to what is incorrect in the situation, and calling on the Sage in everyone's presence to intervene.

Receiving this line may be affirming that a person is sincere in his way of life, and he therefore receives (gathers) the blessings of the Cosmos.

"Great good fortune" also refers to times when the natural order of society arises as each person follows his inner truth.

When this is the case, each individual recognizes and validates the true selves of other people, ending all envy, jealousy, feeling of inferiority, striving for position, hierarchical domination, and the need for force and external control. Then, also, no new spells coming from such ego-emotions are put on people. This natural order of society begins with the individual's consistency in divesting himself of the ego in himself. He also does not fail to say the inner No whenever the egos in others are active, or to ask for the Sage in their presence to intervene. When this practice becomes widespread, all spells that create disorder in a group become deactivated, removing all need for controls to be imposed from without. Because every person's equality and uniqueness is recognized and validated, there is happiness.

By contrast, "great good fortune," as defined by the collective ego in the context of "gathering together," only occurs when the collective ego's controls or rewards are sufficient to keep its order in place.

"Great good fortune" can also refer to a promise given by a human leader that if someone will follow *his* beliefs, he will receive the blessings of the Cosmos. In this case, the line is a warning that following another's beliefs creates a fate.

This line can also be warning a person against relying on someone who considers himself a Sage, and interprets the *I Ching* for others. The Sage does not give tasks to people who give themselves the air of "Master," "Sage," etc. The person can rely on the *rtcm* to inform him whether someone who has experience with the *I Ching* can help him understand it. A true guide will discourage any dependence on himself and encourage those he helps to learn how to communicate directly with the Sage that speaks through the *I Ching*.

A person who seeks out or follows people who give themselves the titles of masters, often labors under spells that put his own commonsense down, such as: "you can't trust your senses/feelings," "what the leaders say is true because you can see it" [calling attention to half-truths that are based on what is seen]. Other spells that keep a person from communicating directly with the Sage may have to do with fears of punishment, or feelings of guilt that arise when he questions his established beliefs;

these spells make him adopt the "comfortable approach," as in, "my guru tells me what to do; I don't have to worry about making mistakes." (*See* p. 697, Freeing Yourself from Spells, and p. 693, Freeing Yourself from Fears.)

Line 5. *If in gathering together one has position, this brings no blame. If there are some who are not yet sincerely following their inner truth, being firm in what is correct is needed. Then remorse disappears.*

Through making continuous efforts in ridding himself of mistaken ideas and beliefs, and thereby uncovering his true self, a person automatically finds himself a center for gathering others around him, whose true natures have been suppressed. There is the danger that they might want to follow him because they have been taught to follow an authority. In this case, they are "not yet sincere in following their inner truth." "Firm and correct" refers to their learning to say the inner No to any dependence on human authority; otherwise there will be remorse.

There will also be remorse for the person who gathers others around him, if he grandiosely concludes from this that it is his destiny to be a leader. It is a Cosmic Principle that a person may not allow the ego to usurp and use the confidence of those who gather around him. When the ego becomes involved, there is the danger that he puts spells and poison arrows on the people around him, to the effect that they establish him as their leader, and they look up to him for recognition and authorization. In this way, what could be a group with a natural order is turned into a group that takes on the hierarchical structure of the collective ego's order. When this happens, the Sage uses the mistake to teach everyone in the situation the consequences of violating the Cosmic Principles of equality, uniqueness, and loyalty to one's inner truth. The person receiving this line may be experiencing those consequences in the form of a fate. In this case, he is informed that he can free himself of his fate by ridding himself of the mistaken ideas listed below. (See p. 692, Freeing Yourself from a Fate.)

This line also refers to how the collective ego appropriates (gathers) a person's Cosmic Virtues and the virtues intrinsic to his nature, and puts them up as virtues that people need to acquire, under its tutelage. The collective ego then turns these virtues into moral requirements that are used by it to suppress the person's true nature. Thus, loyalty, for example, which in Cosmic terms means being loyal to one's inner truth, is turned into loyalty to the collective ego's institutions, regardless of what the person's inner truth tells him.

Some seed phrases in connection with this line spell out values of the collective ego which place a person in conflict with his inner truth: "a good citizen is also a patriot," "my country, right or wrong," "there must be a head of the family/ship/nation, if there is to be order," "someone needs to be in command," "every henhouse needs a rooster," "you must have goals to get ahead in life" (the goals being those of the collective ego), "order needs to be implemented."

These phrases show that the collective ego's order is hierarchical, and made up of rules which are imposed either blindly or factionally, and so are the source of repetitive fates. Only when the seed phrases that justify such structures and rules are taken away, and people's true natures are freed, can the natural order, which is a *feeling* order, emerge. The natural order exists whenever these conditions occur.

The natural order of society can also be called the symbiotic order because it is based on the individual's unity with the Cosmos. When each person brings himself into harmony with the Cosmos, the order that results for the group is also in accord with the Cosmos.

Line 6. *Lamenting and sighing. Floods of tears. No blame.*
This line refers to a person who is despairing because he has been on the path of someone else's truth and has come to its inevitable "dead end." (He was meant to follow his own unique path, with his inner truth as guide.) He entered this path when he accepted the idea (and the spell it put on his inner truth) that "his feelings could not be trusted, and that he therefore needed to follow someone who knows the truth." Having now come to the dead end, he may seek refuge in the belief "that his

only hope lies in the afterlife." This thought gives his body (and his will) the message that it needs to die. With the will to live given up, all the chi energy leaves the body, causing an illness that will lead to that goal. Consciously or subconsciously giving the body such messages is the cause of most cancer. Even flirting with such ideas causes illness that can lead to death.

This line spells out the Cosmic Principle that every life has a purpose, and that to question why he is alive, or to doubt the fundamental purpose of his life creates a fate. Doing so is a luxurious attitude that comes from the human-centered view of the Cosmos.

Just as the natural social order described in Line 5 is a symbiotic one, health is also an unimpeded symbiosis among all aspects of the body. Thus in the brain, for example, there is no natural dominance or superiority of the forebrain over the rest of the brain, nor is there superiority of thinking over feeling. When one part dominates another, an imbalance is created that causes susceptibility to illness.

46. *Pushing Upward/Being Lifted Up by the Helpers*

 K'un
Sun

The Judgment: *Pushing Upward has supreme success. One must see the great man. Fear not. Departure toward the south brings good fortune.*

The Cosmic theme of this hexagram is how inner development leads to the fulfillment of one's life. Supreme success, in Cosmic terms, is achieved through freeing the true self by subtracting, step by step, the false inner program of the collective ego. Each subtraction of a false seed phrase or image initiates a transformation that involves being lifted up by the Helpers of the invisible world.

By contrast, the attainment of supreme success is presented by the collective ego as ascending to a high position (in society, business, spirituality, etc.), through accommodating oneself to the collective ego's values and rules. Success, in ego terms, involves pushing upward through mental effort and external action. In the latter, the person is without the aid of the Cosmic Helpers; he must battle through his difficulties alone. In the course of these battles, he invariably runs into conflict and uses power, and thus creates a fate. Cosmic success is achieved through *inner* action that is directed at bringing oneself into harmony with the Cosmic Way. It is carried out simply, without ambition, and through asking for help. The result is success.

Receiving this hexagram is counsel to make a decision between these two paths. Where he puts his wish, he puts his will: is it the path of his unique destiny that he alone can trod by following his inner truth, or the one laid out by ancient wisdom that has been trodden by others?

"Pushing upward has supreme success" refers to getting past obstructions and difficulties in a specific way: through saying the inner No to their causes, and asking for help from the Cosmic Helpers. "One must see the great man" refers, in this hexagram, to the Helper of Transformation, which is called forth by turning within in meditation, and asking for help. "Departure toward the south" points to the direction in which one finds this help: within, rather than "up," as in heaven. "Fear not" counsels that if a person does this, he can safely let go of the dread he may have of what will happen.

With regard to the individual ego, this hexagram points to its ambition to remain in control of the personality. The thing the ego most dreads is the person's self-examination that would expose its tricks and manipulations; therefore, once a person has decided to undertake the liberation of his true self, the ego's first move is to join the effort with gusto. Just as it had once eagerly set itself goals of brilliance, power, and success in worldly attainments, it now renounces them, and puts up the values associated with self-development that will show it as "modest," "true," "spiritual," and "devoted." It then proceeds, if not halted, to beat the person to death, if necessary, to prove itself "devoted."

It is the purpose of the many ascetic and complicated rituals and practices associated with self-development to divert the person from ever seeing that accessing the Sage is meant to be simple and direct. The lessons with the Sage always have a liberating effect, at every step, whereas self-development through the ego enslaves the person more and more. The ego is ever goal-oriented, and discovering its goal-orientation is one of the ways to catch on to its presence and trickery. Its means of "pushing upward" is one of the upgrade features of the collective ego's program, which allows the ego to adapt to the shifts and turns the person makes as he tries to get free of it.

Sometimes a person receives this hexagram as confirmation of the help that has followed his relating to a situation harmoniously, as after he has said the inner No to wrong intentions on the part of someone, and then turned the matter over to the Cosmos. Being pushed upward refers to the transformation that takes place when he has correctly said the inner No.

Spells connected with this hexagram have to do with traditional interpretations that suggest the desirability of pushing upward on a "ladder of success" (the success defined by the collective ego), and making the effort required to overcome obstructions, as through taking competitive examinations, accommodating oneself to rules and regulations, and integrating them into one's mental program. The person is asked to bend himself around the resulting obstructions, and to stretch himself to tolerate them as "normal," rather than looking into their causes and saying the inner No to them. These spells include phrases such as: "accommodation and integration are part of the civilized way," "you can't fight City Hall," "nothing comes from nothing," "no pain, no gain," "tolerance of ideas means integrating them," "just go with the flow," and "the way to overcome obstructions is to bend to the fact that they are harder than you are."

Many misinterpretations of the traditional *I Ching* come from commentaries that have misrepresented Nature's way, as in this case, where seedlings are pictured as pushing upward through the soil with *effort*; in reality, they are pushed up through the soil by the Helpers of Nature, which achieve things through transformation. From these misinterpretations, false analogies have been drawn and applied to human life as "wisdom taken from Nature." Wilhelm says in his commentary, "Pushing upward indicates rather a vertical ascent—direct rise from obscurity and lowliness to power and influence."

Note: Since all lines contain infinite possibilities of interpretation, one needs to use the *rtcm* to determine if the meanings suggested here apply to the given situation. (*See* p. 736 for using the *rtcm*.)

Line 1. *Pushing upward that meets with confidence brings great good fortune.*

This line describes the true confidence that grows from following our inner truth and finding that we are pushed upward out of our difficulties by the Helpers. This confidence comes from repeatedly experiencing the reliability of the Sage's guidance and help to understand the hidden factors in situations. It happens gradually, through taking small steps of trust by temporarily suspending one's disbelief. The inner growth achieved differs from faith, which requires a person to put aside his commonsense in favor of trusting an abstract concept taught to him by human authorities.

To develop a direct personal communication with the Sage, the person needs to remove the spells that have been put on his commonsense. (*See* below.) Receiving this line is to reassure him of the great good fortune that comes when he builds confidence in this one-to-one relationship with the Sage.

This line may also point to a person's lack of confidence in his feelings, or a doubt that he will receive help from the Sage or Helpers *in time*. Lack of such confidence in his feelings points to phrases operating in his inner program that say, "I can't trust my feelings," or, "if everything depends on the Helpers, how do I know they will come in time?" (*See* p. 689, Freeing Yourself of Seed Phrases and Images.)

This line can also indicate the presence of a self-confidence coming from the ego that gives the person the impression that his undertakings will be supremely successful. He can use the *rtcm* to find out whether this meaning is intended, and if so, the causes of his false confidence.

Line 2. If one is sincere, it furthers one to bring even a small offering. No blame.

This line calls a person to make a "small offering" that will restore him to his wholeness and free him from blame. Small, here, gives the clue that one or more seed phrases are indicated, which are at the root of great trees of thought. The object is not to deal with the whole tree, but to identify and extinguish the seed that has given rise to it. Throughout the *I Ching,* "making an offering" means to divest oneself of a mistaken idea or belief by saying the inner No to it in a short meditation. The offering referred to here is the idea of original sin/guilt, and the beliefs it has given rise to, that, due to their false nature, cause real blame.

The single idea of original sin is such a seed, because it is a slander put upon Nature itself, of which we humans are one aspect. When a person possesses this idea, which has given rise to the belief that the self is divided into spirit, mind, and body, he wants to push himself up and out of his slandered animal nature. This impulse to escape his own nature provides the entire basis of the hierarchical view of the universe, and of the human effort to escape the influence of the body by becoming spiritual, meaning "non-animal," or "incorporeal" (without body). The idea of humans as potentially spiritual provides the basis for seeing humans as being at the center of the universe. All these derivative beliefs, which come from the one belief that a person's original nature is flawed or tainted, separate humans from the Cosmic Unity, and are the real causes of blame. This is because the demonization of any part of one's nature causes that part to become perverted.

The way for a person to get out of his difficulties is not to sacrifice any part of his nature, but to divest himself of the above beliefs, and the seed phrases which give rise to them. By firmly rejecting them, he draws the Sage and the Helpers from retirement to push him upward out of his difficulties.

This line can also refer to the help that pushes the person upward. It may come as an unexpected and unusual event that some people would call a miracle or "supernatural"; it is the ordinary way Nature creates transformations, when it is not blocked by our fixed ideas of how things are "supposed" to work.

Line 3. *One pushes upward into an empty city.*

This line is similar to Line 3 of Hexagram 3, *Making a New Beginning*, which speaks of a person who hunts deer without the aid of the forester (the Sage), who knows where the deer are, and how to kill them. Such a person only loses his way in the forest, which represents the demonic sphere of consciousness created by the collective ego. Here, the empty city refers to a place from which the Helpers have withdrawn. This means an institution, an imagined solution, a direction, or an attitude which does not contain the possibility of progress, because of the entirely mental approach used there, that ignores them. The line may also refer to a person's demanding or presumptuous attitude toward the Sage, or the Helpers.

The "empty city" is also a metaphor for the emptiness of hoping. Hoping is never in harmony with the Cosmic Way, because it is focused on the future, due to the assumption that there is no help in the present. The person hoping does not realize that he can receive immediate help if he will say the inner No to hoping, and ask the Cosmos for help.

The empty city may also refer to the place, such as an imaginary heaven, for the fulfillment that he deems to be unattainable on the earth. This amounts to a statement that he has ruled out the possibility of help coming, in this life, from the Helpers. No amount of hope will bring about a satisfactory conclusion, so long as such views, and the fears and doubts that are behind them, prevail. What must be addressed are these fears, doubts, false convictions, and his reliance on hoping. Then, the Sage and the Helpers will be freed to come.

Line 4. *The King offers him Mt. Chi. Good fortune. No blame.*

"The King offers him Mt. Chi," refers to a person's progress toward reunification with the Cosmic Whole. Through ridding himself of the errors mentioned in the previous lines, the person is "lifted up"—reunified with the whole through transformation. The King here refers to the Helper that lifts him up out of his difficult situation.

When, however, Mt. Chi is taken as a symbol for a "sacred" mountain, the line can indicate that a person needs to free himself of the self-image of "being spiritual." The person who has climbed Mt. Chi flatters himself that he has attained spiritual enlightenment, and a connection with heaven. In his mind, "climbing the sacred mountain" is the spiritual journey that will free him of the earthiness of his nature, and thereby bring about his wholeness. The half-truth of this idea is obvious when we ask, "wholeness of what?" A person who seeks to elevate himself out of his body is not achieving wholeness, for wholeness is to fully embrace all of one's being. This embrace is possible only by divesting oneself of all beliefs that divide the personality up into parts, and all hierarchical views that place one part as higher than, or superior to, another. When a person elevates himself above his body, which connects him with the source of the very life, what he unifies with is death. The mind and "soul" draw all their energy from the person's true nature. The mind is a part of the psyche. All parts of the body/psyche are different kinds of consciousness, that are meant to function in complementary ways to enhance life. (*See* Glossary: Soul.)

Transformation occurs when a person says the inner No to these ideas and beliefs which flatter the mind and separate the person from his unity with Nature. Such self-flattery denigrates the earth and all things natural.

Line 5. *Perseverance brings good fortune. One pushes upward by steps.*

Pushing upward by steps points to the way we make true progress. Every mistaken idea we have ever entertained, including those from our earliest childhood, remains in our mental program until such time as we bring it into full consciousness and reject it. This process is carried out under the guidance of the Sage that alone knows the next step which is appropriate for each individual. The process continues until the mental program is fully deprogrammed, and the person is his true self once again. A certain dedication and perseverance is required, but all is made easier when we ask the Helper of Self-Examination to bring the ideas to mind and to erase them.

Perseverance, in its ego-meaning, is often associated with images such as "putting your nose to the grindstone," or pursuing something doggedly. Such an attitude is one which allows the ego to be the hunter of the ego, something that certainly will not lead to success. The steps the Sage wants us to take have a constancy that is free of pressure. The Sage and the Helper of Self-Examination do all the "scheduling" for us, bringing the lessons to us one after the other in the form of life situations. In this way, the life situations are corrected, while the lessons are being learned as part of the economy and practicability of the Cosmic Way. When a person finds himself asking, "Is there something I need to correct today?" when no problems exist, he is being too ambitious. He needs only to respond to questions and situations that come to his attention, to progress smoothly. Otherwise, he is meant to enjoy his life.

The line also points to phrases which assert that "inner work is difficult," or that one "cannot meditate." (*See* Hexagram 52, *Meditating*.) Self-examination can indeed be easy, if the person rids himself of the seed phrases that misrepresent perseverance. They assert that "anything worthwhile requires hard work, asceticism, and rigorous discipline," a view which projects itself into reality. Correctly viewed, perseverance is the process whereby a person consistently brings himself into harmony with the Cosmos, because it allows him to throw off one burden after another. The goal is not that of climbing upward to *attain* wholeness, as through cultivating abstract virtues, engaging in positive thinking, or following someone's footsteps, nor is it climbing upward to attain heaven itself. It is rather a stepping *down* from all pretenses and ambitions that require such efforts. Thus, the humble person allows himself to be pushed upward by the Helpers. A phrase that often undoes the good results is, "it can't be that easy." Doubts of this kind and other efforts of the ego to denigrate self-correction need to be intercepted immediately, and deprogrammed.

Line 6. *Pushing upward in darkness. It furthers one to be unremittingly persevering.*

"Pushing upward in darkness" refers to blind impulse, driven by the ego. A person presses forward in a goal-oriented way under the conviction that some progress will be achieved. As mentioned in the general text of this hexagram, we are not meant to be goal-oriented toward a mentally conceived end. Because such efforts exclude the Helpers, the most such a person can achieve is a temporary conformity to his wishes, or the attainment of an ego-goal.

The person receiving this line is counseled to seek out and deprogram hidden seed phrases that have formed themselves into imps, which push him to act impulsively. The imps then cause him to invest in false enthusiasms (*see* Line 3). The common theme behind these phrases is the attainment of "supreme success." If the goal is money or fame, the imps drive the person to sell his dignity to attain it. If the goal is spiritual perfection, the person may sacrifice his health, friends, or possessions. The careful path of following one's inner feelings by small steps never elicits this kind of enthusiasm.

"To be unremittingly persevering" here is incorrect advice, when it is taken to mean "constant effort," the reason being that no room is given for the Helper of Transformation to do its part. It is the one that helps the correct effort along, and completes the awareness through transformation. Effort "furthers" only when the person moves forward after having gained clarity, or when there are clear indications from the Helpers that it is time to take inner or outer action.

A person often receives this line when he has made a great effort to follow the Sage's counsel, but has not achieved the expected result. This is because the ego has ambitiously taken charge and made him slavishly follow each word of the *I Ching* text, while chastising him for every mistake. This has blocked both the Sage and the Helper of Transformation. To free these Helpers, he needs to say the inner No to his slavish efforts at pleasing the Sage, as if the Sage were his superior.

This line can also refer to a person who thinks that he has been spiritually awakened. To bring himself back into harmony with the Cosmos, he needs to free himself of the self-image of the awakened person.

47. *Oppressing/Exhausting*

 Tui
K'an

The Judgment: *Oppressing. Success. Perseverance. The great man brings about good fortune. No blame. When one has something to say, it is not believed.*

Oppressing/exhausting refers to a condition of oppressing or of being oppressed, of exhausting or of being exhausted, a state that we often call depression. A person may receive this hexagram even when his depression is scarcely recognized as such and he only goes about yawning and being tired, without any apparent reason.

The message given by this hexagram in the word "success" is that the condition, with all its destructive effects, can be ended if the person will relate to it in the correct way, as explained below. Certainly, the person in a state of depression or exhaustion, upon hearing these words, might find them hard to believe, because the ego in him says that there is " no other way" or "no way out."

Oppressing/exhausting primarily refers to situations that continually exhaust a person's reservoir of chi energy, or life force—the energy drawn from his true self, and given to him at birth. Under normal conditions, the reservoir would be continuously replenished by the person's harmonious contact with others and with Nature, through his feelings. However, the social conditioning by which he has developed an ego, or perhaps certain traumatic experiences, have cut him off from his feelings and from the ability to have the healthy exchanges he needs with Nature and with people. Furthermore, the ego in him, which is a parasite in his psyche, constantly sucks on the reservoir of chi energy that the true self possesses. This ends with the person becoming starved for chi; the feelings of exhaustion he experiences are due to the true self's fears of being extinguished through loss of chi.

Oppressing secondarily refers to the influence of doubts implanted in the psyche by the collective ego during youth. These doubts suggest that help from the Cosmos is either insufficient to cope with the difficulties at hand, is not forthcoming, or simply does not exist. They further assert that the person himself is unable to cope with the difficulties and that the only help available is what the institutions and ideologies of the collective ego have to offer. Once these doubts have been activated, every possible threat on the horizon comes to mind, creating a mountain of seemingly insoluble difficulties.

At the core of this problem is a sleight-of-hand trick played by the collective ego. It switches our natural recognition of our reliance on the Cosmos (from which we receive everything we need) to a false dependence on the collective ego, through its assertion that we are, by our natures, insufficient. Our need to cooperate with the Cosmos is due to the interdependence that exists between all aspects of the Cosmic Whole. The collective ego would call this a fault, whereas the person who is in harmony with the Cosmic Whole experiences this interdependence as a fulfillment and blessing.

Interdependence with the Cosmos does not have the bad taste that comes from being dependent on the collective ego, because the Cosmos does not have strings attached to its gifts. Likewise, the Cosmos does not supervise our behavior with a judgmental attitude. The person himself is the entire source of the feelings of blame that he experiences when he betrays his true nature. Thus, being in harmony with the Cosmos is the source of a person's true *inner independence* from the collective ego and its oppressive ways.

The exhausting effect of doubt needs to be recognized, so that the phrases and images it consists of can be deprogrammed. The following is a list of mistaken ideas and beliefs about oneself, about life, and about the nature of the Cosmos, which are expressed as oppressive views, or doubts. Included also are self-images that lead to lifestyles that are oppressive. All of these ideas, beliefs and self-images can form spells and poison arrows that effectively lock him into an inner prison.

• **To be good means to be self-sacrificing.** This allows others to draw endlessly on a person's chi energy, and creates a situation of co-dependency. It prevents both sides from asking for help from the Cosmos. A similar idea is: **life has meaning only through self-sacrifice.** This idea, fostered by the collective ego, when followed through, leads to the extinction of the true self, leaving what is elsewhere in this book referred to as a "walking dead person." (See Glossary: Walking Dead Person.)

• **A person has no right over his own inner space.** This allows others to repetitively encroach into his inner space and steal his energy.

• **A person is solely responsible for his success.** This allows the ego to climb to great heights, only to experience its inevitable collapse. The resulting depression comes from the ego's reaction to failure.

• **A person's natural inhibitions block him from experiencing life.** This leads him to constantly override his natural inhibitions, causing him to enter a downward vortex that ends in despair.

• **The body is a servant to the mind.** This leads a person to indulge in work-overload and can lead to chronic illness or burnout. (*See* Hexagram 16, *Enthusiasm.*)

• **The body's needs are unimportant.** This leads to neglect of the body in one way or another, causing its consciousness to suffer, which is the depression experienced.

• **A person's identity is determined by what he surrounds himself with.** This causes his personal space to become overcrowded, either by people, animals, or objects, or overgrown with plants.

• **A person's freedom and independence come from his external circumstances.** He is therefore cast into depression when those circumstances suddenly change.

• **Love does not last, or does not exist.** This leads to relationships that are based on deals, and therefore take, rather than generate, chi energy, causing depression and exhaustion.

• **Help is not, or may not be available from the Cosmos for me.** This causes him to make deals that compromise his dignity, or cause him to sell himself and his capacities short.

• **No one is sufficient unto himself.** This causes him to look up to others, thus giving them his chi energy. (*See* Hexagram 16, *Enthusiasm*, Line 3.)

• **The belief in passivity.** This belief has been traditionally read into the *I Ching* as the way to success. It leads a person to endlessly tolerate others' ego demands and caprices, thereby to being oppressed. Such endless perseverance has the wrong effect of condoning other peoples' wrong behavior. This idea of an absolute passivity has come from reading the word "perseverance" as an abstract command to endure evil conditions, or make an unremitting effort, beyond the limits of commonsense.

• **A person who has invested heavily in a self-image of "being the best"** can fall into deep depression when toppled or exposed.

• **Spells a person puts on himself or others by saying "he is unable to do this (or that),"** depress or repress his ability (Helper) to do those things.

• **Promises of any kind** create depression, because they are based on the human-centered pretense that a person has absolute control over his future. They bind him rigidly, so that there is no room for growth and for responding to changed circumstances. Furthermore, making promises invites a fate that will overturn them.

• **It is necessary to defend and to justify one's inner truth in words.** The person who does this throws his chi energy away, and becomes exhausted through empowering the ego in himself, which is the element making the defense. Such a person may be seeing himself as the "valiant defender of truth," and does not realize that Cosmic Truth needs no defense.

Generally speaking, depression is a state in which a person's *will* is acted upon by thoughts and emotions that form a negative energy vortex. Once a person steps onto the edge of this vortex, which happens whenever he entertains any of the above thoughts, beliefs, or self-images, he is pulled downward farther and farther until he finds himself in a pit of despair/exhaustion. This is the opposite of the effect described in the preceding hexagram, *Pushing Upward*, where the Helpers lift a person up. In every situation of oppression, the prison is first and foremost an inner one, for even in the most desperate circumstances, the person who does not allow his will to waver draws all the energies of the Cosmos to his help and protection.* Thoughts and emotions that pull a person into the vortex are: "it is too late to rectify matters," "I'm beyond help," or "the situation cannot be changed." Self-accusations cite one's "inadequacy," "defective nature," and "inability of having a relationship." Distrust, likewise, generates its own group of negative thoughts that make a person feel deprived or discarded, as in "everything is a lie." Beliefs in Fate as an arbitrary and inevitable force cause a person to see himself as "ill-fated." Such beliefs give rise to expressions such as, "Nobody cares whether I live or die," "people don't care," "the only thing to look forward to is death," and "the world is evil."

Freeing oneself from depression is a process of saying the inner No to each and every negative thought or emotion that approaches. This exercise builds and rallies a person's will to stand up to the difficulties of the moment. Soon he finds that the assault of the negative force, which comes in waves, diminishes in power. Throughout this process, the Sage continues to offer him encouragement and inner nourishment. This resoluteness allows him to look for spells and poison arrows from which he needs to free himself. In looking for and deprogramming spells, phrases, ideas, and beliefs, he finds that the collective ego is the prison, and the individual ego the gatekeeper; dispelling takes them apart, piece by piece, thus depriving them of their power. Once again, the person is able to breathe the clean, fresh air outside the prison, and to see and feel the bountiful, beautiful Cosmos, with which he is reunited.

This road to recovery is expressed in the words, "the great man brings about good fortune." The great man refers to the Sage that helps break the spells. It also helps us recognize that the ego is an interloper in the psyche, and not the true "I" it pretends to be, when it takes over to speak for the personality. It is the envious rival and enemy of the true self, constantly busy undermining and repressing it. Furthermore, it only uses the

---

*One is reminded of Dostoyevsky's account of the Russian prince who was put in prison by the Czar, and who sang every day in his cell, to the amazement of all his fellow cellmates.

psyche as a springboard to attain recognition for itself. As an instrument of the collective ego and a parasite within the psyche, it will walk over the corpse of its host, if necessary, to attain its goal of either gaining the collective ego's recognition or its pity; the first through attaining fame and immortality, the second through living up to the self-image of being "the poor victim of a hostile Fate."

The depressed person may need to form one or more hexagrams, and with the help of the *rtcm*, identify the phrases and images which form the problematical beliefs. (*See* p. 689, Freeing Yourself from Seed Phrases and Images, and p. 697, Freeing Yourself from Spells and Poison Arrows.)

Note: Since all lines contain infinite possibilities of interpretation, one needs to use the *rtcm* to determine if the meanings suggested here apply to the given situation. (*See* p. 736 for using the *rtcm*.)

Line 1. *One sits oppressed under a bare tree and strays into a gloomy valley. For three years one sees nothing.*

"One sits under a bare tree" shows a person in a state of depression for one or more reasons. In one example, a person's efforts may have turned out to be fruitless (the "bare tree"), and he is accusing himself of being guilty for having failed. The effect of guilt is that it collapses a person's will to live, and on this account is life-threatening. Guilt is a term that has no Cosmic basis, but was invented by the collective ego to keep the individual under its control. This line tells the person that his failure is a fate that has been caused by his having acted against his true nature. It further tells him that his present fate can be ended the moment he recognizes and frees himself from the mistaken ideas that have caused it. (*See* p. 692, Freeing Yourself from a Fate.) It is also telling him that he needs to stop blaming himself, otherwise he will create another fate. (*See* p. 50: Guilt, Blame, and Shame.) It will help if he is aware that the ego has a vested interest in keeping him attached to feeling guilty, therefore will suggest such phrases as, " it is impossible to rid oneself of guilt," or "you can only get free of it through making big self-sacrifices." He must reject such rationales by saying the inner No to them. (*See* p. 696, Freeing Yourself from Guilt.)

509

This line also applies to the person who has created a fate for himself by adopting the idea (a spell) that "there is no meaning in life." Continuing to rationalize about the meaning of his life brings him to one dead end after another (the meaning of "For three years one sees nothing"), and prevents the Sage from revealing the meaning of his life to him. He needs to free himself from the spell caused by those original words.

This line also applies to the person who is allowing the ego to rant in his psyche in "dark terms" that find fault with everything. He allows it because he is still unaware that it is not his true self speaking, but an interloper that needs to be silenced with a firm will, by saying the inner No to each of its phrases.

Line 2. *One is oppressed while at meat and drink. The man with the red knee bands is just coming It furthers one to offer sacrifice. To set forth brings misfortune. No blame.*

This line shows a person who, although he does not lack outer nourishment, including material comforts, is psychically oppressed. The cause for his oppression can be his dissatisfaction with the commonplaces of life (the meaning of life as defined by the collective ego), which have absorbed all of his attention, and obscured his life's true meaning. The Sage has been coming to him in dreams and/or meditations to make him aware that his life has a Cosmic purpose which the Sage can help him fulfill, if he will allow it. (The red knee bands here are a reference to the Sage, and to the often odd guises in which it shows itself in dreams or meditations, e.g., as limping.)

The cause of oppression can also lie in a number of mistaken beliefs a person has about his own nature, the most oppressing being that his "animal nature is evil, or is the cause of evil." As has been pointed out in the main text of this hexagram, it is through his animal nature (bodily nature) that a person is connected with the Cosmos, the source of his chi energy. By putting a spell on his animal nature, he has demonized it, and the chi energy is blocked. The above-mentioned spell can be accompanied by a guilt spell that makes the person feel guilty every time he gives bodily expression to love. This feeling of guilt can be conscious or completely subconscious, but in any case it draws on the reservoir of chi energy that has been given to his true self at birth by the Cosmos. The reference to sacrifice in this line points to the fear of his true self of being sacrificed to his feelings of guilt.

Reference to the "man with the red knee bands" can also indicate a Cosmic intervention by the Sage when a person is unconsciously giving assent to the execution of his true self, because he thinks himself guilty for living. The intervention comes perhaps as a dream or an experience in meditation that shows him that his true self has become a stranger to him. For example, he may be seeing himself giving his consent to an execution, either his own, or another's.

The guilt spell has its roots in his having been told that his animal nature is the source of evil. If he will free himself of that idea and its associated guilt spell, he will be freed from all blame (the meaning of "no blame"), and from the fate he has created. Otherwise, the misfortune indicated, the extinction of his true self, will run its course. (*See* p. 697, Freeing Yourself from Spells, and p. 696, Freeing Yourself from Guilt.)

This line can also refer to a person who has become one of the "walking dead," through consenting to the execution of his true self. He continues to live only by drawing chi energy from other people, animals, food, and from objects in his environment that are dear to him. (*See* Glossary: Walking Dead Person.)

This line is also given to a person who has been coping with a difficult situation with help from the Sage (the "meat and drink" received), to help him understand why the situation lacks visible progress. Behind his depression is the ego, which is saying, "I will only follow the Sage's advice if the situation changes right away." Sacrifice here means to say the inner No to the ego and its demands, and reopen his mind. This will free him of the ego's oppressive influence.

Similar interferences of the ego occur to keep a person from starting to cooperate with the Sage, and thus prevent the person from obtaining the "meat and drink" offered by the Sage: "maybe it would be better if things did not work out," "it's not possible to get rid of my ego, and it might not even be desirable," "maybe I won't be able to afford the change," "maybe we wouldn't like each other after all," etc.

The line may also point to ideas that feed the ego, by claiming to help the person develop his higher nature (as by becoming a hero) and shed his lower nature. The idea of developing his higher nature is associated with public recognition for doing good works: achieving victory in war, or victory over ignorance, as defined by the collective ego. The ego is similarly fed by a person's identification with the heroic, as by reading novels, or by identifying with social groups that perform good works. The inflation of the ego that occurs through a person's identifying with others blocks the renewal of his own chi energy that would come from his honoring his own true nature. To free the flow of his chi energy, he needs to free himself from the spell he has put on his true nature by dividing it into higher (heroic/good) and lower (non-heroic/evil) aspects. Such a division has placed a guilt spell on his "lower" nature. (*See* p. 697, Freeing Yourself from Spells, and p. 696, Freeing Yourself from Guilt.)

Line 3. *A man permits himself to be oppressed by stone, and leans on thorns and thistles. He enters his house and does not see his wife. Misfortune.*

"Oppressed by stone" is a metaphor for a person who looks at the external world as "the only thing there is," and therefore fails to take into account that its underlying structure is the Cosmic Consciousness. It is as if such a person is blind, and his blindness isolates him from all the sources of help that come from the invisible world. His belief is like a stone that weighs heavily upon him, because it makes him think he has to "do it all himself." This belief, which leaves him both helpless and hopeless, is the cause of his depression.

Leaning on thorns and thistles is a metaphor for the constant prickling of the doubts that accompany untruths and half-truths. They are doubts a person has about his own nature, the identity of the Sage, the efficacy of following his inner truth, or whether there is an appropriate answer to the situation at hand. The untruths and half-truths behind such doubts need to be identified, with the help of the Sage and the *rtcm*, and deprogrammed through saying the inner No to them. It is never necessary to live with doubt and uncertainty, since the Sage is ever present to help the person see the matter with clarity.

Being oppressed by stone also refers to people who construct or adopt philosophies based solely on thinking and fantasizing, as their guiding principles, as is the case with materialistic or idealistic philosophies. What renders such constructions lifeless and oppressing, is their purely mental nature, which is divorced from any feeling understanding of Nature's ways. These philosophies survive mostly because they flatter the mind's image of itself as "superior" to feeling. Another example is the belief that the world is divided into spirit and matter, with spirit being conceived as a thinking consciousness that has importance or purity, and all other things as having importance only inasmuch as they serve the thinking consciousness. In this thinking, everything outside the thinking consciousness, including all animal species, plants, and the earth itself, is reduced to "matter." The misconceptions that come from such thinking divorce a person from the Cosmic Whole, and prevent him from receiving the life-renewing chi energy that would otherwise come through his feeling connection with the Cosmos. Particularly affected is the person's ability to love and to care. Beliefs that oppress a person's caring also oppress his creativity.

A related belief that causes oppression is one that sees "nothing after death"; it contains the implication that life has a beginning and an end, denying the basic continuity of life as consciousness, whether it is compressed into visible form (body), or exists in an invisible form. (See Glossary: Death.)

A person can also receive this line when, after putting a matter in the hands of the Sage or the Helpers, he has then interfered in their transforming it by falling back on conventional answers and solutions. This line informs him why the problem has not been resolved; it is also saying that he may not acquire Cosmic help so long as he persists in interfering.

Line 4. *He comes very quietly, oppressed in a golden carriage. Humiliation, but the end is reached.*

The carriage, in the *I Ching*, is a metaphor for the Helpers of the invisible world that help a person make natural progress. This line shows the Helpers oppressed because the person does not acknowledge their existence. Instead, he allows the ego to lead his affairs by relying on conventional means of protecting himself or making progress, such as by relying on policies, contrivances, or other uses of power. If he continues in this way, he will create a fate.

With a slight change of emphasis, the golden carriage can refer to a person who is forced to go the conventional route, e.g., hire a lawyer, as in divorce. However, because he recognizes that employing this kind of help is only an outer necessity, and that success really depends on the Helpers, a good end is reached, despite the humiliation of having to follow this process.

The line can also indicate a person who is weighing whether it is correct to give up his dependence on rational thinking and follow the way of the Sage. Although he has had good experiences in following the Sage's guidance (the golden carriage), he feels guilt because what he has experienced does not coincide with his previous beliefs. This conflict is the cause of his depression. If he recognizes that guilt is a mistaken idea of the collective ego, and asks the Sage to help him end the spell that guilt has created, he can end the conflict and its humiliating consequences.

Being oppressed in a golden carriage can also refer to a person who has a fixed negative image about what will happen in the future. He imagines a bad outcome to the present train of events, or thinks the worst about someone, to harden himself against him. These fixed ideas are the golden carriage mentioned, in that they keep the person from being disappointed when he fails in achieving his goals. This extremely common mindset is often accompanied by the rationalization, "I always expect the worst, and if something good happens, it's a pleasant surprise." Having such views insures that the goals will not succeed. The person needs to free himself from the power that exists in negative thinking by saying the inner No to it and by making his attitude neutral in regard to the future. (*See* p. 680, Centering Yourself.)

The golden carriage is also a metaphor for the help the Sage can draw from the Cosmos on behalf of a person. Here, however, the Sage is kept in waiting because the person is arrogantly presuming that he has a right to be helped, and is regarding the Sage as his servant. Being deprived of help, the person becomes depressed.

Line 5. *His nose and feet are cut off. Oppression by the man with the red knee bands. Joy comes softly. It furthers one to make offerings and libations.*

"His nose and feet are cut off" indicates that a Cosmic Helper has intervened against a demonic element in a person's psyche. At first the person feels this as "being oppressed" or punished by a higher power, whereas in reality a Helper is restraining him from a desire that would create danger for him. "Offerings and libations" is a metaphor for counseling the person to apologize to the Cosmos for incorrectly blaming it. Apologizing does not mean to get on his knees, or prostrate himself, but simply saying from his heart, "I am sorry." It is only the ego that would demand a person to throw away his dignity.

The metaphor of the nose in the *I Ching* stands for the inner sense of smell which normally tells a person that something in his situation "smells bad." This protects him against being irresistibly attracted to a dangerous idea coming from the ego in himself or in another. When a person regards his mind as a reliable judge of ideas and people, and disregards his feelings as unreliable, his inner sense of smell becomes demonized and made inoperative. This exposes him to the danger of falling into an unqualified attraction to the dangerous idea or person. The nose being cut off means that the Helper that counters demonic elements has intervened on his behalf to bring him back to his inner sense of smell, which has now caused him to recognize that he is "fed up" with the situation—a correct response.[*]

The metaphor of the severed feet can indicate that the Helper that counters demonic elements has put a firm grip on the imp that is blaming the person's feelings of oppression on the Cosmos, by saying it has led him in the wrong direction. The inter-

---

[*] In German, the expression is not "fed up," but "I have my nose full."

vention of this Helper has now put him back in touch with his commonsense—the meaning of "joy comes softly."

This line may refer to one or more beliefs which are put forward by such imps: that life on earth, or in a body, is "hell," and a punishment, or that the universe is hostile, or that he is ill-fated. What the person sees as punishment is the automatic Cosmic reaction to his discord. This reaction functions like a law of physics, in that the person meets the limits that apply to human behavior. Cosmic limits are like invisible walls people bump into when they act outside the limits set for humans. These limits actually serve to protect them from their egos, and to bring them back to their senses. The cutting off of the nose and feet refers to the humiliation a person feels on bumping into his limits.

Such a person can correct his situation if he recognizes his true place in the Cosmic Whole, and rejects the ego's arrogance in proposing that limits do not apply to him. Joy comes softly when he begins to take his true place in the Cosmic Whole.

Line 6. *He is oppressed by creeping vines. He moves uncertainly and says, "Movement brings remorse." If one feels remorse over this and makes a start, good fortune comes.*

Creeping vines refer to the tentacles of negative thought processes that return a person to depression after he has become free of it. Specific negative thoughts that pull him back into old patterns of thinking come from teachings he has learned previously from the collective ego, or from people who have represented its viewpoint. This happens because he has not fully validated his ability to listen to his own inner truth. As long as he validates these others as more important than himself, he will "move uncertainly," and fear that listening to his inner truth will bring remorse. If, as the line says, he feels remorse over this degraded view of himself and makes a new start by consulting his collected inner feelings, he will gather the support of the Cosmos to help him find the correct way.

This line can also refer to a person who has been intimidated through conditioning into feeling a collective responsibility for what his family, nation, or species has done. His only responsibility is to say the inner No to what others do that he *feels* to be incorrect, and thereby to withhold his inner assent. In this way, he remains free of blame. It is likewise correct for him to refuse acceptance of others' attempts to blame him, in a case where he has not inwardly participated in what is incorrect.

"Creeping vines" is also a metaphor for the guilt a person may feel because he is following the *I Ching*. The creeping vine is his suspicion that its values are subversive to the collective ego, and that he is therefore betraying it. What he must realize is that it is the collective ego and its values that undermine the Cosmic Harmony and the natural order of society. An example is the Cosmic Virtue of loyalty to one's inner truth. The collective ego appropriates this loyalty by setting it up as a virtue that he "needs to develop." What it means is that the person "should" be loyal to the collective ego's values. The collective ego demands that he renounce his inner truth, whenever it conflicts with loyalty to his partner, family, nation, race, or creed. However, only by following his inner truth can he be in harmony with himself and with the Cosmos. If he will reject his mistaken guilt, he will free himself from those tentacles and the oppression they cause. (*See* p. 696, Freeing Yourself from Guilt.)

48. *The Well*

 K'an
Sun

The Judgment: *The Well. The town may be changed, but the well cannot be changed. It neither decreases nor increases. They come and go and draw from the well. If one gets down almost to the water and the rope does not go all the way, or the jug breaks, it brings misfortune.*

Here is presented a metaphorical well, whose water represents the Cosmic Principles revealed by the Sage. It is accessed in the manner of a hand-dug well, by putting a jug tied to a rope, down to the water and drawing it up. The entire process is also a metaphor for the way a person accesses the truths of life through connecting with his own inner truth. Putting the rope down far enough describes the sincerity of effort required. It seems obvious that the jug should not be cracked, but it is mentioned here to make the person aware that if he is to be successful in drawing up the water (understand the messages received from the Sage), the jug (his attitude) needs to be clean, empty, and free of prestructured beliefs. Finally, it is not enough simply to look at the truths; to be nourishing, they need to be applied to his life.

The water of the well also represents knowledge and learning generally, whether it is from the Sage, or what a person has learned in life. "The town may be changed, but the well cannot be changed" tells a person that, while he may change his beliefs, his inner truth remains constant. Because his inner truth is always with him, and the Sage nearby in his presence, his "town" is complete. His learning can take place anywhere, and the Sage can use every situation to teach him.

The Sage teaches that everything we learn about the Cosmos is but a "handhold" to a broader understanding yet to be attained. This is due both to the limits humans have in regard to understanding something so vast as the Cosmos, and to the limitations created by language, which occur the moment we write things down as "truth." When the understanding of the moment, which is always relative to the situation at hand, is put into too definite words and phrases, the effect is to put a frame around that understanding which shuts out further questioning, new perceptions, and broader explanations. Thereafter, new situations tend to be interpreted within the old frame. This is also true for handholds of understanding, the moment we fail to see that they are but temporary positions that prepare us to move on.

In learning from the Sage, the frame the student comes with is constantly enlarged by suspending these old frames, in order to go beyond them, to see the broader view. We can understand the way language limits perception by considering that the language used by Aristotle to explain Nature's ways held the world's scientific thinking in a vise until the experiments of Newton shattered that way of explaining things. Newton's verbal explanations, in turn, held science in yet another vise of thinking, until Einstein began to speak in relative terms. In each case, the science of the time, although limited, proved applicable in many instances, but when taken as final doctrine, prevented or inhibited further discoveries. When we look for the reason that the discoveries of these men halted further learning for so long a time, we find it in the fact that the collective ego grasped their achievements and monumentalized the men themselves, in order to give yet one more "proof" of human superiority, and to create an atmosphere of awe in the face of "great men." Forgotten is the fact that such men were often the first to acknowledge that they "received their insights" from "something beyond themselves," or at least through a process that they considered mysterious and fortunate.

The student often approaches the Sage with a fixed set of beliefs that inhibit his understanding until new experiences show him their limitations. Thus, with each new experience, the student gains a partial new understanding (a handhold) that is always a preparation for a yet broader view. He eventually begins to recognize that there is never a final fixed point of reference, and that each day of learning provides new handholds.

Human learning in cooperation with the Sage is one of the ways in which the Cosmic Consciousness evolves. Participating in this evolution is a person's destiny, and is felt as personal fulfillment. Key to this evolution is the fact that every situation is unique. Discovering that uniqueness and expressing it in appropriate words adds to the Cosmic Knowledge. The pressure of the collective ego to confine human experience only to *its* preexisting and "approved" explanations is contrary to this evolution, and to the Cosmic purpose. On this account, a person feels that confining himself in this way stifles and defeats his own life's purpose.

When wisdom is taken to mean *absolute knowledge*—formed beliefs that cover not only the broadest spectrum of human behavior and activity, but also pretend to give a complete understanding of how the Cosmos functions—it is in conflict with the Cosmic Way. This is true particularly of ancient wisdom whenever it proceeds from a human-centered view of the universe.

A notable exception among the ancients were the writings of Lao Tzu, whose views allowed for the permanent expansion of learning, and discarded the human-centered view.

The Sage gives the metaphor of the well to indicate how humans, through the *I Ching*, can access their own inner truth, which is the source of all true wisdom. It is a record, as well, of the understandings attained through consulting the *I Ching*, by humans such as King Wen, the Duke of Chou, and Confucius, among others. Inasmuch as the insights attained by these people are taken as handholds, and not as doctrine, they provide the most modern reader with insights into his own behavior.

"When the rope does not go all the way" forewarns of the danger that comes when ancient wisdom, which is based on knowledge of the heart, is converted into absolute truth. Then, its connection with the heart, and its ability to serve as a medium of communication between the student and the Sage, gets lost. All ancient wisdom contains truths, but when those truths are deprived of their metaphorical quality, they can no longer connect the person with his inner truth, and nourish his heart. When people take the text literally, it loses all usefulness and relevance, and becomes a prison for the mind.

The phrase "they come and go and draw from the well," refers to the *I Ching* as a source of dependable nourishment to which they can freely come and go. Whether a person draws from the well is entirely a matter of his free will. It is dependable because it requires "going within" to search out what feels harmonious and what does not.

This metaphor can also be read incorrectly to mean that the stability of written ancient wisdom is such that the generations can come and go in the stoical attitude: "what my fathers believed is good enough for me." Such a person does not draw upon his inner truth, but upon the traditions and thinking of his forefathers. This makes him unable to understand the messages of the *I Ching*. The cracked jug, which represents his prestructured attitude, allows all the water to leak out. Such a person is under the influence of the collective ego, which has a vested interest in maintaining a fixed set of "truths," and the *status quo*, but especially those beliefs that protect its hierarchical structure and its dominance over Nature.

The man-made well also points to the attempt of the collective ego to replace a person's inner truth, the treasure with which everyone is born, with written texts that spell out the meaning of life.

Receiving this hexagram often is to inform the person that it will be impossible for him to access his inner truth if he believes that he already knows the "correct way." To communicate with him, the Sage only requires that he temporarily suspend his beliefs. Then, what he learns from the Sage will be the knowledge of his own heart, from which his beliefs have isolated him. At some other time he may be required to dispense with those beliefs, but not until he has himself experienced them as inadequate or mistaken, and only when he is ready to do that. Often this happens when the belief itself is the cause of an illness, or other galling problem in his life.

Note: Since all lines contain infinite possibilities of interpretation, one needs to use the *rtcm* to determine if the meanings suggested here apply to the given situation. (*See* p. 736 for using the *rtcm*.)

Line 1. *One does not drink the mud of the well. No animals come to an old well.*

"Mud" can refer to a person's allowing himself to be absorbed in fears, trivialities, negative thoughts about life, doubts about himself or other people, without stopping to say the inner No to the ego, which is their source. Mud also refers to these and all other kinds of ego-emotions, such as grievances, which the person is holding in his heart.

The well here is also a metaphor for the heart. An "old well" is one which has repetitively harbored ego-emotions, and thus has "shrunk" in its capacity to love or care; these ego-emotions may have encased the heart in an iron-maiden of sorts,* which prevents it from expanding when the opportunity to love occurs.

---

* An iron maiden was a torture device used by the British on prison ships during the mid 19ᵗʰ century; it was smaller in size than the person who was forced into it.

521

Because people sense when a person's heart is thus hardened, or shrunk, they avoid any sincere interaction with that person. The Cosmic Helpers, likewise, withdraw.

When the well is taken as a metaphor for a "spiritual path" that has been defined by humans, the line warns the person that the nourishment available in those beliefs has been muddied by time, and is full of pollutants. It is a warning that drinking this mud will create a fate.

Mud describes the half-truths inserted into ancient wisdom by the collective ego throughout the intervening ages, to take advantage of the good reputation and credibility of ancient wisdom, and thereby find acceptance. These half-truths reflect the hierarchical and human-centered view that competes with the Cosmic Order.

This line calls attention to half-truths that stand in a person's way to understanding the messages given by the Sage. The person is counseled to review the basic premises of his beliefs, especially their human-centered presumptions. He may be viewing the Sage as a hierarchical authority, or else see himself as such, and the Sage as beneath him. He may be requiring that the Sage "prove" itself to him. Such attitudes allow only the mud of the well to come through, reflecting the ego in himself.

A person may also receive this line when he is embroiled in mistaken ideas about life and death, such as, that death is the *end* of life. His idea of death is the mud indicated. These mistaken ideas may cause him to question the purpose of his life, a mistake described in Line 1 of the previous hexagram, *Oppressing/Exhausting*.

Spells connected with this line may have been created by phrases such as: "Life has no meaning," "what you see is all there is," "the real life is in the afterlife," "we are born as sinners," or "life is suffering."

Line 2. *At the wellhole one shoots fishes. The jug is broken and leaks.*

When the metaphor of the well is taken to mean the *I Ching*, going to the well to shoot fishes means the person is making a wrong use of the *I Ching*. He may have an attitude of superiority in approaching it, in which case the Sage will inform him that his attitude is incorrect, and then give him this line if he continues. His lack of openness is pointed to as a "jug that is broken and leaks," meaning, regardless of the good nourishment the Sage gives, he will not be able to take it in.

"The jug is broken and leaks" can also mean that a person's prefixed views have blocked his understanding the Sage's counsel.

The idea of going to a well to shoot fishes points to the way incorrect thoughts project themselves into reality. This happens when a person hypothesizes or expects a particular result (as in an experiment, or when going to a meeting, he expects conflict to arise). His projected expectation becomes an element in the situation that forms and distorts its outcome. To avoid such distortions, the person needs to say the inner No to all such expectations and hypotheses, and maintain a neutral and open mind. In and of themselves, hypotheses are not bad things. Putting them to the Sage is the way we learn the inner, or Cosmic Truth. A great many people convey ideas as truth, when in fact, they are hypotheses. The swiftest and best way to know whether they are true, is to put them to the Sage, through the *rtcm*. This line may be informing a person that he is misinterpreting the messages of the Sage for the reasons given above.

It can also be informing a person who is using the *I Ching* for divination that telling the future is not its purpose. Its purpose is to help him correct those attitudes that are negatively influencing his future, as by creating Fate.

Shooting fishes also describes the person who approaches the *I Ching* with the assumption that it will support established ancient wisdom, such as the idea "that life is ruled by changes," and that "things function through the interaction of opposite forces." In this case, the fishes represent foreign elements that have been projected onto the truths of life. People who see the world in terms of opposites see the light and the dark as opposing forces rather than complementary energies; they likewise see the male and female as having "opposite" natures, and all other things in similar categorical terms.*

This line also points to a corrupting belief (the fish) held in the psyche, which is responsible for perversions and evil that are falsely attributed to human nature: the belief that man's animal nature is the source of evil in the world. This belief, as a poison arrow, injects its poison into each person's psyche as an "inextinguishable guilt," or lack, which he must overcome. It is therefore the source of all striving, competition, feelings of self-hate and self-blame, and due to its emphasis on sexuality as evil, is also the source of sexual perversion and compulsive desire on the one hand, and self-righteousness, on the other.

Evil is not inherent in a person's nature; it is the consequence of the distortion of his nature caused by mistaken ideas. The first step a person needs to take in his efforts to liberate his true nature, is to get rid of the idea of guilt. (*See* p. 696, Freeing Yourself from Guilt.)

Line 3. *The well is cleaned, but no one drinks from it. This is my heart's sorrow, for one might draw from it. If the king were clear-minded, good fortune might be enjoyed in common.*

This line points to a person who, through studying with the Sage, understands the Cosmic Principles sufficiently, but hesitates to follow them, through fear of becoming guilty for disobeying the collective ego's shoulds and musts. This means that he has not freed himself from the fear of becoming guilty. Fear of becoming guilty is one of the safeguarding and reinstalling features of the collective ego's program, that has been installed in the psyche during childhood with considerable force. If not deprogrammed, prevents the person from accessing the nourishment coming from his inner truth.

Similarly, the line can refer to a person who has read the *I*

---

*These ideologies, which came from the animistic religions of China, were inferred to exist in the *I Ching* lines by the yin/yang school, around 400 BC. The yin/yang school saw yin and yang as opposite forces that drive change. (*See* Hexagrams 1 and 2 for a clarification of this subject.) Seeing the Cosmos and Nature as composed of opposing forces has also accompanied Western thinking, especially after the time of Aristotle, whose logic was an "either/or," good or evil system.

Ching's advice and understood it subconsciously, but has disdained or distrusted it, or has lacked the courage to put it into practice. Consequently, the benefit that would have gone to everyone involved in the situation is not enjoyed. If he recognizes the rationales that cause him to distrust his inner truth, the situation can be corrected. Among these rationales are phrases such as, "I will lose everything" (whereas in reality he would only lose the ego), and "how can that ancient book be of relevance for my present day situation?" The "ancient text" is not to be taken as maxims of truth, but as a medium through which the Sage can speak, by pointing to the seed phrases and images that create the person's misunderstandings.

Sometimes the words "the well is cleaned but nobody drinks from it" inform a person that he can trust his inner truth and follow it without harm.

Line 4. *The well is being lined. No blame.*

"The well is being lined" is often confirming that a person has truly understood a Cosmic lesson that gives him a larger understanding of how the Cosmos functions. "Being lined" means the understanding is still in the process of surfacing in his consciousness.

Because the water of the well is a metaphor for a person's inner truth, lining the well means to take away what prevents him from accessing it. Here, attention is drawn to a person's fantasy life, which is causing him to misinterpret what comes from his inner truth. An example is a person's interpreting an image seen in meditation in the context of the ancient heroic myths, whereas his inner truth is attempting to show him a demonic figure that represents a mistaken idea, belief, or self-image he holds. He needs to use the *rtcm* to verify the correct meanings in these images, and also to learn the *I Ching* way of meditating. Because the fantasy life comes from a person's ego, acting upon it creates a fate. (*See* Hexagram 52, *Meditating.*)

Receiving this line can inform a person that the fate he is experiencing is "lining his well." It is showing him, through the adversities he is experiencing, the negative effects of his fantasies. His fate will end when he has learned the lesson.

The well being lined is also a metaphor for the process of conditioning by the collective ego in which the idea of guilt or shame is introduced into the child's psyche. It is accompanied by thoughts such as, "I am born as a sinner," and "I must not do anything to shame my family." These ideas put poison arrows on his true nature which make him look at himself either as his enemy or his potential enemy.

Lining the well can also be a metaphor for self-development, when it is viewed as cultivating the "higher self." Then, self-development becomes the cultivation of a flattering self-image, such as that of the "good person," the "modest person," the "spiritual person," or the "superior man." Such self-images have the effect of creating a rigid structure (a spell) into which the true self is squeezed, and held prisoner. Such images hold the person within the definitions of good given by the collective ego. Because these definitions are abstract standards that are impossible to fulfill, the person's failure to attain them invariably leads to self-blame. The words, "no blame" indicate that he is free of blame; all he needs to do is rid himself of the poison arrow of blame, and the self-images he has adopted. (*See* p. 691, Freeing Yourself from Self-Images, p. 697, Freeing Yourself from Poison Arrows, and p. 50, Guilt, Blame, and Shame.)

Line 5. *In the well there is a clear, cold spring from which one can drink.*

The "clear cold spring from which one can drink" is the truth that springs from a person's experience of both the outer and the invisible world. The situation is one in which he has been doubting that truth. This line is given to tell him that to maintain his relationship with the Sage, he needs to make a clear choice to follow the light of his inner truth, as revealed by his own experiences.

The line is also saying that true satisfaction and nourishment come from doing a thing for its own sake and not with any motive. In whatever way a person devotes himself with sincerity to a task, he will find all the Helpers he needs to complete it.

The truth experienced by following one's inner light contributes to the constant evolution of Cosmic Truth by adding a fresh taste to it, whereas following an already lit path is like eating predigested food that adds nothing to the Cosmic Evolution.

In another meaning, this line can indicate a person who is evangelizing "universal truths" or "absolute truths." He has taken up the standard of "high moral values" and seeks to bring them to the rest of the world in the name of some idealism. He may be trying to set himself up as a leader in order to obtain followers, whose chi energy he constantly draws to himself. He proceeds by embracing their hopes for peace, prosperity, equality, justice, etc., and merging them into one belief that also integrates all the world's great beliefs to unify all mankind. However nobly expressed, his views require the individual to suppress his own inner truth, and his personal relationship with the Sage, in favor of the leader. None of his views is in harmony with the Cosmos, because they are based on the human-centered view of the universe, and on the fiction that his idealism expresses "the truth." Receiving this line can point to the person being influenced as described above, due to a spell created by the idealistic beliefs the leader has convinced him to accept. Among these are, "all great beliefs are based on the same truth and come from the same source," "the kernel of great beliefs holds the solution," "integration will remove all differences," "the world needs hope," "in their hopes, all humans are alike," "humans need to hold together in their search for the truth," "after all, we are one big human family," and "humans need to work together to solve the world's problems." (*See* p. 697, Freeing Yourself from Spells.)

Line 6. *One draws from the well without hindrance. It is dependable. Supreme good fortune.*

Receiving this line is to make a person aware that through relating to life from his heart and all his senses, he is connected with the source of life and with everything he needs.

It is also a hint to the person who has separated from his heart and his senses that he needs to recognize his separation in order to reconnect with the source of life. If he has demonized his senses through denigrating his animal nature as the source of evil, he needs to seek out, with the help of the *rtcm*, all the phrases in his internal program that have put spells on his bodily nature, and rid himself of them. (*See* p. 697, Freeing Yourself from Spells.) To insure that the spells cannot return, he also will need to rid himself of the guilt spell. (*See* p. 696, Freeing Yourself from Guilt.)

The inner truth that springs from the well can come in the form of mind-flashes (sudden clear realizations), voices heard, or images seen in meditation that always resonate with one's inner truth. Dreams also are an internal communication between one's inner truth and one's body consciousness. Even when one does not mentally understand them, they convey what the body consciousness needs to know, to react in a healthy way.

This line can also refer to a person's drinking from another well—the well of remembered insults, injuries, injustices, guilt, hurt pride, and other negative memories. He feasts on those memories, hoping that by keeping them alive, he will have some effect on the offending persons, so as to bring about his final triumph. Such a well is poisonous only to himself, and since those memories are stored in his heart, they daily shrink his ability to love and care. If continued, it will lead to his becoming a walking dead person.

The well can also stand for the pit of fears created and maintained by the collective ego, to make sure that people depend on the collective ego for protection. The fears are presented as "the basic fears of mankind," and part of the "natural order of things," against which the individual must always defend his home and livelihood. Because these fears conflict with his inner truth by obliterating his knowledge of the invisible world, such a person must constantly reiterate the fears to others, to convince himself of their truth. These fears are imps of the mind that jump from shoulder to shoulder to create mob blindness, hysteria, and wars. Demagogues (people whose egos see such hysteria as springboards to power) feed on and promote such fears. It is necessary for a person who sees such patterns at work around him to say the inner No to them. (*See* p. 693, Freeing Yourself from Fears.)

49. Renewal/Revolution/Ending Fate

Tui
Li

The Judgment: *On your own day you are believed. Supreme success, furthering through perseverance. Remorse disappears.*

The Cosmic theme of this hexagram is renewal. This word is preferable to "revolution" because the context of revolution has to do with the way the collective ego proceeds in making radical changes. Renewal has to do with the way the Cosmos transforms things constantly from within. The difference between the two is that revolution replaces one form of ego-domination by another, while renewal re-harmonizes and reunites aspects of ourselves that have been forced, or oppressively held, apart.

The word revolution also contains other negative connotations: change that goes in the opposite direction, as by raising above what used to be below, tearing down and replacing an old belief system with a new one, or burning out on an old viewpoint (belief system, enthusiasm, etc.), only to replace it with a new one.

Renewal, by contrast, implies the inner action of ridding oneself of decadent beliefs. This action restores the personality to its original strength and capabilities, in such a way as to engage the Helpers. It removes all the impediments that impair the efficient operation of one's naturally perfect inner program. It never replaces one system with another. It only eliminates what is false.

Renewal also refers to the changes that are made in another's consciousness when we say the inner No to the ego in him, and ask the Sage in his presence to displace it. This allows the other to shed the ego-aspect that is active in the particular circumstance, and relate from his true feelings. It is not a permanent change, but it brings out the best in that person during that time, and overcomes obstacles that would appear insurmountable. Relating to others in this way on a daily basis strengthens their relationship with the Sage, enabling them to recognize that the Sage exists, allowing them a glimpse of their true feelings, and to sense that something out of the ordinary has been present in the situation ("the ordinary" referring to the parallel reality created by the collective ego).

Renewal also addresses the way a fate can be ended. The fate addressed by this hexagram has been created by a person's mistaken beliefs about the origin of Fate, as when he sees Fate as the decree of a higher will, as written in the stars, in the lines of his hands, or in a script written by himself before he was born, or when he believes in "death as an inevitable fate." Such beliefs have drawn people to false conclusions about the origin of Fate, and also to false conclusions about how to relate to Fate. They fail to recognize that humans are themselves the creators of their fates through acting upon mistaken ideas and beliefs invented by the collective ego about the Cosmic Way.

A person's fate may be ended at any time by bringing his understanding into harmony with the Cosmos. Otherwise, the fate will run its course, which is a specific time, like that of a prison sentence. The length of time depends upon the degree of obstinacy and rigidity with which the person holds to his mistaken ideas and beliefs. (See p. 40, Fate.)

"On your own day you are believed" can be telling a person that he has the opportunity to end his fate, or that a fate from which he has suffered is coming to an end because it has run its full course. Remorse disappears" refers to the blame that is extinguished with the ending of the fate. The person whose fate is coming to an end is being informed that he needs to examine whether he has any feelings of guilt connected with what caused his fate, and if so, to free himself of them. (*See* p. 696, Freeing Yourself from Guilt.)

Revolution, in the sense of "revolving," i.e., turning around, can refer to the way the collective ego turns Cosmic Truth around to make it fit into its hierarchical ordering. Fate, as a Cosmic Law, is an example of this. Fate is the Cosmic reaction to discord created by the disharmonious thoughts and actions of humans. It is like a law of physics that has nothing personal about it and is easily corrected by a sincere and voluntary retreat of the person from his wrong viewpoint. The collective ego, however, presents Fate as the arbitrary judgment of a supernatural feudal lord that is leveled upon people. This gives the erroneous impression that a person can appeal to the supernatural element and make deals with it to spare himself.

Another example of this turning around of Cosmic Truth is the fact that the collective ego claims that renewal is brought about by making *changes*. The Cosmos, by reacting with Fate, creates *transformation* that restores harmony. A person who follows the collective ego's ideas will mistake the *symptoms* of his problem for its *causes*, and thus only change its symptoms. He puts the emphasis on changing his opinion, appearance, manners, technique, policies or place, etc.

Spells connected with this hexagram have to do with the mistaken beliefs about Fate such as those mentioned above, or that one must use power to make changes, or that true changes can be made by changing one's viewpoint, or by exchanging one human-centered belief for another. Other spells concern mistaken beliefs about how renewal is to occur, as mentioned above.

The particular Helpers associated with this hexagram (in addition to the Helper of Transformation) is the Helper that brings wrong paths to a halt, and the Helper that ends Fate.

Note: Since all lines contain infinite possibilities of interpretation, one needs to use the *rtcm* to determine if the meanings suggested here apply to the given situation. (*See* p. 736 for using the *rtcm*.)

Line 1. *Wrapped in the hide of a yellow cow.*

There is always an opportunity for a person to end his fate, if he is willing to question his beliefs about Fate. "Wrapped in the hide of a yellow cow" is a metaphor for someone who is "wrapped up" in a belief system . The hide represents the tough guardian phrases that justify and protect the mistaken beliefs. They are the first problem a person encounters when there is the need to make inner changes. The guardian phrases prevent him from undertaking self-examination:

• by ridiculing introspection as useless, "it can't be that easy," "it's just more New Age pabulum," "you're way out of your element," "this stuff is crazy," and "inner work is nonsense";

• by frightening him with regard to the consequences of undertaking his self-renewal, "if you dig into fundamentals, you may have to change your whole life," "if you do this inner work, your whole inner balance may get disturbed," and "the truth you find may be terrible";

• by suggesting a person's incompetence, the need for a specialist (shaman, spiritual guide, or master), or simply by suggesting that the undertaking will be too difficult;

• by suggesting that the time is not ripe, "I think I should wait," "you can do this later," or that time will take care of the matter, "you can outgrow the problem," "time will heal it."

All these phrases come from the ego, giving it time to regain its power. (*See* p. 689, Freeing Yourself from Seed Phrases.)

Receiving this line can also indicate that a person has just taken on the self-image (behind which the ego hides) of the "truly spiritual person," possibly informed by some ritual. He needs to realize that this is not in harmony with the Cosmos, and therefore not a way to end his fate. Ridding himself of that self-image, however, can end his fate. (*See* p. 691, Freeing Yourself from Self-Images.)

Line 2. *When one's own day comes, one may create revolution. Starting brings good fortune. No blame.*

Receiving this line indicates that a person is inwardly ready to face the mistaken beliefs that have created his fate. He now needs to ask for help to identify and free himself from them.

This line is the source of the traditional excuse the various regimes in China (and elsewhere) have given for justifying a revolution brought about by force. The Sage counsels that all resorting to changing things by force is against the Cosmic Harmony, and creates a fate for those who proceed in this manner. All mistaken beliefs about (1) the meaning of "revolution," and how it is to be carried out, and (2) how a fate can be ended, are to be corrected by saying the inner No to them and asking for the Helper of Fate to initiate the corrections needed. In all cases involving the Helper of Fate, it is necessary to ask the Sage, through the *rtcm*, whether it is correct to call on this Helper.

Line 3. *Starting brings misfortune. Perseverance brings danger. When talk of revolution has gone the rounds three times, one may commit himself, and men will believe him.*

Trying to get free from an oppressive old way of doing things by rushing to a radically different approach means that one is only jumping from one extreme to another, or as it is often put, from the frying pan into the fire. It is in the nature of radical external solutions to generate each other, keeping people locked in reactionary patterns. In this way a person is prevented from ridding himself of the root of the problem, which would free him once and for all.

The fact that people are ready within themselves to make a fundamental change in their way of life is simply not enough, so long as change has only to do with external conditions. Real changes in the outer circumstances can only come from transformations made within each individual, as this entire volume makes clear.

When a person truly understands this, he will cease trying to correct other people by telling them to follow what is true for himself. Instead, he will say the inner No to any displays of ego in them, thus strengthen their true selves. Then others will gather around correct principles within themselves, and a harmonious order will grow from within.

Line 4. *Remorse disappears. Men believe him. Changing the form of government brings good fortune.*

"Remorse disappears" refers to becoming freed from the oppression of being locked in a fate created by one's mistaken beliefs. "Men believe him" refers to the confidence he inspires in others through having gained the help of the Helpers.

Receiving this line can also warn a person against drawing the conclusion that the phrase, "men believe him," authorizes him to lead others. It can also refer to his aspiring to such leadership. In that case, the person needs to rid himself of his self-flattering presumptions.

"Changing the form of government brings good fortune" refers to turning the leadership of the personality over to the true self. The true self understands that to lead means to follow one's inner truth, as each unique moment requires, and asking for help from the Helpers of the invisible world.

Line 5: *The great man changes like a tiger. Even before he questions the oracle he is believed.*

"The great man changes like a tiger," stands for a person who, with the help of the Sage (the great man), has seen a thing with clarity. As a consequence, the weakness he has been feeling is replaced with a true inner strength and inner independence that draws the confidence of others. This confidence is such that people do not question it, the meaning of "even before he questions...he is believed."

"The great man changes like a tiger," is also a metaphor for the Helper of Transformation that has changed the situation in the realm of the atom, thus creating renewal.

This line can also indicate a person who does not consult the oracle, or who interprets its answer incorrectly, because he *assumes* that he knows what is correct. He therefore creates a fate for himself.

Line 6: *The Sage makes changes like a panther. Without help, one only molts in the face. Starting brings misfortune. To be firm and correct brings good fortune.*

Here, the Sage comes, accompanied by the Helper of Transformation, thus making a needed change in a person complete.

Molting only "in the face" refers to a person who has made a superficial change, as by taking on a new self-image. "Starting bring misfortune" indicates that this kind of change creates a fate.

A person may receive this line when he seeks to compel another, who is behaving badly, to change. Being "firm and correct" tells him that the correct action is to say the inner No, and when the other is encroaching outright, to say an outer No. The problem cannot be solved by any use of force. It is important, in such circumstances, to ask the Sage in the other's presence to intervene with the ego in him.

50. *The Ting*

 Li
Sun

The Judgment: *Supreme good fortune. Success.*

In its Cosmic meaning, the ting is an image of the Cosmic Consciousness as a vessel containing the nourishment for all things that exist. This includes the Helpers that make all things grow and flourish. The ting is also a metaphor for the Cosmic Truth that we learn from the Sage; this truth is always relative, having the soft sheen of jade mentioned in Line 6. Cosmic Truth has no resemblance to the sharp and threatening nature of the abstract ideas put forward by the collective ego as "the truth." The clarity of Cosmic Truth is self-evident, harmonious, and resonant with our true natures, whereas ideas held up by the collective ego as truths present themselves as puzzles in poetic dress, that appeal to the intellect without touching the heart. Often they are half-truths, because they exclude the invisible half of the Cosmic Reality; what parts of the invisible reality they do include are mixed with myths and fantasies that put humans in the center of things. Because the truth of those ideas is not self-evident, they need huge systems of rationales to support them. They also pretend to answer things once and for all, while Cosmic Truth leaves space for the evolution of awareness.

The ting, as a Chinese cultural object, was a sacrificial vessel in which food was offered as sacrifice to the deified ancestors. Any idea of sacrifice is contrary to the Cosmic Harmony because of the connotations that go with that word: it was a primitive form of bribing the gods, with the sacrificed animal being a substitute for a person's own body parts. Sacrifice differed from an offering, which was more to honor ancestors or a higher power, but offerings also have the mistaken implication of there being something higher than oneself, and are connected with the idea of there not being enough (harvest) if one does not make offerings. This view of Nature as stingy, and as withholding its fruits, is incorrect, and inhibits the nourishment from flowing freely. The same applies to the protection and help the Cosmos gives.

A person can receive this hexagram to reveal to him the incorrectness of such beliefs that act as spells, blocking the nourishment, protection and help he needs. Giving up beliefs that imprison the true self, and that prevent a person from being in harmony with the gift-giving Cosmos, can neither be called a sacrifice nor an offering, although the ego would phrase it in those terms, to give the impression that one is sacrificing a part of one's true nature. (*See* p. 697, Freeing Yourself from Spells.)

The ting is also a metaphor for what a person allows to occupy his conscious mind. A person may receive this hexagram as a message to reflect on what he harbors and cultivates in his thoughts. People who have adopted the human-centered view of the universe incorrectly believe that whatever they busy their minds with is harmless. Therefore, they generally ignore the inner disappointment in themselves, which they feel after they have indulged in gossip, vilification, self-righteousness, or have allowed impish, petty thoughts. This disappointment is an inner recognition that they have betrayed their true natures. These indulgences are the "stagnating stuff" that needs to be removed from the ting, as described in Line 1. To neglect this inner cleansing is to invite the fate that arises from the myth-making and talebearing that monumentalize humans.

Other thoughts which need to be removed (because they act as spells) are found in the rational structures created by the collective ego. These structures categorize all phenomena in ways that describe their natures in wrong terms. Such categorizing only puts projections, spells, and poison arrows on the nature of natural phenomena and distorts their behavior. The categorizing of the collective ego puts things into a false hierarchical ordering that ranks one thing or group of things as better and more valuable than another. Such categorizing is contrary both to the uniqueness and Cosmic equality of all things. These hierarchical structures can be found in scientific, esoteric, and religious ideologies. When, for example, bodily systems are ranked in a hierarchical order, parallel systems are created within the psyche, which are then transposed to the body. They then operate in opposition to the natural order and independently of the body's true needs, simply to accommodate the hierarchical beliefs. An example are tumors, and "erratic" cellular growths. These parallel systems can also be seen in Nature, as in the destructive behavior of certain animals (certain microorganisms, or insects), or in the harmful behavior of certain plants. These examples are given to show how human thought, when not in harmony with the Cosmic Way, creates the harmful effects which characterize the parallel reality.

Other types of negative effects are created when alive systems are regarded *mechanically*, as in seeing the cardiovascular system as a web of plumbing, with the heart as its central pump.

At the core of the parallel reality is a thinking that sees man as the measure of all things, and which consequently classifies everything in Nature in terms that circle around man's egotistical needs and desires. Those elements of Nature that suit his purposes he defines as "good." What he regards with indifference, or sees as not benefiting him directly, he defines as "vermin," "pests," or "waste products."

"Supreme good fortune" comes when a person cleans out his inner space of all these negative habits of mind. Other types of habitual and destructive thought include projecting what "ought to happen," and how, when, and why. Shoulds and oughts serve the purpose of superimposing the values of the collective ego upon a person or situation. Thinking in those terms distracts a person from discovering the inner truth of a matter and developing a Cosmic perspective of it. It attempts to force behavior into conventional patterns for that purpose alone, and keeps the person from saying the inner No when it is appropriate.

Another destructive habit of mind is thinking in terms of opposites. This habit traps a person in the dualistic myopia of the collective ego, which sees things as black vs. white, good vs. evil, male vs. female, man vs. Nature, etc. This thinking comes from observing only the apparent world through the sense of outer seeing. Such thinking, which excludes all the inner senses, blots out the Cosmic Reality, which is perceptible only through our feeling awareness. The person who thinks in these dualities is stuck with either/or choices, which are only "between two evils." To escape this narrowness, it is necessary to recognize that thinking in terms of opposites puts spells on things that then keep the person trapped in the parallel reality. The spells keep him from recognizing that everything in the Cosmos is achieved through the attraction that exists between its *complementary* aspects. Nothing in the Cosmic Order includes an inherent opposition between things, because this would not allow its harmony to endure.

Another habit of mind that needs to be cleansed out of the ting is the idea that "you need to become something," such as acquiring a good name in one's social group, a title, an occupation, a standard of living, a proper role in society. This idea falsely implies that a person begins his life as "a nothing," whereas he begins his life fully recognized and validated by the Cosmos. The false idea actively keeps his true nature repressed.

Note: Since all lines contain infinite possibilities of interpretation, one needs to use the–*rtcm* to determine if the meanings suggested here apply to the given situation. (*See* p. 736 for using the *rtcm*.)

Line 1: *A ting with legs upturned, furthers the removal of stagnating stuff. One takes a concubine for the sake of her son. No blame.*

"A ting with legs upturned" is a metaphor for the inner housecleaning that is accomplished through saying the inner No to ideas and beliefs that cause inner stagnation, and prevent a person's further growth.

"Taking a concubine..." refers to the Chinese custom of attempting to acquire a son to support the elders in their old age, when the main wife has been thought to be infertile.

The metaphor as a whole refers to relying on a contrived solution to overcome inner stagnation caused by the ideas and beliefs mentioned below.

As can be seen from the thinking behind the contrived solution, the married couple believe that they must "do it all" to protect themselves in their old age; that is, the Helpers and the entire invisible world are not considered.

Behind all contrived solutions lie doubt or denial of the true way of the Cosmos/Nature to benefit all its parts. These doubts form slanders on the Cosmos and on Nature, and on the person's own nature. They are behind all ideas of a human-centered order of the universe, behind humans regarding themselves as special above all the other things that exist in form, behind the suspicion that Fate is put upon humans by an unkind, uncaring Cosmos, behind the efforts people make to get in good standing with anything and everything that they see as "higher" than themselves, such as human authorities, a higher power, or gods. The net effect of all these ideas for the individual is his isolation from the loving Cosmos, and its myriad Helpers. It is he who, through holding these beliefs, has locked out of his life the Cosmic Helpers, creating the stagnation mentioned. Stagnation also refers to the undefined and persistent feeling of depression that accompanies the cessation of growing and expanding one's awareness.

Contrived solutions only lead to the creation of new problems. What needs to be identified and disposed of are the root causes of the problems, which invariably remain after all contrived attempts to resolve them have been made. An example are certain kinds of medical interventions that are based on a mechanistic view of the body. This view disregards that the body is a feeling consciousness that is sensitive to any mistaken idea about itself. The slander that the body is "a mechanism" that can be treated as such is often the very cause of its reacting with illness. While inviting illness, the slander also disables the body's normal self-healing abilities. The remedy is obvious: to identify and rid the body of the slanders by deprogramming the mistaken ideas and beliefs.

Contrived remedies for problems created by inner stagnation can also include propitiatory prayer, or positive thinking and imaging. Although it may appear that the problem has been resolved through such means, one soon finds that it has only shifted to a new area.

Stagnating stuff includes the numerous images of the Cosmic Consciousness as a God with any of the following features:
• having human form
• having the traits of the human ego (factional, proud, all-

powerful, glorious, vengeful, wrathful, vindictive, unjust, relentless, mental)
• requiring rituals, sacrifices, glorification
• demanding to be loved and honored
• rewarding anyone who is subservient
• a male patriarch, partial to males
• a creator and destroyer
• a judge who constantly watches over the shoulder of one's life
• the administrator of one's fate
• a father who is now merciful, now merciless, now loving, now indifferent,
• someone who makes deals, and with whom one can bargain
• an arbitrary and capricious Force to be feared

"No blame" refers to removing these slanders on the nature of the Cosmic Consciousness. When we take them away, its true nature is able to reveal itself as loving, nourishing, harmonious, brotherly/sisterly, modest, supporting, and just.

Line 2: *There is food in the ting. My comrades are envious, but they cannot harm me. Good fortune.*

"Food in the ting" refers to the second meaning of the word "ting" as someone who possesses and is centered in his true nature. As a consequence, he has inner nourishment from the Cosmos (the Sage and the other Helpers) that people who follow the emptiness of convention or beliefs, lack. They inwardly sense this fact, and are envious. They may also be envious of his connection with the Sage, his creativity, his ability to give expression to his uniqueness, his knowledge about the Cosmic Way, his inner independence and stability, his loyalty to his inner truth, and his refusal to be intimidated by others. His best defense is to remain firm and neutral within himself, while saying the inner No to the ego in them, and asking for Cosmic Protection and help. Then the others will not be able to harm him.

This line can also reflect a person who is teaching the *I Ching* (or who is teaching anything) to another who may be intelligent enough, but is unable to understand. The teacher may be flattering himself that he is treating the other as an equal (thus turning the Cosmic Principle of equality into an abstract principle), and therefore is insensitively presenting the information in the way he himself understands it, but out of reach of the other's understanding. This behavior clearly comes from the ego in him, and therefore invites both envy and hatred that block further communication and give rise to harmful projections. A true teacher recognizes that people have different backgrounds that cause them to have slight differences in the ways they interpret and use words; therefore, he is patient in building an adequate background for understanding. He does this with respect and patience for those who are learning. A teacher who allows a sense of superiority to infect his teaching needs to apologize to the Sage for misrepresenting it, and to rid himself of the ego-aspects that are causing it, such as the self-image of the teacher. He then needs to remove any projections, spells, and poison arrows he has drawn from the other.

This line can also refer to a person who is envious of another because of what the other possesses outwardly. Such a person mistakenly believes that there is such a thing as possessions which one has a right to. A person may possess something, but that does not grant him a right to do whatever he likes with it. The idea of having rights is a purely human construction, because everything a person possesses is either a gift of the Cosmos, or has been stolen from the Cosmos through contrivance or other wrong means. The gifts that come to a person whose attitude is in the right place cannot be taken away; the person can only lose them if he loses his modesty.

This line can also be a warning against boasting of being favored by God, Heaven, or the Sage. To be thankful is one thing, to boast is another.

Line 3. *The handle of the ting is altered. One is impeded in his way of life. The fat of the pheasant is not eaten. Once rain falls, remorse is spent. Good fortune comes in the end.*

"The handle of the ting" refers to a person's psyche, which has been altered by a spell, so that he is unable to obtain nourishment from the Cosmos (the ting here representing the Cosmos as the source of nourishment). The spell prevents him from enjoying life, as symbolized by his not being able to eat the delicious fat of the pheasant. Such a person is envious of others, like the person mentioned in the previous line.

The spell in question has been created by the idea that "life is suffering," together with its many parallel beliefs, "one must do everything oneself," and "you have to be a hero in this life." Other beliefs are, "humans have been expelled from paradise once and for all," "your life is in the hands of an indifferent Cosmos," and "Nature is an enemy that must be conquered." These beliefs draw only misery and suffering to the person who holds them, because they slander the true nature of life, and shut the person off from the nourishment and gifts the Cosmos wants to give. Thus, he negatively impacts not only himself, but also everyone who is closely connected with him, especially those he envies for their freedom from such beliefs. "Once rain falls" refers to the dispersion of the dark cloud of mistaken beliefs about life. This ends the envy and its resulting remorse, bringing the "good fortune" mentioned.

This line can also refer to having an ascetic viewpoint that equates poverty with spiritual virtue. Such an idea makes the Helpers inaccessible ("alters the handle of the ting"), so that one's poverty is assured. (*See* p. 689, Freeing Yourself From Mistaken Ideas and Beliefs.)

Line 4. *The legs of the ting are broken. The prince's meal is spilled and his person is soiled. Misfortune.*
A person can receive this line when he has failed to say the inner No to a transgression by another, or to the servility of the ego in himself through wanting to be liked. This failure has betrayed his inner truth (his "inner prince") and so has soiled his integrity. He needs to seek out the ideas behind his wanting to be liked at such an expense, and deprogram them.

A person can also receive this line when he is caught up in blaming himself for having made a mistake. The self-blame makes him think it is only correct that he "eat the fruit of his sin." From the Cosmic point of view, it is part of learning to make mistakes. The indulgence in self-blame comes from his believing that the damage he has done is irreparable, or that he must accept to be punished for it. This is not true, because a mistake is corrected the moment the person corrects the phrases in his inner program that have misled him. The Sage even protects the student from the consequences of a mistake made while sincerely undertaking his self-correction. In this case, he needs to free himself from self-blame, which otherwise communicates to people around him on the inner level, causing the egos in them to take advantage of him. Self-blame prevents a person from going on with his life, and is the meaning of "the legs are broken."

This line can call a person's attention to the mistaken belief that causes his good intentions to have no effect, which is that the Sage resides in the heavenly spheres. The Sage, as the Cosmic Teacher, resides in the presence of each person. When a person sees another as lacking the Sage in his presence, he tends to disrespect him, and think that he alone has a connection with the Sage. "The prince's meal is spilled and his person soiled " refers to his taking this superior attitude, and then pressing his truth upon the other. It is the Sage in the presence of each person that brings to each the nourishment of his individual inner truth. When someone fails to recognize that the Sage exists in every person's presence, he cannot make meaningful connections with others.

"The legs of the ting are broken" can also refer to a person who is attempting to follow the way of the Sage by assimilating the Sage's teachings within his established beliefs. Inasmuch as these beliefs contain the presumption that "humans are at the center of the universe," the true nourishment will be misconstrued and thus "spilled." "Misfortune" describes the fact that the person cannot enjoy the lessons the Sage would be able to teach him.

The broken legs are also a metaphor for the belief that sacrificing the body elevates one's nature. This idea comes from the ego's ambition to "be spiritual."

Line 5. *The ting has yellow handles, golden carrying rings. Perseverance furthers.*

Here, a person's focus is drawn to the handles by which the ting is carried. The "golden carrying rings" symbolize the real value that accrues when a person has cleaned out the ting (here a metaphor for his thinking and imaging minds) of preconceived beliefs. By clearing his mind, he has made it possible for the Sage and the Helpers to come to his aid. "Perseverance furthers" is a message to say the inner No to the temptation of looking to other beliefs of an opposite nature, after having discarded inappropriate beliefs. Having this temptation indicates that he has still not cleaned out an underlying seed phrase (*see* example below). The handles that make the ting portable are a metaphor for the flexibility of Cosmic Truth to apply to every situation. This flexibility is maintained only when a person keeps his mind empty of all fixed beliefs.

An example is a person who holds the seed phrase that "Nature is wild and needs to be ordered by man." Upon seeing Nature being mistreated by people, he thinks he must come to Nature's aid by trying to correct things on the outer plane. He does not realize that he is acting from guilt, and also from distrust that Nature is equipped to bring itself back into balance. If he will first rid himself of the above mentioned seed phrase (which is a projection, spell, and poison arrow put upon Nature), and then free himself from the projection and spell he has put on himself ("because we humans have caused the problems, we need to fix them"), then the Helpers that restore balance in Nature will be freed. He also needs to say the inner No to his guilt.

The "golden carrying rings" can also refer to a person with a pretentious self-image, to the effect that he has been designated to judge others on God's behalf. Assuming any authority to judge others by categorizing them as good or evil creates misfortune. Perseverance furthers, in this case, refers to the need the person has to rid himself of that magnificent self-image.

The "golden carrying rings" can also refer to the peace that a person believes he is creating by following a "spiritual duty" to "turn the other cheek" to another's bad treatment. By doing this, he gives the other his inner permission to continue, and suffers an increasing loss of self-esteem every time he allows the transgression. He needs to free himself from the mistaken idea that the sacrifice of his dignity and self-respect can ever be correct, or have a good effect. He may also need to say the inner No to his self-image of "the peacemaker."

Line 6. *The ting has rings of jade. Great good fortune. Nothing that would not act to further.*

Here the ting is an image of the intrinsic space each person inhabits. Its "rings of jade" is a metaphor for the Sage that is in every person's presence. When the ego in another is trying to dominate the relationship, the Sage in that person's presence can be asked to intervene to displace the ego, and thereby enable a meaningful connection. The Sage in both his own and the other's presence can be asked to bring whatever Helpers are needed to help with a situation.

"The ting has rings of jade" also refers to a person who carries his connection with the Sage with him wherever he goes, and into whatever he does. This is the meaning of "great good fortune" and "nothing that would not act to further."

Jade also represents an attitude of patience and modesty that comes from seeing the Cosmic view as broader, rather than as higher. This happens when a person has recognized his true place in the Cosmic Order, as fully equal with every other aspect. He recognizes his reliance on the Helpers for all his needs, and includes them in his everyday consciousness. This harmonious attitude brings him "great good fortune," and everything he does acts to further the Cosmic Whole.

True modesty combines the firmness of the inner No in the face of what is incorrect, with a willingness to put matters of justice in the hands of the Cosmos. It trusts that Fate, once activated by the inner No, has the correct measure. The modest person does not fear the way of Cosmic Justice; nor does he engage in partiality, by failing to say the inner No to others, when the situation requires it.

This kind of modesty cannot be adopted as an attitude. It is a Cosmic Virtue that is fulfilled when a person rids himself of all beliefs and images by which he sees himself as special, and which blind him to the dignity of all other aspects of the Cosmos.

51. *Shock*

 Chên
Chên

The Judgment: *Shock brings success. Shock comes—Oh, Oh! Laughing words—ha, ha! The shock terrifies for a hundred miles, and he does not let fall the sacrificial spoon and chalice.*

In this hexagram, the Sage shows the Cosmic purposes of shock. Cosmic shock is distinguished from the shocks that are delivered to the child by the collective ego during its conditioning process.

Cosmic shock has either the purpose of warning a person that his attitude is arrogant, or to tell him the shock is a fate he has created.

Shock can appear as a major event in a person's life, such as an accident, an injury, a shocking diagnosis, or the death of someone close. It can also be the shock of losing one's job after many years of faithful service, or of a divorce.

To the student of the Sage, shock can be as small an event as tripping over a stone, to make him aware that a problem exists in his attitude, such as an exaggerated self-confidence, or that he has adopted a self-image. In the moments after he has tripped, he needs to reflect on what he was thinking, doing, planning, or saying at the time. Simply receiving this hexagram can have the same warning effect for the long time student. In all these cases, shock has the purpose of informing the person of something in the most effective way possible.

The Judgment indicates the correct response to shock: to not allow oneself to be thrown out of one's inner center, or to be collapsed by fear, terror, or the idea of loss. When the shock has been great, affecting many people, the first means of protecting oneself from the successive waves of shock is to remove oneself from identifying with the group as a whole. (*See* Glossary: Group-We.) When a person is directly involved in such an event, his survival depends totally on his responding from his feelings, rather than from his thinking what he (or they as a group) ought to do, or are told to do. An example is someone who is present during the hijacking of an airplane. Experience has proven that when passengers act spontaneously from their feelings, they may thwart the intentions of the hijackers, who depend on the passengers freezing in terror.* Persons unable to act outwardly may also engage the Helpers by saying the inner No to the hijackers, and asking inwardly for help. When a person is only an observer of a shocking event, he needs to activate the Sage and the Helpers, and then bring his focus back to himself, to attain calm.

A shock that affects large numbers of people may contain a fate for some of those involved, or an opportunity for others. It may lead some to examine their relationship to the Cosmos, to enable them to free themselves from a fate, or lead those who have not engaged a fate to free themselves from unpleasant circumstances. Great shocks give the general populace the opportunity to ponder how Fate operates. As for the children of parents who have been killed, as in accidents, it is important to gain a Cosmic perspective of what is perceived as loss. (*See* Glossary: Loss.)

A person may receive this hexagram when he has experienced an unsettling event, which has shaken his confidence in the ordinary ways he has been relating to his life. The shock is to make him aware that these ordinary ways, which he has been taking for granted as correct, have failed to help him in the given situation. It also shows him that the values he has been following are questionable, and that his path has now led him to a deadend. He must first realize that he can go no further in this direction. He next needs to seek help from the Sage to stabilize his reaction to the shock, through attaining inner quiet (*see* p. 680, Centering Yourself.) He next needs to seek out, with the help of the Sage and the *rtcm*, the mistaken ideas or beliefs that have made him take that path, and then free himself of them. Once

---

* An example is that of the "shoe bomber" on a transatlantic flight from England to the U.S. The woman in a nearby seat called the crew's attention to his preparing to light the fuse of the bomb hidden in his shoe. Her action turned the matter around, causing the man to freeze.

freed from the shock and its effects, he needs to beware of any overconfidence that would produce yet other shocks.

The traditional interpretation of shock given for this hexagram has its basis in the collective ego. It presents the image of thunder as a metaphor for any shock that "terrifies for a hundred miles" around, and is interpreted as "a manifestation of God." The benefit of this shock was seen in its ability to produce an "awe in the face of heaven" that reminded the individual of his insignificance, and therefore of his need for protection from something higher than himself. This "awe," presumably produced by heaven was an implied metaphor for the "awesome" authority of the emperor, who was called the "Son of Heaven," and his surrounding feudal lords, who imitated the seeming "power" represented by the noise of thunder.

The phrase, "he does not let fall the sacrificial spoon and chalice," pictured the wise man, who counteracted his fears by making sacrifices to appease the forces of Nature. This image of sacrifice indicates how the collective ego explains shock as an arbitrary demonstration of heavenly power, which needs to be counteracted by a ritual of sacrifice, obeisance, or propitiatory prayer.

From a Cosmic perspective, the steady hand that holds the spoon and chalice amid shock can also be taken as a metaphor for the person who knows the meaning of shock, and asks the help of the Cosmos to show him the way through it.

Cosmic shock, as an expression of Fate, is essentially a mechanism that makes it impossible for the demonic consciousness created by the collective ego to penetrate and destroy the Cosmic Harmony. The ultimate purpose of Fate is to restore harmony to the Cosmic Whole, when it has been disturbed. For the individual, its purpose is to bring him (literally) back from his head to his senses, and to reduce him to an attitude of openness and humility that will help him shake loose the hold of the ego. Its other purpose is to open him up to the Sage, which can help him become aware of his mistaken ideas and beliefs. Often, prior to the shock of Fate, the person has believed himself to be acting entirely correctly, having followed the conventions of what is considered correct. The shock now motivates him to look back over his life, to see how, in seemingly small and un-noticed ways, he has violated the Cosmic Harmonics.

Fate is a circular negative energy created by evil intentions and deeds, and by pride and arrogance. It returns promptly to its source in some form of shocking event or adversity. If, how-ever, it is interrupted in its course, as when the person injured self-righteously fights back, as in a feud, or engages in lawsuits to recover damages, then the person who has done the evil deed is let off the hook of Cosmic Fate. What happens to him then is a matter between the parties. The interfering party, meanwhile, has created a fate for himself by taking Cosmic Justice in his hands. Fate is likewise interrupted if the person injured mag-nificently forgives or excuses the offender (something only the Cosmos can do). Such a person blocks the purpose of Fate: to give the offender the opportunity to correct his errors. The above principle applies both to individuals and groups who take upon themselves to intervene and punish another.

The point at which an individual understands that he has had a part in the fate he is experiencing, and corrects his thinking, is the point at which his fate ends, and he is restored to harmony with the Cosmos, and its protection. Otherwise, the fate con-tinues its full length of time, which is like a prison sentence that has a definite end. It does not get carried over to any future life in a body.

The severity of the Cosmic shock corresponds to the degree needed to wake the person up. It depends on the level of his rigidity, the strength of his attachment to his mistaken ideas and beliefs, and the extent of his arrogance. Human institu-tions can be used by the Cosmos to administer these shocks, but when these humans see themselves as "administrators of Fate," or take on a self-righteous attitude, they bring a fate upon themselves.

Shocks have the purpose of freeing a person from the ego's dominance. Shock is potentially an initiator of transformation. When the person uses the opportunity of shock to examine his attitudes and correct them, the particular ego-element is re-moved in an enduring way. In other cases, repeated small shocks help the student of the Sage understand a particular lesson.

For persons who have turned their lives over to the ego in themselves, and who have not undertaken the freeing of their true selves, shock serves to temporarily freeze the ego, to allow a small step of growth for their true selves. This small space of time allows the true self to perceive that the ego is a foreign element in his psyche that has led him astray, and that his true self, which is temporarily in charge, is capable of leading. The ego will attempt to return by repeating the flattery that it is "his best protection," and by reminding him how it has "so faithfully" served in the past to advance his interests. Its main aim, in making these claims, is to get the true self to once again doubt its ability to lead the personality. Repeated Cosmic shocks reveal to him that the ego has only led him on one false path after another. Through these repeated shocks, the person experiences his own capabilities, and realizes that he can indeed rely on the Sage to guide him.

The *effect* of shock to liberate the true self is the meaning of "Ha! Ha!" in The Judgment. It comes with recognizing that the person is free of the train of fates constantly being created by the ego. Sometimes this Ha! Ha! comes a few years after the major shock, when the person has fully realized all the benefits it has generated. (The feeling is not to be confused with the idea of enlightenment as a final state of advanced awareness.)

Just as saying the inner No undoes a previously said Yes to a mistaken idea, Cosmic shock breaks a spell that has caused a shock in the psyche at an earlier time. The kind of spells connected with this hexagram are those that have allowed the ego to appropriate any of a person's Cosmic Possessions, such as his Cosmic Virtues, his true feelings, and the Cosmic gifts that have been given to him during his life: inventions, insights, gifts of creativity, etc. Shock returns these Cosmic Possessions to the true self. Other kinds of spells that can be broken by Cosmic shock are those put on a person's metaphorical senses.

Shock can also displace the guardian phrases of the collective ego's program, which serve to prevent a person from undertaking the ego's deconstruction. The guardian phrases surround the ego's program much like a castle wall, in that they are phrases that anticipate realizations of its falsity. An example are the "antennae" put out by scientists against any idea that might smack of being associated with "irrational," or with "superstition," and which, if entertained, would injure their standing (pride) as scientists. This rigidity is typical as well of the person defending his idea that faith is the best support of his belief system. In both cases, a rigid wall of complacency is built between the person and the possibility of thinking in new terms. Cosmic Logic is neither rational nor irrational, nor is it to be confounded with superstition. Calling it "irrational" is a misnomer by the ego with the intention of discrediting the Cosmic Logic. Shock enables the person to once again get in touch with his inner truth. Shock jars him free from the ego-assumption that he has it all figured out. Such presumptuousness invariably invites shock.

A person who goes from one spiritual path to another, after finding something disappointing in each, can experience repetitive shocks that tell him he needs to transcend the reactionary pattern in which he is caught. Instead of looking to already trodden paths, he is counseled to look to his own inner truth to guide him. Repeated shocks can also tell a person that he needs to stop relying on set policies and prescribed ways of approaching problems, and to allow himself to be led by his inner truth, as each unique moment requires.

This hexagram also addresses the shocks employed by the collective ego during childhood, in both physical and psychological forms, to condition the child to have reverence and respect for authority. This use of shock has the effect of deeply impressing the psyche with fears, i.e., putting spells on the child. The conditioning, ultimately, has the purpose of transferring the child's inner senses (of correctness, truth, dignity, integrity, self-possession, etc.) from serving his true nature, to serving outer authorities. This transfer is made first to the parents, then to other institutions that represent the collective ego. The parents are made to believe, through their own conditioning, that their failure in this duty will create shame for them in the eyes of the collective ego. The child, for his part, is always told that the shocks are being administered for his own good.

The worst effect of these shocks is to deprive the child of his ability to say the inner No, for this can make him (as the punishment intends) permanently a slave of the collective ego. It is like breaking the horse's will rather than cooperating with the horse. Other effects are the disabilities experienced during adult life ranging from withdrawal, depression, submissiveness, passive-aggressive behavior, to outright rebellion and destructiveness. Indeed the shocks of punishment and domination experienced by children are encountered again and again, in the cyclical repetitions of depression and the psychological aberrations of the adolescent and adult. Nearly every adult, upon reflection, can recognize that shocks administered during his childhood are the source of destructive relational patterns, and recurrent obstructions in his adult life.

Note: Since all lines contain infinite possibilities of interpretation, one needs to use the *rtcm* to determine if the meanings suggested here apply to the given situation. (*See* p. 736 for using the *rtcm*.)

Line 1. *Shock comes—oh, oh! Then follow laughing words—ha! ha! Good fortune.*

This line refers to Cosmic shock. The laughing words reflect the relief felt when the person realizes the freeing purpose of shock. This realization occurs when the rigidity of the ego's defenses (that constitute a spell) has been demolished, and the strength of one's true self has been validated.

Being under shock enables the person to recognize what it is that he can really rely on when worse comes to worse. This realization of his inner truth comes at the moment he needs it.

Because shock frees all the senses, the "Ha, ha!" of relief is also the "Aha!" of recognition.

Line 2. *Shock comes bringing danger. A hundred thousand times you lose your treasures and must climb the nine hills. Do not go in pursuit of them. After seven days you will get them back again.*

This line draws attention to the danger that a person experiencing shock will fall into a hopeless and depressed attitude, caused by the perception of having lost something of great value.

Climbing the nine hills is advice to quiet and center himself. (*See* p. 680, Centering Yourself.)

This line tells him that the shock had the purpose of breaking a spell he was under, which had caused him to lose the real treasures of his life. These real treasures were the joys of love that are expressed in intimacy. The spell consists in the belief that people have a "higher" and a "lower nature," with the lower nature needing to be overcome by developing the higher nature. This spell, by slandering his bodily nature as "lower," has blocked his ability to experience true intimacy, and thus deprived him of the life sustaining chi energy he would otherwise receive from it. (*See* Glossary: Chi Energy.) The spell also has had the effect of blocking his access to his inner truth, making him look to the moral standards held up by the collective ego. This line informs him that the shock has freed him from this spell. The mention of "seven days" tells him that he will gradually begin to realize his new freedom.

Line 3. *Shock comes and makes one distraught. If shock spurs to action, one remains free of misfortune.*

Here a person is distraught by either his own fate or by witnessing someone else's difficulties, due to a fate. He needs to realize that the shock has the purpose of getting both the person affected by it, and the observer, to reflect on what the fate wants to tell either of them. Once he understands the message, then he will be able to do what is appropriate to free himself or the other from the fate. Often what is needed is that he free himself from his mistaken views of the origin of Fate (adopted from the collective ego). These views blame Fate on the Cosmos, Nature, or another person, and so avoid seeing that its origin is in a mistaken view. Quite as often, a person will deny that his human-centered view of the universe is the cause, and that this view has given him the mistaken idea that Cosmic Limits do not apply to him. Whenever a person is involved in, or is in close proximity to, a shocking event, he needs to ask himself why he is there. This line reveals the Cosmic Principle that being a witness to an adversity has a Cosmic purpose which the person needs to seek out.

A person may also receive this line when he has a fate in the form of an illness that will not heal, despite all treatment. A search for the cause may reveal that he has been accusing his body for not being able to heal the illness. This problem has two aspects: (1) The person needs to recognize that his illness is a fate which can be extinguished, if he will seek out its cause. (*See* p. 692, Freeing Yourself from a Fate.) (2) He needs to say the inner No to any phrases by which he has been blaming the Cosmos, or doubting the self-healing abilities of his body. The self-healing abilities of the body and psyche are connected to the person's consciousness: so long as he has mistaken ideas about the origin and purpose of Fate, his self-healing abilities are blocked. The same applies when the person blames his body for the illness, for not functioning properly, or for causing him humiliation or disgrace. Doing so puts a spell on the very Helpers he needs for healing.

This line can also refer to a person who, on seeing something shocking, goes on and on about its being senseless and a waste. He constantly reiterates these and other negative views about it. Such an indulgence is based on a human-centered view of the universe, whereby the person not only puts himself up as a judge of the way of the Cosmos, he is also ignorant of the Cosmic Way. If he continues in his self-righteous attitude, he will create misfortune. The action indicated here is to say the inner No to his self-righteous attitude.

Line 4. *Shock is mired.*

Shock generally breaks one spell at a time. This is so because every fate has its origin in a particular spell, with the purpose of the fate being to break that spell.

Receiving this line is an indication that more shocks may be needed, because the person is blocked (mired) by a number of spells that form a whole belief system.

The mistaken belief which has caused the shock to be ineffective may concern the very nature of Fate and its purpose; thus that belief defeats the fate's purpose. Under these circumstances, the Helper of Fate comes to renew the shock for however many times is needed for him to understand the message.

Line 5. *Shock goes hither and thither. Danger. However, nothing at all is lost. Yet there are things to be done.*

This line can refer to the return of the ego, after a person has regretted a wrong action that has precipitated a Cosmic shock. The ego returns with rationales justifying his wrong action, and causing him to feel self-righteous. The return of the ego heralds renewed shocks.

The line can also refer to a situation in which two people have been arguing over a long period of time. The shocks that go hither and thither in this case are the blows they impart to each other. Receiving this line is informing them that they have created a fate, which they are now experiencing. "Nothing at all is lost" means that the person reading this line can end the fate by saying the inner No to the ego's desire to continue arguing, and also by saying the inner No to the other person's holding onto his grudge.

Line 6. *Shock brings ruin and terrified gazing around. Going ahead brings misfortune. If it has not yet touched one's own body but has reached one's neighbor first, there is no blame. One's comrades have something to talk about.*

This line shows a person who is under the effect of a severe shock. He is now gazing around for someone or something to blame. However, he needs to understand that what he has been experiencing was a fate that he created himself, even though someone else has administered it. The Cosmos can use people or institutions as "arms of fate." He needs to stop blaming others and ask for help.

The line can also refer to a group that is being subjected to a fate due to an arrogant self-image its members have adopted of being special, and which self-image has caused them to look down on others. Receiving this line is to make a member of that group aware that he needs to rid himself of the group's beliefs that foster such a self-image; otherwise, he will draw the fate it creates for them to himself. Although his comrades will not understand his actions, and may even make him feel guilty for not being loyal to the group, he should pay no attention, but take comfort in being true to himself. To gain Cosmic Protection he needs to say the inner No to their trying to make him feel guilty.

52. Meditating

 Kên
Kên

The Judgment: *Meditating. Turning within to cease depending on others, he enters his courtyard to seek his inner truth. No blame. He brings his back to quiet until clarity appears.*

I Ching meditation is an exercise that brings a person into contact with his primary issues of concern. Its purpose is to make him see them in the light of his inner truth. His inner truth reveals the hidden inner elements within the situation so that he can come to a correct assessment and action.

Meditation also reveals the seed phrases and images that have taken on the form of imps in his psyche, and which manifest as impulses which keep his words and actions from being in harmony with his true self and with the Cosmos. *I Ching* meditation is also the means by which seed phrases and images are deprogrammed, through saying the inner No, and through asking the Sage to lead the deprogramming process.

I Ching meditation is also a directed effort to free the person's true self from projections, spells, and poison arrows that are revealed through the hexagrams, or through the *rtcm*. All projections and spells, and many poison arrows, are made up of phrases and/or images that express a half-truth or untruth about a person's true nature, life, or the Cosmos/Nature, in general. Although it may not be obvious at first, all phrases and images that concern Nature and the Cosmos, also negatively affect the individual's psyche, and the character of his daily life, for they determine whether he lives within the Cosmic Reality, or within the parallel reality created by the collective ego.

I Ching meditation differs from known "meditation techniques," which only bring temporary relief from tension or conflict. Among these are techniques in which the person focuses on a candle, or object of inner focus, such as an image, a sound, a word, phrase, or idea, and other exercises, which either silence the primary issues of concern, or keep them at bay through distraction. The same applies to meditation techniques that "empty" the mind, and then keep it empty through a mental discipline. This latter technique keeps the issues of concern locked in a mental compartment where, despite the great need of the psyche to have them brought into conscious focus and addressed, the person is prevented from doing so. Guided meditations, in which the person is led to visualize images, encourage fantasies instead of helping him access his inner truth. All these techniques give a temporary sense of peace and balance. However, the balance is soon lost when the person stops meditating, because the fundamental seed phrases and images which cause the imbalance still reside in the psyche. The ego likes nothing so much as a temporary solution that enables it to remain in control, and to allow it to further spur a person's spiritual ambition. The danger lying in such temporary solutions to find relief from the anxieties that mistaken ideas create in the psyche, is that the technique may become an addiction.

The first step in *I Ching* meditation consists in "opening the mind" by turning away from all meditation techniques (because none of these involve the Sage or the Helpers of the invisible world) and bringing the Helpers into his meditation. He does so by asking for their help and guidance with the problem of the moment. It is important that he not ask the guidance of any spirit or medium, for in that case, he will not reach the Sage, but a dead person who, for one reason or another, is held in an intermediary place, because of some mistaken belief that has not yet burned out. What the person may receive from such a source is false information.

It is also important that the person avoids using meditation to "get" something he desires. Rather than asking for such things as "peace of mind," the purpose of the meditation is to remove those thoughts and images that trouble his mind. This is done by listening to those phrases and looking at those images that disturb his inner peace, and saying the inner No to them.

Thus, the second step in *I Ching* meditation is the process of cleansing the psyche. This process is made easier by asking the cleansing Helpers to free the psyche of everything that the person is ready to rid himself of at a given moment. These Helpers will then bring into focus images that are keys to understanding the context of his concerns.

A person needs time to allow these images to develop; if, however, they do not occur within half an hour, it is likely that the ego is present "trying to meditate" and thereby is maintaining control over the psyche. It is necessary at this point to say the inner No to its presence and to cease meditating, as a way of retreating from it. It may take several sessions to get past the ego before the person can have a successful meditation, but he must not be discouraged by attempts of the ego to assert that he is unable to meditate, or that it is too difficult.

During the meditation, images may flash into his mind, which he does not understand. It is possible to inwardly ask the Sage what the image means. Often, after a few seconds, the answer comes, either in a word or a phrase which may actually be the seed phrase that is causing the difficulty. Shown in the context of the meditation, its absurdity becomes obvious.

After the meditation has come to an end, the person needs to rid himself of the seed phrases or images uncovered, by saying the inner No to them. The No gives his suppressed inner truth the full support of his conscious mind, and thus heals his psyche of that particular problem. It is important to write down these phrases and images, and to continue saying the inner No to them for three days. (*See* p. 689, Freeing Yourself from Seed Phrases and Images.)

Note: Since all lines contain infinite possibilities of interpretation, one needs to use the *rtcm* to determine if the meanings suggested here apply to the given situation. (*See* p. 736 for using the *rtcm*.)

Line 1. *Keeping his toes still. No blame. It furthers one to remain firmly correct.*

"Keeping his toes still" is counsel to resist taking action in any form. The word "action," throughout the *I Ching*, includes thoughts as well as deeds. This is because incorrect thoughts project negative effects onto people and situations. Thus, this line counsels a person to become inwardly quiet, through dispersing all his present thoughts and worries, as a way of opening himself up to the suggestions and guidance of the Sage.

This line clearly indicates that a particular seed phrase, image, projection, spell, or poison arrow, is active in the situation and needs to be identified and addressed. It is sufficient to close one's eyes briefly and ask the Helpers to bring into one's conscious mind the seed phrase(s) or images that need to be identified and disposed of in order to attain clarity. A person may also ask, through the *rtcm*, whether the element to be found is coming either from inside himself or from someone else. Then he needs to identify the nature of the element, and what *inner* action to take to stop its influence.

Movement in the toes can refer to impulses coming from the ego; they are based on particular seed phrases that consist of stated policies and procedures for doing things. Many of these phrases contain "shoulds;" they drive a person's actions and reactions into pre-structured channels that conform to a particular image the person has of himself. Such impulsive actions differ from the spontaneity and simplicity of action that springs from a person's inner truth.

Seed phrases that drive impulses are: "you need to defend yourself," "you need to be somebody," "you must assert yourself in this life," "if you don't fight back, you'll be ruined," "if you don't do something, nothing will happen." Impulsive movement can also be spurred by a person's impatience with ambiguity. Seed phrases behind this difficulty are, "someone has got to put their foot down," "you can't just do nothing," "it is better to act than not to act," and "if somebody doesn't do something, things will never change."

A person can also receive this line when he is caught in the spell that "he is an impulsive person." This spell is causing him to act impulsively. (*See* p. 697, Freeing Yourself from Projections and Spells.)

The impulse to do something may also be coming from guilt that is part of the person's belief system. "No blame" is to make him aware that the idea of guilt has no Cosmic validity. (*See* p. 50, Guilt, Blame, and Shame, and p. 696, Freeing Yourself from Guilt.) "It furthers one to remain firmly correct" is also a warning not to impute guilt to another person or thing.

It is also possible that a person receives the line to make him aware that he is drawing spells and projections from others, because he is attached to a particular self-image. An example is the person who has the self-image of the "likable person." He unconsciously is trapped in behavior to please others, for which the egos in them only despise him, causing them to send the projections mentioned. To free himself from this pattern, he needs to deprogram that self-image. (*See* p. 691, Freeing Yourself From Self-Images.)

Line 2. *Keeping his calves still. He cannot rescue him whom he follows. His heart is not glad.*

The "calves" in this line have to do with the exercise of power, whether it be external power, power through speech or acts, or internal power, through thought. This line concerns a person trying to get someone to conform to the standards and values of the collective ego, thinking this will rescue him. The person may be using leverage, contrivance, pressure, or guilt to achieve his goal. The line counsels him to "keep his calves still," meaning to back away from such efforts, because he cannot rescue anyone by pursuing him. Such a person first needs to deliver himself from his belief in the values of the collective ego that keep his true self imprisoned.

In regard to meditation, this line refers to a person's incorrectly using the energy of his meditation to sway others, to bring them around to his beliefs. Such intentional efforts are not in harmony with the Cosmos. He needs to say the inner No to such a practice.

"His heart is not glad" refers to a person who wants to be rescued by another. He holds the idea that he is incomplete in himself, and that there is no help other than what people can give. This idea keeps him separated from the true source of help (the Helpers of the invisible world), and causes him to continuously feed off the caring energies of another who believes that it is his job to rescue others. The person who acts on the self-image of being a "rescuer" unconsciously projects his doubt that others lack the resources within themselves for their recovery. This doubt puts a spell on them that hampers their ability to ask for help from the Cosmos.

This line counsels the person who has the self-image of the "rescuer" that whatever idea motivates him to fulfill this role, be it guilt, duty, love, loyalty, or some other abstract virtue, these motives will draw people to him who wish to live off his chi energy. Ridding himself of this false motive will cause the other to eventually seek true help from the Helpers, or seek another "rescuer." The person desiring to be rescued is most likely under a spell put on him in childhood that only a higher authority such as a parent or master has the ability to rescue him. The help that can be given this person is to identify and break the spell that prevents him from asking the Helpers to come to his aid. (*See* p. 697, Freeing Yourself from Spells.)

The line can also address a person who is under a guilt spell and, at the same time, is trying to free someone else who is under the same spell. A person under such a spell is not able to help anyone until he has freed himself. (*See* p. 696, Freeing Yourself from Guilt.)

Keeping the calves still also refers to forcing the body into uncomfortable positions, with the idea that doing so is the correct way to meditate. Such efforts come from beliefs that the body is the source of evil and must be disciplined with force if one is to achieve spiritual development. This idea falsely divides one's wholeness into mind and body, with mind/spirit seeking mastery over the body, an idea that puts spells both on the body and the mind. The goal of meditation is not mental/spiritual control over the body, but ridding oneself of spells such as these that prevent one's inner harmony.

Line 3. *Keeping his hips still. Making his sacrum stiff. Dangerous. The heart suffocates.*

"Keeping his hips still" can be a metaphor for a person who is trying to use his will to force results through mental concentration. Such an approach is based on the belief that humans are the ones who are meant to make everything happen; it therefore excludes the Helpers.

This line can also refer to a person who, in meditation or in his life, listens to his mind rather than to his body, and thus suffocates the feelings that come from his heart. The consequence is that his heart cannot find rest, a condition that leads to exhaustion and to all kinds of heart problems.

Receiving this line can also indicate that a person is still harboring worries, anxieties, and doubts. If so, he needs to say the inner No to each one and turn it over to the Helper of Transformation. (*See* also Hexagram 14, *Possession in Great Measure*, Line 2, that speaks of a "big wagon for loading.") Through disengaging from these negative emotions, he will find peace, and allow the solutions to his problems to come as insights.

This line can also address a person who practices meditation ambitiously by meditating for long hours, or by going on austere retreats. The Sage retreats in the presence of all ambition, and whenever a person decreases his dignity by taking on a servile attitude toward anything or anyone he perceives as "higher" than himself, he may believe that his efforts will please or impress the Sage, as would be the case with a human teacher or authority. The help the Sage gives is meant to free his true self from its arrested development during childhood, to grow up to maturity, which includes validating his original completeness. It does not seek to keep him in an inferior position typical of the feudal mindset. The inner No needs to be said to such practices, and to the belief that is behind them.

The line can also warn a person not to throw his dignity away to save a relationship that is dominated by the ego in his partner. He needs to withdraw and not feed the ego with his chi energy, until the other has corrected himself.

The line can also refer to a person who is trying to prolong his life in a body, beyond his time. In doing so, he oversteps the Cosmic Limits that apply to humans. Living in a body is not a matter of right, but a Cosmic gift, and part of a person's life experience. A person continues his life in an invisible form after death, as long as there is no interference with the transformation of his life, coming from mistaken beliefs about death.

Line 4. *Keeping his trunk still. No blame.*

"Keeping his trunk still" counsels regular examination, in meditation, where the heart is in relation to the rest of the body: whether it is neglected by paying attention only to the mind, to one's looks, to one's physical condition, etc. This regular examination enables a person to keep his heart healthy.

It is also important to examine what condition the heart is in: is it rigid, dried-up, swollen, open, or closed? Does it contain foreign objects, such as seeds or worms? The latter stand for seed phrases and images that need to be identified with the help of the Sage. Worms stand for thoughts that are "eating away" his wholeness. (See p. 689, Freeing Yourself from Seed Phrases and Images.) In all such cases, a person needs to ask the Sage to mobilize the Helpers needed to restore his heart.

Such worms can mean the heart is filled with guilt. The person needs to understand that guilt has no Cosmic basis. (*See* p. 50, Guilt, Blame, and Shame.) The words "no blame" are to make him aware that there is no cause for blame (in the sense of guilt). (*See* p. 696, Freeing Yourself from Guilt.)

The metaphor also refers to using meditation or prayer to fulfill certain intentions. In this case, the heart is under the ego's influence, and its efforts to control an outer situation. The ego's desires need to be distinguished from the natural inclinations of the heart. Lovers, for example, naturally want to be in each other's company, but the ego desires to possess and control the partner according to its image of what is correct. Ego-based desire, which comes from a human-centered view of the universe, puts a spell on the gift-giving nature of the Cosmos. It is like holding one's hands out for a *specific* gift (something one thinks or fantasizes will fulfill one's need), rather than asking the Cosmos to supply the correct solution for the situation.

The Sage is blocked when a person prays for a specific goal, which he takes for granted as correct. For example, a person who prays for another's healing when that person's illness is due to a fate, takes on that person's fate. (See p. 692, Freeing Yourself from a Fate.) It would be better to ask for help to free that person from his fate. In regard to praying for peace, such praying bypasses the essential inquiry into the inner causes of the conflict. Only through such inquiry can a person address these causes and say the inner No to them, thus initiating transformations. The inner No also penetrates to other peoples' true selves, strenghtening them to stand up to the ego in themselves. Praying for peace has only the selfish purpose of returning the situation to nonthreatening and non-harmful, so that the person may feel comfortable about it.

When the ego controls meditation, it seeks to have "esoteric" experiences, and to turn the meditation toward its specific goals. This blocks the Sage's coming with insight and help.

Line 5. *Keeping his jaws still. When the words have order, remorse disappears.*

"Keeping his jaws still" counsels a person who is being pressed by the ego's fears, doubts, feelings of guilt, desires, impatience, or other causes of restlessness, to hold back from speaking until he has freed himself from these elements in meditation. So long as he allows them to operate in his psyche, his words and actions create negative results. "The words have order" and remorse disappears when he has eradicated these unruly elements.

This line also counsels a person to be careful that his words reflect the intrinsic worth of things, rather than reflecting only their appearances. He is conscientious in refusing to slander a thing's true nature. (*See* Hexagram 58, The *Joyful.*)

The line can also address a situation in which one person diminishes another's sincerity, as by distorting what he says, or treating it as trivial or banal. The correct response is to say the inner No to the other's action, turn the matter over to the Cosmos, and inwardly retreat from the situation.

Line 6. *Noblehearted keeping still. Good fortune.*

This line can be a confirmation that a person has rid himself of guilt, or that a fate caused by guilt has ended. He therefore experiences a true peace of the heart.

A person may also receive this line to tell him that when he wants to meditate and is sincere and open, he can ask the Sage to keep his thoughts or negative emotions still, so that he can look at them inwardly and rid himself of them.

In another meaning, this line can address a person who is trying to achieve peace of the heart, but employs the wrong means: he lets another off the hook of his ego-behavior, instead of saying the inner No to him. Doing this means acting from the self-image of the "noblehearted person." Such behavior shows that both people are caught in a co-dependency, in which the two egos support each other. Co-dependencies are based on spells, and can be resolved by ridding oneself from these spells. Then good fortune can come. (*See* p. 697, Freeing Yourself from Spells.)

53. *Developing the True Self*

 Sun
Kên

The Judgment: *Developing the true self. The maiden is given in marriage. Good fortune. Clarity brings duration.*[*]

Developing the true self is the process described by this hexagram as "gradually, increasingly"[**] affirming the true self as the leader of the personality. This is done by the systematic step-by-step removal of the seed phrases and images that make up the ego. In this process, a person's sense of wholeness, which had been divided and distorted by the collective ego, becomes restored. Coinciding with this restoration is the person's return to unity with the Cosmos. As this removal progresses, the true self, which was arrested in its development during childhood, grows up. Its growing up is symbolized by the development of a young wild goose from a gosling to a fully fledged goose, which development is pictured in the lines. The wild goose was tradi-

---

[*] *Li Chên*, the two Chinese characters in The Judgment, are the same as those in Hexagrams 1 and 2, where *Li* refers to clarity, and *Chên* refers to duration.
[**] Karlgren cites *Tsien* as one of the ancient names of this hexagram, meaning "gradually, increasingly." (Dan Stackhouse, *Original I Ching, A Self-Awareness Practice*, 1997.)

tionally interpreted as a symbol of conjugal fidelity. In Cosmic terms, however, the development of the goose is a metaphor for the development of a person's loyalty to his inner truth, which occurs through freeing himself from false loyalties to another person or institution.

The process by which the ego is decreased, layer after layer, can only safely take place under the guidance of the Sage, because only the Sage knows how much the psyche can accomplish at any given time, and the order in which the different aspects of the ego's program need to be removed, to avoid psychological problems.

The process leads through many "handhold understandings" toward increasing clarity. It is like climbing a rockface: each handhold allows an increase in the overall view, with no one view being definitive.

All actions through which a person's wholeness can be restored are carried out on the inner plane. The action most frequently employed is the saying of the inner No to what is false. The inner No is a person's normal response to statements that are obviously false, such as, "The moon is made of green cheese." However, because speech often contains statements that are half-truths which seem to be true at first glance, they are often absorbed into our inner programs by default, simply because we have not perceived their implicit falseness. This is particularly true of certain ideas about human nature, fostered by the collective ego, such as the self-doubt created by the statement that evil is due to man's animal nature. This self-doubt, and the belief that the individual is not good enough, in and of himself, keep the true self a child, full of fears, doubts and guilt. All mistaken ideas that a person has taken into his inner program remain in effect until the day he says the inner No to them. As elements of a false program in his psyche, these ideas comprise the source of the distortions and perversions of his original nature, which is in harmony with the Cosmos because it is an integral part of it.

It is important and correct to say the inner No to all ideas and beliefs by which the collective ego *appropriates* our Cosmic Virtues, and turns them to its use. This happens, for example, when our natural loyalty to our inner truth, which would make us say the inner No to each incorrect situation, is replaced by the duty to be loyal to people, groups (the group-we), and their beliefs, even when it involves going against our inner truth. As can be easily seen, betraying one's inner truth is the true source of evil in society, because the inner No is withheld on the basis of partiality to the particular group. Other Cosmic Virtues that are similarly appropriated, but this time by declaring them to be part of our "higher" nature, are discipline, kindness, perseverance, and conscientiousness. Before this appropriation, these virtues operate in relation to the harmony of the circumstance. Afterwards, they become dedicated to the ego-interests of the group. This is achieved by turning them into *absolute* or *abstract* virtues. Their opposites—disloyalty, wildness, unkindness, impatience, and superficiality, are then attributed as vices to our "lower" nature.

Saying the inner No to every aspect of the ego-program engages the Helper of Transformation, which removes the negative effects on the brain caused by having ingested its false phrases. The effect of this transformation, which takes place in the atomic realm, even changes the chromosomes in the body that have been affected; therefore, the change is enduring.

Changes in the psyche, created by any other means, as by forcing oneself to "become" something through discipline, positive thinking, pressure, cajoling, or contrivance, do not last and must be continually reinforced. They are part of the collective ego's program of "self-development," which consists in working at repressing one's "lower" nature with its so-called "instincts and drives," which it sees as the source of evil. The words "instincts" and "drives" are formulations derived from incorrect observations made of human behavior, after a person's wholeness has been divided and part of it demonized. While the one part is flattered and elevated as superior, the other is demonized as the source of evil. This whole process—*the very act of division itself*—has put a spell upon both the bodily nature, causing it to behave in perverted ways, and the mind. The perversions caused by the spell are then called "animal drives." The slander is put not only upon the self, but upon Nature as a whole.

567

What is often overlooked in this picture is what happens to that part of the psyche which, upon being flattered, begins to think of itself as "developed," "superior," and therefore "spiritual;" or if modesty is considered to be the hallmark of spiritual development, it will think of itself no less proudly as "modest," or "humble." All of these become *images* of self that are to be "achieved" through *work* on the self. What these images all have in common is that they are but pretensions that repress the true self. The key feature that betrays the presence of the ego is the "work" feature that accompanies self-development. That it is work (hard effort) shows the difficulty of repressing the true self, which is born with a full quotient of Cosmic chi, and naturally equipped to express its uniqueness. Constant force must be applied to "keep it down." Although the person then has the comfort of being in conformity to the group-we, he is all the while pitting himself against Nature and the Cosmos itself. The work involved in developing the self-image against such obstacles is revealed in the extreme conscientiousness that characterizes spiritual ambition. This hard work contrasts with help that comes from Nature and the whole Cosmos, and with the joy, relief, and release a person experiences each time he rids himself of a false inner phrase or image. While effort is involved in seeking out the seed phrases and images that make up the ego's program, his effort is exponentially aided by the Cosmos, and leads to enduring results. The only thing that makes this effort difficult is when he believes the ego's protests that "it is hard work," and "negative work" (here referring to saying the inner No).

Learning to say the inner No is the key to bringing the true self to maturity. It is the means by which the true self distances itself from the false leadership of the ego within. The inner No also establishes the necessary boundaries around the self, to stop the encroachment of the egos in other people. The inner No validates the person's dignity and integrity, authorizes the true self's existence, and reclaims its true place in the personality. The inner No, said to the ego in another, has the further function of communicating to the other's true self, so that he, too, can succeed in liberating himself.

Much of the conditioning process of the collective ego involves intimidating the true self into an inability to say the inner No. For this reason, a person first needs to ask, through the *rtcm*, whether his ability to say the inner No has been partially or completely blocked. If so, he needs to free himself of that impediment. (*See* p. 677, Saying the Inner No.)

The inner No is to be said to the appearance of the ego in any of its forms, either in oneself or in others. When it is said to another, it is to be combined with a retreat into reserve and neutrality until the ego in him is no longer dominant. One can relate to him safely only when his true self is again present. To hold onto the inner No beyond this time, however, is to take on the task of punishing that person, something that comes from the ego in oneself. Allowing this reverses the transformative effects of the inner No.

The ego shows itself in all displays of arrogance, temper, demand, inequality, expectation, guilt, blame, unfeeling behavior, unkind acts, partiality, careless disregard of others, indifference, envy, jealousy, vindictiveness, vengefulness, idle curiosity, slander, gossip, contrivance, self-righteousness, self-pity, and all self-images, including that of the good person. In whatever ways a person takes on a role or self-image, he betrays his true nature to the benefit of the ego. The reward for such behavior is always the recognition the ego gets from the collective ego, or group-we, or from the ego in others. Therefore, when saying the inner No to another, it is important to avoid eye-to-eye contact as well as any form of confrontation, since either of these affirms and gives energy to the ego to continue. In addition, saying the inner No supports the person's true self that has been imprisoned by the ego.

The maiden given in marriage is a metaphor for the mind (the two frontal lobes) when it is married to the inner senses. In the correct functioning of the mind, the sensations coming from a person's commonsense (the consensus of all his senses) are compared to his inner truth (memories of what Cosmic Harmony feels like), and sent to the imaging mind, where the sensations are formed into images; these images are then translated by the word-mind into words that express inner truth.

This is a correct marriage of the mind with all a person's other innate capabilities, and is manifested in the centered self. No part of this process can be bypassed to create the centered self. The creation of the ego disrupts this process, and leads the mind to increasing estrangement from the person's true nature.

In the healthy psyche, the commonsense serves both to keep us from drifting into error, and to protect us from spells and projections coming from others, among other dangers. However, our commonsense is hindered by phrases and images we have accepted that demonize some senses as lower, and exaggerate others as higher. Such ideas put spells on both, causing the senses of outer seeing and outer hearing to become virtually the only active senses of perception; this deprives us of the clarity that comes when all the senses are combined in a complete consensus. The primacy given to the outer senses of seeing and hearing is one of the primary steps in the perversion of our original nature, causing us to focus on the appearance of things and hearsay about them. The inner senses, which tell us when things "smell bad," have a bad taste, and feel inappropriate, are shut off. The spell also blocks our access to inner truth.

Another effect of the spell created by assigning primacy to outer seeing and hearing is the enslavement of the two frontal lobes (the thinking mind and the imaging mind) to the purposes of the collective ego. The thinking mind is given the enormous burden of providing all the rationales the ego needs, regardless of their truth. Because the ego thinks in terms of opposites, every ego-rationale is countered by another, creating endless inner debates in the mind about what is right and what is wrong. Such constant activity, and the futility of these debates, which are based purely on what is seen or heard, block access to the person's inner truth.

The marriage of the maiden represents the point in a person's development when his thinking and intuitive minds, also called the "intellect," are ready to be freed from their bondage to the ego, and reunited with the person's true nature, which is his animal nature. When a person has thus securely reestablished his loyalty to his inner truth, the maturation of the true self can be said to be complete.

Note: Since all lines contain infinite possibilities of interpretation, one needs to use the *rtcm* to determine if the meanings suggested here apply to the given situation. (*See* p. 736 for using the *rtcm*.)

Line 1. *The wild goose gradually draws near the shore. The young son is in danger. There is talk. No blame.*

The wild goose's drawing near the shore is a metaphor for the true self in the beginning of its liberation from enslavement by the ego. The shore is a metaphor for a place of safety where the goose can hide itself in the reeds and bushes. Drawing near the shore means that while the true self is not yet free of its bondage, the person has nevertheless made progress in overcoming the ego in himself, by refusing to listen to its loud voice. He has also made progress through freeing himself of the guilt spell that was put on his animal nature. "The young son is in danger" refers to the person's rational mind that is still under the influence of the ego, and continues to attack him with the doubt that his true self is capable of leading the personality. This is the "talk" referred to. "No blame" is saying there will be no blame if he stands up to the ego by saying the inner No to its attacks. An important part of growing up is standing up to the ego, and not being intimidated by its loud noises.

Line 2. *The wild goose gradually draws near the cliff. Eating and drinking in peace and concord. Good fortune.*

The cliff represents yet another step of progress in the development of the true self. The doubts mentioned in Line 1 have been overcome, so that the person has gained a new measure of confidence to enjoy the nourishment of the Cosmos. This is his good fortune.

The collective ego expects that the developed person should "naturally" share his nourishment with others. (*See* the second part of Wilhelm's commentary to this line.) However, sharing one's Cosmic Nourishment with another when the ego is present is a throwaway of self, and a throwaway of one's Cosmic gifts. One may correctly share such gifts only when another's true self is present, and when a true inner connection exists. Even then, they are to be shared only in proportion to the other's receptivity and openness.

This line also wants to make a person aware that the nourishment he experiences in the true love relationship is a valid, healthy expression of love. Such nourishment can never come from sexuality practiced independently of feelings of true love, for that is when sexuality becomes perverted, whether in marriage or outside of it.

The ability to love is damaged when love is divided into divine (good) and earthy (evil) aspects. It is the healthy expression of love in sexuality that renews a person's life-force. The marriage of the maiden mentioned in the main text is also a metaphor for the sexual union of two people's true selves.

Line 3. *The wild goose gradually draws near the plateau. The man goes forth and does not return. The woman carries a child but does not bring it forth. It furthers to fight off robbers.*

The plateau is not the wild goose's natural habitat. The metaphor therefore suggests that the true self has been drawn into a dangerous place by ideas that would rob it of its sovereignty, making it difficult for the person to return to his true nature.

A person may receive this line when he has acted from the belief put forward by the collective ego that doing the work of self-development means working on developing his higher nature under the guidance of a human master. He does this in order to become a person of spiritual rank. By his thus aspiring to become an image, his true self is held back from developing further (held to a plateau). The woman stands for his receptivity to the Sage, which in this case is shut off through following a human master; therefore his true self remains a child. "It furthers to fight off robbers" informs him that it is not too late to resist the ego's false leadership.

A person may also receive this line because he has literally interpreted the *I Ching's* counsel to take action, and thus has only created more difficulties. Now, the ego, which has led him to the incorrect interpretation, seeks to blame the unfortunate results on the Sage. The *I Ching's* counsel to "undertake something" always means *inner* action, specifically saying the inner No to what is incorrect, both in oneself and in others. The woman represents the true self that would have known what the Sage meant, if he had only listened to his inner truth.

This line calls attention to an authority spell the person is under, that causes him to remain in a child-parent relationship instead of growing up. He needs to seek out a self-image he holds of being inadequate, and as needing a human authority figure to tell him what is right and wrong, and deprogram it. (*See* p. 691, Freeing Yourself from Self-Images.)

Line 4. *The wild goose gradually draws near the tree. Perhaps it will find a flat branch. No blame.*

The flat branch represents those times in life when the person who is bringing his true self to maturity is placed in difficult situations. People formerly in his circle resent that he no longer takes part in their ego-activities. They misunderstand his behavior and challenge him to explain or defend himself, in attempts to draw him into ego-confrontations. He needs to say the inner No to their incorrect behavior, then ask the Sage in their presence to intervene with their egos. Thereafter, he allows events to develop without interference (he rests on a flat branch), and remains reserved with them until the Sage has intervened. Acting in this way removes all blame from the situation, for there is no longer any basis for discord.

Line 5. *The wild goose gradually draws near the summit. For three years the woman has no child. In the end nothing can hinder her. Good fortune.*

The summit represents a person's having ascended the ladder of spiritual success erected by the collective ego, only to find that he was mistaken in taking that path. By recognizing that he has allowed the ego to fool him through flattery, he repudiates it and hastens back to his true self. This brings him into harmony and unity with the Cosmos and the Helpers, that now welcome him into their circle. His recognition that he needs their help has freed them to come to his aid.

"Three years" is a reference to the fate the person had created for himself, which has either expired, burned out, or been ended through his having corrected himself. The fate was created by his acquiescing in what the collective ego called self-development. "No child" refers to the hindrance this created to the growth of his true self.

Line 6. The *wild goose gradually draws near the cloud heights. Its feathers can be used for the sacred dance. Good fortune.*

From the Cosmic viewpoint, the metaphor of the cloud heights means "out of the clouds," out of the grasp of the ego, with its delusions, flatteries, fears, and doubts— out of confusion and disorder, and into clarity. Here, the true self is pictured as emerging to lead the personality, with all parts of the person unified into a single being, and a single psyche. The person is whole, complete, and in harmony with the Cosmos.

The line can also indicate a person who has reached the goal of self-development as defined by the collective ego. The metaphor of the goose's feathers being used for the sacred dance points to a person's having sacrificed his animal nature in order to overcome his body's supposed evil influence. The self-flattery of being taken into the "heavenly realm" after having conquered his lower nature is the good fortune imagined. However, in "leaving the earth far behind," as Wilhelm's commentary puts it, he is actually leaving behind the source of his life-force; the earth is the living entity and consciousness that nourishes a person in every possible way. Beliefs that demonize the earth and our connection with it are the source of illness and untimely death. By cutting himself off from his bodily nature, which, through his feelings, connects him with the earth's life force, he becomes a person "without a head" as described in Hexagram 8, *Holding Together*, Line 6, or a walking dead person. He lacks the ability to further connect with the Cosmic Whole. (*See* Glossary: Walking Dead Person.)

The collective ego has erected its own monument of spiritual perfection: the perfected person who has fought evil in himself, and then crusaded against evil in the world. The definition of evil is whatever the collective ego has designated as such, at any given moment: poverty, crime, chaos, etc. In this effort, the hero must necessarily see culprits that must either be overcome and repressed, or extinguished. These ideas have given rise to the great Crusades, wars, and Inquisitions of Western history, and the genocides that have occurred worldwide.

The Sage teaches us that the word "culprit" has no Cosmic basis. Evil comes only from the mistaken ideas that each individual holds in his psyche. Each individual is solely responsible for what he permits to reside in his psyche, for inasmuch as he allows these ideas within himself, he separates from the Cosmic Whole. Chief among these destructive ideas are the ideas of there being a culprit, and of original fault. These ideas must not be allowed to give rise to outer action or to hostile thoughts, but are to be deprogrammed by each person's saying the inner No to them.

54. *The Marrying Maiden/An Untenable Situation*

   Chên
Tui

The Judgment: *The Marrying Maiden. Undertakings bring misfortune. Nothing that would further.*

The Sage uses this hexagram to illustrate the Cosmic Principle that the Cosmos provides us with everything we need to live a good life, if we bring ourselves into harmony with its principles.

The "marrying maiden" is used as a metaphor to describe the person who, being conditioned to think that the Cosmos does not provide for him, believes that he must make deals in order to get what he needs in life: deals with people, with God, and with Fate—to get relationships, money, health, a job, a nice place to live, etc. This is a bleak view which comes from misunderstanding the nature of the Cosmos. It is behind the expression, "one must deal with life." The person who holds this view ignores the possibility that everything he needs can come to him as a gift from the Cosmos, if he brings himself into harmony with its principles. By only looking at life as a process of making deals, such a person compromises his true nature in every situation, and constantly creates misfortune for himself.,

The "marrying maiden," being an ancient reference to a con-cubine, is also a metaphor for the untenable situations that re-sult when a person sacrifices his integrity by adopting a belief, in the hope that it will safely lead him, without his having to think for himself. Such a person is making the following deal: "I will take on this belief and follow what it says to do if it will get me what I want." Such an attitude is out of harmony, because it reveals a person who does not want to grow up and take his true place in the Cosmos as a responsible individual. He wants to remain in the comfortable lap of being told what to do, with-out any judgment by his commonsense, or else he wants to fol-low traditional thinking, as when he indulges in the idea of "un-conditional love" that feeds, tolerates, and encourages all ego-behavior.* His commonsense would warn him that there is noth-ing so hard as the consequences of making compromises that throw away his true self and his dignity. Many people approach the Sage with the demand for unconditional love, with the re-sult that the Sage cannot relate to them, until they return to humility. A related mistaken belief is that a person thinks he must do something special, or be something special, to get what he wants from life, or from the Sage. For example, he may be-lieve that he will get what he wants if he is virtuous, or if he does the right thing, or has the right appearance. Thus, through trying to "be" these things, he works at developing the corre-sponding self-images. These become rigid rules of behavior for him— rules that put his personality in a spell.

By nature, every person possesses all the virtues that enable him to relate harmoniously to life. Therefore, he does not need

---

* The idea of both conditional and unconditional love comes from the collec-tive ego, and reveals its thinking in terms of opposites. Giving love *on condi-tions* is the ego's way of withholding love until it gets what it wants. True love is a Cosmic gift to a person's true self, and is meant to flow from there to others'true selves, and back to the Cosmos, in a complete circle. This Cosmicgift is never meant to be thrown away at the ego because the ego is outside the Cosmic Harmonics. The collective ego has invented the idea of *unconditional love* to rob the true self of its very life force, under the pretense that it is "spiri-tual" to extend one's love to everyone, regardless of the ego's presence.

to memorize virtues that he must apply, regardless of the circumstances. In following his natural virtues, he is loyal only to his inner truth. This is his true guiding light.

Phrases that fix the personality in this way are: "If I do this, I will get that," "if I pull the right strings, work hard enough, stand for the right values, prove myself, play the game right..., I will get the right partner, job, place to live, etc." Others have to do with raising children: "a child must be trained in virtue; this is a parent's job" and, "spare the rod, spoil the child."

Other phrases concentrate on having the right appearance, thereby creating self-images: "If I wear the right clothes, perfume, makeup, drive the right car, belong to the right political party/organization, if I have the right degree, title," etc., or "if I (or my children) come from the right family, class, cultural background," such and such should happen.

All these self-images are culturally created values that act as spells framing the personality, and drawing the person into untenable situations. The spells create fates for him, and everything he undertakes on the basis of those self-images creates misfortune, thus the words, "undertakings bring misfortune," and "nothing that would further." The misfortunes come when the person least expects them.

In relationships, the deals people make involve complementary self-images that attract one another. Thus, a person with a particular self-image will attract a person whose self-image "fits" his. Thus, each one is attracted to precisely the person he needs to disillusion him about the desirability of his self-image. He experiences the perfection of his self-image as a growing burden, which leads him finally to the point of burnout. (*See* Line 1.) [Burnout is the exhaustion of a deluded enthusiasm. The person follows that enthusiasm with ever-increasing frustration until it simply can be followed no more. What burns out is the person's will to continue on that path. Burnout is a corrective function built into the will that finally saves a person from exhaustion of his chi energy.]

The person who believes in making deals believes that life can be manipulated by mechanical means. The Cosmos, as the origin of life, is a system of consciousness, and not a set of mechanics, therefore it cannot be manipulated. It is a system of harmonics that is synonymous with a person's inner truth. The person who is connected with his inner truth draws the Sage and the Helpers of the invisible world, which fulfill his needs. Through depending on deals, he loses their help, and as a consequence creates a fate, a fact that makes his life hard. If he frees himself from his erroneous perceptions, he will begin to experience the help that comes from the Cosmos when the Helpers have been freed, in the form of a true love relationship, the right job, the living situation that suits him, etc. When the Helpers of creativity are freed, the creative chi energy within the person is revived, making him come fully alive.

Receiving this hexagram calls a person to recognize that through making deals, he has created a fate, and that he needs to rid himself of the spells that keep him bound to the untenable circumstance. This must be done before any outer action can be taken, because he will be outwardly free to leave that situation only when the inner spell has been broken.

A person may also receive this hexagram when he has made a decision to "get along with" someone whose ego is dominant, just to keep peace, or to maintain appearances, or for similarly superficial reasons, in lieu of stating outright that the situation is incorrect, and taking inner action. Such action may include withdrawal into reserve, saying the inner No to the other's incorrect behavior, and asking the Sage for help.

If a person is unable to leave a wrong situation, as in the case of a person in prison who is subjected to unjust treatment, it is important for him to maintain a strong consciousness that the situation is incorrect, say the inner No to it, and inwardly ask for help. That brings the help needed to transform the situation from within.

Note: Since all lines contain infinite possibilities of interpretation, one needs to use the *rtcm* to determine if the meanings suggested here apply to the given situation. (*See* p. 736 for using the *rtcm*.)
P

Line 1. *The marrying maiden as a concubine. A lame man who is able to tread. Undertakings bring good fortune.*

Here is pictured someone who has agreed to put herself in

the place of a concubine through making a deal to marry or accept a partner who does not wish to grow up (here called a "lame" man). She has accepted the deal because she has flattered herself with the self-image of being the one who "helps others" (be it people or animals). Because the partner has lost his connection with the Cosmos through choosing to remain undeveloped, this has caused him to look for someone to feed him the chi energy that is constantly diminishing. Thus she is enslaved to supply his chi from her own source, something that in the end exhausts her supply of chi, as well.

The self-image of the person who helps others can be a spell composed of phrases such as: "he/she/they need me"; "I'm the only help he/she has," "what would they do without me."

Phrases that characterize the people they help can also be a spell. Such phrases are: "He/she is the only one I can rely on," or "he/she is the only one for me." These spells make each person falsely dependent on the other until such time as the spells are broken, or burn out. (*See* main text.)

Getting rid of the spells is the undertaking that brings good fortune. This frees the Sage and the Helpers to help both parties who were bound together by the spells. (*See* p. 697, Freeing Yourself of Spells.)

The Cosmic Principle enunciated by this situation is that a person who has made a deal that compromises his dignity, inner truth, or self-respect, is not obliged by the Cosmos to see that deal through. He also needs to free himself of any feeling of guilt that may result from his withdrawing from the deal, and must not accept any blame from the partner.

Line 2. *A one-eyed man who is able to see. The perseverance of a solitary man furthers.*

The "one-eyed man" can be a metaphor for the person who has made a deal with Fate by accepting his suffering. His deal is based on the idea that if he accepts and endures suffering in his life on earth, he will not have to suffer in the afterlife. Similar deals are pacts one makes with God "to do this or that, if...." The person is described as one-eyed because he can only see the possibility of suffering. What he cannot see is that with the help of the Sage and the Helpers, he can get to the root causes of his suffering and end it.

The line can also point to a person who sees himself as "being loyal." His view of loyalty in relationships is that the two partners are halves of a whole, and that they are meant to think, act, and feel as one. "The perseverance of a solitary man furthers" calls attention to the error of this idea, since each person is whole in himself, and no person is meant to lose his integrity by blending it into the personality of another. Neither should his loyalty be such as to put loyalty to the other above his loyalty to his own inner truth. Receiving this line is to say that the person's Helper of Integrity has been imprisoned by this belief. To free this Helper, he needs to rid himself of that belief, and to pledge his loyalty only to his inner truth.

Spells created by this belief contain phrases that pledge loyalty to anything but his inner truth, and to ideas such as, "it takes two to make a whole." Pacts a person has made with Fate or God need to be treated as spells. (*See* p. 697, Freeing Yourself from Spells.)

Line 3. *The marrying maiden as a slave.*

The marrying maiden as a slave can be a metaphor for a person who has sold his integrity to get something, such as recognition or endorsement for being kind, selfless, etc. He gives himself, regardless of the circumstances, because he thinks it would be unkind to say No. However, no person is obligated to remain in a situation that has been bought at the expense of his integrity. To regain his dignity he needs to free himself of the self-image of the "kind," or "selfless" person.

In a related circumstance, a person may be giving love on the condition that he will get something, but the consequence is that he suffers because he is being drained of his life force. (*See* footnote to the main text.) Such a person has the self-image of "being greathearted" which makes him give himself while sensitivity is lacking, thus feeding the ego in the other. To free himself from this untenable situation, he needs to say the inner No to the idea of "unconditional love," and free himself from the self-image. (*See* p. 691, Freeing Yourself from Self-Images.)

This line can also describe a person who thinks he can enhance his creativity or knowledge by using others as tools for this purpose. This can also apply to the person who thinks he can use the *I Ching* as a tool to this end, thereby attempting to turn it into the slave of the ego. However, the *I Ching* does not allow anyone to use it in such a way, but counters by leaving that person to his own ego-devices. All he gains is abstract knowledge that has no beneficial application to his life. To correct himself the person needs to say the inner No to such motives and activities, and apologize to the Cosmos.

A person may receive this line when he has compromised his principles because he thought he had no other choice. Now that he is aware that such a compromise was unnecessary, he is being informed that he can rectify the situation by apologizing to his integrity, and going on with his life. He needs first, however, to discover the mistaken idea that led him to believe he had no other choice, and deprogram it.

Line 4. *The Marrying Maiden draws out the allotted time. A late marriage comes in due course.*

The marrying maiden in this line is a metaphor for the self-image of the "patient person." This self-image is based on a seed phrase, such as, "life will reward me with what I want, if only I will be patient." To end his endless waiting, he needs to rid himself of the seed phrase.

A related self-image is that of the "pure/chaste person." The person with this self-image imagines the body as being the "vessel" for the soul, and thus puts a spell on his body as untouchable. The "marriage" envisioned is to take place in the afterlife, hence the words, "a late marriage comes in due course." Such a self-image puts a spell on the body, causing frigidity. To become free of this spell, it is necessary for the person to rid himself of the mistaken idea that sexuality stains the body. It is also necessary to rid himself of the idea that the body should serve as the vessel for the soul. (Also *see* Line 5.)

Line 5. *The sovereign I gave his daughter in marriage. The embroidered garments of the princess were not as gorgeous as those of the serving maid. The moon that is nearly full brings good fortune.*

In contrast to the previous hexagram, the daughter mentioned here "who has been given in marriage" is a metaphor for the person who accepts an inferior position as his or her lot in life. This person has the self-image of being "dependent," "worthless," or "handicapped," therefore "destined" to take an inferior position. This kind of "thinking poor" about himself keeps him locked into inferior positions.

The "sovereign I," in this line, represents the collective ego, which has "fathered" the idea that humans have a "soul," as a way of attributing an eternal life to the ego. The soul is said to be that part in a person that is "eternal." Giving his daughter (the soul) in marriage is a metaphor for the vow a person makes to devote his energies to his soul, through spiritual development. When a person embraces this idea he makes his body into the serving maid of the soul. The embroidered garments stand for the high reputation the person receives in this life for his devotion. However, this metaphor makes it clear that the serving maid, as the body, possesses what the princess, as the soul, does not: it is the body that is real, and part of eternal Nature, while the soul is not because it is a construct of the ego.

As for when people see themselves in the love relationship as "soul mates," this emphasis on the soul denies that the true love relationship is not between two souls, but between two people's true selves. The emphasis on their souls puts their true selves in a spell that becomes their inner prison. One of the seed phrases of this spell is: "our souls are bound together by destiny."

"The moon that is nearly full brings good fortune" points to hopes related to the soul. The person who puts his hopes in the soul keeps his true self imprisoned; therefore, he cannot experience the fulfillment of all his needs that would come to him as gifts from the Cosmos every day. He only focuses on hopes of good fortune coming at some time in the future.

Line 6. *The woman holds the basket, but there are no fruits in it. The man stabs the goat, but no blood flows. Nothing that acts to further.*

582

This line can have many possible meanings, all of which circle around the principle that doing something for appearance's sake leads to results that are empty of their promises.

The line can point to a marriage based on two complementary self-images, rather than being a unity between two people's true selves. Such a relationship lacks nourishment, as indicated by the basket that has no fruits in it; it also lacks sincerity, as indicated by the image of a superficially performed ritual. One of the partners may have the self-image of being the one who "sacrifices all for the relationship," while another believes it is his duty to sublimate himself to the will of the other, and carry it out. In both cases, the people have imprisoned their true selves by having adopted these beliefs.

Other self-images that imprison the true self are that of the "dutiful person," the "socially responsible person," and the "religious person." Phrases and pacts connected with these images are: "it is a woman's duty to follow her husband's will"; "it's a man's duty to fight and die, if necessary, for his family, country, and beliefs"; "to be loyal to another unto death"; "to share everything with another, regardless..."; "to be true to all the pacts one has made." To free his true self, the person needs to rid himself of all pacts and promises to behave in a certain way for any length of time. (*See* p. 697, Freeing Yourself from Spells.)

Also of concern are pacts or contracts a person has made with another, or with God, in which he promises to do something or give up something in return for security against a variety of threats. In this regard, he may have adopted the self-image of the smart businessperson who believes security lies in well-made contracts, be they marriage or business contracts. Phrases supporting this point of view are: "it's better to have everything spelled out on paper," and "you never know unless you have a contract," and "the smart person nails things down." What he gets through his pact-making is not security, but a fate, and the imprisonment of his true self and his integrity. To benefit from the protection of the Cosmos he needs to recognize that he has an incorrect view of life that "what you see is all there is." His view creates fates which continually confirm it. He can end his fate by ridding himself of the slanders he has put on life, and by freeing himself from his self-image, and from the pacts he has made, as well as any feelings of guilt connected with them. (*See* p. 692, Freeing Yourself from a Fate, and p. 691 Freeing Yourself from Self-Images.)

The "woman holds the basket but there are no fruits in it," can also be a metaphor for a person who has learned from the Sage how to heal others (the basket), but does not apply it to himself. "Stabbing the sheep" refers to his having given it a try, but without success (no blood flows). The reason for his difficulty is that he has the belief that if he is to be able to heal others, he ought to be able to heal himself, and so is embarrassed. This bit of ego-pride has created a spell that blocks his being able to apply what he has learned to himself. He needs to free himself from the spell of "needing to be perfect." (*See* p. 697, Freeing Yourself from Spells.)

55. *Abundance*

 Chên
Li

The Judgment: *Abundance has success. The king attains abundance. Be not sad. Be like the sun at midday.*

This hexagram shows the difference between abundance as a Cosmic Principle and abundance as defined by the collective ego. Cosmic abundance refers to a variety of things:
- abundance of caring feelings
- abundance of prosperity and progress
- abundance in regard to life and its limitlessness
- abundance in the forms in which life takes place, whether they be visible or invisible
- abundance in caring, help and nourishment for all the needs of life
- abundance in our Cosmic Possessions

- abundance in help to bring us back into unity with the Cosmic Whole
- abundance of gifts, such as the gift of love
- abundance in Cosmic patience with humans
- abundance of space for creativity, such as for the expression of life
- abundance both of inner and outer space
- abundance of space for evolving our consciousness
- abundance in the Sage's teachings
- abundance of health

Unlike the traditional idea of abundance, Cosmic abundance is beyond linear or cyclical limitations: it is not followed by times of lack or decay because it is continually insured through transformations.

The collective ego defines abundance solely in terms of what a person possesses on the outer plane. Typically, this kind of abundance is seen in the context of the human-centered universe, where humans are the only purpose which Nature and all things in the universe are meant to serve. For humans, abundance means power and influence, titles, wealth, possessions, knowledge, wisdom, public recognition, rights and privileges, and the right to believe anything a person chooses, and do anything he has the power to do. Even this view is ironic, because as history shows, abundance in all these things is inextricably dependent upon a hierarchical ordering of society, meaning that abundance is available only for the few at the top, at the expense of those at the bottom. This abundance creates an overabundance in the human population, which is necessary to uphold abundance at the top, therefore it also creates an abundance of poverty, sickness, perversion of natural values, and damage to Nature and the natural order. Necessary to this system are an abundance of mistaken ideas about the Cosmic Way, an abundance of fears and fantasies, and an abundance of human power, arrogance, and ignorance, to keep the system under control.

An image connected with this abundance is "culture at its height." History incorrectly attributes all the great achievements of culture to humans. What is omitted from this description is the fact that every significant achievement is a gift of the Cosmos. Discoveries such as penicillin are a case in point. The discovery came entirely as a laboratory accident; nevertheless, the man who was working on the project was subsequently credited and honored with the Nobel Prize for the discovery. The *I Ching* makes us aware that in all such cases where the person, after having been helped, either claims the achievement for himself, or inwardly accepts the collective ego's recognition for his discovery, the good effect of the discovery gradually dissolves. Penicillin was one of those "Nature's Helpers" that through being treated wrongly, has waned in its overall effectiveness because the Helpers are gradually retreating from it. The Helpers will return when a person asks them to help him when applying the remedy.

While the collective ego would say, "abundance (in terms of possessions, power, etc.) is the measure of success," we are guided to see that the words "abundance has success" refer to an *attitude* that leads to success. True modesty is the attitude that constantly draws the help of the Helpers. The consequence is the abundance of gifts the Helpers bring. Modesty occurs when a person recognizes the beneficial nature of the Cosmos, and the fact that all the gifts and blessings of his life come from that source. This attitude is attained when a person rids himself of all the mistaken ideas of what abundance is, and how it comes about.

He also needs to delete from his inner program negative phrases and images that block abundance, such as "there is nothing but poverty in the world," "life is hard," "abundance cannot be for everyone," "abundance does not last," "it's a jungle out there," "it's a dog-eat-dog world," "the rich get richer, the poor get poorer," "it is easier to pass a camel through the eye of a needle than that a rich man may enter the Kingdom of Heaven," "to be spiritual is to be poor," etc.

"The king attains abundance" reflects the feudal view that "abundance is for the rich and powerful." This view makes poor people believe that they are not meant to have abundance, and to accept the phrase, "that's the way things are." "Be not sad" can be the consoling phrase of the collective ego, with the implication being, "you will get your reward in the afterlife." Such phrases, which accept poverty as one's "natural" condition, disable the Helpers, so that the phrases become self-fulfilling prophecies. When not inhibited by mistaken ideas, the caring nature of the Cosmos would have us live in abundance, having all we need for our well-being. When we recognize that being fulfilled has to do with a healthy relationship with Nature and the Cosmos (which also provides us with nourishment, help and protection, and also material possessions in abundance), a feeling of self-worth, and a recognition of the greatness that lies in small things, there is no need for greed (the building up of large funds for security), outward display of possessions, power over others, or for protection by security systems. A person who focuses on these things is unaware of the continuous fates he is creating, the purpose of which is to rob him of what he has actually stolen from Nature and from the Cosmos by acting upon his human-centered view.

"Be not sad, be like the sun at midday" can also be the words of the Sage, telling us that although things look bleak at the moment, we are on the way to abundance, due to the help of the Helpers.

Spells connected with this hexagram are created by phrases implying an acceptance of the inevitability of poverty, bad health, mistreatment by others, or any other negative condition. Such phrases and beliefs shut out the help available from the Helpers. This hexagram tells him that by deleting these spells, he will experience abundance as freedom from those conditions. (*See* p. 697, Freeing Yourself from Spells.)

The hexagram also counsels that a person is not meant to meekly accept his fate, but rather to understand its lesson and thereby free himself from it. All fates can be extinguished. (*See* p. 692, Freeing Yourself from a Fate.)

Note: Since all lines contain infinite possibilities of interpretation, one needs to use the *rtcm* to determine if the meanings suggested here apply to the given situation. (*See* p. 736 for using the *rtcm*.)

Line 1. *When a man meets his destined ruler, they can be together ten days, and it is not a mistake. Going meets with recognition.*

The "ruler" in this line can refer either to the Cosmic Consciousness or to the collective ego.

The line is saying that when a person is in harmony with the Cosmos, he experiences all things as abundance. He is nourished by the beauty of the flower, the light of the sun, the refreshment of the rain, and when deprived of these, is able to hear the inner music of the heart. When he is in this state of inner harmony, help pours in from the Cosmos.

When a person is in unity with the Cosmic Consciousness, he is subject to a different realm of time, which is unlimited in nature. "Ten days" expresses this relative quality, and says that abundance depends on the person's remaining in harmony, for when he listens to the ego's whisperings, he allows it to appropriates to its glorification what has been received. This initiates the eclipse described in the following lines, causing the person to lose all he has gained. The words "it is not a mistake," refer to his vigilance to quell these attempts by the ego at their onset. "He does not wait a whole day," as it is put in Hexagram 16, *Enthusiasm*, Line 2.

When the line refers to the collective ego, the reference to ten days is to the time limit put upon the success a person gains through following its ways. It points to the inevitable fall that follows upon every rise; for example, the fall of the ancient empires and their leaders (Rome), the fall of modern dictators (Napoleon, Hitler, Stalin), the fall of "great" republics," or the decline of rich families, making the point that everything that depends on the collective ego is ephemeral in its success.

"Going meets with recognition" refers to the collective ego's idea that immortality is achieved through doing deeds that cause one to "go down in history." Often this line addresses a person who has this hidden desire.

In relation to the relativity of Cosmic time, this line points to the idea of immortality as falsely implying the existence of mortality. In turn, mortality defines life's purpose in terms of greatness or insignificance. All these ideas cast a melancholic light on life that stops its abundance.

Receiving this line also points to phrases of the collective ego about what makes a person great. Examples are: "Hard work is the path to greatness," and "he that serves the greater glory of God will himself be made great." Such phrases need to be discarded through saying the inner No to them. Doing so will re-unify the person with the Cosmos.

Line 2. *The curtain is of such fullness that the polestars can be seen at noon. Through going one meets with mistrust and hate. If one rouses him through truth, good fortune comes.*

The curtain refers to the darkening effect of a solar eclipse. It is so complete that the stars of the dipper can be seen at noon. The picture is a metaphor of a complete misunderstanding.

This line calls attention to the chief cause of misunderstanding: the false use of language, which creates misunderstandings about life and the Cosmic Way. The curtain is a metaphor for the veil that is drawn over the Cosmic Truths by mistaken beliefs and their expression through language.

The false use of language starts with words that have come from thinking which is not based on feeling. Such words are removed from the specific to the abstract, from practical everyday life to the clouds. The resulting misunderstandings eclipse commonsense, creating a reverse world. Language is meant to express the feelings of inner truth, which is in harmony with the Cosmic Truths; false language diverts the person to considering the ego's endless rationales that support its lifeless abstractions. An example is the way the collective ego flatters and then harnesses the intuitive mind to create and maintain the myths which support its dominance. The legendary emperor Fu Hsi, monumentalized as the "creator of culture," due to his having "invented" fishing, agriculture, and the *I Ching*, is an example. The myth served both to elevate humans over other creatures, due to their cultural achievements, and to justify the need for rulers (thus the feudal system itself). Through such myth-making, language has been perverted, blocking its true function to express inner truth.

"If one rouses him through truth...." is speaking of a person who is under the spell of myths. It is saying that an opening can be created in his understanding, if another asks for the Sage in his presence to intervene and make him realize that all the conventional answers given him by his beliefs have not provided him with the real help he needs. It makes him ready to hear his own inner truth, and to engage with the feeling intelligence of the Sage, which harmonizes with his own commonsense.

The curtain can also refer to prejudices a person has, for example, about what is ancient. He may either disregard the *I Ching* as the work of a primitive culture, or he may believe it to be a "pure" source of wisdom, just because it is ancient. Either prejudice prevents the student who consults the *I Ching* from benefiting from the help it can give, when he uses the *rtcm* to clarify the intended meaning with the Sage.

In the first case, he believes that his intellect is the only thing he can trust and therefore may even despise the Sage (*I Ching*) before he knows what it is. In the second case, the curtain refers to the pedestal on which the person has put the *I Ching*. He looks at it as a sacred text that must not be questioned. This attitude keeps him from discovering how he can learn from the alive consciousness that speaks through it, and from putting what he learns to use in his life. In both cases, the person lives entirely in his head, having divorced himself from his feelings. Such an attitude creates a fate.

Line 3. *The underbrush is of such abundance that the small stars can be seen at noon. He breaks his right arm. No blame.*

Here, the eclipse of understanding is total: the inner program, installed in a person's psyche by the collective ego, is so full of explanations of the fundamental nature of the Cosmos, that were the truth so plain as the nose on his face, the person could not see it.

The half truths which are at the basis of all belief systems, need a huge body of rationales to dismiss the objections commonsense would normally make if the person were to look at the belief's basic premises. The rationales distract him from noticing the absurdity of these basic premises. He is likewise prevented from examining these premises by a number of taboos that say he would become guilty if he questioned them.

"He breaks his right arm" refers to a person whose commonsense has been made ineffective, due to conditioning during his youth. It also refers to inhibitions installed through fear of punishment, that have disabled his ability to say the inner No. Thus, he is stuck in the psychic problems created by his belief system. In order to free his commonsense, he first needs to free his ability to say the inner No. (*See* p. 6775, Saying the Inner No.) Then he needs to deprogram the following half-truths: (1) the poison arrow that he was born with original fault/guilt; (2) the spell saying "that the eyes alone can see the truth"; (3) the spell that says, "thinking is superior to feeling." (*See* p. 697, Freeing Yourself from Spells and Poison Arrows.) He may ask the Sage, through the *rtcm*, whether any other spells or poison arrows are contributing to keeping his commonsense imprisoned.

As long as a person is under the influence of the above-mentioned spells and the poison arrow, he is not consulting the Sage at all, but is reading the *I Ching* as a book of ancient wisdom, extracting from it only that which supports his beliefs. The "small stars" refer to his seeing everything but the truth. To make sure that he correctly understands what the Sage wants to tell him, he needs to use the *rtcm*.

"No blame" counsels that there will be no more cause for blame if he corrects his way of consulting the *I Ching*.

Line 4. *The curtain is of such fullness that the polestars can be seen at noon. He meets his ruler, who is of like kind. Good fortune.*

This line can refer to a person who is dying or has died. His death needs to be understood as the end of a fate that he had created by holding to mistaken beliefs about life and death. His death, however, brings the good fortune that with the end of his fate he is reunited with the Cosmic Consciousness. What rules is the ultimate unity of the Cosmos, which supersedes life and death. This Cosmic help comes just when a person recognizes his greatest need for help. What is shown here is the abundant love the Cosmos has for everything that is a part of it.

The belief that death eclipses life leads to the final eclipse of a person's inner light, as described in Line 6 of Hexagram 36, *Darkening of the Light*. However, the Law of Fate precludes that anyone should get lost in "eternal darkness." This mistaken belief is fostered by the collective ego to threaten people into compliance with its moral rules. (*See* Glossary: Death.)

Line 5. *Lines are coming, blessing and fame draw near. Good fortune.*

Because a person has achieved a correct understanding of the Cosmic Principle of Abundance, and has rid himself of his respective mistaken beliefs, lines of Helpers are coming, bringing blessings. "Fame" here, although wrongly named, refers to the recognition and validation given to a person's true self by the Cosmos in the form of material gifts in abundance. Thus, the line states the Cosmic Principle that inner clarity is the prerequisite to prosperity.

This line also addresses the collective ego's idea of blessings: as fame a person achieves by seeking out other humans, with whom he hopes to achieve great deeds. His fault lies in his ambition. This line wants to make him aware that the "blessings" he has been expecting from the Cosmos are not forthcoming, because he has created a fate. It can be extinguished if he rids himself of the self-image of the heroic person.

"Lines are coming" can also refer to a person who believes in personal and global prophecies given by fortune-tellers, or prophets. While each person comes into this life with a set of inner directives (symbolized by the pole star), his life is not spelled out in detail, or predetermined. Often, he will lose sight of his directives, but the adversities created by this make him reflect, and pull him back toward them, without any guarantee that he will fulfill them. The Sage in each person's presence, and his Personal Helper, are ever-present to help him fulfill those directives, but everything depends upon what he wills himself to do, and whether or not he asks for the help available.

"Lines are coming" can refer to the momentary glimpses a person receives, throughout his life, which tell him of his destiny. These glimpses enable him to put all the seemingly disparate interests, pursuits, and events of his life into a meaningful perspective. The events have only been waiting for the liberation of his true self, to be seen as the "perfect preparation" to bring his uniqueness to full expression. This perspective shows the ultimate economy of the Cosmic Way: nothing in a person's life is wasted *if* he is willing to see everything as a preparation for the final fulfillment of his life in a body.

Line 6. *His house is in a state of abundance. He screens off his family. He peers through the gate and no longer perceives anyone. For three years he sees nothing. Misfortune.*

Here, abundance refers to a person's arrogant self-image of being the one "who did it all." It may be that he sees himself as the virtuous and capable helper, who credits himself with the good that has been achieved. He therefore appropriates the Cosmic gifts to his personal advantage, using them to his glory, or to gain power over others. "Misfortune" refers to the fate he has created as a consequence.

This line can also refer to a person who amasses wealth and power through his contrivance and cleverness. Such a person has stolen his wealth from the Cosmos and from Nature. Through his blind arrogance and self-absorption, he is described here as "no longer perceiving anyone." This, and "peering through the gate" mean that he sees others only as tools to serve his interests. "Misfortune," as above, refers to the resulting fate. The words "three years" refer to the spell he has placed on his senses of inner and outer seeing.

A person can also receive this line because he is putting a spell on someone else by characterizing him as "blindly arrogant," or through envying ("peering through the gate") his abundance of wealth, power, or knowledge. By doing so, he also puts a spell on himself. The line can also refer to a person who exploits Nature by looking at it as an object, the only purpose of which is to serve his interests. He not only creates a fate for himself, he also puts a spell on the things he exploits.

This line can also indicate that a person is under an abundance of spells. To rid himself of them, he needs to ask the Sage for guidance to identify them. This might involve asking for one or more hexagrams.

This line also refers to the person who, although blessed by the Cosmos, focuses on negative things, and therefore can no longer see things as they truly are. In doing so, he loses his connection with the Cosmos which is the misfortune mentioned.

56. *The Wanderer*

 Li
Kên

The Judgment: *The Wanderer. Success through the small. Being firmly correct brings good fortune to the wanderer.*

The Sage uses the image of the wanderer to describe the person who is on the path of freeing and bringing to maturity his true self. He is a wanderer because he must make this journey alone, with no one between him and the Sage, as his teacher. He no longer looks to his family as the authority, but makes his own decisions based on his commonsense, even at times when he is totally misunderstood by those around him. Following the *I Ching* has often been experienced as a lonely path. This is true only when the *I Ching* is viewed as something lifeless, as book of ancient wisdom. When the student develops his personal relationship with the Sage—the alive consciousness that speaks through the book—he finds himself in the company of a wonderful and trustworthy friend, thus no longer feels lonely. The difficulties he experiences thereafter occur only when he doubts the good intentions of the Sage, or misunderstands why the Sage must retreat in the face of the ego.

His journey has the purpose to bring to expression his uniqueness, and thereby fulfill his destiny. This occurs through his experience of the Cosmic Truths.

This hexagram states the prerequisite for the wanderer's fulfilling his destiny: that he develop an understanding of his true place in the Cosmic Whole as an equal to all its other aspects. It is from this understanding that modesty, which keeps him in harmony with the Cosmic Way, springs.

"Success through the small" refers to the success that comes from including the Sage and the Helpers in his daily life. The "small" are the transformations that take place in the atomic realm, due to the activity of the invisible Helpers, when a person takes them into account in all that he does.

Among these Cosmic gifts and the help he receives are: a true relationship with the person who suits him, good health, a place to live, the job that fulfills him, and material wealth. He is meant to enjoy them. They are given to nourish him, teach him, and help him express his uniqueness. He realizes that if he allows the ego to appropriate these gifts through attachment, he decreases the Cosmic Whole and creates what the *I Ching* calls *blame*. Then he loses them as gifts of the Cosmos, and they cease coming. His losing them is expressed in Line 3 in the words "the wanderer's inn burns down." The inn is a metaphor for these gifts of home, and sustenance that he receives while in a bodily form. The image of an inn is a reference to the temporary function of these gifts, to fulfill his needs of the moment. The inn, as the temporary abode of the wanderer, is the complement to his "property" which is defined in Line 2 as his dignity and self-respect. By complement is meant, the two are drawn together through attraction.

The wanderer describes the person who has undertaken the liberation of his true self, while in the middle of the world created by the collective ego. He may be estranged from those around him, because they do not understand his process.

He differs from them, in that he is not inwardly attached to his possessions, because he knows where they come from, and knows that his needs will be answered. Thus, he is secure and centered within himself.

What guides the wanderer on his path is his *inner truth*. He is free to experience his Cosmic Possessions as part of his learning process. This freedom includes making mistakes that come from not understanding, and therefore not respecting the Cosmic Harmonics that rule the Cosmos as a whole. The Cosmos gives him all the help he needs to return to his path, before the deviations become too great. A deviation, or dissonance from the greater harmony, is felt as a tension that tells him that he needs to look for its cause, and to correct himself. All dissonances are caused by mistaken ideas put forth by the collective ego. Their purpose is to lure him back into *its* way of life. In order to return to the Cosmic Way, the person needs to seek out the seed phrases and images that underlie the mistaken ideas in question, and delete them from his inner program. They may exist in the form of projections or spells. (*See* p. 689, Freeing Yourself from Seed Phrases and Images, and p. 697, Freeing Yourself from Spells.) When dissonances come from the egos in other people, he needs to say the inner No to them. Correcting dissonances, as they occur, is the meaning of "being firmly correct brings good fortune to the wanderer."

The Cosmic wanderer differs from the person who has adopted an image of himself as being on a spiritual journey. A person may receive this hexagram to inform him of the difference between following the path of his inner truth, which has never been trod by anyone before him, and following a path which has been laid out for him by another, and which the many are treading. While the Cosmic wanderer seeks to fulfill his uniqueness, the spiritual wanderer is seeking to fulfill a self-image of goodness, or perfection.

A person may also receive this hexagram when he has forgotten his true place in the Cosmos, through having adopted the human-centered view of the universe, and other mistaken ideas and beliefs that stem from that view.

Adopting the human-centered view of the universe leads to an attachment to the apparent world as the only reality, and the only thing that gives meaning to his life. Or, it means looking at life on the earth as something that needs to be transcended in exchange for a better life in the hereafter. The human-centered view of the universe also distorts a person's relationship with the Sage. It either makes him think that he can command the Sage as a sort of genie, whose purpose it is to supply his wishes, or it makes him see the Sage as a Higher Power that has authority over him.

Among the mistaken ideas addressed by this hexagram are those that express the human-centered view of the universe, but specifically those that exclude the Helpers of the invisible world and a person's relationship with them. Examples of such ideas are:

- "Our bodily existence is all there is"; this leads to attachment to the material world.

- "Human beings are divided into body, mind and soul," leading to a person's developing his "higher/spiritual" nature at the expense of the rest of his being.
- "Man stands as the centerpoint between heaven and earth," with heaven and earth being conceived as separate places, and heaven being superior to earth. This idea divides the Cosmic Whole, demonizes the earth, and makes a person long to leave his body and the earth behind.
- Ideas that define the purpose of life as being to perfect the moral standards created by the collective ego; these ideas are coupled with the threat of death and damnation, if the individual should follow his inner truth instead.

When the wanderer, as one who is following the Sage's teachings, gives way to the collective ego's threats and follows its standards, he loses his inner home. This is described in Line 6 in the words, "the wanderer's nest burns down." A person may also lose his inner home when he sacrifices his true self to fame, glory, material considerations, or spiritual perfection.

Wilhelm informs us that "strange lands and separation are the wanderer's lot." This is a bleak view of human life in a body. It suggests that humans have been cast out of Eden by an unfriendly Cosmos, whereas in fact, all separation and estrangement from the Cosmos are created by the individual himself when he follows the collective ego's false values, and in doing so, creates fate after fate for himself. Wilhelm's statement is an example of how the collective ego reverses cause and effect.

This hexagram makes it clear that help is available from the Cosmos, at any given time, to end a person's fate and separation from the whole. No one is meant to carry impossible burdens, nor is a person's progress meant to be stopped by insurmountable obstructions due to spells, projections, or poison arrows (put on him either by himself or by others). If a person is hindered by these problems, he can identify the mistaken ideas that have caused them, with the help of the *rtcm*, and ask for help to free himself of them in the here and now, according to the instructions given in the Appendix.

The traditional commentaries to this hexagram mention lawsuits, in relation to the text of the traditional *I Ching*, which is called The Image. These lawsuits, which can be outer conflicts, begin as *inner* wars and conflicts that are accompanied by spells, projections, and poison arrows. Participating in them creates a fate, whereas saying the inner No to them and turning them over to the Helpers, leads to transformation and the end of the fate. (*See* Hexagram 6, *Conflict.*)

The wanderer can also be a metaphor for a person who, having become estranged from his true self, wants to learn from the Sage. Such a person's true self is at the stage of development it had attained when it was abandoned and imprisoned in childhood. Due to this estrangement, the person is like a child learning about the world. If he will put aside his distrust in the benevolent nature of the invisible world, he will be shown everything he needs to know to make progress on his path in the inner and the outer world.

Note: Since all lines contain infinite possibilities of interpretation, one needs to use the *rtcm* to determine if the meanings suggested here apply to the given situation. (*See* p. 736 for using the *rtcm*.)

Line 1. *If the wanderer busies himself with trivial things, he draws down misfortune upon himself.*

This line can call attention to a fate a person has created by busying himself with concerns of the collective ego. Among such trivial concerns are judgments based on the human-centered view of the universe:

- about justice, crime, and the supposed guilt of others
- about supposed rights and privileges
- attributing catastrophes to weather, or Nature, when they have been the result of expectations projected onto Nature
- gossip and idle curiosity about others' relationships, including the intimate affairs of animals
- blaming one's fate on an outside cause, rather than seeing its cause in oneself
- watching whether others are conforming properly to the moral and behavioral standards (the oughts and musts) of the collective ego
- preoccupying oneself with things afar rather than with what lies directly in front of one

• dismissing things of real significance (such as money) as mundane, in favor of working on a spiritual self-image.

When a person does not understand the Cosmic Way and has created a fate due to his incorrect views, the ego in him will seek to put the blame on something or someone else, the Cosmos, life, Nature, or even his true self, rather than having the ego itself recognized as the cause; in addition, it may put a heavy burden of guilt upon the person. The person needs to catch onto this tactic of the ego before it plunges him into yet another fate. (*See* p. 689, Freeing Yourself from Mistaken Ideas and Beliefs, and p. 696, Freeing Yourself from Guilt, and p. 692, Freeing Yourself from a Fate.)

The line can also refer to a person who feels guilty for possessing something while others have nothing. Possibly he has been taught as a child to take on guilt for the starving children in the world, human maltreatment of animals, trees, the earth, etc. It is one thing to care about all these things, and act responsibly in regard to them, but it is another to allow guilt to drive one to fulfill the image of the "compassionate person." Striving to fulfill this self-image keeps the person from saying the inner No to wrong conditions and their causes, and from asking for help from the Helpers, which are truly able to correct these conditions through transformation.

Line 2. *The wanderer comes to an inn. He has his property with him. He wins the steadfastness of the Cosmic Helpers.*

Here the wanderer, the person who is on the path of his inner truth, is in the midst of others. The "property" he has with him consists of his dignity and self-respect. In keeping with his self-respect, he holds to the others only as long as they hold to their own dignity and self-respect. So long as he maintains this guideline, he draws the Cosmic Helpers of the invisible world to help him in all that he does. This line states the principle that it is modesty and sincerity, when combined with dignity and self-respect, that draw the Helpers into one's life.

This line can also point to seed phrases that lead a person to throw away his dignity and self-respect to get something: "there is no help coming from outside, therefore one has to make compromises," "there is no such thing as Helpers," "you can't wait around for something you can't see," "how do I know they will come?"

Line 3. *The wanderer's inn burns down. He loses the steadfastness of the Cosmic Helpers. Danger.*

The "inn," or gift of sustenance to the wanderer, has "burned down" because the person has betrayed his self-respect and dignity by tolerating the arrogance and indifference of others around him. He has done this in order to get along with them, instead of saying the inner No and retreating inwardly. His lax attitude has caused the Cosmic Helpers mentioned in Line 2 to retreat, and if persisted in, will create a fate, which is the danger mentioned.

This line describes the principle that the wanderer cannot take for granted that he will be protected and furthered by the Helpers when he carelessly betrays his inner truth. He can correct himself if he retreats in time from his overconfidence.

Line 4. *The wanderer rests in a shelter. He obtains his property and an ax. My heart is not glad.*

Here, the wanderer whose inn has burned down, in the previous line, has had the benefit of a Cosmic intervention (the shelter mentioned). In comparison to what he has lost, the shelter is minimal. His heart is not glad because the ego has been trying to blame his loss on the Sage, and to discount everything he has learned through following his inner truth, as invalid or worthless. The property and ax remind him that this knowledge has not been lost, is still valid, and if he will put aside his pride, and regret his mistake, he will be restored to the Cosmic Harmony.

This line notes that once a person has begun to learn from the Sage and to follow the path of his inner truth, abandoning that path to return to the world of the collective ego makes him feel miserable (another meaning of "my heart is not glad.") The ego tries, at this point, to prevent his return to his inner path by interjecting some form of self-doubt, blame, or shame. He needs to free himself of these elements by saying the inner No to them.

That is all he needs to do to regain his "inn."

This line can also point to someone who believes that he will be "sheltered" if he follows the rules of the collective ego. The "ax," in this case, refers to the fact that the property he attains, through playing the ego's games, must always be defended from the thieves and intruders who would take it away. Because he has turned away from Cosmic Protection, his heart is never at peace.

This line can also apply to a person who takes shelter in incorrect ideas, which, like a faulty roof or floor, fall through when he begins to rely on them. Such ideas include a mechanistic view of the world. An example is the use of medications that seek to cure solely through chemical means, rather than by addressing the fundamental issues of consciousness which create susceptibility to illnesses. Spells, projections, or poison arrows may be at the root of the problem. (See p. 694, Freeing Yourself from Some Health Problems.)

Line 5. *He shoots a pheasant. It drops with the first arrow. In the end this brings an office.*

Here the pheasant refers to the self-image of one who has fully adopted the human-centered view of the universe. He thus views himself in the image of God, or of the "superior man." He has played God through:
 • judging others as evil
 • assuming that he has the power to forgive
 • encroaching into others' spaces
 • indulging in the use of power
 • acting as if he possesses rights over other people and things
 • believing he has been given the power to authorize others

In allowing this self-image of superiority, the person has separated from the Cosmic Whole and engaged the Cosmic warrior, whose business it is to shoot down all arrogance. The mention of "an office" is informing the person that it is not too late to retreat from his arrogant self-image. If he does so, he can enter the service of the Sage. (*See* p. 691, Freeing Yourself from Self-Images.)

Other versions of playing God occur when a person places all his respect in the achievement of knowledge. Such a person believes that attaining mastery gives him power, and thus he invests all his energy in developing the self-image of the master. A phrase connected with this self-image is: "There are no limits to what you can do with your mind." This self-image also gives rise to the idea that the person is morally free to do any experiment on any thing.

The office given a person by the Sage is the task which enables him to fulfill his destiny. This does not necessarily mean that he has to change the outer circumstances of his job. He can serve the Sage in whatever position he is in. He is counseled by this line to free himself from the "fear of having to change." (*See* p. 693, Freeing Yourself from Fears.)

Line 6. *The bird's nest burns up. The wanderer laughs at first, then must lament and weep.*

In this line, the bird refers to the wanderer, and the nest to the place within himself where he feels at home. When, through sacrificing his true nature he obtains a more prestigious home (fame, possessions, or the hope of glory in the afterlife), the wanderer first laughs. Receiving this line is to make him aware that he will soon come to recognize that in abandoning his modesty and simplicity, he has lost everything of real value, causing him to lament the loss of his true home.

This line can also refer to a person who has been experiencing a fate, but because he is truly sorry for the effects of his arrogance on others, his fate has been brought to an end. Thus, he is once more united with the Cosmic Whole.

"The bird's nest burning up" can also point to the mistaken idea of the phoenix rising from the ashes, which implies that one has to lose everything in order to be cleansed of the mistakes one has made. A similar idea is that a person's body must die in order for the person to enjoy eternal life, or union with God. This idea creates a fate, because it violates the Cosmic Principle that every mistake can be corrected simply by identifying and rooting out the mistaken idea or belief that has caused it. (*See* p. 689, Freeing Yourself from Mistaken Ideas and Beliefs.)

It also denies the fact that life in a body, while being subject to time and space, is nourished, protected, and helped by the Cosmic Consciousness at all times, when the person brings himself into harmony with it.

57. The Penetrating

 Sun
 Sun

The Judgment: *The Penetrating. Success through what is small. It furthers one to have somewhere to go. It furthers one to see the great man.*

In this hexagram the Sage describes the Cosmic Principle of Penetration. It has several fields of application:
- penetration is the way our thoughts penetrate through the light to the Sage when we ask for help, and is the way the Sage's thoughts penetrate to us as insights, intuitions, mind-flashes, and correct responses to emergency situations;
- it is the means by which our thoughts get to the root causes of problems;
- it is the way our thoughts communicate with others' inner truth;
- it is the means by which the inner Yes and inner No reach all parts of our own psyche and body;
- it is how the inner Yes or inner No, when said to others, communicate to their inner truth;
- it is the way the inner No corrects projections, spells, poison arrows, and negative thoughts by meeting them in the realm of consciousness, and by initiating transformation;
- it is the way chi is transmitted to our hearts from the Cosmic source, to renew our life force.

Penetration describes the way the smallest correct thoughts communicate sympathetically through inner channels between people. It contrasts with the way the smallest incorrect thoughts and intentions communicate by disharmonious vibrations that are felt by a person's various senses. Such vibrations also communicate a person's doubts, fears and feelings of guilt.

Penetrating to the root causes of problems is the undertaking shown by the lines of this hexagram. It is the way the person consulting the Sage goes about finding incorrect phrases and images in his inner program, that act out in his life in the form of impulses and irrational behavior, and which can cause him inner distress, illness, and a fate.

Correct thoughts and feelings that penetrate invisibly to others' inner truth are loving and caring thoughts, and also gratitude or embarrassment. They can also be conscious inner messages that warn another that he will create a fate if he continues in his wrong acts, or tell him that he can ask for help from the Cosmos. Conscious thoughts that come from inner truth can also make someone aware of a mistaken idea or belief, without any need for them to be spoken aloud.

When the inner Yes and inner No are said to one's body cells, they heal conditions of ill health. The inner Yes is said to affirm the importance of the cells and to validate the senses they contain. The inner No is said to the phrases that have diminished the importance of certain body parts, as when the mind or soul are elevated over the body. Such conscious affirmation of the body by the mind reopens the channels through which the body receives its chi nourishment.

The inner Yes is likewise said to the love one feels for another, and to the other's true self. The inner No is said to all aspects of the ego in oneself or in another. The inner No penetrates to the true self, and strengthens it.

The inner No, said as a conscious acknowledgment of one's feelings of inner truth, penetrates to the invisible world of the Helpers, engaging them in the need of the moment. The Helper that is most activated by it is the Helper of Transformation. This is one of the meanings of "success through the small." Also, when the conscious mind acknowledges the inner feeling of needing help, this is the modesty that draws the Sage to his side.

Penetrating also describes the ability of a person who is connected with his feelings of inner truth, to discern thought which is of Cosmic origin, from thought which is the activity of the fantasy and rational minds. It is also his ability to recognize half-truths or untruths through his inner senses. Generally, these "feel" incomplete, or "questionable;" thus, the person ponders them. But when the riddle in them is "swallowed" as wisdom, instead of being rejected until thoroughly understood, then the person ignores his feelings. These distinctions are made by the commonsense. Commonsense, however, is often held under a spell created by seeing the body, with its myriad senses, as "animal," therefore "inferior." The commonsense is also blocked when the guilt spell surrounding the fact that one has an animal nature is in place.

The words of The Judgment, "It furthers one to have somewhere to go" refer to asking questions of the Sage that lead to penetrating to the inner truth of a matter. All ideas that people take for granted as true need to be questioned. People often consult the Sage to find out what to *do*. They transpose their feudal idea of the father to the Sage, hoping to be told whether their ideas and plans will bring good fortune/success or misfortune/failure. The Sage will indeed answer, but the person may misunderstand the answer and act incorrectly, if he does not know *why* an idea, plan, or attitude brings good fortune or misfortune. If he is to succeed enduringly, and not simply be tricked by the ego, he needs to penetrate to the basic principles or laws that underlie all existence: the Cosmic Harmonics. Penetrating to the basics leads to the clarity of view pictured by the Chinese ideogram "*I*," in the name, *I Ching.** Like laws of physics, these basic laws set the parameters or "correct limits" that apply to human thought and action. To go against them or to exceed them is like trying to fly without wings.

With the help of the Sage, a person can penetrate to these basic principles; they are reflected in his own inner truth. Only when a person understands these principles can he know whether his thoughts and actions will lead to a success that endures, or to misfortune. Gaining clarity to understand the inner truth of each situation is the first goal of consulting the Sage.

---

*One meaning of the ideogram for "*I*" is "clarity" as indicated by its reference to the "sunlit side of the mountain" as compared to the shaded side.

The phrase, "it furthers one to see the great man," is counsel for the person receiving this hexagram to make the Sage of the *I Ching* his teacher. The way the Sage teaches is through the penetrating influence of inner truth; penetration "breaks through" into a person's consciousness as a realization, just when he is ready for that particular realization. The Sage does not exceed what the student is ready to perceive, or superimpose knowledge upon him; neither does it engage in inner argument or reasoning, or engage in any effort to "prove" the validity of its counsel. It only engages in cooperation with the student's receptivity and openness, after he has recognized the trickery of the ego. It leads him to experience the Cosmic Truths for himself, within the context of his daily life situations; thus the person helped feels the *personal* essence of that truth, its harmony, and its resonance with his whole being. Through this process of daily learning, his confidence in his inner truth, which had been shattered or eroded through the conditioning process of the collective ego, is gradually reestablished. Gradually, then, his true self grows up and becomes a mature adult.

Receiving this hexagram may be telling a person that he needs to penetrate to the root of the problem at hand, by asking the Sage to help him understand what he needs to know. He is being counseled to understand its inner meaning, as well as its outer components. At the root of all interpersonal problems lie false seed phrases and/or images that are embedded in people's hearts. In particular, he needs to look for fears and doubts that were created in childhood.

As noted above, this hexagram also wants to make the person receiving it aware of the penetrating/transforming effect of saying the inner No to incorrect actions in himself and in others. (*See* p. 677, Saying the Inner No.)

The way ego-driven thoughts and feelings communicate from one person to another is quite different: they communicate in the form of vibrations given off by pressure, fear, doubt, and gossip. Negative thoughts gain acceptance by others through creating fears that cause them to doubt their inner truth. Negative thoughts and feelings can also take on the form of mental demons that jump from shoulder to shoulder, whispering into each person's ear. These fears and doubts open the door to unpleasant experiences and difficult situations. They also put spells and projections upon the person and those around him, keeping them trapped in their unfavorable behaviors.

Bad intentions of an aggressor register in the intended victim as an inner warning. Whether the person warned acts on his inner sense of caution depends on whether he habitually dismisses it. "Success through the small" refers to listening to those small warnings. Generally speaking, people with bad intentions sense through their inner feelings those persons around them who habitually dismiss their inner sense of caution, and are drawn to them.[*]

In another example, the desire of a person who is actively looking for a mate is communicated by vibration. Since the desire comes from the ego in him, rather than from his inner truth, he sends the message that his inner space is an "open house" to all prospective candidates. Those he draws are the exact complement to the ego in himself. This mental approach contrasts with the person who asks the Cosmos to bring him the person who is correct for him in all respects, and turns the matter over to the Cosmos. He will find the person who complements his true nature.

A person may also receive this hexagram when his negative inner thoughts are jumping onto another, with the effect of repelling him, or inciting resistance. His thoughts are instigating the negative reaction, causing the person to behave exactly as he has been projected to behave. Moreover, such thoughts can create a fate. (*See* p. 697, Freeing Yourself from Projections.)

Note: Since all lines contain infinite possibilities of interpretation, one needs to use the rtcm to determine if the meanings suggested here apply to the given situation. (See p. 736 for using the *rtcm*.)

Line 1. *In advancing and in retreating, the perseverance of a warrior furthers.*

This line warns a person that in contemplating just the ap-

---

[*] An old Chinese proverb says, "Harm enters only where fear makes the opening."

pearances of things and drawing the superficial conclusions to which this leads, he will create spells or projections. The ego is ever busy in this kind of activity, keeping the observations focused on the plane of the apparent, because doing so keeps the person from consulting his inner feelings and commonsense. In this manner, the ego maintains control of the personality. Perseverance of "a warrior" refers to his being on guard against the quick conclusions the ego likes to draw, and maintaining contact with his inner feelings.

An example is the phrase or realization: "I am getting older." If the person is not inwardly alert, this statement will draw to mind images and traditional beliefs about aging, which have to do with going toward death, and in the process, being attacked by various ailments and the shrinking of his abilities. Adopting these images puts projections and spells upon himself. The unfortunate consequences are guaranteed, once the projections or spells have been programmed into the psyche.

This line warns the person to be on guard to listen to the kinds of preconceptions that have entered his mind about a given situation, and to reject them all by saying the inner No to them.

Advancing and retreating with the perseverance of the warrior also describes the way a person says the inner No to another's incorrect behavior. Advancing refers to saying the inner No, and retreating means turning the matter over to the Helpers and disengaging. The perseverance of a warrior represents maintaining an open awareness of the situation.

Line 2. *Penetration under the bed. Helpers are used in great numbers.* Good fortune. No blame.*

"Under the bed" is a metaphor for a projection or spell that is influencing a person or situation without his being aware of it. A spell may have been put on him or another at a prior time, which is now causing either ill health or behavioral problems. The line counsels the person to "penetrate" to the phrases and/

---

* The traditional reading referred to "priests and magicians." The former were discarded by the Sage and the latter were pointed out to be a misnomer for the Helpers; they, for their part, do not achieve their results by magic, but by transformation created in the atomic realm of consciousness.

or images of the spell, by identifying when it was installed, by whom, and then to evoke the memory of the time, so that the phrases become evident. The Helpers are the ones that are needed to break it. (*See* p. 697, Freeing Yourself from Spells.)

In the case of all spells which affect a person's health, looking for relief from traditional sources, either in medicine, religion, science, or in the esoteric field, will at best only drive the symptoms to a new location, so long as the seeds of the problem have not been removed from that person's psyche.

Line 3. *Repeated penetration. Humiliation.*

"Repeated penetration" refers to seeking a solution to a problem by employing one traditional or conventional means of help after another. "Humiliation" refers to the fact that none of the remedies available from these sources is of help, because the decisive factor is the Sage that alone can activate the Helpers needed.

By seeing the decisive help as coming from humans alone, a person obstructs or imprisons the Sage, and thus prevents it from helping him with the particular matter at hand.

Often, the problem at hand is caused by the very phrases and images a person has adopted that dismiss the Sage or slander Nature, including his own nature. Examples are phrases about the Sage: "How can you trust something invisible?" "How do you know you can acquire the Sage's help?" "This is a matter that only people can decide," "the Sage is just another belief," "it's all just more smoke and mirrors," "coins cannot connect you with the Cosmos," "Helpers are a delusion," "the invisible world is a fantasy world," "there's no relationship between thought and hard fact," "you are relying on pure faith/fluff." Other examples are phrases referring to public matters or politics: "What can you do when the power belongs to the authorities?" "Only authorities can influence authorities," "I don't care about the means, what counts is the end," "you have to take matters in hand and do this yourself." Still other phrases are in regard to illness: "Nature's means are unreliable," "nature is at fault," "it's a natural defect," "you are born with some defect (including the idea of original sin)." In all such situations, it is wise to use the *rtcm* to see if projections, spells, or poison arrows need to be identified and removed.

This line also refers to a person's repeatedly falling back on doubt about the Cosmic Way. It is not faith or trust that is needed (as suggested by the collective ego), but the suspension of disbelief that makes an opening for the Sage to come to help.

Line 4. *Remorse vanishes. During the hunt three kinds of game are caught.*

"Remorse vanishes" refers to having found and eradicated the root cause of the problem at hand—in seed phrases and images, which have created projections or spells.

"Three kinds of game" refer to the multitude of seemingly unrelated problems that were created by the projection or spell, which have now been resolved.

Three kinds of game can also refer to the three kinds of causes for a condition of ill health: (1) spells or poison arrows, (2) Fate, and (3) incorrect treatment due to a mistaken assessment of the causes.

Line 5. *Being firmly correct brings good fortune. Remorse vanishes. Nothing that does not further. No beginning but an end. Before the change, three days. After the change, three days. Good fortune.*

"Being firmly correct" refers to the steps involved in freeing oneself from projections, spells, and poison arrows. It requires saying the inner No (a) to the person who has cast the projection, spell, or poison arrow, be it someone else or oneself, (b) to the person who has unwittingly accepted it, be that someone else or oneself, and (c) to each phrase and/or image that comprises the projection, spell, or poison arrow. The last step (d) is to ask the Sage and the Helpers to delete it. Afterwards, it is appropriate to thank the Sage and Helpers for their help. This procedure is repeated for at least three days and is the meaning of the phrase, "Before the change, three days." "After the change, three days" refers to the time needed for the effect to take place. The word "change" refers to the transformation that is brought about by saying the inner No.

"No beginning but an end," refers to the absolute end brought to the negative element that has been in the psyche for a long time, as if without beginning.

"No beginning but an end," also refers to the way to end disharmony: by realizing that there is no such thing as a culprit; there are only mistaken ideas. Branding someone or something as a culprit freezes that person in their behavior through putting a spell on him. Then one side blames the other, and vice versa, creating an ongoing warfare. To end the warfare, one needs to say the inner No to the idea of there being a culprit, and to free the other from the spell. Through this act, both the vicious circle and the war are ended, restoring Cosmic harmony.

This line also refers to the necessity of putting an absolute end to the imps, dragons, and demons that compose the ego and which rampage through the psyche in demonic form. (*See* Glossary: Demonic Sphere of Consciousness.) They have not been discussed much in this volume because by giving them names, their existence as objective entities is empowered. When we see them only as aggregates of consciousness that are composed of faulty seed phrases and images, they become disempowered. Then, each phrase and image which composes them can be removed from the psyche through the inner No and with the help of the Helpers. This removal disperses the clouds of disharmonious thought and deconstructs the imps, dragons, and demons, leaving us free of their demonic effects.

Line 6. *Penetration under the bed. He loses his property and his ax. Perseverance brings misfortune.*

"Penetration under the bed," in this line, is a metaphor for a person who is searching out the causes of his fate. "Under the bed" is a place where people have traditionally stored things; it here refers to his sorting through his past experiences for clues, by categorizing them in the collective ego's terms of good or evil, right or wrong. So long as he does this, he will miss finding their inner truth, and assign the wrong causes. Continuing in this manner will create a new fate.

Losing his "property" refers to his disregard for his natural possession of commonsense that would help him find the true causes of his fate. Losing his "ax" refers to his disregard for the ability of his word mind to make a correct decision (when it is free from spells, and from being harnessed to the defense of the traditional beliefs). When free, the word mind is able to distinguish what is true from the Cosmic standpoint and what it not, and to make the necessary decisions that require his independent judgment; when free, it also enables him to give the correct names to things. (*See* Hex. 58, *The Joyful.*)

In following what the collective ego calls "good and evil," "right and wrong," a person also believes that the good and the right must be defended and promoted. This leads to employing force and resorting to the courts of law. Resorting to power invariably creates a fate.

A person may receive this line as counsel to ask the Sage to show him, in meditation, the inner truth of the matter.

58. The Joyful

 Tui
Tui

The Judgment: *The Joyful. Success. Perseverance is favorable.*

The trigram *Tui*, doubled in this hexagram, has been traditionally associated with two images: the still water of the lake, and the stagnant water of the swamp. Here, the Sage pointed to "still water" as representing the conditions that bring about true joy, and "stagnant water" as the conditions that pervert it. The still water thus represents the Cosmic Principle of Joy.

Defined further, the still water of the lake represents the liquidity and stillness of the mind that make insight possible. Liquidity means not fixed in one's views, while stillness is the absence of ego-emotions and preconceived ideas. Liquidity and stillness make a person receptive to the liquid light that enables instant communication with the Sage through mind-flashes. A mind-flash occurs when the liquid light transforms Cosmic

Consciousness (which exists as a *feeling*) into words or images that express the Cosmic Truth needed in the moment. It is to be noted that mind-flashes are but one of the myriad ways in which the Sage is able to communicate.

The stagnant water of the swamp characterizes the demonic sphere of consciousness and its perverting qualities, which lead to rigid attitudes. Its "joy" is the perverted joy that results from the demonizing of what is natural in us.

Legge translates the success indicated in The Judgment as "the pleasure of (inward) harmony." Fiedeler uses yet another meaning of the Chinese word *Tui*, calling the hexagram "Der Austausch," meaning "The Exchange." "The Joyful," as we were guided to name this hexagram, conveys the sense of relief and joy that comes when an incorrect name that has been given to something, placing a spell on it, is exchanged for a name that describes its essence, freeing it from that spell. A thing's true name is found by asking the Sage to be shown its true nature. It comes from inner reflection rather than from only looking at its outer appearance. The same principle applies to finding the inner truth that correctly describes situations.

The image of true joy is embodied in the vision of the calm lake with its mirrored surface. When things are called by their true names, they feel recognized for what they truly are. That brings them joy and the peace that resolves the inner anxiety and self-doubt created from being called by a wrong name. It also brings joy to the person who names them correctly, because a feeling of unity is created between them. The still lake is also a metaphor for a situation where the words and images express its inner truth.

"The Joyful" also expresses the activity of finding, with the help of the Sage, the words that express the inner truth of situations through putting questions to the Sage.

"Perseverance" refers to questioning *all* the names humans have given to things, and the qualities attributed to them, by putting them to the Sage, since correcting our use of language is one of the primary functions of the oracle. Since both the names and qualities attributed to things contain (often hidden) assumptions, these assumptions need to be questioned, together with our unreflective use of language altogether. It is this unreflective use of language that allows the collective ego to superimpose its human-centered view and false values upon the individual, and thereby maintain its power. Making the effort to rectify language is essential because the whole parallel reality created by humans is due to wrong words and the false use of language. Among the most common false assumptions are:

• **that we humans are "special" because we have the ability of language.** The *I Ching* shows us that this ability is unique but not special, because every aspect of the Cosmos has been given unique abilities;

• **that the words we commonly use to describe things are correct.** When we receive answers from the Sage that we do not understand, it is time to ask, through the *rtcm*, whether our question contained a word that has no Cosmic basis (meaning, it contradicts the Cosmic Way). One may ask, "Is there a problem with a word I used?" If the answer is "yes," the first step is to identify the problem word or words. Finding the correct word often answers the entire question. To find the correct word, we must give the Sage the opportunity to show that word in a larger context, as for example, by developing one or more hexagrams. An example of how we misname things is when we call the help coming from the Helpers a "miracle," or "magic," or regard it as "supernatural." Their help is the normal way Nature accomplishes its tasks when we have not interfered with it or blocked it;

• that **problems need to be resolved solely on the outer plane**. This assumption is often hidden when we ask, "What can I *do* about this problem?" The Cosmic Way to correct problems is to take action first in the realm of consciousness, as by saying the inner No, or calling on the Helpers for help. After having done this, we may then ask, "am I also meant to do something on the outer plane?"

• that the *I Ching* **contains moral rules of conduct**. Moral rules of conduct put spells on people's Cosmic Virtues. What is needed is to liberate oneself from superimposed moral rules which block and pervert true joy.

"Perseverance is favorable" points to the necessity to always make sure that we have understood the Sage's message correctly, rather than merely assuming that we have. For this purpose we use the *rtcm,* as explained on page 736.

A major problem that inhibits joy in life is naming the Cosmic Consciousness "God," *when* that word is connected with images that present a mistaken view of the Cosmos. When, however, God is seen as the "all" which includes all that exists, and means only loving energy, then that idea *is* in harmony with the Cosmos. Not in harmony is an image of God in human form, God as the supreme authority, God as the authorizer and protector of the collective ego, God as a monarch or judge, a wielder of power, and as possessing characteristics and emotions common to the ego in humans. Also discordant is the image of God as having given man the job of being overseer of God's property (the earth). These ideas of God are essentially Western in origin. While there was no specific concept of God in the Chinese tradition, the role that "heaven" played in authorizing the Emperor, resembled these mistaken Western ideas of God.*

A major problem with the ideas of God and heaven is that they show the Cosmic Consciousness ordered like a feudal society. It is an image of the invisible world created to support humans' arrogant view of themselves.

A student of the *I Ching* who is unaware of the above- mentioned problem ideas, easily makes the Sage into a figure of authority, thus creating a false distance between himself and the Sage. In this relationship, he sees himself as "little" or "insignificant." Such projections on the Sage and on himself make it difficult for the Sage to approach him in the friendly, personal way that is natural to the Sage. If the student rids himself of all his projections, the presence of the Sage is felt as true joy, and he himself is no longer caught in the grip of being the eternal child.

---

* Each Chinese family honored and paid tribute to its chief ancestor, but there was no overall God. Heaven, and not a specific being, was seen as the origin of all things. Heaven and earth were seen as the "all" which operated on principles of harmony. The person who put himself up in a god-like position was the emperor, who decided that his power gave him the job of administering heaven's will on earth. It is to be noted that the action of declaring himself a "god" was also taken by the Roman emperor Augustus.

The same joy comes when a person acknowledges the Helpers of the invisible world as companions and friends. When we begin to experience and recognize the Sage and the Helpers in our daily lives, we also begin to experience the loving, generous nature of the Cosmos. We shut out its love when we give it false names, attributes, and identities.

Those of us who come from Western religions to consult the Sage tend to see the Sage as the founder or figurehead of a religion. Such a view is spurred by the ego-need to make the Sage into a comfortable, father-like figure that belongs to our family or clan. Various lines in the *I Ching,* especially in Hexagram 13, *Associating with People,* address this appropriation of the Sage by the individual ego as partiality. The Sage is neither a father nor a partisan *of any clan.* Behind this tendency is the fear of damnation that accompanies any thought of "turning away from the God of one's fathers." The Sage, knowing the depth of the underlying fear, gives the person time to develop the confidence needed to trust the Sage enough to reject this threat. (*See* Hexagram 18, *Recognizing and Correcting the Causes of Decay.*)

True joy also comes when a person recognizes his own true nature and embraces it fully. This is different from the feelings of self-contempt that dwell in a person who has obtained power and recognition through deceiving others. This self-contempt is projected outward as a contempt for those who have believed his deception. Invariably, with time, this "joy," that has come from "being seen as special" by the collective ego, deflates and must again and again be reinflated, until such time as it burns out altogether. At the point of burnout, the person is left with a feeling of emptiness, because he now sees the falseness and vapidity of the collective ego's recognition.

Finally, the Chinese ideogram *Tui* shows how fear and sorrow are dispelled, when the correct names for things are found. This is also to say that fear and sorrow are always the consequence of misunderstanding the nature of things. When we realize the unity of the Cosmic Whole, and that it functions through harmony, we realize that nothing in its nature gives cause for fear and sorrow. Fear and sorrow come from accepting spells projected upon us, by ourselves or by others, or from assigning wrong names to things. Dispelling these spells is the undertaking that brings us joy. It is done through taking away the wrong names, by saying the inner No to them, and finding their correct names with the help of the Sage.

Note: Since all lines contain infinite possibilities of interpretation, one needs to use the *rtcm* to determine if the meanings suggested here apply to the given situation. (*See* p. 736 for using the *rtcm*.)

Line 1. *Contented joy. Good fortune.*

Contented joy refers to a state of awareness that is free of expectation and/or of projection. (*See* Hexagram 25, *Innocence/ Not Expecting/Not Projecting.*)

This line refers to the state of the newborn child. Although it does not yet use language, it has the perfect inner feeling program needed to live life in harmony with the Cosmos, free of expectation and projection.

This state differs from that of the adult who has learned to use words to describe reality and to construct belief-systems. Receiving this line may indicate that the words he uses to name things do not express their inner truth; therefore, he is in conflict with these things. The problem can be resolved by finding their correct names. This happens, for example, when a person calls the Cosmic Consciousness God and attributes to it all the ideas already associated with the word God, as listed in the main text. Giving the wrong name to a thing puts a spell on it.

Line 2. *Sincere joy. Good fortune. Remorse disappears.*

"Sincere joy" refers to submitting the names by which we call things to the Sage, to see whether they are correct. When we find the correct name for that which has been misnamed, the doubt and fear that are inspired by that incorrect name disappear. That is the good fortune referred to.

Receiving this line makes a person aware that he has drawn false conclusions due to misnaming something, or to having accepted wrong names given by others. To carry on the example given in Line 1, when we misname the Cosmic Consciousness God, certain fears are aroused that come from seeing it as an authority figure that has power over us. When we realize that the Cosmic Consciousness is neither higher, nor uses power, but helps us reunite with its harmony, there is no place for fear.

Line 3. *Coming joy. Misfortune.*

This line refers to drawing false conclusions about the Cosmic Way from looking only at the negative *appearance* of something, as when we conclude that life is suffering, or, that joy is to be attained only in the future or in the afterlife. The misfortune is the fate that is created by such a belief, as it projects itself into reality. Such a belief also puts a spell on the person's Cosmic gifts, making it impossible for him to enjoy them. For example, these gifts include his ability to receive and express love in all its aspects, and to ask the Cosmic Family for help with all his needs.

The person can correct this problem and the fate he has created, by ridding himself of all the beliefs having to do with joy coming in the future or in the afterlife. Beliefs in joy coming in the afterlife are based on the division of the Cosmos into heaven and hell, with earth and Nature being on the hell side of this division. Heaven, in this picture, is associated with the expected joy of being in the presence of God, the king of heaven. Such beliefs demonize the Helpers that comprise all aspects of our earthly nature, as well as those of Nature generally. When freed of this demonization, they give us the sense of well-being and wholeness which is the true joy defined by this hexagram.

The person who builds his life on hopes of future joys misses out on living his life altogether. The person who lives his life in the moment draws the Helpers to his side. By recognizing their presence in his daily life, he constantly experiences joy.

As for the person who has experienced misfortune, if he will let go of his negative thoughts and emotions about it and go on with his life, without expectation and without regret, he will find himself accompanied by the Cosmic Helpers.

Line 4. *Joy that is weighed is not at peace. After ridding himself of mistakes, a man has joy.*

This line refers to a person's allowing the ego in himself to weigh and choose what it prefers, rather than allowing the Cosmos to give him what is correct.

For example, a person may be weighing whether to settle for a relationship at hand that is incorrect. Or, he may be compromising his dignity and integrity by accepting inequality, insensitive treatment, or other unfair conditions, in order to get along. The ego, in urging such acceptance, suggests that "you can wait forever without getting what you really want," and "better the bird in the hand than two in the bush." Such a relationship cannot lead to inner peace. If he says the inner No to such phrases and suggestions and corrects his mistake, he will make it possible for the correct relationship to happen.

This line also refers to weighing, through asking the Sage, whether a word or a phrase expresses Cosmic Truth. Often it is only a matter of adding or omitting one word that turns a Cosmic Truth into a half-truth.

Receiving this line can indicate that we have failed to subject our primary beliefs to such questioning; thus we have allowed our ego to weigh and choose what *it* prefers.

Line 5. *Sincerity towards disintegrating influences is dangerous.*

"Sincerity towards disintegrating influences" refers to judging the nature of things in terms of "good and evil." Doing so divides the wholeness of Nature into opposing parts that fight each other. The person receiving this line is made aware that the question he has put to the Sage implies that Nature or the Cosmos in general are divided into good and evil parts. This assumption is incorrect. The Cosmos is a system of harmony. Only the parallel reality created by the wrong use of language is characterized by opposites. (*See* Glossary: Good and Evil.)

This line can also refer to a person's thinking he has rights which he must protect; behind this idea is the hidden assumption that humans are at the center of the universe. When a person is in harmony with the Cosmos, there is no need for rights, as the Cosmos protects what he truly possesses. The same hidden assumption is at work when a person decides that he will trust the Sage's advice only when its answers agree with his own views. Such an approach will be ignored by the Sage, so that only false or misleading answers will be received. This is the source of the danger mentioned.

Line 6. *Seductive joy.*

What is "seductive" is the short-lived joy that comes from the self-admiration of the person who, seduced by the ego, imagines himself to have been given the special task to name things according to his own whims. The result is that he puts spells on them, creating suffering for them and a fate for himself.

There is also a certain seductive joy in putting oneself up on a pedestal to judge others and their ways. Since indulgence in such joys comes from the ego, with its "knowing better," it creates inner wars between people. These wars can be stopped by saying the inner No to the ego in oneself. Judging others is the way the collective ego keeps its order going. Fear of being judged intimidates people, keeping them from following their inner truth. The collective ego succeeds in these tactics through calling people and things "culprits," when, from the Cosmic viewpoint, there is no such thing as a culprit. The word "culprit" puts a spell on them. It also creates a fate both for the one who creates the spell, and for the one who accepts it, either knowingly or unknowingly. (*See* Glossary: Culprit.)

Receiving this line indicates that a person is putting spells on things and on his situation by misidentifying and misnaming them. This person believes he is at liberty to give verbal expression to his fantasies, be it through writing or speaking, thereby exercising a harmful influence on things. An example is the storyteller who uses his word and image minds to gain power over other people's minds by stimulating their ego-fantasies, rather than to reflect to them their inner truth. Such a misuse of his abilities creates a fate. (*See* p. 692, Freeing Yourself from a Fate.)

Finally, true joy comes when we free the intuitive and word minds from being harnessed by the ego and made to serve its purposes. Once freed, they are restored to their original functions, with the intuitive mind having the function of forming images of inner truth, and the word mind of rendering these images into words.

59. *Dissolution/Dissolving*

 Sun
K'an

The Judgment: *Dissolving brings success. The king approaches his ancestral temple. It furthers one to cross the great water by being firmly correct.*

The Sage has pointed to the main theme of this hexagram as dissolving one's attachment to the collective ego, with the aid of the Helper of Dissolution. Differing types of ego elements require different treatments, in order to free oneself of them. This hexagram speaks of those that require dissolving, such as rigidity, and what the Sage has identified as "balls of conflict."

Rigidity occurs when a person becomes attached to a set of rules that tell him what to think, what to feel, and what to do, instead of listening to his inner truth, which would connect him with his sense of what is harmonious and what is discordant in each given situation. Rigidity is the result of dependence on the collective ego. The collective ego spells out and applies its rules and regulations to all circumstances; the individual internalizes these rules as "right and wrong" and "good and evil."

A person's attachment to the collective ego is expressed by his thinking in terms of the "group-we," as in saying, "We are one big family," whether it refers to a marriage, family, community, spiritual group, people in a corporation, or a whole nation. Thinking in those terms diverts the individual from being in touch with his own inner truth, and forces him to place his dependence on the values and rules that have been defined by the his group. This shows that the group-we is a group-ego.

Dissolving one's attachment to the collective ego is the meaning here of "crossing the great water by being firmly correct." The great water, in this case, is a metaphor for the river of fears and self-doubts, on the one hand, and flattery and vanity, on the other, created by the collective ego to keep the person trapped in his feeling of need to belong to the group. Dissolving this attachment is achieved by identifying the seed phrases and/or images that hold him to the group-we, saying the inner No to them, and asking for the Helper of Dissolution to dissolve them.

The collective ego says that if the individual dissolves his attachment to its groups, order in society will dissolve with it, and chaos will reign. However, just the opposite is true, as the natural order of society becomes liberated. This order produces cooperation, creativity, and harmony between humans and the Cosmos; therefore, help comes to them in all forms from the Cosmos. The striving, competition, conflict, and exercise of power that constantly create suffering and chaos in the social order, are no longer needed.

The individual's feeling of belonging to the group is carefully cultivated by the collective ego through the introduction of fears and self-doubts, by his being told he is insufficient, in and of himself, on the one hand, and through a flattery that gives him the feeling of being special and protected by the group, on the other. However, this unity is only an illusion, which contains no real fulfillment but instead leads the person to suffer the fate of that group. Helping the individual to free himself from these false bonds to the group is part of the greater Cosmic Plan to reunite him with the Cosmic Whole.

The feudal interpretation of the purpose of dissolution, as explained by Wilhelm, is actually the opposite of its Cosmic meaning. The importance of this interpretation is that it provides us with clues to the mistaken beliefs we need to dissolve in order to free our true self from the grip of the group-ego. The collective ego's argument, that "egotism is what divides humans from one another," is used to assert that a person's holding to his inner truth will prevent him from joining the group-ego—something that is necessary if the existing feudal-based order of society is to be maintained. According to Wilhelm's commentary, the integration of the individual into the group is accomplished through the performance of "splendid religious ceremonies and sacred music," which have the purpose of impressing the individual that the king alone possesses the human connection with heaven. Wilhelm comments that this display stirs the individual's emotion in a way that it is "shared by all hearts in unison," awakening in him "a consciousness of the common origin of all creatures."

This description shows the sleight-of-hand logic employed by the collective ego, in that the identification with the group-we is achieved through the creation of awe—the awe arising from the individual's personal insignificance. The awe also contains the perception that the group to which he belongs is "awesome" and that he, who is otherwise insignificant, is honored (flattered) by being made a part of it. The consequence is that his identification with the group dissolves his loyalty to his inner truth and transfers it to the group-ego and its values. By dedicating himself to the group's "high goals" and "great general undertakings," he shifts his sense of self to the group-ego, and thus loses his inner independence.

Wilhelm's description enumerates the very emotions that leaders (who choose to represent the collective ego) mobilize in preparation for wars, that team leaders mobilize to play gladiatorial sports, that gang leaders mobilize to loot and kill, etc. Indeed, they are the ego-emotions that are aroused and employed by demagogues of every kind. The moment the individual relinquishes himself to such emotions is the moment in which he abandons his ability to feel his inner truth. It is when his feelings of what is harmonious and discordant are replaced by mental considerations of "right and wrong," or "good and evil." Thereafter, of course, his group is always on the side of the right and the good, and pitted *against* something—either another group, or Nature itself. This "collision" mindset is also implied in the word "feud" that is intrinsic to feudalism.

Also implied in the creation of the group-ego is the assertion that the interests of the individual necessarily collide with the interests of the group (which the collective ego calls "the whole," thereby putting itself in the place of the Cosmic Whole), and that individuality must be dissolved in its favor. This puts the individual who refuses to be part of the group-ego in a position of being feared by those who are dedicated to the group.

As the lines of this hexagram make clear, the individual can go along with a group only so long as the group itself is in harmony with the Cosmos. He must retreat and say the inner No when an action, or course of action, does not correspond with his inner truth. A society can launch itself on a fateful course only when its people fail to say this inner No, either through being led to think that they cannot do anything about it, or when they acquiesce in its course. Failing to say the inner No gives the leaders an inner permission to continue. When the inner No is said firmly by the people throughout, the leaders cannot continue.

The second field in which dissolving is the correct means, is in regard to "balls of conflict." A ball of conflict exists when a person sees "no way out" of his situation. An example is a situation in which two people are inwardly connected in a love relationship, but are separated by a history of mutual accusing and blaming, because they did not know how to recognize and relate to the egos in themselves. Any attempt to revisit, or sort out that history only produces more alienation. There is nothing to do with this history but to dispose of it entirely by asking the Helper of Dissolution to dissolve it. Another example is a person who is caught in feelings of guilt and self-blame. The ego continuously throws these feelings, like a ball, at the person, so that he remains absorbed in their details. Like the Gordian Knot, they cannot be resolved, because every argument triggers a counter argument, each of which is managed by the ego. Dissolving, again, means turning the entire ball over to the Helper of Dissolution, after saying the inner No to the idea of trying to solve it.

Once the problem has been dissolved, a transformation shows itself in myriad ways: a person who normally does no small acts of kindness suddenly does them; another has sudden changes of opinion; another will momentarily make a decision in accordance with his inner truth; or, the precise solution will come as a mind flash; in sum, this momentary intervention in affairs by the Helper of Dissolution creates what people experience as "sudden and unexpected help that comes from the Unknown," and what people often call "miracles," or the "penetrating insights" that are needed for the situation.

The Helper of Dissolution also dissolves obstructions within the body, when the person rids himself of the ideas that have caused them. Among such obstructions are plaque in the veins, and hardening of the arteries caused by self-blame.

Spells connected with this hexagram have to do with the idea that to be true to oneself is identical with being "selfish," and betrays the interests of the group. Since these spells automatically include the guilt spell that accuses a person of being disloyal to the group if he follows his inner truth, the guilt spell must be extinguished first, otherwise it will reinstate the other spells taken away. Phrases that form spells are: "You are selfish if you don't support your group," "loyalty to your family (country, family, class, race, etc.) comes first," "loyalty requires personal sacrifice on behalf of your group." The guilt spell says, "you are guilty, if your first loyalty is not to the group." (*See* p. 697, Freeing Yourself from Spells.)

Note: Since all lines contain infinite possibilities of interpretation, one needs to use the rtcm to determine if the meanings suggested here apply to the given situation. (See p. 736 for using the *rtcm*.)

Line 1. *He brings help with the strength of a horse. Good fortune.*

"He" in this line refers to the Sage that brings help to connect a person first with his commonsense, and then with his will that has the "strength of a horse." This strength is needed for the individual to separate himself from the pull and demands of the collective ego. It is his commonsense that, when he is helped by the Sage to feel it, enables a person to "keep his own counsel," that is, to listen to and follow his inner truth, even when the pressures are great to prevent him from doing so. This line thus states the Cosmic Principle that bringing one's will in line with one's inner truth leads to good fortune.

This line is also about dissolving feelings of alienation that are in their beginnings. Dissolving, as indicated in the main text, requires saying the inner No to doubt that encroaches into the heart, causing it to harden. It is the doubt in one's natural inner ability to successfully meet the situation at hand. It needs to be counteracted by recognizing and validating one's ability to ask the Sage for help. One may first have to remove the slanders that have devalued one's feelings, and say the inner No to one's pride, which would prevent one from asking the Sage for help.

Receiving this line can also indicate that spells, put either on oneself or on another, are creating the problems observed. The problems are solved not by wrestling with them, but by removing the spells, which are their causes.

Spells connected with this line have to do with a person's identity being connected with his particular group, be it family, class, race, nation, etc. Phrases may be, "they are my people," "that is the group that supports me," "my country right or wrong." Images may have to do with an identification with a place, as in "my place," "my town," "my land," "a man's home is his castle, and there he is King."

Other spells may cause a person to look in the wrong direction for help, as "looking upward" (*see* Hex. 16, Line 3), or "sideways," as to other people. The spells are caused by beliefs saying that help lies in those directions. These beliefs cause the person to fix his gaze outward, and thus miss the fact that the route to Cosmic help always lies within himself. This route is not to be equated with channeling, in which communication with a spirit is made. Such a connection is restricted to a communication between the person's rational mind and the spirit, while his feelings are excluded. Connection with the Sage can only be made through the heart, and that is why, when a person cries out with sincerity for help, the help always comes. (*See* p. 697, Freeing Yourself from Spells.)

Line 2. *At the dissolution he hurries to that which supports him. Remorse disappears.*

Dissolution here refers to a person who has been undertaking to free his true self, but upon being confronted with pressures from the collective ego, has either betrayed his integrity, or is about to do so. If, at this juncture, he listens to the proddings of his commonsense, his remorse at having considered abandoning his inner truth will disappear. "Hurrying to what supports him" refers to his asking for the Sage's help to disperse the pressure created by the collective ego.

The pressure this person is under may come in the form of threats or guilt. Threats may include, "if you don't serve us, you won't get our support," "Your security depends on us." Guilt includes ideas such as, "you owe it to your family, country, race, creed, etc." The person may likewise be pulled by his vanity into the delusion that the group will bring him the happiness, security, or recognition that he seeks. All these ideas are the source of the pressure mentioned, and have been stored in his psyche since childhood. If followed, they will keep his true self a child, imprisoned in his psyche.

This line also refer to the loss of a person's commonsense because one or more of the senses have been demonized. For example, his sense of smell may have been traumatized by an intimidating experience in the past, causing him to have compulsive behaviors. Frequently, such compulsive behaviors are due to toilet accidents that have been associated with guilt. In this case, a certain smell was connected with the experience that one might call the "smell of intimidation." Whenever the person encounters that odor again, he experiences the same symptoms of anxiety that he felt at the time, but often in a different form, such as sickness of the stomach or palpitations of the heart.[*] Receiving this line is counsel for the person affected to go through the necessary steps to remove the spell and then ask the Sage to free him from the memory of the traumatizing smell. This will restore his commonsense and bring an end to his symptoms. (*See* p. 697, Freeing Yourself from Spells.) If, in the meantime, he has himself stepped into a position of authority, he also will need to free himself from the self-image and spell of being an authority.

The phrase "he hurries to that which supports him" has often been misinterpreted as advising one to rush toward an opposite point of view, after having hit a dead end with a previous outlook. For example, a person who has always taken a rational approach to be the measure of all things now hurries to an irrational or impulsive approach. Neither approach has anything to do with his commonsense, which encompasses the totality

---

[*] The symptoms may be less acute, or vary depending on the original stressor; they are especially encountered in cases of post-traumatic stress disorder.

of his inner and outer senses. This is what he needs to rely on now. If he seeks sincerely to know the advice that corresponds with his commonsense, he can use the *rtcm* to find out.

In terms of a person's life, this line speaks of what supports him. Invariably, it is Cosmic love that supports him, whether he lives alone or with others. This love is meant to come through another human being, but it comes to him as well when he is alone, if he is open to receive it. In this sense, a person is never alone. A person may receive this line when his love relationship with another has come to an end. Hurrying to what supports him refers to his remembering that Cosmic love can come to him directly as well as through another. He need not hesitate, therefore, to allow the relationship to fall away, and go on with his life. If he does not remember that the Cosmos is the source of all love, then he will certainly hesitate to leave behind the failed relationship. It is also important, on leaving behind a relationship, to ask the Sage, through the *rtcm*, if it is correct to dissolve the inner channel that has existed between himself and the other. Then the remorse disappears that would otherwise accompany the end of the relationship. (*See* p. 687, Closing an Inner Connection.)

"Remorse disappears" refers to the disappearance of any residue of regret holding him to the other, or any feelings of hopelessness that accompany the mistaken belief that he will be "all alone." If these causes of remorse are not addressed and rejected, their continued presence in his psyche may drive him to avoid intimate relationships, turn to ascetic practices, or to seek "divine love," as explained in the next line.

Line 3. *He dissolves his self. Remorse.*

This line makes it clear that any time a person sacrifices his true self to a group-ego, he creates remorse. As mentioned in the general text, the idea of self-sacrifice is based on the assumption that the individual's interests necessarily collide with the egotistical interests of the group, which the collective ego calls the "whole." What is not said is that "the general good" is falsely equated with the interests of a particular group (family, clan, nation, creed, etc.). If the person follows this appeal, he sacrifices his true self to a group-ego, and thus loses his connection with his inner truth and the Cosmic Whole. When the individual is in harmony with his true self, his needs are in harmony with the Cosmic Whole; then the interests of everything connected with the Cosmos are furthered by his following his inner truth.

This line may address a person who feels remorse about having failed in a relationship, or who may have lost the support he has depended on in the past, and now jumps to the conclusion that he is guilty for having failed. He now hurries to the idea of redeeming himself by dissolving his true self, which he has presumed to be guilty. Being an ego idea, this is an attempt of the ego to dissolve (get rid of) his true self. However, as guilt has no Cosmic basis, there is no need for redemption. Freeing himself of the idea of guilt also collapses the idea of redemption and the ego's ploy.

This reveals the circular and self-consuming logic of the ego: how one mistaken idea finds its support in another mistaken idea that had been offered as an answer to the problem created by the first idea. In this manner, an array of mistaken *beliefs* is created that support the ego's power over the individual. Another illustration of this mechanism is the false solution proposed by the ego for a person's hopelessness. (*See* Line 2.) The hopelessness is caused by the mistaken idea that if a person follows his inner truth, he will be left all alone. He is then told that there is hope, if he will dissolve (sacrifice) his self. This "solution" is derived from the idea that by divorcing ourselves from our bodily need for love, we will find nourishment in divine love. Cosmic love differs from what the collective ego calls divine love, in that it is undivided: it includes the body with its need for chi nourishment. (*See* Line 2 about the ways Cosmic love can be received by a person, either through a relationship, or all by himself.) The term "divine love" is based on the false division of a person's wholeness into body, mind and soul. The problem of such a division is discussed in Hexagram 23, *Splitting Apart*. A person needs to free himself of the mistaken idea that he is split into these parts. (*See* p. 689, Freeing Yourself from Mistaken Ideas and Beliefs.)

This line can also describe a person who has been following the path of his inner truth but is now seeing himself as "weird," a "loner," or as a misfit, just because others have called him these names. He now thinks that the answer lies in doing whatever he can to get rid of (dissolve) his true nature, in order to fit in with the group. Through despising himself, he has accepted the projections put on him by the others. He needs to free himself from these projections to regain his self-respect, which will also re-unite him with the Cosmos. (*See* p. 697, Freeing Yourself from Projections.)

Line 4. *He dissolves his bond with his group. Supreme good fortune. Dispersion leads to accumulation. This is something that ordinary men do not think of.*

This line is stating that if a person is willing to ask the Cosmos to help free him from bonds he has accepted that tie him to the egotistical interests of a group, he gains Cosmic Protection, which is the good fortune referred to.

The term "group" can also refer to a group of mistaken ideas that form spells. An example is "thinking poor": that poverty and self-denial are hallmarks of spirituality. Regarding one's true needs as a bother to the Cosmos, so that one does not ask for help to satisfy them, is misunderstanding the generous nature of the Cosmos and its willingness to help us in all that we need. The *I Ching* comments: "This is something that ordinary men do not think of."

"He dissolves his bond with his group" can also refer to a love relationship that needs to be ended. (Also *see* Line 2.)

Dispersion that "leads to accumulation" refers to dispersing the neurotic pride that blocks reunification with another. Receiving this line can be informing a person that his pride is the only thing standing in the way of reunification. Pride is a complex system of defensive ideas adopted during childhood to protect the child from the constant inner anxiety created by having been told that in and of himself he was a "nothing." The defensive complex is an autonomous unit that is not readily dismantled, because in actuality it is an interwoven, self-supporting system of rationales—a ball of conflict (*see* main text). The person can only get rid of it by turning it completely over to the Helper of Dissolution. The consequence of this decision is the unity with the other that the true self longs for, and the flowing in of Cosmic love that is released.

Line 5. *His loud cries are as dissolving as sweat. Dissolution! A king abides without blame.*

Pictured here is a situation that has disintegrated: a marriage has ended, a corporation's contract with another company has failed, the ruling government has fallen, etc. All appears to be chaos. Then, changes are made to shore up the marriage, the contract, or the government, by compromising, making reforms, and appearing to be more receptive to the people's real needs. When the smoke of the turbulence has passed — lo! the same system has been reinstalled. Nothing substantial has changed. How is this to be explained? By convincing the people that "anything is better than chaos," the ruling egos remain in place. This is the "unifying" idea the collective ego employs to keep itself from being dissolved, and is what it would call "the king's abiding without blame."

This line is also given as an answer to an individual's disintegration, which is evident, for example, in his inability to sleep. As a solution, the collective ego would propose that he must "unify his body, mind, and soul." As mentioned in the previous line, what is truly needed is to restore his wholeness by ridding himself of the idea that he is divided into these three parts.

Line 6. *He dissolves his blood. Departing, keeping at a distance, going out, is without blame.*

This line is about dissolving hatred and other violent emotions that arise when someone is identified as a wrongdoer; if indulged in, these emotions would lead to bloodshed. A person is made aware that he needs to say the inner No to seeing the collective ego, or his group, partner, etc., from which he wants to set himself apart, as the locus of evil. Any opposition would only keep him attached. By distancing himself from accusing feelings, he avoids a worsening of the problem. If a person has regarded something or someone as the focal point of his, or the public's problems, he needs to dissolve the spell that he has created. (*See* p. 697, Freeing Yourself from Spells.)

This line also refers to a person's need to distance himself from thoughts that create despair, such as the thought that death is the end of life. (*See* Glossary: Death.)

60. *Limitation/Self-Limitation*

 $\dfrac{\text{K'an}}{\text{Tui}}$

The Judgment: *Limitation. Success. Galling limits must not be persevered in.*

The Sage here describes the Cosmic Principle of Limitation, which states that limits apply to all of existence. Particular attention is paid to the difference between true and false limitations, as they apply to humans. At the border of all Cosmic Limitation is Fate; its purpose is to put a person back within his true limits, which are set by the Cosmic Harmony.

The Principle of Limitation makes us aware that humans, as aspects of the Cosmic Whole, are *equal* to each and every other species, organism, and particle of existence, each of which has its own dignity, consciousness, and worth within that whole. In this regard, humans are not "free," in the egocentric sense asserted by the collective ego, to do anything they want with other species, creatures, individuals, or Nature itself. Human freedom thus is held within the framework of respect for every other entity of existence. So long as that respect is in place, human freedom is enormous. Respect is part of the Cosmic Principle of Modesty. For example, as Hexagram 58, *The Joyful*, makes clear, humans are not free to give fantasy names to things that fix them in spells. Neither are humans free to invent and use words and images that limit the Cosmic Consciousness in its ability to communicate with humans.

True limitation also reminds us that we are not meant to accomplish tasks and goals without the help of the Helpers of the invisible world, and that we are dependent on the whole for all our needs. Acknowledging this dependency is not something to regret but to rejoice in, because engaging the Helpers gives us both a feeling of relief that we do not have to "do it all," and because it enables us to partake in the Cosmic blessings.

Cosmic limits ensure that a person can bring his uniqueness to expression within the framework of the Cosmic Whole. This happens when he takes his true place as an equal in the Cosmos. By contrast, the false limits put on a person by the collective ego repress his uniqueness and creative self-expression, and replace it with the fantasy and illusion of being special. This illusion, in turn, initiates Fate.

The false limitations exercised by the collective ego, through its feudal power structure, seek to press all individuals into its molds, since conformity is the only way it can maintain its order. Tremendous pressure is put on individuals who do not fit into these molds, to cut out of themselves whatever does not fit. This process, by which the growth of humans and of Nature is limited, is accompanied by the casting of projections, spells, and poison arrows on both. In such ways, the collective ego interferes in the evolution and harmony of the Cosmos.

Other limitations put on the individual by the collective ego consist of rigid moral rules that repress and deny his animal nature. They are among the "galling limits" mentioned in The Judgment. This repression is the result of beliefs that divide a person's nature into animal (lower) and spiritual (higher) aspects, with his animal nature being designated as the source of evil. The demonizing of the person's animal nature has a far-reaching effect in that it blocks all his inner senses. With his inner senses blocked, he is no longer able to perceive that it is his very animal nature which connects him with the life force. Another effect is that his perceptive abilities become limited to the sole senses of *outer* seeing and hearing.

"Galling limits" also refers to ideas a person has adopted that amount to "thinking poor." Such a person feels guilty for being "well-off," because he associates spirituality with the *appear-ance* of humility. Such ideas slander the gift-giving nature of the Cosmos. Related to these are the false limits a person puts on himself by striving to develop his "higher" or spiritual nature through ascetic practices (*see* Line 6).

Receiving this hexagram is often to tell a person that he has exceeded the Cosmic Limits for humans, and thereby created a fate. Fate is a law of physics, in that it is a Cosmic response to the disharmony created when a person exceeds his true limits. Having created a fate, he has deprived himself of the help of the Helpers. He can free himself of this fate if he rids himself of the ideas that have created it. Among these ideas are phrases such as: "we have to do it all," and "there is no help."

This hexagram also is given to make a person aware that his belief that life has a beginning and an end has set false limits on his life that, if not deprogrammed, will be carried out as a projection. (*See* Glossary: Death.)

"Limitation" also calls a person to rid himself of mistaken assumptions about the nature of physical phenomena that limit or prevent him from learning about their true nature. We are speaking here of assumptions which are based only on what is seen with the outer eyes (thus excluding, for example, the existence of the Helpers of the invisible world), and that can be measured with some mechanical device. Such assumptions are often the result of what humans have hypothesized to be true, and then projected into reality.* Experiments that are undertaken to prove a hypothesis only prove that the power of projection is at work. (*See* Hexagram 31, *Influencing.*) The only correct way to examine a hypothesis is to put it to the Sage. The Sage can then show the hypothesis within the framework of the Cosmic Way by pointing to one or more hexagrams.

Among the mistaken conclusions that have been drawn from

---

* As Erich Schumacher points out in his book, "*Small is Beautiful: Economics as if People Mattered* (Harper and Row, 1973): "The sciences are being taught without any awareness of the presuppositions of science, of the meaning and significance of scientific laws, and of the place occupied by the natural sciences within the whole cosmos of human thought. The result is that the presuppositions of science are normally mistaken for its findings." P.99.

uncritically swallowing people's projections are:

- that in Nature there is such a thing as "dead matter";
- that there is such a thing as "random chance" (in terms of the Cosmic Way);
- that the Cosmos works through opposite forces (example: that good and evil are both parts of the Cosmos, and that good fights the evil);
- that the ego is a natural and essential part of the personality;
- that there is a force of repulsion at work in the Cosmos;
- that certain things in Nature are inherently evil.

All of the above phenomena are true only inasmuch as they are part of the parallel reality created by human projection. They do not describe Cosmic Reality.

In regard to "dead matter," Hexagram 2, *Nature*, shows matter to be compressed consciousness. In regard to "random chance," every experience of consulting the *I Ching* shows that probability theory and theories of happenstance do not apply; but these theories do apply when the person is outside the Cosmic Harmony. The entire *I Ching* is a demonstration of the interrelatedness of everything in the Cosmos. As to the "force of repulsion" Hexagram 8, *Holding Together*, shows that the Cosmos is held together as a system of harmony solely through the force of attraction between complementary aspects. There is no "opposite force" in the Cosmos. Everything in the Cosmos is held in its intrinsic space by a feeling consciousness.* This is true as much for birds flying in a flock as it is for the planets being held in an orbit. As to regarding some aspects of Nature as evil, the *I Ching* makes us aware that nothing in Nature is evil to start with; anything that is observed as "evil coming from nature" is actually the result of human projections that have demonized one or another of Nature's helping aspects.

This hexagram also speaks of self-limitation as necessary to define a person's intrinsic space. It means defining and adhering to what feels correct and harmonious, while rejecting all

---

* That the material aspect of the Cosmos is composed of feeling consciousnesses explains the obvious objection that a person might make on observing the reaction of putting the N pole of one magnet near the N pole of another: they simply do not feel compatible in that relationship to each other.

aspects of the ego, in oneself and in others, whether it be in the form of thoughts or deeds. This is done, not by telling others what to do, for that is outside one's proper limits, but by refusing to join behaviors and actions when they feel inappropriate, and by refusing to accept treatment from others that would betray or decrease one's dignity. This rejection is always made through saying the inner No, or an outer No, if necessary. This is what The Judgment means by "being firm and correct."

This hexagram also calls attention to the way a person's fixed beliefs limit his gaining a broader view of the Cosmic Way. Fixed beliefs put a frame of fixed dimensions around a person's picture of life. By deciding to accept this picture as complete, synapses in the brain are blocked that would otherwise allow the Sage to teach him. It is as if his mind is like a bank of full postal boxes that contain his final opinions on every subject. This condition has brought his growth to a halt and locked his true self and its learning abilities in a prison. Such a person experiences his life as being full of obstructions. The obstructions have the purpose of waking him up to this problem.

Receiving this hexagram may be calling a person to rid himself of any one of the mistaken ideas listed above. He can identify them by consulting the Sage through the *rtcm*.

Note: Since all lines contain infinite possibilities of interpretation, one needs to use the *rtcm* to determine if the meanings suggested here apply to the given situation. (*See* p. 736 for using the *rtcm*.)

Line 1. *Not going out of the door and the courtyard is without blame.*

"The courtyard" symbolizes the contained society of the collective ego, and its rules and customs. Upon becoming aware of its devices, it is a person's tendency to want to see that social structure as responsible for all evil, and to separate from it in an antagonistic way. Doing so would be "going out of the door." Here, however, the line says that "*not* going out of the door" is "without blame." This means that a person is not meant to set himself apart, together with others like himself, as a faction against the collective ego, because that would be staying within the same feudal mindset he thinks he is leaving behind.

The mistake of antagonistically fleeing the existing social order is the result of thinking in opposites, and either/or alternatives: "either you are within the society or you are divorced from it."* To live within the society and still be true to himself, a person needs to distinguish, with the help of his commonsense, what in the societal rules is arbitrary and purely abstract, and what is consistent with his inner truth. The real difference between a society dominated by the collective ego and a natural society lies in whether that society incorporates the Helpers or excludes them.

This line also is saying that we are not meant to leave society to become hermits in Nature, but to consistently say the necessary inner No's toward encroachments of the collective ego onto the natural social order; for evil in society exists only when we fail to say those inner No's.

The person whose true self is fully matured gathers likeminded people around him, and thus has a salutary effect on his environment. He forms the core of a natural society without having to erect a formal organization, since he is connected with the others through his feelings. His inner truth penetrates to their inner truth and draws the Cosmic Helpers into their lives. Influencing others in this way is without Cosmic blame.

This line can also be received by a person who is trying to evangelize others to "his" truth, carried by the desire to establish a "new society." In seeing himself as the founder of a new society, he adopts a self-image and thus incurs Cosmic blame.

Another self-image addressed by this line is that of the person who believes that he is without blame because he has been "good," meaning he has followed all the rules and standards of the collective ego. He, too, has adopted a self-image and incurred Cosmic blame. (*See* p. 691, Freeing Yourself from Self-Images.)

---

* An example is the Puritans, who on coming to America, believed they were leaving behind the causes of evil that they attributed to monarchy. What they brought with them, fully intact, was the very same self-righteous feudal attitude they left behind, along with the very same institutional structures, with monarchy being replaced by a religious oligarchy; thus, even in our modern language, the term "Puritanism" came to mean a specific or idiosyncratic form of tyranny.

Line 2. *Not going out of the gate and the courtyard brings misfortune.*

Here is presented a circumstance where the group or organization, of which a person is a part, is about to create a fate. In such a case, he is not obligated to remain in that group. It is rather his duty to say the inner No to its intentions, and to leave that group, in order to avoid becoming involved in its fate. "Leaving" in this case, is meant to include outer action. This can apply to a partnership, a group about to commit a crime, or a national group getting involved in a war. Upon receiving this line, a person needs to ask the Sage, through the *rtcm*, whether "leaving" (after having said the necessary inner No) is the appropriate action for him to take. A person who says the inner No to his group's evil intentions puts himself under Cosmic Protection. This protection, however, is ensured only when he removes himself from the space in which the fate created by the group will take place. Also, he will enjoy the Cosmic Protection only so long as he abstains from self-righteously trying to correct the others.

Firmness in refusing to participate in what is incorrect is what limits evil in the world. The Helper of Transformation is activated just by his saying the inner No.

Line 3. *He who knows no limitation will have cause to lament. No blame.*

This line concerns the half-truth that "man is born free," and describes the person who believes he has the freedom to do or think as he pleases, and therefore allows the ego to run rampant. Such a person neither recognizes the natural limits of human thinking and action, nor the fate that is generated by disregarding Cosmic Limits. Such an idea comes from the human-centered view of the universe, through which humans see themselves as "special." This view separates the person from the Cosmic Whole, and when acted upon, creates a fate. This line makes it clear that a person is responsible for everything he thinks and does, and that he needs to rid himself of the seed phrases, "man is born free," "man is born special, with the right to rule Nature" and all the images that go with those phrases.

"No blame" refers to the Cosmic Harmonic that no blame is incurred when a person voluntarily accepts the Cosmic Limits, at the core of which is modesty. (*See* Hexagram 15, *Modesty*.)

Line 4. *Contented limitation. Success.*

"Contented limitation" refers to a person who recognizes his limits, and his true place in the Cosmos, therefore knows that he is not meant to "do it all." Because his attitude is in harmony with the Cosmos, he gains the cooperation of the Helpers of the invisible world, and what he undertakes has success.

A person may receive this line to show him that through correctly limiting himself as indicated, he achieves his goals easily.

Line 5. *Sweet limitation brings good fortune. Going brings esteem.*

"Sweet limitation brings good fortune" refers to the nourishment that comes when a person limits himself to following his inner truth. Inner truth is naturally in harmony with the Cosmos, and nourishes a person's self-esteem with chi energy.

"Going brings esteem" refers to the self-esteem gained when a person leaves behind his mistaken ideas, and the flattering goals of the collective ego that promise the esteem of others. This phrase also refers to the person who holds to his inner truth during times of turmoil. He finds, to his surprise, that he gains the esteem and respect of other people's true selves.

"Going brings esteem" can also point to the mistaken idea promoted by the collective ego, that a person cannot "live as an island to himself," and that he needs to gain the esteem of others. Or, he may be told that there are times when it is necessary to compromise his values to get along with others. When a person discards such ideas, he finds that he is in the good company of the Helpers of the invisible world.

Line 6. *Galling limitation. Perseverance brings misfortune. Remorse disappears.*

This line can refer to the person who has limited his view of reality to what is apparent: "What you see is all there is." This idea projects itself into reality for this person, making his life a galling experience. If, however, he will rid himself of this idea, he will be able to experience the underlying harmony that gives rise to all beauty and joy in life. Then the fate caused by his having limited his perception in this way will be extinguished.

This line can also refer to sicknesses related to the gallbladder that are caused by the above false belief in mere appearances. Mistaken beliefs, such as this one, set up false systems in the body that inhibit or block its natural functioning. If the person so affected rids himself of this belief, he will be freed from its negative effects.

"Galling limitation" also refers to the ascetic practices people undertake in their ambition to fulfill the images associated with "being spiritual." It also refers to the extreme limitations a person puts on himself to fulfill any self-image, whether it be that of the athlete, the hero-warrior, the top executive, or the person who sees himself as "the responsible one." Such sacrifices of the body to a self-image create a variety of adverse reactions in the body, which has been enslaved to those purposes. Freeing himself from those self-images and the ambition to perfect them removes the adverse effects, and ends the remorse. (*See* p. 691, Freeing Yourself from Self-Images.)

Remorse is a Helper, whose function it is to help a person recognize that he is the one who has created his fate, and that it is he who needs to remedy its causes. It is important, therefore, that a person does not try to ease another's feelings of remorse.

A person having remorse needs to be aware that the ego will attempt to seize this feeling and turn it into guilt, which it then puts on the person's true self. It does this to distract him from recognizing that it (the ego) has been the very element that is responsible for the remorse.

61. *Inner Truth*

 Sun
Tui

The Judgment: *Inner truth. Pigs and fishes. Good fortune. It furthers one to cross the great water. It furthers one to be firm and correct.*

In this hexagram, the Sage speaks of inner truth in two fundamental ways: as the "treasure chest of inner truth" that each person is born with, which he is meant to rely on, and as the truth within situations, which must be found before a correct decision can be made about how to relate to them. In regard to the latter, decisions made purely on the external appearance of a situation create a long chain of negative consequences that include continuing conflict, entanglements, injustices, and a litany of further misunderstandings.

"Pigs and fishes" is a metaphor for the totality of our physical senses, which, when combined, speak as our commonsense. "Good fortune" refers to the result of going by one's commonsense in the conduct of one's life. The totality of our senses comprise, for example, the inner seeing of meditation that leads to insight, and outer seeing, as when we look at the world around us. Other inner senses not often considered are inner listening, as in phrases that come as mind-flashes, inner smelling, as when a person is said to follow his nose, or when "something smells wrong," or inner taste, as when we say "life has a good taste," or, "that experience leaves me with a bad taste," and inner feelings, as when something feels harmonious or discordant.

Commonsense combines the perceptions of the inner and outer senses and then compares them with our inner truth. Every person possesses inner truth. It is the primal memory of what Cosmic harmony feels like, that we possess before we develop any memories of images and words. This memory is stored throughout our body in the chromosomes of each cell, and constitutes our "treasure chest of inner truth."

Inner truth is a reliable guide, which the commonsense employs to find out what is harmonious or disharmonious. Commonsense is expressed in the psyche as a feeling of Yes or No, a feeling which is to be trusted and followed. Following one's commonsense leads to the "good fortune" mentioned, for commonsense is in harmony with the Cosmos. Recognizing the nature of things from our commonsense is what brings clarity. This contrasts with the mistaken idea fostered by the collective ego that it is our intellectual abilities alone that bring clarity. (*See* Glossary: The Senses.)

What helps a person assess the inner truth of a situation is his listening first to the Yes or No conveyed by his commonsense. He can then consult the Sage to understand the situations' particulars, with the help of a hexagram and the *rtcm*.

The inner truth of each situation is unique and cannot be known purely from looking at its appearance. That is because the truth of each moment is shaped by the private thoughts of each person in it. Furthermore, the presence of projections, spells, and poison arrows needs to be known. Indeed, the present moment is often influenced by negative elements that have been put on people in the past, and which are still acting out. The inner truth of a situation can only be found with the help of the Sage. Learning it and saying the inner No to the disharmonious elements in that situation initiates transformations; transformations, in turn, lead to duration, whereas changes made through external efforts cannot endure.

"It furthers one to cross the great water" stands for recognizing and counteracting dangerous ideas that have formed poison arrows, and are blocking us from accessing the truth that lies within ourselves. "Being firm and correct" refers to the process of identifying and ridding ourselves of these spells.

Among the dangerous ideas that prevent access to a person's inner truth are those that say: "truth is only to be found outside ourselves," "truth is difficult to find," "intelligence helps one find the truth," "truth can be found through gaining knowledge," "truth can be found through following a spiritual leader," "to look within oneself for the truth is dangerous," "when it comes down to the base of all beliefs, the truth is the same, and it is one truth."

Inner truth in one person has the ability to energize another's inner truth, without external effort. Also, when a person is in harmony with his inner truth, he is protected and defended by the Cosmos. A person who is not in harmony has "holes" in his natural defenses, which stimulate unsavory elements in others. These holes are inner conflicts stored in his psyche, which have made him doubt his inner truth. The egos in other people know intuitively in which areas of awareness these holes exist, and rush to take advantage of them.

Note: Since all lines contain infinite possibilities of interpretation, one needs to use the *rtcm* to determine if the meanings suggested here apply to the given situation. (*See* p. 736 for using the *rtcm*.)

Line 1. *Being prepared brings good fortune. If there are secret designs, it is disquieting.*

"Secret designs" here refers to a person who has a specific intention, which he is about to carry out.

This line advises a person that he needs to be prepared for another's intention to encroach into his space, and into his learning process, to influence him according to his opinions, or even according to his desire. It can also concern a person who believes, after having found his own inner truth about a matter that concerns others of his group, that it is his duty to bring them to his own understanding. Such a person does not trust that others can get in touch with their own inner truth, because he views them as ignorant, or undeveloped. His view puts a projection, spell, or poison arrow on those around him and on the situation. If the person about to be encroached upon will say the inner No to the other's intention, he will remain free of these negative influences.

Similar "secret designs," which come from a person's looking down on Nature, cast projections, spells, and poison arrows on Nature. The person is unaware of the harmful effects of his attitude, and that by casting harmful views on Nature, he is also harming his own nature. Receiving this line counsels him to review his back-of-the-mind thoughts about Nature and rid himself of them. An example is someone who looks at nature as "matter" which he can manipulate and extinguish at will, and as something that needs to be controlled. Such a person looks at his body in the same way, as a vehicle which *he* occupies, and whose purpose is to "get him about," and fulfill his desires. This view of Nature demonizes it and leads to illness.

This line can also be warning a person of a projection or spell that has been placed on him by another which is making him say or do things he does not want to do. The projection or spell consists of the prediction that he will behave in the precise ways indicated, or "always" say certain things at given times. If he inquires of the Sage (through the *rtcm*) who the person is, and what has been projected on him, he can deprogram the projection or spell by saying the inner No to it. (*See* p. 697, Freeing Yourself from Projections and Spells.)

Line 2. *A crane calling in the shade. Its young answers it. I have a good goblet. I will share it with you.*

This line is a metaphor that describes how the conscious thought of one person (symbolized by the crane), when it is in harmony with his inner truth, penetrates involuntarily and without intention to the inner truth of another person ("the young" here symbolizes every person's inner truth). It does so out of the sight and hearing of the ego in another. Its effect is to strengthen the other's true self (the meaning of sharing the good goblet), therefore weakening the ego.

The penetration can also refer to the inner No or to an inner message said to another, such as "help is available if you will ask the Sage for it." The inner No and the appropriate inner messages initiate transformation through inner truth.

The crane can also be a metaphor for the Sage that comes to a person when he is in need, nourishing and supporting him. It does this through other people, through the inner voice, and through meditation.

In its negative meaning, the crane in the shade can be a metaphor for a person who is looking for disciples (the shade here referring to his dark motives), by saying, "I want to share the good message with you." If one follows that person, one would get involved in his fate. Receiving this line may be to alert a person to this danger, or that he may already be under the spell of that phrase, and needs to free himself of it. Such a spell blocks a person's inner truth and brings him under the control of the other. He needs to realize that this person is not speaking from his inner truth, but from something that he himself has been told. In addition to freeing himself from the spell put on his inner truth, he may also need to free himself from a poison arrow that has come from the belief that he was born with original sin/blame/guilt. Generally, it is the presence of this belief that draws people to look up to others who promise to lead them to redemption. (*See* p. 697, Freeing Yourself from Spells and Poison Arrows.)

Line 3. *Now he sobs, now he sings. If he stops beating the drum, he finds a comrade.*

Here, a person "sobs and sings" alternately, as he moves from hope to despair. He would like to follow *the* truth, but does not realize that the only real truth is his *inner* truth, which does not consist in words and phrases, but in his feelings of what is harmonious and what is discordant. Because he is looking for an *absolute* truth outside of himself, he finds only hope and despair. He may be running from one book of wisdom to another for relief, while what he needs to do is deprogram the idea that truth lies in words and phrases.

The hope and despair mentioned above may also refer to a person's anticipation of his own death. In order to attain peace, he needs to discover the inner truth that death is not an end to life. The fact that he is not at peace indicates that he is not in harmony with his inner truth. To stop beating the drum means to say the inner No to his belief that death is the end of life. Then the comrade, his inner truth, is freed, bringing him true happiness. (*See* Glossary: Death.) In order to free the access to his inner truth, he may also need to ask the Sage to remove the poison arrow of original sin mentioned in the previous line.

Line 4. *The moon nearly at the full. The team horse goes astray. Blame.*

The "moon nearly at the full" represents half-truths that are implicit in the situation, which will lead the person concerned astray, causing blame.

Pictured here is a team of horses, one of which has gone astray, bringing progress to a halt. This metaphor concerns a person who is experiencing a fate. That one of the horses has gone astray suggests that the less experienced student, who is being taught by the Sage to trust his inner truth, has fallen prey to doubt.

This person has been tempted by others, who want him to follow a belief system by making him think it is identical with his inner truth. He may have adopted the idea that all belief systems point to the same truth and can be integrated to achieve harmony. The problem, however, lies in equating *any* established belief system with a person's inner truth. All belief systems are human-created and based on half-truths and myths which place humans as the central masters of the universe. Such a belief imagines humans as "holding the reins" of the universe. These beliefs act as frames-of-reference that *shut* synapses in the brain, imprisoning Helpers of the invisible world, and blocking the help of the Sage. By contrast, inner truth creates *new* synapses to allow ever-broader realizations and understandings.

The team of horses can also be a metaphor for the two aspects of our life force: the light and the dark. They can become divided when a person looks up to another, or up to a group, system, or belief. The division prevents the commonsense from being able to create transformations, as described in Hexagram 16, *Enthusiasm*, Line 3.

The team horse's going astray can also represent a situation in which a person's mental faculties are turned to the service of the ego, leading the whole personality astray. When this occurs, the harmony of the team, that is to say, of the whole psyche, is lost. When the mental faculties lead, they put projections, spells, and poison arrows on people and on the person himself, causing blame, and, if continued, lead to a fate.

This line can also refer to a person's using the *I Ching* for ego-purposes, as when he reads the hexagrams and lines to confirm the viewpoint of the ego.

The team horse goes astray can also refer to a person's forgetting his dependency on the Sage as the source of his inner independence. This happens when he credits the good things that have happened to his own doing. He forgets his relationship with the invisible world, thus incurs blame, which is experienced as feelings of isolation.

A person can also receive this line when he has either assumed he knows what the problem is, or that he knows the truth of the matter, and so does not need to understand more. This is the ego's work, preventing him from looking deeper for the problem, and preventing him from discovering that not he, but the ego in him is in charge of his personality. So long as the ego leads, the person's efforts to solve the problem will go in the wrong direction. The person can determine, with the help of the *rtcm*, if this is true. It can also help him gain a true assessment of the problem and find its true causes. To prevent himself from continuing to follow the ego, he needs to find the phrases that make him a slave of its authority.

Line 5. *He possesses truth, which links together. No blame.*

This line expresses the way inner truth creates an inner link between people. In this inner link, there is no blame.

This line also makes us aware that inner truth links our physical makeup together harmoniously. As mentioned in the main text, inner truth is imprinted in the chromosomes of each cell of the body. When, however, a person receives the poison arrows mentioned in Lines 3 and 4, or certain other poison arrows created by mistaken ideas (as mentioned in Hexagram 16, *Enthusiasm*, Line 3), the chromosomes become altered, blocking his inner truth, diminishing the functioning of his commonsense, and creating abnormal bodily conditions.

This line may also speak of the person who *thinks* he possesses *the* truth and therefore thinks he is without blame. What such a person misses is that "the truth" as fixed and immutable words, thought to be applicable to every circumstance, does not exist. If he relies on such truths to link him with others, he will succeed only in acquiring a mental link with them. Because this link makes no connection between their hearts, the unity is a fiction.

Line 6. *Cockcrow penetrating to heaven. Perseverance brings mis-*

fortune.

This line describes a person who blindly follows the path of a leader, and crows that he is "in the know," or thinks that he has discovered a truth. In reality, however, he has only discovered a half-truth. Half-truths are statements in words that cannot be confirmed by inner truth. (*See* Glossary: Half-Truth.)

The crowing cock can also refer to someone who forces his habits and beliefs on others, and attempts to make them move according to his rules. Such a person opens wide the door to Fate, which is the meaning of "perseverance brings misfortune."

62. *Preponderance of the Small*

Chên

Kên

The Judgment: *Preponderance of the Small. Success. To be firmly correct furthers. Small things may be done; great things should not be done. The flying bird brings the message: It is not well to strive upward, it is well to remain below. Great good fortune.*

In this hexagram, the Sage shows how paying attention to the "small" seeds of events leads a person to success. Our attention is called to the common tendency, due to conditioning, to allow the ego to identify situations in *its* terms, so that we miss the salient points. It does this to keep our focus only on the external factors. The "small," in this context, refers to the trivial (external) aspects of situations rather than their essentials.

To overcome the tendency to focus on trivialities, we are counseled to give a preponderating attention to the *conceptual framework* we are using to describe the situation at hand, for this framework has caused us to misidentify its essentials. When a situation is identified in the terms of the collective ego, the conceptual framework is always too small.

"To be firmly correct" refers to saying the necessary inner No's to these incorrect conceptions. "Small things may be done" points to the person's having limited his influence on the situation by having come to a wrong conclusion about it. The "small things" he can do amount to making changes that will not last, instead of initiating transformations that will bring duration. "Great things should not be done," together with the advice not to strive upward, refers to holding back from trying to force his wrong conclusions on the situation. "Good fortune" refers to his correcting his misconceptions.

The image employed in the lines of this hexagram is of the little bird that is just hatching.* It represents a correct conception that is materializing from a person's inner truth; it is just in the process of forming into insight. At first it is a vague feeling that, given time, can form into an image that becomes an insight with many ramifications. One notices this in the creative writing process, where the writer is visited with a quick glance of an image; this image is the beginning of his putting pen to paper, and as he allows it to unfold in its many ramifications, he follows it until it emerges into a complete and whole picture. Correctly understood, it is a process of unfolding, much like that of a flower; all of the petals are tightly wrapped up in the bud and are "there," but they attain completeness of expression and realization only by allowing the process to continue undisturbed. Interference by the ego, while the insight is unfolding, distorts this process and brings it to a sudden halt. The ego interferes by seeing that it can use the insight as an instrument to fulfill its opportunistic desires. Because the halt does not allow the insight to complete itself, incorrect conclusions are drawn. Such hastily drawn conclusions (the kind that we "jump" to), are the result. Invariably, they are delusions.

The metaphor of the "flying bird" mentioned in The Judgment calls to mind a bird that has already left the nest. It is one of the metaphorical senses, warning the person of a deluded conclusion. It comes "from the gut," saying that something is wrong, and that he needs to ask to be shown the inner truth of

---

* This image is a continuation of the image suggested by the ideogram for "truth" given in the preceding Hexagram, 61, *Inner Truth*, which is a picture of a bird's foot over a fledgling. The ideogram suggests the idea of brooding. In Hexagram 62, the bird, representing inner truth is, so to speak, in the process of "hatching."

the matter. Conclusions drawn from seeing only the outer situation form abstract ideas that are not connected with the person's feeling consciousness. It is only in the realm of feelings that he can get a full sense of the reality of the circumstance.

The traditional interpretation of this hexagram speaks of giving preponderance to that which would satisfy the ancestors (or tradition): preponderance to grief over their loss, to obedience toward their customs, and to "fixing one's eyes more closely on duty than the ordinary man" (Wilhelm), this duty being what would honor the ancestors, and satisfy the oughts and shoulds connected with societal authority. All of these inner dictates come, of course, from the collective ego, which is the origin and guardian of the individual ego. (*See* p. 40, The Collective Ego.) An obsession with duty serves to divert the person from being in touch with his true feelings.

Spells connected with the themes of this hexagram are those put upon the individual by the collective ego, in the form of guilt for listening to his true feelings. The guilt is an inner tape recording that reminds the person, whenever his feelings say No, or even when he has no feeling at all, that he should be having another or at least some emotion. For example, a person may not experience "appropriate" feelings of sorrow when a parent, friend, or spouse dies, and as a result feels guilty. The person needs to say the inner No to this inner command to feel something he does not feel, and a No to the collective ego that has been posing as the authority on what is proper to feel. He needs as well, to dispel the guilt spell that has been put upon him. (*See* p. 697, Freeing Yourself from Spells.)

Other spells have to do with all those societal commands that demand one to pay attention to outer form: to observe all the small details of behavior that ingratiate one with others upon whom one depends (observing birthdays, attending ceremonies, giving appropriate gifts to balance accounts, and giving credence to rank). This is not to say that birthdays cannot be observed or gifts given, when the desire to do so comes from the heart. But a feeling of obligation prevents the person from acting from his true feelings.

Note: Since all lines contain infinite possibilities of interpretation, one needs to use the *rtcm* to determine if the meanings suggested here apply to the given situation. (*See* p. 736 for using the *rtcm*.)

Line 1. *The bird meets with misfortune through flying.*

The bird that has flown too soon refers to a person's allowing the ego to interrupt and appropriate the emerging inner truth, to fly away with it, and put it to its purposes. It prods the person into getting "carried away" by an ego-enthusiasm.

Inner truth needs time to emerge. It is a feeling that is either directly transformed into action, or is transformed into an image, and then into words; it is when it first begins to be formed into words that the ego attempts to grab it. When the process is allowed to come to expression free of the ego, the words never lose their connection with the underlying feeling, which remains their guiding force.

When the ego hears the first phrase formed from the image, it uses the imagination to place the insight within the context of its preestablished beliefs. It then uses the rational mind to formulate the necessary supporting rationales. Thus the ego makes "insight" conform to existing beliefs. The misfortune is that the person loses the emerging inner truth that would keep him in touch with reality.

A person may also receive this line when he has correctly "remained in the nest" because he has not yet attained clarity. Others criticize him for doing this, making him feel that something is wrong in his "nature," because he does not come to the quick conclusions they do.

The line may also refer to a person who has correctly left the nest (home, family), as he needs to do. He is being blamed for something that gives no just cause for blame. An example is a person not quite of age who has left the nest. Judged by appearances, he is considered "foolish," whereas in inner terms he may be quite ready to make his first steps outside the nest.

In these latter two cases, the person's "nature" is blamed for being either too slow or too rash, impulsive, etc. Such false judgments can put projections or spells on him that need to be removed. (*See* p. 697, Freeing Yourself from Spells.)

This line can also refer to instances in which the earth and

Nature are blamed for what is deemed evil in the world: for Fate, for death, etc. Such ideas seek to drive the person into an escape from the earth, toward an imagined "heaven." This fantasy of fleeing the earth and life has falsely made heaven and earth into opposites and has put spells on the earth, creating a fate for the person who accepts the delusion. To extinguish the fate, the spells that the person has put on others and on Nature need to be removed. Since he is a part of Nature, the spell also affects himself. (*See* p. 692, Freeing Yourself from a Fate.)

Line 2. *She passes by her ancestor and meets her ancestress. He does not reach his prince and meets the official. No blame.*

"She passes by her ancestor and meets her ancestress" refers to the person who has been disappointed with one belief or tradition (the ancestor) and thus has gone to an opposite belief or tradition (the ancestress). The Sage (prince), that he would like to meet, is not reached, because the Sage is not to be found in opposite beliefs and traditions. The official that he meets is the fate he has created for himself by having adopted the opposite belief. "No blame" refers to ending the fate by ridding himself of his mistaken belief.

This line may also refer to a person who is reproaching himself or another for failing to comply with correct form, which he sees in terms of "right" or "wrong." The traditional interpretation of this line describes a woman who deviates from the standard form by following her feelings. Thus, there is no blame. An example is a mother who decides matters affecting the family from her feelings of what is correct, rather than asking the eldest son what to do, who believes himself to be the rightful "head of family" following his father's demise. The line may be making a person aware of a blame spell that is being put on him by someone who believes he has been "passed by" or ignored.

"She" in this line can also refer to a Helper that acts as an arm of Fate. The fate has affected the body (the "ancestress"), which the person is now blaming as "my evil body." "He" (who does not meet the prince) refers to the rational mind that, in service to the ego, has reversed cause and effect in trying to explain what is happening. It accuses the body, while in reality the cause of the problem is a mistaken belief promoted by the collective ego. It is in the nature of the ego to reverse cause and effect in this way.

This line can also refer to "passing by," or neglecting one's duty to say the inner No to the ego. Failing to say the inner No, be it to the ego in oneself or in another, when the circumstances require it, can create a fate. The same applies to one's duty to free oneself or another from projections, spells, and poison arrows that are active in a given situation.

Spells connected with this line include those phrases and ideas which put the body down in favor of the mind, such as: "The mind has to control the body." "The mind knows what the body needs." "The mind is willing, but the flesh is weak." "The body creates nothing but problems," "mind over matter," "mind is master, body is servant."

Line 3. *If one is not extremely careful, somebody may come up from behind and strike him. Misfortune.*

This line refers to a fate that has struck a person "from behind," indicating that the cause is to be found outside himself. The fate is actually due to spells or poison arrows that have been put upon him by someone else, and that have manifested as illness, injury, pain, or chronic ailments.

To be extremely careful is counsel to avoid assigning wrong causes for the problems, such as by blaming himself. With the help of the *rtcm,* he can identify the source (in persons living or dead), and rid himself of these influences, in order to end the fate. (*See* p. 692, Freeing Yourself from a Fate.)

This line can also refer to a person who acts unreasonably or compulsively due to a spell. The spell consists of a seemingly insignificant seed phrase, such as, "he is unreasonable" or "he is compulsive," or, "he always (or never) does that," or "that's the way he is."

Other spells referred to by this line are those created by seed phrases in a person's inner program that put down an aspect of the Cosmos as insignificant. These can be phrases of disbelief, such as: "There is no such thing as invisible Helpers," "that is a problem the Helpers cannot solve," "the universe does not care about me," "what counts is my mind, or my soul, not my body," "the body dies but the soul lives forever," "a person's sexuality, as one of the lower instincts, needs to be sublimated in favor of one's higher nature," "one's bodily nature does not matter." Spells are also created by humans when they regard the Helpers as too small for the task. In truth, it is the Helpers alone that are able to break spells and complete transformations around the world.

Line 4. *No blame. He meets him without passing by. Going brings danger. One must be on guard. Do not act. Be constantly correct and firm.*

"No blame" refers to reacting in the right way to an injustice done by others: by finding the inner truth of the situation, with the help of the Sage. Danger comes if the person fails to do this and instead allows the ego to attach itself to blaming the other, naming him the guilty party or culprit. In the Cosmic sense, there is no such thing as a guilty party, or an object of hatred; naming a person as such is to get entangled in the fate the other has created by his wrong deed. (*See* Glossary: Culprit.)

"He meets him without passing by" refers to the Cosmic Law of Fate: all evil deeds create a fate that returns to the doer. It does so sooner if no one takes hold of it by attaching himself to blaming the wrongdoer, or by attempting to "make justice happen." A vindictive attitude comes from thinking, "there is no one to defend me but myself"; it shuts out the Helper of Justice that would ensure that the situation is rectified. This does not mean that the person injured should deny the evil nature of the deed, or the fact that it has occurred. His duty is to say the inner No to the person's wrongdoing, and then turn the matter completely over to the Cosmos. It remains "on the Cosmic books," so to speak, until the fate has been extinguished. A fate is extinguished either when it has run its full course, in terms of time, like a prison sentence, or when the person himself has recognized and regretted his deed and rid himself of the mistaken ideas that have led him to do it. Whether he has corrected himself is not something other humans can determine, as this correction takes place within the heart of that person, out of sight.

"Going brings danger. One must be on guard" refers to a

person's failing to rid himself of a self-righteous attitude that causes him to indulge in vindictiveness. Vindictiveness is the ego's attachment to blame, and comes from having a self-image of being morally superior to another by nature. Part of that self-image is the idea that the person has the right to judge another as tending to be "good" or "evil," because that person belongs to a particular family, class, race, or religion. Vindictiveness can also have its origin in the idea that humans are the center around which the universe revolves, and stand in the place of God to judge affairs. Human pride is another cause of vindictiveness, as when a people (or country) holds itself up as powerful and "advanced," and regards those who rebel against its oppressions as criminals. The inner No needs to be said in all cases of self-righteousness and vindictiveness.

The words "no blame" may be reassuring a person who has been falsely blamed for something, and who is receiving another's poison arrows, that he bears no blame. It is also telling him not to allow himself to get involved in an inner war with that person by blaming him, but to turn the matter over to the Cosmos. "Be constantly firm and correct" tells him not to accept any guilt the other may wish to put on him, and to free himself from the poison arrows. (*See* p. 697, Freeing Yourself from Spells and Poison Arrows.)

Line 5. *Dense clouds, no rain from our western territory. The prince shoots and hits him who is in the cave.*

"Dense clouds, no rain..." indicates that a person has missed the point in his judgments and decisions. Metaphorically speaking, he has concluded, from seeing dense clouds, that there will be rain, and has acted accordingly. An example is the person who, on seeing the stock market move up "a tick," decides that "now is the time to invest." "No rain" indicates that his assumption, based on momentary appearances, was incorrect. The prince is a metaphor for the person's exalted self-image as a decision-maker. What he has "shot down," through shooting into the dark of the cave, is the Sage, that has the ability to show him the inner truth of the situation that would enable him to make a decision from inner clarity.

It is possible that the person has consulted the *I Ching*, but has not asked, through the *rtcm*, "have I understood the message correctly," and thus has missed the point. "Shot down" here means that the person has dismissed the Sage's help and acted on his own, as when he reads the *I Ching* messages of the lines and hexagrams to match his preexisting beliefs.

Line 6. *He passes him by, not meeting him. The flying bird leaves him. Misfortune. This means bad luck and injury.*
"He passes him by, not meeting him," refers to missing the point. "The flying bird leaves him" states that a person's inner truth, although it is no longer an inexperienced fledgling, has been lost.

This line may point to a person who has learned that the Sage is available to help him find the inner truth, and who has enough experience of the Sage's trustworthy counsel to "fly"; nevertheless, he has allowed the ego to return in the form of a false self-confidence. "He passes him by" refers to his bypassing the help of the Sage. Receiving this line is meant to make him aware that his arrogance has created a fate. If he then recognizes that he has allowed certain phrases of the ego to return, and rids himself of them, the fate can be ended, and he can return to harmony with the Cosmos.

This line can also refer to a person's monumentalizing a mistake, by believing it was something no one "should" make. Behind this is the ego, which has made a small mistake into a big issue, which the person either then becomes vindictive about, or for which he blames himself excessively. Such a person has missed the point that in making the effort of freeing the true self, mistakes are necessary, and are not the cause of blame if the person recognizes his mistake and corrects himself. Sincerity keeps mistakes from leading to harm or embarrassment, and they are swiftly forgotten in other people's memories.

"He passes him by" can also refer to the rational and imaging minds that, when acting in the service of the ego, bypass Nature's Laws, causing the "bad luck and injury" mentioned. This happens, for example, when these minds have been flattered by the collective ego into believing they are superior to the rest of the body. This view puts spells on both these minds and on the body, creating health problems by disabling the body's abilities to regulate itself effectively. It is like the proverbial centipede who tries to think "how to walk," and is suddenly unable to move its legs harmoniously. When not blocked, the feeling consciousness of the body has all the abilities it needs to be healthy, to feed itself properly, and to recover from injury—all without thinking. (*See* p. 697, Freeing Yourself from Spells.)

63. *After Completion*

 K'an
Li

The Judgment: *After completion. Success in small matters. Perseverance furthers. At the beginning good fortune. At the end disorder.*

Exactly what is it that makes success endure? The Sage addresses this question in the theme of this hexagram, which concerns that which makes the success achieved through one's efforts endure. This is what defines the Cosmic meaning of completion.

As in Hexagram 64, the word "completion" refers to *completing* all the steps of an undertaking that has Cosmic approval, *through transformation.* A person's efforts to bring to completion any goal require the Helper of Transformation. The person may engage in consistent efforts, be guided by the Sage, correct his attitudes, and say the necessary inner No's; thus, he puts in his one-hundred percent effort. At this point, he must turn the matter over to the Helper of Transformation and leave it to the Cosmos. Then, the Helper of Transformation, together with other Helpers of the invisible world, makes the necessary changes on the primary level of consciousness, transforming the situation. No great achievement can attain enduring success in any other way.

"Completing" also means fulfilling one's true uniqueness,

through freeing and bringing to maturation the true self, with the aid of the Sage and the Helpers.

"Success in small matters" can be read in two ways: (1) that one has reached a small, or partial, success in regard to one's undertaking; or (2) that enduring success is to be attained through consistently ridding oneself of the "small" seed phrases and images that comprise the ego and prevent the personality from achieving its full potential.

This hexagram can be saying that while certain seed phrases and images have been removed, and a transformation has occurred, other seed phrases or images are still present, which threaten to undermine the success achieved. An example is having said the inner No to a parent who has encroached into one's affairs. But because the person has been trained to feel guilty for saying No to a parent, the guilt enters to undo the No, and undermine its beneficial effects. The person needs to rid himself of the poison arrow of guilt he has accepted. (*See* p. 695, Freeing Yourself from Poison Arrows.)

A person may also receive this hexagram when, after making some outer changes, he has achieved balance among conflicting forces. However, because he has not dealt with the cause of the conflict, all he has achieved is a teetering situation like that of being on a tightrope, which requires constant attention and effort to keep the various contradictory forces balanced. In the end, such a situation can only end in exhaustion and failure, which is the meaning of "at the end, disorder." An example is the person who uses meditation only to calm himself. But, as soon as he leaves this state of rest, he is quickly agitated again, because the worries he displaced return. The true purpose of meditation is not a temporary escape but to seek out the causes of the imbalance (false phrases in one's inner program) and rid oneself of them. Only then does the peace become enduring.

In regard to balancing opposing forces, Cosmic forces do not oppose each other. The Cosmos maintains harmony through the attraction that exists between *complementary* forces. The idea of opposing forces originates in the demonic sphere of consciousness, and needs itself to be deprogrammed.

"After completion" can also concern a person who has

achieved success in the form of great wealth, fame, or a top position. Or, he may have externally engineered his life in such a way that he now feels secure. However, this security is based on a false self-confidence and pride. "At the end, disorder," points to the fate he has created through having achieved his success without the aid of the Helpers. His failure is pictured in the image of the fox that, having nearly crossed over the ice, at the last minute falls in and gets its tail wet. Here, the tail represents the "small detail" of the Helpers, which he has left out of his calculations. It also indicates the considerations of things unseen that he has left behind, but which follow him, like the tail.

The hexagram also warns the person who has achieved great progress due to his sincerity, against allowing the ego within him to appropriate the success by saying "I did it," "I have it made," or other such thoughts of self-congratulation. Such phrases need to be treated as spells.

Other spells connected with this hexagram have the words "always" or "never" in them, which prevent transformations. An example is a spell put on a person that asserts he will *never* change, that he will *always* make that mistake, or implies that he *is* such and such a person "by nature," implying, "always that way." Poison arrows that reflect hopelessness or helplessness also block transformations.

Note: Since all lines contain infinite possibilities of interpretation, one needs to use the *rtcm* to determine if the meanings suggested here apply to the given situation. (*See* p. 736 for using the *rtcm*.)

Line 1. *He brakes his wheels. He gets his tail in the water. No blame.*

The metaphor, "he brakes his wheels," can refer to the person's bringing his progress to a halt through indulgence in wanting, wondering, and worrying, at the base of which is doubt. He may be wondering, for example, why, after having put in his effort to achieve his goal, success still remains aloof. He may be asking himself whether, in following the Sage, he has been deluding himself. He needs to understand that the goal can only be brought to completion by his turning the matter over to the Helper of Transformation, and letting go of it entirely. He needs also to say the inner No to any attempts of the ego to supervise the completion. There will be no blame if, at this point, he corrects his attitude by saying the inner No to his doubts, and acts as counseled.

Other meanings of "getting his tail in the water," mentioned in the main text, include trying to reach completion without the Helpers, and forgetting to take into account unseen factors, that follow him, like the tail.

Line 2. *The woman loses the curtain of her carriage. Do not run after it; on the seventh day you will get it.*

Wilhelm comments, "when a woman drove out in her carriage, she had a curtain that hid her from the glances of the curious. It was regarded as a breach of propriety to drive on if this curtain was lost." In this line, the metaphor is used to indicate a loss of the protection and help given by the Sage when a person has put his trust in the wrong kinds of protection (force, arms, power, symbols, etc.).

Riding in a carriage, in this line, speaks of a person who is riding above the ground, out of contact with his commonsense. This causes him to lose his connection with reality and to put his trust in his fantasies. Without his commonsense, he loses the protection it gives him against being deceived by others.

The carriage can also symbolize a wrong way of making progress. Here, the progress has bypassed the help of the Sage and the Helpers, through the person's acting from a vain self-image. Consequently, he has lost the Cosmic help and protection he needs, and thus invites encroachment. This reveals the Cosmic Principle that the person who is free of a self-image does not invite encroachment. If he will rid himself of his self-image and return to humility, he will again draw the protection and help of the Sage. (*See* p. 689, Freeing Yourself from Self-Images.)

This line also makes us aware of the Cosmic Principle that the things we desire are free to come to us only when we have detached from wanting them. In running after what is lost, we only lose our self-esteem. Nothing worthwhile can be retrieved or attained in this way. To truly understand this principle, we need to be aware that everything in the Cosmos has consciousness and responds to consciousness. Consciousness that is in harmony with the Cosmos, i.e., that comes from one's dignity, invites the harmonious response of the Cosmos, whereas acting from any ego-desire invites a rebuff.

The reference to seven days states the Cosmic Principle that what truly belongs to a person (his dignity and self-respect) can be recovered within a relatively short time, if he corrects his attitude. The word "loss" has Cosmic meaning only when we speak of losing self-esteem, self-worth, clarity, and Cosmic protection, help, and nourishment. These inner losses, which are the only real losses, can be retrieved by correcting one's attitude.

This line can also refer to guilt that undermines what a person has achieved in cooperation with the Cosmos. He had attained that cooperation through deprogramming his mistaken beliefs. Now that the problem has been resolved, he returns to his beliefs through feeling guilty for having abandoned them. (A related problem occurs when partners who have separated fail to close their inner connection with the help of the Helpers. Guilt for having broken vows or promises will keep them bound together in a way that is destructive to both.) (*See* p. 694, Freeing Yourself from a Guilt Spell, and p. 684, Closing an Inner Connection.)

The carriage can also symbolize reliance on hopes to "keep going." All hoping is a response to underlying fears or doubts: the fear of not getting what one needs, and the doubt that one's efforts will lead to happiness. Such fears and doubts cannot be resolved by hoping, which is pure fantasizing. Fears and doubts come from the ego and need to be addressed by identifying the seed phrases and images that give rise to them. Then, they need to be deprogrammed. Once these ego-emotions have been addressed and they no longer influence the heart, help comes from the Sage and the Helpers to help us fulfill all desires of the heart.

Line 3. *The illustrious ancestor attacks the devil's country. After three years he conquers it. Inferior people must not be employed.*

In its Cosmic meaning, this line refers to the persistence over a period of time that is necessary if a person is to succeed in deconstructing the ego in himself. This process must proceed phrase by phrase and image by image, as these are brought into consciousness in relation to his everyday circumstances. It is not possible to attack the ego as an entity in itself, for it is a complete program of phrases and images that has installing features, protecting features, upgrading features, and reinstalling features. Its deconstruction is carried out with the aid of the Helpers. The persistence must be such that it wears the ego out. The person who believes that it is enough merely to shrink it, or that he is capable by himself to contain it, or keep it small, falls under the teasing phrases put forward by the ego itself. This is why the line warns against employing inferior people. "After three years he conquers it" refers to this persistent effort. "Three years," does not refer to an actual time, but is saying that the ego can indeed be conquered, and that it is not indomitable, as it tries to make us believe. The term "illustrious ancestor" refers to the deepest sincerity in making this effort.

In the meaning given by the collective ego, the "illustrious ancestor" is the collective ego itself, which has appointed itself as the correct authority to fight evil in the world. The collective ego defines the devil's country as anything connected with "animal nature." On this basis, it claims that if a person follows his true nature, he will undermine the social order. Such a claim distracts the individual from seeing how the collective ego, through its conditioning activities, undermines the natural order of society and the harmonious way in which human nature operates in society, when not conditioned by the machinations of the collective ego. Indeed, the "inferior people" mentioned are these mistaken ideas and beliefs, and the "devil's country" is the true name for the demonic sphere of consciousness created by the collective ego.

This line can refer to a person who, in following the path of freeing his true self, suddenly sees himself as undermining the social order (created by the collective ego), and therefore feels guilty. He is unaware that he is reacting to a guilt spell put on him during childhood, that is keeping him under the collective ego's control. He needs to free himself from that guilt spell, and to recognize that it is the collective ego that undermines the natural order of society.

A person can also receive this line when he desires to discipline or discredit another, by bringing the matter between them into the open. Doing so, however, is to employ inferior people: by causing the other to lose face, he only hardens the ego in him. Such an attempt comes from the ego in himself, which acts from self-righteousness. Bringing the matter into the open only destroys his first intention to have a good effect. Responding to another's incorrect behavior through saying the inner No achieves the correct effect, without defaming the other person's character.

Inferior people can also be a reference to what a person falsely considers to be inferior in himself and is therefore trying to discipline. For example, he may be trying to rid himself of his animal nature by disciplining his body through ascetic practices, such as excessive time spent in meditation, sitting in contorted positions, or abstaining from giving sexual expression to love. In reality, the inferior people are the poison arrows he has put on his animal nature, which need to be removed because they prevent the renewal of his life force. (*See* p. 695, Freeing Yourself from Poison Arrows.)

Line 4. *The finest clothes turn to rags. Be careful all day long.*

The "finest clothes" mentioned is a metaphor for a person's having become free of one or more self-images. His success, however, will turn again to rags if he indulges in any self-congratulation, as in thinking he is superior. "Be careful all day long" is counsel for the person to keep aware of his inner thoughts, and on guard against any new self-image that may tempt him.

A person can also receive this line when it appears that he is about to succeed in his undertaking. The line counsels him, however, that he has not rid himself of one or more seed phrases that, if left in place, will undermine his success. The phrase may be "I did it,"— an attempt by the ego to claim credit for what was achieved by the Helpers. He needs to say the inner No to that idea, otherwise the success will "turn to rags," meaning its good effects will dissipate.

This line may also call attention to the person who, after

achieving success, cannot shake off his doubt that transformation makes it truly endure. Such a person may believe that "ups are followed by downs" as being the way of life ("rags to riches, riches to rags"). If he persists in projecting this belief, indeed, his fine clothes will turn to rags.

This line can also refer to the person who thinks he has followed the *I Ching*'s counsel, but it is now apparent that he was not successful. The cause is that his sincerity was halfhearted, so that he has glossed over the remaining issues standing in the way of success. Such a person may have a variety of false phrases in his program, such as, "whatever you do it is not enough" (behind which is "the Cosmos only puts up obstacles for us"), "no one is ever going to appreciate what you do" (looking to others for approval) and "nobody is perfect" (implying that putting 100% effort into the task is impossible). These kinds of phrases cause a person to approach his life halfheartedly.

This line can also warn a person of another who appears to have corrected himself, but who is not yet trustworthy. He therefore needs to remain cautious and reserved until the other has truly corrected himself. He may also need to ask the Sage for protection from that person's wrong intentions.

This line can also refer to the person, who, upon undertaking his study with the *I Ching*, believes the task consists in developing his "higher self." This idea creates many misunderstandings in his readings of the text, and creates a barrier between him and the Sage, because this idea is based on a division of his wholeness into a "higher" and a "lower" self. (*See* Glossary: Spirituality.)

The image of "the finest clothes" can also be a metaphor for a "magnificent attitude," by which a person magnanimously "plays God" by taking it upon himself to forgive, admonish, or condemn others. He thereby condemns another by telling him, "you have really failed this time," or he lets another off the hook of his fate by telling him that what he has done is, "okay," or that he forgives him. Such ideas come from the human-centered view of the universe that has put man in the role of representing God (or heaven) on earth. Paradoxically, this view can cause a person to allow others to run roughshod over him. Such pretensions of possessing power come only from the ego, and bring about the fate referred to above as "rags." The person can end his fate if he will rid himself of this magnificent self-image and the seed phrases that have created it, and if he regrets his arrogance. (*See* p. 689, Freeing Yourself from Self-Images.)

Line 5. *The neighbor in the east who slaughters an ox does not attain as much real happiness as the neighbor in the west with his small offering.*

This line has to do with the seed phrases and images that underlie the magnificent attitude mentioned in Line 4. Such an attitude is based on seeing humans as charged by heaven or by God with the duty to condemn or forgive others. This idea is also used to authorize persons, groups, or institutions to have rights over other species and things. In the Cosmic system of harmony, a person has only the duty to forgive himself for his mistakes, once he perceives and corrects them, and the duty to say the inner No to all aspects of the ego in himself or in others.

The ox, traditionally an animal of sacrifice, is mentioned here as a metaphor for a person's having sacrificed his animal nature, believing it will placate the "higher powers." While proud of his sacrifice, he also envies others who go about their lives simply, and are happy. He therefore thinks the Cosmos, or life, is unjust. Receiving this line can be to make him aware that he has acted on the mistaken idea that he has a higher and a lower nature, which idea has created a fate. Freeing himself from it, and from the self-image of the spiritual person, will free him from his fate, and bring happiness back into his life. Getting rid of such ideas that slander his wholeness is the small offering referred to. (*See* p. 687, Freeing Yourself from Mistaken Ideas and Beliefs.)

This line also addresses the idea of sacrifice in general, whether it be to gods, higher beings, or sacrifices made to ideas or institutions. Originally, sacrifices were made to placate a "higher power," or induce it to be benevolent. It was plainly an attempt to make a deal with these powers. Such sacrifices are foreign to the Cosmic Way, for bargaining is the way of the collective ego, and there is no higher power with which to negotiate. Humans can reunite with the Cosmic Harmony through the simple act of perceiving and correcting their mistaken ideas.

Line 6. *He gets his head in the water. Danger.*

"He gets his head in the water" refers to a person who has begun to look back with longing and regret, after having crossed the great water, and separated from the human-centered vision of the world.

For example, a person who has freed his true self has now adopted the idea that he has "left his friends and fellows behind." He now thinks he must "haul them across." He is unaware that dissolving his bond with his group (the "group-we," as it is put in Hexagram 59, *Dissolution*, Line 4) is the only way to dissolve his adherence to the *values* of the collective ego, and the individual egos around him. It does not mean abandoning the others' true selves or those with whom he is inwardly connected. The Sage resides in everyone's presence, and is available to help, if asked. However, the idea that it is one's duty to save others comes from the human-centered belief that humans have to "do it all." This view obliterates the existence of the Sage and the Helpers. Danger refers to the fate that is created by such an exaggerated self-importance.

The line also applies to the person who has been blessed by the Cosmos, but allows the ego to suggest that his life is now lacking excitement. The ego is thus slandering harmony as being "too tame," and giving one "nothing to strive for." Listening to these voices of the ego creates a fate, the danger mentioned. The same danger is also created by self-satisfaction. The truth is that life in harmony with the Cosmos is far more inspiring and full of wonders than the treadmill drudgery of living within the parallel reality.

Danger can also refer to someone who believes he has conquered the ego in himself once and for all. While it is possible to conquer the ego, the ego is the first to suggest that it can be conquered through means other than deconstructing it as mentioned throughout this volume. The person who boasts that he has conquered his ego has lost touch with his commonsense, and is under the control of the ego.

64. *Before Completion*

 Li
K'an

The Judgment: *Before completion, success. But if the little fox, after nearly completing the crossing, gets his tail in the water, there is nothing that would further.*

The Sage has indicated the theme of this hexagram to be our cooperation with the Helper of Transformation that brings our undertakings to completion.

Receiving this hexagram is saying that the student who has nearly completed a step in the process of freeing his true self, needs to deal with residual fears or doubts which are addressed in the lines. After having dealt with them, the Helper of Transformation can bring his efforts to completion. This Helper is the "vehicle for crossing the great water" mentioned in Line 2.

A person may receive this hexagram when he has done his 100% in achieving his goal; then he needs to recognize that he can go no further, and turn the matter of its completion over to the Helper of Transformation. The situation is like that of the musician who has practiced assiduously, has done all he could to understand the feeling the composer wished to communicate, and is now about to begin the performance. By turning the whole matter over to the Cosmos and asking for help, he finds himself guided and playing on a level that is quite beyond his ordinary abilities. He simultaneously performs and enjoys his performing, and it is endowed with the genius of the Helper of Transformation. While the feeling is "magical," it is the natural way the Cosmos performs when we get out of its way.

The young fox represents the student who, upon beginning the path of liberating his true self, is inexperienced in the ways of the Cosmos. The fox, as an animal, represents the student's ability, within his own nature, to meet with all circumstances, including standing up to the ego in himself, and to the fears and guilt the collective ego has instilled in his psyche. Important among his natural abilities is the ability to ask for help from the Sage and the Helpers. The young fox's tail stands for his residual fear, "what if I don't succeed," which is one of the last attempts the ego makes to prevent the crossing. Getting the tail in the water refers to listening to such fears, for then, indeed, he cannot free himself from the influence of the collective ego.

The great water is a metaphor used throughout the *I Ching* for all the doubts, fears, and feelings of guilt the collective ego has trained into the individual, to keep him within the parallel reality. Crossing the great water refers to a step in the process of freeing the person's true self, by which he returns to the Cosmic Reality. Making this crossing is the dual task referred to above: the student does his half by deprogramming the mistaken ideas of the collective ego; the Helper of Transformation completes the other half.

Crossing the great water can also refer to completing any kind of undertaking, whether it be the process of bringing relationships into harmony, writing, performing, meditating, or doing a difficult mechanical task. A successful completion is always a cooperative relationship between the person on the one hand, and the Sage and the Helpers on the other. (The beginning student needs to avoid trying to identify and name the Helpers because too often, his inexperience will categorize them in ego-terms which come from fantasy. Wrong names block their true functioning. Their correct names may come as mind-flashes, and can be checked with the *rtcm*.)

A person receives this hexagram to inform him of the effort that is still needed on his part to make the crossing possible. The first part of his effort consists in becoming centered within himself. (*See* p. 678, Centering Yourself.) When he has cleaned his inner space as described in that exercise, he next asks the Sage and the Helpers to give him the insight of what he needs to do, and to bring the help needed to make that possible. When he has finished these tasks, he then turns the matter over to the Sage and the Helpers for completion.

After turning it over, he needs to keep any doubts, expectations, and wondering about it dispersed, and separate from the ego's tendency to focus his inner eye on the matter. This letting go needs to be complete, especially in regard to the time required for the transformation to take place.

Spells connected with this hexagram are created by beliefs that isolate a person from the Helpers. Among them is a person's belief that the Helpers do not exist. It is not necessary to believe in the Helpers, but for transformation to become possible, it *is* necessary to deprogram the beliefs that disable them. These beliefs say: "I can/must do it all myself." "What is our intelligence for?" "There is no help." Such beliefs act as spells.

Other spells blocking transformation have to with the belief in *changes:* "*All* that is needed to make success happen is a change" (a change in partners, jobs, scenes, engineering, policies, etc.). The belief in changes ignores the fact that transformation, which is true change, can only be brought about by the Helpers. Other spells that block transformation have to do with beliefs in initiation: "one needs to become initiated [as by a human master], into the mysteries that lead to mastery."

Note: Since all lines contain infinite possibilities of interpretation, one needs to use the *rtcm* to determine if the meanings suggested here apply to the given situation. (*See* p. 736 for using the *rtcm*.)

Line 1. *He gets his tail in the water. Humiliating.*

"He" in this line represents a person who, having nearly crossed the river of his fears, doubts, and guilt, now hesitates to listen to the ego's last plea, "how will you cope with the world out there without me?" "I have been your faithful friend," "I am a part of your personality: you can't get rid of me...without harming yourself." These last pleas of the ego, which were part of the original installing features of the ego-program in the psyche, are now replayed, if the person has never deprogrammed them. Their only purpose is to pull him back into the parallel reality. Once he listens to them, other reinstalling features of the program are activated.

If the person will now say the inner No to these phrases, and ask the Helpers to deprogram them, the transformation will take place, although he will feel some humiliation for having listened to these fears.

The line can also indicate that the healing of a health problem cannot be completed because a person has failed to ask the Helper of Transformation to complete the healing. Or, he may have overlooked one or more phrases or images that have created the health problem. The line can also describe a regression that has occurred after an initial improvement in his condition. This may be due to his thinking certain thoughts, such as "it can't be that easy," or "now I can do whatever I like" (meaning, return to old bad habits).

Line 2. *He brakes his wheels. Being firmly correct brings good fortune.*

"He brakes his wheels" is a suggestion that the person has been making progress in a wagon or carriage, which has been appropriate for his passage across land. However, now, since this part of his journey has been completed, with the next step requiring him to cross water, the appropriate vehicle is a boat. This means that whereas his effort consisted in doing *his* full share, now, the completion, done by the Helper of Transformation, adds the other half.

The message given is that the person can halt in his efforts, because he has done enough. He now needs to ask the Helper of Transformation to complete his goal. He remains firm that his goal is correct, and turns the matter over to the Cosmos by becoming neutral about how the transformation will take place, in what form, and in what time.

"Being firmly correct" warns against fantasizing about the outcome. If a person has been doing this, it may be necessary to deprogram the projections and spells he has created, or other spells that have prompted him to indulge in fantasy. (*See* p. 695, Freeing Yourself from Projections and Spells.)

Crossing the great water can also be a metaphor for healing an illness with the help of the Sage. Thoughts that impede the progress include spells created by inner comments of the ego, such as: "It's silly to be tossing coins, I am above that," "it's not proven by science," "it only works when you believe in it, I don't believe in that kind of hocus pocus." The ego will employ every tactic, especially those appealing to vanity, to keep a person from healing himself with the help of the Sage, for that means to free himself of certain aspects of the ego in himself. Another "logic" employed by the ego is its assertion that the "true way" of healing must necessarily be hard and complicated; at the same time, it would assert that if the person follows the Cosmic way of healing, it should be an instantaneous and impressive "miracle," or at least only a matter of two days and no effort; if it takes any longer, it is "simply too hard." The intended conclusion is that if the Cosmic Way does not "work right away," and "is not thorough and complete," a person should return to the conventional way that the collective ego recognizes.

Finally, the crossing can refer to the passing over that is commonly called death. To make this crossing smooth and timely, the vehicle needed is comprised of certain Helpers, which a person can ask on another's behalf, to help him make the crossing. A timely crossing means that the purpose of the person's life in a body has been completed. Receiving this line can be an indication that the time has come to ask these Helpers on behalf of another person. One can determine this by asking the Sage through the *rtcm*. (*See* Glossary: Death.)

Line 3. *Before completion, attack brings misfortune. It furthers one to cross the great water.*

After having done his self-correction, the person is advised not to make a further assault on the goal by trying to make it happen. Instead, his next step is to center himself, let go of the matter completely, and turn it over to the Cosmos. (*See* p. 678, Centering Yourself.) He neither thinks, fantasizes, nor worries about whether or how the transformation will happen (for this, too, would be an attack on the process); thus he does not generate any negative consciousness that would interfere with the completion process.

Revealed here is the Cosmic Principle that progress is made while a person is going on with his life and while he is keeping up his efforts at self-correction. Progress halts when he puts his life on hold, and waits with expectation.

Line 4. *Being firmly correct brings good fortune. Remorse disappears. Shock, thus to discipline the devil's country. For three years, great realms are awarded.*

This line refers to a person whose goal has been to reunite with another, after the relationship has fallen into a misunderstanding. He has corrected himself thus done his share of preparing for the transformation. The "devil's country" stands for the misunderstandings that remain. Through the intervention of the Helper of Transformation, a shock has jarred the other free from the ego, allowing his true self to lead his personality. This line informs the person observing the changes taking place in the other that they are real and will endure, because they have been created through transformation.

"For three years, great realms are awarded" refers to subsequent transformations to be expected, which will free up more and more of that person's true nature. This process is also accompanied by an increasing good influence he has on others, and on the situation. All remorse for past mistakes is wiped away.

This line shows the principle that people are not changed by altering themselves externally. It is only when transformation has taken place that the heart is cleansed and restored to its original state; then, the person is no longer in the grip of "the devil's country."

Line 5. *Perseverance has brought good fortune without remorse. The transformation is complete. The light of the Sage is true. Success.*

The victory over the ego has been won, because the person has been firmly correct in saying the necessary inner No's, and has deprogrammed the spells, projections, and poison arrows active in the situation. He has thereby initiated the aid of the Sage and freed the Helpers needed to complete his undertaking. He needs only to keep free of claiming the victory as his.

In regard to healing, this line informs the person that his healing is complete.

Line 6. *There is drinking of wine in genuine confidence. No blame. But if one wets his head, he loses it, in truth.*

This line shows a person whose confidence in the Cosmic Way has been justified. Just at this point of victory, there is the danger that he may fall into overconfidence, which is the last attempt of the ego to undo the success achieved. This would happen if the person flattered himself that the success was his own doing, and thus eliminate the role of the Helpers.

The person is also warned by this line to avoid any assumption that he has conquered the ego within himself, once and for all. Such an assumption might tempt him to relax back into a careless, easygoing acceptance of what is incorrect.

Losing one's head is also a metaphor warning of the danger of becoming a walking dead person through allowing a "drunken" attitude. Drunkenness is a metaphor for a person's careless indifference to the moral contradictions of the collective ego, an indifference which insists on defending its point of view. (*See* Glossary: Walking Dead Person.)

Authors' Note: Just as we were completing this book, the Sage made us aware that the first three lines of this hexagram describe the final preparation for the completion that occurs in Line 4, and is confirmed in Line 5. The old belief that "completion never occurs in the *I Ching*," because it shows constant changes to be the rule of life, is incorrect. This belief, written into the traditional versions of the *I Ching,* has robbed the book of one of its greatest messages—that victory over the ego is possible. While the ego will always attempt to creep back in, the person who has liberated his true feelings will have the help he needs from the Sage to keep the ego dismantled.

Part III

Appendices and Glossary

Appendix 1

How to Strengthen and Free the True Self

The Inner No

The inner No is a Cosmic Principle and thus has a Cosmic function. Its function is to *transform* a discordant situation from *within*, thereby taking care of a problem in the atomic realm, or realm of consciousness.

Saying the inner No is the correct way of decreasing all *active* aspects of the collective and individual egos, either within oneself or in others. The inner No does this by deprogramming the individual phrases and images that make up the ego and that also give rise to ego-emotions. Deprogramming deletes a Yes to mistaken ideas and beliefs you have formerly accepted, either consciously or unconsciously. The inner No is said to each of the ego's phrases and images as they are brought into your consciousness, usually with the help of the Sage. The inner No is also the means by which projections, spells, and poison arrows are extinguished in the psyche.

Saying the inner No to ego-activities in another person gives his true self the message that allowing the ego to lead his personality is unacceptable. It also gives his true self the necessary strength to say No to the ego in himself. Unlike the outer No, which often comes from self-righteousness. and only raises the ego's opposition, the inner No goes around the ego, therefore avoids the loss of face which arouses the ego's hatred. Failure to say the inner No gives the person's true self the impression that his ego-behavior is permissible.

Saying the inner No is to consciously affirm what our commonsense and feelings have already recognized as incorrect. The No is said from the heart as an inner renunciation of what is incorrect. In this way, mistaken, or disharmonious ideas that we have previously accepted, are expelled from all the body cells, in which some of them may have made their homes.

Failure to say the inner No, as when we excuse, or let someone "off the hook" of his mistakes, creates what the *I Ching* calls "misfortune." The same applies to failure to delete projections, spells, and poison arrows that we have put on ourselves, others, or any part of Nature.

The inner No is most effective when said three times with inner resolve (but unaccompanied by hostile emotions): "No, No, No."

Situations that require saying the inner No:

The inner No is said to every *active* aspect of the ego in yourself or in another. You may use the *rtcm* to verify that it is appropriate. The inner No is said:

- *to attitudes* or behaviors: self-righteousness, self-pity, demands, competitive behavior, temper, threats, encroachments, idle curiosity, blaming yourself or others, and any belief in power, or the use of power;
- *to ego-emotions*, guilt, desire, fear, anger (when seized by the ego), boredom, envy, pity, etc.;
- *to self-images* of all kinds, including "the modest person," "the spiritual person," "the superior man," etc.;
- to *mistaken ideas and beliefs*, and the *rationales* that support mistaken ideas, thereby keeping the ego in place. An example of a rationale is the thought: "It cannot be that easy to decrease the ego by saying the inner No";
- to *images that support mistaken ideas*. Example: the image of "going downhill, deteriorating, getting certain illnesses" connected with the idea of "getting older."

The above mentioned ego-aspects are often based on *seed phrases* and *images* that need to be identified with the help of the *rtcm*. (*See* p. 689, "Seed Phrases and Images.") It helps to keep in mind that by saying the inner No to each seed phrase or image, a Helper is set free. Each freed Helper then brings into your conscious mind more phrases and images that can then be deleted, because it wants other Helpers to be freed as well. In this way, you gradually get down to the very root phrases and images on which whole belief-systems are built.

Inability to say the inner No

From working with individuals in seminars and private consultations, we realized that a majority of the people were suffering from a partial or total inhibition to say the inner No. The reason lay in standards of goodness adopted in childhood conditioning which inhibited them from expressing their feelings of inner truth. This goodness, defined by the collective ego, means "never saying No." It also means being tolerant of other people's misbehavior, or even submissive, when they are persons of authority. Both rewards and punishments are applied to fix this conditioning in the child's psyche.

When, for example, a child *felt* that something the father has said was untrue, and objected by saying No, the child was punished. The punishment was repeated until the child no longer said No to authority. In some cases there was only the threat that "something awful would happen," that blocked the child's ability to say No. In other instances, simply the fear of becoming guilty sufficed. When disablement to say No has been caused by a traumatic experience, the person may be helped by another to become free of this problem. The actual event needs to be recalled and identified with the help of the *rtcm.*

Restoring the ability to say the inner No requires several of the following steps (identify which are needed in the specific case, by using the *rtcm*):

(A) Say the inner No, No, No to the idea of becoming guilty for saying the inner No to authority, when its demands did not correspond with your inner truth.

(B) Say the inner No, No, No to the person who carried out the punishment or pronounced the threat. (This may have been a parent, a teacher, or the collective ego in general).

(C) Say the inner No, No, No to the punishment or threat itself in its verbal and image form.

(D) Ask the Sage for help to remove the disablement.

(E) Give yourself the message and permission that saying the inner (and sometimes an outer No) is needed to define yourself.

(F) Thank the Sage for its help.

The steps (A)-(F) need to be repeated daily until you receive the ok, through using the *rtcm*, that the matter has been successfully resolved by the Sage and the Helpers.

Saying the inner No to aspects of the ego:

(A) Make sure, with the help of the *rtcm*, that the inner No is all that is needed in the given circumstance. If it is not enough, you may have to deal with the issue as a projection, spell, or poison arrow, all of which are described on p. 697.

(B) Identify the exact elements that need to be deprogrammed. These elements can include an ego-emotion or attitude, a phrase, an image, or a self-image. Then say No, No, No to it (the element, phrase, or image involved). Example: No, No, No to my envy. No, No, No to "I wish I had such a nice car," or: No, No, No to the self-image of 'being the one who is in the right.'"

(C) The above steps need to be repeated daily until you are informed, through the *rtcm*, that the matter has been successfully dealt with by the Helpers.

After having said the first inner No, it is important to really let go of the matter; otherwise you remain attached to the problem and prevent the Helpers from dealing with it.

After having said the inner No to someone's ego-behavior, make sure that your heart remains open, but neutral. If you notice that it has closed, ask for help from the Helpers to re-open your heart.

Centering Yourself

To be centered within means to be in harmony with your true self, and therefore with the Cosmos.

Centering means to take your true place in the Cosmic Order by recognizing and saying the inner No to all ways in which you see yourself as special, or above any of the other aspects of the Cosmic Whole. It is to recognize and validate your interrelatedness with everything in the Cosmic Whole, and your dependency on the Sage. It is to recognize the human-centeredness of petty grievances, dissatisfactions, annoyances, and other aspects of the ego which prevent you from seeing the good things in life.

Centering yourself enables the Sage to teach you whatever you need to know about your situation, and to deepen your understanding of the nature of things, and of the Cosmic Way. It is achieved through a brief meditation in which you turn over to the Helpers everything that is bothering you at the moment.

Step 1: Suspending your disbelief: This means stopping the "yes, but..." thoughts of disbelief that attempt to fill up your inner space and crowd out the Sage, by saying the inner No to them. If these thoughts appear in meditation as figures, regardless of size, ask the Helpers to take care of them.

Step 2: Loading things onto the wagon of the Helper of Transformation. This is a reference to the wagon mentioned in Line 2 of Hexagram 14, *Possession in Great Measure.* You may see it in a different image that is personal tor you; allow whatever other image comes to your mind that serves the same purpose of "removing" from you what is false. Load onto the "wagon" whatever is bothering you at the moment, and let go of it. This frees up your inner space, enabling the Sage to reply and address the problems in the most efficient way. Turn over any of the following kinds of mental elements:

- self-images that come to mind, including being the rescuer of others;
- your intellect, its criticisms, and analyses;
- negative and positive emotions, such as worry, anger, desire, vindictiveness, hate, grief, melancholy, compassion, love, sadness, since they would interfere with the centering process;
- fear that you might be doing something that will make you guilty;
- ideas about how to meditate;
- self-blame, guilt, and blame of others. Turn over the idea of there being a culprit—be it yourself, others, or anything. Not even the ego is a culprit. (*See* Glossary: Culprit.);
- all ambition, and the image of striving upward toward some degree of perfection;
- the idea that freeing your true self is some kind of hard work and/or ascetic practice (*see* Glossary: Work.);
- seeing your body in a degraded way.

Having turned over the relevant things, you then envision your inner space as a circle around you, or a room which you have cleaned out. This is your intrinsic space. Now possess it as yours, as not belonging to anybody but yourself. At this point you are free of attachment. Having come to this point, remain quietly in your inner space to allow the Sage to enter, if and when the Sage will. Leave that entirely up to the Sage.

Continue until you feel it is time to stop meditating. If this time exceeds twenty minutes and nothing has happened, it is enough. Inner cleansing is the most important thing you have achieved. Continuing the practice each day without expectation that something will happen, will make it possible for the Sage to enter. If you stay, through some inner feeling that you have not done enough, the ego has already entered, with its ambition, to control the process. Then it is time to stop and make a renewed effort later. With repeated practice and cleansing, the ego will be successively diminished in power.

Activating the Helpers of the Invisible World

"It furthers one to employ helpers," is the advice given in Hexagram 3, of the Wilhelm version of the *I Ching*, which has the name, *Difficulty at the Beginning*. This is the only place in that version that mentions the name "Helpers." In other places the Helpers are only obliquely referred to as "people, who are specialists in their fields," as "friends that come," as a "big wagon for loading," a "vehicle for crossing the great water," or simply as "he."

What are the Helpers?
The Helpers are aspects of the Cosmic Consciousness, and as such, are *invisible. (See* p. 33.) The Helper we are most familiar with is the Sage, as the Cosmic Teacher. The Sage also helps to break spells, free other Helpers that have become disabled or imprisoned, and it calls in other Helpers for all sorts of needs.

All the Helpers in their totality maintain and restore the Cosmic Harmony through nourishing, healing, protecting, and furthering everything that exists. The correct way to distinguish the names of Helpers is by their *functions*. There are Cosmic Helpers, and the Helpers of Nature, and a large group of other kinds of Helpers that form a person's natural makeup: they are his Cosmic Virtues, talents, and abilities to learn things. Every person also has a Personal Helper assigned to him to help him fulfill his destiny, while living in a body. Fulfilling one's destiny means to develop and bring to expression one's unique talents. When a person brings himself into harmony with the Cosmos by freeing the Helpers of his body and psyche from the spells and poison arrows created by mistaken ideas and beliefs about his true nature, all his Helpers "grow up" and cooperate in a big symphony. Specific Helpers are mentioned in every hexagram.

There are also Environmental Helpers, Weather Helpers, and various other Helpers that form the "yellow lower garment" of Nature (*see* Hexagram 2, *Nature*, Line 5), which is a metaphor for the feeling consciousness of Nature.

The Helpers do not operate through power, but through the force *of attraction between complements.* They are various forms of chi energy, which also have intelligence. Some form its light, others its dark aspect. Since both aspects complement and attract each other, they constantly create more chi energy, which is to say that new Helpers are generated for new tasks, as the need arises. This explains how inventions are brought about that further the wellbeing of the whole. The Helpers operate in the realm of the atom, changing things in their fundamentals. Because of this, their activity is totally effortless.

The Helpers are activated when we call upon them for help. However, they can only respond if the requests are in harmony with the Cosmos, and do not come from the ego. Each Helper is an expert in its field. Once called into action, the Helpers must be given a free hand as to how they accomplish the task. Any interference by the ego causes the Helpers to retreat and abandon the task.

Because everything the Helpers do has the goal of furthering the Cosmic Whole, what they do takes varying lengths of time, since many things must be harmonized. Sometimes the result is immediately felt, as when a spell or projection is released; at other times the result is dependent on the release of another, as yet undetected block, or spell. Sometimes the goal cannot be completed, as when a guilt-spell is left undetected and not deprogrammed.

The person helped must ensure that the ego in him does not appropriate what the Helpers' achieve, as by claiming he was the one who brought about the benefit. When this happens, the benefit gradually wanes.

The Helpers are hampered in coming to our help when we give them names which diminish them, or when we elevate them, as by calling them angels. As a result, some Helpers become blocked or imprisoned, others retreat, and others, which are

slandered, become demons in the psyche. When they are immobilized or imprisoned, people feel helpless and abandoned.
The Cosmos may intervene in some situations, as through Fate,
to make the person aware that his Helpers are blocked. The *I
Ching*, and the *rtcm* can be used to help us free the Helpers to
fulfill their natural functions, and restore us to the correct attitudes that activate them.

How to Activate the Helpers:
   Step 1: recognize that help is available from the Cosmos for
every need.
   **Step 2: understand that the help can be given only to the per-
son who is modest and sincere.**
   **Step 3: say the inner No to any ego-element in yourself ac-
tive in the situation.** This activates the Helper of Transformation, and strengthens your true self.
   **Step 4: ask for help to understand what blocks the help you
need.** Keep in mind that it may be a projection, spell, or poison
arrow that you need to identify in all its components. (*See* p.
687, "Freeing Yourself from Mistaken Ideas and Beliefs," and p.
695, "Freeing Yourself from Projections, Spells and Poison Arrows.")
   Step 5: delete the mistaken idea or belief, or the projection,
spell, or poison arrow. This frees the Helpers that were blocked
or demonized, to resume their original functions.
   Step 6: thank the Helpers after they have completed their task.

Attitudes and Mistaken Ideas that Block the Helpers
   As the Helpers can function only in accordance with the Cosmic Principles of Harmony, all ego-based attitudes, and all mistaken ideas about their nature, block their ability to help. If,
upon discovering an incorrect attitude or mistaken idea, you
feel guilty for it, you first need to say the inner No to your feelings of guilt, because they come from the ego in you. Incorrect
attitudes and mistaken ideas are extinguished by saying the inner No to them. Among such attitudes and ideas are:
   • The idea that humans are born without help. This idea is the
      collective ego's attempt to rule out the existence of the in-
      visible Helpers altogether;
   • The idea that there is a hierarchical order among the Help-

ers. Such an idea goes against the Cosmic Principle of Equality of all aspects of the Cosmic Whole;

• The idea that the Helpers are "spirits." The Sage wants us to use the term spirits only for demons. They are products of the mind when it operates *without feeling*. The Helpers of the invisible world, however, are all part of the feeling consciousness of the Cosmos;

• An attitude of waiting for help, after having asked for help. Help comes while you are going on with your life;

• An attitude either of superiority, servility, reverence, or adoration toward the Helpers. Such attitudes also go against the principle of equality and dignity of all aspects of the Cosmic Whole;

• Making offerings or sacrifices of any kind. They imply that we need to make deals with the Cosmos or its Helpers, or that they can be bribed;

• A demanding attitude, which comes from the idea that humans are special, and have rights;

• A ritualistic approach, implying that one needs to create a special environment to invite the Helpers. It violates the simplicity and modesty with which the Helpers joyfully fulfill their functions. A ritualistic approach makes them retreat, and draws false Helpers created by one's imagination, or suggested by the collective ego;

• Thanking the Helpers in a ritualistic way for doing their normal job. Again, this goes against the normality with which Nature joyfully provides us with everything we need; (Recognizing this principle teaches us not to expect thanks for things we do to help others. It is only the ego that asks for special recognition of what one has done.)

• Supervising the Helpers after we have asked them to help. Any watching them with the inner eye, or putting demands on them as to what the outcome should be, or when it should occur, comes from the ego, and causes them to cease helping;

• Shame or embarrassment about asking the invisible Helpers for help. These are emotions that come from the ego, while it is in control of the psyche. Behind them are ridiculing phrases, such as, "you're a fool to speak to the air."

Freeing Yourself from Ego-Emotions

The presence of any ego-emotions blocks the ability of the Sage and the Helpers to help you. Different inner actions are required depending on what kind of ego-emotions are involved. The following groups need to be distinguished:

• **ego-anger, and ego-desires.** Both are true feelings that have been seized by the ego. True anger is generated through being treated unjustly. It is a Cosmic energy that comes to your defense. (See Hexagram 26, *The Taming Power of the Great.*) When it has been seized by the ego it is magnified into self-righteousness. Our natural desires are to be recognized for who we truly are, to have a love relationship that truly suits us, to have a home, job, food, etc. Ego-desire is to be someone special, or to be approved of, or exalted by others, or to want to possess something (the latter giving rise to possessiveness, envy, or greed). Our natural desires draw the Cosmic Helpers and the Helpers of Nature to fulfill them, whereas the ego appropriates these desires by making us believe we have to make deals, or become something special, or have to use power to procure what we need. *To free yourself from these ego-emotions,* imagine, in meditation, that you are putting them, and all the seed phrases and images connected with them, in the "Cosmic dumpster."

• **Feelings of guilt, fears, doubt, hatred, and blame** (both self-blame and blame of others) are to be put on the wagon of the Helpers. This act on your part, enables the Helpers to dispose of those feelings through transformation. (*See* p, 678, "Centering Yourself.")

• **Hurt pride, hopes and expectations** can be erased from your inner program by saying the inner No to them.

The Three-Minute-Rule

Three minutes refers to the amount of time that the ego's energy can be maintained when it is deprived of chi energy. Within the self this term refers to a firm and unwavering inner No that is said to the ego three separate times: in the interval of the three waves of assault it makes, the first being a large wave, the second half its size, and the third only a ripple. The same applies to an inner No said to another. Sometimes, when all the circumstances warrant it, an outer No is said as well. The ego, having a bully nature, and operating from a bravado, seeks to dominate by fooling the person that it is powerful. It does all it can to hide the fact that it cannot withstand a determined resistance. As in the case of all bullying activity, calling on the Helpers of Fate may be necessary to "bloody the bully's nose," which temporarily shocks it into quiescence.

Closing an Inner Connection

When an inner connection no longer exists between two people, the inner channel of that connection needs to be closed; otherwise, it can be used by the ego to project negative thoughts and emotions onto the partner, and to suck on his life force. The closing of the inner connection is done by several invisible Helpers. Before this can be done, however, you need to ask, with the help of the *rtcm*, whether there are still any ego-emotions on your part that need to be eradicated (*see* above), and/or whether any spells, projections, or poison arrows are still in place, be they on yourself or on your partner, or on the relationship between you. (Very common are guilt-spells, or spells that have to do with inner pacts. They are created by phrases such as, "I will always love you," "I will never leave you...")

After having done the above, you simply ask the Helpers, in meditation, to dissolve the inner connection.

Dissolving the inner connection does *not* mean that you must not, or cannot, love the other person's true self anymore. It only means that you are making the necessary inner adaptations to the changed circumstances.

Retreating from Conflict or Opposition

Retreating is a discipline by which you withdraw inwardly from an argumentative attitude, whether with yourself, another, the Cosmos, Nature (or any part of it), Fate, life, or the individual or collective ego.

The word "opposition" has no Cosmic validity. Everything in the nature of the Cosmos is based on the principle of *harmony*. Therefore, when you see anything or anyone as your opponent, enemy, or adversary, it is a sign that you have separated from the Cosmic Harmony and are engaging in an inner war, be it through thoughts, words, or action. Continuing on this path always leads to humiliation. (*See* Hexagram 6, *Conflict*, Line 1.)

Withdrawal from inner conflict first requires relinquishing the demand of the ego in yourself for a resolution to its arguments. To do this, say the inner No to seeing another person or *anything* as an opponent. Second, ask the Sage in your presence for help. If you have been engaged in a conflict with a *person*, also ask the Sage in the other person's presence to take over the situation. (It is also helpful to practice asking for this help before any situation of counseling, or group meeting.) Calling on the Sage in every person's presence is one of the meanings of the *I Ching* term "it furthers one to see the great man."

Retreating is also the correct reaction to another's ego display, or temper. The retreat begins with retreating from the ego in yourself by saying the inner No to its attempts to seize your anger. Next, disengage from eye-to-eye contact (for the ego in a person derives its energy from being recognized in another's eyes) until the person returns to humility.

The argument or conflict from which you need to retreat can be either inner or outer, as:

• when you watch an evil deed with your inner eye and make a judgment that the other person doing it *is* evil;

• when you argue inwardly with another's statements or ideas;

• when you fasten on a subject or person with worry, or anticipate possible negative consequences.

Retreat does not mean you smother feelings of dissent. It means to first say the inner No, when there are clear feelings of wrongdoing, and then let go of the subject by putting the matter in the "hands" of the Cosmic Helpers, or the Sage, after asking them to take care of it. This means you give over to the Helpers your anger, and your sense of being handled unfairly or insensitively. You also give over to them any desire that the other should be punished.

Such a retreat does not show on the outside, and makes no attempt to be noticed; sulking is not a retreat, but a display intended to make a point. It only shows that the ego in you is still attached to the conflict. A retreat has only one aim: to disengage entirely from the energies of the ego, both in the other and in yourself, and to consistently avoid further involvement. If the other persists, it is perfectly appropriate to temporarily pretend submissiveness to disperse any further involvement. Sometimes a firm outer No is needed to signalize one's determination not to participate in any further discussion.

Retreating has the effect of transforming the energies of your anger into Helpers that will show themselves in exactly the right way at the right time.

Retreat into inner neutrality and saying the inner No is the correct reaction to all ego-encroachment.

Freeing Yourself from Seed Phrases and Images and from Mistaken Ideas and Beliefs

Seed phrases is the name given in this book to the basic premises on which mistaken ideas and beliefs of a more complex nature are built.

Examples:

- "Humans are at the center of the universe and are superior to everything else." This idea is responsible for the myriad human misconceptions about their place in the Cosmos and is the root cause for humans' separation from the Cosmic Unity. (This unity is maintained through the fact that all aspects which make up the Cosmos are *equal.*) This idea is also the origin of all hierarchical ideas which have been put on the Cosmic Order, the Human order, and the order of the self.

- "A person has a higher and a lower self." This idea divides the original wholeness of the self up and places the two parts in a hierarchical order. With his wholeness divided, the person no longer functions as a harmonious whole, a fact that has a wide range of disastrous consequences for his health.

- "Humans are born deficient (with original sin/fault/guilt; man's animal nature is the source of evil)."

All Seed Phrases are accompanied by *images* that need to be deprogrammed simultaneously. In a short meditation (two or three minutes), ask the Sage and the Helpers to extinguish the seed phrase in question. If images come to mind, ask for them to be extinguished, as well. With the help of the *rtcm*, ask each succeeding day whether you need to repeat this procedure, until you receive a No.

689

Mistaken ideas are the by-products of the seed phrases mentioned above. They have been carried from generation to generation through conditioning, and are reinforced by all the institutions of the collective ego. The ideas that follow are among those stated as *absolute truths* that are not be questioned:
  • Fate is a punishment for having an animal nature;
  • We are born without help from any source outside the societal fabric (implying that there is no help, but what we can see);
  • What you see is all there is;
  • The mind is superior to the body (or mind over "matter"); thinking is superior to feeling/sensing;
  • Nature (including human nature) needs to be controlled;
  • It is man's task to bring order to the "ten-thousand things" of existence by categorizing and naming them;
  • A person becomes guilty when he questions any of the above ideas which have been accepted by his group since ancient times.

Mistaken beliefs are elaborations or extensions of the abovementioned or similar ideas. An example is the belief that goodness in a person has to be developed. It is an extension of the idea that humans are born deficient. This belief, in turn, becomes the basis for the whole program of conditioning established by the collective ego. When one or more mistaken beliefs are combined with the other mistaken ideas mentioned above, they form a *belief system.*

All mistaken ideas and beliefs are to be treated as *poison arrows,* because they poison the true nature of a person or thing by demonizing it. Because mistaken beliefs are derived from mistaken ideas, the main ideas behind them need to be identified and deprogrammed. This can mean that you need to remove several poison arrows. By using the *rtcm,* try to identify all the mistaken ideas that form the root of the belief in question.

In view of the role that the idea of guilt plays in making sure that the mistaken ideas are not questioned, you first need to free yourself of it by saying "No, No, No to the idea of guilt." (For a correct understanding of guilt *see* p. 50: Guilt, Blame, and Shame.)

690

Freeing Yourself from Self-Images

To free yourself from a self-image you need to recognize that there are basically four kinds of self-images behind which the ego in you hides:

- those connected with *virtues, duties, and responsibilities* (they are often associated with what is defined as the "superior man" in the Confucian overlay of the *I Ching* text);
- those connected with *professions;*
- those connected with *social position* (family name, wealth, etc.) that make the person feel special over others, and those connected with *titles* (academic, military, religious, administrative, governmental, or inherited titles in the form of social position, etc.);
- negative images connected with low social position due to economics, or being the son/daughter of a disgraced person
- mental fixes caused by *attaching oneself to an idea,* such as "I am allergic to…" or to an emotion, "that kind of thing makes me angry."

Step 1. Identify those self-images you possess, using the *rtcm*.

Step 2. Understand that all self-images are in conflict with your true nature. They are, in one way or another, compensation for having been made to feel, as a child, inferior, or born insufficient, or guilty. The self-images have been adopted in the childish hope of redeeming you in the eyes of those who taught you that you were not good enough. They can be the obvious images of the hero, the noble or the great-hearted, the high-minded, elevated, good, superior, or spiritual; or they can be the more subtle ones of the sunny child, the helpful child, the artistic child, the quick-learning child, the brave child, the go-getter, the industrious child, the kind child. The child that does not fit into these models may be fixed as the bad child, the rebel, the bete-noir, a no-good, an outsider, a difficult or obstinate child, or the slow-learner, the clumsy, sickly, serious, lazy, or silly child. Or he may have been given a nickname that fixes him in a particular image. The adult adopts other self-images that accompany their professions, titles and degrees, or their more lowly positions in life. In all cases, the self-images diminish the worth of the person's true nature.

691

Step 3. Ask, through the *rtcm*, whether the self-image needs to be treated as a spell. If not, you can simply reject it by saying the inner No to all its manifestations, and turning it over to the Sage. It is helpful to ask to be shown, in meditation, all its aspects. Remember that all ploys of the ego to resist being deprogrammed cannot withstand a firm determination to rid yourself of it.

You will also need to deprogram false emotions that are attached to self-images. These emotions will arise to gain your pity for the prospective loss of the self-image. Another of the ego's tricks is make you feel guilty for giving up what has been so carefully cultivated (by getting you to invest in it). This resistance occurs in all cases of co-dependency, whether it is a co-dependence on family, country, church, or employer. Co-dependency with your family can arouse the fear of being abandoned by them. Thinking of yourself as dependent on them (rather than on the Cosmos) disables the Cosmos from being able to help you. Often co-dependency is founded on spells that need to be eradicated. (*See* p. 697, Freeing Yourself from Spells.)

Freeing Yourself from a Fate

To understand the Cosmic meanings of Fate, *see* p. 40. Fate is applied through certain Helpers of Nature that have been demonized by spells and poison arrows created by the mistaken ideas and beliefs in question. The fact that Nature applies Fate has often been the cause of the mistaken idea that Fate *originates* in Nature, with Nature falsely getting the blame. The person who wishes to free himself from his fate, may also have to remove a poison arrow of blame he has put on Nature, including his own bodily nature. When a person rids himself of the mistaken ideas and beliefs that have created his fate, he frees the Helper of Transformation to extinguish his blame and his fate.

A fate can be ended by ridding yourself of its causes through following the steps below:

Step 1. Use the hexagrams and lines to help you identify the cause of your fate/suffering, which is either caused by a self-image, a mistaken idea or belief, or a projection, spell, or poison arrow.

Step 2. Having determined which is the cause, see the corresponding section for the method needed to free yourself.

Note: You need to be aware that the collective ego will seek to hold you in the parallel reality, under its control. On setting out to free yourself from your fate you may hear it whispering in your mind: "It can't be that easy," or "Fate must be fought," or, "you have to humbly accept your fate." You need to say the inner No to such phrases at the outset, otherwise they will undermine your undertaking.

Freeing Yourself from Fears

First, distinguish between small and big fears. An example of a **small fear** is the phrase, "I am afraid I'll never learn this..." This phrase is an imp, demon, or dragon in the psyche, which seeks to keep its place by imprisoning the Helper of Insight. The seed phrase behind this fear is the idea that you are born insufficient in and of yourself; this idea has imprisoned your native abilities. To free yourself from its influence, you need find out which element is involved (imp, demon, or dragon), and say "No, No, No" to it, and to the phrase. In getting free of the fear, you release the imprisoned Helper. Myriads of such small fears imprison our inner Helpers.

Big fears cause obstructions both in the brain and in the body. Often the solution to a problem lies right in front of you, but your fears make it invisible. Fears create a restricted frame of reference that close out anything that does not fit into that frame as "outside the accepted bounds." Thus they shut down your receptivity, and the ability of the Sage to teach you. In terms of the brain, fears close synapses that would otherwise open up your ability to perceive the reality of the situation, and to react appropriately. This is referred to in Line 5 of Hexagram 39, *Obstruction*, as "friends come."

Humans are not *born* with fears, except when spells have been put on the unborn child. All other fears are the result of the mistaken ideas and beliefs mentioned above, that have been adopted during childhood conditioning. The most basic fears are caused by the following seed phrases or images:

- the image of the invisible world of the Helpers as a threatening unknown/abyss/place of eternal darkness;
- the image of hell-fire as a Cosmic punishment;

693

- the idea of Judgment Day (damnation by an arbitrary God);
- mistaken ideas about the nature and purpose of Fate;
- images of death: of being annihilated, terminated, or devoured (such images also cause a fear of life, because life is constantly overshadowed by the threat of death);
- the image of being abandoned and isolated, based on the phrase, "there is no help except what you receive from other people";
- the phrase, "life is suffering";
- the idea of guilt.

Other fears may arise from traumatic experiences during childhood or adolescence. The experience is stored in "shorthand form" in the body as a memory chip. This memory chip is a compressed form of the words, images, feelings, smells and tastes that accompanied the experience. In this compressed form, the fear is stored as a particular protein in the amygdala (a gland in the brain), and replicated in certain body cells (particular organs, muscles, nerves, blood cells, bones, etc.). Thus, when certain elements within this complex are encountered later on— as for example in hearing certain words, or coming across a particular smell—an unwanted reaction is triggered. The reaction may be an unreasoning fear, a compulsion to do something, or one or more physical symptoms, such as irritation in the stomach, heart palpitations, nervous disorders, skin outbreaks, allergies, tremors, headache, involuntary muscular reactions, muscle pain or spasms. The components of the traumatic experience always need to be viewed as having formed a *spell* or a *poison arrow*, and treated accordingly. To complete the treatment, ask the Sage to free you from the sensory perceptions that accompanied the experience, and from the guilt you have put on yourself in the context of that experience. (*See* p. 697, "Freeing Yourself from Projections, Spells, and Poison Arrows.")

Freeing Yourself from Some Health Problems

A health problem (mental or physical) is always an indication that a person has become separated from his unity with the Cosmos. Freeing yourself from health problems is a matter of identifying the mistaken ideas and beliefs, and/or the presence of projections, spells, and poison arrows, that have caused your separation. It is our animal nature that helps us live our lives in harmony with the Cosmos. It is composed of innumerable natural Helpers, which draw the Cosmic Helpers needed in any given situation. Any ideas that slander our animal nature put spells on our natural body Helpers and become the source of our susceptibility to illness.

Among the chief mistaken ideas that make a person *susceptible* to illness are: "I am susceptible to…" or "he/she is susceptible (or weak, always getting sick, genetically impaired, etc.)…." Other ideas, which damage our natural wholeness, need to be deprogrammed as spells. They are:

• our animal nature (meaning our bodily nature) is the source of evil;
• we are guilty for having an animal nature;
• we have a higher and a lower nature;
• there is no help from the invisible world to cope with life.

Once the spells that have made you susceptible to illness in general have been removed, you need to discover the specific cause(s) of your illness or ailment. They are usually to be found in projections, spells, and/or poison arrows (either put on you by yourself or by someone else), or in a fate you have created. (*See* p. 697, Freeing Yourself From Projections, Spells, and Poison Arrows.)

After identifying and removing the *inner* causes, it may be necessary to complement the treatment by applying natural remedies. You can ask the Sage, through the *rtcm*, which remedy would help best and how long it needs to be applied.

Deprogramming an illness can involve dealing with several layers of causes. The Sage guides you in the best sequence for removing these layers. One becomes aware that other layers exist when an improvement does not result in a complete healing. A problem can also return for the following reasons:

• when you dismiss or diminish the help you have received from the Helpers;
• when you allow feelings of guilt for having been healed;
• when you allow back-of-the-mind doubts (coming from the ego) which suggest that you have not been completely freed of your problem;
• when you are on the lookout for the problem "to come back";
• when you arrogantly assume that, after having been healed, you can resume a luxurious life style, etc.

In all these cases, saying the inner No to the incorrect thoughts (and retreating from any incorrect action based on such thoughts) will correct the problem.

Many, but not all problems can be resolved by following the above instructions. It is possible, for example, that a person has an unconscious resistance to getting well. This can be due to certain fears, or feelings of guilt:

- the belief that he does not deserve to be healed because he has been "a sinner";
- the fear that he will lose the love of the person who has been taking care of him (a co-dependence issue);
- the fear to lose the control his illness has given him over others around him;
- the fear to lose certain benefits that are connected with being ill or disabled.

Pain is an expression of alarm created within the consciousness of the body cells involved. Its purpose is to make the person aware that he has been injured and that he needs to identify and free himself from the cause of that injury. The cause may be a projection, spell, or poison arrow (or any combination of them), either put on himself or by others, or it may come from feelings of guilt the person is harboring. To regard pain as something that needs to be fought only makes things worse, because the cause of the injury remains untouched, and the body is viewed as an enemy. If you have already demonized the pain by viewing your body as your enemy, you need to first remove the poison arrow created by this view.

The correct reaction to pain is to talk to your body and reassure it that you are going to ask the Cosmos for help. Then reassure your body cells in a loving way, embracing and comforting them, as you would embrace and comfort an injured child.

Next, identify any projections, spells, and poison arrows, of which the pain wants to make you aware. (*See* p. 697, "Freeing Yourself from Projections, Spells, and Poison Arrows.") Then ask the Sage to draw all the Helpers needed.

Freeing Yourself from Guilt and Self-Blame, or Blame put on Others

The presence of guilt, and the self-blame or blame of others that it creates, always betrays the presence of the ego. The concept of guilt has no Cosmic basis. Its sole purpose is to keep you caught in the parallel reality created by the collective ego. (*See* p. 50, Guilt, Blame, and Shame.) Freeing oneself of guilt is done by saying: "No, No, No" to the idea of guilt, or "No, No, No to blaming myself." Then "remorse disappears."

Cosmic blame occurs when a person has betrayed his true nature. It is extinguished the moment you rid yourself of its cause (a self-image, a mistaken idea or belief, or a projection, spell, or poison arrow).

Blame put on another person, as by pointing to him as a "culprit," always takes on the form of a spell and poison arrow, and causes the other (consciously or unconsciously) to project the blame back in the same form. Both spells and poison arrows need to be removed in the order in which they have been put on.

For example, a blame-spell and poison arrow are removed from one of the parties involved by saying, "No, No, No to myself for having put a blame spell and poison arrow on (name of the receiver), and No, No, No to (name of the receiver) for having accepted that blame spell and poison arrow."

Freeing Yourself from Projections, Spells, and Poison Arrows

Projections, spells, and poison arrows consist of phrases and images that are not in harmony with the Cosmos. All projections, spells, and poison arrows bring harm not only to the person who receives them, but also to the sender. They differ in specific ways, as described below:

Projections consist of imps or demons that are projected into a person's psyche through negative thoughts or spoken words. The person can also put them on himself.

They can cause headaches, or compel a person to say something he does not believe, simply because someone has imagined him to have those kinds of thoughts. Mutual projections occur frequently in relationships. Projections coming from a third party can cause sudden arguments in relationships. To find such hidden sources of disharmony, it is helpful to ask, through the *rtcm*, whether any projections are coming from without.

Projections differ from spells in that they are usually of a temporary nature. Their effect can last only up to about a week.

Projections can be:

- Thoughts of vengeance or "justice." Example: "He will pay for having done this to me."
- Thoughts based on arbitrary wishes. Example: "I wish she was here now. She would know what to do."
- Certain phrases that contain the word "must": "You must obey your parents."
- Common sayings can act as projections. Example: "You never know..." Such a phrase projects a doubt upon the situation that opens the door to unwanted elements, such as making a person take precautions to defend or protect himself rather than inquiring about the inner truth of the situation.
- Certain phrases that have shoulds in them. The projection gets renewed every time a person thinks that phrase. Example: "I should not drink coffee." (Implying that coffee is bad for my health.) This is a projection the person puts on himself *and* on the coffee, with the effect that he cannot enjoy coffee any more. The effects of his projection are (a) that it creates guilt in himself whenever he drinks it, and (b) that it demonizes the consciousness of the coffee. These negative effects can be undone, if he removes his projection, as indicated below.
- Projections by manufacturers put on foods and drinks, and on the consumers. They are caused by egotistical desires to get consumers addicted to the product, or to give the product the appearance of being "special," "top rank," etc. Such projections add a demonic element to the product that can cause a headache or digestive problems. These problems disappear after removing the projection. One needs to identify the intention that was projected onto the food or drink.
- Projections put on foods or drinks and their consumers through genetically altered ingredients. Such projections can cause a headache or digestive problems, all of which disappear after deprogramming the projection. As in the previous paragraph, one needs to identify the intention that was projected onto the product, and the fear behind it, such as

698

"not getting enough of the market share."

Spells can consist of a single word that has no Cosmic basis, or of one or more phrases. Self-images can also be spells. A spell is always accompanied by ego-emotions. Spells have the effect of fixing a person, or parts of his personality, through words or phrases. The consequences can be compulsive or other neurotic patterns of behavior that prevent a person from developing his uniqueness. Spells can also create a fate for that person in the form of illness, that can even lead to his death.

Two spells, which are the basis of other spells are created by the ideas:

- that "in and of ourselves we are born inadequate to deal with life," and therefore must look to the social fabric around us for our needs, because "that is all there is." (This idea represses our feeling connection with the *Cosmic Consciousness* into a sphere of consciousness called the "subconscious.")
- that "our animal nature is the source of evil in the world," and that because we have it, we are born with an inextinguishable "sin" or "guilt."

Spells can fall into the following categories:
- Spells consisting of a *single word* that misidentifies a thing or creates a negative consciousness that is contrary to the Cosmic Harmony. Such a word is "guilt." (*See* p. 50: Guilt, Blame, and Shame.) **The Guilt-spells it creates are the most destructive spells,** because they block the Helper of Transformation in a person. They also act as door-openers to other spells and projections. Another is the word "culprit." (Also *see* Glossary: "Culprit.")
- Spells consisting of one or more *seed phrases* that assert a thing *is* this or that way. Example: "Life *is* suffering." This phrase puts a spell on the person's life who has accepted that idea;
- Spells consisting of a *self-image.* Example: The self-images of the "wife," or "the good person," "the superior man," etc., locks the person into the behavior demanded by that image. Another example: "He/she *is* a bad/irresponsible/lazy/

silly/great-hearted/kind... person." Such statements put a fix on a person's nature causing him to behave in the way defined; it would be correct to say, "he *acted* irresponsibly... or in a kind way";

- Spells created by certain phrases that contain the words *always* or *never*. Examples: "I never do the right thing," "you will never change," "I will always love you," or phrases that generalize a unique experience: "It will always be that way";

- Spells created by *associating one thing as intrinsically connected with another*, as in "hearing loss = eating sugars" or "arthritis = eating acidic foods." The spell, in this case, is put on the sugar, or the acidic food. Thereafter, the foods in question have the expected effects until the person removes the spell;

- Spells created by *deeply ingrained beliefs that give rise to hopes and fears*. Once these beliefs have become part of a person's inner program, they continuously get projected back into reality. Hopes and fears are mentioned together because every phrase that expresses a hope is based on a fear. Example: "I hope times will get better." The person needs to seek out the phrase that describes his fear. It may be the phrase, "there is nothing one can do, but hope for the best." This phrase denies the existence of the Helpers of the invisible world, giving the person a feeling of helplessness. If not deprogrammed, the fear (and not the hope) will project itself into reality;

- Spells created by certain *mistaken ideas*, such as the idea that "the Cosmos is unknowable." Such a phrase puts a spell on the person's inner truth and on his Learning Helpers, and opens the door to putting all kinds of threatening fantasy projections on the Cosmos.

- Spells created by certain *common sayings*. Example: "You can never get enough." Such a phrase can cause an eating disorder.

- Spells created by the *"three w's": wishing, wondering, and worrying*. Example: "I wish my son would do better at school," "I wonder why he is not doing better...," "He may never be successful in life." Another example: The wish to become "like" (or unlike) someone else whom one admires, or rejects. Example: "I want to become like aunt Grace," or

"I don't want to become like my father." Such wishes take away a person's uniqueness, in that they connect her/him by *likeness* with the other person. A strong dislike of another person can make one rush to put oneself in an opposite box (with the result of going away from oneself). The same happens when one likes someone a lot and therefore identifies with him.

Poison Arrows are thoughts projected into the psyche and body of oneself or another, that create a poisonous reaction in his body. They are felt immediately in the body, either as a sharp pain, as a crick in the back, or a sting in the heart. Some poison arrows date from years back, even from the time in utero. When not removed, they always cause physical illness.

The following are some of the most common causes of poison arrows:

- *Guilt*: "I am born a sinner," "I am guilty for having an animal nature." "I am guilty for... (anything)"; (*See* also p. 50, Guilt, Blame, and Shame.)
- *Comparisons of all kinds.* They injure a person's unique abilities and prevent him from expressing them. They also create a fate by projecting a foreign image on him that, consciously or unconsciously, he tries to live up to. Example: "He has the will of a Napoleon";
- *Envy,* which is a certain form of comparing oneself with another. Example: "I envy her for having had children." This projects poison arrows, both on oneself and on the other, and creates a fate for the person sending the poison arrow; here, the fate can prevent the woman, who is envious, from actually having a child. The envy is an expression of her self-doubt that she is capable of having a child;
- *The strong wish to become "like" someone else* whom one admires, or the wish *not* to become like someone else for various reasons; (This can also create a spell; to determine which, use the *rtcm.*)
- *Commonly held presumptions about what is "typical."* Example: "Men are ... that way";
- *Inherited diseases,* when they contain a comparison, are caused by poison arrows. Example: "You have inherited your father's heart problem," or "she has inherited her mother's

bad genes." Such a poison arrow actually alters a person's chromosomes and disables his self-healing abilities;

• *Misnaming of parts of the body and their functions* as in viewing the body as a system of mechanical functions and calling the heart a "pump." Such a mechanical view blocks the Helper of the Heart from fulfilling its function, which is to draw chi energy, or life force, from the Cosmos. Another poison arrow is created by seeing the heart is the *source* of the love given to another. This poison arrow allows the ego to dominate the feelings that come through the heart, causing the heart to harden;

• *Speaking of an illness, or disability as if it were part of one's nature:* "my" arthritis, or "my" hearing loss. The person needs to keep in mind that its *cause* is a *foreign* element in his body and psyche;

• Poison arrows are also produced by *practices of black magic,* which intentionally seek to harm another or take revenge. However, they are not limited to acts of black magic, but include various shamanic practices that require dancing and beating drums, and any other techniques used to arouse emotions to a frenzy and pitch that cause *hypnotic effects.* They can also include prayers that pray for vengeance upon others, or for justice by a godhead that is perceived as partial;

• Poison arrows created by *traumatic experiences;* (For a detailed discussion *see* above: "Fears.")

• A poison arrow created by viewing one's body as an enemy when it has reacted with pain, or with an ailment or illness; (See p. 694, "Some Health Problems.")

• When certain landscape features are called "evil," or "negative," or seen as imbued with "dragon energies," only because they are not favorable for human settlement, it puts a poison arrow on them.

Deprogramming Procedure

While projections, spells, and poison arrows differ from each other, they are deprogrammed by the same method. Nevertheless, it is important to find out, with the help of the *rtcm,* which one, or which combination of the three, is active in the given situation, since each problem or illness may be caused by a different combination of them. Finding the name, i.e. "projection," "spell," or "poison arrow," that corresponds with their characteristics attracts the particular Helper or Helpers needed to deal with the situation.

The steps to freeing yourself from a projection, spell, or poison arrow are as follows:

Step 1. Identify the originator (yourself or another person who put it on you). It may help to ask at what age it was put on you (it could have occurred *in utero*, at birth, between 1-10 years, 10-20 years, 20-30 years, etc.).

Step 2. Identify the words, phrases, and/or images that have formed the projections (P), spells (S), or poison arrows (PA), and write them down. If necessary, ask the Sage, in meditation, to reveal the situation or what you need to know; this need take only up to five minutes.

Step 3: In a short meditation, during which you may open your eyes, if needed, follow the steps below in regard to the phrases or images you have written down:

(**A**) Say: "No, No, No to .... [name of the originator] for having caused the trauma, or put that P, S, or PA on me."

(**B**) Say: "No, No, No to myself for having accepted that P, S, or PA."

(**C**) Say: "No, No, No to ... (here say the phrase, in its original wording, of which the P, S, or PA consists, as for example: "Life is suffering." When more phrases are involved, repeat the "No, No, No to every phrase), picturing that it gets wiped out in your psyche.

(**D**) Clarify, with the *rtcm*, whether you need to ask the Sage or the Helpers, or both, to free you from that P, S, or PA. Then ask them to do so.

(**E**) With the help of the *rtcm*, ask for the next three (sometimes more) days, whether you need to repeat the procedure (not more than once per day). In rare cases, it can take up to six days to completely free yourself from a P, S, or PA.

(**F**) When the work has been done, thank the Helpers for their help.

The same procedure applies to a P, S, or PA you have put on someone else.

Appendix 2

Glossary of Cosmic Terms and Words Created by the Collective Ego

Animal Nature: In the Cosmic sense, humans are part of the animal kingdom. It is our animal nature that gives us our Cosmic Dignity and connects us, through our inner senses and feelings, with the Cosmos. The human desire to be "special," because we have language, however, has led to the idea that our "self" is divided into a "higher" and a "lower" nature, the latter being our animal nature. The term animal nature is often used as a synonym for "bodily nature," but has in particular been connected with our sexuality. The slanders that have been put on our sexuality and on our animal nature as a whole, by calling it "lower," or viewing it as the "source of evil," are the subject of many hexagrams because they are the first cause for humans' separation from the Cosmic Unity. The *I Ching* shows that every person can reunite with the Cosmos by removing the slanders put on his animal nature. (In particular, *see* Hexagram 38, *Separating/Opposition.*)

Burnout: Burnout refers to the exhaustion of a deluded enthusiasm. The person follows that enthusiasm with ever-increasing frustration until it simply can be followed no more. What burns out is the person's will to continue on that path. Burnout is a corrective function built into the will that finally saves a person from the exhaustion of his chi energy.

Chance: Chance, in the sense of "random chance," has no place in the Cosmic Order. It is a term that describes what happens when a person has lost his Cosmic Protection. It thus also describes the parallel reality created by the collective ego. Chance as a vagary implies what the *I Ching* calls Fate. Fate itself, however, is not delimited as a vagary that strikes randomly. It is an automatic reaction of the Cosmos to a continuous violation of the Cosmic Harmonics. It is always specific to what is needed

705

to open a person up to the possibility of correcting the mistaken ideas and beliefs that have created his fate. (*See* p. 715, "Fate and Destiny.") Chance, in the sense of "good luck," also belongs in the parallel reality. The terms "good fortune" and "success" in the *I Ching* do not refer to good luck, but to Cosmic gifts and blessings, and to the prospective success of an undertaking when the Helpers have been included.

Chaos: There is no such thing in the Cosmos, because the Cosmos by its very definition *is* Order. Chaos is created by the collective ego through the introduction of words and abstract concepts that have no Cosmic basis. Chaos characterizes the demonic sphere of consciousness. The idea of a "primordial chaos" from which order was created by man or by a godhead in man's image is part of the collective ego's myth that serves to justify the control of Nature by humans.

Character: This word has no Cosmic basis. It is used by the collective ego to appropriate the Cosmic Virtues every person is born with. The collective ego denies our Cosmic Virtues (kindness, modesty, loyalty to our inner truth) by saying that we are born deficient. It then says that we have to "develop character," meaning the development of abstract standards of kindness, modesty, loyalty, etc. Character is the sum total of a person's self-images.

Chi Energy: There are different kinds of chi energy, which the Sage has taught us to distinguish as follows:
   • the life force that animates all of existence;
   • the will, which is the sum total of a person's or animal's psychic energy;
   • the electric energy that enables things outside the body to move.
Together, these different kinds of chi energy form the Cosmic Consciousness. In the terminology of the *I Ching* they are made up of the myriad of Helpers of the invisible world. All kinds of chi energy have a light aspect and a dark aspect which complement each other. Everything that exists in the Cosmos comes

from the attraction between these complements. The word Helpers reflects the fact that chi is not a mechanical energy, and that the Cosmos does not work as a system of mechanics, but operates as a system of interactive helping energies. The Cosmos is primarily a *feeling* consciousness, with most of its Helpers operating through feelings.

Everything in the Cosmos is imbued with **life force**, with the exception of crystallized forms (although they also have a specific kind of consciousness). The transformation of life force into visible life forms occurs in the sphere of the atom. With regard to humans, every person is born with a reservoir of life force in every body cell. This life force is part of his "inner truth," which is also *his feeling memory* (in the form of imprints, or DNA) of what Cosmic Harmony feels like. Under normal circumstances, the life force is constantly renewed, in the atomic realm, through the person's contact with his feelings and the totality of his senses. The life force brings Cosmic nourishment to the person's whole being. It is felt as a caring and loving energy that makes him feel one with the Cosmos. Another function of the life force is to heal illness and injuries. Its ability to do so, however, is often impeded by the slanders that have been put on humans' animal nature. Because the Cosmos does not entertain any relationship with the ego in a person, the only way for the ego to exist is to steal that person's life force. Various hexagrams describe how this is done in the same way a parasite lives off its host. (*See* in particular the following hexagrams, in this order: 23, *Splitting Apart*; 36, *Darkening of the Light*; 26, *The Taming Power of the Great*; 9, *The Taming Power of the Small*, 33, *Retreating/Hiding*; 34, *Using Power*; 1, *The Cosmic Consciousness*, and 2, *Nature*.) If not stopped in its activities, the ego will destroy its host (the person's true nature). The main cause that keeps a person locked in the grip of the ego is guilt. Guilt is an invention of the collective ego for the one purpose only: to gain access to Cosmic energy via a person's feelings of guilt.

The will, which is the sum of a person's or animal's psychic energy, is located in the nerves in the back of the neck. Under healthy conditions, the will is aligned with all his inner senses. When the senses perceive a situation as harmonious, it means that the situation is under the protection of the Cosmic Harmonics and receives the coordinated support of the Cosmic Helpers. This is felt as a strong *pull* to follow what feels harmonious. When a situation feels discordant, the will is directed (by the inner senses) toward saying the inner No to what is discordant. The inner No transforms the split created by what is discordant, in the realm of the atom, thus returning the situation to harmony. This situation is described in Hexagram 23, *Splitting Apart*, Line 6, where the chi energy (as will), after having been split apart by mistaken ideas, has been transformed and is therefore able to carry the true self forward on the path of his destiny. When, however, the will has been harnessed by the ego (*see* Hexagram 28, *The Preponderance of the Great*), it is employed to suppress the person's true nature, and deprive him of his life force.

Chi energy, as the **electric energy that enables things outside the body to move,** is the product of the interaction between the Cosmic Helpers and the Helpers of Nature. It can be pictured as an energy circuit that is constantly self-renewing.

Collective Ego: The collective ego is the parent of the individual ego. The collective ego is the name given to the totality of mistaken ideas and beliefs about the nature of the Cosmos, about human nature, and about the human place in the whole. The visible side of the collective ego is found in the social structures and institutions that have been erected to support the human-centered view of the universe. Since it is a false construct that has no Cosmic Reality, the collective ego depends totally on the life energy it steals from people's true natures. To do so, it creates the individual ego, a false mental program that is introjected, phrase by phrase and image by image, into the psyche of the young child, where it begins to live a life of its own. (Also *see* above: Chi Energy.) (For a more detailed description *see* p. 42, The Collective Ego.)

Commonsense: is a consensus of all the senses. The commonsense comprises the five commonly known senses and the metaphorical senses. In humans, the commonsense is the "inner judge," which discerns what is in harmony with the person's inner truth (and therefore also in harmony with the Cosmos) and what is not. Its judgment is based on the inner senses, and is in the form of a *feeling*. Another function of the commonsense is that of being the Helper of Transformation (this applies only to humans). This function is referred to in Hexagrams 15, *Modesty*, 16, *Enthusiasm*, 17, *Following*, and 21, *Biting Through*. As part of our animal nature, the commonsense gets blocked when a person's animal nature has been slandered as "lowly," or as "the source of evil." (Also *see* below: Senses.)

Cosmos: Cosmos is the appropriate word to describe the Cosmic Whole. The Cosmic Whole consists of the invisible Cosmic Consciousness and the visible world of Nature. The Cosmic Whole is a system of harmonics, which is described in all its aspects in Hexagrams 3-64 of this volume. All consciousness, which exists both in the forms of feelings and thought, finds expression in the Cosmic Whole, both that which is harmonious and that which is discordant. However, the core consciousness of the Cosmos is only harmonious. Discordant consciousness, which is generated only through a false use of language, has no place in the core consciousness. It creates its own sphere, a place of separation and isolation from the Cosmic Whole, which we have called "the demonic sphere of consciousness." The latter competes with the Cosmos and seeks to replace it with a human-centered, purely mental order which is hierarchically structured, with humans occupying the top position. (See Hexagram 1, *The Cosmic Consciousness*.) From its place of isolation from the Cosmic Whole, the negative energy of the collective ego continues to operate in a destructive way on humans and on Nature. The visible side of the demonic sphere of consciousness is the "parallel reality" of the collective ego. Living in the parallel reality deprives people of Cosmic Protection and of the help it gives to every aspect that is in harmony with it. Without Cosmic Protection, people create fates, often referred to in the *I Ching* as "misfortune." One of the purposes of Fate is to help a person reunify with the Cosmic Whole. (*See* p. 715, "Fate and Destiny.")

The Cosmos is not identical with what humans have called "the universe." The idea of a universe has been created by the human-centered view. As such, it constitutes the demonic sphere of consciousness and the parallel reality of the collective ego.

Creator: is a human term that comes from a reductionist imagination that sees the Cosmos as having a beginning and an end—that is to say, the Cosmos as seen in the myopic framework of linear time. Being a creation, a creator is also imagined, and not surprisingly, it is one with human features. While the term reflects the myth-making activity of the collective ego, it does not apply to the *originating activity* of the Cosmic Consciousness. Everything that exists on the visible plane is an expression of an individual aspect of the Cosmic Consciousness *in form.* Thus, Nature is not a creation of the Cosmic Consciousness but *its expression in form.* Humans originate in the Cosmic Whole and return to it. Creating, in its true sense, refers to a person's bringing to expression the unique abilities and talents he has been given by the Cosmos. When these abilities and talents are appropriated by the ego, they falsely "create" the demonic sphere of consciousness and the parallel reality that competes with the Cosmos.

Culprit: There is no such thing as a culprit in the Cosmic Order. The word is a creation of the collective ego, and a "seed of evil," because it implies thought in terms of *opposites.* It also implies the existence of *guilt,* another ego-invention. (*See* p. 50, Guilt, Blame, and Shame.) The word also suggests that the evildoer or problem identified lies in the *nature* of the person or thing, which is untrue. All evil originates in false mental programs that have been introjected into the human psyche by the collective ego. These programs suppress a person's true nature and demonize his Helpers. However, the Sage that exists in the presence of every person, can be called upon to bring his wrong actions to a halt. When a person sees another as a culprit, a spell and poison arrow are put on the Sage of the one called a culprit. This perpetuates the combat of the opposite forces created by the use of that word.

The word "culprit" needs to be deprogrammed as a spell and a poison arrow. Although the collective ego is the source of blame, even *it* is not to be regarded as a culprit, because doing so would only energize it. (*See* p. 687, Retreating from Opposition and Conflict.)

Death: When applied to processes in Nature, death marks the transformation of a person, animal, or plant from visible form into an invisible form of existence within the Cosmic Whole. Life is an ongoing process from non-form into form, and from form into non-form. Everything in Nature is Cosmic Consciousness compressed into a unique form, which allows it to have experiences, and to set free its multiform consciousness. These various kinds of consciousness, we are informed by the Sage, are the invisible aspects of every living thing. Applied to a human being at the end of his visible form, the person's aggregate consciousness, if it has fulfilled its uniqueness, is transformed back into the invisible realm, where it continues to live in its unique identity and take on new tasks. Those individuals who have not realized their uniqueness are reabsorbed, again through transformation, into the Cosmic Consciousness, in their original undeveloped state of innocence. Thus, there is no "loss" involved when life in a body ends, and there is no reason to fear the transformation back into non-form. Those who have not developed their uniqueness or fulfilled their destinies are given another opportunity to do so, by being returned once more to human form. The Sage has made it clear that these persons do not labor under any remnants of the former life in a body. Each person comes into his human form free and clear, innocent, and able to make an entirely new start.

It may happen that before the transformation has become completed, the deceased may contact a relative to inform him of something, as for example, that he needs to let go of any feelings of guilt toward the deceased. Guilt would keep him attached to the deceased, preventing both from making progress. When he says the inner No to his guilt, the transformation can be completed.

When a person's true self is kept imprisoned by the ego, it has the fear that it will die without having fulfilled its destiny, and that it will have bypassed all its opportunities for growth. This fear is expressed in dreams of being enrolled in a school and coming up to examination time without ever having attended the classes. Another very real fear of death, connected with the presence of the ego in a person's psyche, is the true self's fear that it will fall into total oblivion, or that it will be executed by the ego. This fear is experienced in dreams of being ritually sacrificed, of being executed by a death squadron, or of going to the doctor to receive a lethal injection, etc.

Finally, there is the fear of death held by the ego. Indeed, the ego is the only thing that dies when a person's life *in the body* ends. Because it is not part of the Cosmic Whole, but a foreign element in the psyche, the ego sees death as loss and an end, and as a final punishment. All ideas of a last day of judgment, or of eternal punishment, come from the ego; they have no basis in the Cosmic Reality. Because the ego does not want to die, it has created the idea of there being an immortal soul, which the person must develop at the expense of the body. The concept of soul is the ego's attempt to gain eternal life. Because the person's true nature has eternal life, there is no need to *strive* for "immortality."

When the time has come for a person to die, because the purpose of his life has been completed, a team of Helpers can be called upon to help him make that step in Harmony with Nature: the Helper of Death, the Helper to Free him from the Fear of Death, the Helper to Make Death Swift and Easy (to overcome the effects of the platitude that death is difficult and hard), the Helper of Acceptance of Death, and the Helper of Seeing his Inner Truth. How long it will take the Helpers to complete their task depends on the obstinacy with which the ego in the person clings to the body. The person who wants to help another in this way *always* needs to ask the Sage whether it is correct for him to do so. If he simply goes ahead without asking, the ego in him has taken charge of the action, which creates blame for him. It would not harm the other person, because the Helpers do not associate with the ego.

Demonic Sphere of Consciousness: The demonic sphere of consciousness is composed of imps, demons, and dragons created by the false use of language, and is so named because it fights the Cosmic Consciousness. The use of false words in describing the Cosmic Reality leads to mistaken ideas and beliefs: about the nature of the Cosmos and its ways, about life, about Nature, about human nature, and about the place of humans in the Cosmos. Because human thinking and imaging have the ability to either express the person's inner truth (which is in harmony with Cosmic Truth), or to produce fantasies and myths (which happens when the person isolates himself from his feelings of inner truth), humans have the ability to create a false consciousness. The false thoughts and emotions coming from this false consciousness project themselves into reality in the form of projections, spells, and poison arrows. The product of the demonic sphere of consciousness is the parallel reality created by the collective ego, which can be described as the *domain of suffering*. As a sphere of consciousness, it exists outside the individual, but seeks to gain access to the individual's psyche through the conditioning process that the collective ego initiates during childhood. It is the source of all individual egos, which, in turn, are needed to keep it alive.

The demonic sphere of consciousness is totally dependent on the life energy it gets from people's true natures, via the egos in them. To steal a person's life energy, the collective ego makes the individual believe that he lacks the ability to cope with life, and that the institutions of the collective ego are the source of all his needs. It also makes him believe that he needs to cultivate a kind heart toward others who are in need. Based on the lie of personal lack, the collective ego thus succeeds in stealing the person's life energy, to keep its false system alive. The economic cycle of the collective ego, as one might call it, relies on three kinds of demonic elements that form a complete system: they have been mentioned above as imps, demons, and dragons.

The imps have the function of separating the person from his feelings of inner truth, to make him rely on thinking and fantasizing. They thus remove the person from the Cosmic Reality. The demons fulfill the function of appropriating the person's

713

true feelings and putting them in the service of the ego, where they become ego-emotions. This is true for natural anger and desires, which become feelings of self-righteousness, and of having rights. By putting a person's true feelings in the service of the ego, the Cosmic energy that is contained in them is turned into negative energy that the ego uses to control the personality. The controlling function is exercised by dragons. The main dragon in a person's psyche is the *dragon of guilt*. Guilt is an invention of the collective ego to keep the individual permanently under its control. This is why guilt is said to be an inextinguishable stain. (Also *see* p. 50, Guilt, Blame, and Shame.) The economic cycle of the collective ego is broken, and the demonic sphere of consciousness is weakened, by every individual who frees himself first from the idea of guilt, and then from all the spells that have imprisoned his true self, and thus have separated him from his unity with the Cosmic Whole.

Drives: Contrary to commonly held opinion, drives are not part of a person's true nature. They need to be seen as a result of the slanders that have been put upon humans' animal nature. These slanders that hold a person's animal nature to be "lowly," or "the source of evil," are spells and poison arrows that demonize his animal nature. Once demonized, it acts out in demonic ways. Under healthy conditions, the bodily expression of love is an act in which all the senses participate. However, when *guilt* is put upon the sexual expression of love, all the senses become unable to participate; they are replaced by a false sense, which is the sense of titillation. While the titillation is heightened by feelings of guilt, it is quickly satisfied, leaving the sexual expression of love empty of feelings, except a slight feeling of disappointment. This disappointment accompanies an inner realization that the experience has lacked the chi energy that the body needs; it is also accompanied by a loss of self-esteem.

Duty: a word that has no Cosmic basis. The collective ego has created the idea that the individual has duties: first toward his parents, then to his community, nation, and to God. Duties have two purposes: (1) to make sure that he is loyal to them instead of being loyal to his inner truth, and (2) to create guilt. Duty and guilt are inseparable; together, they "hold" the individual to the institutions of the collective ego. The Cosmos, as Hexagram 8, *Holding Together*, shows, holds all its aspect together through the force of attraction, another name for which is *love*. A person is by nature attracted to what is cosmically correct.

Ego: The individual ego is that composite of self-images and their supporting rationales that a person develops in the course of his childhood conditioning. The child is told that he needs to develop an ego (self-image), which is then referred to as his "self" or his "character," in order to get along in the world. The ego is thus based on inferiority instilled in the child by asserting that he is "insufficient in and of himself to cope with life," and that there is no help for him other than what he can get from the institutions of the collective ego. In order to be accepted by these institutions, he is told that he needs to "develop his character," i.e., accept the values and rules of the collective ego. (For a detailed description *see* p. 46, The Development of the Individual Ego.)

Expectation: Expectation is a mental focus that tends to eliminate everything in its field of vision that does not seem to directly to pertain to what is desired or expected. It causes a person to see what he desires or expects to see. The same thing happens when we expect the Sage to confirm our existing beliefs. The Sage cannot mirror our inner truth when we have imposed such a set of limits on what we are willing to see or hear.

Fate and Destiny: Fate is the term used in this volume to describe the adversities created when a person violates the Cosmic Harmonics. Fate is an automatic reaction of the Cosmos to such violations.

The word destiny describes the true purpose of an individual's life in a body, to bring to maturation his true self. When he is in harmony with the Cosmos, he receives all the help he needs from the invisible world to express his uniqueness, and to develop his Cosmic gifts: his abilities and talents. Through fulfilling his destiny, he also contributes to the constant evolution of the Cosmic Consciousness, because he realizes the various kinds of consciousness he is born with.

Fate is that part of the Cosmic Harmonics that ensures the continuation of harmony. It also has the purposes: (1) to compensate for the damage done to the Cosmic Whole; (2) to bring the person (literally) back from his head to his senses; and (3) to make him aware of his mistaken ideas and beliefs, and (4) to reduce him to an attitude of openness and humility that will help him shake loose the hold of the ego. The severity of Fate corresponds to the degree needed to wake him up; this depends upon the degree of his rigidity, the strength of his attachment to his mistaken ideas and beliefs, and to the degree of his arrogance.

Fate comes to an end when it has fulfilled its purposes. It can be reached in different ways: (1) by bringing the person to the state of burnout, in which he sees how his mistaken ideas have led to a dead-end; (2) when he has of his own accord sought its causes and rid himself of them, or (3) when the fate has run its full course of time. In this latter case, the person may not have corrected his viewpoint, but the fate has run out its time, like a prison sentence. (*See* p. 692, Freeing Yourself from a Fate.)

God: When the word God is used to describe the Cosmic Consciousness as only a loving energy, then the word is in harmony with the Cosmos. It is problematic, however, *when* it is connected with images that present the "all" as an image in human form, as the supreme authority, as the authorizer and protector of the collective ego, as a monarch or judge, a wielder of power, or as possessing characteristics and emotions common to the ego in humans. Also discordant is the image of God as having given man the job of being the overseer of God's property (the earth). These ideas of God are essentially Western in origin. While there was no specific concept of God in the Chinese tradition, the role that "heaven" played in authorizing the Emperor resembled these mistaken Western ideas of God. A major problem with these latter ideas of God and heaven is that they show the Cosmic Consciousness ordered like a feudal society. It is an image of the invisible world created to support humans' arrogant view of themselves.

Good and Evil: The *I Ching* makes it clear that the Cosmic definition of good and evil is fundamentally different from the definition given by the collective ego. "Good," in the Cosmic sense, is what is in harmony with the Cosmos. Everything is good by nature; human original nature, too, is whole, complete, and good, including our animal nature, which is not something separate. "Evil" comes into the world with the *false use of words,* because such words create a field of false consciousness, which we have called "the demonic sphere of consciousness." This happens, for example, when we classify a person as *being* either right or wrong, good or evil, or when we accept the idea that a person's animal nature is the source of evil. Then, we make a judgment about his *nature,* or essence. Calling a person *evil* puts a spell on him that creates an *inextinguishable stain.* This stain can, however, be removed by the Helpers of the invisible world. In a broader sense: when we say that Nature is wild (implying that it is unpredictable and threatening), the word "is" fixes Nature in a spell. We need to realize that Nature is more than meets the eye: it is a *feeling consciousness* that reacts sensitively to any slander that is put on it through the use of false words. Calling Nature "wild" demonizes its harmonious consciousness and makes it act wild. The evil never lies in the nature of anything that is part of the Cosmic Whole. False words that describe the mere appearance of something are the "seeds of evil." Such words are created when we separate *thinking* from our *feelings of inner truth.* This happens when thinking is elevated as superior over feeling. The *I Ching* shows that the Cosmic Consciousness is primarily a *feeling* consciousness, and that every person is connected directly with it through his feelings. When he connects with his feelings, they tell him the *inner truth* of what he is experiencing. Doing this allows him to call things by their true names.

Evil, thus, is neither part of the Cosmic Consciousness nor of

Nature. The Cosmic Consciousness—and Nature as its visible expression—operate on the principle of harmony. Harmony is possible only when all parts of the Cosmos recognize their feelings as that which holds them together, and when they give expression to their feelings. The true function of words is to give expression to feelings that are in harmony with the Cosmos. Words that do not fulfill this function create the *demonic sphere of consciousness*, which actually fights against the Cosmos and against Nature.

Evil arises with the development of the ego and the repression of the true self. It thus separates a person from the Cosmic Whole. Evil is contained in every ego-based intention, and comes from all thoughts and actions that are based on a human-centered view of the Cosmos. Evil manifests in every assertion of rights and privileges, every aspect of arrogance and temper, every encroachment into the private inner spaces of other beings, including the consciousness of the Helpers, the invisible aspects of the Cosmos, or the consciousness of animals, plants, and even of stones, or the various elements such as fire, water, wind, and earth. Such encroachments have to do with the peering of the ego into the nature of things with idle curiosity, in order to be "in the know" and thus attain power and control. Good can be defined as all that belongs to one's true nature and its perfect program that needs no intention. This nature relates intrinsically with the consciousness of all things.

When a person goes against his true nature, he creates blame in the Cosmic sense of that word. If he continues, he also creates a fate. Both blame and Fate can be extinguished at any time by freeing oneself of their cause. This happens when the person recognizes his error and rids himself of the mistaken idea/belief in question. Doing so requires saying the inner No to the false idea and asking the Helpers of the invisible world to free him from his fate. As can be seen from the above, everything in the Cosmos is directed toward maintaining and restoring the harmony of the whole. The Cosmos offers humans every possible source of help to see our errors in the light of our inner truth, and to show us how these errors, and their evil consequences, can be corrected.

Good Fortune: a standard term in the *I Ching* that points to Cosmic blessings and gifts that are given to a person because he has a correct view toward possessions. These possessions can be insights, help to achieve his tasks, or possessions in the most literal sense.

Good fortune as an augury in the line means that harmony will be achieved through following the counsel given.

Group-We: another term for "group-ego." Identifying with a group (family, creed, culture, nation, etc.) causes a person to lose his uniqueness. Also, by taking on the values of the group, he puts loyalty to the group above being true to himself. Doing so binds him to the fate of that group. (*See* Hexagram 59, *Dissolving*, Line 4: "He dissolves his bond with his group.")

Guilt: The Sage has made it clear that the word guilt, and all ideas related to it, do not have a Cosmic basis. This includes the idea of original guilt or sin, as well as the idea that we become guilty for whatever we do or fail to do. The idea of guilt, associated with the image of an inextinguishable stain, is an invention of the collective ego to keep the individual under its control.

Throughout its text, the *I Ching* gives evidence that the Cosmos does not hold anything against us forever. Moreover, making mistakes is considered to be an essential part of our learning process. Going against our true natures creates Cosmic blame, which can be corrected by regretting our mistake and extinguishing the mistaken idea that caused us to make the mistake. If we continue making the same mistake, we create a fate. But even a fate only runs for a limited period of time; the end of the fate extinguishes the Cosmic blame. Like blame, a fate can be ended at any given moment by correcting what has caused it. (*See* p. 692, Freeing Yourself from a Fate, and p. 50, Guilt, Blame, and Shame.)

Half-Truths: A half-truth is comprised of a phrase which presupposes something without stating what that something is. Half-truths find their appeal in that they appear to answer the broad riddles of life. All belief systems are based on half-truths. Example: "In the beginning was the word." The phrase leaves all its particulars to the imagination. In the beginning of what, one needs to ask, and what was the word referred to that caused the beginning? The phrase gives the false impressions (1) that there is such a thing as an absolute beginning, and (2) that it began with a word, and (3) that a "creator" spoke that word, making everything happen. Because humans are the only species that speaks in representative language, the phrase further implies that humans must have some special connection with the creator, thus a "special place" in the order of things: all this from one phrase! In that one phrase is contained the basis to justify the human-centered view of the universe. Such half-truths are generally surrounded by taboos that say they are not to be questioned. The taboos ensure that people who question these half-truths become guilty for doing so.

Helpers: The Helpers mentioned in the *I Ching* are not human beings, angels, or supernatural figures; they are individualized aspects of the Cosmic Consciousness and of Nature, and as such, are invisible. Every Helper fulfills a specific function within the harmonious flow of the Cosmos. (For a detailed description *see* p. 33, The Helpers as Helping Aspects of the Cosmos, and p. 682, Activating the Helpers.)

Hero: The hero is a self-image that is rooted in the human-centered view of the universe. It is the basis of *all* self-images, and the individual's attempt to define himself as special. In the Cosmic Order, no one thing is "special." The idea that the world needs heroes denies the existence of the Helpers of the invisible world, that alone have the ability to maintain and restore the harmony of the whole. The idea of the hero is always associated with human achievement, i.e., either through divine assistance or the use of power, contrivance, or mental cleverness. However, all these means contradict the Cosmic Harmony. Acting from the self-image of the hero or heroine creates fate after fate.

Instincts: The word "instincts" describes a person's inner and metaphorical senses. These senses are instrumental to getting a correct sense of what feels harmonious or discordant in a situation. (Also *see*: Senses.) However, when a person has accepted the view that his nature is divided into "higher" and "lower" parts, his instincts, as part of his animal nature, become slandered, and act out in demonic ways. (Also *see*: Drives.)

Light and Dark: The light and the dark are the two complementary aspects of chi energy. The light penetrates the space of the dark, while the dark attracts the light. In this manner, they give rise to "the ten thousand things" of existence. (*See* Hexagrams 1 and 2.) The collective ego falsely defines the light and the dark as *opposing* forces. When this view is projected upon things, they actually combat each other, thus giving rise to the demonic sphere of consciousness. By deprogramming this mistaken view, the two forces become harmonized by the Cosmic Helpers.

Loss: Loss, in relation to death, is an idea that has no Cosmic basis. Its use in this context has the negative effect of separating a person from his loved ones (which may include his animal friends), who, as "intelligences," live on in the invisible world. Were it not for this idea or loss, these intelligences would otherwise be present as Helpers and Protectors when he needs them. Looking at them as "lost" puts a false barrier between himself and them. The person with a correct attitude toward them recognizes their presence, but does not dwell on them as "gone." He goes on with his life in the knowledge that they are there when he needs them, and that they are watching out for him. If a person has shut them out through regarding them as lost, he needs to deprogram the image of them as lost, and to accept them once more into his life. It is also important that he not look at them as "spirits" or "ghosts." Spirits are entities created by human projections, which are outside the feeling consciousness of the Cosmos. Ghosts are the forms of people who have become stranded between the visible and invisible worlds for various reasons, the most common being that death has come to an adult before he was inwardly ready. The formation of a ghost, it needs to be added, is a rather uncommon phenomenon. A ghost can be released from being stuck in this in-between place in the same manner as freeing someone from a projection and poison arrow; in this case, the projection or poison arrow is the image or phrase that the person is "stuck," or "lost."

Misfortune: the standard term used in the *I Ching* to indicate the result of a person's acting from the ideas or beliefs of the collective ego. Misfortune can, but does not necessarily, indicate a fate.

Poison Arrows: a form of hostile thoughts, or thoughts that injure the uniqueness of something. They can be projected either onto oneself (or a part of one's body), onto other people, animals, plants, or any other aspect of Nature. In all cases, they create a poisonous reaction in the thing injured. It is important to recognize a poison arrow and free oneself (or another) from it. (*See* p. 697, Freeing Yourself from Projections, Spells, and Poison Arrows.)

Projection: In its general meaning, a projection is any thought that does not come from a person's true feelings. While thoughts that come from true feelings *penetrate* to the inner truth of others and have a beneficial effect, thoughts that are of a judgmental nature, or come from intention, have a harmful effect. Also, wishes and imaginations, based on arbitrary dislikes act as projections. Projections can occur between the partners of a relationship, or can be attacks upon a couple by other interested parties outside their relationship, most often from members of their respective families. (*See* p. 697, Freeing Yourself from Projections, Spells, and Poison Arrows.)

Psyche: The word "psyche," in *I Ching* terms, refers to the invisible aspect of a person's whole being. The psyche is *complemented* by the body as the visible aspect of the personality. Together, psyche and body form a harmonious whole. The psyche, more specifically, refers to the *total consciousness*, including the *subconscious* and the *unconscious*.

The consciousness of the total psyche goes far beyond the consciousness of the two frontal lobes of the brain that we normally think of as "consciousness," and which mainly centers around perception gained through outer seeing and hearing. The consciousness of the psyche includes a person's *feeling* consciousness, which is partly unconscious and partly repressed into his subconscious.

The *unconscious* includes the *feeling consciousness* of the autonomic nervous system. (It is influenced, most often negatively, by the thinking consciousness, when the latter has come under the influence of the ego. This happens, for instance, when we "put down" the body as lesser, and suppress its capabilities into the subconscious.) The unconscious consists of what the *I Ching* calls Helpers that connect us with the feeling consciousness of the Cosmos (and of Nature). These Helpers coordinate all aspects of the body's functioning with the world outside ourselves. The unconscious also includes other Helpers such as our Cosmic Virtues (modesty, sincerity, loyalty to our inner truth, etc.), our natural abilities (such as to learn, to ask for help, and to say the inner No), and our senses, both physical and metaphorical (the latter being our "sense of wholeness," "sense of truth," "sense of fairness," "sense of dignity," "sense of limits," "sense of caution," to name a few). Some, and even all of these Helpers can have been made ineffective through having been appropriated or imprisoned by the ego, or made to deviate from their original functioning through the demonizing of our animal nature.

The *subconscious* is not a natural part of the psyche. It is created by the formation of the ego, when the child's connection with his feelings, natural abilities, and inner truth gets suppressed. The subconscious is the inner prison into which everything is flung that is deemed as "undesirable" by the ego. It also contains the deepest true fears and self-doubts that are the result of his being isolated from his true feelings, and thus being isolated from his connection with the Cosmos. Also residing in the subconscious are false feelings of guilt and ego-inspired fears. These fears, self-doubts and feelings of guilt take on demonic forms that are sometimes seen in meditation and dreams as imps, demons, and dragons. The characteristics of the *imps* are that they seem cute, mischievous, clever, shrewd. They are behind a number of "imp" words, such as *imp*ulses, *imp*udence, *imp*roper, *imp*erative, *imp*ressive, etc. The imps are words, seed phrases and images that have taken on a life by the simple fact that we have not said the inner No to them, but have accepted them into our minds. They gain their power through impressing us with their *imp*ortance, cleverness, etc. They take on identities, either by speaking in the mind as "I" (as in "I will do this heroic thing"), or by adopting the voice of an authority that speaks to us in commanding phrases, such as "you must do this!" or reprimanding us, "you shouldn't be doing that!" They are deprived of their power over us when we consciously deprogram the words, seed phrases, and images of which they consist, by saying the inner No to them. The *demons* can be fears, doubts, or feelings of guilt that haunt the psyche with repetitive phrases or worries; they can also be ego-emotions. *Dragons* are full-fledged *control* elements created by belief systems which take power when we accept those belief systems as true.

The Sage made us aware that humans are not without help from the Cosmos in coping with the harmful consequences of their false use of language. One of the Sage's functions is to watch over the borderline between a person's subconscious and his conscious mind, to prevent the fears from literally driving the person "crazy." When a person follows the guidance of the Sage, the Sage will bring into his conscious mind only those demonic elements he can cope with at a given time. The Sage also determines the best order in which the contents of the subconscious are to be faced and deprogrammed. This brings up the question why some people do get overwhelmed by their fears, as in schizophrenia, cases of deep depression, etc. This happens when the person has developed a particular neurotic complex, called the "God Complex." The idea that a "higher power" is watching over one's hopes and fears projects an image on the Sage that slanders the Sage's true nature and blocks its ability to help. A person who wants to help another who is suffering from such a complex can deprogram it by eradicating the idea mentioned. (This idea needs to be treated as a projection, a spell, and a poison arrow.)

The imps, demons, and dragons remain operative in the psyche until such time as the words, phrases, images, and beliefs that comprise them are deprogrammed.

Note: As imps, demons, and dragons would like to have autonomous identities that make people feel helpless against them, it is better to reduce them to what they really are: simple words, phrases, and images.

Punishment. This is a word created by the collective ego to describe *its* idea of "correcting" a person, or an animal, by using force. The Cosmos corrects people in ways that are in accord with the Cosmic Harmonics. These Cosmic reactions are always directed at reconnecting a person with his true self, by keeping the ego in him in check. It is the ego that perceives the Cosmic correction as "punishment."

Sacrifice: The idea of sacrifice violates a number of Cosmic Principles, such as the Principles of Justice and of the Equality and Dignity of all aspects of the Cosmic Whole.

The Cosmos gives its gifts freely to the person who is modest. Cosmic Justice respects a person's dignity; in fact, a part of its function is to restore a person to his dignity which he has "thrown away," as by thinking that he has to make deals with a "higher power."

The idea of sacrifice comes from the feudal view of the Cosmos as having a hierarchical order with an all-powerful and judgmental entity at the top that needs to be pleased, bribed, or soothed. Since everything is an equal part of the Cosmos, no one part requires the submission, reverence or sacrifice of another part.

Senses (The): The senses include a person's five physical senses and a number of "metaphorical" senses. As to the five physical senses known as smell, hearing, taste, touch, and seeing, some of them have, in addition to their obvious characteristics, what may be called figurative characteristics. Their function is to tell us the inner truth or untruth of a matter. Thus the sense of smell can, for example, "smell" authority (since authority is not part of the Cosmic Order, but belongs to the demonic sphere of consciousness and therefore smells intimidating); it also smells danger or the hidden incorrectness of a situation, as when we say that something "smells foul" indicated by a wrinkling of the nose. Among the five senses, the sense of smell is the keenest in sensing the *hidden* state of affairs. Next in this ability is the sense of taste. The common expression that something is "unsavory" leaves no doubt about the crass inappropriateness of someone's behavior, nor does the perception that something tastes cloyingly sweet leave a doubt about the presence of ego-flattery or obsequiousness. Even though the suspicious odors or tastes are not noticeable to the outer senses, they register in our consciousness, if we have practiced awareness of them. Listening to our inner senses requires practice. The word "listening" draws attention to the next sense involved in perceiving the inner truth or untruth of a situation—the sense of inner hearing. Its function is to bring what has been smelled or tasted into the person's conscious mind. When the sense of inner hearing gives the message that something does not "sound" right, the figurative sense of touch comes into play: its function is to compare the perception with the person's sense of inner truth. The Sage informs us that every person is born with a memory of what Cosmic harmony *feels* like. This memory is his inner truth. When the figurative sense of touch compares a perception that does not "sound" right with this memory, the result is perceived as dissonance, an inner feeling that something does not "feel" right.

At this point the person's "metaphorical" senses come into play. Their function is to automatically trigger the correct reaction to the disharmonious situation. The metaphorical senses include a person's sense of appropriateness, his sense of loyalty to his inner truth, his sense of fairness or neutrality, his sense of equality (being equal to all things), his sense of caution or danger, his sense of dignity, his sense of integrity, or wholeness, his sense of inner quiet, his sense of innocence, his sense of Cosmic blame for betrayal of his true self, his sense of the dignity of all things, and his sense of what his Cosmic duty is. One of the general characteristics of the metaphorical senses is their *sim-*

plicity. It lies in their ability to allow a person to react harmoniously and appropriately to disharmonious circumstances without the *necessity of thinking.* They keep him *centered and complete within himself.* Their full abilities are unleashed when a person consciously validates their importance, or, in other words, pays them his full respect. The result is self-respect in its true meaning. The task of *human* self-development, as the Sage makes us understand, has to do with developing one's awareness of the workings of the inner senses and the metaphorical senses and to consciously engage one's sense of *inner seeing* to gain an inner picture of the disharmonious situation. This inner picture may be showing the opposite of what the situation appears to be on the outside. Gaining an inner picture of the situation allows a person to actually *see* the disharmonious results of a false use of words that creates imps, demons, and dragons.

The sense of inner seeing can also be engaged unconsciously, which occurs when a person is dreaming. However, a person needs to distinguish between dreams that come from his inner truth, and those that come from his subconscious. He can employ the *rtcm* and any needed hexagrams to decipher them, if the Sage indicates that they have a message of importance for him. (*See* above, "Psyche," for a definition of the subconscious.)

Although the metaphorical senses may be under various spells, they continue to work on behalf of the whole personality as best they can. Those parts not directly under the spell try to make up for the functions of those that are.

Many of the metaphorical senses are located in the muscle tissues throughout the body. They bring about involuntary reactions such as blushing, retreating, fleeing, and also advancing along the line of no resistance; the latter is another term for saying they work through transformation. However, this can happen only when they are not under a spell. One of the functions of a person's metaphorical senses is to protect him from harm coming from outside that threatens his completeness. In short, they enable him to do the right thing at the right moment.

Soul: The word "soul," when used to describe that which is "immortal" in a person (as in the expression: mind, soul, and body), is a creation of the collective ego. The collective ego has created words that support its mistaken idea that a person is divided into parts, some of which are mortal (the body), while others are not. The problem lies in the idea of "mortality." (*See* above, Death.) When used to describe a person's true self, in the sense of *essence*, one needs to be aware that it is his very animal nature that *is* his essence.

Spell: A spell can consist of a single word that has no Cosmic basis, or of one or more phrases, or of a false image. Spells have the effect of fixing the thing they are put upon, causing it to behave in the way attributed to it by the spell. When a spell is put on a person, or parts of his personality, the consequences are numerous: it can fix him in compulsive or other neurotic patterns of behavior that prevent him from developing his uniqueness. Spells can also create a fate for that person in the form of illness. (*See* p. 697, Freeing Yourself from Projections, Spells, and Poison Arrows.)

Spirit: We were advised by the Sage that this word has been incorrectly used by the collective ego to divide a person's wholeness into mind, body, and spirit, and to incorrectly designate spirit as "higher" than body. It is used correctly, however, when it is used to refer to a person's life-force, in the sense what animates him, since what animates him has to do with his animal nature.

Spirituality: This word, being a derivative of "spirit," in the incorrect use indicated above, is often used by the collective ego in regard to a person's "self-development." In this idea, the spirit is regarded as "higher," and what needs to be developed at the expense of his "lower," or animal nature. Spiritual development thus has the goal of separating the person from his animal nature in order to attain some abstract standard of perfection. Since it is our animal nature that connects us with the Cosmos, spiritual development leads a person only farther away from his unity with the Cosmic Whole. By contrast, self-development, as described in the *I Ching*, is achieved by freeing oneself from all ideas that falsely divide one's original wholeness. (*See* Hexagrams 23, *Splitting Apart*, and 27, *Nourishing*.)

Ironically, people who speak of spirituality often associate this term with the idea of a new relationship with Nature or with "holistic" thinking. What they do not realize is that by "thinking about" being holistic, they miss out on *living* holistically. Living holistically means to be one with the Cosmos. This unity does not come about by "uniting" body, mind, and soul, but by ceasing to see ourselves as divided into these parts. This can be achieved by saying the inner No to the idea that we are so divided. We *are* a unity by nature.

Success: as a standard term in the *I Ching*, refers to the positive result achieved through cooperating with the Helpers of the invisible world.

Supernatural: What the collective ego calls "supernatural" is actually the *normal* way of Nature when a person cooperates with it. The use of this term only shows a lack of understanding of the way the Helpers of Nature function. The same is true for what people call "miracles." Using such terms to describe the result of the Helpers' activities gives credit to a wrong source and causes the Helpers to withdraw from the situation. Calling a healing that was achieved with the aid of the Helpers "a miracle" can lead to a regression. This negative effect can be reversed by deprogramming the word miracle as a projection and spell, and by asking the Sage to call in all the Helpers necessary to correct the situation.

Transformation: the way by which Nature achieves everything harmoniously. Transformation occurs in the realm of the atom, which is also the realm of consciousness. The realm of the atom is chi energy, which is composed of the light and the dark. Transformation compresses Cosmic Consciousness into the forms of Nature, and also decompresses the forms when they have completed their experiences.

Applied to humans, transformation is felt when one is released from the bondage of a spell, projection, or poison arrow. The feeling is similar to what may be described as the simultaneous lining up of all the images of the slot machine when the jackpot is hit. The transformation affects the psyche and the body simultaneously. Transformation occurs without resistance; it is what is described in Wilhelm's commentary to the main text of Hexagram 57 as "penetration," which produces "willing consent." (Also *see* p. 52, Transformation versus Changes.)

True Self: True Self is the name given by the Sage to that which constitutes a person's true nature. In its natural state, the true self is in harmony with the Cosmos. It is completely endowed by the Cosmos with everything the person needs to live his life in a body in peace, harmony, and joy. A person's true nature is animal nature; it is totally good and undivided.

When, through the activity of the collective ego, a person's nature is divided into parts, with one being defined as "superior," and the other as "inferior," or as "the source of evil," spells are put on his animal nature that cause it to act in perverted ways. Thus, the true self becomes "the stranger within." Many hexagrams show the evil consequences of these spells, and point to the necessity of freeing the true self from them. (Also *see* p. 47, The True Self.)

Verbal Logic: The term verbal logic is used to define a kind of logic that is based only on thinking, to the exclusion of feeling. (By contrast, Cosmic Logic is based entirely on feeling, but can also express itself in words.) It can be said that the collective ego owes its whole existence to verbal logic. Because verbal logic has no Cosmic basis, it needs a huge system of justifying phrases (rationales) to support its basic premises. To establish its basic premises, verbal logic relies on a single physical sense: the sense of outer sight. It explains things only by looking at their outer appearance, and then drawing fantasy conclusions. Thus, it can be said that verbal logic not only depends on the thinking mind, but also on the image mind to "fill in" with fantasy and myth what cannot be seen with the outer eyes.

Walking Dead Person: This term refers to a person who has totally separated from his feeling consciousness, disdaining his feelings and his body. Each person is born with a certain amount of chi (inner light) that invigorates and supports him during his life in a body. Under healthy circumstances, his chi energy is constantly renewed through contact with his feelings of inner truth, which, in turn, connect him with the Cosmic Whole. His chi is also replenished by Cosmic love as it is received either directly from the Cosmos, or through being truly loved by another person. His chi energy is decreased by ignoring and suppressing his true feelings, and by rejecting the Cosmic gift of love when it comes to him. If neglected long enough, his inner light dwindles to a mere set of coals. Often, at this point, he experiences a major life crisis, in which he perceives the state of his inner light. If he then further neglects it, the light becomes extinguished and he becomes a "walking dead person." The Sage calls such a person one "without head" because he lacks the ability to further connect with the Cosmic Whole.

People may continue in this state for many years, stealing chi energy from other people by creating sympathy and attention. They may also draw chi from objects, but especially from crafts and art objects into which the craftsmen and artists have poured their chi. When a person realizes, through using the *rtcm*, that he is being drained of chi energy in this way, he needs to inwardly disconnect from and remain neutral in the presence of a walking dead person, to prevent giving away his energy. It is also important that he not view that person as a culprit, as that too would give him energy. Because the Sage is in the presence of every person, it is helpful to ask the Sage to call in the Cosmic Army to kill the demonic elements that have taken over the other's body, and to revive his true self.

Appendix 3

How to Consult the Sage through the *I Ching* Oracle

Preparing Yourself

There are some prerequisites to successfully consult the oracle:

- First, you need to know **what it is you are communicating with**. The *I Ching* oracle is an alive consciousness, and not "just a book." What speaks through it is the Sage, or Cosmic Teacher. It is activated by inwardly asking for its help to attain clarity.

- Second, it is necessary to have a **sincere and modest attitude**.

- Third, **an open mind is essential**. If you are suspicious of the Sage, the Sage will retreat before you have begun. The same is true if you are feeling in conflict with life, because some shock or disappointment has happened. Before you consult the Sage, put aside your inner conflict, together with any wanting, wondering, or worrying, to free your mind of all opinion and activity, for if your mind is already full, how can there be any space left for the insight the Sage wants to give?

- Fourth, be aware that **the answer you need may lie outside the confines of your question**. When this happens, the retrospective-three-coin method (*rtcm*) described below can provide you the clues to understanding the answer.

Asking your Question

Most people, on consulting the Sage, have a deep inner question, whether they have phrased it or not. The answer of the Sage will invariably be to this inner question. Thus, if a person "plays" with the oracle by asking some superficial question, he may not understand the answer.

The best way to approach the Sage is to get in touch with your inner question. If your inner question is about money matters, and you think money is too mundane a matter to take to the Sage, you might be surprised to find that the answer is actually concerning your mistaken attitude toward money. When you are concerned about someone else's bad behavior, the answer will point to the *inner* truth of the situation. The *rtcm* is the best way to determine who and what the Sage is addressing.

When you consult the oracle daily, you may want to leave it to the Sage to draw your attention to any problem you are not consciously aware of. In this case, you can ask, "Please show me what I need to know for today." The answer given may either be about a specific problem, or teach you a general lesson about life. If you consult the oracle only when you are in trouble, you are learning "the hard way." If you consult it regularly, you can learn about the Cosmic Way in many joyful lessons.

Your consultation consists basically of two steps: In step 1, after having put forth your question, you develop a hexagram which is one of the 64 hexagrams. In step 2 you use the retrospective-three-coin method (*rtcm*) to make sure that you have understood the oracle's answer.

How to Develop a Hexagram

A hexagram consists of six lines. The lines are obtained by throwing three coins—each throw resulting in a line. Count the head side of the coin as three and the tail side as two. A throw can result in one of the four following possibilities as you add up the total value received:

$$2 + 2 + 2 = 6 \quad \text{— —} \quad \bullet$$
$$2 + 2 + 3 = 7 \quad \text{———}$$
$$3 + 3 + 2 = 8 \quad \text{— —}$$
$$3 + 3 + 3 = 9 \quad \text{———} \quad \bullet$$

The lines composed of all even or all odd numbers (values 6 or 9), that have been marked with bullets, are called "changing lines." These lines contain the pertinent messages given by the Sage. They are read within the context of the general theme of the hexagram.

Example:

1. Shake three coins (pennies are fine) and let them fall. The total value of heads and/or tails gives you your first line.

2. Start drawing your hexagram from the bottom up. Imagine you are building a house, starting with laying the foundation. If, for example, your first throw showed 3+3+2=8, draw a broken line at the bottom.

3. Continue in this fashion until you have built your hexagram

Line 6: ——
Line 5: — —
Line 4: — — •

Line 3: — — •
Line 2: —— •
Line 1: — —

4. To identify the number of your hexagram, divide the hexagram in the middle as shown above. The bottom three lines are called the "lower trigram," and the top three lines the "upper trigram." Using the key on the inside back cover, find the trigram that looks like your lower trigram on the vertical column of trigrams. Then find the trigram that looks like your upper trigram on the horizontal row of trigrams. The above example hexagram consists of the lower trigram **K'an** and the upper trigram **Ken**. The number where the two columns intersect represents the number of the hexagram you have received. In the above example it is # 4. Now find Hexagram 4 in Part II of this volume. Its name is "**Youthful Folly.**" In reading the oracle, you first read the hexagram's general text and then read the changing lines.

5. The above shows you have received Lines 2, 3, and 4, as "changing lines." (In writing this new version of the *I Ching*, we were advised by the Sage not to follow the tradition found in other *I Ching* books of developing a second hexagram by changing the lines. The reason for this is twofold: first, the Sage clearly prefers simplicity, and second, the retrospective-three-coin method (*rtcm*) explained below, enables you to thoroughly un-

derstand the hexagram and the changing lines. The changing lines point to a problem or misunderstanding that needs to be addressed in the way the line counsels; freeing yourself from the cause of the problem (see Appendix 1) is the true meaning of a "changing line.")

Interpreting your hexagram

1. Note its **name**. In rare cases the name contains the whole message.

2. Next, read **The Judgment**. It is written in metaphorical terms and represents the actual oracle message. The purpose of a metaphor is to allow multidimensional meanings. It is the nature of a Cosmic oracle to refer to things on many different levels: literal or figurative. This volume differentiates the Cosmic meaning from the traditional meaning attributed to a hexagram. [To fully understand how this volume differs from traditional versions of the *I Ching* it is necessary to read Part I.]

Using the above sample hexagram, The Judgment reads: *Youthful folly has success. It is not I who seeks the young fool; the young fool seeks me. At the first oracle I inform him. If he asks two or three times, it is importunity. If he importunes, I give him no information. It does not further to persevere.* The Cosmic Principle described by this hexagram concerns the way the Sage, or Cosmic Teacher, relates to a person who approaches the *I Ching* showing how he may best communicate with it. If he has an ego-attitude, the Sage will give him an answer that makes him aware that he needs to correct it. If the questioner persists in his immodest attitude, the Sage retreats to maintain its dignity; thereafter, he will only receive hexagrams that confuse him. The commentary to The Judgment gives a number of hints as to how the ego may interfere in approaching the oracle. It also indicates how to correct an ego-attitude.

3. Next, read the texts of the *changing lines* you have received. In the above example, they are lines 2, 3, and 4. Each line describes in detail a particular aspect of the main theme of the hexagram. Here, the lines show how the Sage relates to the person who seeks to learn, but is still under the domination of his ego. Line 2 reads: *To bear with fools in kindliness brings good*

fortune... The line may be telling you that the Sage expects that you come with misconceptions about the Cosmic Way, and that it wants you to know that in learning, mistakes are inevitable, and no cause for regret or blame, so long as you are sincere. It also takes into account your fears, and will help you to free yourself of them, which is the good fortune indicated. Line 3 reads: *Take not a maiden who, when she sees a man of bronze, loses possession of herself. Nothing furthers.* This line wants you to be aware that the Sage does not make decisions for you, but by confirming your inner feelings of truth, helps you to have the confidence to follow your inner truth. The maiden who loses possession of herself does so by turning her life over to an authority outside herself (the man of bronze). Line 4 reads: *Entangled folly brings humiliation.* This line may be seeking to make you (or someone you are concerned about) aware of a fate you have created by following a mistaken belief, and that you have the choice to follow it to the point of burnout (the humiliation mentioned), or to end it. The Sage can teach you how to end it through gaining an understanding of what caused it, and correct the cause.

4: While reading the main text of your hexagram and the specific changing lines indicated by your throws, **certain words or parts of the text may draw your particular attention.** They most likely contain the message of the Sage with respect to your situation. If nothing resonates during your reading, the hexagram may be referring to someone else with whom you are connected and the influence he is having on your situation. The *rtcm* described below can be used to clarify whether the hexagram refers to you or to someone else.

The Retrospective-Three-Coin Method (*rtcm*)

The *rtcm* is a method used in conjunction with developing a hexagram, to clarify precisely the message intended by the Sage. To this effect you put forth hypotheses about the meaning of the metaphors mentioned in The Judgment and Line texts. The commentaries to the hexagrams, within this volume, are meant to give hints as to these meanings, or to explain the Cosmic

Principles you need to understand and observe in order to successfully deal with your situation.

As indicated by its two-line-structure, the *I Ching* oracle originated from a simple method, such as tossing a single coin, to ask a question that could be answered as either Yes or No. To the ancients Yes meant 'it is okay to go ahead with what you are doing or planning,' while No meant that it is not okay. In time, this led to a recognition of sorts that Yes also meant, "the object of your question is in harmony with the Cosmos and will therefore lead to success/good fortune," or No, "something about your questioning is out of harmony with the Cosmos, and will lead to misfortune if you continue." It was just such a method that led to the two primary answers the *I Ching* oracle gives: good fortune/success or misfortune/remorse. The larger picture in which these Yes's and No's fit, is the system of Cosmic Harmonics which is revealed in the 64 hexagrams and their lines.

The Retrospective-Three-Coin Method is based on the same principle as tossing one coin to get Yes or No, except that three coins are used to give more possibilities. The Sage, in our experience, is not comfortable with a narrow and absolute Yes or No. It wants a broader band or spectrum in which to answer which enables it to qualify its response by suggesting "yes, but..." or "no, but..." to describe relatively the individual situation. The three coins allow for this relative kind of answer.

In this method, we have designated the head sides of the coin to mean Yes, and the tail sides to mean No. In tossing the three coins, you can receive as an answer, "Yes, Yes, Yes," which is taken as a definitive Yes, or two heads and one tail, which are read as "basically Yes." Two tails are read as "basically No," and three tails as "definitively No." Receiving three tails can also have a number of other meanings, some of which are mentioned below.

This method is best used to verify, after forming a hexagram, whether the understanding you have come to is actually the understanding meant by the Sage. It is important to make sure that your ego is not in charge because in that case the Sage retreats and you are actually communicating with your ego.

After casting a hexagram, and having allowed the text to speak to you, you may have felt a particular resonance in one or more places. If you are not quite sure what to make of the answer, you can propose hypotheses of what you think the text might be saying: "Is this...(stating your hypothesis)...what it means?" When the reply is a definitive Yes (three heads) you don't need to go further, you have hit the main point. If it is two heads, it can either mean, "yes, but your question was not quite to the main point," or "yes, keep going in this direction with your questions." Use the three coins to verify whether your direction is to the point. If it is the right direction, you may only need to proceed further by putting forth any remaining questions, until you have obtained a complete understanding. When you believe you have understood it thoroughly, you can ask, "Do I need to go further?" If it says "No," it means just that, but it may also mean, "That is enough for now." All learning, we begin to understand, is a temporary platform to new understandings of increased breadth and depth. We find, through this method, that there is no such thing as an ultimate truth, and that truth is always relative to the moment.

Some things of importance we have learned from using the *rtcm*.

1. Only certain versions and translations of the *I Ching* contain the necessary metaphorical language which enables the Sage to speak. One of these is the Wilhelm translation, which has been one of the basic texts used for this volume.

2. The Sage, in responding to the questioner, does not use the same parts of the oracle text each time to mean the same thing. The *rtcm* helps you determine the unique meaning of the moment.

3. The longtime student of the *I Ching* often assumes that he understands the oracle, because he has internalized its text over many years of reading it. If this applies to you, your attitude prevents the Sage from being able to show you broader vistas through allowing new meanings to come out of the standard metaphors. These new meanings would also help you in your circumstance of the moment. Using the *rtcm* to ask, "do I correctly understand what the Sage is saying in this hexagram to-

day" frees the Sage to open your eyes to these new meanings.

4. Because it can happen that you read the *I Ching* text to justify what you already believe, or to hear what flatters you, the *rtcm* helps you avoid such self-deceptions if you ask with an open mind.

5. The *rtcm* helps you clarify the causes of feeling ill, or unwell. Since such feelings may be due to projections, spells, or poison arrows, it is always best to ask about them. They may be caused by the ego in yourself, or come from someone else. You need, therefore, to ask whether the influence is coming from yourself or from someone else. If from someone else, you can identify the source (one person or several people). Clarifying its source also helps you to become aware of any negative feelings you may have that are the result what the other(s) may be projecting on you. A short meditation (up to five minutes), in which you ask the Sage to help you identify any thoughts or ego-emotions coming from inside or outside, can be of help. You can then ask, by using the *rtcm*, about every phrase or image that comes to your mind, whether it is part of the negative influence you are feeling.

Some Guidelines to Your Questioning Process

It is helpful to start with questions that are general and proceed to the specific, always narrowing in on the subject and its particulars. For example:

Begin with identifying the subject: who or what the hexagram is talking about. It is incorrect to assume that it is always about yourself. Keep in mind that receiving several changing lines in one hexagram can refer to different people in the situation; therefore ask: "does this changing line refer to me?" If not, move outward, from persons closest to you: "does it refer to a member of my family?" If not: "a friend?", "a public person?" "a group?" "Is it about the situation I've been thinking about" (money, health, work situation, someone's comment), "is it referring to nothing specific, but is informing me of a Cosmic Principle?"

The time element. "Is it referring to a situation in the past?" "present?" "future?" "Is it referring to something now in process?" Keep in mind that receiving several changing lines can be intending to give you an overview over a situation you have gone through and which is still having an effect on you now.

Is it an inner or an outer situation? If it is an inner situation, "is it about my attitude toward someone?" or "is it about my attitude toward the Sage, or the oracle that needs correction?" This can include mistrust, arrogance, ambition, knowing better, vanity, pride, or subservience. Any of these attitudes held toward the Sage need to be corrected before it can answer any further questions. Correcting is done by saying the inner No to the ego in yourself and its haughty attitude, and apologizing to the Sage. If it is an outer situation, "is it about my job?" "my family?" "my friends?"

The end of the oracle session is determined by asking, "is this all I need to know now?" If the answer is Yes, then it is good to thank the Sage for the help received. If No, ask whether you need another hexagram, and continue the process of questioning as before.

Some Other Important Considerations:

Because the Sage never answers the same question twice, it is important to keep a written record of your questions. (You may want to use a 'shorthand' for the answers: ++, +++, - -, - - -.) If you ask a question that is not identical to a question previously asked, but still means the same thing, it is the same as asking twice, and the answer given will be the reverse of what it was formerly. Answering in this way is one of the ways the Sage indicates its withdrawal when you persist in doubting its answer.

Sometimes we remain on the wrong track in our questioning, indicated by a long string of No's. In this case the Sage is not withdrawing, but waiting until we find the right direction. It such cases it can be helpful to ask, "Do I need another hexagram to get the right direction?" If it again says No, it is time to ask, "Should I discontinue questioning at this time?" If again it says No, ask, "Is the answer so simple that I am overlooking it?" Then we inwardly ask for help from the Sage to get the right direction. This often leads to a "mind flash"— a phrase or image that is the precise help needed.

It is our experience that the Sage often wants to point only to a part of the text. The *rtcm* is helpful to find that part. Sometimes the oracular line texts are relevant, but not their commentaries. Sometimes only a single word will contain the Sage's message. Sometimes the Sage wants to make you aware of an incorrect interpretation in the commentary. The *rtcm* allows you more quickly to find the parts and phrases that are relevant, and what they are referring to.

Using the *rtcm,* the messages take shape through a cooperation between the Sage and your intuitive feelings of what it is saying. The reasoning and rationalizations that typify a purely mental approach to the oracle come from the ego. A purely mental approach converts the readings into trivialities, and reads into the text what the questioner wants to hear. Many of the problems people experience in consulting the *I Ching* come from being too mental and isolated from their intuitive abilities.

The *rtcm* is also helpful when someone tells you with authority what "the truth" of a matter is. Ask the Sage, using the *rtcm,* rather than accepting without question what the other says. If necessary, pursue the matter further by casting a hexagram to understand it in its full context. Often something seems true because of the way things appear outwardly. Working with the Sage reveals the *inner* truth of the matter. The same is true when you think you have understood something correctly. Ask if it is so, and do not merely assume you have.

The Cosmos is primarily a feeling consciousness. Your ability to sense the truth is one of your greatest assets, yet many people have been divorced from this ability by having been conditioned to doubt their inner senses. If you give the Sage enough space, it can help you reconnect with your sense of inner truth and to learn to trust it. That is the whole purpose of the *I Ching*: to help you trust your true self with all its myriad natural abilities. To learn, you only need to ask. The Sage does not get tired of your sincere quest to know what is cosmically true and what is untrue.

Be aware that sometimes you may not be ready (through lack of awareness of how the Cosmos operates) to understand the answer to a question. For this reason, try to avoid asking monumental questions such as, "what is my destiny?"

Some dangers in using the *rtcm*: (These are the same dangers you experience in consulting the *I Ching* by traditional methods, except that in using the *rtcm* you tend to run into them right at the beginning. This gives you the opportunity to correct your attitude rather than having to learn "the hard way.")

Being slavishly dependent on the Sage: The Sage will not make decisions for you that you can answer by asking your commonsense. For example, don't ask, "is it time to get out of bed now?"

Putting the responsibility for your life on the Sage: Avoid asking questions such as, "should I take the job offered?" It is best to follow your inner feelings about it. If your question about taking the job comes from a doubt whether you are able to fulfill it, or whether there is a hidden catch in the situation, then it is appropriate to ask the Sage about these issues of doubt, and to understand the inner truth of the situation, rather than simply wishing to be told what to do.

Idle curiosity is an inappropriate attitude and motive for asking the Sage anything. The convenience of the *rtcm* may tempt you to ask questions of this sort, but the Sage will not answer them, because they come from the ego's desire to "be in the know" and to be in control. Ego-based questions cause the Sage to retreat, thus making the answers unintelligible. If you suspect that you are doing this, you can ask, "Was I asking that from idle curiosity?" The answer to this question can be trusted.

Questioning to resolve inner conflict: When you do not like an answer you have received from the Sage and try, through further questioning, to get a better one, it is an indication of inner conflict caused by the resistance of the ego in yourself. The only thing to do when you are full of questions of conflict, is to retreat and disengage from questioning until your sincerity and modesty have returned.

What to do when you believe the Sage has retreated?
This situation is frequently encountered when you are still in

the beginning stage of learning how to use the *rtcm* correctly. It is indicated by your receiving either a series of No answers, or by receiving contradictory answers. The reason for this situation may be that you have fallen into either one of the dangers mentioned in the section above. It is part of your learning process to make mistakes, and the Sage's retreat has one purpose alone: to make you aware of a mistake so that you may correct your attitude. Correcting your attitude is carried out by saying the inner No. For example, you may say, "no, no, no to my idle curiosity," or "no, no, no to my thinking that I know better." Then, apologize to the Sage. Apologize in the same manner as you would to a person whom you respect as your equal. (Please read carefully the examples given in the Appendix: Activating the Helpers of the Invisible World, subsection: Attitudes and Mistaken Ideas that block the Helpers.) If you are blaming yourself for having made a mistake, the ego has entered the stage, and you need to say the inner No to its blaming you. Another frequent mistake that comes from childhood training, consists of projecting images of a punishing authority onto the Sage. Although the Sage is our Cosmic Teacher, it is also our friend. Again, the situation can be corrected by saying the inner No to such images, and apologizing to the Sage.

Example of how the Sage can teach you a Cosmic lesson

After the completion of the 64 hexagrams in this book, Hanna was looking for a sample lesson that would show how the *rtcm* can be employed in learning from the Sage. As she was browsing through the "daily notes," the Sage made her aware that it wanted to give her a new lesson. This experience is typical of the Sage's way: it always wants to give you a gift by teaching you something new:

"I started with developing a hexagram, and received Hexagram 55, *Abundance,* Line 3: *The underbrush is of such abundance that the small stars can be seen at noon. He breaks his right arm. No blame.*

"Is it a lesson concerning me personally?-- (= no, no) (In reading the commentary to this line, my attention was drawn to its talking about belief systems.) Do you want to point to the effect of belief systems? ++ (= yes, yes) The effect they have on particular Helpers?-- The effect they have on a person's chi energy?++ Is the metaphor of the broken right arm a hint?-- Is the hint contained in "the underbrush?"++ Does the abundance of "underbrush" stop the flow of chi energy coming to that person from the Cosmos?-- Does the underbrush stand for rationales supporting the belief systems?-- Does it stand for the chaos created in the person's chi energy?-- Does the underbrush stand for ready-made explanations of how the Cosmos works?++

"Is the word "works" a problem?"++ Would the word "functions" be a better word?++ Is one of the problems with "work" that it is based on a mechanical view?++ Is there still another problem with it?+++ That it implies "effort?"++

—**The first point of the lesson concerns: ready-made explanations of how the Cosmos functions, with the main problem being beliefs that see it as a set of mechanics.**

"(Here, I remembered that the way of the Cosmos is to achieve everything through transformations, and that transformations occur through the complementary action of the light and the dark in the atomic realm, where there is no resistance. The light and the dark, together, form what is called chi energy.) Is there any other problem with the word "work?"--

"(My next inner question was: Where is the connection between the false assumptions people hold about the way the Cosmos functions—by looking at it as a set of mechanics, that achieves things through effort—and a person's chi energy? I realized in writing this question down that any set of mechanics, in order to achieve something, *uses up* energy. So, when people think of the Cosmos in such terms, they also assume that the Cosmos uses up energy. However, what we have learned about transformations is that they actually generate chi energy while things are being achieved.) Is my assumption correct that the Cosmos, in achieving things, actually generates more chi energy all the time?-- Should I say "the Cosmos generates *new* chi energy as it goes?"++ Is that the main meaning of Hexagram 42, *Increasing*?+++ And of course also one of the meanings of

Hexagram 55, *Abundance?*+++

"Applied to a person's chi energy, does the person's mechanical view of the Cosmos block him from receiving the Cosmic chi energy?-- Is there a problem with the word "block?"++ Does his view cause him to use up chi energy?++ Because he looks at his own makeup as a set of mechanics?++ Can that be the cause of depression?++

—**Second point: that looking at one's body as a set of mechanics uses up chi energy and leads to depression.**

"Do you want me to throw another hexagram?++

"I then got Hexagram 4, *Youthful Folly*, Lines 1 and 6.

"Line 1: *To make a fool develop, it furthers to apply discipline. The fetters should be removed. To go on in this way brings humiliation.* (This line mentions mistaken beliefs that disable the Helper of Transformation, that renews a person's chi energy.) Is it about these beliefs in general?-- About a particular one?++ The belief that "the mind knows how the body functions?"++ Does this belief need to be treated as a spell?++ Also as a poison arrow?-- Is there anything else I am meant to understand from this line?+++ (The commentary to this line also mentions that such mistaken beliefs create health problems, which have the beneficial effect of returning a person to his senses.)

"Do you want to draw my attention to this part?++ Is it that the health problem actually restores a person's commonsense?++ (We have learned from the Sage that our commonsense is our Helper of Transformation. When this Helper is able to function in a healthful way, our chi energy gets renewed through transformation. At this point I was able to see the connection to the metaphor "his right arm is broken," which is a reference to the person's commonsense being injured. I now realized that the Sage was showing me how our nature can heal itself by way of an illness.) Have I understood enough from this line?-- Does the illness break the spell that has been put on the body by the mistaken belief?++ Is there a danger that the person will put the same spell back on his body, if he does not inquire about the cause of his illness?++ Is it time to go to Line 6?++

"Line 6: *In punishing folly it does not further to commit trans-*

gressions. The only thing that furthers is to prevent transgressions.
Are you pointing to the wrong view people have that an illness
is a Cosmic punishment?++ Have I understood enough?++

"**Summary:** The Sage was showing me how the mistaken beliefs—that seeing either the Cosmos or the body as operating as
a set of mechanics—puts a spell on our natural ability to renew
our chi energy. The lack of chi energy then leads to illness (a
fate). However, the illness actually breaks the spell, thus restores
our ability to renew our chi. The Sage pointed to the Cosmic
Principle of Transformation as the vehicle for the renewal of
chi energy, and to Fate as having the function (among other
things) of restoring our ability to renew our chi energy.

"To me, this lesson, once again, showed the loving and caring
nature of the Cosmos in correcting our mistaken beliefs. It also
shows the abundance of patience the Cosmos has in waiting
until we are ready to open our minds to a true understanding
of its ways."

Hexagram Key

TRIGRAMS UPPER / LOWER	Ch'ien	Chên	K'an	Kên	K'un	Sun	Li	Tui
Ch'ien	1	34	5	26	11	9	14	43
Chên	25	51	3	27	24	42	21	17
K'an	6	40	29	4	7	59	64	47
Kên	33	62	39	52	15	53	56	31
K'un	12	16	8	23	2	20	35	45
Sun	44	32	48	18	46	57	50	28
Li	13	55	63	22	36	37	30	49
Tui	10	54	60	41	19	61	38	58